Why Do You Need this New Edition?

5 good reasons why you should buy this new edition of *Case Studies in Abnormal Behavior!*

1. **Brand new cases!** Brooke Shields (Post-Partum Depression); Seung-Hui Cho (School Shooters); Marilyn Monroe (Female Psychosexual Dysfunction); Muhammed Ali (Pseudo-Parkinson's Disease); Christina Ricci (Anorexia Nervosa); Alfred Kinsey (Sexual Deviation); Albert Einstein (possible Dyslexia/Learning Disorder).

2. **New and updated** cultural material, making this edition the most culturally diverse edition yet!

3. **Updated and further integration** of *DSM-TR-IV* helps students gain a relevant and comprehensive understanding of the major DSM disorders.

4. Each case contains the full background material relevant to etiological, diagnostic, and therapeutic considerations.

5. Significant family and social history data give students a clear picture of how specific behavior patterns are generated and maintained.

PEARSON

To Monika Meyer Hubbard:
Still quite a case and still delightful
RGM

To Bonnie and Bill
CMW

Case Studies in Abnormal Behavior

EIGHTH EDITION

Robert G. Meyer
University of Louisville

L. Kevin Chapman
University of Louisville

Christopher M. Weaver
U.S. Dept. of Veterans Affairs–Palo Alto & Stanford University

Boston   New York   San Francisco
Mexico City   Montreal   Toronto   London   Madrid   Munich   Paris
Hong Kong   Singapore   Tokyo   Cape Town   Syndey

Series Editor: Michelle Limoges
Editorial Assistant: Christina Manfroni
Marketing Manager: Kate Mitchell
Production Editor: Patrick Cash-Peterson
Editorial Production Service: Black Dot Group
Composition Buyer: Linda Cox
Manufacturing Buyer: JoAnne Sweeney
Electronic Composition: NK Graphics
Cover Administrator: Elena Sidorova and Jennifer Hart

For related titles and support materials, visit our online catalog at www.ablongman.com.

Between the time website information is gathered and then published, it is not unusual for some sites to have closed. Also, the transcription of URLs can result in typographical errors. The publisher would appreciate notification where these errors occur so that they may be corrected in subsequent editions.

ISBN-13: 978-0-205-59416-0   ISBN-10: 0-205-59416-6

Library of Congress Cataloging-in-Publication Data
Meyer, Robert G.
  Case studies in abnormal behavior / Robert G. Meyer, L. Kevin Chapman,
and Christopher M. Weaver. — 8th ed.
      p. cm.
  Includes bibliographical references and index.
  ISBN 0-205-59416-6
  1. Mental illness—Case studies.   2. Psychology, Pathological—Case studies.   I. Chapman, L. Kevin.
II. Weaver, Christopher M.   III. Title.
  RC465.M44   2009
  616.89—dc22
                                                        2008002483

Printed in the United States of America

10   9 8 7 6 5 4 3 2 1   11   10   09   08

CONTENTS

PREFACE

Research articles in abnormal psychology necessarily focus on specific theories and experiments; texts in this area are concerned with integrating a vast array of literature on historical, descriptive, research, diagnostic, and treatment issues. Some texts do a good job of bringing in "chunks" of case material to demonstrate particular points. However, textbooks cannot do justice to their other goals if they provide any significant number of cases in depth. *Case Studies in Abnormal Behavior* fills this niche. This book helps the reader regain a sense of how the whole person experiences and reacts to the diverse factors studied in abnormal psychology. The abstract and conflicting concepts of this field can thus be seen in the context that eventually counts—the totality of an actual person who has the disorder.

Many of the cases in this book are of people who are well known for one reason or another (e.g., John Lennon, Princess Diana, and Presidents Reagan and Clinton) or who played an important role in the evolution of the field of psychology (e.g., Anna O.). A number of these and other cases presented are based on actual, recent cases, though not in the public record. Identifying details have, of course, been changed to protect people from even a small chance that they would be recognized. Aside from those in the public record, most cases originated from our own experiences or were donated by colleagues. We have also included several classic cases originally published in journals or early manuscripts. These cases either make an original point or demonstrate a particular point of view (e.g., as in the Cases of the Three Little Fellows, Hans, Albert, and Peter, in Chapter 3).

Readers will note that cases that are provided by us and that are not public figures are assigned names with a logical or mnemonic (i.e., sounds like) relationship to the syndrome being studied—for example, Agnes Agoraphobia. Granted, though this may at times sound a bit corny, we have nevertheless found it to be a helpful technique for most readers. Students have found this to be a useful device, since it adds clarity to classroom discussion and it enhances the remembrance of the cases if needed during a test.

Readers might also note the high number of case studies in this book. Feedback from our students and from other professors and their students indicated that case studies in most other books were too long and included irrelevant detail (and in a couple of cases, much too short). The majority of cases in this book contain the full details of background material that are relevant to etiological, diagnostic, and therapeutic considerations, and yet, hopefully, they are not overly long. This allows us to provide a full spectrum of case studies, perhaps more than in any previous case study book. It also allows us to detail cases from all categories of the *Diagnostic and Statistical Manual* (DSM-IV-TR) of the American Psychiatric Association, to provide contrast cases within the major categories, and to present some other cases that deal with other important patterns. Also, new material from the Text Revision version (2000) of the *DSM*—that is, the *DSM-IV-TR*—is included as well.

Relevant and detailed family and social history data are presented in almost all of these case studies, since such data give the reader clearer ideas about how specific behavior patterns were generated and maintained. A few of the case studies have little background data, such as in the case of Harry (in Chapter 15), in which an abrupt organic trauma is the focus of disorder. In cases such as Harry's, we present more detailed information regarding present behavior and the responses in psychological evaluations. Other cases have less background data if it seems less important for some other reason—for example, when it seems clear that genetic factors dominate the development of the disorder, as in the case of Virginia Woolf (Chapter 7). All cases go through to a natural conclusion, even though it may not always be termed a success. As in most experiences, much can be learned from failure.

We thank those individuals who have helped with this book. Much appreciation is extended to Michelle Limoges, my Allyn and Bacon editor, for her support and advice. Our thanks, too, to the reviewers of this eighth edition, and to Corey Pallatto for her help with copyediting and developing the index.

We would also like to acknowledge the help in writing some of these cases, as denoted in prior editions, and in this edition from Dustin Morris (female psychosexual dysfunction); Kristy Matala (postpartum depression); Melissa Gordon (school shooters); Scott Forbes (Albert Einstein); Mary Hundley (Alfred Kinsey); Jennifer Cundiff (anorexia nervosa). We also appreciate the extensive help from the senior author's daughter, Monika Meyer Hubbard, and his wife, Peggy, in organizing this edition.

—RGM
—LKC
—CMW

INTRODUCTION AND MAJOR HISTORICAL DEVELOPMENTS

If you always think the way you always thought, you'll always get what you always got.

—Anonymous

For centuries, spiritual and crude biological models dominated thinking about abnormal behavior (Larson, Graham, & Baker, 2007). More recently, the field of abnormal psychology has evolved through many theoretical orientations. In the first half of the twentieth century, the Freudian psychoanalytic model, already developing a more broad-spectrum psychodynamic orientation (Kohut, 1977; Schwartz et al., 1996; Weston, 1998), clearly dominated the study of abnormal psychology in North America. At the same time, the seminal behavioral studies of John Watson and Mary Cover Jones established behaviorism as an important influence in the study of abnormal behavior. Behaviorism, and more specifically, behavior therapy, was coming into bloom in the 1950s and 1960s (Ayllon & Azrin, 1968; Wolpe, 1958), and then merged with the cognitive therapies in the 1980s and 1990s (McCullough, 2002). Concurrently, a "third force" also was emerging, marked by diverse theories, many new psychotherapies (Garfield, 1981; Piper et al., 2002), and a varying and differing interest in diagnosis and etiology. At the same time, psychodynamic theory was further diversifying and showing a renewed concern for experimental verification (Silverman & Weinberger, 1985; Wachtel, 1997; Weston, 1998). Behavior therapy, meanwhile, was (1) becoming less wedded to theory (Lazarus, 1971), (2) expanding its concern back to at least some aspects of the mind under the influence of the cognitive-behavior modifiers (Dattillo & Freeman, 2008; Beck, Freeman, et al., 1990; Meichenbaum, 1977), (3) developing into a broader perspective on environmental variables under the social learning theorists (Bandura & Walters, 1963; Mischel, 1969), (4) being forced by the pressure of managed care and national health insurance issues into an emphasis on shorter-term and more focused therapies (Piper et al., 2002), and (5) facilitating the overall trend in the mental health field toward a greater emphasis on the experimental verification of assessment and intervention techniques (Dilalla, 2004; Ray, 2004).

Teachers and practitioners alike have reflected the increasing sophistication that is inherent in this maturing and diversification process. Very few would now argue that any one technique or theoretical approach answers all or even most of the diagnostic, etiological, and treatment questions that arise. Certain theories and techniques have more relevance to certain disorders. In this vein, it is interesting that the "sphere of relevance" of an approach is most closely centered on the original group that was studied or treated when the approach came into being.

Freud's specific theories became less relevant as society lost some of the repressions of the Victorian era (possibly only to take on repressions in other dimensions). Carl Jung's treatment techniques, which focus on uncovering "spiritual" yearnings and on creating a sense of meaning, arose primarily in the therapy of middle-aged males who had "made it big" financially and in their careers, but who lived the feelings expressed in the songstress Peggy Lee's classic refrain, "Is that all there is to that?" Just as the client-centered therapy techniques of Carl Rogers seem most appropriate to bright "psychologically minded," and introspective clients (similar to the graduate ministerial and psychology students he first worked with), the behavior therapist's "token economy" is most effective when dealing with clients who are institutionalized and who show marked deficits in basic social and interpersonal skills.

Concomitant with this growing awareness that no one theory or technique holds all the answers is the concept that a number of diverse techniques may be necessary to handle any one case most efficiently. This multimodal approach, first thoroughly developed as a concept by Arnold Lazarus, is an underlying assumption in this book.

The eclecticism inherent in the ideas stated here is another assumption in this book. Hopefully, this allows a broad-based acceptance of many cause-paths to disorder, as well as a more comfortable melding with most specific theories and an absence of an "ingroup" language.

In order to put some of the prior comments in perspective, and to provide a historical framework for the book in general, the following quote is a synopsis of those important historical developments related to mental disorder.

> *The only reason I have dabbled in psychology here is to demonstrate to you that you can use it to arrive at whatever conclusions suit you best. It all depends on who uses it. Psychology tempts even the most responsible and serious people to create fictions, and they cannot really be blamed for that.*
>
> —Defense Attorney Fetyukovich's closing argument
> from Fyodor Dostoyevsky's novel, *Brothers Karamazov*

Major Historical Developments Related to Mental Disorder

Western Society

Early Greeks—Hippocrates (460–377 b.c.)—(a) Provides a focus on the brain as the site of disorder, (b) emphasizes life stressors.

Romans—Galen (2nd century A.D.)—(a) Conceptualizes the hospital as a treatment center, (b) the first thorough classification of disorders.

Age of Crusades—(a) Physicians obtain higher-status social class and greater intellectual influence, (b) the rediscovery of Greek and Roman texts, as well as contact with Near Eastern and Oriental influences, offer new perspectives on abnormal behavior.

1347—From this year to the end of the fourteenth century, the Black Death ravages Europe, destroying lives and signaling the beginning of the end of the "medieval period" in its primary reliance on theological explanations of everyday behavior.

Renaissance (1500–1650)—(a) There is a beginning rejection of witchcraft, (b) naturalistic explanations of emotional disorder attain wider acceptance, (c) in the late fifteenth and early sixteenth centuries former leprosariums are converted into the first asylums or "madhouses."

Enlightenment (1700–1800)—(a) More humane care, (b) keeping of case histories and rudimentary statistics.

Late 1700s—Jean-Baptiste Pussin and then Phillipe Pinel free mental patients from their chains at LaBicetre, a hospital in Paris.

1810—Friedrich Koenig, a German working in London, harnesses steam power to produce the "fast" printing press (i.e., to power a cylinder over a paper sheet lying on a bed of inked type, instead of hand pressing a flat weight on it as was done when Gutenberg invented the first printing press in approximately 1450). Koenig's discovery allows for a much faster dissemination of ideas nationally and internationally.

1865—Gregor Mendel publishes his influential theories of genetics.

1879—Wilhelm Wundt, a professor of physiology at the University of Leipzig in Germany, establishes the first laboratory for the experimental study of psychology.

1883—Emil Kraeplin's influential textbook on psychiatry likens mental disorder to physical disease.

1891—The first description of psychosurgery is published by Dr. Gottlieb Burckhardt, director of a Swiss asylum. This approach was later popularized by Dr. Egas Moniz, a Portuguese psychiatrist, whose 1936 monograph first described the lobotomy. Moniz was awarded the Nobel Prize in medicine in 1949 for this work.

1893—Sigmund Freud, with Josef Breuer, publish the first chapters of *Studien uber Hysterie*. Hypnosis is used to produce spontaneous verbalizations that are theorized to break down psychological repressions, leading to catharsis, and "cure." These concepts parallel the earlier theories of Johann Christian

Heinroth (1773–1843), who asserted that mental illness springs from the conflict between unacceptable wishes and the guilt generated by these wishes.

1905—The first publication of a true IQ scale, the Binet-Simon Scale.

1921—The first publication describing the Rorschach Test. Hermann Rorschach, a Swiss psychiatrist, while riding in the country, had noticed that what his children saw in the clouds reflected their personalities.

United States

Early colonial period—There is a regression to witchcraft and demonology.

1693—The peak of the witch-hunting trials in Salem, Massachusetts.

1773—The first U.S. hospital specifically for mental patients—in Williamsburg, Virginia.

Late 1700s—"Moral therapy" becomes popular.

1812—Benjamin Rush, a signer of the Declaration of Independence and the "father of American psychiatry," writes the first American textbook on psychiatry. He also invents the "tranquilizing chair," a kind of immobile straitjacket.

1842—Dorothy Dix takes a position as a school teacher in a prison. The conditions she encounters stimulate her to become the major reformer of the mental health movement in the nineteeth century.

Circa 1850—Hospital reform movement begins to generate provision of more humane treatment.

Late 1800s—Medical model increases its influence.

1892—The first meeting of the American Psychological Association (APA). In 1925, APA incorporates and eventually adopts its first formal ethics code in 1953.

1892—Responding to an invitation from William James to direct the psychological laboratory at Harvard, Hugo Munsterberg, who had been a student of Wilhelm Wundt, engages in activities that arguably allow him the title "Father of Forensic Psychology," including his 1908 book, *On the Witness Stand*. Munsterberg is also considered the "Father of Industrial Psychology."

1896—Lightner Witmer, often called the "Father of Clinical Psychology," establishes the first psychological clinic in the United States at the University of Pennsylvania.

Circa 1900—Morton Prince pioneers the use of hypnosis in reintegrating (i.e., "fusion") a multiple personality in his case of "Miss Beauchamp."

Early 1900s—Freudian model increases its influence, especially stimulated by Freud's lectures delivered at Clark University in 1909.

1907—Clifford Beers writes *A Mind That Found Itself*, the story of his long-term struggle with his own mental illness and the treatments he encountered. The widespread popular response to his book furthered the reform movement inherited from the efforts of Dorothy Dix.

1913—John Watson publishes his influential manifesto, "Psychology as a Behaviorist Views It." Sometimes referred to as the "Father of Behaviorism," he argues that psychology should abandon the study of consciousness, laying the groundwork for the behavior therapists and for later theorists such as B. F. Skinner. In about 1920, Watson goes to work for an advertising agency and helps to develop advertisement that encourages women to smoke cigarettes.

Early to mid-1900s—Behavioral model increases its influence.

1923—In *Frye* v. *United States* (295 F.1013(D.C. Cir.)), a federal appeals court establishes the standard of "scientific acceptance" for the admission of information based opinions from an expert witness (from all fields, not just psychology) into trial testimony. This remains the standard until 1993, when the Supreme Court, in *Daubert* v. *Merrill Dow Pharmaceuticals*, appeared to allow a much less stringent "helpfulness" (to the court, e.g., the jury) standard in federal trials, an influential though not compelling standard on state courts as well. See Research in the Courts in Chapter 1.

1936—The first psychosurgery in the United States, a frontal lobotomy, by Dr. James Watts and Dr. Walter Freeman, in Washington, DC.

1939—The first publication of the Wechsler-Bellevue Intelligence Scale, the predecessor of the various Wechsler measures of intelligence, the most popular forms of the IQ test.

1943—The first published version of the Minnesota Multiphasic Personality Test (MMPI), devised by Starke Hathaway and Jovian McKinley. It is revised as MMPI2 in 1989.

1946—The first true computer, developed by John Mauchly and J. Presper Eckert, ENIAC (Electronic Numerical Integrator and Computer) is demonstrated at the University of Pennsylvania. In the 1970s, in a patent dispute, a court held that the Atansaoff-Berry computer, built at Iowa State University, was first. But since that ABC computer was only designed to solve parts of linear equations, experts agree that ENIAC deserves the title because of its general applicability. Two essential concepts evolved out of ENIAC: the idea of "stored programs" and the programming tool known as an "if statement." When it was fully operational, ENIAC filled a 30- by 50-foot room, but a $30 calculator today has more computing power.

1951—The first nationwide television broadcast, by Edward R. Murrow.

1952—The first edition of the *Diagnostic and Statistical Manual of Mental Disorders* is published by the American Psychiatric Association. *DSM-IV,* the fourth edition, is published in 1994, and a text revision form (*DSM-IV-TR*) is published in 2000.

1950s and 1960s—Humanistic and cognitive models increase influence; and the advent of a new class of psychotropic drugs, the phenothiazines (e.g., chlorpromazine [Thorazine]), for the first time allow chemical control of psychotic behavior.

Early 1960s—Community Health Act of 1963 and the mental health centers that are subsequently developed change care delivery structure; the related "deinstitutionalization" of patients generates an exodus from the centralized state hospital systems.

1968—Association of Black Psychologists is formed.

2000—Francis Collins, leader of the Human Genome Project, and J. Craig Venter of Celera Genomics independently, yet with some collaboration, complete the first analysis of the human genetic code. The code consists of 3.15 billion letters that provide the instructions for all human genes. Although the code varies among individuals by only about 1 percent, these differences are crucial to the development, and hopefully the control of, many of the physical and mental disease processes in humans.

1980s–present—"Corporatization" of mental health care delivery and the advent of "managed care." Those who pay for services (or their administrators, such as health maintenance organizations [HMOs] and preferred provider organizations [PPOs]) capture the system from those who deliver the services. There is a continuing interest in universal health care, but likely with only modest coverage for mental health.

2008–present—Psychologists are increasingly seeking and attaining prescription privileges. New Mexico and Louisiana were the first states where this has occurred. Also, there is an emphasis on defining empirically validated therapies for specific disorders, i.e., developing a "standard care."

2011–14—Likely publication of *DSM-V*.

> *America is one of the few places where the failure to promote oneself is widely regarded as arrogance.*
>
> —Gary Trudeau, Cartoonist Author of *Doonesbury*

An Outline of the Cases

The first chapter's case in this book, that of O. J. Simpson, clearly highlights the social, legal, and political issues inherent in defining abnormality and subsequently applying that label to an individual. The second chapter, on theories and techniques, first presents the case of Danielle, who manifests a most common problem—a persistent though not constant moderate level of anxiety, several simple phobias, and some allied mild depression. After Danielle's case is detailed, there is an analysis of the etiology and treatment that could be expected from the seven major overall theoretical viewpoints: Psychoanalytic-psychodynamic, Behavioral, Cognitive, Information Processing and Systems Theory, Humanistic-existential, Multicultural, and Biological. The chapter closes with a multimodal treatment approach, wherein techniques from a variety of theoretical perspectives are blended together to treat a case of exhibitionism.

The third chapter, but the first to focus on a specific syndrome, is concerned with anxiety disorders. After a discussion of those three little fellows (Hans, Albert, and Peter) who are classic, early cases in the psychodynamic and behavioral traditions, more severe cases are presented—specifically, Agoraphobia and Obsessive-Compulsive Disorder. This chapter closes with a relatively recent, though now often-used, addition to the *DSM:* Post-Traumatic Stress Disorder, which is considered an Anxiety Disorder.

Chapter 4 combines Dissociative Disorders and Sleep Disorders, since the altered state of consciousness in each provides some interesting contrasts. Dissociative Disorders are exemplified by the case of Anna O., considered the first case in the psychoanalytical tradition, and here seen not so much as a case of hysteria but as a case of multiple personality. Sleep Disorders are exemplified first by a sleepwalking case and then one that combines a disturbance of the sleep-wake cycle with insomnia. Chapter 5 looks at Somatization Disorder (in the case of Empress Alexandra Fedorovna, the wife of the last Czar of Russia, at the time of the communist revolution) and Psychogenic Pain Disorder, commonly observed subtypes of the Somatoform Disorders.

Chapter 6 is concerned with severely disruptive syndromes: Schizophrenic and Paranoid Disorders, as seen in cases of Undifferentiated Schizophrenia and Paranoid Schizophrenia (here exemplified in Freud's classic case of Daniel Paul Schreber). Schizophrenia is a subgroup within the overall conceptual category of "psychosis," which essentially designates a loss of reality contact. The three schizophrenia cases allow a contrast between Paranoid Schizophrenia, the most well-integrated form, and Undifferentiated Schizophrenia, in which the functioning has especially deteriorated. These two forms are then compared with a case of schizophrenia with a positive outcome—that of Nobel Prize winner John Forbes Nash, the focus of the movie *A Beautiful Mind*. The other category of very severe disorders, the Affective Disorders, are detailed in Chapter 7 in cases of Major Depressive Disorder (the case of Joseph Westbecker—a workplace violence case that was also the first major civil trial focusing on the drug Prozac), Postpartum Depression in the case of Brooke Shields, and Bipolar Disorder (the case of Virginia Woolf, a famous writer and a pioneer in the women's movement), and again both of these are often psychotic-level disorders.

In combination with the case of exhibitionism from Chapter 2, the full spectrum of Psychosexual Disorders is seen in Chapter 8. In addition to a case of sexual addiction (the case of William Clinton), a classic general paraphiliac (the case of Jeffrey Dahmer), cases of both male and female sexual dysfunction are noted, as well as a case of Gender Identity Disorder. Then, Chapter 9 (Substance Use Disorders) discusses three of the most common disorder patterns in society: Alcohol Dependence (in the case of Betty Ford), Prescription Drug Abuse (in the case of Elvis Presley), and Nicotine Dependence (in the case of Dr. S.).

Complementing the discussion of addictive patterns in Chapter 9, Chapter

10 discusses eating disorders, with the cases of Karen Carpenter and Christina Ricci focusing on anorexia nervosa, and that of Princess Diana on bulimia nervosa. Chapter 11 has four of the more important personality disorders: the Histrionic, Antisocial, Schizoid, and Malignant Narcissism patterns. Ted Kaczynski, known more popularly as the Unabomber, illustrates the Schizoid Personality Disorder. The antisocial diagnosis is discussed in the case of Theodore Bundy. Malignant Narcissism is discussed in the cases of Hitler, Stalin, and Hussein. This complements the discussion of Paranoid Personality Disorder in Chapter 6 and Borderline Personality disorder in Chapter 17. Somewhat related issues are then found in Chapter 12 (Disorders of Impulse Control), seen in cases of a Borderline Personality Disorder Associated with Rape, Pathological Gambling, and Kleptomania (the cases of Winona Ryder and John Lennon).

Violence patterns are found in several cases throughout this book (e.g., in the cases of O. J. Simpson [Chapter 1], Jeffrey Dahmer [Chapter 8], and others). In Chapter 13, the issue of violence and its causes is specifically addressed in the case of Jack Ruby and the case of the first well-documented serial killer in the United States, and then two cases of family violence. In Chapter 14, the cases of Developmental Language Disorder, Attention Deficit Disorder with Hyperactivity, and Early Infantile Autism point to three of the most critical disorders that emerge in childhood. The Oppositional Disorder and Separation Anxiety Disorder (associated with school phobia) cases then document two common maladaptive channels for the strivings of identity and independence that are often a concern in middle childhood and adolescence. Another case focuses on school shooting. The last case focuses directly on the identity crises and identity disorder.

Chapter 15 offers four cases in which a clearly defined organic factor has caused psychological symptomatology. The first case documents a person's disorder and then virtually complete recovery of psychological functioning subsequent to having an entire half of the brain surgically removed. The second case examines Parkinson's and Pseudo-Parkinson's Disease in the case of Muhammed Ali. The third focuses on Alzheimer's disease, and the fourth case—that of Daryl Renard Atkins—deals with the Supreme Court considering issues of mental retardation and its relationship to the death penalty.

Chapter 16 is concerned with the interaction of psychological disorder and legal issues. Providing a transition from the prior chapter, discussion focuses on the all-important issue of how to discriminate true disorder from malingering, and discusses Munchausen by Proxy, a form of Factitious Disorder, in the case of Marna. The last case, that of John Hinckley, who attempted to assassinate President Reagan, examines the legal concepts of insanity, incompetency (to stand trial), and involuntary civil commitment as it relates to predicting dangerousness. The last chapter focuses on the development of positive mental health.

The full spectrum of cases provided by this book should develop an awareness of the diversity inherent in the modern study of abnormal psychology.

1 Concepts of Abnormality

Adultery: Consensual non-monogamy.
Corrupt: Morally challenged.
Looters: Nontraditional shoppers.
Drug addicts/alcoholics: People of stupor.
Sadomasochists: The differently pleasured.

A few entries from Henry Beard and Christopher Cerf,
The Official Politically Correct Dictionary and Handbook

The first case in this book, that of O. J. Simpson, dramatically highlights some of the problems in merely defining abnormal behavior. A traditional method of defining abnormal behavior has been to use statistical norms. However, this only establishes extremes and does not per se discriminate between positive and negative patterns or characteristics. Also, some widespread patterns (e.g., drunk driving, anxiety) may be labeled as normal because of their commonness.

Defining *abnormality* as the absence of optimal or ideal characteristics is another possibility. The problem, however, is then simply shifted: What is "optimal" and who decides (Meyer & Weaver, 2006; Schneider & Leitner, 2002)? Also, most normal individuals are not that close to "ideal."

In any case, most people will generally agree that abnormal behavior is behavior that significantly differs from some consensually agreed upon norm and that is in some way harmful to the differently behaving person or to others. More specifically, components of a judgment of abnormality often include the following descriptors:

Deviant	*Deviant* refers to behavior that differs markedly from socially accepted standards of conduct. In many cases, the word has negative connotations.
Different	*Different* also suggests behavior that varies significantly, at least statistically, from the accepted norm, but it does not usually have negative connotations.
Disordered	*Disordered* implies a lack of integration in behaviors; the result may be impairment of a person's ability to cope in various situations.

Bizarre   *Bizarre* suggests behavior that differs extremely from socially
                 accepted norms. In addition, it connotes inadequate coping
                 patterns and disintegration of behavioral patterns.

If we like a man's dream, we call him a reformer;
if we don't like his dream we call him a crank.
—William Dean Howells, Writer (1837–1920)

The *DSM*s

The general framework for this book is in the diagnostic terminology of *DSM-IV-TR* (American Psychiatric Association, 1994). Even though there are valid criticisms of the *DSM*s (Greenberg, Shuman, & Meyer, 2004), it is the official document of the American Psychiatric Association, it is approved by the American Psychological Association, and it is well respected by all varieties of mental health workers, both nationally and internationally. The first *DSM* was published in 1952, *DSM-II* in 1968, *DSM-III* in 1980, and *DSM-III-Revised* in 1987. There were numerous changes from *DSM-III-R* to *DSM-IV-TR*, published in 1994, with further changes in *DSM-IV-TR* in 2000 (American Psychiatric Association, 1994, 2000). Indeed, the simple listing of changes took up 28 pages in the *DSM-IV-TR* book. A concise list of some of the more important changes is as follows: Only the Personality Disorders and Mental Retardation remain on Axis II; Rett's Disorder, Childhood Disintegrative Disorder and Asperger's Disorder have been added as Childhood Disorders; there is no separate category of Attention Deficit Disorder, it is subsumed under ADHD; there is now a separate overall category of Eating Disorders; there are now two separate Bipolar Disorders, with Bipolar Disorder I referring to the traditional, severe form, where both recurrent manic and depressive patterns are observed; the phrase "outside the range of normal human experience" has been deleted as a criteria for PTSD, and the related category of Acute Stress Disorder has been added; the term Multiple Personality Disorder has been changed to Dissociative Identity Disorder; Passive-Aggressive Personality Disorder has been deleted as an Axis II Personality Disorder but has been retained in revised form as a "Criteria Set . . . for further study"; two new patterns in "other conditions that may be a focus of clinical attention" are "Religious or Spiritual Problem" and "Acculturation Problem."

Rates of Mental Disorders

There have been numerous efforts over the last several decades to effectively apply definitions of abnormality to determine overall rates of mental disorder. Earlier endeavors provided some useful data. However, the first major study is known as the Epidemiologic Catchment Area (ECA) study wherein, researchers interviewed 17,000 individuals in five different cities/areas. They found a 33 percent lifetime prevalence rate, with anxiety disorders as the most common disorder type. They also looked at rate differential among different geographic areas: schizophrenia, organic brain disorder, alcohol and drug abuse, and antisocial personality disorder were highest in the central city, less so in the suburbs, and lowest in rural areas; depression was somewhat evenly distributed; somatization disorders, panic disorders, and some affective disorders were a bit higher in rural/small town areas. The only disorder more common in the suburbs was obsessive-compulsive disorder (Robins & Regier, 1990).

A subsequent set of two studies, the National Comorbidity Study (NCS) and the NCS-R, was even more extensive than the ECA. They had numerous methodological improvements and "sampled" the entire U.S. population (Kessler, Berglund, Demler, Jin, & Walters, 2005). They concluded that the lifetime prevalence rate of having any *DSM-IV-TR* disorder is approximately 45 percent. However, because they did not include schizophrenia, eating disorders, autism, or several of the personality disorders in this specific assessment, it is reasonable to infer that the lifetime prevalence rate of mental disorders is over 50 percent. Because these were better designed studies than the EPA study, one has to give more credibility to the 50 percent figure. In the NCS and NCS-R studies, anxiety disorders are the most prevalent category, and the most common specific disorders are major depression, specific phobias, and alcohol abuse. Of course, some of the disordered individuals included in these statistics manifested the disorder only briefly and/or mildly. These studies also found a high but variable level of comorbidity (two or more disorders in the same person at the same time). Half of those with a severe disorder had a comorbid disorder, while only 7 percent of those with a mild disorder had a comorbid disorder.

In general, all of the major studies suggest that overall median age of onset is less than 25 years of age. There has been an increasing prevalence of emotional disorder in persons born after World War I, especially for affective disorders (Reinecke, Washburn, & Becker-Weidman, 2008). Also, it is estimated that about 20 to 30 percent of those diagnosable as mentally ill never receive any treatment. And only about 20 percent of these receive care from mental health specialists; most receive it from medical practitioners other than psychiatrists.

Issues relevant to these points, issues, and statistics will occur throughout this book, and several are especially evident in this first case of O. J. Simpson.

> "Is Adolf Hitler crazy?" Bohner asked eventually—the sort of damn-fool question too many people ask as soon as they hear a man is a psychologist.
> —Len Deighton, Goodbye, Mickey Mouse (1982, p. 136)

A Presumably Normal Person Potentially Viewed as Pathological

The famous, or infamous, case of O. J. Simpson highlights many of the conceptual and diagnostic dilemmas that often confront mental health professionals. What sort of psychopathology, if any, led to his behavior within the episode of June 17, 1994?

Was he a psychopath? Did he deteriorate into some sort of psychotic state at some point? On what dimension(s) is he reasonably construed as normal or abnormal?

The Case of O. J. Simpson

O. J. Simpson literally and figuratively ran to the forefront of the American consciousness. We first knew him as a dazzling running back at the University of Southern California (USC), where he won the Heisman Trophy. Then he went to the pros with the Buffalo Bills and the San Francisco 49ers where he was the first running back to gain 2,000 yards in one season and was named to the Pro Football Hall of Fame in 1985. We next saw him running through airports in Hertz Rent-A-Car commercials, during the time when he also had some previously forgettable roles in movies such as *The Towering Inferno* and *The Naked Gun* and was a commentator on *ABC Sports Monday Night Football*. However, he had become an American icon, or, as one television executive commented, "He was Michael Jordan before Michael Jordan."

Tragically, the last time his running was highlighted in our consciousness was when we saw him running on Friday night, June 17, 1994, when the nation watched the police pursue him in his white Ford Bronco, along with his friend Al Cowlings, in an almost funeral march down a Los Angeles freeway. In sum, until June 17, 1994, the public's perception of O. J. Simpson, in addition to appreciation of his substantial athletic talent, was of an easygoing, articulate individual—that is, as normal, if not much more normal, as anyone in the public eye. After that date, information kept accumulating to suggest a very different picture.

O. J. was born on July 9, 1947, and was named Orenthal James Simpson, the name Orenthal coming from an obscure French actor. His early childhood appears to have been relatively unremarkable, although his father had abandoned the family when O. J. was just a toddler. A reaction against his awareness that his father was both gay and dysfunctional may in part explain O. J.'s alleged "macho" patterns. His mother, Eunice, a strong and supportive figure throughout his life, raised O. J. and his three siblings by working as an orderly on a psychiatric ward.

Ironically, the boy who was to grow up to be one of the greatest running backs in football history was called "Pencil Legs" as a child and had to wear leg braces until age 5 because of a diagnosed case of rickets along with a calcium deficiency. He remained pigeon-toed and bowlegged, and his deformed extremities contrasted with his large head, subjugating him to taunts such as "Headquarters" and "Waterhead."

However, as O. J. developed into adolescence, he moved from defense to offense. Although he was probably never a hard-core delinquent, he came close. In junior high school, he became a bully, and at age 14, he joined a "fighting gang," the Persian Warriors. He received his sexual initiation from the gang's "ladies auxiliary," and also managed to get caught stealing from a local liquor store. The myth is that a talk with baseball legend Willie Mays pushed him back onto a positive path. Reality is that his mother's directing him toward a small private Catholic school placed him with a much more positive peer group and also allowed him to attain a more positive identity by demonstrating his emerging athletic skills. He did so, leading the city in scoring his senior year.

Recruiters came flocking. But, contrary to image, O. J. was never overly bright, nor was he a good student, and he didn't have adequate grades for a major college. So he enrolled in the City College of San Francisco. He starred in football and was able to get grades that were at least adequate (and, in those days, adequate wasn't much) to accept a scholarship at USC. There, he became an All-American, won the Heisman Trophy in 1968, and gained "polish." He learned to dress well, to talk well, and to communicate an amiable and easy-going image. However, he was not a student-scholar and dropped out before earning his degree. But he went on to stardom while a pro and then gradually developed into an American icon, a beloved and almost universally recognized hero.

O. J.'s private life was less admirable. He was reputed as a chronic womanizer, but he told us that his devout Baptist wife "brings the Lord into our house and helps me when I sway" (and he swayed a lot). Although he stayed married for 11 years to Marguerite, the marriage was marked by several separations and by O. J.'s womanizing. He also reportedly abused Marguerite. He denied this. He was believed, as was often the case (Kubany, McCaig, & Laconsay, 2004).

He reportedly had a drug problem. He clearly did use marijuana. A Buffalo television station reported that the owner of a bar that Simpson frequented stated that O. J. had been snorting coke during his years with the Bills and twice came very close to being busted. In any case, O. J. was believed—at least by the NFL. He told *Playboy* magazine that he had experimented with drugs (marijuana) only once, as an adolescent, but that he "just pretended to take a hit." Even President Bill Clinton didn't try to say he "only pretended," just that he didn't inhale. Clinton was not believed; O. J. was.

In the most publicized abuse incident, on New Year's Eve of 1989, during his second marriage, a hysterical and severely bruised Nicole came out of the bushes in a bra and underpants to report "He's going to kill me" to the officers responding to a 911 call. When O. J. came out, he said, "I got two women and I don't want that woman anymore," shouted at the officers, and drove off. But Nicole later refused to testify, and charges were dropped. O. J. told Frank Olsen, the CEO for Hertz (who paid O. J. a great deal as its advertising spokesperson), and the public that it was only

an argument and was "no big deal and there was nothing to it." Olsen, Hertz, and the public believed. We all wanted to believe, and our behavior may be a form of abnormal behavior, as it is certainly maladaptive.

O. J. had met his second wife, Nicole Brown, then 18 years old, in June 1977 at a nightclub where she was waitressing. This was just before celebrating his tenth wedding anniversary with Marguerite, who was carrying their third child. O. J. and Nicole were quickly involved, but O. J. and Marguerite were not divorced until later, in 1980. The relationship with Nicole was stormy from the beginning, as he was very controlling (and she no doubt contributed in some fashion) and was easily made jealous, although he was reportedly already consistently unfaithful to her. When Nicole became pregnant in 1985, they worked out a complex prenuptial agreement and were married. The child was born on October 17, 1985. Nine days before, the police made their first documented response to a distress call at 360 Rockingham. O. J. had knocked the front window out of the car with a baseball bat, and the responding officer found Nicole sitting on the hood of the car. Nothing came of it. During the next four years, until the New Year's episode, Nicole made at least 8 and up to 30 distress calls. (It is unclear how many there were because no charges were filed.)

After the New Year's episode the marriage went further downhill, marked by drug and alcohol abuse by both O. J. and Nicole and by public and private conflict. The divorce was finalized in October 1992. Nevertheless, O. J. and Nicole periodically reconciled and split up from that time until Nicole was killed late Sunday night of June 12, 1994.

There is evidence that just prior to the killings, O. J. was getting clearer messages from Nicole that there was no longer any chance whatsoever of a reconciliation. Also, at 7:00 A.M., 15 hours before the killings, Paula Barbieri, a model who was dating O. J., left a message on his phone recorder that his relationship with her was also over. Though this was not revealed until after the criminal trial, another model, Gretchen Stockdale, testified

(continued)

The Case of O. J. Simpson   Continued

during the first trial, but outside the jury's presence, that O. J. had left her a phone message about three hours before the slayings, saying he was "finally . . . totally unattached with everybody."

Much of the data would at least suggest that O. J. killed Nicole, along with Ronald Goldman, who was returning a pair of sunglasses she had left at a restaurant. Goldman was also a friend of Nicole's and possibly a lover. Note that O. J. did make a pledge to continually work to find the true killer; appar-

ently he feels certain that the killer will most likely be found on a golf course in Florida. Despite significant enough evidence to hold O. J. civilly accountable for the murders of Nicole and Mr. Goldman, many still hold on to the belief that O. J. was innocent or in some way had deserved a break. Not surprising to others, O. J. has continued to have significant legal problems, including his 2007 arrest on charges of kidnapping, armed robbery, and assault with a deadly weapon for his alleged involvement in a robbery at a Las Vegas hotel.

Standards of Proof

As most readers are aware, O. J. Simpson was unanimously found "not guilty" (note that once there is a trial a criminal suspect is never formally found to be "innocent") of the criminal charge of murder (Meyer & Weaver, 2006). However, he was subsequently and unanimously found legally responsible in the civil trial by a different jury for the deaths of the two victims. Some commentators have argued that race played a factor, since the jury in the criminal trial was largely black, whereas in the civil trial, it was all white. Although that may be the case, certainly a critical factor was the different standards of proof required (i.e., "beyond a reasonable doubt" for most criminal trials and a "preponderance of evidence" [for most, assume this means just over 50 percent] in the civil trial).

O. J. Simpson's difficulties in the child custody area highlight the third legal standard of proof (i.e., "clear and convincing evidence"). This third standard is intended to fall between the other two and thus applies to quasi-criminal procedures (i.e., where there is an imposed loss of one's constitutional rights). This standard could apply only to such procedures as the termination of parental rights—upheld in the 1982 Supreme Court case of *Santosky* v. *Kramer* (455 U.S. 745), later dramatized in the movie *Kramer vs. Kramer* starring Dustin Hoffman and Meryl Streep—or in civil commitment cases, where one is placed in a mental hospital because he or she has been found to be both mentally ill and imminently dangerous to self or others.

Diagnoses and Syndromes

Whether he did kill Nicole or not, O. J. Simpson's overall behavior was certainly abnormal at times. Did it warrant a formal *DSM-IV-TR* diagnosis? Both O. J. and Nicole probably suffered from substance abuse and codependency. There is evidence that both experienced periods of significant depression and/or anxiety, and that O. J. was evidently suicidal after the incident. In addition to a *DSM-IV-TR* diagnosis, patterns of abnormality, or syndromes (as opposed to *DSM-IV-TR* diagnoses) may apply "the battered spouse syndrome" and "codependency." A *DSM-IV-TR* diagnosis is generally accepted as having more credibility and validity than a syndrome (Greenberg, Shuman, & Meyer, 2004).

Many such syndromes have appeared (or been publicized) in recent years. Some, such as the battered spouse syndrome (BSS), have at least stood the test of time. Others have surfaced only momentarily, quickly to disappear.

Battered spouse syndrome (BSS) (then the battered *woman* syndrome) defense was first successfully employed in 1977 in *State* v. *Grieg*. This Yellowstone County, Montana, court allowed testimony about the violence a woman had experienced in her marital relationship and how this might have made her psychologically unable to leave her husband. The jury voted to acquit, on self-defense. Since that time the BSS has been used in numerous cases, with varying success. It has often been intermingled with the concept of the *DSM-IV-TR* diagnosis Post-Traumatic Stress Disorder (PTSD) (Melton et al., 1997) (see Chapter 3). The early use of PTSD (a diagnosis accepted in the *DSM*s) and, to a lesser extent, of BSS (a syndrome) in the legal arena often portrayed the victim client as severely disordered, almost psychotic-like at times, as a result of the trauma. More recently, both PTSD and BSS have been portrayed as "normal" or expected responses to a severe trauma (Kubany, McCaig, & Laconsay, 2004).

A *syndrome* is defined in *Webster's Third International Dictionary* as "(1) a group of symptoms or signs typical of a disease, disturbance, condition or lesion in animal or plants; (2) a set of concurrent things: concurrent." Various other definitions of *syndrome* contain most of the same elements, with the general idea being that a syndrome is a group of behaviors or events that is reported or observed with consistency. For the specific issues here, syndromes are reports of observed patterns of behavior that are predictably precipitated by some event.

There are difficulties conceptually with defining behaviors as abnormal in any syndrome. First, there is the clear implication that in some way or degree, a consequent critical behavior has been compelled. For example, when establishing the BSS in an assault or murder case, the clear purpose is to void some degree or even all of the perpetrator's responsibility for the behavior. The standard argument, at least by implication, is that the establishment of the syndrome's existence de facto mutes or voids responsibility. At the same time, it is evident that (1) only a minuscule percentage of battered spouses ever criminally assault or murder their abusers, (2) there is no clear variable or set of variables that differentiates those who do from those who don't murder, and (3) if there is a valid case for the behavior as self-protection, the availability of the more legally acceptable self-defense claim negates the need for the establishment of a syndrome.

To highlight the positives and problems of syndromes as a quasi-diagnosis, I have presented on several occasions (Meyer & Weaver, 2007) for consideration the issue of the possible validity of the "estranged spouse syndrome" (ESS). One of the clearest and most well-known examples that appears to demonstrate this syndrome is O. J. Simpson, as all of the essentials of the syndrome are seemingly found in his case:

1. One spouse (O. J. [A]) is evidently still in love with or emotionally dependent on the other (Nicole [B]).
2. B is disengaging from A, but, because of ambivalence, concern for A's feelings, fear of A, and so on, B provides mixed messages.
3. Some event or series of events transforms A's intellectual understanding that there is a disengagement into an emotional or "gut-level" awareness that it is "over."
4. A becomes severely emotionally disrupted by a sense of loss, often confounded by feelings of shame, humiliation, betrayal, jealousy, and so on.
5. Depression, anxiety, and anger grow in A in a variable admixture.
6. In some cases, personality predispositions of A (and often to some degree in B as well) combine with a catalytic event, such as seeing B with a new lover or losing another important relationship (possibly facilitated by easy access to means and the use of disinhibiting substances), causing emotional arousal and disruption to peak, and very likely to spill into anger and on occasion into homicidal and/or suicidal ideation and behavior.

The point is that one can argue that the ESS—and for that matter, a number of other patterns of behavior—shows the consistency required of a syndrome. I also believe one could establish that the ESS shows a consistency that is at least equal to that of the BSS (Meyer & Weaver, 2007). The dilemma, then, is whether "consistency" of behavior should allow inference that the behavior was to some degree "compelled," and, in turn, to allow a perpetrator to argue less or even an absence of responsibility for a related act. Legal cases have generally accepted this "compulsion based on consistency" in clear cases of BSS, but not very often in most other syndromes. The dilemma is confounded by the fact that there is little scientific data to allow definitive conclusions; thus, political issues may dominate. (See the discussion, later in this chapter, on the admission of scientific evidence into the legal arena.)

Perceptions of Abnormality

It is interesting that sociopolitical assumptions are often critical to a judgment of abnormality (Greenberg, Shuman, & Meyer, 2004). In earlier times, certain similar behaviors in a person of prestige might be termed "romantic" rather than abnormal. For example, although the renowned music composer Hector Berlioz composed his *Symphonie Fantastique* out of his love for the Irish actress Harriet Smithson, he had not succeeded in meeting her by the time that work was introduced in December 1830. He became engaged to a 19-year-old pianist, Camille Marie Moke, just before he left for Italy as a Prix de Rome fellow early in 1831. In April, he received an unpleasant letter from his fiancée's mother, announcing Camille Marie's marriage to another man. Berlioz wrote in his memoirs that he was so outraged that he determined to return in disguise and kill them all: "As for subsequently killing myself, after a coup on this scale it was of course the very least I could do." People saw this as a demonstration of Berlioz's romanticism rather than abnormality, in part because of the attitudes of the time and also because he never actually did it. In fact, he eventually married Harriet. Truly, there are times when a judgment as to deviance is "in the eye of the beholder."

> *Applied psychology will . . . become an independent experimental science which stands related to the ordinary experimental psychology as engineering to physics. Politicians, military officers, and even clergymen have awakened to the utility of psychology; the lawyer alone is obdurate. . . . The lawyer and the judge and the juryman are sure that they do not need the experimental psychologist. They go on thinking that their legal instinct and their common sense supplies them with all that is needed.*
>
> —Hugo Munsterberg, *On the Witness Stand* (1908)

Guidelines for Judging Abnormality

General guidelines have evolved throughout history, modern research studies, and across most cultures that are consistently relevant to a judgment of abnormality. These criteria can be summarized as follows:

- Some recurring behaviors that seem indicative of potential, developing, or existent mental disorder are (1) inability to inhibit self-destructive behaviors, (2) seeing or hearing things that others in the culture agree are not there, (3) sporadic and/or random outbursts of violence, (4) consistent inability to relate interpersonally in an effective manner, (5) persistent academic and/or vocational failure, (6) anxiety and/or depression, and (7) inability to conform to codes of behavior whether one verbalizes a desire to do so or not.
- The most consistent criteria for deciding whether any specific individual is abnormal are (1) the deviance (or bizarreness) of behavior from the norms of that society, (2) the continuity and/or persistence of disordered behavior over time, and (3) the resulting degree of disruption in intrapersonal and/or interpersonal functioning.
- The continuum of behavior ranges from clearly normal adjustment to definitely abnormal adjustment. Many people's behavior belongs in that middle area where judgments about abnormality are difficult. A specific abnormal behavior pattern is seldom inherited genetically, but genetic factors may play a part in predisposing a person to abnormality of one sort or another.
- The causes of any one abnormal behavior pattern are usually multiple.
- Indicators of abnormality are not necessarily obvious or flagrant. In many cases, the signs are uncommon and/or subtle.
- Both long-term and transient social value systems affect judgments as to whether a person is abnormal.
- A psychological handicap often has a more negative effect on interpersonal relationships than does a physical handicap.
- The label of psychological abnormality often remains with a person even after the disorder no longer exists. Such a label, people's expectations and responses, may prolong the psychological disorder.

■ In most societies, there is a substantial overlap between judgments of mental abnormality and criminal behavior (i.e., the same specific behavior may receive either label, depending on who is doing the labeling).

I am starved for love and I almost believe wicked science is guilty.
—Letters of Albert Einstein

The Scientific Method

A prominent change relevant to mental health that has evolved especially in modern times is the recognition of the need for scientifically valid information (Larson et al., 2007). As Table 1.1 shows, all research methods can be useful. For an excellent example of how a natural event observation can be both scientifically valid, see the section on etiology in Alzheimer's disease in Chapter 15. In most instances, the idea, or the model, or the paradigm must eventually be validated via a well-designed experiment.

The evolution of scientific knowledge typically occurs in the following sequence: (1) general ideas and insights; (2) observations, often in clinical cases; (3) initial theories; (4) hypotheses; (5) operational definitions; (6) experiments; (7) new theories and models or paradigms; (8) new hypotheses; (9) further experiments; and (10) new models or paradigms, and revised theories.

TABLE 1.1 Positive and Negative Aspects of Research Methods

Method	Positive Aspects	Negative Aspects
Case Study	a. Generates new theories b. Records rare situation c. Inexpensive and easy to carry out	a. Highly subject to selective and observer bias b. Cannot generalize the results c. Cannot determine any true cause
Natural Event Observation	a. Allows study of major event and overall cause b. Is not artificial	a. May introduce observer bias and/or disturb a natural event b. Cannot repeat the event; difficult to generalize any results
Correlational Design	a. Allows quantification and b. Need not be artificial, although often is	a. Cannot define the specific cause replication
Experiment	a. May control, insolate, and define specific causes b. Allows manipulation of variables, repetition, and generalization	a. May become overcontrolled or too focused, thus becoming artificial and missing the reality of the issue b. The control that is available is subject to unethical methods and abuse of subject rights
Model or Paradigm	a. Provides new insights and hypotheses and coherence between specific issues	a. Attachment to model may blind one to data that are contradictory

A *theory* is a statement about the probable relationship among a set of variables. It organizes existing knowledge of a phenomenon, provides a tentative explanation for the phenomenon, and generates predictions (hypotheses) about the phenomenon. A *hypothesis* is a prediction of some relationship between variables, or of an experimental result. After data have been collected, a theory may be arrived at inductively. *Induction/inference* is the process of drawing a general conclusion from a set of specific instances or statements (i.e., the process of using events or statements to draw a conclusion that is *probably* true).

After a theory has been constructed, hypotheses are arrived at deductively. *Deduction* is the process of drawing specific conclusions for a general statement (i.e., the process of using events or statements to draw a conclusion that must be true). In deduction, if the premises are true, the conclusion must be true; if the conclusion is false, then at least one premise is not true; if the conclusion is true, the premises *might* be true. Hypotheses may be tested with research. If the hypotheses are not borne out, the theory has been deductively *falsified* (the theory, as it is, cannot be true). If the hypotheses are borne out, the theory has been inductively supported (the theory is consistent with the new data, but some other theory may also predict the same results). Logically, a theory can be falsified, or proven wrong, but can never actually be truly and definitively confirmed. In summary, a good theory (1) accounts for most or all available data, (2) predicts new findings, (3) is subject to testing and falsification, and (4) is *parsimonious* (i.e., it should be as simple as possible).

Type I and Type II errors can be confusing. Those who are confused by the distinction might feel like the old sea captain who, on each and every morning when out at sea, would arise, have a cup of coffee, open a small drawer in his desk to which only he had a key, peruse a piece of paper, and then take the helm. This went on for over 40 years. Then, one day, he gracefully died at the wheel. The other ship's officers all rushed to his room and forced open the drawer, only to find a piece of paper on which it was written "Starboard is to the right, port to the left." In any case, a *Type I error*, or a false positive, tells a person something (e.g., a treatment technique) works when it doesn't; or in the legal arena, there is a conviction of an innocent person. A *Type II error*, or a *false negative*, says a procedure does not work when it actually does; in legal lingo, a guilty person is found not guilty.

Issues about the validity of various research studies are common in most fields, certainly including psychology. The following information suggests ways one might go about obtaining more valid research.

> *Replication:* A major fault in many fields is the acceptance of findings from unreplicated studies (or worse, only from clinical case observation), especially when the original finding was obtained by someone with a vested interest in that finding and/or a related theory. Science makes much of its progress in a plodding fashion, not just by new insights and innovative research.

The Use of Adequate Control Groups: Indeed, some research has only an assumed control group. Often, more than one type of control group is needed but is often not included.

Adequate Sample Size: If sample size is not adequate, a few extreme responses can distort the data so as to make it appear there is a group effect of some significance, even if most of the group changed only minimally.

Representative Samples: Using Psychology 101 students is defensible in many stages of research, but samples that represent society as a whole need to be considered before any significant generalizations can be attempted.

"Blind" Participants: One of the biggest problems in psychological research is the relative lack of experimenters who are blind to the purpose of the study. This lack may be acceptable at the initial stages of a research program, but it should be controlled for in later stages. To the degree feasible, and within the constraints of reasonable informed consent, research participants should also be blind to the purpose of the study.

Dualistic Thinking: Always tempting, this type of thinking simplifies things to separate the self into mind and body, psychology and biology. The Law of Parsimony does state that if two hypotheses are equally powerful in explaining data, one should prefer the simpler hypothesis. But, many times—not only in science but also in areas such as courtroom trials—one accepts the less explanatory but simpler physiological reasoning. An excellent example of a study demonstrating mind-body interdependence is that of Schwartz and colleagues (1996), as discussed in the case of Bess in Chapter 3.

Reasonable Levels of Significance: The traditionally accepted .01 and .05 levels of significance were not set in stone by some god of research, but are accepted as a result of consensus decision rules. As such, they may not always work well. For example, in an exploratory study using a small number of participants, reaching a significance level of only .15 may be valuable, as it can be used to refine the research to a point where a higher significance level may be appropriate.

Clinical versus Statistical Significance: Although empirically validated findings are much more valuable than clinical case generated findings, the difference between "statistical significance" and "clinical significance" is sometimes overlooked. For example, a relaxation technique may produce an average decrease of two points of blood pressure, hardly of clinical significance. But, if the sample size is huge, this will attain "statistical" significance, and may confer some undeserved validity on the relaxation technique.

Giving Credence to Pseudoscience

Unfortunately, the media often give much attention to the claims of a pseudoscience, such as astrology. There are several markers of a pseudoscience. First, personal testimonials and anecdotal evidence, including clinical experience, are often used as a means of proving hypotheses. Second, pseudoscience emphasizes the confirmation of—rather than the refutation of—hypotheses. Eminent scientists, such as the physicist Richard Feynman, assert that the hallmark of a true science is bending over backward to prove oneself wrong. Pseudoscientists often ignore or inappropriately dismiss evidence that contradicts their theory. In fact, they are inclined to place the onus of proof on critics rather than on themselves. Third, pseudoscience tends to use scientific-sounding terms that are intended to impress rather than explain. Last, pseudosciences have little or no "connectivity" to other sciences or reputable intellectual disciplines, and do not build on or contribute to existing scientific knowledge.

Research and the Courts

A critical societal issue is how the findings of science are brought to bear on issues in the courtroom (e.g., the acceptance of DNA evidence, or the rejection by most courts of the results of polygraph tests). The standard that has dominated this issue is the "Frye Rule," established by a federal appeals court in 1923, and stated as, "It is sufficiently established to have gained general acceptance in the particular field to which it belongs."

In 1993, in *Daubert* v. *Merrill Dow Pharmaceuticals* (113 S.Ct. 2786), the Supreme Court established a new, theoretically less stringent standard, verbalized as a "helpfulness standard" (i.e., the decision rule is whether the information is viewed by the judge as helpful to the trier of fact). This standard is mandatory in federal courts. Although it has been adopted by some state courts, states may retain the more restrictive "scientific acceptance" standard. The more restrictive standard does help juries from having to cope with the questionable value of "fad" or "junk science" findings. Curiously, the *Daubert* decision *suggested* possible guidelines for deciding whether evidence was valid, but the Supreme Court emphasized that not all, or even any, of these guidelines need be used by the judges. However, over time, trial judges have been inclined to use most or all of the guidelines, making the *Daubert* criteria [upheld in *Kumho Tire Co.* v. *Carmichael*, 119 S. Ct. 1167 (1999)] more restrictive, and thus possibly less helpful, than the Frye Rule. Also, both the *Kumho* and the *Daubert* decisions have brought an emphasis on the trial judge as the "gatekeeper," who decides whether expert witness testimony is admissible in an individual case. Since trial judges vary widely in their knowledge of both the scientific method and the relevant content area, *Daubert* has brought a degree of chaos to these decisions.

2 Theories and Techniques

There is today a diversity of approaches to the assessment and treatment of mental disorders. Many of these treatment techniques can be blended into multimodal individualized intervention programs. This chapter begins by discussing the case history of Danielle. It then examines how the major theories would explain how these problem patterns came about and what they would each propose as the primary treatment plan.

Multiple Theoretical Views on Moderate Anxiety, Depression, and Simple Phobias

Complaining that he suffered from acrophobia, which is the abnormal fear of heights, the athlete said, "I went to Paris and visited the Eiffel Tower last year. I started going up and then I quit. I couldn't stand the height."

The athlete was Billy Olson, who had just set a world indoor pole vault record of 19 feet, 5-1/2 inches.

—*Sarasota Herald Tribune* (February 11, 1996)

The case of Danielle is concerned with a most common pattern—one that includes some simple phobias as well as persistent although not constant moderate anxiety and depression. Many people at one time or another suffer from similar disorders. However, many do not seek professional treatment, for a variety of reasons ("It costs too much to see a shrink"; "I don't think they could help me"; "That kind of stuff is only for people who are really crazy"; "Nobody in my family has ever gone to a psychologist so I just couldn't go to one"; etc.). However, such attitudes are especially unfortunate here, as the prognosis for controlling problems such as Danielle's is good.

After the presentation of Danielle's case history, discussion will focus on how the major theories (psychoanalytical-psychodynamic, behavioral, cognitive, information processing systems, humanistic-existential, and biological) would approach the etiology and treatment of her disorder.

The Case of Danielle

Danielle, who has just turned 26 years old, presented herself to a university-based psychology clinic with complaints of problems with her work and marriage, as well as just being generally unhappy. A structured interview and several psychological tests were administered. What emerged was a picture of a young woman who had suffered from a variety of phobias as well as varying degrees of depression and anxiety throughout most of her life. Yet, from most perspectives, she had usually functioned within the normal range on most dimensions. She had a normal childhood, and both Danielle and her parents would have characterized her as reasonably well adjusted and happy. Her grades were above average throughout grade school and high school, and although Danielle struggled academically in college, she did manage to graduate with a business degree, with a major in marketing. She started to work on her MBA but felt "just burnt out" with school. So she quit to take a lower-echelon job in the marketing department of a large firm in a major city about 300 miles from the area where she grew up and went to college.

Danielle was introduced to her future husband shortly after moving to that city, and they were married after a brief but intense courtship of four months. This intensity waned almost immediately after the marriage ceremony, and they settled into a routine marked neither by contentment nor by obvious problems. They seldom fought openly, but they developed increasingly "parallel lives," wherein interactions (including sexual ones) were pleasant but minimal.

Embedded in this overall life structure were the difficulties that had moved Danielle to come to the clinic. Ever since she had been little, Danielle had been afraid of snakes and insects, especially spiders, and from her high school years onward, she became anxious if closed in for any length of time in a small room (claustrophobia). She also reported that she occasionally experienced periods during which she would feel anxious for no reason that she could put her finger on ("free-floating anxiety") and then, more rarely, would become depressed. Once, when she was in college, the depression became severe enough that she considered suicide. Fortunately, her roommate was sensitive to the crisis. She made sure Danielle went over to the campus counseling center, and Danielle's upset diminished quickly enough for her to quit therapy after three sessions.

More recently, Danielle had experienced the episodes of anxiety and depression more consistently, and it was clear that her husband didn't have much interest in hearing about all this. Also, she still had the phobias. She could live with the fears of the snakes and spiders, although they substantially reduced her ability to enjoy outdoor activities. But the claustrophobia had worsened, making some of the meetings required by her job very difficult for her.

Danielle's history was not grossly abnormal in any dimension, but there were aspects that could be related to her developing problems. Although Danielle's birth was normal, she was noted to be a "fussy" child and seemed to startle more easily than did her two younger brothers. Also, her mother was a rather anxious person and on a few occasions had taken to her bed, obviously somewhat depressed, blaming it on "female problems." Both parents obviously loved and cared for all the children, but Danielle's father was not one to show affection very often. He demanded good performance, in both the academic and social areas, and a lack of performance usually meant some form of direct punishment as well as emotional distance from him.

Case Analysis

An analysis of this case will be made from the perspective of each of the major theories, and some other more specific details that emerged in Danielle's case will be discussed as appropriate. The discussion of each of these theoretical perspectives on etiology and treatment will not be presented in great detail. Also, the most commonly accepted theories and treatments for anxiety and depression will be discussed again in the later sections of this book that focus on those problems.

The Psychoanalytic-Psychodynamic Perspective.   Psychoanalysis is the approach originally devised by Sigmund Freud and then elaborated by his early and more orthodox followers (Larson et al., 2007). As changes in theory or technique were introduced by persons who still followed the essential points of Freudian theory, these splinter schools (developed first by individuals such as Adler and Jung and later by Klein, Horney, and Sullivan and more recently by Kernberg, Gill, Bion, Ricoeur, Arieti, Silverman, Shafer, Kohut, Mahler, and others) were usually termed *psychodynamic* (Schwartz et al., 1996; Wachtel, 1997; Weston, 1998).

However, virtually all of those theorists would see Danielle's problems as developing out of an inadequate resolution of conflicts that could have developed in one of the hypothesized stages of development that each person, as represented through the "ego," must proceed through to reach maturity (the oral, anal, phallic, latency, and genital stages). Conflicts in the Oedipal phase (a prelude to the genital stage), interpreted as the male child's desire to sexually possess the mother and get rid of the father (the Electra phase is analogous in the female) are seen as crucial to a number of patterns. (See the discussion in Chapter 3 of Little Hans.) Underlying tension leaves the person anxious without an explanation for this feeling (Fenichel, 1945), the free-floating anxiety experienced by Danielle.

Regarding depression, Karl Abraham's early classic papers (Abraham, 1916) provided the basis for the orthodox psychoanalytic view. He theorized that depressed individuals, unable to love, project their frustrated hostility onto others and believe themselves to be hated and rejected by other people. Abraham related depression to orality and explained loss of appetite and related symptoms in terms of an unconscious desire to devour the introjected love-object. Thus, introjection (rather than the projection that psychoanalysts see as central to the paranoid process) is the psychopathological process, and the depressive's self-reproach can therefore be seen as an attempt to punish those newly incorporated components of the self.

Psychoanalytic treatment involves techniques like (1) "free association" (having the person say whatever comes into mind, without censoring it—a more difficult task than it may initially appear); (2) analysis of dreams; (3) analysis of the feelings the client develops toward the therapist (transference); and (4) attempts to develop insight into the sources of the anxiety and depression. All of this is directed toward gaining a rational, objective attitude toward the self, with symptom relief or happiness as secondary and possibly not realizable goals. Orthodox analytic treatment, which is practiced by very few therapists today, would have the analyst sitting behind the client, who is on a couch, seldom either confronting or responding to the client at any length. To the degree that the therapy is less orthodox, and thus more likely to be termed psychodynamic, the therapist is more likely to face the client, confront issues more directly, and in general interact more. The insights that are attained, along with the accompanying release of emotion (catharsis), theoretically act to decrease the anxiety and depression and thus allow the development of more mature and effective coping patterns.

The perspective inherited from Freud has been rightly criticized for being difficult (and sometimes impossible) to empirically validate. However, in a landmark paper, Weston (1998) has described findings in various disciplines such as developmental, social, and cognitive psychology that support psychoanalytic theory in general. He has described several of Freud's central postulates that have received substantial empirical support, including (1) the preponderance of feelings, motives, and thoughts are unconscious; (2) childhood and early development play a critical role in personality and adult relationships; (3) mental processes, including emotion and affect, often operate in parallel, and can be in direct opposition to each other; (4) mental representations of the self and others influence social interactions and may generate psychological symptoms; and (5) mature personality development involves learning to regulate sexual and aggressive impulses, and from a dependent to an independent state.

The Behavioral Perspective.   Early efforts by behaviorists to explain the development of anxiety and phobias were essentially efforts to translate psychoanalytic thought into the language of learning theory. However, beginning with John Watson and Mary Cover Jones (see the discussions of Little Albert and Little Peter in Chapter 3), early practitioners such as Joseph Wolpe and Arnold Lazarus and later theorists such as Clark Hull and B. F. Skinner, the explanation of the development of anxiety and phobias was in terms of conditioning principles. Thus, anxiety is a learned response that now is unpleasant but that was appropriate at the time of learning. However, the avoidance inherent in the response prevents the corrective learning of newer, more adaptive responses.

From the behavioral perspective, the two major ways in which the anxiety responses and phobic patterns (and the depressive responses) are learned are *modeling* and *direct experience learning,* which are then amplified by mental and behavioral rehearsal. An examination of Danielle's history revealed that modeling played a significant role in the development of her anxiety and phobic responses with regard to snakes and insects. As is the case with most people who have such fears, there was no actual, naive traumatic encounter with one of these creatures. Rather, Danielle's mother, as well as her aunt who often babysat her, would shriek with horror at the sight of a spider, or even the suggestion that a snake might be in the vicinity. At some level of consciousness, Danielle assumed that if these gigantic and all-powerful adults (from the perspective of a small child) were so afraid of these beings, she ought to be, too. Her responses, copied from her model, were accepted and reinforced by those around her. Note that the differential stereotypical reaction to such responses in boys may explain why such patterns are not so usually evident in males. Also, boys are more likely to be encouraged to have actual encounters with these potential phobia sources. In any case, although modeling can often be an efficient way of learning, as it does save the time and possible pain of trial-and-error learning, sometimes, as with Danielle, modeled patterns may promote maladaptive behavior.

The simple phobias, of which Danielle's fears of snakes and spiders are good examples, often have simple and specific targets. Since some of these fears likely had an evolutionary value for the human species (e.g., avoidance of poisonous snakes, etc.), some theorists believe this is evidence that there is a greater *preparedness* to associate anxiety responses to these stimuli, and this contributes (along with the modeling) to the overall learning process here.

On the other hand, direct experience learning was critical to the origin of Danielle's claustrophobic pattern. When she was young, her usual punishments were spanking, being made to stand in the corner, or a withdrawal of reinforcers (staying up late, TV, etc.). However, if she really upset her mother, Danielle would be forced to stay in a small, dark closet until she was quiet and her mother felt calmed down. On a couple of occasions this took several hours. The anxiety and discomfort of the situation, compounded by Danielle's fear of the dark and sense of uncertainty about what was going to happen to her, produced a panic response. Panic includes a sense of loss of control, the most anxiety-generating experience of all. Direct experience learning is a potent factor in the development of many phobias.

Regarding depression, the general theories of the early behaviorists were first refined into an overall theory by Ferster in 1965; the general concept is that depression can result from either of two processes (Ferster & Culbertson, 1982), which do not necessarily exclude parallel biological issues. In the first, an environmental change (e.g., loss of job, death in the family) sharply lessens the level of incoming reinforcement, and no new methods of obtaining reinforcement have developed. Danielle's college depression immediately followed the break-up with her boyfriend. They had always spent a great deal of time together, so this abrupt loss of reinforcement precipitated the depression in that instance.

Behaviorists also note that depression can occur from a pattern of avoidance behavior. This is when a person's attempts to avoid aversive situations have become so strong that they preclude behaviors that bring reinforcement; that is, these behaviors are used to avoid anxiety.

From a treatment perspective, behavior therapists have pioneered some of the most successful treatments for phobias and anxiety, even using such approaches as group therapy (Saiger, Rubenfeld, & Dluhy, 2008). The most commonly used technique, however, has been exposure therapy, especially in the specific form of systematic desensitization therapy (SDT). Typically, the therapist first develops a relaxation response, sometimes through drugs but more commonly and controllably through some form of relaxation training. A hierarchy of anxiety-producing stimuli is then produced and presented, and may be enhanced by virtual reality technique—for Danielle, this involved closed spaces, snakes, and spiders (Wolpe, 1973).

In each case, Danielle would be asked to describe the most anxiety-arousing situation she could think of in each category. That scene (e.g., "snakes crawling over my body") would receive a score of 100. A scene that brings on little or no anxiety (e.g., "hearing my professor mention snakes") would receive a 0. While remaining relaxed, the client is gradually moved through each hierarchy in imagination (*in vitro*), and then some live tasks (*in vivo*) may be introduced (e.g., asking Danielle to handle a snake or sit for a period of time in a small closed room).

An alternative behavioral technique for phobias or anxiety is *flooding*, or *implosion therapy*, which attempts to maximize anxiety rather than minimize it, as is done in SDT. Usually carried out in a few longer-than-usual sessions, the technique asks the person to imagine more and more anxiety-producing scenes (e.g., snakes crawling in and out of body orifices). Virtual reality procedures are being used to enhance this method. The theory is that the anxiety will eventually peak and then extinguish, with the consequence that the phobia gradually lessens.

As for Danielle's depression, modern behavior therapists would emphasize getting her in touch with more interpersonal contacts and sources of positive reinforcement (Horowitz, 2004). For her, this could mean returning to active sports and learning social skills so that she could have more rewarding interpersonal interactions. Since depressives tend to be overwhelmed by tasks, breaking a goal down into subtasks and short-term goals (the "graded-task" approach) is useful.

Also, behavior therapists would help Danielle survey her present range of activities. Since depression tends simultaneously to lessen activity in general and increase the percentage of nonpleasurable activities, contracting, modeling, and stimulus-control techniques could help to reverse this process.

Morita therapy, developed by a Japanese professor named Morita, is an approach that combines both behavioral and cognitive elements, as is evident in these two quotes from David Reynolds (1984), long one of the foremost interpreters of Eastern psychotherapy techniques to Western cultures:

> Behavior wags the tail of feelings. Behavior can be used sensibly to produce an indirect influence on feelings. Sitting in your bathrobe doesn't often stimulate the desire to play tennis. Putting on tennis shoes and going to the courts, racket in hand, might. (p. 100)

> Awareness, awareness, awareness. That is where we live. That is all we know. That is life for each of us. (p. 4)

A Morita therapist would (1) attempt to bring a regular routine into Danielle's life; (2) deemphasize talking about the historical antecedents to her problems; (3) emphasize the growth possibilities in all experiences, including pain and failure; (4) try to get her to begin to function "as if" she was psychologically healthy and competent; and (5) emphasize bringing both attention and awareness into all facets of her day-to-day functioning.

The Cognitive-Behavior Perspective.   Since *cognition* refers to a person's thinking pattern, any theorists who talk about disordered thinking patterns as critical to the development of psychopathology can be considered to be cognitive theorists, and now are more commonly referred to as cognitive behavior therapists (Dattillo & Freeman, 2008). In that general sense, psychoanalytic and psychodynamic theorists also have a cognitive perspective (Wachtel, 1997).

However, a more focused emphasis on cognition as central to the development of anxiety is found in the pioneering works of people such as Albert Ellis and George Kelly and such later therapists as Donald Meichenbaum and Aaron Beck. Kelly's theory of "personal constructs" notes that people develop certain beliefs, of which they may be consciously unaware, that cause them anxiety. Ellis (2002) similarly has commented on how people adopt such belief-rules as "I must reach a high point of success in whatever I undertake" or "If I ever show aggression or upset to those people close to me, they won't love me." (Not surprisingly, no one can ever fully live up to such standards, and anxiety and depression quite naturally ensue.)

Aaron Beck, the winner of the 2004 Grawemeyer Award for outstanding contributions to psychology, focused on the development of depression from cognitive beliefs, and the theory evolved from an initial study (Beck & Valin, 1953) that indicated that themes of self-punishment occurred with great frequency in the delusions of psychotically depressed clients. Beck would not disagree with the psychodynamic theorists that an early traumatizing event could predispose an individual to depression. However, the major focus is on distorted thought patterns. Beck and others note that depressives have developed thought processes that simultaneously (1) *minimize* any positive achievements; (2) *magnify* problems with "catastrophic expectations" (i.e., "making mountains out of molehills"); (3) tend to view issues in extremes, (i.e., to *polarize* their ideas, seeing only in black or white, no greys); and (4) *overgeneralize* to a conclusion based on little data, (e.g., one or two events). These tendencies are often compounded by a sense of "learned helplessness," a view that one cannot do anything to really control or change one's world. Low self-esteem, lessened activity, negative mood, and self-punitiveness follow (Reinecke et al., 2008; Alford & Beck, 1997; Barrett & Meyer, 1992; Beck & Valin, 1953).

As for intervention, Albert Ellis, who was functioning as a cognitive-behavior therapist before anyone even used that term, would directly challenge his client's irrational beliefs. For example, Danielle believed that she could never again be happy, and that if she were to leave the marriage, no one would ever find her attractive again. Ellis (2002) would directly confront these beliefs, exploring what the implications and consequences would be if indeed these irrational hypotheses were true. This would then be followed by challenges to act in accord with the more rational beliefs that the client has now labeled as more likely to happen.

Beck also tries to help clients bring their beliefs and expectations into consciousness and/or clearer focus, although he is a bit less confrontational than Ellis in this process. He then helps them explore new beliefs. Meichenbaum (1986) goes a step further by first helping clients eliminate negative subvocal verbalizations (e.g., "When things in my life do not go the way I want them to, it is bad or terrible"). He then helps the clients develop alternative sets of positive self-statements (e.g., "When things don't go my way, it may be unpleasant, but it's not the end of the world. Sometimes things do go my way; sometimes they don't") to use by consciously and periodically repeating to themselves. Such therapists readily agree with the clients' protests that they will not believe what they are saying. However, if they persist, it does have an effect. Helping client engage in positive imaging of successful and competent behaviors, possibly through hypnosis, can help here as well.

Information Processing and Systems Theory. Modern variations of the cognitive approach, pioneered by people such as Noam Chomsky, Walter Mischel, George Kelly, and James Grier Miller, are information processing, the sociocultural perspective, and systems theory, and they often overlap. They are obviously influenced by evolving concepts from computer science and from interdisciplinary studies, and they share a belief in two seemingly paradoxical concepts: (1) Emotional disorder is a universal human experience, even in many of its specific manifestations; and (2) the pattern and experience of emotional disorder can be strongly influenced by the amount and types of information that are obtained from the persons, families, and society around that individual, while the diagnosis and treatment are likewise affected by that information. Paradoxically, high use of the Internet has been associated with increased interpersonal withdrawal and depression. Consider this information processing example described by Mischel (1986):

> A boy drops his mother's favorite vase. What does it mean? The event is simply that the vase has been broken. Yet ask the child's psychoanalyst and he may point to the boy's unconscious hostility. Ask the mother and she tells you how "mean" he is. His father says he is "spoiled." The child's teacher may see the event as evidence of the child's "laziness" and chronic "clumsiness." Grandmother calls it just an "accident." And the child himself may construe the event as reflecting his "stupidity." (pp. 207–208)

Information theorists use the terms of computer science—for example, "*hardwired* for sex" (it is built in genetically) or "brain *software*" (information provided from the outside that is developed into what George Kelly referred to as a "personal construct," a personal myth about life, such as, "Your family members are the only people that you can really trust").

Psychological disorders are discussed as disorders of *input* (e.g., faulty perception), *storage* (e.g., amnesia from brain trauma), *retrieval* (e.g., selective recall as in paranoia), *manipulation of information* (e.g., via defense mechanisms), and *output* (e.g., the "flight of ideas" in mania). There is also a focus on how individuals *encode information.* For example, aggressive young males as well as those who watch a large amount of violent programming on television (and these groups do overlap somewhat) are more likely to encode neutral behaviors of others as threatening. Similarly, when males receive messages from their environment (e.g., "When women say 'no' and they don't appear very angry, they really mean 'yes'"), they may be more likely to misinterpret signals or statements from women they are interested in, a fertile situation for date rape.

Sociocultural theorists such as Thomas Szasz, who pioneered the concept of the "myth of mental illness," and R. D. Laing take this a step further to propose that the cause of abnormal behavior is to be found in society rather than in the individual who manifests a disorder. They look to the conflict and stress engendered by social problems (e.g., poverty, discrimination, social isolation) or the messages embedded in a society's overall structure as the explanation for psychological disorder. For example, Laing often speaks of "unjust societies"as creating psychological disorder in the oppressed. The weakness of the sociocultural perspective has always been trying to explain why certain individuals in the same conditions are affected with manifest disorder, while others are not.

The Humanistic-Existential Perspective.   From a humanistic viewpoint, anxiety and depression are a result of cultural and social structures that impede the full expression of the personality (Everly & Lating, 2004; Maslow, 1954; May, 1981; Rogers, 1961). The psychodynamicist sees these emotions as determined early in development and maintained by defense mechanisms. The behavioral therapist argues that they are a function of experience with a variety of conditions that results in patterns being learned, unlearned, and relearned throughout life. However, the humanist sees anxiety and depression as inevitable as long as societies thwart a person's goodness and inborn drive for self-actualization. Anxiety and depression are therefore functions of the society and will continue until the right kind of social atmosphere is made available (Schneider & Leitner, 2002).

Two conditions often implicated by the humanists are a repressive society and/or poverty. Poverty obviously limits the options a person can take, not only in development of the self but also in remedying disorder and deficit. Within a repressive society, fear of self-expression forces the individual to adopt constricted or disordered response patterns, with anxiety or depression as a common concomitant response.

Humanists emphasize that the person receiving treatment should not be considered a "patient," but instead is a "client," putting more emphasis on equality in the relationship. Curiously, the word *client* derives from the Latin word for an underling who leans on a patron in a fawning, subservient manner—so perhaps a better word is needed.

Humanists would contend that because the individual is forced to sacrifice to social demands that are inconsistent and arbitrary, the defense strategies that he or she adopts reflect the irrational nature of the society. Anxiety and depression may therefore be a prerequisite for existence in a chaotic world (May, 1981).

Because of the limitations and constraints of society, pure humanists may not focus very much on the concerns of an individual client. They often feel their energy is better directed at righting the original causes. Indeed, Carl Rogers, the founder of nondirective, or client-centered, therapy, virtually ceased doing any individual therapy in favor of working with whole subgroups from the perspective of a humanistic educator and social engineer. Directly attacking conditions generated by poverty would not be relevant with Danielle, although it might be with some other cases in this book (e.g., see the case of Abby in Chapter 13 on family violence and child abuse). It is true that some aspects of Danielle's problem might be relevant to change by humanistic social engineering, but it is unlikely there would be enough benefits to directly help her in any immediate sense.

Some parts of the community psychology movement are quite consistent with the humanistic approach. The idea here is that a change in social conditions, through educational efforts or a redirection of social variables, will change the level of disorder (or more likely, act to prevent emergence of that disorder in persons vulnerable to it in the future).

Existential psychotherapists such as Viktor Frankl and Medard Boss are more concerned about the individual "choices" of the client. Like cognitive therapists, they would directly confront the distorted beliefs of the client, probably placing more emphasis on the absurdity or paradoxes inherent in the particular individual's conditions in the world (Frankl, 1975). At the same time, they might well change the focus of the problem from the original causal conditions—be they social forces, biological disorder, early environment, or whatever—toward the choices the individual has to make in the here and now (Boss, 1963). This focus on the present is also a constant theme in Gestalt therapy, which has strong existential and cognitive components (Bongar & Beutler, 1995).

Although existential theories are most closely associated with European philosophy and psychology, they are not unknown in other cultural traditions. For example, the Akan people of Ghana believe that all people are endowed with the capacity for correct thought and correct action, and emphasize that each individual is ultimately responsible for his or her own life situation, a central tenet of existentialism. A technique termed *Sunsum*, or *NTU*, is a primary principle of the Bantu people and focuses on personal responsibility. A related saying ("Mmo'denbo' Bu Musuo Abasa So," translated as "If you try hard, you will always break the back of misfortune") was the central theme of the 1997 International Convention of the Association of Black Psychologists.

With Danielle, an existential therapist would likely point out that preoccupation with her anxiety and depression allows her to escape responsibility for making choices in her world. The "parallel life" that has been established in her marriage could go on indefinitely, as do many "conflict-habituated" marriages. Making authentic choices can change these and similar patterns. But those choices leave the person open to the burden of responsibility for their consequences. An existential therapist would try to get the individual to stop evading any important choices and their consequences (Frankl, 1975).

Existentialists are also likely to have their clients squarely face the responsibility for past choices or, as is often the case, the results of avoiding a choice (Boss, 1963). This commonly entails "guilt," and existentialists emphasize the difference between neurotic guilt and true guilt. *Neurotic guilt* is the experience of anxiety and depression from situations that the person had no part in bringing about, such as restrictive early parenting practices. *True guilt* entails the acceptance of responsibility for conscious choices or a lack of choosing and the willingness to live with a full acceptance and awareness of the consequences that cannot be changed, with efforts now being made to right any negative effects that can be changed. Here, anxiety and depression, especially the free-floating anxiety that Danielle occasionally experienced, are seen as possible symptoms of the avoidance of authentic choices and true guilt.

The Biological Perspective.   Anxiety and depression from the biological perspective are seen as conditioned by a person's physiology (Dattillo, Davis, & Goisman, 2008; Andreassi, 2000; McCullough, 2002; DiLalla, 2004). Also, some physiological conditions may be genetically determined. In Danielle's case, there are indicators that she may have had some genetic disposition to developing anxiety responses; she was a "fussy" child, was easily startled, and had an anxious mother.

The fact that Danielle's mother had apparently been depressed would lead to the suggestion that Danielle's occasional depression had a strong genetic component. However, this, of course, would have allowed Danielle to model the behavior as well, and she would have suffered the "contagion effect," wherein depressives increase the depressive patterns in nearby normals. Findings that (1) children who experience a clinical depression in childhood or (2) adolescents who have frequent multiple unexplained physical symptoms are more at risk for clinical depression in adulthood may fit the biological model.

The major biological theories of depression are typically a variation on the theme that depression reflects an alteration in the level of brain transmitters (chemicals that facilitate nerve transmission to the brain), such as norepinephrine or serotonin. This may be moderated by proteins such as P11 that regulate how brain cells respond to serotonin and dopamine. For example, the brain releases dopamine when a reward is attained, and this dopamine release generates positive feelings. The curious part is that more dopamine is released to the degree that the reward is unexpected, which may explain the pleasure obtained in such diverse activities as gambling and fishing. However, it should be remembered that a variety of external or psychological conditions (e.g., situationally generated stress or anxiety, prolonged inactivity, prolonged low sunlight conditions, and various substances such as caffeine and the "beta-blockers" used to treat high blood pressure and heart pain) can produce physiological changes that in turn generate depression (Johnson, 2008). Evidence does show that genetic variables play a part in significant endogenous (internally generated) depression. However, all indications are that major components of Danielle's depression were exogenous, or reactive to the situational problems in her world.

The traditional biological treatment for anxiety emphasizes chemotherapy with the drugs usually referred to as the "minor tranquilizers"—for example, meprobamate (Equanil) or the benzodiazepenes such as diazepam (Valium) (Bezchlibnyk-Butler & Jeffries, 1999). However, psychological techniques, such as relaxation training, can also be effective in reducing even the physiological components of anxiety.

For depression, the biological theorist has *traditionally* used one of two major chemotherapies, the MAO inhibitors and the tricyclics, for any significant depression. Both have significant side effects (MAO inhibitors may produce toxic cardiovascular and liver reactions as well as problematic interactions with certain foods;

tricyclics may produce dizziness as well as heart and gastrointestinal disorders). Both require trial-and-error adjustments (titration) on dosages, and both take from several days up to several weeks to show an effect. Some believe that these drugs deal with differentially generated depressions (i.e., the tricyclics for norepinephrine-based depression, MAO inhibitors when it's serotonin based). Also, tricyclics seem to work better with depressives who show some delusional characteristics, and are helpful for chronic pain patients who are depressed. Other newer drugs (e.g., the selective serotonin reuptake inhibitors [SSRIs] such as Lexapro) offer fewer side effects and different modes of action (see Table 7.1 in Chapter 7). When depression accompanies physical pain, which is not uncommon, duloxetine is a drug of choice. In any case, research does indicate that all of these drugs, when they are effective, act at least in substantial part by increasing the frequency of activity-related behaviors, and they only indirectly and unpredictably change interpersonal and cognitive components (Nathan et al., 1995).

Because not all severe depressions react positively to chemotherapy, and because it is a delayed reaction even when they do, electroconvulsive therapy (ECT) and, less commonly, psychosurgery are sometimes used for depression. These interventions seem to be useful with severe, acute depressions, especially where there is a suicidal component, since the delay in the developing effects of the antidepressants then is even more problematical. Even in the relatively small proportion of cases where ECT and psychosurgery are effective, one needs to balance any gain with the irrevocable nature of this type of intervention and the several potentially severe side effects. A newer biological approach that offers promise is "vagus nerve stimulation." In this treatment, a pacemaker-like device the size of a pocket watch is implanted in the body. It sends small electric shocks into the vagus nerve in the neck. This approach has improved mood in a number of severely depressed patients who have not responded well to other treatments.

The Multicultural Perspective.   Some disorders show a remarkable consistency across cultures (e.g., schizophrenia); in others, the content of the pattern is affected by one's culture (e.g., the named characters [Jesus Christ, Allah] in a delusional system; see Chapter 6). It is also true that in some instances, both the pattern and content of a disorder are set by the culture, as in the examples shown in Table 2.1.

In addition, some mental health care (often not enough) is provided in virtually all cultures. For example, in Bregbo, a fishing village near Abidjan, Ivory Coast, in Africa, there is a monument to Albert Atcho, a legendary healer known as the Prophet. With his large starfish-shaped rings, Atcho, who died in 1990 at the age of 84, is said to have cured thousands of people, sons and daughters of the rich and poor alike, who streamed to his home from far and wide. Although Atcho's powers were considered by his constituents to be a gift of God, his techniques clearly blended a warm and supportive acceptance, much like Carl Rogers's "unconditional positive regard," hypnotic-like suggestion techniques, and the facilitation of catharsis and commitment by way of a lengthy confessional process. The various types of mental health providers found in the United States and most Western countries will now be considered.

TABLE 2.1   **Culture-Bound Syndromes**

Numerous patterns of aberrant behavior and troubling experience are recognized mostly in specific localities or societies, and may not be linked to an official diagnostic category. Here are some of them:

Pattern	Where Recognized	Description
Amok	Malaysia; similar patterns elsewhere	Brooding followed by a violent outburst; often precipitated by a slight or insult; seems to be prevalent only among men
*Anorexia nervosa	United States and some other Western cultures	The culture-bound aspect is reflected in the disproportionate occurrence in upper-middle and upper-class white females
Ataque de nervios ("attack of nerves")	Latin America and Mediterranean	An episode of uncontrolled shouting, crying, trembling, heat in chest rising to the head, verbal or physical aggression
Bilis, colera, or muina	Many Latin groups	Rage perceived as disturbing bodily balances, causing nervous tension, headache, trembling, screaming, etc.
Boufee delirante	East Africa and Haiti	Sudden outburst of agitated and aggressive behavior, confusion, and mental and physical excitement
Brain fag	West Africa; similar symptoms elsewhere	"Brain tiredness," a mental and physical reaction to the challenges of schooling
Dhat	India; also in Sri Lanka and China	Severe anxiety and hypochondria associated with discharge of semen and feelings of exhaustion
Falling out or blacking out	Southern United States and Caribbean	Sudden collapse; eyes remain open but sightless; the victim hears but feels unable to move
Ghost sickness	Native American tribes	Preoccupation with death and the dead, bad dreams, fainting, appetite loss, fear, hallucinations, etc.
Hwa-byung	Korea	Symptoms attributed to suppression of anger (insomnia, fatigue, panic, fear of death, depression, indigestion, etc.)
*Koro	Malaysia; related conditions in East Asia	Sudden intense anxiety that sexual organs will recede into body and cause death; occasional epidemics
Latah	Malaysia; Indonesia, Japan, and Thailand	Hypersensitivity to sudden fright, often with nonsense mimicking of others; trance-like behavior
Locura	United States and Latin America	Psychosis tied to inherited vulnerability and/or life difficulties; incoherence, agitation, hallucinations, possibly violence

TABLE 2.1 Culture-Bound Syndromes

Mal de ojo ("evil eye")	Mediterranean and elsewhere	Sufferers, mostly children, are believed to be under influence of "evil eye," causing fitful sleep, crying, sickness, fever
*Multiple Personality Disorder (MPD)	United States	Though a controversial position, many experts view MPD as a culture-bound phenomenon
Pibloktoq	Arctic and subarctic for Eskimo communities	Extreme excitement, physical and verbal violence up to 30 minutes, then convulsions and short coma
*Qi-gong psychotic reaction	China	A short episode of mental symptoms after engaging in Chinese folk practice of qi-gong, or "exercise of vital energy"
Shen-k'uel or shenkul	Taiwan and China	Marked anxiety or panic symptoms with bodily complaints attributed to life-threatening loss of semen
Sin-byung	Korea	Syndrome of anxiety and bodily complaints followed by dissociation and possession by ancestral spirits
Spell	Southern United States	A trance in which individuals communicate with deceased relatives or spirits; not perceived as a medical event
Susto ("fright" or "soul loss")	Latin groups in United States and Caribbean	Illness tied to a frightening event that makes the spirit leave the body, causing unhappiness and sickness
*Taijin kyofusho	Japan	An intense fear that the body, its parts, or functions displease, embarrass, or are offensive to others
Zar	North Africa and Middle East	Belief in possession by a spirit, causing shouting, laughing, head banging, etc.; not considered pathological

*Included in the official *DSM-IV-TR* system.
Source: Adapted in part from *Diagnostic and Statistical Manual of Mental Disorders,* Fourth Edition (Washington, DC: American Psychological Association, 1994).

The Various Mental Health Professionals

Just as there are various theories and techniques, there is a variety of mental health professionals. This can be confusing to laypersons and even professionals, such as judges. For example, in *Jaffee* v. *Redmond* (116 S.Ct.; 64 L.W. 4490, June 13, 1996), the Supreme Court created a new "evidentiary privilege" that supported confidentiality in federal cases for psychotherapy clients of clinical psychologists, psychiatrists, and clinical social workers. The Court did not support it for other types of social workers, or any type of counselor, citing lack of definition of the speciality and/or weak credentialing-training requirements. In any case, the following is a list of the various titles.

Clinical Psychologist: Has a master's degree and a Ph.D. or Psy.D. in psychology, with specialized training in assessment techniques (including psychodiagnostic tests) and research skills, along with skills in intervention, is increasingly (depending on the state) allowed to prescribe psychotropic medications

Counseling Psychologist: Has a Ph.D. or Psy.D. in psychology; traditionally, though not necessarily, works with adjustment problems (e.g., in student health or counseling centers) not involving severe emotional disorders

Experimental Psychologist: Has a Ph.D.; provides much of the basic and applied research data that allow one to progress in the study of human behavior

Clinical Social Worker: Has a master's degree in social work, sometimes a B.A., and very occasionally a Ph.D., with a specialized interest in mental health settings

Psychiatrist: Has an M.D., with a specialization in emotional disorders, just as other physicians might specialize in pediatrics or family medicine

Psychoanalyst: Usually has either an M.D. or Ph.D., with a training emphasis in some form of psychoanalytic therapy

Psychiatric Nurse: Has an R.N., sometimes with an M.A., with specialized training for work with psychiatric patients

Pastoral Counselor: Has a ministerial degree with some additional training in counseling techniques, to help clients whose emotional difficulties center on a religious or spiritual conflict

Specialty Counselor: A technician of the mental health field; often has no higher than a bachelor's degree, and sometimes less than that, but with specific training to assist in the treatment of a specific focus problem (e.g., alcohol and drug abuse problems, or sexual problems)

> *"That's nice," she said. But seeing him struggle she wanted to laugh. What a misshapen and ridiculous thing the penis was! Half of them didn't even work properly and all of them looked pathetic and detachable, like some wrinkled sea creature-like something you'd find goggling at you and swaying in an aquarium.*
>
> —Paul Theroux, *Doctor Slaughter* (1984, p. 140)

An Overall Perspective on Treatment Change

Early studies of psychotherapy include work by such pioneers as Carl Rogers (the first person to audiotape a therapy session for research purposes) and Tim Leary (yes, the Timothy Leary of LSD 1960s notoriety, and the godfather of Winona

Ryder [see Chapter 12]) and the first meta-analytic studies of psychotherapy (Smith, Glass, & Miller, 1980). Seligman (1995) and others have reviewed these studies, including a massive study by *Consumer Reports* and another meta-analysis by Bickman (2005), to generally conclude the following:

1. Psychotherapy is effective; the average person who is treated is about 75 percent better off than untreated control subjects.
2. Long-term treatment is better than short-term treatment.
3. No specific treatment modality is clearly better for some disorders.
4. Medication plus psychotherapy is not consistently better than psychotherapy alone.
5. The curative effects of psychotherapy are often more long term than those of medication.
6. The effective use of psychotherapy can reduce the costs of physical disorders.
7. There is no clear evidence that psychologists, psychiatrists, and social workers differ in *treatment* effectiveness.
8. All three of these groups are more effective than counselors or long-term family doctoring.
9. Clients whose length of therapy or choice of therapy was limited by insurance or managed care did worse than those without such limits.
10. Approximately 5 percent of persons who seek treatment do get worse, usually not markedly so (Nolan, Strassle, Roback, & Binder, 2004).

Prochaska, DiClemente, and Norcross (1992) have provided a useful model for change behaviors. Although designed originally to respond to substance-abuse behaviors, it is helpful for responding to virtually all disorders. They conceptualize change as occurring in five stages:

1. *Precontemplation:* The person avoids any confrontation of true issues and generally denies realistic consequences.
2. *Contemplation:* There is at least some acknowledgment of responsibility and problematic consequences and at least a minimal openness to the possibility of change, although effective change has not yet been instituted.
3. *Preparation:* This is the decision point. There is enough acknowledgment of problematic behaviors and consequences that the person can make the required cognitive shift to initiate change.
4. *Action:* There is a higher sense of self-liberation or willpower, generating sets of behaviors toward positive coping and away from situations that condition the undesired behavior.
5. *Maintenance:* Efforts are directed toward remotivation and developing skills and patterns that avoid relapse and promote a positive lifestyle.

The following, adapted from Prochaska, DiClemente, and Norcross (1992), lists the major change processes that are embedded in the various treatments and theories. They are listed in the order in which they occur in the overall change process: Consciousness raising is more likely to occur in the precontemplation and contemplation stages, and self-disclosure and trust are more likely to be central to the action and maintenance processes.

Consciousness Raising: Increasing information about self and problem: observations, confrontations, interpretations, bibliotherapy

Dramatic Relief: Experiencing and expressing feelings about one's problems and solutions: psychodrama, grieving losses, role playing

Environmental Reevaluation: Assessing how one's problem affects physical environment: empathy training, documentation of effects

Self-Reevaluation: Assessing how one feels and thinks about oneself with respect to a problem: value clarification, imagery, corrective emotional experience

Choice and Commitment: Choosing and committing to act or believing in the ability to change: decision-making therapy, New Year's resolutions, logotherapy techniques, commitment-enhancing techniques

Reinforcement Management: Rewarding one's self or being rewarded by others for making changes: contingency contracts, overt and covert reinforcement, self-reward

Self-Disclosure and Trust: Being open and trusting about problems with someone who cares: therapeutic alliance, social support, self-help groups

Counterconditioning: Substituting alternatives for problem behaviors: relaxation, desensitization, assertion, positive self-statements

Stimulus Control: Avoiding or countering stimuli that elicit problem behaviors: restructuring one's environment (e.g., removing alcohol or fattening foods), avoiding high-risk cues, fading techniques

Sociopolitical: Increasing alternatives for nonproblem behaviors available in society: advocating for rights of repressed, empowering, policy interventions

CHAPTER

3

The Anxiety Disorders

Everyone experiences anxiety at one time or another. In the anxiety disorders, anxiety is either consistently experienced or at least occurs when the person attempts to master the symptoms. Some disorders formerly referred to as *transient situational disturbances* are now included among the anxiety disorders in the Post-Traumatic Stress Disorder and Acute Stress Disorder (a new addition in *DSM-IV-TR*) categories. These are the Anxiety Disorders categories: Agoraphobia, Social Phobia, Specific Phobia, Panic Disorder, Generalized Anxiety Disorder, and Obsessive-Compulsive Disorder.

Agoraphobia, as seen in the case of Agnes, the second case in this chapter, is a fear of being left alone or finding oneself in public places in which one could be embarrassed and unable to find help in case of sudden incapacitation. In a *social phobia*, people fear and avoid situations in which they might be open to scrutiny by others. They are afraid of being embarrassed or humiliated and often avoid such situations as public speaking or being called on in class. The simple phobia diagnosis is often referred to as a *specific phobia*, and is the focus in the first set of cases, The Three Little Boys. In a *panic disorder*, the person experiences recurrent, unpredictable panic attacks. The *generalized anxiety disorder* is characterized by consistent physiologically experienced anxiety without a primary syndrome manifesting phobias, panic attacks, obsessions, or compulsions. The diagnostic emphasis is on muscle tension, apprehension, and autonomic overreactivity. The *obsessive-compulsive disorder*, discussed in detail in the upcoming case history of Bess, is a relatively common and debilitating disorder that is often difficult to treat.

The post-traumatic stress disorders are reactions to psychologically traumatic events that would elicit symptoms in most people (e.g., rape or assault, kidnapping, military combat, and disasters). The characteristic response involves reexperiencing the traumatic event, depressive and/or withdrawal responses, and a variety of autonomic symptoms, and it is described in the cases of the September 11, 2001, attacks and Paul, found at the end of this chapter.

Fear has many eyes and can see things underground.
—Miguel de Cervantes (1547–1616)

The Three Little Boys: Hans, Albert, and Peter

A Study on Anxiety

Hans, Albert, and Peter are all young boys who became famous in the mid-1920s as a result of being experimental-clinical subjects of Sigmund Freud, John Watson, and Mary Cover Jones, respectively. Freud published his theory of the origin and cure of anxiety based on information learned from Little Hans, whereas Little Albert and Little Peter were used to demonstrate the origins and cure for anxiety according to learning theory.

Freud's study of Hans (Fernald, 1984), a 5-year-old boy born in 1903, was the first published case analysis of a child. Freud used the case of Hans published in 1909 to illustrate his theory of childhood sexuality, the Oedipal complex, and the origins of neuroses. Freud only later postulated an aggressive drive (Larson et al., 2007), so he used this case of Hans to demonstrate that "the motive force" of all neurotic symptoms of later life is based on conflicts around the sexual drive. Also, before Hans, Freud's theory was applied only to adults. By studying a child, Freud strengthened his conviction that people are born with universal conflicting urges that form the basis of neuroses. Just as Freud's theory explained the origin of Hans's phobia, Freud believed the phobia was cured when Hans was presented with and understood the reasons for his fears. Thus, Freud's theory both explained and cured Hans of his phobia (in theory).

The Case of Little Hans

Even though Hans was one of Freud's most significant case studies, he saw the boy in person once. Responding to Freud's encouragement to provide information about those who have neuroses, Hans's father wrote Freud numerous letters detailing the boy's behavior and statements. The more salient facts will be recounted here.

At age 3, when Hans showed an interest in his "widdler" (penis), his mother told him if he touched it she would have it cut off. Later, responding to his unclothed mother who asked him why he was staring at her, Hans said he wanted to see if she had a penis, which he thought would be as big as a horse. His mother indicated that she did have a penis. Still at age 3, Hans witnessed the circumstances surrounding the birth of his little sister.

Hans heard his mother groaning and saw bedpans full of blood. He said, "But blood doesn't come out of *my* widdler" (Fernald, 1984).

Numerous accounts described Hans's preoccupation with the penis. He commented that his baby sister had an extremely small one, which Freud construed as meaning it had possibly been cut off. When Hans was 4, he asked his mother why she did not touch his penis when powdering him, to which she responded that it was not proper. He answered, "But it's great fun."

Finally, at age 5, Hans had developed "a nervous disorder." He protested having to walk on the streets because he feared that a horse would bite him. Freud responded to this report that what Hans really wanted was to go to bed with his mother, where he occasionally slept. Hans's father told Hans that horses do not bite, to which Hans responded that he overheard his friend's father warning his friend not to touch the white horse or it will bite. Eventually, Hans was afraid of all large animals. He told his father that his fear was so great that he touched his penis every night. His father told him to stop touching his penis and his fear would disappear. When Hans said he stopped touching his penis, his father retorted, "But you still want to." Hans agreed.

Freud referred to the information that Hans's father shared with his son about his penis and wishing to sleep with his mother as "enlightenment," which Hans just needed to accept in order to recover. As the facts about Hans's case unfolded, it became apparent that his father planted Freud's notions into Hans's mind and then reinforced his son for reporting facts that concurred with the theory. When Hans said he was afraid of the horse's black bridle, Freud interpreted this as being afraid of the father's black moustache. An ensuing conversation from father to son was as follows: "You'd like to be Daddy and married to Mummy; you'd like to be as big as me and have a moustache; and you'd like Mummy to have a baby. . . . Would you like to be married to Mummy?" Hans replied, "Oh, yes."

Freud and Hans's father, who was one of Freud's most devoted followers, paid attention to information from Hans that supported the psychoanalytic theory. An extreme example of this was when Hans told his father that his younger sister was white and lovely. In order to fit this statement into Freud's concept of sibling rivalry, his father construed Hans's statement as hypocritical and insincere.

Even though Freud was aware of the contrived nature of the information, he interpreted Hans's phobia as an Oedipal conflict that came out when Hans did not touch his penis. The more intense sexual arousal that followed is the genesis of Hans's phobia. The libidinal longing is transformed into anxiety.

In summary, Freud interpreted Hans's story as originating in a sexual desire for his mother, and when his father prevented this, Hans hated, feared, and wished to murder his father. Because there was no way to express it, Hans's sexual desire for his mother turned into anxiety. The anxiety also served the purpose of keeping Hans near his mother. Afraid that his father would cut off Hans's penis if his desires were known, Hans transferred his fear of his father to a fear of horses. Finally, and most remarkably, Hans's anxiety finally disappeared because he became aware of and understood his Oedipus complex.

The Case of Little Albert

Not to be outdone by Freud, an American psychologist in the 1920s known as the Father of Behaviorism, John Watson, performed his own anxiety-inducing experiment (Watson & Rayner, 1920) after being awarded a grant of $100 in 1917 to study reflexes and instinct in human infants. Watson called the infant "Little Albert" so that he would be compared with Little Hans. Watson's article on Albert is the earliest known explanation of anxiety that is based on learning theory.

Before conducting his experiment, Watson exposed 9-month-old Albert to various stimuli to see his reaction. Albert showed no distress at a rat and a rabbit; however, he was upset at the noise of a hammer hitting a steel bar behind his back. Watson waited two months, and then when Albert was 11 months

(continued)

The Case of Little Albert Continued

old, Watson startled him with the same distressing loud noise behind Albert's back whenever he played with a small white laboratory rat. After the noise was paired with the rat an unreported number of times, Albert became upset in the presence of the rat, even when there was no noise (when not allowed to suck his thumb). In addition, because Albert also exhibited this anxiety when exposed to a sealskin coat, Watson concluded that the fear extended to other furry animals and objects. Many accounts of Watson's study state that Albert's fear of the rabbit had been removed. In actuality Albert's mother removed him from the hospital, so there was never any chance to remove the phobia. Hence, if in the year 2010 you meet an old man in his 90s named Al, with a fear of small furry animals, you could ask him if he ever knew Watson.

Watson declared the experiment a success because he produced a phobia in a child solely through the use of conditioning. He chose to overlook the fact that Albert showed no signs of fear if permitted to suck his thumb. Critics pointed out that generalizing Albert's phobia to all furry objects may have been too broad a conclusion when all that occurred was Albert "fretting" around a sealskin coat. Watson never exposed Albert to a cotton coat to compare the reactions. Others who tried to replicate Watson's specific results have generally failed. Despite this, the contribution made by Little Albert to the field of psychology was demonstrating that anxiety could be conceptualized in terms of classical conditioning.

The Case of Little Peter

Behavior therapy proceeded with publications by Mary Cover Jones (1924) who, with guidance from Watson, experimented with classical conditioning to cure phobias. On a daily basis, Jones treated Peter, one of her most serious cases, for two months. She called him "Little Peter" to join the Freud-Watson line of research and sought to show that the conditioning process could be used to eliminate fears. Peter, a 3-year-old boy, had a fear of white rats, rabbits, fur, cotton, wool, and similar items. During his first session, Peter, while sitting in a high chair, was eating candy when a rabbit in a cage was placed four feet away from him. Peter immediately began crying and begging that the rabbit be taken away. After three minutes, he again started crying about the rabbit, and it was removed.

Gradually the duration of "rabbit time" increased and the proximity of the rabbit to Peter decreased as he exhibited an increasing tolerance to the rabbit's presence. Two months later, in Peter's last session, his behavior was markedly different. Standing in a high chair while looking out of a window, Peter asked, "Where is the rabbit?" (Jones, 1924, p. 389). The experimenter placed the rabbit at his feet. Peter patted the rabbit and tried to pick it up but it was too heavy. With help from the experimenter, Peter was able to hold and play with the rabbit. After treatments ended, Peter continued to show no fear when exposed to similar small animals.

Jones cautioned that this method is delicate because just as she was able to pair food, a positive stimulus, with the rabbit, a negative stimulus, the opposite result could have occurred, attaching the anxiety associated with the rabbit to the sight of food.

Summary

Taken together, Hans provided Freud with a psychoanalytic basis to explain both cause and cure for anxiety; Albert was Watson's source for explaining anxiety through classical conditioning; and Peter provided information to support classical conditioning as a way to extinguish anxieties. Today there are multiple theories about the origins and preferred treatments of the various types of anxiety. We have seen here the psychoanalytic and behaviorist theories applied to anxiety. In addition, there is cognitive therapy, which utilizes schemata and the concept of thought distortion as the fundamentals for change.

The origins of Albert's phobia can be attributed directly to the classical conditioning performed by Watson. In general, it appears that environmental stimuli play a large part in the development and maintenance of anxiety. Some modern theories assert that Hans's and Peter's phobias likely started with a negative reaction to an environmental stimulus, whereas others pursue more genetic and biological origins.

The "exposure" treatments such as systematic desensitization therapy (SDT) are commonly used and are effective with a wide variety of phobias. This type of treatment can be adapted to group treatment and does not require a substantial number of sessions. If SDT is done in a group, the experience has the added advantage of providing real-life modeling from the other members of the group. Cognitive-behavior modification, social skills training, anxiety management techniques, and "exposure" treatments are most commonly used, as well as psychotropic medication (Whybrow, 1997).

Occasionally other symptomatology surfaces after behavioral treatments have dealt with the specific referral symptom. This need not be considered an indication of symptom substitution because, in most instances, the other pathology has always been there. When the more debilitating primary symptoms are relieved, the person can turn his or her attention to other problems. Secondary gain patterns also often occur with the phobias. For example, Hans received a great deal of attention and reinforcement from his father for reporting his sexual urges and other symptoms of his phobia.

Agoraphobia

> *The problem with television is that people must sit and keep their eyes glued to a screen: The average American family hasn't the time for it. TV will never be a serious competitor of broadcasting [radio].*
> —*The New York Times* (1939) (Television was introduced April 30, 1939)

Agoraphobia (literally meaning "fear of the marketplace") is especially marked by an irrational fear of leaving one's home and its immediate surroundings. It is often preceded and accompanied by various panic attacks. The specific *DSM-IV-TR* diagnoses are Agoraphobia without History of Panic Attack, Panic Disorder, and Panic Disorder with Agoraphobia. *Agoraphobia* is specifically defined as the avoidance (or endurance with distress) of any situation, particularly being alone, where people fear they would be embarrassed and/or could not be helped or get in touch with help in the event of a panic attack or having panic-like symptoms (Pollard & Zuercher-White, 2003). These fears pervade their worlds, and, as a result, they avoid being alone in open spaces or avoid public places. As a result, their normal behavior patterns and experiences are severely disrupted. Freud suffered from a mild form of agoraphobia (Larson et al., 2007).

The *DSM-IV-TR* offers the specific diagnoses of Panic Disorder with Agoraphobia or without Agoraphobia. To diagnose either type of panic disorder, the *DSM-IV-TR* requires (1) recurrent unexpected panic attacks and (2) at least one of these attacks being followed by at least a month by one or more of (a) persistent anticipatory concern about attacks, (b) worry about implications or consequences of having an attack, or (c) a resultant significant change in behavior.

In order to diagnose a panic "attack," the *DSM-IV-TR* requires a specific episode of the fear and/or discomfort and the presence of at least four of the following symptoms during most of the attacks: (1) palpitations, pounding heart, or accelerated heart rate; (2) chest discomfort; (3) choking sensations; (4) feeling faint or dizzy; (5) feelings of unreality or depersonalization; (6) paresthesia (numbness or tingling); (7) hot or cold flashes; (8) sweating; (9) shaking or trembling; (10) nausea or abdominal distress; (11) fear of dying; or (12) fear of going crazy or losing control.

On occasion, panic attacks may last for hours, although typically they last for a period of about 15 minutes during which the person literally experiences terror. They present a high suicide risk (Bongar, 2002). About one-third to one-half of such individuals develop agoraphobic patterns. The disorder seldom first emerges after age 45 or before age 14, and modal ages of onset are late adolescence or the mid-30s. If age of onset of panic disorder occurs prior to age 20, it is 20 times more likely that the person has a first-degree relative who has suffered a panic disorder. Consistent with this, genetic factors play a part. The disorder is recurrent and episodic, with about half of these cases becoming chronic (Dattillo & Kendall, 2008).

The Case of Agnes

Agnes is a thin, reasonably attractive 43-year-old white female who was brought to the community mental health center in the eastern seaboard city in which she lived. Her 22-year-old daughter brought her in, stating that Agnes was driving her crazy with requests that she accompany her everywhere. Agnes reports that she has always been a "tense" person, has experienced agoraphobic symptoms off and on during the last seven years, but the intensity has increased substantially in the last six months.

For the past four years, Agnes has also suffered with what she refers to as "heart disease." She has often taken herself to a cardiologist, complaining of rapid or irregular heartbeats. The physician always reassured her that he saw no pathology and believed that it was probably a result of anxiety and tension. He advised her to exercise regularly and prescribed tranquilizers for any severe episodes of anxiety. Agnes occasionally uses the tranquilizers, but not to any significant extent. It is interesting that she has never experienced any of the symptoms at home, even though she does rather heavy housework without any assistance.

The agoraphobic pattern took a severe turn for the worse six months ago during the middle of winter, while Agnes was visiting her daughter. Her daughter had taken her own child to a movie, leaving Agnes alone in their home. There had been a severe snowstorm the day before. It was difficult for cars to get about, and Agnes became fearful that she was isolated. She tried to call her sister, who lives in a nearby city, only to find that the phone was dead. At this point, Agnes began to panic, noticed her heart beating rapidly, and thought she was going to have a heart attack. When Agnes's daughter eventually came home after the movie and some shopping, Agnes was extremely distraught. She was lying on the couch, crying and moaning, and had started to drink to try to lose consciousness. After her daughter returned, Agnes continued to drink, and with the added reassurance of her daughter, she managed to fall asleep. When she awakened, she felt better and refused to seek help for her fears. In the last six months, she has had other similar experiences of near panic at the thought of being alone.

Agnes's husband, who is a sales representative for a national manufacturing company, spends a lot of time on the road. When he is home, he is no longer willing to listen to Agnes's complaints. But the problem is not as apparent then, since Agnes relaxes considerably when her husband accompanies her on outings. Even though she can acknowledge that her behaviors are absurd and not warranted by demands in her environment, Agnes is still compelled to perform within this pattern. As is often the case with agoraphobia, Agnes shows an accompanying level of depression, since she has a sense of helplessness about controlling the events of her world. In that sense, she reflects the phenomenon referred to as "learned helplessness."

Agnes did not have a difficult or unhappy childhood. Her father was very authoritarian and discouraged rebellion in his children, although he was otherwise warm and affectionate with them. He had a moderate drinking problem and was particularly prone to whip Agnes's older brother when he was intoxicated. This older brother was the one family member who was overtly rebellious and independent. Her mother was passive and submissive and manifested mild agoraphobia herself, although she would never have been allowed to seek professional help for her condition.

Throughout her school years, Agnes was described as a "good student" and "teacher's pet." She had one or two girlfriends with whom she could talk about her worries, but she was not active socially. She did not participate in school activities and was not very outgoing with other students. Because Agnes was somewhat plain in appearance, she was not "pulled out" of her withdrawal by any males who might have shown some interest. When free of school and schoolwork, she assisted her mother in domestic duties.

Following high school graduation, Agnes took a job as a secretary with hopes of saving money for college. She did not make enough at first and had to remain at home. When she was 20 years old, she met her future husband at a church gathering, and they were married within the year. She continued her work as a secretary in order to help him finish his last year of college. Her husband was stable and undemonstrative and, like her father, a bit authoritarian. Agnes thus found it easy to become passive and dependent in response to him. She continued to long for a college degree but never made any real efforts to pursue it. After the birth of her daughter, she had another pregnancy, which ended in a miscarriage. This upset her so much that she refused to think of becoming pregnant again. Throughout the early years of her marriage, Agnes was stable in her functioning and only occasionally showed nervousness or anxiety. Yet, as noted, she has shown increased problems in recent years.

Etiology

A number of factors in Agnes's background make it understandable that she would eventually develop an agoraphobic response. First, she had always been timid and shy; it is probable that genetic temperament factors at least partially influenced her development in this pattern. But the pattern was also greatly facilitated by her parents. Her father was clear in what types of behaviors he expected. He did not want any rebellious behaviors, particularly from his daughter, and was quick to suppress any show of such behavior. On the other hand, he was affectionate, and his affection was clearly reserved for times when deference to his authority was apparent. Agnes's mother was a classic model for agoraphobic behavior. She was deferent and passive, and at the same time showed anxiety coping patterns that had an agoraphobic quality to them. She also kept Agnes involved in domestic activities through late adolescence, which did not encourage her to experiment with new and independent roles.

Her lack of physical attractiveness precluded Agnes from being drawn out of her developing withdrawal patterns by attention from males, and her lack of social or athletic interests reinforced her lack of attention from peers. When Agnes eventually married, her husband's similarity to her father's authoritarianism facilitated passive and dependent behaviors. Even though she hoped someday to return to college and develop a career, she never made any efforts to bring this to fruition. It is probable that her husband would have quashed this desire.

Agnes's miscarriage precipitated her first panic-like response, but it was controlled by the structure of the hospital and the sedative medication she received. The miscarriage was a tremendous threat, since it was in the area of child care that she had found her primary source of self-definition. She carried a fear of reexperiencing this panic, and as a result avoided future pregnancies while throwing herself into the care of her home and daughter. It is interesting that although Agnes's husband demanded passivity in his wife, he allowed and reinforced independent and even masculine behaviors in his daughter. Such behaviors provided him with a companion in fishing and golf, skills his wife had never considered developing. This allowed the daughter to escape the cycle that had been passed to Agnes from her mother and probably from other women in the family history before her. Her daughter's independence, however, stressed Agnes because it threatened her own sense of being needed. As her daughter became more independent, Agnes became more liable to anxiety, which then channeled into agoraphobic responses. The heart palpitations and slight arrythymias that naturally accompany anxiety in many individuals provided her with another focus for her anxiety. However, she was not classically hypochondriacal (Meister, 1980), since she did not seek out a variety of physicians to look at her symptoms, she did not present a wide variety of symptoms, and, in general, she attended to the comments and advice of her physician.

Once she had experienced a true panic reaction, Agnes was then sensitized to anticipate a fear of helplessness—a very frightening feeling. As a result, she engineered a wide variety of behaviors to keep her from reexperiencing panic. The patterns she developed were initially successful, since remaining at home kept her calm. But such a pattern required giving up much in the world, including the support of her husband and daughter, who increasingly found her behaviors tedious and irritating. As this occurred, she became more isolated, thus coming closer in actuality to the feeling of being alone emotionally and to the consequent panic she feared so much.

The specific diagnosis that Agnes received was Agoraphobia with Panic Attacks. Incidentally, it should be noted that some of her behaviors might also have suggested the diagnosis of Avoidant Personality Disorder. But there is very little concern about the symptoms in the avoidant personality. The person may be socially isolated and passive yet seem less concerned about this behavior and evidences little apparent desire to change it.

Treatment Options

A number of treatments are potentially useful in dealing with agoraphobia. Cognitive behavioral and the behavioral treatments have received the most research attention and support in treating all of the anxiety disorders (Dattillo & Kendall, 2008; Roth, Eng, & Heimberg, 2002). This is especially so for those referred to as "exposure treatments"—that is, they have a common goal of the elimination of maladaptive anxiety by exposing the client to fear-producing stimuli (Chambless et al., 1996). For example, an exposure program for agoraphobia would help the client gradually enter those situations (e.g., specific enclosed places, shopping malls, bridges, tunnels, etc.) that such clients typically avoid the most.

Applied relaxation can be useful with the panic component (Dozois & Dobson, 2004). After a relaxation technique—such as progressive muscle relaxation—is learned, any word (e.g., *spoon*) is conditioned to become a cue for the relaxation, so that eventually the effects of the well-learned relaxation pattern work as a counterconditioning procedure to anxiety. Also, the passivity and timidity common to agoraphobia make assertiveness training a helpful adjunct.

Medication can be helpful, especially for the panic component (see Table 3.1). The benzodiazepines, tricyclic antidepressants (especially imipranine and clomipranine), and the monoanine oxidase inhibitors (MAOs) have been proven effective and were the traditional choice, although the problematic side effects of the MAOs made them a less common choice (Bezchlibnyk-Butler & Jeffries, 1999). More recently, selective serotonin reuptake inhibitors (SSRIs), such as Prozac and Paxil, and related drugs such as Effexor, have been approved by the Federal Drug Administration (FDA) for the treatment of the panic component. Unfortunately, without other interventions, there is a substantial relapse rate for the panic component within 6 to 12 months after discontinuance of these medications.

Secondary gain patterns especially occur with agoraphobia. For example, Agnes's controlling response toward her daughter is this kind of side effect. Insight-oriented psychotherapy can be helpful in breaking the dependence roles that so often interfere with the agoraphobic's development of new responses.

Agoraphobia is difficult to treat. Two of the more effective traditional exposure

TABLE 3.1   Antianxiety Drugs

Name (Generic/Trade)	
Benzodiazepines	**Nonbenzodiazepines**
diazepam (Valium)	buspirone (Buspar)
chlordiazepoxide (Librium)	propanolol (Inderal)
chlorazepate (Tranxene)	hydroxyzine (Vistaril)
halazepam (Paxipam)	mirtrazapine (Remeron)
lorazepam (Ativan)	triflupromazine (Vesprin)
alprazolam (Xanax)	doxepin (Sinequan)
oxazepam (Serax)	duloxetine HCL (Cymbalta R)
clonazepam (Klonipin)	
quazapam (Doral)	

techniques for it are *implosion* (or *imaginal exposure*) *therapy* and *flooding* (now termed *in vivo exposure therapy*). *Graduated exposure therapy* is also commonly used now; in this technique, the goal is to keep exposing the individuals to the feared stimulus, allowing them to experience as much anxiety as they can tolerate, until they can begin to make both approach and mastery responses. Since the treatment process is likely to be a long one, group treatment techniques, along with bibliotherapy (reading specified self-help books) can be helpful (Pollard & Zuercher-White, 2003). Since the spouse of an agoraphobic may have a vested interest in the client staying agoraphobic (although this is typically denied consciously or unconsciously), marital or family therapy may be necessary.

The goal of implosion or imaginal exposure therapy is to maximize one's anxiety, whereas SDT attempts to keep it at a minimal state while the person gradually confronts the feared stimuli. G. Gordon Liddy, former Watergate personage and now an author and radio commentator, in an interview in the October 1980 issue of *Playboy*, gave a vivid description from his youth of a self-administered flooding technique:

> For example, to conquer my fear of thunder, I waited for a big storm and then sneaked out of the house and climbed up a seventy-five foot oak tree and latched myself to the trunk with my belt. As the storm hit and chaos roared around me and the sky was rent with thunder and lightning, I shook my fist at the rolling black clouds and screamed, "Kill me! Go ahead and try! I don't care! I don't care!" . . . I repeated this kind of confrontation over a period of years, mastering one fear after another. I was afraid of electricity, so I scraped off an electrical wire and let ten volts course through me.

The Treatment of Agnes

The "exposure" treatments of implosion therapy (imaginal exposure) or flooding (in vivo exposure therapy) are ideal for agoraphobics, such as Agnes, who already show a moderate ongoing level of anxiety. Implosion therapists attempt to maximize anxiety and yet keep the person in continued confrontation with the feared stimuli so that the anxiety peaks, or, in the language of the behaviorist, "extinguishes." A cognitive explanation for the extinction phenomenon asserts that the person has simply discovered that the expected catastrophic events do not occur, even under maximal stimulus conditions (Roth, Eng, & Heimberg, 2002). As a result, the person becomes aware that there is nothing that warrants his or her extreme fear and so the individual gains an increased sense of control.

Agnes was scheduled for an open-ended implosion session, one without a built-in time limit. This type of session is standard, since it is difficult to predict how long it will take the anxiety to peak. Agnes was asked to imagine different variations of her greatest fears, such as being left alone, being helpless, and going into a panic. The therapist then used graphic and vivid language throughout the session to maximize the images in Agnes's imagination. Agnes had been told ahead of time that this technique would bring on anxiety, but she had to commit herself to stay with it, with the assurance that the therapist would be there with her. She did so, and even when the scenes produced intense anxiety, she continued to hold the scenes in her imagination. If she had not done so, the result would have been counterproductive rather than simply neutral. The following excerpt is from the dialogue used in her first treatment session:

> **THERAPIST:** Agnes, keep imagining the scenes just like you have been doing—you're doing very well. I want you to imagine yourself at your daughter's house. It is a cold bleak day. The wind is howling and all of a sudden the electricity goes out. Imagine that intensely. You rush to the phone and pick it up only to realize the phone is also dead. Now you realize that with the electricity off, the furnace will not turn on and it is gradually getting much colder.
>
> **AGNES:** I'm scared, I don't want to see that. Can't we stop?
>
> **THERAPIST:** No, remember you must go on and keep these images in your mind. You're feeling colder. It's getting darker and now your heart starts to beat wildly. It's not beating right. You can feel it going wrong. You're really scared now and you know that no one's coming back home.

This type of suggestion—along with scenarios of being abandoned as an old person, suffering a lonely death, and having another miscarriage—was suggested throughout the three sessions it took for Agnes to begin to be able to face her fear and make some new and positive steps. Her anxiety peaked and then lessened several times in those three sessions, as more than one peak and fading phase is usually required. Once Agnes began to feel more confident, she was included in group therapy and also had a few marital therapy sessions with her husband. She recovered significantly over a period of five months. Although over the years she is likely to have occasional return bouts of at least a mild form of the agoraphobia, her increasing confidence and positive behaviors predict that she will be able to bounce back and handle those situations.

Comment

In Agnes's case the following factors contributed to her debilitating agoraphobia: (1) a probable temperamental predisposition toward excessive organismic arousal to stress, (2) her mother's modeling of mild agoraphobic symptoms, and (3) her father's contingent affection. Against these historical factors, Agnes's response to the miscarriage in her second pregnancy was her first experience with extreme anxiety. She was frightened by the magnitude of her experienced distress and immediately decided to avoid (with certainty) another experience of overwhelming helplessness by refusing to become pregnant again. The typical mild anxiety that pervades the agoraphobic's life between panic episodes was exacerbated in Agnes's case by her own daughter's independence, which threatened Agnes's sense of being needed. These variables, combined with Agnes's limited social development, resulted in an inability to cope with her loneliness and anxiety, except through increased withdrawal and fearfulness. Her family's impatience with Agnes's symptoms increased her isolation and encouraged her manipulation of her daughter's affection.

Obsessive-Compulsive Disorder

Shoelaces had to lie flat against his shoes. Going on or off the field he would run by the right side of the goalpost only. First step up the stairs had to be with the left foot. Before going into a game the first time he'd have somebody slap his shoulder pads exactly three times. The long white sleeve of the sweatshirt we wear under our jerseys always had to be visible. He always sat in the last row of the plane—claimed it was safer . . . shall I go on?

—William Kienzle, *Sudden Death* (1985)

For Obsessive-Compulsive Disorder (OCD) the *DSM-IV-TR* requires evidence of either obsessions (recurrent and persistent thoughts, images, or impulses experienced at some point as inappropriate and intrusive; absorb at least one hour a day; cause distress; are not just an excessive response to real-life issues; attempts to resist; and the thoughts are recognized as one's own) or compulsions (repetitive behaviors that are somehow a product of an obsessional pattern, accompanied by behaviors designed to change the situation, and these behaviors are not realistic for such an endeavor). The obsessions or compulsions must then be recognized as excessive or unreasonable.

Obsessives will usually try to ignore or suppress their obsessions, which often results in an accumulation of distress and anxiety. Subsequently, this anxiety is neutralized by the corresponding compulsions. Others may accept their condition and learn to incorporate their compulsions into their daily routine. Unfortunately, their unique lifestyle often ends up harming their general functioning. Often, OCD is chronic and accompanied by some disruption in personal functioning. The prognosis is guarded, since close to 50 percent will persist in some of their symptomatology, even with treatment. A common comorbid pattern is depression.

In 1660, the English bishop, Jeremy Taylor, provided an excellent description of a developing obsessive-compulsive pattern in referring to William of Osery as having "read two or three books of Religion and devotion very often. . . . [He] had read over those books three hours every day. In a short time, he had read over the books three times more. . . . [He] began to think . . . that now he was to spend six hours every day in reading those books, because he had now read them over six times. He presently considered that . . . he must be tied to 12 hours every day" (Pitman & Orr, 1993, p. 4).

As Freud emphasized in his comment (1906–1908), "Sufferers from this disorder are able to keep their suffering a private matter," OCD is often hidden. As a result, OCD has traditionally been thought to be relatively rare, but more recent estimates suggest it occurs at about a 2.5 percent lifetime prevalence rate in the general population. Many who might be willing to report phobic anxiety would be more distressed to disclose that they think and act in ways they cannot control. About 25 percent of OCDs are clearly obsessionals. According to the *DSM-IV-TR*, age of onset for males is typically between age 6 and 15 years old, and ages 20 to 29 for females. The most common symptom clusters are (1) washers, (2) sinners/doubters, (3) checkers, (4) counters/organizers, and (5) hoarders. The severe perfectionism found in some OCDs can be a risk factor for suicide, especially in crisis. The most common obsessions seen by clinicians are repetitive thoughts of contamination or of violence, scrupulosity and/or doubts about religion and one's duties, and self-doubts. The most common compulsions include checking behaviors, repetitive acts, and handwashing. The disorder does not include compulsions to perform behaviors that are inherently pleasurable, such as alcohol indulgence or overeating.

Obsessive-Compulsive Disorder is occasionally initially confused with Tourette's Syndrome, which is marked by a seemingly compulsive utterance of various words (often obscene) or grunts. It has been asserted that the great composer, Wolfgang Amadeus Mozart, suffered from Tourette's because Mozart's letters often included curses focused on the buttocks and defecation. Others have noted that it would have to be proven that this behavior was "out of control" to establish a diagnosis of Tourette's.

Obsessive-compulsives tend to be more intelligent and to come from a higher social economic class than do other neurotics. This characteristic makes sense, since the minor variants of this disorder, such as meticulousness and persistence, are efficient and productive, particularly in a society that is so immersed in the idea of external achievement (van Oppen, Hoekstra, & Emmelkamp, 1995). They do not reasonate to the idea that "only seekers find, but never while seeking."

The Case of Bess

Bess is an attractive 27-year-old, upper-middle-class woman. She lives by herself in a well-kept apartment in one of the best sections in town. Yet, she has few friends, and social activities play a small role in her life. Most evenings she works rather late and then comes home, fixes her own dinner, and reads or watches television until she gets ready to fall asleep. Frequently, she needs alcohol and a sleeping pill to get to sleep. She is an only child; her parents were divorced when she was 10 years old. She was primarily raised by her demanding mother, having only sporadic contact with her father. Bess is a successful accountant for a large manufacturing firm and spends a lot of time at her work. She is very perfectionistic, but of course in the field of accounting this is generally regarded as functional.

Bess's mother often expressed her love for her daughter and spent a great deal of time with her. At times, it was as if she had no other activities in her world that could give her a sense of meaning. Yet, Bess does not recall the time with her mother as filled with warmth or fun. Rather, her mother focused on activities in which Bess could "improve herself." She was constantly setting up lessons for Bess to take, and they would usually fight over whether Bess was really trying hard enough at these lessons. When home, her mother consistently emphasized the virtues of cleanliness and neatness. They struggled between themselves over these issues. Her mother would constantly nag her for not having the things in her room "in order." Bess would work at this task when she was ordered to do so, but the minute her mother took her attention away, Bess would allow things to get disorderly. Her mother continually emphasized to her that this attitude would hurt "when she got older," yet she never made it clear how.

Bess's mother showed an inordinate concern about cleanliness. She made sure that Bess washed her hands thoroughly each time Bess went to the bathroom or for any reason touched herself in the genital area. Her mother was repulsed by the smell of the bathroom and had a variety of deodorants and incense candles available to counteract odors. Anything rotten or dirty was lumped into this category and was immediately cleaned and deodorized. Like most individuals, Bess had times as a child when she felt unhappy. When she expressed these feelings to her mother, she would immediately try to talk Bess out of the feelings (e.g., "I love you so much, and spend so much time with you, so how can you be unhappy?"). If Bess further expressed her unhappiness, it would quite clearly upset her mother.

Bess enjoyed visiting her father, who lived in a nearby city. He was more relaxed about the world, although he had not been very successful and had moved through a series of jobs. He was generally a happy person and attended to Bess when she was there, although he seldom kept in contact when she was absent. Her mother was never happy when Bess went to see her father and subverted this contact whenever possible. She never failed to take the chance to point out to Bess how her father's "laziness" had brought him nothing from the world and implied that he did not support them the way he should.

In various ways, Bess resisted her mother at home, but she lived out her mother's value system in school. She worked very hard and was meticulous in her preparation of assignments. Because she was higher than average intellectually, she consistently succeeded in school. At the same time, she was seen as a "do-gooder" and was not popular with her peers. She did not get involved in class activities and spent most of her time preparing her lessons and then doing chores around the house.

She also was quite active in the Methodist church, in which her mother raised her. This was generally a positive experience for Bess, although there were occasions when she became very upset about whether she had been "saved" or whether she was a "sinner." The upset usually passed quickly as Bess pushed herself further into her schoolwork or into any activity prescribed by her church for dealing with these concerns. As Bess moved into late adolescence, she became more and more beset by erotic fantasies. She was never totally sure whether this was against the rules of her church, but she supposed it was. Bess tried to control these fantasies by getting involved in repetitive tasks or other kinds of activities that distracted her attention. She particularly became a fan of crossword puzzles and jigsaw puzzles. These would occupy her for hours, and her mother was happy to buy her the most complex available. But occasionally, the erotic fantasies arose at a time when Bess had few defenses available, and she would then engage in orgiastic bouts of masturbating.

Bess had surprisingly little difficulty interacting with males on a friendship basis. Yet, she never seemed to know how to deal with the romantic and sexual issues. As a result, she seldom dated anyone for any length of time. She did become enamored of a boy at a nearby college when she was a senior in high school. He constantly pressed her for sex, and she refused. However, one night she gave in when they had had too much to drink at a party. They then had sex virtually every day for a couple of weeks, at which time Bess began to fear pregnancy. It turned out her fears were well founded, to the horror of her mother when she was told. She immediately arranged an abortion, never allowing Bess to think out whether this was what she wanted. After the abortion, she took Bess on a trip to Europe, during which time she strictly chaperoned her. When they returned, the boyfriend had found another lover, as Bess's mother had hoped.

Bess slipped into the role of "top student," received many honors, and then easily moved into the consequent role of "up-and-coming young career woman." Her job absorbed most of her time, and it was clear that she was a rising star in the firm she worked for. Bess continued to have vague anxieties about dating, marriage, having a family, and other related issues. She handled these anxieties by throwing herself even harder into her work. At the same time, however, she began to experience symptoms that focused around the issue of cleanliness, a pattern not dissimilar from her mother's.

This concern with cleanliness gradually evolved into a thoroughgoing cleansing ritual, which was usually set off by Bess touching her genital or anal area. In this ritual, Bess would first remove all of her clothing in a preestablished sequence. She would lay out each article of clothing at specific spots on her bed and examine each one for any indications of "contamination." She would then thoroughly scrub her body, starting at her feet and working meticulously up to the top of her head, using certain washcloths for certain areas of her body. Any articles of clothing that appeared to have been "contaminated" were thrown into the laundry. Clean clothing was put in the spots that were vacant. She would then dress herself in the opposite order from which she took the clothes off. If there were any deviations from this order, or if Bess began to wonder if she might have missed some contamination, she would go through the entire sequence again. It was not rare for her to do this four or five times in a row on certain evenings.

As time passed, Bess developed a variety of other rituals and obsessive thoughts, usually related to using the toilet, sexual issues, or the encountering of possible "contamination in public places." As her circle of rituals widened, her functioning became more impaired, for the rituals consumed enormous amounts of time and psychic energy. She was aware of the absurdity of these behaviors but at the same time felt compelled to go through with them and did not constantly question them. Finally the behaviors began to intrude on her ability to carry out her work, the one remaining source of meaning and satisfaction in her world. It was then that she referred herself for help.

Etiology

From a biological perspective, studies using brain scans, typically PET scans, find that four brain structures "lock together" in OCDs; that is, they become overactive in unison. One structure is the orbital frontal cortex, situated just over the rear of the eye socket, which operates as the brain's error-detection circuit. The orbital frontal cortex alerts the rest of the brain when something is wrong and needs to be taken care of. In Obsessive-Compulsive Disorder, the orbital frontal cortex is hyperactive, so one keeps correcting what he or she thinks is not right, like checking to see the stove is turned off over and over.

Connections to the caudate nucleus and the cingulate gyrus—structures deep in the brain's core—give the person the feeling something is deadly wrong. They make one's heart pound and one's gut churn with anxiety. The thalamus, the brain's relay station for sensory information, also tends to act in unison. When one becomes more active metabolically, the other three structures do, too, which is not the case in healthy people. The caudate nucleus is usually active in people with Obsessive-Compulsive Disorder. Patients who respond positively to selective serotonin reuptake inhibitors—such as Paxil—also show a lessening of activity in the caudate nucleus. Just as important, the caudate nucleus also becomes less active in OCD clients who respond to psychotherapy (Schwartz et al., 1996), as noted later in the treatment of this case.

Freud's view of obsessive-compulsive individuals was that these persons were still functioning at the anal-sadistic stage of development and that conflicts over toilet training were critical in their development. This theory has some face validity (or apparent truth) in many cases, including Bess's. However, these common concerns about dirt related to toilet training could occur simply because this is one of the first arenas in which parent and child struggle for control of the relationship. It is also usually the first period in which whole sequences of parental behavior are integrated and modeled by the developing child. Hence, it is easy for these types of concerns to become the content of obsessive-compulsive features. It is also clear that these issues are not relevant to a substantial number of obsessive-compulsives.

Obsessive-compulsives usually model much of their behavior from parents. A common learned defense against anxiety for the obsessive-compulsive is intellectualization (talking around the core issue of a conflict in order to avoid its gut-level impact). This pattern is effective in many areas, such as school and work. But when it is used to deal with anxiety, it is not effective in the long run, as it does not actually serve to gain corrective information and because these rituals require large amounts of time and energy.

Bess's development shows most of these factors. Her mother was a thoroughgoing model for obsessive-compulsive behavior, and Bess had no significant access to other models. Her mother was also adept at inculcating guilt, and, in addition, voided any of Bess's attempts to dissipate her conflicts by voicing and sharing her concerns and upset. Bess's pattern of religious involvement furthered the development of guilt, and, as is common with most adolescents, sexual concerns provided a ready focus for the conflicts.

The rituals that the obsessive-compulsive develops serve to distract the individual from fully confronting the experience of anxiety or the feeling of a loss of control (van Oppen, Hoekstra, & Emmelkamp, 1995). Bess had long ago learned that involvement in academic subjects not only brought her inherent rewards but also at the same time served to distract her from her conflicts and impulses. She feared that if she gave in to the unacceptable impulses, she could not control her behavior. As a result, she often vacillated between control of impulses and constant indulgence, as was evident in her masturbation patterns. Like many obsessive-compulsives, Bess feared that if she let down her guard and followed her impulses, she might never again regain control, and "control" is important to obsessive-compulsives. Hence, any activities that served to distract her were welcomed. Her obsessive interest in crossword and jigsaw puzzles is an instance of an individual trying to distract oneself in activities that are often pleasant accompaniments to a full life. Her ritual cleansing was another way of distracting herself from the void of meaning in her world and from the anxiety that was always at the edge of her awareness. Yet, as she most feared, she gradually lost control of these patterns, and they began to dominate her world, even to the point of interfering with the area that had always provided meaning and satisfaction to her—her work.

Treatment Options

A wide variety of treatments has traditionally been applied to the obsessive-compulsive personality. In actuality, none has achieved spectacular success, as OCD is difficult to treat, probably because the conflicts and anxiety have already been well covered over by the obsessive-compulsive patterns. Also, such individuals seem to fear the passivity (i.e., loss of control) implied by the "patient role."

Psychoanalysts have had some success with the obsessive-compulsive personality. However, the danger with this psychoanalysis is that the obsessive-compulsive individual has had a long history of using intellectualization as a defense mechanism, and the technique of free association in psychoanalysis easily lends itself to the abuse of intellectualization. Only if the therapist can skillfully keep the client away from this pattern can psychoanalysis be helpful (Wachtel, 1997).

However, most (Chambless et al., 1996; van Oppen, Hoekstra, & Emmelkamp, 1995) recommend a clear and consistent program of *response prevention* (e.g., taking all soap and towels away from a handwasher) combined with constant *exposure in vivo* to the eliciting stimuli to promote extinction in the context of firm and consistent support. A demanding but affirming therapy relationship is the core of an effective treatment program for the compulsive aspects of the disorder. An additional behavioral technique that has been of help is "thought stopping," presented in more detail in the discussion of transvestism (in Chapter 8).

Cognitive-behavior modification can also be effective. Schwartz and colleagues (1996) confirmed that cognitive-behavior modification can reverse the OCD's physiological "locking up" of brain structures, especially in the connections of the caudate nucleus to the orbital frontal cortex, as described earlier in the section on etiology. Clients learned to relabel their obsessive urges as such, rather than simply giving in to them. Instead of saying, "I have to wash my hands again," they were trained to say, "I'm having an obsessive urge or a compulsion again." Clients were instructed to explain to themselves why the urges and the sense of dread persisted, reminding themselves that they had a disorder that caused the feelings and thoughts. Then, instead of giving in to the urge, they intentionally engaged in 15 minutes of an activity they could be absorbed in and found enjoyable or productive. They might practice a musical instrument, or take a walk, or knit. This shifts their attention away from the compulsion, a step that is crucial in altering the brain's circuitry. The therapy, in which sessions were held once or twice a week, for 10 weeks, often culminates in the clients' ability to dismiss their urges as symptoms as soon as they feel them. Finally, the urges themselves diminish. For people who are willing to try it, the benefits last in at least 80 percent of the cases.

This study (Schwartz et al., 1996) is also especially noteworthy in its demonstration that psychological techniques can produce physiological changes in the brain, here using positron emission topography (PET), an antidote to the dualistic mind-body thinking that tempts everyone at one time or another.

In some cases, "paradoxical techniques" have been used. For example, the client is asked to go ahead and purposefully proceed with the unwanted thoughts and behaviors, but exaggerating them. Doing these behaviors on purpose, in varying patterns, seems to give a client a greater sense of control over the behaviors, and therapy can build on this developing sense of control.

Psychosurgery is traditionally reputed to be successful in some cases of obsessive-compulsive disorder, but in actuality it is seldom effective.

Medication is often useful, especially where depression is a comorbid pattern. Clomipranine was the first drug to win official FDA approval for the treatment of OCD, and it is still usually the drug of choice, although it has more side effects than most other drugs of choice here (Bezchlibnyk-Butler & Jeffries, 1999). More recently, SSRIs—such as Prozac, Zoloft, Paxil, and Luvox—have received FDA approval for inclusion in the treatment of OCD.

> *If you mean to keep as well as possible, the less you think about your health the better.*
>
> —Oliver Wendell Holmes, *Over the Teacups*

Bess's Therapy

Although the classic regimen for OCD is response prevention and exposure, Bess's therapist chose to start the treatment with cognitive-behavior modification, as described in the prior section, and thought stopping (which can be construed as a form of response prevention). In the thought stopping, he first asked Bess to let the obsessions just flow freely and to raise her hand to let the therapist know when she was doing so. Some time after Bess had raised her hand, the therapist shouted "Stop" and then asked Bess to examine her consciousness. Naturally, the train of obsessions had been disrupted. They did this several times, and then the therapist asked Bess herself to shout "Stop" whenever she felt herself in the midst of these obsessions. She was then asked to practice this in her own natural world and was given a small portable shock unit to amplify the effect. Whenever Bess shouted "Stop" to herself, she also gave herself a moderately painful electric shock from this unit, which she had strapped inconspicuously under her dress. This thought stopping demonstrated to Bess that her obsessions could actually be controlled. In that sense, it was the basis on which her therapist could train her in new, positive behaviors.

Together, these techniques helped Bess substantially diminish the obsessive-compulsive patterns within four months. She and the therapist also continued to work on the void of positive activities in Bess's life. She was in therapy for approximately two years before she achieved what she considered to be an adequate success. Even so, at various points in the ensuing years, Bess occasionally experienced a reemergence of the concerns that she had experienced. On one occasion, she did return for several therapy sessions in order to work these through, although she was usually able to deal with any residual patterns using the skills she had learned in the original therapy sessions, plus training in new skills to cope with these impulses.

Comment

The obsessive-compulsive disorder is at least initially experienced as a distressing loss of control over one's thoughts and actions and is usually somewhat incapacitating. However, a degree of obsessiveness can be productive, and balancing that productiveness against losses in other areas of life is a cost-benefit decision. For example, Dom Capers, who has been a National Football League head coach, is a productive obsessive. The description of his earlier years as the defensive coordinator in the early to mid-1990s with the Pittsburgh Steelers indicated that he worked 100-hour weeks, up to 20 hours daily, during the football season. He arrived at the office each morning at 6:30. The only night he left before 10 was Friday—"date night" with his wife, Karen. Steelers' players called him a workaholic, an exacting perfectionist. Capers's mother, Jeanette, says he's been that way since the day he was born. His brother, Julius, recalls Capers precisely mowing neighbors' lawns in their hometown of Buffalo, Ohio, trimming the sidewalks by hand with a fork. He would always emphasize that nothing should be left to chance, the obsessives' credo as they try to gain certainty in an uncertain world.

Post-Traumatic Stress Disorder

> *The one thing I remember about Christmas was that my father used to take me out in a boat about 10 miles offshore on Christmas Day, and I used to have to swim back. Extraordinary. It was a ritual. Mind you, that wasn't the hard part. The difficult bit was getting out of the sack.*
>
> —John Cleese, British comedian

The essence of the *traditional* post-traumatic stress disorder (PTSD) diagnosis, as it was conceptualized during the Vietnam conflict, was a delayed distress response pattern to a very atypical and significantly traumatic event, an event such that most people would have very negative and disturbed responses. However, the more recent views of the concept, as reflected in the *DSM-IV-TR*, downplay the "delayed" and "very atypical" components (Friedman, Keane, & Resick, 2008).

The requirements for a *DSM-IV-TR* diagnosis of PTSD are quite complex, possibly reflecting the combination of high controversy and the common use of the diagnosis in the legal arena. The *DSM-IV-TR* requires (1) exposure to a traumatic event in which there is actual or threatened serious trauma or threat to self or others *and* there is intense fear, helplessness, or horror (or at least disorganized or agitated behavior in children); (2) persistent style of the event as evidenced by at least one of the following: (a) recurring and intrusive distressing recollections, (b) recurrent distressing dreams, (c) acting or feeling as if the event is recurring, (d) intense psychological distress at cues (internal or external) that symbolize or resemble the event, (e) psychological distress as well as physiological reactions to such cues; (3) persistent avoidance of stimuli associated with the event and a numbing of responsiveness as evidenced by at least three of these: (a) efforts to avoid related feelings or thoughts, (b) efforts to avoid related activities, places, or people, (c) inability to recall an important event component, (d) reduced participation in significant activities, (e) feelings of detachment or estrangement from others, (f) restricted affect range, or (g) sense of a foreshortened or physical future; (4) two or more persistent, post-trauma symptoms of arousal, from (a) difficulty falling or staying asleep, (b) irritability or anger outbursts, (c) difficulty concentrating, (d) hypervigilance, or (e) exaggerated startle responses. The symptoms listed in points (2), (3), and (4) must be expressed for at least one month and the condition must cause significant distress or impairment in general, daily functioning. Unfortunately, since the diagnosis depends so heavily on self-report, it is relatively easy to malinger this disorder (Boyd, McLearen, Meyer, & Denney, 2007).

A critical predictor of a later PTSD is evidence of dissociation, such as blanking out or reporting or appearing to be "in a daze" at the time of trauma. (This dissociation may appear to onlookers to be a calm, nonstressed response.) In addition, a greater likelihood of developing PTSD as well as a more negative prognosis can be evidenced by lower intelligence; prior patterns of impulsive, social withdrawal; irritability and/or impulsivity; early patterns of depression and later diagnoses of major depression and/or a family history of depression; substance abuse; significant delay before seeking treatment; secondary gain; and detachment or denial patterns.

The Case of Paul

The 9-11 Attack

On the morning of September 11, 2001, a horrific terrorist attack of unprecedented magnitude violently devastated the twin towers of the World Trade Center as well as several adjacent buildings in New York City. In Washington, DC, the Pentagon was also attacked and damaged. The overall death toll was close to 3,000 people.

Paul had just turned 5 years old one month before the tragedy. His parents had a big birthday party for him, figuring that at age 5, a child's memories begin to etch life events with more clarity than before. They had a magic show, clowns, balloons, cake, and ice cream, and had invited all of Paul's little buddies from kindergarten and their neighborhood in Long Island. Paul had an enjoyable day playing with his friends, but he particularly enjoyed the companionship of his older brother, Tom. He looked up to Tom who, at the time, was beginning second grade. Paul's mother, Sandra, worked in the south tower of the World Trade Center, located in lower Manhattan. She was a member of the World Trade Center Association (WTCA), located on the 77th floor. Paul's father, David, who had formerly served in the United States Air Force for 15 years, was now an assistant chief at the New York Fire Department.

On that infamous morning, one month after Paul's fifth birthday, Paul and his family got up to what at first seemed to be just another day. David always left for work early, to be at the firehouse at "0600." Paul was always expected to be ready by 7:30, after he had finished his bowl of Captain Crunch and brushed his teeth. He then would hop into the car and ride along with his mom to drop Tom off at school. Twice a week, Paul would be taken to his grandparents' house. Unfortunately, that September 11th was one of the other three days of the week when Paul went to a kindergarten, located a bit over one block north of the World Trade Center. By 8:15 A.M. Sandra had made sure Paul was safely in his classroom. Paul and his mom kissed good-bye and parted ways with ample time for her to make it to her 9-to-5 job at the World Trade Center, only a block away.

At 8:45 A.M. that Tuesday morning, American Airlines flight 11, hijacked from Boston, slammed into the World Trade Center's north tower in Manhattan. Eighteen minutes later, United Airlines flight 175, another Boeing 767 hijacked from Boston, crashed into the World Trade Center's south tower. Several desperate people could be seen with the top half of their bodies hanging out of the towers' windows; a number of the occupants jumped, apparently trying to escape what seemed to be an even worse fate. At 10:05 A.M. the weakened south tower collapsed into the ground, triggering immediate chaos as hundreds of emergency workers tried to clear people out of the city. Approximately 25 minutes later, the north tower imploded into itself in a matter of seconds, releasing a tremendous cloud of debris and smoke. The impact was felt within a radius of several miles, severely damaging several of the surrounding buildings. From a distance, shocked onlookers could only watch in horror, as immediate bystanders frantically attempted to outrun the wave of smoke and debris that chased them. The streets of lower Manhattan were quickly covered by a thick layer of ash and soot, resembling the aftermath of Mt. Saint Helens' explosion in the early 1960s. Almost as a symbolic signature of the merciless terrorist attack, a trail of smoke billowed toward the Statue of Liberty. The attack on the World Trade Center was part of an overseas terrorist plot against the United States, almost certainly masterminded by Islamic fundamentalist Osama bin Laden. In addition to the pair of hijacked planes that devastated the World Trade Center towers, two other aircraft were hijacked that same morning. One plowed into the west wall of the Pentagon in Washington, DC, and the second one crashed about 85 miles southeast of Pittsburgh, Pennsylvania, presumably headed toward Washington, DC, as well. Approximately 250 people were killed as a result of these two crashes.

Tons of rubble and debris piled up into a morbid mound of destruction in the heart of New York City. Fire departments, rescue and crisis teams, nurses, doctors, and paramedics found few signs of life. Most of the fortunate but few survivors suffered burns, broken limbs, and critical wounds. Hundreds of desperate family members and friends appeared at the scene in the days to follow to begin a long and usually futile search for their loved ones.

Upon realizing what had happened, Paul's grandparents picked up Tom from

(continued)

The Case of Paul Continued

school and frantically tried to drive into Manhattan. Unable to get through traffic or reach anyone through the phone lines, they returned to their home in Long Island, uncertain if Paul, Sandra, or Dave were alive. Hours passed before anything was known about them, until there was a phone call from the hospital telling the grandparents that Paul was in intensive care. For some reason, Paul's kindergarten building was not evacuated immediately after the planes hit; presumably, authorities thought the children would be in less danger if they remained temporarily inside the building and stayed out of the already chaotic streets. Once the towers collapsed, it was too late, and the impact devastated the kindergarten before anyone could safely exit the building. Two firefighters had pulled Paul from under a metal file cabinet. The child was in shock and had four broken ribs and first-degree burns on both his legs. Doctors later said the file cabinet likely saved Paul's life by shielding him against falling debris. Paul's parents were not that fortunate: Dave was among the 200 firefighters who were engulfed by the collapse of the north tower; Sandra's body was never found.

Paul's Background

Paul's background was a normal, healthy one—somewhat resembling the American dream that is often depicted in Hollywood films. His family lived in a middle-class suburban neighborhood in Long Island. Paul's parents had been happily married for 10 years and had respectable, stable jobs. Paul and his brother Tom, never had any major health complications. They were both cheerful and obedient boys, and were brought up with strong values such as honesty, respect, and generosity.

Paul was far from being a problem child. His friends were mostly neighbors and fellow classmates from kindergarten. Paul was a leader; he had many of the fun ideas, and would often make up the rules of the game, yet he was popular with his peers.

Paul was devoted to his father, and his favorite game was to play "war" with his dad. He wanted to know all about what it was like to be in the Air Force. They used to suit up in USAF uniforms, go up to the tree house in the backyard, and "start their engines." When he was not shooting down enemy planes with his father, Paul enjoyed cooking with his mom and playing with his brother. Tom was protective of his little brother, and would patiently listen to Paul read his first storybooks. Some nights, if it was all right with Mom and Dad, they would spend the night up in the tree house.

Post-Trauma

Everything changed for Paul after the 9-11 tragedy—his family, his outlook on life, and certainly his personality. The catastrophe may have spared Paul's life, but it robbed him of his childhood innocence and his self-confidence. For a while, Paul seemed more confused than affected by the whole situation. Kronenberger and Meyer (2001) mention that very young children may react indifferently to the death of a close one, perhaps because of their limited understanding of the permanence of death. However, as time passed, Paul and Tom were living their new lives with their grandparents. Tom became even more protective toward Paul. He might have felt guilty for not being by his little brother's side that morning. Tom endeavored to put a smile back on Paul's face, but his efforts met with little success.

Paul often spent weeks without saying more than a few words at a time. He carried a look of helplessness and disappointment. It was hard to get him interested in the activities that would amuse most kids his age. He never went back up to the old tree house, nor did he ever wear that USAF uniform that he once loved so much. He even refused to eat any of the dinners that were once "standards" cooked by his mother.

Paul never asked any questions about the day of tragedy. He didn't need to ask why all his friends from kindergarten never stopped by to play again. It was hard for him to adapt to his new home, a different school, and an altered life in general. Although he gradually recovered physically, emotionally he seemed to become increasingly detached with time, and fell deeper into a depressive state. Periodically, he woke up in the middle of the night screaming and shivering, but he could not verbalize any of his feelings.

In general, Paul spent most of his time playing alone with Lego blocks. But when he finished a construction, he then smashed it down with the stretched palm of his hand, pretending it was an incoming airplane. He apparently perceived this as the way life was—buildings crash, families die, and there is no use getting attached to anyone.

Paul's grandparents later described to his doctors how Paul used to "space out" on the rare occasions when somebody around him would mention his parents and the tragic memories of that morning. This reaction, later identified as *dissociation,* seemed just like Paul's "state of shock" in which the two firefighters found him the day of the attack.

Another characteristic that Paul developed was a tendency to display sudden outbursts of anger, unfortunately often elicited by attempts from relatives to approach him in a caring fashion. On a subconscious level, he did not want to relive the pain of losing a loved one, so he remained emotionally distant and inhibited. Perhaps the saddest of all transformations in Paul's character was his loss of affect, especially for Tom. Paul shut his brother off emotionally, as if he was an unimportant stranger.

Diagnosis

Paul was diagnosed with Post-Traumatic Stress Disorder, as PTSD may occur at any age, including childhood (American Psychiatric Association, 1994, p. 466). Obviously, Paul's case was filled with *potentially traumatic experiences:* survival of a violent act of terrorism, personal injury and burns, morbid and gory visual stimuli, and, most significantly, the abrupt loss of close loved ones. It is generally accepted that trauma generated by deliberate violence is likely to have longer-lasting mental health effects than trauma caused by natural disasters and accidents.

Several instruments that exist to assess PTSD in children older than 8 years of age have proved to be psychometrically satisfactory and useful in research and clinical settings (Ruggiero, Morris, & Scotti, 2001). Even though Paul's age of 5 does not fit in the range of such assessment measures, the nature of his traumatizing event and his consequent symptomatology allow for an unmistakable diagnosis of chronic PTSD. Nevertheless, some assessment measures were taken to confirm the already intuitive diagnosis for Paul. His results on the Children Behavior Check List (CBCL) and the Teacher Report Form (TRF) showed elevations on the Anxious/Depressed, Attention Problems, and Withdrawal scales. Furthermore, the clinician-rated Children's PTSD Inventory was utilized to assess Paul, and it clearly revealed the presence of PTSD symptoms. Finally, in a child self-report questionnaire, the Behavior Assessment System for Children (BASC),

Paul's responses elevated the Anxiety, Atypicality, and Locus of Control scales, indicating symptoms related to fear, intrusive thoughts and behaviors, and lack of control, respectively (Kronenberger & Meyer, 2001).

Symptomatology

Typically, children with PTSD experience a mixture of intrusive and avoidant symptoms (Friedman et al., 2008), including nightmares, exaggerated startle, agitation, and disorganized behavior. Other characteristics occasionally seen in PTSD children are dissociation and anger (Dell & O'Neil, 2008). Flatness, avoidance, and withdrawal have all been suggested as the key symptoms presented by children with this disorder (Kronenberger & Meyer, 2001).

Paul's post-trauma persona is a detailed depiction of PTSD symptomatology. Aggressive outbursts and tantrums were present, possibly as a means of detachment and isolation. Loss of affect was evident, especially toward his brother, Tom. Paul consistently reenacted the traumatic event through play. He experienced episodes of dissociation, especially when he was exposed to familiar memories of the tragedy. Paul also had problems sleeping and suffered from anxiety and depression. An almost antisocial type of avoidance and disinterest emerged, yet Paul experienced elevated arousal and fear, which Pfefferbaum and colleagues (1999) described as significant predictors of PTSD in those children exposed to the Oklahoma City bombing in 1995. Increased anxiety and exaggerated startle responses were also evident, as was a decrease in the verbalization of feelings.

> *The trouble about always trying to preserve the health of the body is that it is so difficult to do without destroying the health of the mind.*
> —G. K. Chesterton, *On the Classics*

Treatment Options

The first step in treatment for PTSD is crisis counseling (Rainer & Brown, 2008). A degree of PTSD symptom reduction has occurred in some adults with the use of hypnotherapy, but no definitive empirical support yet exists for hypnosis as the primary treatment of choice. Similarly, pharmacotherapy has failed to establish clear efficacy, despite some positive results with beta-blocking agents and alpha agonists. Tricyclic antidepressants and antihistamines may be useful for reducing depressive and sleep symptoms, benzodiazepines may serve to treat hyperarousal and anxiety, and fluoxetine (Prozac) may minimize other PTSD symptoms such as denial/avoidance and depression. At the same time, one should always be conservative in the use of psychotropic medication with children.

Although psychodynamic interventions for children with PTSD have proved inconclusive due to methodological limitations, play therapy naturally permits symbolic expression and allows access to emotional conflicts associated with trauma.

Nondirective or minimally directive play therapy is frequently used with younger children with PTSD. The establishment of a safe, structured, but permissive environment frees the child to show his or her most influential thoughts and feelings. In many cases, these will include issues related to the traumatic event. Common feelings and behavior are aggression, anger, destructive impulses, detachment, and injury/illness. The therapist facilitates by providing support and by acting as a safe person during the child's acting-out of the threatening thoughts, emotions, and beliefs. In many cases, after repetitive playing out of the themes related to the traumatic event, the child is able to change play to other topics, signaling that the trauma has less of an effect on his or her immediate thoughts and feelings. (Kronenberger & Meyer, 2001, pp. 257–258)

With adults, the combination of anxiety management training (AMT) and educational techniques has received the greatest amount of empirical attention with trauma-exposed individuals. Anxiety management training includes relaxation and social-skills training, cognitive restructuring, distraction techniques, and biofeedback. Exposure-based techniques (EBT) have also been recognized, with AMT, as the two most efficacious interventions for PTSD. Exposure stops the reinforcement that is attained by avoiding trauma-related stimuli. For the treatment of children, systematic desensitization and graduated exposure are recommended, in contrast with implosion and flooding, which generally elicit extreme levels of distress (Ruggiero et al., 2001). Exposure-based techniques are generally a popular choice for treating younger children because the events they encounter typically occur in controlled settings (e.g., sexual/physical abuse). However, Paul's case was not amenable to such an intervention because the stressor was of such magnitude and had so many facets that it could not be replicated in a controlled setting (Everly & Lating, 2004).

The Treatment of Paul

The level of psychopathology in PTSD patients is often proportional to aspects such as severity, frequency, and duration of the event. Clearly, due to the severity of the stressor, the level of Paul's psychopathology would be expected to be extremely high. Therefore, Paul's treatment has had to be broad and delicate, and will quite likely be a lifelong process.

First of all, an atmosphere of support from Paul's remaining family and friends has been fundamental throughout treatment. This support exists in response to thorough crisis counseling and education about PTSD that was provided to the significant others in Paul's life (Rainer & Brown, 2008). It has also been important for family members to provide Paul with structure. An activity schedule with defined roles is one form of offering such structure. Giving him helping roles with proper direction helps him feel safe and important; this also helps to keep him distracted from trauma-related memories. Although hard to do at first, it was advised to minimize Paul's exposure to any form of media related to the incident. Affective modeling has also been recommended, specifically to Tom and his grandparents. If they interact in a warm and calm fashion, Paul is likely to regenerate a sense of normalcy, comfort, and safety.

It was decided to treat Paul with a combination of the two most empirically efficient approaches: AMT and EBT. In addition, play therapy is being employed as a way for Paul to release his emotions and express his unarticulated thoughts in an indirect and unintrusive manner.

Paul is being patiently trained to relax when he feels aggressive outbursts developing. Through cognitive restructuring, he is beginning to accept the tragedy and its consequences. Progressive strategies such as *integration of the experience* and *processing the traumatic experience* are key elements in Paul's cognitive rehabilitation. He is learning the technique of distraction when confronted with disturbing cues that otherwise would likely elicit dissociation or anxiety attacks. Social skills are helping Paul to slowly immerse himself in social settings again. The psychotherapeutic technique of *articulation of affect* (e.g., expressing feelings, learning empathy, giving and receiving compliments, etc.) is aiding Paul in progressively crumbling the emotional wall that he had built around himself, and will eventually permit him to open up to the people who love him.

In exposure-based therapy, desensitization was used to overcome the fear of buildings, explosions, and other morbid images. Paul was asked to imagine himself in situations similar to his traumatic experience. Slowly, Paul learned to use breathing and relaxation techniques to better assimilate such situations. His cognitive reframing skills and trauma integration training allowed him to perceive these situations from an observer's point of view. If he felt safe, Paul was asked to describe what the situation felt like in detail. By helping him verbalize his original fears, the negative feelings and emotions that were manifested as anger outbursts or anxiety states eventually faded away. Systematic desensitization has proceeded with visual stimuli (e.g., picture images of his parents, the skyline of New York City, injured/burnt individuals, fires, and explosion videos) and audio stimuli (e.g., bombings, airplanes, and explosions). Also, because of the severity of his situation, for a period of time Paul was prescribed antihistamines to help with his sleeping problems, as well as fluoxetine for the treatment of denial and avoidance symptoms.

Paul has begun to understand that what occurred was an exceptional act, and his progress is evident in the gradual modification of his play pattern. Through play therapy, Paul has learned to build Lego buildings without the urge to destroy them. The therapist created a toy city with several buildings of various sizes and dozens of "people" figurines inside and outside the buildings. The therapist has been representing all the safe and harmless people who work in buildings and walk around buildings every day. Paul has learned to feel safe playing in a representative "society" where terrorism is not the norm. He has come a long way emotionally, but still benefits from psychotherapy and counseling sessions and will likely require that for the foreseeable future. In 2004, the Office of Naval Research provided four million dollars to fund research on the use of virtual reality techniques to treat PTSD. It is now combined with cognitive behavior modification to treat the estimated 15 to 30 percent of Iraq conflict veterans who suffer some degree of PTSD.

Flashbacks are manifested as dissociation states that may last from a few seconds up to days (Friedman et al., 2008). During these episodes, the person behaves as if the traumatizing event was recurring. In both adults and children, flashbacks are commonly reported in cases of PTSD, but they can be malingered in order to bring a claim of PTSD into the legal arena. The dramatic quality of flashback symptoms is certainly impressive; the difficulty is in deciphering the veracity of such reports. The following criteria are typically characteristic of true flashbacks:

- The flashback is sudden and unpremeditated.
- The flashback is uncharacteristic of the individual.
- There is a retrievable history of one or more intensely traumatic events that are reenacted in the flashback.
- There may be amnesia for all or part of the episode.
- The flashback lacks apparent current and specific motivation.
- The current trigger stimuli reasonably resemble the original experiences.
- The individual is at least somewhat unaware of the specific ways he or she has reenacted some of the prior traumas.
- The individual has, or has had, other believable symptoms of PTSD.

The principles of crisis intervention that have been employed in cases of combat exhaustion in the field also provide an excellent overall framework within which to provide emergency treatment for post-traumatic stress syndromes. *Immediacy* refers to the early detection and treatment of the disorder, with an emphasis on returning individuals to their typical life situations as quickly as possible. *Proximity* emphasizes the need to treat the individuals in their ongoing world by avoiding hospitalization. *Expectancy* is the communication of the therapist that although the patients' reactions are quite normal, it still does not excuse them from functioning adequately; the "sick role" is not reinforced (Meyer & Weaver, 2007).

4

The Dissociative and Sleep Disorders

The dissociative disorders are marked by a sudden disruption or alteration of the normally integrated functions of consciousness. This disturbance is almost always temporary, although it may wax and wane, particularly in amnesia and fugue. With the exception of the depersonalization disorder, the dissociative disorders occur rarely, and consideration must be given to the faking of this type of disorder in order to avoid some social or moral responsibility (Boyd et al., 2007; Melton et al., 1997).

The various subcategories are Psychogenic Amnesia, an acute disturbance of memory function; Psychogenic Fugue, a sudden disruption of one's sense of identity, usually accompanied by travel away from home; Dissociative Identity Disorder (Multiple Personality), the domination of the person's consciousness by two or more separate personalities (the classic and in many ways the most severe of the Dissociative Disorders, as demonstrated in the case of Anna O.); and Depersonalization Disorder, a disturbance in the experience of the self in which the sense of reality is temporarily distorted.

There is also a category referred to as Other Dissociative Disorders, which is simply a residual category. The patterns most commonly included in this diagnosis are those of persons who experience a sense of unreality that is not accompanied by depersonalization and who also show some trance-like states.

It can be argued that the Depersonalization Disorder, also referred to as the Depersonalization Neurosis, is not appropriately included in this general category, as there is no substantial memory disturbance. Yet, there is a significant disturbance, albeit temporary, of the sense of reality, and thus the identity is certainly affected.

The sleep disorders are included in this chapter since they are analogous to the dissociative disorders in that they also involve an altered state of consciousness. Sleep, however, though an altered state, is of course a normal process, and in parallel fashion, the disruptions are usually not as severe as they are in the dissociative processes. There is a wide variety of possible disturbance patterns, and the cases here deal with the most common and important patterns: sleepwalking (Sam) and insomnia (Ilse).

You want to go where everybody knows your name.
—The Theme Song of *Cheers*

Multiple Personality Disorder

The *DSM-IV-TR* uses the term *Dissociative Identity Disorder;* I will use the more universally recognized term of *multiple personality disorder (MPD). DSM-IV-TR* defines MPD as the presence of two or more distinct personalities within one person, each of which is relatively complete and integrated and maintains its own pattern of behavior, thinking, and social relationships. Each of these entities may be dominant and control behavior at different times or in different situations. Usually, the core personality is passive, dependent, guilty, and depressed, but the alternates may be hostile, controlling, and self-destructive. At times, the more authoritative alternates may allocate time to the others. Similarly, aggressive or hostile personalities may place the others in uncomfortable situations. Multiple Personality Disorder is the most extreme of the dissociative disorders. Although persons exhibiting psychogenic fugue typically experience only one "switch" to another personality, multiples experience many personality alternations over an extended period of time. The alternate personalities generally serve important functions that the core personality cannot manage for itself. Unfortunately, many people believe that MPD is closely related to schizophrenia, possibly because this latter term literally means "split mind."

No disorder has proven more fascinating to the public than MPD—for example, consider Robert Louis Stevenson's classic novel *The Strange Case of Dr. Jekyll and Mr. Hyde*, completed in six cocaine-fueled days and nights (Durrant & Thakker, 2003). Two more recent books dealing with the topic, *The Three Faces of Eve* and *Sybil*, became best-sellers and were subsequently made into movies. Despite the attention that popularizations have received, MPD remains one of the least understood psychological disorders, in part because reliable reports in the professional literature are quite rare.

It is difficult to judge the incidence of MPD. After the celebrated case of Mary Reynolds, described by S.L. Mitchell in 1817, only 76 cases were reported in the ensuing 127 years (Taylor & Martin, 1944). Since 1944, the number of reported cases increased somewhat, with Winer (1978) finding over 200 documented cases. A few modern theorists have suggested that a significant proportion of all psychiatric patients are multiples, but most researchers or clinicians would find this concept unbelievable (Dell & O'Neil, 2008). Thigpen and Cleckley (1984), as well as Weissberg (1993), have suggested that much of the apparent increase here may be due to the glamour that accrues to both patients and therapists claiming the disorder—that is, it is iatrogenic, a result of the treatment itself. On occasion, people may attempt to escape accusations of criminal behavior by presenting themselves as a "split personality." Of the cases documented to date, the majority are women.

An additional complicating factor stems from the very nature of MPD. In most cases, the core personality is completely unaware of the alternates, though the reverse need not be true (Kluft & Fine, 1993; Spanos, 1996). Since the alternates usually have specific roles, they are unlikely to seek treatment on their own. The core personality is often aware of "blackouts" or lost time but is unlikely to discuss these problems with anyone. When multiples do enter treatment, it is often for reasons other than the primary disorder, such as suicide attempts or criminal behavior (Reinecke et al., 2008). The most common diagnoses initially given are major depression and schizophrenia. Most multiples are identified as such only after some extended contact with mental health specialists who eventually observe one or more of the alternates in vivo.

A history of having suffered amnesia or other dissociative experiences or borderline personality disorder pattern is mildly predictive of a future multiple personality disorder (Chu et al., 1999), as is a history of physical or sexual abuse (especially repeated traumatic incest). Stress and/or significant personal loss is an important precipitating factor, as are difficult developmental or social transition points. New personalities are usually a crystallization into a personality of opposite facets from the original one.

Anna O. is critical to the development of psychoanalytic theory and then the later psychodynamic therapies; indeed, she is considered the first patient of psychoanalysis. Specifically, she is the first patient with whom the cathartic method was employed. In light of the evolution of modern diagnostic concepts, it is increasingly evident that Anna O. suffered from MPD, in addition to or instead of the traditional diagnosis of Anna as "hysteric" (Weissberg, 1993).

Also, although many professionals believe Anna O. was a patient of Freud's, he never saw her. Rather, she was a patient, for about 18 months between November 1880 and June 1882, of Josef Breuer, Freud's early mentor and collaborator. Breuer and Freud both viewed Anna O. as a classic case of hysteria. However, Weissberg (1993) has argued persuasively that although there are hysteric components, Anna O. is most accurately seen as a multiple personality, with the possibility that the MPD was at least in part induced by Breuer's treatment. Some difficulties in assessing this case stem from the fact that Breuer did not write up the case until 10 years after he had terminated treatment with her.

The Case of Anna O.

Anna (actually Bertha Pappenheim), an unmarried 21-year-old woman from a prominent Jewish family in Vienna, first consulted with Breuer at the end of November 1880 with the initial complaint of a persistent cough. Breuer used hypnosis to elicit memories to reconstruct the events that led up to referral. This included Anna's reaction to childhood and, more recently, to her distress around caring for her father while his health gradually failed. In July 1880, he developed a pleuritic abscess, probably caused by tuberculosis—the possible cause of Anna's symptoms as well.

As is often the case with seriously disordered individuals, any success and/or acceptance of the initial complaint allows elaboration into numerous allied symptoms—in Anna's case, vision and hearing problems, neck weakness, headaches, and anesthesia of her right arm and leg. She then became mute for two weeks, and soon thereafter revealed two distinct personalities that apparently switched back and forth without warning. Anna's first, or usual, personality was a bit melancholy, in part because, as is common with MPDs, she experienced gaps in consciousness, mood swings, and even possible hallucinations. As is also often the case with MPDs, the second personality has a more antisocial quality, what Anna termed "naughty." It was also often abusive toward others, and occasionally generated odd, rebellious behaviors, such as tearing buttons off of bedclothes.

After Anna's father's death on April 5, 1881, she (1) stopped recognizing anyone except Breuer, (2) would communicate only in English (her second language), and (3) would eat only if fed by Breuer. As is evident, this first Freudian was hardly orthodox in his therapeutic technique. Each and every day, Anna would become somnolent in the afternoon (probably autohypnotically), and after sunset, Breuer would formally hypnotize her or she would do the autohypnosis, and would then recount her hallucinations/dreams of that day and then awaken "calm and cheerful."

Yet, Anna's condition worsened, and she became suicidal. On June 7, 1881, she was moved to a house outside Vienna, where she could be monitored more closely. Breuer now visited her most days, occasionally resorting to pleading to get her to talk. She would sometimes talk only after thoroughly feeling Breuer's hand to make sure it was him, asserting she could not recognize him visually. Though her symptoms had at first worsened, they now calmed somewhat—Anna attributed this to the "talking cure" of reliving her memories under hypnosis—and Anna moved back to Vienna.

However, Anna's personalities again changed more dramatically, and Breuer could now elicit a personality shift by showing her oranges (the only food she would eat during the first part of her illness). It was in this period that after avoiding water for six weeks, Anna, while hypnotized, recalled her disgust when she saw a dog drink from a water glass. When she awoke from the hypnosis, her hydrophobia disappeared. Breuer now had the insight to recognize this as *catharsis*, a basic principle of psychoanalytic technique, and systematically used it on her many other symptoms. Most disappeared, and in the process Breuer discovered they had all started the summer her father fell ill. Breuer and Freud later theorized that

Anna's feelings about this had been "strangulated" (later termed "repressed"), only to come out later in her various symptoms, and then relieved by "insight" as well as "working through" by analyzing dreams and talking into "abreaction," and eventual catharsis, bringing a cure.

Though many of these symptoms cleared, Anna's alter personality appeared again in the spring of 1881, something Breuer called a "disagreeable event." Breuer last saw her in June 1882 and stated that she now enjoyed "complete health." But, possibly reflecting his Victorian ethics, or his pride, or his reported panic, or all three, he neglected to note that in their last session, Anna had told him she was pregnant with his baby. After calming her down by inducing a hypnotic trance, Breuer arranged for his own immediate departure to Venice with his wife for a second honeymoon. Anna was not pregnant. Freud later used his belief that Breuer had misunderstood Anna's sexual attraction to Breuer to develop his concepts of transference and countertransference.

She "was institutionalized for a year following her therapy with Beuer" (Larson et al., 2007). Documents were later obtained from Anna's file at the Bellevue Sanatorium in Kreutizlingen, where she had been hospitalized in July 1882 for morphine addiction, indicating periodic inability to speak German (her first language), absences of consciousness, and feelings of "time missing." Anna also showed two separate personality states at least five years after termination.

Consistent with the concept that abuse is often (though not always) found in the histories of those who later manifest MPD, there were indications that Anna had been sexually abused, and that she was certainly emotionally abused by her mother. As an adult, she showed a consistent preoccupation with as well as active efforts in her social work career against Jewish men who abused women. Some believe that Anna was also generally emotionally abused, in that her needs to be independent were stifled by her father, by the family's Orthodox Jewish practices, by her mother and brother who eventually excluded her even

(continued)

The Case of Anna O. Continued

from the care of her dying father, and by society's repressive reaction at that time toward bright and intellectually curious women. Ironically, Anna maintained a lifelong disdain for psychoanalysis, and the Nazis later used Anna's journalistic exposé of wealthy Jewish slave traders as anti-Jewish propaganda.

However, Anna did eventually recover and overcome her addiction. In 1895, she became the director of a Jewish orphanage in Frankfurt, Germany. She went "on to a successful career as Germany's first social worker,

an author of short stories, a playwright, and a champion of women's rights" (Larson et al., 2007, p. 274). In 1904, she founded a League of Jewish Women, the first organization of its kind. And in 1907, she began a home for unwed mothers. Committed to the causes of women and children, she can be considered an early feminist. She wrote, "If there is any justice in the next life, women will make the laws and men will bear the children!" In 1954, the West German government issued a commemorative postage stamp in her honor.

MPD Controversies

Most experts believe there are true MPDs, with these qualifications (Dell & O'Neil, 2008; Thigpen & Cleckley; 1984; Spanos, 1996; Weissberg, 1993):

- Although a few therapists seem to come up with many "multiples" in their practice, most therapists seldom see such cases.
- Not only have there been significantly more reports of cases of MPD, but also in recent decades, MPDs report a significantly greater number of secondary personalities, or "alters."
- The diagnosis of MPD is to some degree culture bound, and the great bulk of cases have been observed in the United States.
- The diagnosis has another possible culture-bound bias in that the vast majority of MPD cases are female.
- In the majority of cases, the diagnosis of MPD emerges only after a period of therapy, usually employing hypnosis (and often self-hypnosis) and with a therapist who is sympathetic to (if not an active advocate for) the idea of multiples.
- Many proponents of MPD argue that separate "alters" (or personalities) may influence the MPD's general behavior without actually emerging or being observable to others, thus making any kind of independent corroboration impossible. If so, the concept of MPD must be placed in the realm of philosophy or religion rather than of science.
- As in the case of Anna O., the great majority of information derives from anecdotal testimony and case reports, and remains unverified by scientific methods. However, much of this information is repeated often enough to take on the veneer of truth.

- Some of the supposed scientific findings about MPD that are commonly repeated by believers are spurious. For example, advocates consistently assert that different personalities show different physiological patterns (e.g., in EEG patterns and in psychological test response patterns). However, normals can show similar differences when they are in different emotional states, and persons who attempt to simulate different personalities show EEG differences similar to those found in different MPD personalities. Also, some scientific findings—for example, that many MPDs report a history of childhood abuse—are generalized to the point of becoming inaccurate (e.g., "many" becomes "most" or even "virtually all"; or a history of abuse becomes specified as a history of sexual abuse, etc.).

Etiology

Dissociative processes are a part of normal functioning, although the propensity for their use varies among individuals. Many kinds of stressful events, such as natural disasters and combat fatigue, can produce extreme dissociative phenomena. The extreme manifestations seen in some cases of MPD stem from long-term stress, often associated with severe trauma and/or abuse.

Multiple Personality Disorder can also be seen as a learned response within the family (Horowitz, 2004). Research suggests that in most instances, at least one parent is severely disturbed, as was the case with Anna O. Many multiples report the dissociation of the first alternate in early childhood, often before the age of 6. This first dissociation establishes a pattern wherein sudden stresses elicit further alternates that arise to meet these new challenges. Cases of "super-multiples," with over 100 alternates, have been reported but are understandably given little credence in professional circles.

Individuals are more susceptible to developing a multiple personality if they (1) were abused as children; (2) are under significant stress; (3) have had somewhat contradictory personality factors; (4) have experienced maternal rejection; (5) are impressionable, suggestible, and/or dependent; (6) tend toward overdramatic behaviors; and (7) have accepted unrealistically high standards of performance.

Many persons find it difficult to imagine the underlying mechanism of dissociation. It seems implausible that truly distinct personalities could share the same neural patterns. The most promising explanation for this phenomenon appears to be a state-dependent learning (SDL) model. An organism's state at any given time is a function of conditions in the environment as well as physical and psychological conditions. Information learned under certain conditions is best recalled in the exact same state and may be inaccessible under a different state. Idiosyncratic cues, such as the oranges in Anna O.'s case, may then call out an alternate personality. Thus, dissociation is an extreme form of SDL. Multiples may acquire memories and behaviors while in a state of extreme stress and are later amnesic for this information while in a more normal state (Chu et al., 1999). Once the stressful state is reinstituted, the memories and behavior return, and may appear to belong to a different person. This model would help explain why alternate personalities tend to be very emotionally responsive, whereas the core personality seems affectively blunted or drained. It would also explain why alternates seem to have specific functions and tend to appear only in situations that call for that function.

Treatment Options

The classical treatment approach with MPD (indeed, in that sense originating with Anna O.) makes extensive use of hypnotic techniques (Meyer & Salmon, forthcoming; Weissberg, 1993). Because hypnosis is often viewed as a structured or purposeful form of dissociation, it can help to make the transition from one alternate or ego state to another more predictable and manageable. An alternative explanation holds that the hypnosis merely produces a placebo effect, giving the client a rationale to give up dissociative symptoms. The usual strategy is to elicit each of the alternates, while audio- or videotaping, and discover their peculiar memories and characteristics to gain a working knowledge of the elaborately divided self-system of the client. Next, the therapist negotiates with each alternate for some kind of therapy contract. This process often meets with considerable resistance, because some alternates may be very hostile, destructive, or negativistic, whereas others may be immature, egocentric, or seductive toward the therapist. Eventually, each alternate must be convinced that he or she stands to gain from being integrated into a whole person.

The process of *fusion*, or joining of two or more alternates, is often dramatized in popular accounts of MPD. It can be seen as a more elaborate effort to help the client reconcile conflicting motives and ideas, as is common in many types of therapy (Dell & O'Neil, 2008). Hypnosis may be used to contact the alternates and encourage them to become active at the same time (Meyer & Salmon, forthcoming). Some clinicians make videotapes of the alternates and show them to the others during a waking state. The order of fusion generally follows two patterns. Alternates that dissociated at the same time or serve similar roles are brought together first. The therapist then attempts to reconcile remaining personality fragments with the core personality in roughly the order in which they split off. This process may involve hypnotic age regression of the core personality to the appropriate time period.

Some therapists have attempted to use antipsychotic drugs in treating multiples, but these efforts have had limited success. Anti-anxiety medications may be useful during periods of extreme stress as the process of fusion is underway.

Comment

Many clinicians have noted that MPD can often be an iatrogenic disorder, one that is superimposed on a variety of amorphous complaints by the therapist's suggestions that multiplicity would explain the client's condition (Spanos, 1996; Weissberg, 1993). Since many of these persons are frightened by their experiences, they might be particularly vulnerable to such suggestions. A second reason for skepticism about the concept of MPD stems from the occasional attempts of malingerers to escape criminal responsibility by presenting themselves as "split personalities." Most clinicians do accept the notion of MPD in principle, but most would argue that this disorder is very rare and difficult to diagnose (Spanos, 1996; Thigpen & Cleckley, 1984; Weissberg, 1993). Unfortunately, the rise in reports has stemmed primarily from the work of a relatively small number of clinicians and researchers who have a great deal of their professional identity invested in the concept. Knowledge of this puzzling disorder would be greatly enhanced by increased involvement of mainstream psychologists and psychiatrists who could bring more diverse perspectives to bear on the problem.

> *The little girl did not want to go to sleep in a neighbor's house unless the bedroom door was left open. "Why, you're not afraid of the dark—a big girl like you?" the neighbor teased.*
> *"Yes, I am," the little girl cried.*
> *"But you're not afraid of the dark at your house."*
> *"I know," answered the little girl, "but that's my dark."*
>
> —Anonymous story

Sleep Disorders

Sleep is an important part of life. People sleep for different lengths of times at different ages. Newborns need from 13 to 16 hours of sleep a day. As a rule, sleep needs then start to decrease so that those who are past 50 years of age need about 7 hours. Also, we require more sleep when we are sick, stressed, or have been involved in strenuous activities, and women need more during menstruation and pregnancy (Harsh & Ogilvie, 1995).

There is great variety in sleep disorders, just as there is in normal sleep patterns. Many adults will suffer a period of chronic insomnia at some point in their lives. In the *DSM-IV-TR* the sleep disorders are divided into (1) Sleep Disorders Related to Another Mental Disorder (e.g., a mood or anxiety disorder); (2) Sleep Disorder Due to a General Medical Condition; (3) Substance-Induced Sleep Disorder; and (4) the focus of this chapter, Primary Sleep Disorder. The Primary Sleep Disorders are subdivided into the Dysomnias (abnormalities in the amount, quality, or timing of the sleep cycle) and the Parasomnias (sleep-related abnormal events, such as nightmares).

The Dysomnias include (1) Primary Insomnia (307.42) (at least one month of difficulty initiating or maintaining sleep, with life impairment, and not better explained by other sleep or other disorders); (2) Primary Hypersomnia (307.44) (at least one month of excessive sleepiness, less if recurrent, and life impairment, etc.); (3) Narcolepsy (347) (at least three months of daily and irresistible attacks of refreshing sleep that include at least either catalepsy or recurrent intrusions of REM sleep into the sleep-wakefulness transition); (4) Breathing-Related Sleep Disorder (780.59) (evidence of a sleep-disrupting breathing condition); (5) Circadian Rhythm Sleep Disorder (307.45) (impairing and persistent or recurring excessive sleepiness or insomnia due to a mismatch of the sleep-wake cycle to the individual's circadian rhythm and/or environment requirements; can be further specified as Delayed Sleep Phase Type, Jet Lag Type, Shift Work Type, or Unspecified Type); and (6) Dysomnia NOS (307.47).

The Parasomnias are Nightmare Disorder (307.47) (impairing and repeated sleep awakenings, with recall of extended and very frightening dreams, with rapid reorientation upon awakening); Sleep Terror Disorder (307.46) (impairing sleep awakenings, usually with a panicky scream, intense fear with related autonomic signs, relative unresponsiveness to comforting, with little recall of the dream); Sleepwalking Disorder (307.46) (impairing repeated sleepwalking episodes, with unresponsivity in the episode, relatively quick reorientation, and amnesia for the episode); and Parasomnia NOS (307.47).

The critical diagnostic recommendation is that any apparently serious sleep disorder should be evaluated at a sleep disorder center; a thorough evaluation should include some observation and physiological monitoring, ideally of at least a couple of nights of sleep.

The two cases presented here detail three of the most important and common patterns: sleepwalking disorder in the first case and chronic insomnia and disruption of the sleep-wake cycle in the second. The first case (Sam) focuses on sleepwalking.

Little or no research has been done on the control of sleepwalking, although as early as 1968, Silverman and Geer eliminated one patient's nightmares by systematic desensitization. Most people do not view sleepwalking as more than an unavoidable nuisance. Even in the case presented, it was not the sleepwalking per se that was the problem, since the patient had walked in his sleep at a regular and high rate for nine years.

It is no small art to sleep: to achieve it one must keep awake all day.
—Friedrich Nietzsche, *Thus Spake Zarathustra* (1885)

The Case of Sam

Sam, a 24-year-old white male, came to therapy at the instigation of his wife. During a recent act of sleepwalking, he took down a shotgun, loaded it, and prepared to fire at imaginary burglars. His wife awakened to find herself looking into the end of the gun. Luckily, her screaming did not stimulate him to fire but rather woke him up. She insisted that he see someone the very next day. He had previously walked in his sleep four to five times per week without incident ever since he was 15 years old. His wife had tolerated this, only occasionally complaining of being awakened by his fumbling about.

From talking to Sam and his wife, all indications were that Sam had a very normal and happy childhood. He had no more than the usual childhood diseases, was obviously loved and well cared for by his parents, and never showed any childhood maladjustment.

Sam did casually mention that since his first year of college, he had always suffered anxiety before taking tests and had resorted to tranquilizers with little success. He said he was now becoming more anxious as time loomed for his bar examination.

Associated Features

There is no indication that psychological disorder is common in the background of persons with a sleepwalking disorder (Pressman & Orr, 1997). However, as with Sam, episodes become more frequent when the person is under stress or is fatigued. The incident with the shotgun had brought Sam to treatment, but similar aggressive or destructive incidents were never observed in Sam's history. Such incidents seldom happen with sleepwalkers.

Similar to Sam's, most sleepwalking episodes usually last anywhere from 2 to 3 minutes up to 30 to 40 minutes. Episodes usually occur in the nonrapid eye movement period—that component of sleep that typically contains the EEG delta activity (sleep stages 3 and 4).

Sleepwalkers often just sit up, make a few movements, and then go back to sleep; only on occasion does the episode proceed to actual walking. When they do walk, they show a blank stare (which can appear eerie or frightening), are poorly coordinated, can see and maneuver around objects, and usually are amnesic for the experience, which is the dissociative component.

Sleepwalking usually begins in and is most common in childhood, and approximately 15 to 20 percent of the population have sleepwalked at least once. There may be a genetic component, since the disorder does tend to run in families, and it is more common in males (Harsh & Ogilvie, 1995; Pressman & Orr, 1997).

The Treatment of Sam

The following recommendations, as adapted in part from Gilmore (1991), were first presented to Sam in a handout to take home:

1. Use no drugs, alcohol, or caffeine, and use no psychotropic medications unless prescribed by a physician who is aware of the potential of such medications to exacerbate sleepwalking. Avoid any over-the-counter cold remedies or diet pills that contain stimulants.
2. Remove and/or dismantle any lethal weapons from access by the sleepwalker.
3. Take special precautions, such as placing locks on doors and windows, tying one's ankle to the bedpost, and placing a "kiddie fence" by the bedroom door.
4. Sleep on the ground floor.
5. Get treatment for depression and/or other concurrent emotional problems.
6. Learn stress management skills and obtain skills and reassurance to lower anxiety, and consider marital counseling for related stress.
7. Maintain a regular sleep-wake cycle and get adequate sleep at regular intervals.
8. Get a complete assessment by an expert in sleep disorders who can monitor physiological measurements.

Relaxation techniques were employed with Sam, especially as there seemed to be a possible relationship of the gun incident to the test anxiety. A seven-item hierarchy of anxiety-arousing situations was agreed upon, ranging from "hearing about a friend who has a test," through "trying to study several days before the tests," up to the most anxiety-including item, "receiving the test paper and looking it over."

Sam said his wife was a light sleeper and often awakened during the sleepwalking because her bed was close to his, and the only exit from his bed was along a narrow aisle between the beds. He agreed to have her bed moved into contact with his so that he would have to wake her by crawling over her. His wife purchased a loud whistle, which she was instructed to keep by the bed and to blow anytime she was awakened by his sleepwalking. She was to chart each act of sleepwalking and how long it took him to react to the whistle.

Since Sam's bar exam was one month away, he was seen twice a week for systematic desensitization (see the case of Danielle in Chapter 2), for a total of 10 sessions (five weeks). In the meantime, he had dismantled the firing pin of his shotgun. Sam sleepwalked four times during the first week. His wife immediately blew the whistle and woke him. He sleepwalked five times the second week, twice the third, and no more from the fourth week. He had no negative reaction to the whistle.

During the first week, he was still unable to study effectively. However, in the second week, he accomplished the amount of studying he felt necessary. This change persisted, and there was a minimum of felt anxiety. He passed his bar exam with a mark somewhat higher than he expected, even under optimal conditions.

At a three-month follow-up, Sam reported he had walked in his sleep twice more, but each time, when his wife had blown the whistle, he had awakened immediately. At a one-year follow-up, he reported only two more such incidents. He had had no problem studying or concentrating in his law work.

We now turn to an even more common problem: insomnia and the disruption of the sleep cycle.

> *Mr. Answer Man, what is the existential equivalent of infinity?*
> *Why, insomnia, Sandy, good old insomnia.*
> —Norman Mailer, *Of a Fire on the Moon* (1970)

The Case of Ilse

Ilse is 42 years old and has two well-adjusted children, ages 21 and 19. The older is married and lives across town from her, and the younger is a sophomore at the state university some 90 miles from the medium-sized eastern seaboard city where Ilse lives.

Ilse had married while in college and almost immediately became pregnant with her first child, but she did finish her B.S. and R.N. degrees. The marriage had its problems but had been generally satisfying to her and lasted until Ilse was 34. At that time, her husband had rather abruptly announced that he had become involved with another woman and did not want to continue the marriage.

Ilse was emotionally shattered, but within a year she recovered. She had been working part-time as a nurse, but immediately took a full-time job. As the children grew older, she added some occasional part-time jobs, and with the aid of child support and judicious investing, has become financially stable. She has developed a wide range of outside interests and a number of good, close friends and would be considered happy by both herself and her friends.

However, since adolescence, Ilse has been troubled by occasional bouts of disturbed sleep that have increasingly bothered her over the last several years. Most often, she goes to sleep without much trouble, but awakens after 90 minutes or so. She then is unable to get back to sleep very easily, sometimes going the rest of the night without any decent sleep. At other times, she can't even get to sleep in the first place, and spends the night moving about, getting only snatches of sleep. Also, during especially stressful periods in her life—for example, change of work hours or problems with her boyfriend or one of her children—she has a nightmare, often awakening with a scream from a vivid and frightening dream, usually shaking and in a cold sweat.

Ilse consulted with her physician, an internist, who gave her an array of physical tests, told her she was fine, and wrote her a prescription for some sleeping pills that she advised her to take only if she needed them. They did prove useful when she took only one on a particularly stressful night (e.g., before leaving town on a long trip). But Ilse would occasionally take them for a number of nights in a row. They would knock her out the first night or two, then would do little more than make her sleep deeply for three or four hours, after which she had even more consistent difficulty returning to sleep than she had experienced before using the pills.

She returned to her internist, who told her there was really nothing more that she could do, and she referred Ilse to a neurologist. The neurologist gave her several other tests, told her she was fine, and prescribed another brand of sleeping pill, with much the same result as before. Ilse was disappointed and upset. She tried several techniques that she had read about in nursing journals. Unfortunately, she was also siphoning off a few sleeping pills at a time for her own use from the patients on the general medicine ward where she was a supervisor, and occasionally took these for a few nights in a row. Almost nothing helped her, probably because she was randomly mixing pills and techniques.

The sparse follow-up data available suggest that Ilse's problems continued. From her own subjective perspective, she is likely to see her problems as worsening, since she will need somewhat less sleep anyway as the years go by. It's regrettable that Ilse's case occurred before clinics that were specifically designed to treat sleep disorders became more common. It's very likely that if there had been one to refer her to, the outcome would have been more positive.

Treatment Options

Though Ilse has occasionally experienced nightmares, the primary issues are her delayed or advanced phase sleep cycle disorder (i.e., awakening after three to four hours of sound sleep with problems going back to sleep) and her insomnia (the inability to get to sleep in the first place). Such sleep disorders can be secondary to other psychopathology or be caused at least in part by externals such as allergies, aging, types of food eaten (e.g., too much caffeine), or side effects of medications (Andreassi, 2000; Harsh & Ogilvie, 1995), but none of this appears applicable to Ilse.

The humorist and old-time movie star W. C. Fields once said that the best way to get a good night's sleep was to go to bed. He should have added "at a regular time every night, and within a regular routine." He should have also advised that if you do not fall asleep within 15 to 30 minutes, you should get up, and come back to bed only when you actually feel sleepy. The important point is to consistently associate the bed with falling asleep. Note that if you awaken in the middle of the night, it is usually better to keep your eyes closed and stay in bed for a while, as you will likely fall back to sleep. People with problems like Ilse's should not work in bed or read or watch TV for long periods of time while in bed. They should establish a set routine and stay with it.

A sleep clinic would then have looked at other issues with Ilse. After an initial interview and review of medical records, a physical exam and a battery of questionnaires and psychological tests would be given, along with a polysomnogram. A polysomnogram, through electrodes attached to the face and head during an actual sleep period, records brain waves, muscle movements, and eye movements. Data from all of these pinpoint any abnormalities. If no great abnormality is located, then eating, exercise, and napping patterns are considered, and suggestions for other potentially useful techniques are made.

As noted, the first goal would be to help someone like Ilse establish a regular bedtime routine. Regarding eating patterns, Ilse would be advised that a late heavy meal often has a negative effect, but a small portion of food at bedtime is positive for most people, especially certain types of food. Specifically, foods that are high in the amino acid L-tryptophan (e.g., milk products, poultry, tofu, and eggs) have been found to aid sleep. Also, sweet, starchy foods high in natural carbohydrates (e.g., bread, bananas, and figs) help liberate the L-tryptophan. The process is even further facilitated by a small portion of foods high in both fat and carbohydrates (e.g., peanuts, walnuts, and avocados).

Napping and exercise patterns also need to be assessed. *Napping* has been defined as an unconscious 25-minute rest without pajamas, and it does seem to be an aspect of the body's natural biorhythms. It helps those who need it to catch up on their sleep, but naps late in the day can facilitate an insomniac pattern. Exposure to bright light later in the evening or when getting up at night can disrupt the biorhythms that govern sleep. A disrupted biorhythm leading to sleep disorder can often be evened out by controlled exposure to intense light, usually early in the morning, or dosages of melatonin. It's also helpful to get in the habit of not only going to bed at the same time every night but also getting up at the same time every morning.

People who get little or no vigorous exercise are more prone to insomnia and sleep cycle disorders. Good vigorous exercise three or four times a week, at least three to five hours before bedtime, helps develop more restful sleep patterns, and it is even better if it is carried out in the morning or early afternoon.

Other techniques have been found useful with certain people, such as (1) yoga or other slow stretching exercises and/or a warm bath two hours before bed (as your body temperature naturally returns to normal, you'll tend to become drowsier); (2) a period of "quiet time" before bed; (3) slow, repetitively melodic music; (4) a repetitive sound, such as a white-noise machine or calming music (not a new technique, one of the most famous piano pieces by Johann Sebastian Bach, the "Goldberg Variations," was specifically composed to control a Count Kaiserling's insomnia); (5) a nose bandage that allows one to breathe easier, especially if allergies are a factor; (6) a distracting, repetitive internal dialogue (e.g., "counting sheep"); (7) certain herb teas (e.g., chamomile, valerian, periwinkle); (8) use of certain vitamins, especially the B vitamins and calcium, magnesium, and potassium. Medication (see Table 4.1) can be helpful as a short-term mechanism. Relaxation training and/or biofeedback training may help, and psychotherapy can reduce the stress and conflicts that lead to sleep disruptions similar to those that Ilse experienced.

TABLE 4.1   Sedative-Hypnotic Drugs

Name (Generic/Trade)

Benzodiazepines	Barbiturates	Other Sedative-Hypnotics
flurazepam (Dalmane)	secobarbital (Seconal)	chloral hydrate (Noctec)
temazepam (Restoril)	methobarbital (Mebaral)	zolpidem tartrate (Ambien)
triazolam (Halcion)		zaleplon (Sonata)
estazolam (ProSom)		ethchlorvynol (Placidyl)
quazepam (Doral)		ramelteon (Rozerem)
midazolam (Versed IV)		eszopiclone (Lunesta)

5 The Somatoform Disorders

Persons with somatoform disorders, like those with the factitious disorder (see Chapter 16), manifest complaints and symptoms of apparent physical illness for which there are no demonstrable organic findings to support a physical diagnosis. Thus, an accurate diagnosis in this group of disorders can be difficult, especially if there is some reward for malingering (Boyd et al., 2007; Katon, 1993). However, the symptoms of the somatoform disorders are not under voluntary control, as are those of the factitious disorder. The diagnosis of somatoform disorder is therefore made when there is good reason to believe that the person has little or no control over the production of symptoms. The factitious disorder is more common in men; somatoform disorders occur more frequently in women.

> *There's a fly to deep center field. Winfield is going back, back. He hits his head against the wall! It's rolling toward second base!*
> —Jerry Coleman, San Diego Padres broadcaster

Somatoform Disorder Subcategories

There are five major subcategories of the somatoform disorders: Somatization Disorder, Undifferentiated Somatoform Disorder, Conversion Disorder, Psychogenic Pain Disorder, and Hypochondriasis. There is also a catch-all category, Atypical Somatoform Disorder, in which individuals are placed if they fit the general criteria for somatoform disorder but not the specific criteria of the other five major categories.

Somatization Disorder

The chronic though cyclic multiple somatic complaints that mark the subcategory of the somatoform disorders are not primarily due to any physical illness. Yet, they may be mixed with other symptoms derived from an actual disease, so arriving at this diagnosis is initially difficult (Johnson, 2008; Morrison, 2002). This disorder is discussed in the first case in this chapter, along with the Undifferentiated Somatoform Disorder.

The symptoms of both of these disorders are often presented in a vague but exaggerated fashion. Incidentally, this dramatic component was the linkage between the traditional diagnostic terms *hysterical neurosis* and the *hysterical personality*. Fortunately, the *DSM-IV-TR* terminology did away with some of the confusion inherent in these labels. Hysterical personalities are now referred to as having a histrionic personality disorder (see the case of Hilde in Chapter 11). Hysteria is typically subsumed under one of the somatoform disorders, usually as a conversion disorder that is still sublabeled the Hysterical Neurosis, Conversion Type.

Conversion Disorder

The *DSM* describes conversion symptoms as "pseudoneurological," since they are related to motor and sensory functioning. Therefore, the diagnosis should be implemented only after a true neurological or general medical condition has been ruled out. The conversion disorder pattern is similar in many respects to the somatization disorder. The difference is that in the conversion disorder, there is a specific symptom or a related set of symptoms, and these symptoms either are used for the attainment of some secondary gain or they express a psychological conflict (Dattilo et al., 2008). Conversion symptoms are not under voluntary control. Psychogenic Pain Disorder, which is discussed in detail in the upcoming case of Pam, can be considered a subcategory of conversion disorder where the specific symptom is simply pain.

With some of the psychosexual dysfunctions (see Chapter 8), it may be difficult to decide whether the problem directly expresses a psychological issue (and is thus technically a conversion disorder) or whether it is a physiological response to anxiety. In actuality, it may be a mixture of both. For these reasons, as well as for convenience, all of these cases are included in the psychosexual disorders.

A conversion disorder is still referred to as a Hysterical Neurosis, Conversion Type, and such individuals are said to manifest *la belle indifference,* an attitude in which there is little concern about the apparent serious implications of the disorder. Persons with a conversion disorder appear to be aware at some level that their complaints do not predict the dire consequences that others might infer from them. Although indifferent to their presenting symptoms, a pattern of emotional "ups and downs" (lability) in response to other stimuli is commonly noted. The attitude of *la belle indifference* is not found in all conversion disorders. Some people develop their symptoms under extreme stress and manifest that stress quite directly. Yet, even in these individuals, anxiety seems to dissipate over the duration of the disorder in favor of a focus on physical symptoms.

Hypochondriasis

The *DSMs* have consistently suggested that the essence of this disorder is in the unwarranted preoccupation with having a medical condition. This preoccupation is rooted in the exacerbation of insignificant bodily changes. Hypochondriacs unreasonably interpret normal or relatively unimportant bodily and physical changes as indicative of serious physical disorder. They are constantly alert to an upsurge of new symptomatology, and since the body is constantly in physiological flux, they are bound to find signs that they can interpret as suggestive of disorder.

In one sense, hypochondriacs do not fear being sick; they are certain they already are. Hypochondriasis is a relatively common pattern from adolescence to old age. It is seen most frequently in the 30- to 40-year age range for men, and the 40- to 50-year range for women (Meister, 1980). Meister also believes that there are many "closet hypochondriacs," who do not constantly go to physicians yet are heavily involved in health fads, checking of body behaviors, and discussion of their concerns with close friends (who may relish the quasi-therapist role). These closet hypochondriacs would not earn a formal *DSM* diagnosis, as they do not fit some of the specific requirements, such as seeking out medical reassurance and going through physical examinations. Nonetheless, they manifest the disorder.

A number of common factors have been observed in the development of hypochondriasis:

- Most hypochondriacs have a background marked by substantial experience in an atmosphere of illness. This could include identification with a significant other who was hypochondriacal or early exposure to a family member who was an invalid.
- Hypochondriacs often have had a strong dependency relationship with a family member who could express love and affection normally or intensely during periods when the hypochondriac was ill, yet was distant or nonexpressive at other times.
- Hypochondriacs often channel their psychological conflicts and their needs for existential reassurance into this pattern. As a result, the hypochondriac pattern of behavior may mask a midlife crisis or some other challenge that is not being met effectively.
- A certain subgroup of hypochondriacs is postulated as having a predispositional sensitivity to pain and body sensation. This could be stimulated by prior physical disorder in systems in which the hypochondriacal pattern is now manifest.

All of these factors are naturally facilitated by reinforcement of the hypochondriasis in the client's world. Avoidance of tasks or demands because of being sick is often noted here. A most entertaining portrayal of this disorder is presented by Woody Allen in his 1986 movie, *Hannah and Her Sisters*.

Now we'll turn to a case on the Somatization Disorder, and then to a common pattern within the somatoform disorders, the Psychogenic Pain Disorder.

Father Theodosius, representative of the Russian Ecclesiastic Mission in Jerusalem, when pictured in a white robe and a black head-dress, was asked about the afterlife. He said, "When I die, I'll go to heaven. That's what I'm working on. What do you think I'm dressed like this for?"

The Case of "Alix" (Empress Alexandra Fedorovna)

Alix Victoria Helena Louise Beatrice, Princess of Hesse-Darmstadt, was born on June 6, 1872, in Darmstadt, a medieval German city near the Rhine River. She was named "Alix," the closest euphonic rendering of "Alice" in German, after her mother, Princess Alice of England, the third of Queen Victoria's nine children.

In a letter to the Queen, Alix's mother described Alix as a "sweet merry little person, always laughing," and everyone quickly took to Alix's nickname of "Sunny." Since her godparents were Tsar Alexander III of Russia as well as the future King Edward VII of England, it's not surprising she had an early entree into contact with royalty across Europe as well as the Russian imperial family.

At least until age 6, Alix had the idyllic childhood that people fantasize is characteristic of nobility. When she was 6, an outbreak of diphtheria swept through the palace where she lived, eventually killing her 4-year-old sister. Then, apparently stressed from taking care of her sick children, Alix's mother, Princess Alice, also fell ill and died, at age 35. After the tragic death of her mother, Alix's sunny disposition darkened, and henceforth, a hard shell of aloofness often covered her emotions.

She first met her future husband, Nicholas, the future Tsar Nicholas II of Russia (of the Romanov family), when, at age 12, she traveled to St. Petersburg, Russia, for the marriage of her sister to the younger brother of Tsar Alexander III. Five years later, in 1889, when she visited her sister in St. Petersburg, Alix and Nicholas met again, and apparently fell in love.

Though still somewhat aloof with groups of people, Alix was a generally happy person whose life was normal and unpretentious, at least for a princess. In 1889, she rejected the marriage proposal of Prince Albert Victor, heir to the throne of England, who later died tragically at age 28. In 1894, she accepted the marriage proposal of Nicholas II.

In October 1894, Tsar Alexander III reported distress from headaches, insomnia, and weakness in his legs. At first, there was little concern. But he worsened and a little over 10 days later, on November 1, 1894, he died at age 49. Nicholas, now age 26, and Alix were married on November 26, one week after the funeral. Then, after a long period of mourning and preparation, Nicholas was crowned tsar (actually "Emperor and Autocrat of all the Russias") on May 26, 1896. He was the richest man in the world and ruler of almost one-sixth of all its land. Alix became the Empress Alexandra Fedorovna.

There was intense pressure and expectancy that Alexandra would produce a son, as only a male could become an heir to the throne. In mid-November 1895, Alexandra went into labor, and cannons were fired, 300 cannon shots to announce the birth of a boy. They stopped firing at 101, announcing the birth of Grand Duchess Olga. At two-year intervals, three more daughters were born: Tatiana, Marie, and then Anastasia, in 1901, the same year as the death of Queen Victoria of England.

Then, on August 12, 1904, Tsar Nicholas II was able to write in his diary, "A great never-to-be-forgotten day when the mercy of God has visited us so clearly. Alix gave birth to a son at one o'clock. The child has been called Alexis." The joy in the royal family was unbounded, but only until six weeks later, when Nicholas II wrote, "A hemorrhage began this morning without the slightest cause from the navel of our small Alexis." Within months, the terrifying suspicion of both parents was fulfilled; Alexis had hemophilia. Some historians would later argue that this defect in this tiny infant would be the critical factor in toppling Imperial Russia.

Hemophilia is an inherited blood-clotting deficiency, transmitted in a sex-linked recessive Mendelian pattern. Thus, although women carry the defective genes, they almost never suffer from the disease. It is a disease recognized from ancient times (e.g., in the Egypt of the Pharaohs, a woman was forbidden from bearing more children if her firstborn son bled

(continued)

The Case of "Alix" (Empress Alexandra Fedorovna) Continued

to death from a minor wound). It has been termed "the royal disease," and Queen Victoria, who was a grandmother, aunt, and so on to most of Europe's royalty, turned out to be a hemophilia carrier.

Alexis was a charming, chubby, blonde, blue-eyed boy. He was constantly attended by guards, restricted from many activities, and doted on continuously, especially by his mother, who felt enormous guilt over "producing" his condition. Crisis after crisis occurred, even after the slightest bump or fall, with Alexis often enduring great pain and/or being near death. In 1912, an injury was exacerbated by the trauma from the jolts of a carriage ride, and he again almost died. He was allegedly saved through the intervention of the monk, Father Gregory Efimovich (known as Rasputin, from a Russian word for "dissolute"). Rasputin eventually gained great power with the royal family, especially with Alexandra. Rasputin allegedly controlled Alexis's bleeding through hypnosis, but criticism of his influence over her was a rallying cry for revolutionaries. Nicholas was apparently not as taken by Rasputin as some have believed, but was willing to put up with him, once commenting, "Better one Rasputin than 10 fits of hysterics a day," reflecting Alexandra's deepening emotional disorder.

Many factors took an emotional toll on Alexandra. She still suffered from sciatica, a severe pain in the back and legs that she periodically experienced since childhood. Her pregnancies were all difficult. But all of this paled before the emotional battles with her son's hemophilia. During these crises, she would sit all day and night with Alexis, often observing him in great pain. After the crisis, she would collapse, lying on a bed or couch for weeks, moving only in a wheelchair. In 1908, she began having episodes marked by hyperventilation, anxiety, and/or fatigue. She reported a variety of other physical symptoms at other times, including headaches and nausea, and also fainted on several occasions. She

attributed virtually all of these symptoms to "an enlarged heart" and "a family weakness of blood vessels." Episodes were common. In 1911, she wrote, "I have been ill nearly all the time." Evidence for this pattern continued periodically until her death.

The political revolution fomented by revolutionaries such as Alexander Kerensky, and then carried through by Vladimir Ilyich Ulyanov (known as Lenin), gradually swept into power. In mid-March 1917, Tsar Nicholas II abdicated in favor of his brother, who in turn almost immediately abdicated. Tsar Nicholas II and his family were exiled to Siberia.

On July 17, 1918, apparently in order to destroy any lingering hopes of a return of the Romanov dynasty or any royalty, the imprisoned tsar and his family were executed, along with four retainers who had shared the family's captivity: a cook, a valet, a maid, the family dog, and the Romanov's physician. Yakov Yurovsky, the Bolshevik officer in charge of the Romanovs' captivity, was a photographer by vocation. He asked the 11 prisoners to stand in two rows against the wall of the room, as if for a family portrait. Satisfied with his arrangement, he then called in the killer squad—six Latvians and five Russians—who immediately crowded into the narrow door that faced the captives. As Yurovsky finished reading a brief statement that ended with the words "The Ural Executive Committee has decided to execute you," the shooting began. The brutality of the carnage that followed is unequaled in the recent annals of royal executions.

The tsar was killed on the spot, as were the Empress and Grand Duchess Olga, neither of whom could finish making the sign of the cross. Other members of the group were less fortunate. Because the Czarevitch and the three remaining sisters wore corsets thickly sewn with some 17 pounds of jewels, for long moments bullets fired at their chests continued to ricochet around the tiny room like hail, failing to kill them. First mystified, then enraged, the executioners finished off their victims with bayonets and rifle butts. It was so vicious that some of the imperial party's skulls, in the words of a forensic expert, were "crushed as though a truck drove over them." The bodies were then dumped in a mineshaft and grenades were thrown in. However, since rumors about the bodies were still circulating, they were moved the next day. But the truck broke down near Yekaterinburg, the city in the Urals where the execution took place, so the executioners tried to burn two of the smaller bodies. It took so long that they put the other bodies into a pit and poured sulfuric acid on them. Curiously, in 1977, Boris Yeltsin, the future president of Russia, who was then a Communist Party chief, organized the destruction of the massacre site—a further attempt to wipe out the memory of the monarchy from the psyche of the Russian people. A black marble cross now marks the site.

In 1992, the remains were exhumed. Definitive DNA tests in Britain and the United States identified the remains of Nicholas, Alexandra, and three daughters. In 2007 the bones of both Alexis and Marie were tentatively identified. Also, a chest with 38 pounds of crown jewels that had been smuggled out of the palace has never been found. The remains of the family were reburied in the Imperial family vault in the Cathedral of St. Peter and St. Paul, in St. Petersburg, Russia.

The Diagnosis

It is not surprising that Queen Victoria is associated with this case. Somatoform disorders were common in the Victorian era, and were the source of much of Sigmund Freud's theorizing in that period.

Let's first consider which specific somatoform disorder would apply here. In order to diagnose a somatization disorder, the *DSM-IV-TR* requires evidence of a history of physical complaints occurring over several years, resulting in seeking treatment or a significant life impairment, with evidence that the physical symptoms began before the age of 30. The clients must also report over the course of the disorder, four pain symptoms, two gastrointestinal symptoms, one sexual symptom, and one pseudoneurological symptom, and either (1) these symptoms cannot be directly explained by a medical condition or substance or (2) if there is a relevant medical condition, the response is excessive, and it is not a Factitious Disorder (see Chapter 16). The Somatization Disorder is thought to be diagnosed rarely in males, but approximately 1 percent of females are alleged to have this disorder at some point in their lives.

On the other hand, in order to diagnose the Undifferentiated Somatoform Disorder, the *DSM-IV-TR* requires only one physical complaint, again not directly explainable by a substance or a general medical condition, or being an excessive response if there is a medical condition; causes a life impairment; lasts at least six months; and is not better accounted for by other mental disorder diagnoses.

It is evident that Alix's condition would at least warrant the diagnosis of Undifferentiated Somatoform Disorder. She showed numerous physical symptoms not attributable to any true medical condition, and these symptoms persisted over many years. It is probable that she would also earn the more specific diagnosis of

Somatization Disorder. There's no evidence that Alix ever showed a sexual symptom within this pattern, but a lack of disclosure in this regard would be consistent with the tenor of those times. In any case, Alix quite clearly suffered some form of a classic somatoform disorder.

Causes

As to the possible causes of this disorder in Alix, several factors likely played a part. The psychological trauma from her mother's death and the atmosphere of illness that surrounded this episode no doubt influenced her in this direction. Her periodic bouts of sciatica also helped set the stage (Morgillo-Freeman, 2008).

Significant stressors after the engagement and marriage were periodic rejection by the Russian people because she was "German" and the intense expectancy that she would produce a son. The precipitants were followed by the crushing disappointment upon learning of Alexis's hemophilia. Then, for the rest of her life, there were the constant crises around Alexis's health that required huge expenditures of both physical and emotional energy.

Additionally, in the Victorian period people communicated about their distress through the vehicle of descriptions of physical disorder, a pattern still observed today in many elderly patients. There were no psychiatrists or counselors as they are known today. People were not encouraged to talk about their emotional feelings or problems; indeed, more often they were discouraged from doing so.

All of this was certainly a fertile ground for the production of a somatoform disorder (Morrison, 2002). Factors such as (1) childhood or adolescent trauma within an atmosphere of illness, (2) experience with an actual physical illness, (3) depression, (4) major physical and emotional stressors, and (5) the inability to articulate or communicate one's distress in psychological terms are still common precipitants.

Treatment Options

Today, a treatment regimen for any of the Somatoform Disorders, and especially the Somatization Disorder, could include various components (e.g., psychotherapy, biofeedback, group or support group therapy, etc.). Whatever techniques are employed, however, the following core principles (Katon, 1993; Morrison, 2002) should govern the treatment plan: (1) the suffering should be accepted as real (though real does not always mean a physical cause), but it is often hard to find a treating physician with this attitude; (2) there should be regularly scheduled visits for "treatment" so that production of a new disorder is not required as an "admission ticket"; (3) after a thorough physical, constant recourse to more and more obscure lab tests should be avoided; (4) anti-anxiety or sleeping medications should seldom be prescribed, especially since they can be addicting; (5) never prescribe pain medications "as needed"—prescribe them only for short, defined periods; (6) above all, get clients moving, psychologically and physically—never prescribe rest, for rest and inactivity are always counterproductive for them; and (7) families should be involved in the treatment—they can be taught to help get the client to exercise and avoid inactivity, and they can learn to respond supportively yet without encouraging "pain" or "disease" talk. These principles can also be effective in the treatment of the next disorder discussed: pain disorder.

> *They breathe truth that breathe their words in pain.*
> —William Shakespeare, *Richard II* (1596)

Pain Disorder

Psychogenic pain disorders are similar to conversion symptoms that center on an experience of pain for which there is no plausible physiological explanation. Often, the pain may be initiated by some real traumatic event, such as an accident. In other cases, the pain merely asserts itself gradually until it is entrenched in the sufferer's lifestyle (Katon, 1993).

Conversion disorders differ from the factitious disorders in that the conversion sufferer is not consciously aware that the symptoms experienced are unreal (i.e., have no physical basis—but pain is commonly reported in both patterns). The notion that pain, sometimes serious and debilitating pain, is all in one's head is sometimes difficult to accept (Dell & O'Neil, 2008). It is important to note that the experience of pain takes place not at the perceived site of discomfort, but in the brain, and a variety of central nervous system operations may influence pain experiences. Techniques such as Lamaze (for childbirth) are based on the assumption that appropriate attitudes and emotions can minimize pain. Psychogenic pain often seems to be the flip side of this process, with conversion-prone persons experiencing intense symptoms with minimal provocation.

Until the 1800s, a variety of florid conversion disorders was relatively common. Some patients would mysteriously lose sensation in all their extremities or suffer sudden seizures. Recent advances in medicine have made it possible to easily debunk these extreme displays, and they have nearly disappeared. Relative to these sorts of conversion disorders, the incidence of psychogenic pain has increased dramatically, perhaps because vague, diffuse pain symptoms are far more difficult to identify as inaccurate. Psychogenic Pain Disorder thus presents a special diagnostic challenge that requires the collaboration of psychologists with medical specialists, who are often the first to encounter the psychogenic pain symptoms.

> *Look for a long time at what pleases you, and for a longer time at what pains you.*
> —Collette, French novelist (1873–1954)

The Case of Pam

Pam was 38 years old when first seen at the pain clinic. She reported that she had suffered from recurrent hip pain since her early teens, linked to a car accident that occurred when she was 17 years old. Her regular physician, a gynecologist, had referred her to an orthopedic surgeon some time previously, but this evaluation yielded no conclusive explanation for the ongoing pain. Her hip pain was sporadic, sometimes confining her to bed for a day or two. On the other hand, she and her husband had recently taken a skiing vacation with no ill effects.

Pam also reported frequent headaches, which she characterized as "migraines, definitely." Like her hip pain, the headaches were an intermittent problem, sometimes being quite severe while later disappearing altogether for several weeks. The headaches had begun about two years previously, shortly after Pam and her family had moved into the area. Again, Pam was referred to a medical specialist, a neurologist, for evaluation. The neurologist noted that her description of the headaches did not correspond to a typical migraine pattern, and he was unable to find a plausible explanation for them. He initiated the referral to the pain clinic in cooperation with Pam's gynecologist.

Finally, Pam had recently seen a daytime television show that described premenstrual stress (PMS), and she suggested that this would explain both of her problems as well as several new infirmities. The gynecologist reported that this possibility had already been considered and did not account for Pam's problems. Hence, "functional" or psychogenic factors would need to be evaluated.

Etiology

At the pain clinic, Pam was seen by several health care personnel. Thorough medical, psychological, and social histories were taken, and numerous psychological and medical tests performed. Finally, a multidisciplinary team reviewed all the available data and found that a variety of psychological factors probably served as the primary sources of both the headaches and the hip pain.

Pam was the second youngest of four children, and her position ensured that she received little individual attention from her parents. Her younger sister was pampered as the baby of the family, while her older brother excelled in sports. Because he was several years older, his achievements seemed to overshadow those of the younger children. This effect was heightened by the attitudes of Pam's parents, who felt that males should be competitive and outgoing, and rewarded this behavior in a variety of ways. They also expected their daughters to strive for success, but in more traditional female roles, such as music and academics. Pam came to adopt a traditionally feminine view of herself and confined herself to these outlets.

Pam described her parents as cool and aloof. They rarely showed affection toward one another or toward their children. On the whole, the family had little social contact with others in the community, except for formal events centering on church and school activities. Pam and her siblings found that emotional displays of any kind made their parents uncomfortable, and so learned to hide their feelings. Pam recalled that her parents seemed more caring and tender toward her whenever she suffered a childhood illness, such as the measles.

Pam's father spent little time with the family, instead devoting himself to his career. The children were troubled by their father's absence, but Pam's mother quashed any complaints. She shamed the children for complaining while their father was working so hard to be a good provider. The children suspected that their mother also resented the father's absence, but she never expressed this directly. Instead, she behaved with superficial charm toward her husband. Whenever he did wish to spend time with her, she suddenly became tired or ill, thus frustrating his limited attempts at intimacy. Pam came to adopt her mother's style of suppressing frustrations with others, only to express them in indirect ways. This pattern depended in part on her expectation that she would be made to feel guilty if she voiced her discontent overtly.

According to Pam, her mother suffered a variety of gynecological problems and frequently consulted her physician. On occasion, her vague complaints would require that she stay off her feet for several days. During these episodes, the father would demand that the children do nothing to upset their mother, thus indicating that he believed the illnesses were stress induced. He behaved solicitously toward his wife until she felt better, then frantically threw himself back into work to "catch up." A predictable cycle was established, with the mother becoming ill and dominating the family briefly, only to have things return to normal as soon as she felt better. Pam learned firsthand that ill behaviors could be effective in gaining attention (and control) from otherwise disinterested family members.

Pam was an attractive girl who reached puberty rather early. She was initially pleased by her resulting popularity and became involved in a variety of school-related activities. Upon entering high school, she hoped to begin dating, viewing this as a logical extension of her social life. Consistent with her parents' reluctance to confront many aspects of human intimacy, they did not discuss sexuality with her, and she was quite naive about the role it might play in dating. Despite her parents' attempts to screen her boyfriends, Pam inevitably dated boys who pressured her to become sexually active. Surprised by these advances, she resisted anything more than light petting at first. Eventually, she became involved in a long-term relationship and in this context she felt less inhibited. She found the warmth and intimacy of these interludes a welcome change from the emotional coldness of her family. While she began to enjoy more sexual experimentation, she had moral reser-

vations about these activities and experienced considerable emotional conflict as a result. Ultimately Pam and her boyfriend progressed to having intercourse in the backseat of his car. Following one of their initial encounters, when Pam was age 17, they were involved in a car wreck on the way to her parents' home. Each sustained a variety of minor injuries, and Pam complained that her right hip was stiff and sore. Physicians found no sign of injury, and suggested that this pain would go away in a few days.

Despite these predictions, Pam's hip pain continued and came to interfere with many of her activities, including dating. After several months, the boyfriend began dating someone else, and Pam's pain gradually subsided. This relationship had produced considerable conflict for Pam, but her "injury" provided her with an indirect means of escape. She did not have to break off the relationship herself or insist that the boyfriend stop pressuring her for sex. It is not unusual for conversion symptoms, including psychogenic pain, to symbolically reflect the underlying anxieties that they mask; in this case, Pam's hip pain had localized near the genital area.

After high school, Pam continued to live at home while attending a local community college. Her grades would have permitted her to attend a more prestigious institution, one that her parents preferred and one that would have allowed her to remain within their control. Pam resented the implication that her educational advancement should give way to their wishes, but she protested little. She met her husband through the community college, and they married after a brief romance. In many respects, this liaison served as an escape from her parents' domination, and was particularly effective, since they did not approve of her husband-to-be.

Pam reported that her husband, John, is a very conventional, hard-working individual. He has an M.B.A. and works for a local bank in an administrative capacity. Like Pam's father, John puts in considerable overtime and seems to have little involvement with his family. His expectation is that Pam will take care

(continued)

The Case of Pam Continued

of all the domestic duties while he will be the "breadwinner." The couple has three children, ranging in age from 9 to 15. The children participate in athletic and artistic activities in addition to attending a private school. The family is comfortably upper-middle class. Pam perceives the demands placed on her as onerous and would like to escape some of these. Her pain experiences may help her to do this.

When asked about the strengths and weaknesses of her marriage, Pam had difficulty in identifying any strengths, other than that she believes her husband is "substantial." She feels that their relationship lacks much real emotional commitment. Pam was able to identify one area of conflict. The family had moved every two to three years because John felt that it was necessary to advance his career. At present, Pam is very comfortable with her home and social circle. Although she finds it difficult to make friends, she has become close to several people in the community and is resistant to another move.

Pam was uncharacteristically adamant about her position when John once again mentioned "moving on" approximately two years ago. She felt guilty for this outburst and resolved not to act so hot-headed in the future. Her recurrent headaches began shortly thereafter. Pam now has some realization that she can tell when John wants to discuss moving, and it appears that her headaches serve to preempt these overtures. They may also provide an escape from the many demands her children place on her.

Treatment Options

The treatment principles discussed in the case of Alix, concerning a somatization disorder, are equally applicable here. Because a broad range of factors may contribute to psychogenic pain, many types of interventions have been employed with some success (Katon, 1993). One group of approaches centers on confronting the lack of a plausible physiological explanation for the pain, while at the same time pointing up the psychological "rewards" for the pain experience. Techniques associated with reality therapy and confrontation-insight therapy may be useful. Such confrontations must be carefully managed, however, to prevent flight from treatment. Since these persons often find intense relationships anxiety provoking, they instinctively withdraw from therapists who attempt to cut through their superficial defenses.

Cognitive–behavioral techniques provide a second major line of attack (Morgillo-Freeman, 2008). Merely changing the client's environment to eliminate secondary gains may serve to reduce the frequency or intensity of psychogenic pain experiences. Hypnosis has been proven to be effective (Meyer & Salmon, forthcoming). Also, biofeedback has been found to help alleviate many types of pain, even if no clear pathophysiology exists. Contracting with clients to increase the number of activities they attempt may divert attention and energy away from the pain experience. These efforts are consistent with the finding that many persons experiencing psychogenic pain may be clinically depressed. Depressed persons also tend to benefit from attempting a wider range of activities.

A third general approach entails training the client to relate to others in more positive and explicit ways. Often, their pains and illnesses serve to gain attention and caring from others or to absolve clients of responsibilities they find overwhelming. Assertiveness or social-skills training may help the individuals express their needs clearly, thus reducing the need for more manipulative behavior. Work on problem solving or related issues may help clients manage demands adequately.

A new line of drugs may help here. The neurological site of chronic pain is in a small class of spinal cells, less than 2 percent of spinal cord volume. When a substance termed SP-SAP, a biochemical marriage of a toxin and a compound that activates the chronic pain cells, was injected into rats, all chronic pain symptoms ceased, without side effects or impairment of any other functions. Applications to humans appear imminent. Also, it is common that psychogenic pain may overlay a degree of actual pain and/or may be associated with depression. A relatively new drug, duloxetine, has proved to be particularly effective with pain associated with depression. It is chemically similar to the fluoxetine (Prozac), except that duloxetine affects both serotonin and norepinephrine, whereas Prozac primarily affects serotonin.

The Treatment of Pam

Pam's evaluation at the pain clinic took weeks to complete. During this period, she was asked to keep a journal of her pain experiences and a variety of other activities and events. Once the team had determined that her pain was primarily psychogenic, the journal data were helpful in pointing out many contributing factors. She was gently but firmly confronted with the possibility that her hip pain and headaches served several purposes of which she was unaware. Since some of the pain was related to actual trauma, and some depression was noted, duloxetine was prescribed, and appeared to help her.

During the initial phase of therapy, Pam was encouraged to explore several characteristics of her early life that predisposed her to pain disorder. She came to recognize that her passivity and dependency, inability to confront negative emotions, and guilt proneness stemmed from the family milieu in which she was raised. Subsequently, she was encouraged to explore ways in which she might be reenacting the patterns of behavior her mother had used in her own marriage.

Homework assignments for Pam initially focused on increasing positive activities outside her usual domestic drudgery. Special emphasis was placed on health-related behaviors such as exercise and diet. Subsequently, she felt healthier and more energetic—factors that greatly reduced her expectations that she would be ill or in pain. Biofeedback was useful in giving her more of a reality-based perception of physical sensations and symptoms. She also contracted to increase contacts with her friends. It was far more inconvenient to have a headache or sore hip when it would conflict with a luncheon engagement or some other pleasurable activity.

Pam's skills in relating to others came under scrutiny in the course of therapy. Social skills and assertiveness training methods were used to enhance her ability to make appropriate requests of others, to express her opinions openly, and to refuse requests politely.

John was also brought into the therapy effort. It was noted that he shared a number of his wife's attributes, including difficulty expressing emotions and passivity in confronting problems. It became apparent that the family's repeated moves had been motivated not so much by career necessity as by John's inability to confront normal difficulties in the workplace. The ongoing but veiled conflict over an impending move was subsequently reduced. A brief but intensive course of couples therapy helped both Pam and John become better able to work out potential problems quickly, rather than experience ongoing anxiety over their lack of resolution. The couple also found that their relationship became more emotionally passionate, and John found that he wanted to spend more time with his wife. Pam's need to gain attention through incapacity was thus negated.

Ultimately, Pam made a very successful recovery from two recurrent and debilitating problems. Her treatment was facilitated by the multidisciplinary nature of the pain clinic. Many persons experiencing psychogenic pain have been told by an acquaintance or family member that "it's all in your head," and hence refer themselves to a variety of medical specialists in an attempt to validate their pain experience. These persons often receive treatments that they do not need, such as analgesic medications, which are basically ineffective. They easily habituate to or even become addicted to medications, so they should never receive medications "as needed," but only for short, circumscribed periods. Side effects and iatrogenic health problems may be the result. As with the factitious disorder (see the case in Chapter 16), it is important that these persons be identified rather than left to flounder in the conventional medical system.

Comment

Persons who suffer with psychogenic pain seem to fall along a continuum ranging from those whose pain is primarily a reflection of some type of psychological conflict to those whose symptom production is dominated by secondary gain. Most conversion disorders involve each motif to some degree, as was the case with Pam. Her hip pain initially arose as a result of intense internal conflict. It was apparently prolonged because it was so effective in eliciting secondary gains. Once the pattern of illness behavior and concessions from the environment is established, it is common for these persons to acquire additional symptoms. New complaints often arise in the face of new demands or if the old symptom is discredited somehow. Also, complaints that are difficult to verify empirically may serve as the catalyst for conversion symptoms.

The Nocebo Effect

The nocebo effect could be implicated in at least part of the symptom picture seen in some cases of somatization (including pain) disorder. Experts have long recognized the placebo effect (that patients improve because they believe they will); the opposite (nocebo) effect may be equally powerful: Patients get sick because they believe they will.

The nocebo phenomenon may also be responsible for occasional outbreaks of what has been called "epidemic hysteria," in which numerous people in a group (e.g., students in school) suddenly begin to experience similar symptoms of illness, though no physical cause is found. Seventy-eight such outbreaks of illness were documented in Quebec between 1872 and 1972. Because the symptoms are triggered by patient beliefs does not make them less real or less costly to the patients, and the possibility that expectations could be a major factor in illness should be taken seriously.

The brain mechanisms by which the placebo and nocebo effects work are now being elucidated. It appears that the stimulation of the insular cortex in the brain can produce serious effects on the heart, including ventricular fibrillation, or uncontrolled fluttering, which can lead to severe symptoms and even death. Thus, chemical components in the brain might stimulate the insular cortex and produce such a reaction.

6 The Schizophrenic and Delusional (or Paranoid) Disorders

Especially severe forms of psychopathology—characterized by perceptual, cognitive, affective, communicative, motor, and motivational disturbances and specifically denoted by a loss of contact with reality—are termed *psychoses* (Cullberg, 2006). Some psychotic reactions are obviously associated with brain disruption due to physical causes such as diseases of the nervous system, brain tumors or injuries, toxic drug or chemical reactions, or circulation disturbances. More prevalent are the functional psychoses that do not stem fully and directly from a known physical trauma to the brain, although a biological factor (e.g., genetic) may be an important or even a primary cause. There are three major classifications of functional psychoses: Mood (Affective), Schizophrenic, and Paranoid. The Mood (Affective) Psychotic Disorders, which are discussed in the next chapter, are characterized by extreme fluctuations of mood, with related disturbances in thought and behavior. The *DSM-IV-TR* also includes the Schizoaffective Disorder, in which schizophrenic and affective symptoms are both prominent and develop at about the same time.

The primary focus here is on the *DSM-IV-TR* diagnostic categories of the Schizophrenic Disorders and the Delusional (or Paranoid) Disorders. The major symptoms of schizophrenia involve withdrawal from reality, with flat or inappropriate emotional reactions and marked disturbances in thought processes. Delusions, hallucinations, and stereotyped mannerisms are common.

> *All issues are political issues, and politics itself is a mass of lies, evasions, folly, hatred, and schizophrenia.*
>
> —George Orwell (1903–1950)

Schizophrenia has been recognized as a disorder since Morel's (1857) description of a 13-year-old whose intellectual, moral, and physical functions gradually and inexplicably deteriorated over time. Morel used the term *demence précoce* (mental deterioration at an early age); he thought the deterioration was caused by hereditary factors and was virtually irreversible. Several modern theories of the disorder do not differ very much from Morel's views. *Dementia praecox*, the Latin form of Morel's term, was used by Kraeplin (1899) to refer to the rather large class of disorders that has features of mental deterioration beginning early in life. Bleuler (1911) introduced the term *schizophrenia* (split mind) to indicate his belief that the disorder chiefly involved a lack of integration between thoughts and emotions and a loss of contact with reality. Bleuler attained some measure of fame when he diagnosed schizophrenia in Vaslav Nijinsky, one of the most famous ballet dancers of all time.

To apply the overall diagnosis of schizophrenia, the *DSM-IV-TR* (American Psychiatric Association, 1994) requires evidence of two of the following: (1) delusions, (2) hallucinations, (3) grossly disorganized or catatonic behavior, (4) disorganized speech, or (5) negative symptoms, such as affective flattening, alogia, or avolition. But if hallucinations involve voices commenting consistently or voices conversing with each other, or if delusions are bizarre, only one of the symptoms is required. The symptoms must be present for at least one month, and some signs of the disorder must continue for at least six months with or without a prodomal or residual phase. Prodromal and residual symptoms are often present before and after the active phase, respectively. Sometimes these symptoms may be mild manifestations of the positive symptoms, but more often, they are severe manifestations of the negative symptoms. Typical delusions of schizophrenics include somatic delusions, delusions of being controlled, thought broadcasting, and grandiose delusions. Five subtypes of schizophrenia listed in the *DSM-IV-TR* are Paranoid, Disorganized, Catatonic, Undifferentiated, and Residual.

Disorganized Schizophrenia (previously termed *Hebephrenia*) is marked by disorganized speech and behavior and flat or inappropriate affect (often in the form of random giggling). Catatonic Schizophrenia is manifested by extreme psychomotor disturbance, or withdrawal or excitement patterns. Undifferentiated Schizophrenia, as in the case of Sally, involves a variety of symptoms and is often the eventual diagnosis applied to chronic cases. Paranoid Schizophrenia, as in the case of Daniel Paul Schreber, is the least overtly disturbed form of schizophrenia. Paranoid schizophrenia can be contrasted with the other paranoid disorder, as well as with the other schizophrenic disorders (see Table 6.1).

The Delusional Disorder (Paranoia) is a psychotic disorder characterized by the gradual development of a complex, intricate, and elaborate delusional system—in contrast to the more fragmented delusions of Schreber (a paranoid schizophrenic) or the nonpsychotic paranoid personality disorder. The delusional systems in a Delusional Disorder (Paranoia) are usually based on misinterpretations of actual events. Once this (inaccurate) premise is established, other aspects of the delusion logically follow. However, an extensive interview with a paranoid patient may reveal no marked abnormalities if the areas of delusional material are not mentioned. Five primary subgroups (based on type of delusion) are recognized in *DSM-IV-TR:* Erotomanic, Grandiose, Jealous, Persecutory, and Somatic. For example, persons with delusions of grandeur believe they are some exalted being, such as Jesus Christ or the president. Erotomanics believe someone, usually of higher status, is in love with them. Somatic delusions are very irrational beliefs that one has some physical deficit or general medical condition. Individuals who have delusions of persecution feel they are targets of various conspiracies against them.

TABLE 6.1   Paranoid Disorders Compared

Paranoid Schizophrenia	Other Paranoid Disorders
The delusional system is poorly organized and may contain a number of delusions that change over time; schizophrenia and belief system disorder are both fundamental to the abnormality	The irrational beliefs may not be so severe as to constitute a delusion, or, when existent, there are fewer of them, and they don't often change; a belief system disorder is the fundamental abnormality
A generally bizarre appearance and attitude	Appearance of normality
Problems in reality contact	Relatively good reality contact
The delusions are wide-ranging, including persecution, jealousy, grandiosity, irrelevant thoughts	The delusions are usually of persecution or nonreality-based jealousy
Biological factors are generally the significant contributing causes	Psychological factors are generally the primary causes
Depression or other mood disorder is more common	Depression is not very common
Develops later in life	First manifestations occur in adolescence or late adolescence
More common in males	Approximately equal incidence in males and females
More disoriented or withdrawn appearance	Often some reasonably normal-appearing outward behaviors
Often of lower-than-average intelligence	Higher intellectual ability than other schizophrenics
Approximately equal occurrence across cultures	Rare occurrence in many rural non-Western cultures
Tend toward long periods of hospitalization	Proportionately shorter hospital stays
No specific body build	Tend toward mesomorphic body build (the body of the powerful athlete)

Undifferentiated Schizophrenia, a particularly severe level of disorder, can be seen in the first case of this chapter—that of Sally.

> *"Your secret dreams that grow over the years like apple seeds sown in your belly, grow up through you in leafy wonder and finally sprout through your skin, gentle and soft and wondrous, and they have a life of their own . . ."*
> *"You've done this?"*
> *"A time or two." (p. 99)*
>
> —W. P. Kinsella, *Shoeless Joe* (1982)

Undifferentiated Schizophrenia

Schizophrenia exacts a tremendous cost from both society and the persons who suffer from it. Occurrence is approximately equal across sex, although there is frequently a milder course in women as well as a mean later onset of six years. Onset typically occurs between mid-teens to mid-twenties, and is usually a year or two later in those societies where children stay longer within the family environment, for example, India or China. About 1 out of every 100 people in the United States will be diagnosed as schizophrenic at least once in their lifetime. This 1 percent rate has been consistent across cultures and also across the years within U.S. culture (Amminger et al., 1999; Munich, 2002).

The following case, that of Sally, is an example of Undifferentiated Schizophrenia. Sally, a person who eventually shows an undifferentiated pattern, often had shown earlier disorganized, catatonic, or even paranoid patterns. The *DSM-IV-TR* distinguishes this subtype as meeting the positive and negative symptom criteria for schizophrenia, without conforming to the criteria for the Paranoid, Disorganized, or Catatonic type. Most long-term schizophrenics show various symptoms at different times and usually eventually show a mixed and/or varying pattern of symptoms, thus earning a diagnosis of Undifferentiated Schizophrenia (American Psychiatric Association, 1994).

The Case of Sally

Sally did not start life with the best roll of the dice. In spite of physicians' warnings, Sally's mother persisted in her two-pack-a-day smoking habit, even while she was carrying Sally. Also, during her fifth month of pregnancy, Sally's mother suffered a severe bout of the flu. Additionally, there is reason to believe Sally may have inherited some vulnerability to schizophrenia. Her maternal grandfather had always been known in the family as an "eccentric," but people less fond of him preferred to call him "crazy" or "nuts." He had developed a number of unique religious beliefs and also was known in the community for having placed unusual mechanisms on the roofs of his barns, supposedly to bring in "electromagnetic energy" to help his livestock grow. Farming in those days did not demand the organizational and financial skills that it does today, so it provided plenty of room for odd and/or person-avoidant behaviors. He was never brought to the attention of any mental health professionals—indeed, he thought *they* were "nuts."

In general, Sally was slow to develop. She both walked and talked late, but at the same time was an active child. She was never formally diagnosed as "hyperactive" but she clearly was above average on this dimension.

Sally's parents had a marriage filled with conflict, even separating for almost 10 months when Sally was 2 years old. But they did reunite, to enter into what would best be termed a long-term conflict-habituated marriage. They were both devoted to Sally, especially since after two miscarriages after Sally's birth they were advised not to have any more children. Sally's father traveled quite a bit because of his position as a sales coordinator for a farm machinery company. When he was home, he played with Sally a lot. But he could be quite critical if he thought she was not behaving (and later achieving) at the level

(continued)

The Case of Sally Continued

he thought she should be. Her mother, on the other hand, developed an intense, almost symbiotic relationship with Sally.

Sally was of above-average intelligence. However, in spite of her mother's intense coaching and Sally's withdrawal into studying (and fantasy behavior), she was only average or lower in most subjects. It was always as if her thought processes were, as one teacher put it, "just a bit off center."

Sally did have an occasional friend. But her mother's overprotection and Sally's occasional odd behaviors and thought processes kept her out of the flow of activities, and she never made long-term, deep friendships. In fact, when it appeared that Sally had any possibility of having a deep friendship, her mother's intrusions became more pronounced, and the promise of that relationship was destroyed. Essentially, Sally was a quiet and a mildly shy child. Also, because she did not have the feedback inherent in friendships and an active social life, she developed even more odd interests and mannerisms. These in turn served to further distance her socially.

Upon graduation from high school, Sally was allowed to board at a nearby college. However, the stress of being in new surroundings was too much for her. She started talking to herself, and her assigned roommate quickly managed to be moved to another room. One afternoon the dorm counselor found Sally in her room sitting in a chair, staring at the floor. Sally was unresponsive, and her limbs could be moved about and would then stay in place, almost as if she were plastic doll.

Sally was in a withdrawn catatonic state, marked by a condition referred to as "waxy flexibility." She was hospitalized and improved fairly rapidly. She tried to return to school but became more and more reclusive, now often skipping classes. Her mother brought her back home "to take care of her," and Sally degenerated even further, at one point showing a pattern of almost totally unresponsive behavior, interrupted occasionally by periods of giggling and rocking behavior, traditionally termed a *hebephrenic* pattern.

Finally, Sally's father insisted that Sally return to the hospital. She did, but when she showed some improvement, her mother again brought her home and did not continue the recommended outpatient treatment. Sally was able to get a part-time job as a clerk in a nearby store that did a low-volume business, which did not place great demands on her. She spent almost all of her free time at home, doing some jobs around the house and spending the rest of the time in her room.

About this time, her father suffered a fatal heart attack, making Sally's mother even more dependent on her daughter. Sally had now taken to wandering about on her way home from work, possibly as a defense against the intensity of her mother's needs. Her behaviors were also becoming more bizarre. One day the police found her walking in the shallows of a pond in the town park, muttering to herself. They took her to the local hospital, and she was then transferred to a nearby mental hospital.

Etiology

Just as there is a variety of symptoms in schizophrenia, so also may a number of causes contribute to an eventual case of schizophrenia. In one case, certain factors may be primary, whereas in another case, other factors may be more critical. Indeed, it may be more accurate to refer to schizophrenia as "a family of disorders" rather than a single disorder (Cullberg, 2006).

It is also important to remember that there are various types of causes for schizophrenia. The several possible "original" causes for schizophrenia are termed *generic variables;* for example, genetics are one probable generic cause. The most immediate manifestation of the disorder is an information processing deficit, evident in problems in attention, perception, and memory (Munich, 2002). The variables that subsequently produce these symptoms are labeled *mediating variables.* It is also important to note that there are *maintenance variables*—that is, variables that do not generate the disorder or the symptoms (e.g., interpersonal difficulties) but that later serve to maintain and even increase the symptoms of the disorder (Horowitz, 2004).

Various generic, or original, causes of schizophrenia have been proposed. Substantial evidence shows that there is a genetic (hereditary) predisposition to schizophrenia, which may operate as a compelling cause in some individual cases and may be only a contributing factor in others (Cullberg, 2006; Munich, 2002). It is very possible that Sally's eccentric grandfather actually suffered from schizophrenia, although there was never any formal diagnosis.

A critical problem in this case is likely the severe bout of flu that Sally's mother suffered when she was five months pregnant with Sally. Research indicates that trauma from a virus, or even malnutrition, or some other systemic disruption in the second trimester increases markedly the risk for schizophrenia. The theory is that such an event disrupts the migration of cells resulting from the breaking up of the neural subplate, which typically first forms in the second trimester of pregnancy. This subplate then usually dissipates almost entirely within the first month of life, having performed its task of aiming neurons toward their proper location in the cortex. Since by far the major migration of cells through that neural subplate occurs during the second trimester, any disruption at that time is potentially problematic. It can result in an unusual distribution of "guidepost" cells in the brain, leading to atypical and/or faulty neural connections—that is, more a "bad wiring" rather than a "bad seed" or "bad environment hypothesis."

Because of the nature of the symptoms of schizophrenia, any potential cause of brain disorder (genetic problems, birth disorder, trauma, viral or infectious disorder, etc.) may contribute. Even Sally's mother's heavy smoking during the pregnancy could have generated some mild intrauterine asphyxiation, a combination of anoxia (a loss of oxygen to brain tissue) and increased carbon dioxide tension in the blood and tissues, which leads to an acidic metabolic condition that could result in some tissue damage. Any of these original causes can lead to neurological disorder or imbalances of brain chemicals such as dopamine, serotonin, or norepinephrine.

Psychological disorders, such as early psychological conflict or family disorder, can also be a critical variable in the development of schizophrenia. Although most theorists do not see it as an original cause in and of itself, it can certainly be very important in the development, amplification, and maintenance of the disorder. For example, research (Miklowitz et al., 1986) indicates that two environmental factors, intrafamilial expressed emotion and communication deviance, are especially contributory, and they both appear to be operative in Sally's case. *Expressed emotion* refers to a family situation in which parents are emotionally overinvolved and overprotective (as was Sally's mother) or are highly critical (as was her father, at least on occasion).

Communication deviance is a measure of the degree to which an individual is unable to establish and maintain a shared focus of attention with someone while in a dialogue. This could of course result from brain disorder, but it could also result from early conflict or familial disorder. Communication deviance was also evident in Sally's history.

One of the more recent theories about the development of schizophrenia is termed the *prodomal pruning* theory. This theory is based on the well-established observation that as humans move from biological adolescence into adulthood, the point when schizophrenia is most likely to emerge, the normal brain initiates an intense biological form of spring cleaning, disconnecting and discarding many little-used brain circuits, or synapses. This natural pruning of brain cells occurs because there is a much greater need for such circuits to handle the explosive growth of information that occurs in the earlier formative years. Pruning allows the brain to become more efficient and adaptable to the changing mental needs of adulthood. The theory is that the schizophrenic's brain becomes more vulnerable at this transition point because, depending on which genetics and which other disruptive early factors are operating, his or her brain is an overly aggressive pruner, and he or she has more vulnerable and/or fewer nerve links to begin with. Since this pruning is occurring at the same time there are typically pressures on the individual to become more physically and emotionally independent, vulnerability is even greater. One implication of this theory is that rather than wait and react to the emergence of full-blown symptoms, an earlier and more aggressive treatment approach is warranted.

Even with the potential multicausal background of schizophrenia, there are premorbid factors that predict the emergence of schizophrenia as well as a common sequence of what often takes place in the development of schizophrenia.

Premorbid Factors in Schizophrenia

Premorbid factors are those factors associated with, but not necessarily causal to, the later development of schizophrenia. Only a few of the factors listed may be noted in any one case, but they are common across cases:

1. A schizophrenic parent or parents or (a less potent variable) the presence of other schizophrenic blood relatives. (There is approximately a 15-times greater chance of developing schizophrenia when a nuclear [blood relation] family member is schizophrenic. Curiously, having an older biological father slightly increases the risk for schizophrenia, but the age of the mother at birth is uncorrelated with risk.)
2. A history of prenatal (pregnancy) disruption, birth problems, viral or bacterial infections, malnutrition in the mother, exposure to *Toxoplasma gondi* (transmitted from cat feces), or toxic situations in pregnancy, especially if these occur in the second trimester.

3. Slowed reaction times in perception (such as slowness in becoming aware of a stimulus) or very rapid recovery rate of autonomic nervous system after some stress or novel stimulus.
4. Any early signs of developmental and/or central nervous system dysfunction (such as convulsive disorder), hyperactivity, decreased size of temporal lobes, or evidence of enlarged, lateral cerebral ventricles (the spaces between brain tissue).
5. Low birth weight and/or low IQ relative to siblings.
6. Early role as odd member of family or scapegoat.
7. Parenting marked by inconsistency and by emotionally extreme (both positive and negative) responses and double messages; parental rejection particularly when one parent's negative effect is not countered by corrective attention and care from the other parent.
8. Rejection by peers, especially if accompanied by odd thinking patterns, ambivalent and labile emotional responses, or a lack of response to standard pleasure sources.
9. Early behavioral problems, especially noted in play and school; being perceived by both teachers and peers as more irritable and more unstable than other children.
10. An inability to form stable, committed relationships, especially for men. (For example, never-married men have almost 50 times higher odds of developing schizophrenia than men who have married; for women, it is about 15 times higher for never-married than for married.)

Treatment Options

Given the multisymptom nature of schizophrenia, it is not surprising that a variety of treatments is needed just to stop and/or reverse the course of the disorder. Total cures are rare. But many schizophrenics can be returned to a level of at least adequate functioning in their jobs and communities.

Administration of psychotropic medication is necessary in most cases (see Table 6.2). Traditionally, this has been with the phenothiazines (e.g., as chlorpromazine/Thorazine), the butyrophenones, or the thioxanthenes (Bezchlibnyk-Butler & Jeffries, 1999). Drugs such as aripiprazole and olanzapine are now favored, in large part because they produce fewer side effects. Clozapine is also favored because of its effectiveness, but requires constant blood monitoring because of a potentially lethal side effect, agranulocytosis, that occurs in a small percentage of cases. Although extremely helpful in most instances, there are disadvantages to the various chemotherapies: (1) they don't work at all with a sizeable minority of schizophrenics; (2) they work best with "positive" or more benign symptoms, but are less effective with the "negative" symptoms (see discussion later); (3) getting the dosage right is difficult, and overmedication can result; and (4) significant side effects are common, especially with long-term use, which is required in most cases (Buckley & Meltzer, 1995).

TABLE 6.2   Antipsychotic Drugs

Name (Generic/Trade)	
Phenothiazines	**Other Antipsychotic Drugs**
chlorpromazine (Thorazine)	loxapine (Loxitane)
thioridazine (Mellaril)	molindone (Moban)
fluphenazine (Prolixin)	clozapine (Clozaril)
fluphenazine decanoate (Prolixin D)	risperidone (Risperdal)
perphenazine (Trilafon)	olanzepine (Zyprexa)
trifluoperazine (Stelazine)	quetiapine (Seroquel)
	pimozide (Orap)
Butyrophenones	ziprasidone (Geodon)
haloperidol (Haldol)	aripiprazole (Abilify)
chlorprothixene (Taractan)	paliperidone (Invega)
Thioxanthenes	
thiothixine (Navane)	
propranolol (Inderal)	

A variety of other physical treatments is occasionally employed for schizophrenia: electroconvulsive treatment (ECT), dialysis, psychosurgery, and megavitamin therapy. However, there are little data to indicate that these are of any significant help in the treatment of schizophrenia, and there are potentially negative side effects with all of these interventions.

Supportive individual and group psychotherapies (Saiger et al., 2008), possibly abetted by family or marital therapies in certain cases, are usually part of any overall treatment program for schizophrenics. They help to reduce excess expressed emotion, thus allowing a lower dosage of maintenance medication, and they also help to ensure the schizophrenic is compliant in taking medication. It is also not well understood, even by many clinicians, that there is a high rate of suicide in schizophrenia—about 10 times higher than in normals. According to the *DSM-IV-TR* (American Psychiatric Association, 2000), suicide risk factors specific to schizophrenia are male, recent hospital discharge, under 45 years old, problematic employment, and signs of depressed hopelessness. Violence risk factors specific to schizophrenia are younger males with a history of violence and noncompliance with prescribed medications yet abuse of illicit drugs.

To the degree that schizophrenics are at a low level of overall functioning, confrontive techniques may also be helpful in getting them to at least respond. Also, with such severely deteriorated schizophrenics, token economies are useful in modifying a wide range of behaviors, including some of the bizarre mannerisms that distance others; they are also useful in promoting more positive social skills. Milieu therapy (unfortunately at times just a euphemism for the hospital environment) is also helpful in reorienting schizophrenics to more appropriate social behaviors. Other adjunct therapies—such as biofeedback, occupational and expressive therapies, and environmental and nutritional planning—can also be useful.

Training in more appropriate cognitive strategies and in ways to avoid the information processing distortions that occur with schizophrenia are necessary as well.

A most critical step is aiding schizophrenics in making an effective transition back into their families and communities. Indeed, it makes little sense to put forth significant time and effort when the problem first comes to the attention of social agencies or treaters and then provide only a minimum of attention when schizophrenics return from the hospital to the community. Proactive efforts by an aftercare "case manager" (i.e., consistent contact, monitoring, and support, sometimes referred to as "assertive community treatment" [ACT]) can be very effective, although they are seldom applied. They work by helping the client stabilize during crises, apply already learned and new social and coping skills, and make more positive social and vocational contacts.

Negative Symptoms

Negative symptoms (affective flattening, alogia, avolition/apathy, anhedonia/asociality, and attentional impairment) have been found to be directly correlated with a high rate of remission, slow onset, and higher probability of permanent disability for schizophrenics (Cullberg, 2006). Positive symptoms (positive in the sense that they are marked by their existence rather than their absence, as in negative symptoms)—such as hallucinations, delusions, positive formal thought disorder, and bizarre behavior—respond best to the antipsychotic medications. Unfortunately, the positive symptoms are relatively weak and unspecific as predictors of other variables. Two negative symptoms, anhedonia and affective flattening, are the strongest independent predictors of negative outcome. Patients with the poorest long-term outcome tend to show greater increases in negative symptoms during the early years of their illness. Early and progressive negative symptoms may signal a process leading to long-term disability.

Positive Prognostic Signs in Schizophrenia

Assuming that some effective treatment is occurring, the following positive prognostic signs predict to an adequate remission once schizophrenia is diagnosed (Knable, Kleinman, & Weinberger, 1995; Munich, 2002). These variables should be initially considered as correlated factors rather than necessarily explicit causes of such remission:

- Sexual-marital status: married, or at least a prior history of stable sexual-social adjustment. It is not just the support from the relationship but also the monitoring inherent in having someone else in the home.
- The degree to which negative symptoms (discussed earlier) are absent, especially to the degree they are absent early in the symptom picture
- A family history of affective rather than schizophrenic disorder
- Presence of an affective response (elation or depression) in the acute stage of the disorder

- Abrupt onset of the disorder; clear precipitating factors at onset
- Onset later than early childhood
- Minor or no paranoid trends in the disorder
- Higher socioeconomic status
- Adequate premorbid school and/or vocational adjustment
- Premorbid competence in interpersonal relationships
- Short length of stay in hospital
- No history of ECT treatment
- Tendency to be stimulation-receptive rather than stimulation-avoidant
- Lower levels of hostility, criticism of others, and emotional overinvolvement (expressed emotion) upon hospital release

Sally's Treatment

Sally's mother subverted any real treatment at the time of Sally's first two hospitalizations. Thus, Sally was not effectively treated until late in the process of her disorder—not an uncommon occurrence with schizophrenics. In her third hospitalization, Sally was immediately put on chemotherapy—in this case, Thorazine. She was included in an inpatient therapy group and talked to her psychiatrist for a half-hour or so about twice a week.

Fairly rapid improvement was seen in Sally's more obvious symptoms, such as talking constantly to herself, sometimes in an obvious response to voices she heard. However, some of her "negative" symptoms—specifically, her disturbances in attention and thinking—remained. Eventually, she was released back to her mother's care, which meant that, in spite of attempts to deal with her large overlay of social deficits through outpatient therapy procedures, Sally made little progress.

There were several relapses; indeed, the relapses began to be more common. The symptoms were now many and varied, although not always so flamboyant as in some of the earliest episodes, thus now earning her the diagnosis of Undifferentiated Schizophrenia. At the last contact with her therapists, Sally was in the hospital. The prognosis for any substantial cure was poor, and it is probable that she will continue the pattern of going in and out of hospitals and aftercare.

Paranoid Schizophrenia

> *Ninety-nine percent of the people in the world are fools and the rest of us are in great danger of contagion.*
>
> —Thornton Wilder, *The Matchmaker* (1954)

Paranoid schizophrenia is an interesting and severe disorder. In order to apply a diagnosis of Paranoid Schizophrenia, the person must first meet the overall criteria for schizophrenia. The disorder is specifically labeled as Paranoid Schizophrenia when the symptom picture is dominated by preoccupation with grandiose or persecutory delusions, delusions of jealousy (erotomania), or hallucinations (auditory) with a delusional content. See Table 6.1 earlier in this chapter for a comparison of Paranoid Schizophrenia with the other schizophrenias and with the other paranoid disorders.

The Case of Daniel Paul Schreber

Daniel Paul Schreber gained permanent status as a famous psychiatric patient by virtue of the attention given to him by Freud. The only source of information used by Freud in his renowned analysis of Schreber was a book authored by Schreber himself describing his thoughts and beliefs. Before Freud discovered Schreber's book, Freud had kept a woman with a classic case of paranoia in psychoanalysis in order to learn about her condition, even though he believed she was unable to benefit from therapy. When Freud discovered Schreber's work, he became consumed with writing Schreber's case history as a classic example of paranoia.

Freud was captivated by the eloquence with which Schreber wrote of his condition. Phrases used by Schreber to describe his condition such as "soul murder" and "nerve contacts" delighted Freud, who introduced them into his written communications. Every page of Schreber's grandiose descriptions of his affairs and the universe was an opportunity for Freud to amplify the sexual aspects of his psychoanalytic theory. Freud believed Schreber's paranoia caused him to explain the universe as a survival mechanism.

Daniel Paul Schreber was born on July 25, 1842, as a second son and the third of five children into a family of many generations of professionals. There is little direct evidence of what occurred in Schreber's childhood. It is known that he was gifted as a student. His father, Dr. Schreber, was a successful and well-known physician and reformer. One of many books written by Dr. Schreber had to do with how to raise children between infancy and adolescence. Dr. Schreber's first advice in that book, which he asserts with pride he used on his own children, is to put as much pressure on children during the earliest years of their lives in order to avoid trouble later. Dr. Schreber stated that infants should be bathed in cold water to toughen them up, and, to make sure children never cry, parents must startle children from crying by knocking on the bed or simply punish them through physical beatings, until no emotion is again shown. He stated that children should undergo intense physical training and learn to restrain their emotions.

One of Dr. Schreber's favorite topics was making the child have perfect posture at all times. Between ages 2 and 8 especially, children should wear an orthopedic device made of iron intended to create an extremely erect and straight posture. He emphasized that this must be maintained while the child is sleeping, and he created a device with iron rings and a chain to ensure the child's sleeping posture.

In addition to extremely rigorous restraints and exercises, Dr. Schreber's philosophy was to control every waking moment of a child's day. The child should be completely organized and well groomed at all times. If the child does not adhere to each activity at the exact time interval alloted to it, the child is to be denied the next scheduled meal for that day. Harsh physical punishment was recommended if the child deviates from the schedule at all. When the child is punished, the child must hold out his or her hand to the person who is administering punishment to ensure that the child will not be bitter. Dr. Schreber said a list must be maintained on the child's wall, detailing every act of disobedience, and

(continued)

The Case of Daniel Paul Schreber Continued

at the end of each week the child should be punished accordingly. This was also to ensure that the child will not grow up to masturbate.

As a result of the views of their father, Daniel Paul Schreber and his siblings likely grew up in complete passivity, and Schreber was described as nervous in his childhood. In 1858, when Schreber was 16 years old, Dr. Schreber's head was injured when a ladder fell on him. After that, he was known to have severe headaches, hallucinations, and stated homicidal intentions. Dr. Schreber was never the same; some believe that his peculiar behavior following the accident was a nervous breakdown. Three years later, when Schreber was age 19, his father died.

Schreber became a successful lawyer and later an esteemed judge. His older brother, Gustav, committed suicide when Schreber was 35 years old. At age 42, Schreber was defeated in a race for political office. It was after this defeat that he suffered his first mental breakdown. He started having hypochondriacal delusions, such as believing he was emaciated and that he was going to die of a heart attack. During this first hospital stay, which lasted six months, Schreber had speech impediments, two suicide attempts, hypersensitivity to noise, and high emotionality. Even when Schreber was discharged, he believed he had lost 30 pounds (when in fact he had gained 2 pounds).

After his discharge, Schreber spent the next eight years happily with his wife. His only disappointment was that they had no children. He reached the top of his profession when he was appointed presiding judge of the country's highest court. Immediately before this appointment, Schreber dreamed that his mental illness had returned. When his insomnia and anxiety became worse, Schreber contacted Dr. Paul Emil Flechsig, his former psychiatrist. Schreber's condition worsened and he was again hospitalized, this time for eight years. Schreber was 51years old—the same age of his father when he suffered the

blow to the head from which he never fully recovered.

It was during this second hospitalization that Schreber wrote *Memoirs of My Nervous Illness,* a book recording his thoughts, delusions, and hallucinations, written "to acquaint my wife with my personal experiences and religious ideas" so that she would understand his "various oddities of behavior." It is from this book that we have information about Schreber's psychological condition. Schreber's medical records reflect that when he began his second hospitalization, he feared he would soon die and had delusions of persecution. He believed he was a woman and his penis had been twisted off with a nerve probe. He had constant auditory and visual hallucinations. He believed he was being tortured to death and that God spoke openly to him.

Schreber often screamed out of his window statements such as "The sun [or God] is a whore." His thoughts about his body began to change from death and destruction to flowering into the body of a female, which made him pleased to show his doctor his naked chest. He became preoccupied with sexual thoughts.

While Schreber was spending much of his time with ribbons over his naked body in front of a mirror, he was able to write letters to his wife and family, wherein he spoke of his illness with amazing insight. In addition, when he was age 53, Schreber filed and ultimately won an appeal of his permanent commitment, which had been done without his knowledge. Schreber argued he had a nervous illness that resulted from problems that were objectively true. The court found that Schreber was mentally ill but agreed with him that mental illness was not determinative, since he was able to convince the court he could care for himself. In response to the argument that Schreber's intention to publish his *Memoirs* was evidence of his lack of judgment, the court ruled that the publication might be financially beneficial to Schreber and that despite the obvious lack of reality in the book, it did reflect a genuine interest in finding the truth.

The content of Schreber's *Memoirs* alternated between three levels: (1) the history of his illness and his efforts to appeal his order of involuntary commitment, (2) his personal experiences, and (3) his analysis of the cosmos. Schreber received information about the cosmos from souls that spoke to him, but unfortunately not in complete sentences, forcing Schreber to do so, which he said caused him to think compulsively:

> I meet a person I know by the name of Schneider. Seeing him the thought automatically arises "This man's name is Schneider" or "This is Mr. Schneider." With it "But why" or "Why because" also resounds in my nerves.
>
> When humans die God appears and sucks the nerves out of the body to return and be purified. Sometimes God, who sees all humans as corpses, makes a mistake and attaches Himself to living humans. When this occurs, there is danger because some living human nerves have such a powerful attraction that God will not be able to disconnect Himself. If this happened, God would cease to exist and there would be a rip or tear in the cosmic order.

The process of being transformed into a woman was one of Schreber's continuing preoccupations. Even though he believed this process was initiated by Flechsig, as a soul murder, with an intent to make him a prostitute, Schreber said that through a series of miracles, he agreed to become a woman to ensure his survival. He described this transformation in terms of many attacks on his body—for example, the destruction and replacement of his internal organs, the pumping out his spinal cord from his body through the assistance of little men in his feet, and the saturation of his body with female nerves. When he would ultimately surrender to this force, Schreber referred to himself as a joint of pork, and said his ultimate goal was to become pregnant by God.

Schreber's second stay in the hospital ended when he won his appeal of the permanent commitment. Eight years after entering the hospital, at age 60, Schreber went home. He lived there for five years. His mother, with whom he had been living, died, and soon after, his wife had a stroke and died. After his wife's death, Schreber reentered the hospital at age 65 and stayed there until his death at age 69, the same year that Freud's essay on paranoia based on Schreber's *Memoirs* was published.

Schreber's last position was as the president of a panel of judges at the Superior Country Court (court of appeals) in Dresden. Throughout his life, Schreber continued to publicly protest anyone using the devices his father used on him.

Freud's Analysis of Schreber

Freud interpreted Schreber's delusions as a manifestation of paranoia caused by homosexuality that Schreber denied or rejected. Freud used Schreber's writings to formulate a theory of paranoia. The foundation of this paranoia, repression of his homosexuality, took other forms so that Schreber wouldn't recognize his own wishes. Freud believed Schreber transferred his love for his brother and father to Flechsig and God. Freud used Schreber's *Memoirs* to develop his psychoanalytic theory of paranoia. Freud interpreted Schreber's desire to become a woman as a justification for his loss of masculinity and termed this the "father-complex,"

viewing homosexual fixation such as Schreber's as the result of unresolved Oedipal conflict. The threat of castration by Schreber's father caused him to abandon
his mother's love but at the same time identify with her.

Etiology

The onset of schizophrenia late in Schreber's life is consistent with symptoms he
displayed of paranoid schizophrenia. The extreme steps taken by Schreber's father
to control his children and to inhibit normal functioning and expression of feelings
likely resulted in this condition. There were no other schizophrenics known in
Schreber's family history, thus possibly placing Schreber into that small percentage of schizophrenics who may have acquired the syndrome during his life. Schreber's delusions were grandiose and bizarre, and his hallucinations were constant
during his episodes of schizophrenia. His preoccupation with turning into a
woman, his involvement with God and nerves, and his compulsive thinking as a
result of messages from souls all are part of a classic symptom picture of paranoid
schizophrenia.

What is interesting is that even during his most extreme episodes, Schreber
was able to function sufficiently to meet his needs. For instance, he was able to
write a logical, meaningful letter to his wife, describing his illness while he was
experiencing constant hallucinations and delusions. Also, Schreber's successful
appeal of his permanent commitment was seemingly remarkable. These events
are not unusual, however, for the paranoid type of schizophrenics, who are often
able to present themselves in a reasonably normal-appearing manner. Schreber's
high level of intelligence also is not that uncommon in the paranoid type of
schizophrenia.

A factor in Schreber's background that is common in the history of the development of paranoid behavior is the use of harsh and shaming techniques by his
parents to discipline him. As Colby (1977) noted many years ago, the paranoid
individual learns very early to use "symbol-processing procedures to forestall a
threatened unpleasant affect experience of humiliation, detected as shame
signals. . . . In preventing humiliation, the procedures use a strategy of blaming
others for wronging the self" (p. 56). Shaming techniques particularly predispose
an individual to learn to anticipate the possibility of humiliation and thus to
engage in numerous mechanisms to protect the ego from this experience.

Paranoids do differ from normals in terms of how they process information—that is, in their use of projection. Projection was initially hypothesized by
Freudian theorists, in part based on Schreber's case, although they were specifically referring to projection of an inner conflict over homosexual impulses. More
recent formulations have pointed out that it is not necessary to hypothesize a
homosexual conflict; indeed, some paranoids are overtly homosexual, which
directly contradicts this Freudian theory. On the other hand, the Freudian hypothesis of projection of the unconscious as an abstract concept has held up well
through the years (Weston, 1998), and it is clear that many of the paranoid's delusions are projections of internal ruminations and concerns.

Treatment Options

Persons with a paranoid disorder of any sort are seldom likely to be involved in treatment unless coerced some way, such as imprisonment, hospitalization, or pressure from a spouse. This is not surprising. Paranoids are inherently suspicious of many people and trust few. Also, most therapies, particularly for interpersonal problems, eventually require a degree of self-disclosure and the client's willingness to admit vulnerability. These latter characteristics are the antithesis of those qualities that make a person paranoid. Paranoids strongly fear allowing others to see their vulnerabilities and other foibles, as they are then open to a much feared shame experience or even to attack (especially if they have delusions of persecution). Thus, the critical first step is gaining the trust of the client (Cullberg, 2006).

Paranoids who are severely disturbed, and thus either dangerous or somewhat disorganized, are likely to be hospitalized. Some clinicians have administered ECT to paranoids, possibly from the notion that the paranoids will forget the content of their delusions. This treatment has shown little success, which is not surprising, since paranoids greatly fear any sense of increased vulnerability and/or loss of control over their self, which is a probable effect of ECT. Also, there is not much evidence that ECT is of any therapeutic value, except possibly for acute severe depression. The same problems and the lack of positive results have generally been found in the application of psychosurgery to paranoid disorders. However, chemotherapy strategies have been effective in reducing the more bizarre components, and more so with persecutory delusions than with somatic or erotomanic delusions (Buckley & Meltzer, 1995). Long-term psychotherapy is difficult, since the very nature of most treatment approaches (increased self-disclosure and confrontation of the self) are the things the paranoid most fears. Any significant cure depends on the therapist's ability to generate trust in one who is inherently untrusting.

Comment

It is rare for any type of paranoid to come into therapy without significant coercion from others. In order to relate to, or even treat, the paranoid, it is essential to gain the client's trust through empathy, but not through participation in the disorder patterns. It is especially necessary to empathize with and then articulate to the paranoid the consequences of such behavior, such as the sense of being isolated and not understood or the interpersonal rejection that appears unfair to the paranoid.

Ironically, paranoids will frequently be correct in assuming that other people are against them or, as some put it, "A paranoid is a person who has all the facts." Since it is noteworthy that such groups as immigrants, the elderly, and the sensory impaired are somewhat prone to paranoid thinking, it may be more accurate to say, "A paranoid is a person who has all the facts she is able to obtain, given who she is."

Before I built a wall I'd ask to know what I was walling in or walling out.
—Robert Frost, American poet (1874–1963)

As was the case with Sally and Daniel Paul Schreber, there are often long-term impairments in all areas of life. However, in the following true case we see a person with schizophrenia who ultimately attained monumental success.

The Case of John Forbes Nash, Jr.

Sanity is a form of conformity.
—John Nash, Jr.

The remarkable story of John Nash was made popular by the recent blockbuster movie *A Beautiful Mind,* based on the definitive book on Nash of the same title, written by Sylvia Nash and published in 1998 by Simon & Schuster. John Nash is one of the greatest mathematical geniuses of our time, even though he suffered from schizophrenia. In 1949, John established the principles of game theory, but it wasn't until 45 years later, when his schizophrenia was in remission, that he received the Nobel Prize for his monumental contribution to the mathematics of economics.

John Forbes Nash, Jr., was born in Bluefield, West Virginia. Clearly, John had an unhappy childhood. His parents didn't have the best marriage. His mother was loving and nurturing, but his father was emotionally distant. But both parents valued hard work and education. John typically avoided the neighborhood children, often playing in solitude inside his house. He could read by age 4 and skipped half a grade in elementary school. Yet, his teachers focused on his lack of social skills and saw him as an underachiever, overlooking his intelligence. He daydreamed constantly and had difficulty following the simplest of directions.

As John grew older, his parents became concerned about his nonexistent social life. They resolved to try to force him to become more "well rounded," enrolling him in Boy Scout camps, Bible classes, and dance classes, and forced him to get jobs and to go on dates. John did so, but he did not enjoy them. Additionally, some odd behavior patterns were emerging. His mother described an incident in which her son accompanied the family to dinner at the Appalachian Power Company. John spent the entire evening riding up and down in the elevator until it broke. During softball games, he would often stand in the outfield and eat grass. Other reports say that he even enjoyed torturing animals as a child, and often performed chemical experiments with explosives—one time possibly leading to the death of a fellow pupil. Not surprisingly, John was teased horribly as a child.

At the Carnegie Institute of Technology, where he went to study chemical engineering, John's odd behavior continued. For example, his roommate said John would sit and hit a single key on the piano repeatedly for hours, or he would leave a melting ice cream cone on top of his clothes pile. He was aloof, childish, and was experimenting with homosexuality, sometimes jumping into bed with sleeping boys. Yet, John graduated from Carnegie in three years.

Then, in the fall of 1948, John went to Princeton for graduate study in one of the truly elite mathematics programs. While at Princeton, John, at the age of 21, wrote his most famous piece on game theory, the cornerstone of the work that eventually led to his winning the Nobel Prize. He challenged traditional zero sum game theory by proving that in every game there is a different but best strategy for each player, given the strategies chosen by the other players. His game theory caught on later and has been used in everything from poker to economics. In the spring of 1950, John wrote *The Equilibrium Point,* which became known as the Nash Equilibrium. It revolutionized economics, although no one realized this until decades later.

After receiving his Ph.D. from Princeton, John accepted a job at the RAND Corporation.

However, shortly thereafter, in the summer of 1954, he was charged with indecent exposure by an undercover police officer in the men's bathroom at Palisades Park in Santa Monica, California. The police notified RAND, where homosexuality was then reason to prohibit security clearance. He was immediately fired, and officials at RAND made an agreement with the police that John would be leaving the state if the charges were dropped. After RAND, he accepted a position as a professor at MIT. He was described by his colleagues there as an elitist, selfish, and egocentric, and he displayed a number of strange verbalizations and odd behaviors. However, because of his undeniable intelligence and ongoing contributions to the field of mathematics, they respected John. While working at MIT he met Eleanor. After dating for two months, Eleanor became pregnant. John refused to take responsibility for the child and even refused to have his name on the birth certificate. Eleanor was forced to put the child in foster care; John's sister, parents, and colleagues never even knew about the child. Soon after this affair, John met Alicia Larde, one of his students. He dated Alicia for three years before marrying her in 1957. One year later, Alicia became pregnant and gave birth to a son, John Charles Martin Nash. The demands of career, new marriage, and a baby were too much for John, and he began manifesting even clearer psychotic symptoms.

On New Year's Eve 1958, John and his wife attended a costume party; John went as a baby and spent the evening curled up on Alicia's lap. Later that year, he interrupted a lecture to announce that he was on the cover of *Life* magazine as Pope John XXIII because 23 was his favorite number. In 1959, he stormed into the *New York Times* office, claiming that the paper contained encrypted messages from outer space that were meant only for him. MIT was forced to let John go. His functioning continued to deteriorate. Alicia came home one day to find that he had painted black spots all over the walls. She finally involuntarily committed him to a psychiatric hospital, where he

was diagnosed with paranoid schizophrenia. He was prescribed Thorazine and received some psychotherapy. John realized he wouldn't get out until he conformed, so he hid his delusions and was released.

After being released, John fled to Europe, leaving his child and Alicia behind. His goal was to denounce his American citizenship, but he was turned away in Luxembourg. John wandered Europe for nine months before he was deported. In 1961, Alicia had him committed involuntarily to Trenton State Hospital. For five days a week for a month and a half he was injected with insulin so his blood sugar would drop, creating insulin shock. But his symptoms diminished, and he was released after six months. John said much of his memory had been wiped out by the insulin therapy.

In 1962, Alicia divorced John. He had been taking antipsychotic medication, but felt that the medication was interfering with his thinking, so he stopped taking the medication in the mid-1970s. The symptoms of schizophrenia soon returned, especially auditory hallucinations. Nevertheless, around 1970, Alicia moved back in with John and promised never to hospitalize him again. Probably unbeknown to John, the world around him started to realize the enormous importance of his early papers. The Nobel Prize committee began to consider giving the prize to John. The committee members all agreed he deserved it, but decided they couldn't give it to someone who was so emotionally disturbed. In the 1980s, John began to generate his own transformation. He consciously rejected the voices, deciding simply to ignore them. He purposely began to think more rationally and began to work on mathematics again. By the 1990s, his schizophrenia was in full remission without the help of therapy or medication. In 1994, John received the Nobel Prize in Economic Science. In 2001, he and Alicia were remarried. Currently, John is still at Princeton University. His son, Johnny, received his Ph.D. in math from Rutgers and also suffers from paranoid schizophrenia.

7 The Affective (or Mood) Disorders and Suicide

The occasional experience of depression or even of suicidal thoughts (not plans) occurs during the life course of most people. German philosopher Friedrich Nietzsche once wrote, "It is always consoling to think of suicide, in that way one gets through many a bad night." "Indeed, the mood (or affect) disorders seem especially prevalent in modern society (Reinecke et al., 2008; Dozois & Dobson, 2004; McCullough, 2002; Whybrow, 1997). *Affect* refers to the subjective experience of emotion, whereas *mood* designates a consistent and pervasive emotion that influences our view of our world and ourselves. The affective disorders are broadly defined in the *DSM* as primary disturbances of mood and affect in contrast to disordered thinking, which characterizes the other two severe disturbances previously discussed, schizophrenia and the paranoid disorders. Included among the Affective Disorders classification in the *DSM* are symptom patterns that were formerly labeled as Depressive Neurosis and even on occasion as Cyclothymic Personality Disorder. Symptom patterns in this category range from mild to moderate depressive episodes to the psychotic affective reactions.

The major categories are those of Bipolar Disorder (I and II), Major Depression, and the specific affective disorders, which include Cyclothymic Disorder, Dysthymic Disorder, and Substance-Induced Mood Disorder. The Bipolar Disorder, which replaces the traditional term of *Manic-Depressive Psychosis*, is discussed here in the case of Virginia Woolf. Major Depressive Disorder categorizes severe, possibly chronic depression; it is discussed in the case of Joseph Westbecker.

Normal depression is characterized by a brief period of sadness, grief, or dejection in which disruption of normal functioning is minimal. Mild disturbances of mood and thought are manifested by apathy, impaired concentration, and increased guilt. These reactions are often responses to discrete environmental events, such as the loss of an important other (of high stimulus value, although not necessarily loved) or disappointments in career or finances. This depression may require no treatment and often lifts with the passage of time. Moderate episodes (as discussed in the case of Danielle in Chapter 2) are more disruptive to normal functioning and may be associated with distorted cognitions and/or skill deficits that require various psychological therapies. The more severe (and sometimes psychotic) depressive syndrome necessitates a multimodal therapeutic approach, usually including chemotherapy, psychotherapy, and cognitive-behavior modification; some of these techniques were employed in the treatment of Joseph Westbecker.

Major Depressive Disorder Associated with a Suicide Attempt

Well, I think you got anhedonia. It affects maybe one out of a hundred. It means you can't have fun. No kind of fun. Just like you on a golf course. You look like Torquemada's got the hot pliers on your nuts instead of just enjoying the game.

—Joseph Wambaugh, *The Secrets of Harry Bright* (1985)

Depression is a disorder of mood and affect, with these primary symptoms: (1) dysphoria (feeling bad) and/or apathetic mood; (2) a loss or decrease in the potency of stimuli—for example, through the death of an important other (a condition referred to as a *stimulus void*); and (3) *anhedonia*, or a chronic inability to experience pleasure. These symptoms were well described by the noted existential philosopher and theologian Soren Kierkegaard in his 1844 book, *The Concept of Anxiety* (Princeton University Press):

I do not care for anything. I do not care to ride, for the exercise is too violent. . . . I do not care to lie down, for I should either have to remain lying, and I do not care to do that, or I should have to get up again, and I do not care to do that either. . . . I do not care at all. (p. 19)

These primary symptoms are often associated with a various mixture of the following secondary symptoms: (1) withdrawal from contact with others; (2) a sense of hopelessness; (3) rumination about suicide and/or death; (4) sleep disturbance, especially early morning awakening; (5) psychomotor slowing or agitation; (6) decrease in and/or disruption of eating behaviors; (7) self-blame, a sense of worthlessness, irrational feelings of guilt; (8) lack of concentration; (9) lack of decisiveness; (10) increased alcohol or drug use; and (11) crying for no apparent reason.

Virtually everyone has been depressed at one time or another in his or her life. Indeed, it is a normal response to loss or disappointment. But when it persists and/or becomes so severe that it significantly disrupts a person's world, depression becomes pathological. It is estimated that up to one-fourth of the office practice of physicians who focus on physical disorders is actually concerned with depression-based symptomatology. It is noteworthy that about 85 percent of the psychotropic medication dispensed for depression is prescribed by nonpsychiatrists, primarily internists, gynecologists, and family practitioners (Nathan et al., 1995), and now, increasingly, pediatricians (Phelps, 2002). In 2004, the FDA required "black box" warnings on all antidepressant drug containers, stating that the drugs increase the risk of suicidal ideation and behavior in children.

The *DSM* mentions that a Major Depressive Episode may be labeled Mild, Moderate, Severe without Psychotic Features, or Severe with Psychotic Features. Whereas manic disorders and depression with a manic component usually begin before age 30, depressive disorders can begin at any age. Peak occurrence is in the 20–45 age range; episodes in older people are likely to include more severe symptoms and a more precipitous onset. According to the *DSM-IV-TR* (2000), approximately 60 percent of those who have one episode of Major Depression will have a second episode. Predisposing factors include a family history of depression; a depressive episode in childhood (e.g., there is a 75 percent chance of recurrence in later life if a child has a first episode during the period of age 8 to 13); several episodes of reported physical symptoms without a medical basis during the teen years; alcohol abuse; high negative stress; recent losses; chronic low self-esteem; and any history of chronic illness or recent severe physical disorder such as cancer. Comorbid anxiety or panic disorder predicts a more negative prognosis, as does melancholia (a syndrome including such symptoms as early morning awakening and more severe dysphoria in the morning, psychomotor agitation or retardation, loss of ability to experience pleasure, and, occasionally, anorexia). Melancholic features are associated with a family history of depression and also with a better response to ECT and tricyclic antidepressants. One in seven with a major depression will make a suicide attempt, and one in three will develop some form of substance dependency (Nathan et al., 1995; Strupp, Lambert, & Horowitz, 1997).

It is sobering to realize that in nations as separate as the United States, Taiwan, Lebanon, and New Zealand there is evidence that each successive recent generation is growing more susceptible to depression. Of those Americans born before 1905, only 1 percent had experienced a major depression by age 75; of those born after 1955, 6 percent had suffered a significant depression by age 30. Certainly, better recognition is a factor, but so is the stress of modern life. It is estimated in *DSM-IV-TR* that approximately 3 percent of males and 6 percent of females have had a depressive episode sufficiently severe to require hospitalization. However, this "gender gap" is narrowing, especially for those under the age of 40. An important aspect of the greater incidence of depression in females compared to that in males is the accentuation of behavior prescribed by traditional sex-role expectations. Also, abuse early in life, other patterns of victimization, and infertility or a large number of children (especially when the latter is combined with low economic resources) are factors that predispose women to depression. Several other factors predict depression, and more so in women: economic deprivation, low self-esteem, a preoccupation with failure, a sense of helplessness, a pessimistic attitude toward the world, and narcissistic vulnerability.

Dimensions of Depression

The normal-pathological continuum is one way of typing or conceptualizing depressions. Other continuums on which one can categorize different depressions are acute-chronic, agitated-slow, neurotic-psychotic, primary-secondary, and, of course, the unipolar-bipolar dimension that would differentiate Joseph Westbecker's typical pattern of depression (unipolar) from that of Virginia Woolf (bipolar) in the cases in this chapter. Another particularly important continuum is the endogenous-exogenous one. This popular classification system attempts to categorize depressions by cause. *Endogenous* depressions are assumed to originate from internal psychic and physical causes (such as genetics and/or hormonal disruption); *exogenous* depressions are from external causes (such as personal loss). The four traditional behavioral indications of a significant endogenous depression are (1) generally slowed response patterns, (2) early morning sleep disruption, (3) more severe mood problems, and (4) significant weight loss without dieting.

The Case of Joseph Westbecker

Joseph Westbecker is a classic example of an affect disorder, as well as an early and prototypical case of workplace violence. His case also became the first civil (rather than criminal) trial concerning the drug Prozac. Throughout his life, including the first time he checked himself into a hospital because of his disorder, Joe consistently showed four themes central to the diagnosis of affect disorder (depression, suicidal ideation, mania, and anger). He also showed evidence of mania-agitation, but seldom if ever any mania-euphoria.

Ultimately, his affect consumed him. On September 14, 1989, Joseph Westbecker walked unnoticed into the Standard Gravure printing plant in Louisville, Kentucky, where he had worked for 17 years, and killed 8 and wounded 12 of his former co-workers with copper-jacketed bullets from an AK-47 semi-automatic rifle. He then killed himself with a Sig Sauer 9mm pistol.

While this appeared to be an insane outburst, his suicide prevented any close examination of his sanity. However, the consensus of the evidence does suggest that he (1) knew what he was doing at the time, (2) could control at least some of his behavior during the episode, and (3) had at least considered some form of a specific plan almost a year before he carried it out, indicating probable sanity (Meyer & Weaver, 2006).

Joseph's long, downhill slide probably started even before his birth. There is sketchy but reasonable evidence from family history that his genetics at least predisposed him to a degree of mental disorder. His maternal grandmother was twice placed in a state mental hospital, reportedly showing depression, suicidal ideation, and delusions of persecution. But other factors certainly contributed mightily to Joseph's condition. His birth was normal, and nothing untoward was noticed in his first year of life. But just before his first birthday, his father fell while repairing the roof of a church, fractured his skull, and died. His widow, Joseph's mother, was 17 years old. She moved back in with her parents, and her father was appointed Joseph's guardian. But less than a year later, he was killed at his railroad job when he slipped beneath the wheels of a train engine. Then, only two years after that, Joseph's paternal grandfather, the only other adult male figure in his life, died of heart disease.

Although Joe was raised by his apparently dedicated maternal grandmother, there were few financial or emotional resources, and Joseph spent almost a year in an orphanage when he was 12 to 13 years of age. The family also moved many times, and various family and friends occasionally took on a parenting role. His schooling was equally disrupted, and he attained only an eighth-grade education. During that time, he showed both dyslexia and delinquency but eventually did attain a general equivalency high school degree.

(continued)

The Case of Joseph Westbecker Continued

In 1960, Joseph obtained a job at a printing company, and in July of that year he was married. While no one ever characterized Joseph as gregarious or joyful, or even happy for any length of time, the better times of his life were in the years before and just after his first marriage.

Joseph was competent in his job and consistently put in long hours of overtime. But this, along with his personality, took a toll on the marriage. He was also increasingly upset over his wife taking a job outside the home, and in 1978, he moved out, reportedly in the hope that his wife would give up her job. She didn't. There is good reason to believe this was a catalyst for the emergence of clear psychiatric symptoms.

Joseph's mental disorder was first noticed in early 1980 by a physician treating him for bursitis in his shoulder. He referred him to a psychiatric unit at a hospital, where he received one week's inpatient treatment for agitation and depression. The psychiatric summary reported, "He worked 16 hours a day, bar hopped at night, slept only two to three hours and drove himself mercilessly."

About this time, Joseph began another serious relationship. He eventually married Brenda in August 1981. His continuing bouts of depression, problems with stepchildren, and anger toward Brenda's ex-husband (whom he perceived as making money "too easily") kept this from being an especially happy interlude. His anger toward his wife's ex-husband was so severe that he followed him for about a month and later confided the "thought of blowing his brains out, but he always has a witness with him." During the next few years, personal disputes led Joseph to break off relations with both his oldest son and his mother. In 1984, he made the first of what were to be several suicide attempts. His wife told police that seeing him with a gun threatening suicide was the catalyst for her decision to divorce him. They separated in

May 1984, a month after he was released from a psychiatric hospital. But they continued to have a relationship until his death and occasionally lived as husband and wife.

It was about this time that pressures at work increased, and Joseph asked to be excused from working the "folder," a piece of machinery that required sustained concentration and decision making, a request supported by his psychiatrist. Although there is evidence that he seldom, if ever, was asked to work the folder from that point on, management's refusal to state they would never ask him to work it fueled a growing anger toward the company and some of its management personnel. His depression and agitation increased, possibly abetted by a diet centered on cookies and ice cream (sometimes a gallon at a time) and often a dozen or more diet colas a day. Joseph was again hospitalized in March 1987, and in a reply on a sentence completion test to the sentence stem "How do you feel about yourself?" he wrote, "I don't like feeling weak. I feel I've been screwed. I'm angry." His concerns about working the folder continued, and he filed a complaint that he was being discriminated against because of a mental handicap. A human relations committee felt it had no jurisdiction over the case, and the union later was disinclined to support Joseph's case. He insisted he was still asked to work the folder (although again, it's doubtful this was so), and he also complained that co-workers teased him, calling him "Westbecker the whacko, . . . the sickie," and so on. About this time, Joseph began buying guns, reading gun magazines, and occasionally bringing a gun with him into work.

In the summer of 1987, Joseph began seeing Dr. Lee Coleman, the psychiatrist who would treat him for the duration of his life. Dr. Coleman first diagnosed Joseph with Bipolar Disorder, Atypical Type because of the paranoid overtones, and he started prescribing various medications. Nothing worked well.

Joseph's condition continued to deteriorate, and Coleman suggested he go on medical leave. Joseph worked his last day at Standard Gravure in August 1988. Shortly before, he had told Brenda he would like to go there and kill "a bunch of people." The Social Security Administration determined that Joseph was disabled, and it awarded him $892 a month. His behavior over the next year was relatively unremarkable, except that he occasionally divulged plans of revenge (to acquaintances, not his psychiatrist) and bought guns. However, his beloved grandmother suffered a stroke on July 8, 1989, and died on August 5. Joseph continued to see his psychiatrist about once a month. Coleman had by then diagnosed Joseph's condition as a schizoaffective disorder. Three days before the shootings, Joseph visited his psychiatrist, who noted increased agitation and cognitive disruption. During this session, Joseph cried and related that he had been forced to have oral sex, in front of several employees, in order to be excused from working on the folder. There was never any later corroboration of this story, and his psychiatrist believes it was probably a delusion. He advised Joseph to voluntarily check himself into a mental hospital, which he refused to do, and to discontinue the Prozac. The autopsy after the shootings revealed a moderately high level of Prozac and lithium in his blood, as well as small amounts of three other antidepressants and a sleeping medication. His psychiatrist says Joseph was taking these on his own.

The morning of the shooting, Joseph left $1,720 in cash on his dresser (a large amount for him) and left a *Time* magazine of February 6, 1989, which was devoted to "Armed America," on a kitchen table, open to a story on Patrick Purdy (see Etiology section).

He took his bag filled with guns and bullets to the plant, where he moved from floor to floor, killing and shooting people he knew (even some he had apparently liked a bit) and some he didn't know. He did let a couple of people go whom he reportedly knew and liked. Ironically, Joseph never found and killed the people he viewed as his main enemies.

Etiology

Certainly Joseph Westbecker's ultimate, sad legacy was not a product of any single factor. As noted, genetics gave him a bad start. Also, the severe disruptions and losses in his early childhood not only robbed him of a chance to develop the cognitive and personality variables that most people use to effectively overcome emotional burdens but also may have predisposed him to depression. Such early stressors may lead to a later hyperactivity of the hypothalamic-pituitary-adrenal axis, from overproduction of the hormone corticotropin releasing factor (CRF), which in turn leads to an oversecretion of stimulating hormones under stress, facilitating any agitated depression. The lifelong, ambivalent, and often negative relationship with his mother also voided an option to develop better coping patterns and no doubt increased his pain and distress.

As he became increasingly distanced even from those who cared about him, including his oldest son, Joseph's no-better-than-slim chances of turning his life around became virtually nil. This was especially so as he accumulated means of acting out his hurt (a variety of weaponry) and opened himself to influence from the many models of deviance and destruction provided by the media. For example, after the carnage, police found a *Soldier of Fortune* magazine (a magazine for mercenaries, the curious, and, no doubt, some gun and violence groupies) as well as the *Time* magazine, whose cover story focused on Patrick Purdy, who also used an AK-47, killing 5 children and wounding 30 children and adults in a Stockton, California, schoolyard in 1989. The data from researchers such as Phillips (1974) and others (Bartol & Bartol, 2008) make it clear that violence toward others (and suicide) is in part attributable to the quantity and intensity of media portrayals of such acts.

Legal Aftermath: The First Major Civil Trial of Prozac

Joseph Westbecker's "fame" increased after his death when the survivors, along with the estates of those killed, joined to file a civil suit for damages. A number of people alleged to have committed crimes had already tried a "Prozac [or other SSRIs] made me do it" defense in a criminal trial, with no significant success. Dr. Coleman was eliminated early on by the trial judge as an available target for suit. This left Eli Lilly, the manufacturer of Prozac, as the major target, and thus the suit became the first clear legal test in a civil action (liability for damages) of an SSRI's alleged propensity to facilitate violence in some patients.

After 2½ months of testimony, the jury deliberated for hours and came back with a 9–3 decision that found Westbecker totally responsible for the action, thus apparently exonerating Eli Lilly and Prozac. However, it was later discovered that Eli Lilly had secretly given large settlements to all of the attack survivors and their attorneys, and in 1997, the judge officially changed the record from a jury verdict to a simple dismissal of a settled case. Yet, this case set the tone for this type of litigation until 2001, when a Wyoming court awarded $8 million to the estate of an oil-field worker who shot his wife, their daughter, their 9-month-old granddaughter, and then himself (*Tobin* v. *GlaxoSmith-Kline*, CV00-025, June 6, 2001). He had been prescribed Paxil (an SSRI similar to Prozac), but the product information given to physicians in the United States did not include a warning, which was given to German physicians, that in 3 to 5 percent of cases, suicide or homicide could be precipitated and that in potentially suicidal patients or those with insomnia or restlessness, patients taking Paxil should also receive a sedative and be closely monitored (Reinecke et al., 2008). The jury held the drug firm 80 percent responsible; that is, it owed $6.4 million.

Etiology of Depression

A variety of theoretical perspectives on the etiology of depression was presented, along with their related treatments, in the case of Danielle in Chapter 2. In the present case of Joseph Westbecker, both biological and psychological factors are involved, as they are in most serious cases of depression (DeBattista, 1998; Dilalla, 2004; Horowitz, 2004; McCullough, 2002). These external and internal factors usually combine in varying degrees in an actual case of depression to produce a self-perpetuating sequence such as the following:

> Negative environmental condition + biological predisposition $\longrightarrow$ social withdrawal + lowered information processing $\longrightarrow$ inadequate social behaviors + guilt and self-blame $\longrightarrow$ further self-devaluation + social withdrawal $\longrightarrow$ more biological change that facilitates depression

Treatment Options

The reader is referred to the case of Danielle in Chapter 2, as it details the options available for the treatment of depression. As with many cases of major depression, the primary treatments used were chemotherapy (see Table 7.1) and "supportive therapy"—that is, relatively short office contacts that are not based on any particular theoretical orientation. When some form of formal psychotherapy is used with depressives, those generally accepted as the most effective are interpersonal psychotherapy (IPT), which aims at promoting more effective interpersonal relationships, thus improving self-esteem as well, and cognitive-behavior modification (CBM) (Reinecke et al., 2008; Beck, 1976; Horowitz, 2004; McCullough, 2002). Cognitive-behavior modification aims at determining the rules that govern the life of the depressed person. It makes the assumption that "what we do and how we think about it determine how we feel." Brief dynamic therapy can also be effective here (Chambless et al., 1996). Some form of psychological treatment appears to be more effective if the client suffered some clear early trauma, such as abuse or loss of a parent. When an adult is depressed and there is no evidence of

TABLE 7.1   Antidepressant Drugs

Name (Generic/Trade)

Tricyclic and Tetracyclic Antidepressants	MAO Inhibitors	Other Antidepressants
amitriptyline (Elavil)	tranylcypromine (Parnate)	fluoxetine (Prozac)
imipramine (Tofranil)	phenelzine (Nardil)	bupropion (Wellbutrin)
desipramine (Norpramin)		trazodone (Desyrel)
nortriptyline (Pamelor)		sertraline (Zoloft)
protriptyline (Vivactil)		paroxetine (Paxil)
doxepine (Sinequan)		venlafaxine (Effexor)
maprotiline (Ludiomil)		nefazodone (Serzone)
amoxapine (Asendin)		fluvoxamine (Luvox)
clomipramine (Anafranil)		citalopram (Celexa)
trimipramine (Surmontil)		mirtazapine (Remeron)
		escitalopram (Lexapro)
		duloxetine (Cymbalta)
		selegiline (Emsam)

early trauma, medication along with psychological treatment are typically indicated. Some form of "mindfulness training" has proved useful, especially with motivated and less deteriorated depressed individuals (Williams, Teasdale, Segal, & Kabat-Zin, 2008).

With antidepressant medication, CBM, and/or IPT depression is quite treatable. Vast amounts of antidepressants, especially the SSRIs (selective serotonin reuptake inhibitors), are now prescribed, and typically by a physician other than a psychiatrist. This raises concern around the overprescription of all such drugs that are abused in the Orwellian sense of placating the everyday anxieties of life rather than treating true disorders (see Chapter 9's section on prescription drug abuse).

In a similar vein, it has been increasingly recognized that clinical depression occurs in children, and there has been a sharp rise in the prescription of antidepressants for children. But it is also recognized that administering antidepressants to children may increase suicidal and/or violent behaviors (Novak & Pelaez, 2004). Prozac was the first antidepressant to win approval for use with children.

Nevertheless, no matter how much change is attained, relapse is common. Depressives who are most likely to relapse back into depression show (1) a greater number of previous episodes of depression; (2) a higher depression level at the entry point into treatment; (3) a family history of depression, especially with a history of depression in first-degree relatives; (4) poor physical health; (5) a higher level of dissatisfaction with their major life roles; and (6) a definite episode of clinical depression in late childhood or early adolescence. Also, those who receive antidepressant medication do best if they receive consistent monitoring of the effects of the medication, especially during the first three months they are taking it.

Postpartum Depression (PPD)

Postpartum depression (PPD) is a "specifier" in the *DSM-IV-TR* when the criteria for a Major Depressive Disorder, Bipolar I or II Disorder, or to Brief Psychotic Disorder are met and the onset occurs within four weeks after childbirth (American Psychiatric Association, 2000). PPD affects approximately 10–12 percent of women after childbirth (NMHA, 2006). Specific symptoms can include fear of harming the baby, disinterest in the baby, an inability to respond to the baby's needs, delayed maternal bonding, and/or excessive preoccupation with the baby's health. Less than 1 percent of new mothers develop postpartum depression with psychosis, a much more serious type of PPD. According to the *DSM-IV-TR*, postpartum mood disorders *with psychotic features* appear "from 1 in 500 to 1 in 1000 deliveries" (American Psychiatric Association, 2000, p. 422). Symptoms of PPD with psychotic features are similar to those of other psychotic disorders and can include delusions and/or hallucinations.

Postpartum mood episodes are different from "the 'baby blues,' which affect up to 70% of women during the 10 days postpartum" (American Psychiatric Association, 2000, p. 423). These feelings are transient and do not impair daily functioning. The "baby blues" typically subside in about 1–2 weeks following delivery. Of course some women fall somewhere between those with the "baby blues" and those who develop psychotic symptoms. Mood and anxiety symptoms during pregnancy as well as "baby blues" increase the risk for developing a postpartum depression. Women with PPD often have anxiety and panic attacks. Their attitudes toward the newborn can change dramatically, altering between an overinterest in the baby that can interfere with the baby's rest and a fear of being alone with the infant and disinterest and even hostility toward the child (American Psychiatric Association, 2000).

The Case of Brooke Shields

Brooke Shields was born on May 31, 1965, in New York to Frank Shields, a Revlon executive, and Terri Shields, a model. Brooke's parents separated while she was very young, and she was raised by her mother. Although he remarried and had additional children, her father remained involved in her life. She began her modeling career at the age of 11 months, posing for commercials. She was modeling by the age of 3, and at the age of 8 had landed her first acting job. Her mother was her manager for most of her career. This placed Brooke in the public eye for most of her life. Despite Brooke's having a flourishing acting career at such a young age, Brooke's mother attempted to give her as normal an upbringing as she could. Brooke attended school and only occasionally missed class for acting.

Brooke graduated from Princeton University with a degree in French literature. She met tennis star Andre Agassi and married him. They divorced after only two years. She met her current husband, Chris Henchy, a comedy TV writer, in 1999. After dating for approximately two years, they married in May of 2001. They desperately wanted to have a baby. However, things did not happen as planned. The couple had trouble getting pregnant on their own. It was discovered that a surgery that Brooke had several years before to remove precancerous cells resulted in scarring on her cervix, making it difficult for her to become pregnant naturally. At the age of 36,

she began artificial insemination. These efforts also failed. Meanwhile, Brooke was offered a role in the Broadway play *Cabaret* and decided that this would be one of her last opportunities to perform in such a prestigious role. Immediately after returning from her honeymoon, Brooke took the next six months to star in *Cabaret* on Broadway while her husband worked in Los Angeles.

At the end of the Broadway show, Brooke and Chris decided again to try to conceive. Due to the failure of their artificial insemination attempts, they underwent in vitro fertilization (IVF), which involved drug injections, estrogen patches, and surgery. While quite stressful for both of them, the first treatment was successful and Brooke became pregnant but soon miscarried. Also, because of problems with Brooke's cervix, the baby had to be expelled naturally instead of the D & C procedure that is normally performed. This was a painful experience for Brooke, lasting about 12 hours. For the next seven months fertility treatments continued but were unsuccessful. During this time, Brooke began to feel alone and bitter. She desperately wanted to be a mother. In 2002, they went for their last treatment and had agreed to take a break from treatments if this one failed. In August of 2002, Brooke learned she was pregnant again.

Brooke's dad had been diagnosed with prostate cancer, and they had hoped he would live long enough to see his granddaughter. Unfortunately, in April of 2003, he died only

(continued)

The Case of Brooke Shields Continued

three weeks before the baby was born. Brooke's pregnancy was described as "uneventful." However, she was in labor for 24 hours when the doctor decided to order an emergency C-section. On May 15, 2003, Rowan Francis was born with the umbilical cord wrapped around her neck. The baby recovered and was healthy, but Brooke's uterus herniated initially, preventing the muscle from contracting back to normal, causing significant blood loss. Her uterus eventually returned to normal.

However, she spent the next five days in the hospital in agony. She had difficulty breast feeding, and there was a constant flow of people in and out of her hospital room. Eventually, the family members returned to their new apartment. Upon arriving, Brooke felt an "overwhelming sense of panic." She dreaded when her husband would bring the baby back to her. She felt physically exhausted and sick, often experiencing chest pains. She had no desire to hold her baby and felt terribly guilty for feeling this way. Naturally Brooke expected that there would be an instant bond between her and Rowan, but she felt nothing. Instead, she believed that maybe she was not meant to be a mother. A quote from her book, *Down Came the Rain* (2005) illustrates how she was feeling: "My present reality was the antithesis of everything I had expected, and I was desperate for connection and pure joy I thought I would have experienced in motherhood" (p. 80).

Brooke often cried inconsolably and yet was unable to articulate what was wrong. She felt like a prisoner to this child, as if her life were not her own. She had no connection with

Rowan and wanted to die because of this feeling. Brooke would envision herself jumping out of her apartment window and saw images of her baby flying through the air and smashing into a wall. She was afraid to be left alone with the baby, not for fear of harming her, but for fear of not being able to care for her. She hated herself for feeling this way and longed to be "normal" and have a connection with her daughter. Finally, after urging from her family and friends, she spoke to a doctor about her feelings. He prescribed Paxil. Relief did not come immediately. Chris had to return to Los Angeles to work, and Brooke was terrified of being left with the baby. Brooke hired a baby nurse to help her through the week without her husband, and this turned out to be a positive experience. The nurse helped her to establish a routine with the baby and get more rest.

After feeling better for some time and moving back to Los Angeles, Brooke decided to stop taking her Paxil, but she soon realized this was a mistake. She had panic experiences and once got into her car to drive home and had an overwhelming urge to crash her car into a wall. When Brooke returned home for the first time she clearly looked into the possibility that she may be experiencing postpartum depression. She realized that she not only needed the medication, but also probably needed therapy. Brooke began seeing a therapist regularly and continued taking antidepressants. This combination helped her to slowly feel better and enjoy being a mother for the first time.

Brooke's Etiology

Looking at Brooke's history, one can see that she had many of the risk factors for experiencing a postpartum mood disorder. Individuals who go through IVF treatments are more likely to develop PPD, most likely due to the manipulation of hormones during the treatment. In addition, in the past five years before giving birth, Brooke experienced a divorce, a remarriage, a miscarriage, multiple IVF treatments, the suicide of one of her best friends, the death of her father, a new apartment, a traumatic delivery, and her husband leaving to go across the country to work soon after the birth. Her family also had a history of alcoholism, and even though she had never experienced a Major Depressive Disorder in the past, she had experienced strong mood swings during PMS episodes as well as periodic sadness.

Etiology

The exact nature of the cause of PPD is unclear, but research suggests that several factors may increase the chances of developing PPD. In addition to factors Brooke specifically experienced, hormonal changes that occur after childbirth, such as the drop in estrogen immediately following delivery or fluctuations in serotonin, may contribute. Situational stressors such as a lack of sleep due to the presence of a newborn, change in employment, the recent loss of a loved one, or marital discord can all contribute to PPD. A personal history of non-postpartum depression or anxiety, a family history of mood disorder, and inadequate social support and previous PMS episodes may increase the risk for the development of PPD (NMHA, 2006; American Psychiatric Association, 2000).

Treatment Options

The treatments noted for the treatment of depression in general described earlier in this chapter and in the case of Danielle in Chapter 2 are also applicable to PPD. Additionally, direct education and training in parenting and family or couples therapy are typically required.

Comment

There has been increasing recognition of PPD and less severe but related patterns. Much of the credit for this goes to Brooke Shields, who used her fame and visibility to write and speak about these disorders.

Seasonal Affective Disorder (SAD)

Most people on occasion have experienced a touch of "winter blues"; if the blues are persistent and significantly disruptive, the episode may earn a clinical label. Although it can take several forms, by far the most common seasonal affective disorder (SAD) pattern is winter depression (Oren et al., 1994), and that is what *SAD* will refer to herein. This disorder is primarily marked by decreased energy with vegetative changes in appetite and sleep, with related (probably consequentially) negativism and lowered self-esteem. Women are affected three to five times as often as men, and a degree of Premenstrual Dysphoric Disorder may be a comorbid symptom. Estimates are that as high as 5 percent of the population suffer from SAD. Although referred to as "holiday blues," it is clear that SAD occurs in people in the southern hemisphere, where Christmas is a summer holiday. The disorder does occur in children, but severity usually reaches clinical significance when SAD sufferers are in their twenties or thirties. A move to a higher latitude (e.g., moving north in North America) may set off SAD in vulnerable individuals.

The treatment of choice for the most common form of SAD, winter depression, is exposure to light (DeBattista, 1998; Oren et al., 1994). Light therapy works best with clients whose symptoms include increased appetite, hypersomina, craving for carbohydrates, and a worsening of symptoms in the evening. It is less effective when symptoms include melancholic symptoms—that is, anxiety, suicidal tendencies, insomnia, and a worsening of symptoms in the morning. Light therapy apparently acts by affecting melatonin productions and the circadian rhythm. Of course, anyone embarking on light treatment should be cleared by an ophthalmologist if there is any history or indication of eye disease.

Delivery of light can be adjusted on four parameters: intensity, wavelength, duration, and timing. Intensity has to be bright enough to suppress nighttime melatonin production; 2,500 lux is suggested. A standard dosage is 2,500 lux for about two hours, once a day at first, then tapered to once every other day if improvement is maintained.

Traditionally, timing of treatment was not held to be important. However, findings now suggest that the great majority of SADs are "phase-delays" (referring to circadian rhythm delays), indicated by characteristic morning hypersomnia and clear vulnerability to shortened photoperiod exposure (Oren et al., 1994). For the phase-delays, whose circadian rhythms are cued by dawn rather than dusk, light therapy should be administered as soon as feasible upon awakening, with an optimal dose of two hours daily of strong light (2,500 lux) throughout the high-risk season. For phase-advance types, cued by dusk, whose sleep disruption is usually more toward morning, light therapy should be administered at night, preferably between 7:00 and 9:00 P.M. To help orient the circadian rhythms, phase-delays should avoid bright light exposure at night (e.g., in bright malls); phase-advances should minimize it in early morning. Persons with characteristic early morning awakening and early evening fatigue—"advanced sleep-phase syndrome"— should receive light therapy before bedtime. Occasionally, people will shift from one pattern to another, requiring a timing change for the light therapy.

There is some evidence that a treatment that increases the number of high-density negative ions in the air decreases SAD. Also, melatonin, a hormone produced by the pineal gland and available without a prescription, can produce results similar to light therapy. Internal melatonin production usually has a strong diurnal rhythm. It is released primarily and in most cases only at night, as its production shuts down when daylight reaches the eyes and is perceived by the brain; thus, it is seasonally patterned. Manipulation of serotonin levels can also help SAD sufferers, as the supra chiasmatic nuclei, thought to be a critical component in one's "body clock," is heavily endowed with nerve cells rich in serotonin.

Suicide

The annual worldwide rate of suicide is approximately 10 to 20 per 100,000 (10 to 12 percent in the United States), and the rate of suicide attempts is approximately 15 times higher. Suicide rates associated with psychiatric disorders have traditionally been estimated at about 15 percent. However, better data from a more recent study by Bostwick (2000) indicate much lower rates. For patients hospitalized after a suicide attempt or ideation, the lifetime prevalence rate of suicide completion was 8.6 percent; for affective disorder patients hospitalized without specification of suicidality, the lifetime suicide completion rate was 4.0 percent; and for mixed inpatient-outpatient populations, the risk was 2.2 percent. Those in the general population without affective disorder show a lifetime rate of only 0.5 percent or less. In 2001, the Centers for Disease Control and Prevention also reported that in the United States (1) approximately 3 out of 5 suicides were completed with a firearm; (2) suicide is the third-leading cause of death in young people ages 15 to 24, behind unintentional injury and homicide; (3) more people die from suicide than homicide, at a ratio of 1.7 to 1.0; and (4) males are almost four times more likely than females to die by suicide, but females are slightly more likely than males to attempt suicide.

Some severe depressions do not involve suicide, and some suicides do not involve depression (Bongar, 2002). However, very often when there is significant depression, as with Joseph Westbecker, suicide is a concern. There is a long list of famous suicides, including Ernest Hemingway, Jack London, Amadeo Modigliani, Adolf Hitler, Samson, and Cleopatra. However, in general, the typical suicide attempter "profile" is an unmarried white female, with a history of past and recent stressful events (often involving estranged relationships), who had an unstable childhood, and who now has few social supports and lacks a close friend in whom to confide. On the other hand, the typical suicide completer profile is an unmarried or divorced or widowed white male who is over age 45, lives alone, has a history of significant physical or emotional disorder, and probably abuses alcohol.

As noted in Durkheim's types of suicide described next, not all suicides are considered by mental health professionals to be pathological, and in 2006, the Supreme Court upheld Oregon's 1997 "Death with Dignity" Act allowing a physician to assist a suicide by a lethal dose of drugs, in cases that met a number of specific requirements.

Having suffered greatly from the pain of cancer, on September 21, 1939, Freud "requested that his physician Max Schur put an end to his suffering. Schur fulfilled Freud's request by administering an overdose of morphine over a 24-hour period" (Larson et al., 2007, p. 282).

Suicide Types and Prediction. Emile Durkheim (1951) pioneered an emphasis on sociological factors contributing to suicide. Members of certain subgroups lose cohesiveness and feel alienated. His typology of suicidals (anomic [under conditions of normlessness]; egoistic [lack of group ties]; altruistic [suicide for the good of some cause]) is still influential (Shneidman, 1985), as is evident in the following list of types of suicides:

Realistic	These suicides are precipitated by such conditions as the prospect of great pain preceding a sure death.
Altruistic	The person's behavior is subservient to a group ethic that mandates or at least approves suicidal behavior, such as kamikaze pilots in World War II.
Inadvertent	The person makes a suicide gesture in order to influence or manipulate someone else, but a misjudgment leads to an unexpected fatality.
Spite	Like the inadvertent suicide, the focus is on someone else, but the intention to kill oneself is genuine, with the idea that the other person will suffer greatly from consequent guilt.
Bizarre	The person commits suicide as a result of a hallucination (such as voices ordering the suicide) or delusion (such as a belief the suicide will change the world).
Anomic	An abrupt instability in economic or social conditions (such as sudden financial loss in the Great Depression) markedly changes a person's life situation. Unable to cope, the person commits suicide.
Negative self	Chronic depression and a sense of chronic failure or inadequacy combine to produce repetitive suicide attempts eventually leading to fatality.

Clues and Correlates to Suicide.   Suicidal individuals tend to give clues to those around them, and these areas should be the focus of any evaluation. In addition to being depressed, suicidal people are likely to show feelings of hopelessness and helplessness, a loss of a sense of continuity with the past and/or present, and a loss of pleasure in typical interests and pursuits. Conversely, a strong element of perfectionism is a risk factor for suicide, when mixed with depression and a crisis and/or ego insult. "Perfectionistic" suicidals show less response to medication or psychotherapy than do other depressed persons. For one thing, they tend to misinterpret small successes, such as the typical process in treatment, as failures.

The basic suicide risk profile has been consistent over the years: older, white male, live alone, active alcoholism, a loss experience, medical illness, schizophrenia, depression, and a sense of hopelessness. In recent years, add AIDS and a diagnosis of panic attacks or borderline personality disorder. In addition to these factors, suicidal persons are more likely to:

1. Have a personal and/or family history of depression, especially a major endogenous depression, or of psychosis
2. Have had a parent or other important identity figure who attempted or committed suicide
3. Have a history of family instability and/or parental rejection
4. Be socially isolated
5. Have a chronic physical illness
6. Show a preoccupation with death and/or make statements of a wish to die, especially statements of a wish to commit suicide
7. Manifest consistent life patterns of leaving crises rather than facing them (in relationships: "You can't walk out on me; I'm leaving you" or in jobs: "You can't fire me, because I quit")
8. Show a personal or family history of addiction patterns
9. Live alone, or involved (married or similarly occupied) with a loved mate who is interpersonally competitive and/or is self-absorbed
10. Show sudden cheerfulness after a long depression
11. Be putting their affairs in order, such as giving away favorite possessions or revising wills
12. Show some abrupt atypical behavior change, such as withdrawal from family or friends
13. Show a family history of self-damaging acts
14. Have a history of self-damaging acts, often previous suicide attempts (in this context, the first axiom of psychology could well be "Behavior predicts behavior," and the second axiom could be "Behavior without intervention predicts behavior")

The initiation of the suicidal event is apt to be triggered by a major life stress—for example, the experience of a chronic debilitating illness or the loss of an important social support, such as a spouse, beloved relative, or confidante. Violent impulsivity with high-risk mental disorders (e.g., depression, panic) suggests high risk for suicide. There is about a 10 to 15 percent probability that a *serious* attempt will be successful. At the same time, there is some consensus that out of 100 people in the "acute suicidal zone," only about 1 will kill herself or himself within the next year.

The following factors increase the potential for attempted suicide and the probability of completion:

- A cognitive state of constriction—that is, an inability to perceive any options or a way out of a situation that is generating intense psychological suffering
- The idea of death as a catalytic agent for the cessation of distress
- Acute perturbation—high distress/agitation/depression
- An increase in self-hatred or self-loathing, especially if the result of a recent shameful behavior
- Perception of the self as a source of shame to significant others

- Fantasies of death as an escape, especially if there are concrete plans for one's own demise
- Easy access to a lethal means (e.g., as in physicians, who show high suicide rates)
- Absence of an accessible support system (family and good friends)
- Life stresses that connote irrevocable loss (whether of status or of persons), such as the relatively recent death of a favored parent, or even something like retirement, which is particularly important if the person at risk is unable to mourn the loss overtly
- High psychophysiological responsiveness: cyclical moods, a propensity toward violence, and a high need for stimulation seeking in spite of suicide thoughts (high rates of the serotonin receptor 5-HT$_{2a}$ in blood platelets of a potentially suicidal individual add to the prediction of serious intent)
- Serious sleep disruption and/or increased use of alcohol or drugs
- Lack of a therapeutic alliance and/or constructively supportive friendship alliance
- Noncompliance with prescribed psychotropic medication or abrupt cessation of use of prescribed psychotropic medication
- Persistence of secondary depression after remission of primary disorder and/or recent discharge from a psychiatric hospital (in the last three months)
- A history of panic attacks and, even more importantly, recent panic attacks

So, there are many factors; unfortunately, there is no specific value loading placed on these factors. That is, there is no way to plug these factors into an equation to make a suicide prediction in an individual case. Virtually all of these factors derive from studies that looked at long-term prediction, whether suicide would occur over a period of some years. But, in the real world, the predictions that are needed are for the short term. Also, there are virtually no data on that type of situation—that is, whether a person will *imminently* attempt or commit suicide (i.e., within the next several days or so). And imminent suicidality is usually the critical question.

Suicide Prevention

Several things can be done both on a societal and an individual level to lower the incidence of suicide (Bongar, 2002; Phillips, 1974; Phillips, Lesyna, & Paight, 1993; Shneidman, 1985). First, educating the public on the myths and facts of suicide is an important step. Second, there is evidence that suicide-prevention telephone hotlines and centers can at least slightly decrease the suicide rate. Last, suicide prevention at the societal level requires restriction on media publicity about suicides (Phillips, 1974; Phillips et al., 1993).

In Phillips's (1974) initial research endeavor, he compiled a list of suicide stories appearing on page 1 of the *New York Times* from 1946 to 1968 and then examined U.S. monthly suicide statistics from 1947 to 1967, with appropriate corrections for the effects of trends and seasons. He found that U.S. suicides consistently rose significantly just after suicide stories. He termed this the *Werther effect*, after the German author Goethe's fictional hero whose suicide was thought to have triggered imitative acts. Phillips, Lesyna, and Paight (1993) accepted the hypothesis that this effect is caused by imitation and suggestion, after considering and eventually rejecting any reasonable competing explanation—the four most plausible of which are:

1. *The Coroner Explanation:*   In ambiguous cases, coroners may shift unclear suicides into the competing categories of homicide, accident, or undetermined death. If so, the numbers of deaths in these competing categories should decrease after a suicide story, but they don't.
2. *The Precipitation Explanation:*   Suicide stories only hasten suicides that would have eventually occurred anyway. If so, the post-story peak in suicides should be followed by an equal drop in follow-up periods, but that doesn't happen.
3. *The Prior Conditions Explanation:*   A prior social change, such as an economic depression, causes a rise in both publicized and unpublicized suicides, but this cannot explain the consistent correlation of a suicide story and a post-story rise in suicides.
4. *The Bereavement Explanation:*   Grief rather than imitation is the reason for the post-story rise, but if so, nonsuicide celebrity deaths would generate a post-story rise in suicides as well, and they don't.

Other researchers have shown that television movies about fictional suicide can produce the same effect, especially multiprogram portrayals. In fact, the most powerful evidence for the effect of a fictional suicide comes from a clever German study by Schmidtke and Hafner, cited in Phillips, Lesyna, and Paight (1993). In 1981 and 1982, West German television broadcasted a fictional story about a 19-year-old student who killed himself by throwing himself in front of a train. There was a nationwide increase in railway suicides immediately after each broadcast. The increase was highest for young males, the closest in identity to the fictional role model. Here also, other competing explanations did not fit the data. Subsequent data indicated the Werther effect is weak or nonexistent for single program fictional presentations, but does occur with multiprogram presentations. In addition to the identity effect, the phenomenon appears to trigger suicides in statistically predisposed groups (i.e., males, white, unmarried, and people of retirement age).

Several precautions can also be taken for prevention of suicide at the individual level:

1. Attend seriously to people who voice a desire to kill themselves or "just go to sleep and forget it all." About two-thirds of people who kill themselves have talked about it beforehand in some detail with family, friends, or others.
2. Take any complaint seriously. Attend especially to depressed individuals who speak of losing hope. For example, most terminally ill patients who are severely suicidal may give up such intent when they find out there are medications and techniques that will give them control over their pain.

3. To the degree possible, keep lethal means (guns, large prescriptions of sedatives) away from suicidal individuals.
4. Show a personal concern to a suicidal person; a suicide attempt is most often a cry for help. Suicidal individuals need a temporary "champion" who can point them toward new resources, suggest new options, and who, at least in a small way, can diminish the sense of hopelessness.
5. Try to get suicidal persons to perform some of the following behaviors: (a) engage in regular physical exercise, (b) start a diary, (c) follow a normal routine, (d) do something in which they have already demonstrated competence, (e) confide inner feelings to someone, or (f) cry it out. Try to get the person to avoid self-medication and other people inclined toward depression.
6. Make every effort to guarantee that a suicidal person reaches professional help; in the immediate sphere, some form of crisis counseling (Saiger et al., 2008). Making an appointment is a good first step; getting the person to the appointment is the crucial step.

Bipolar Disorder (Manic-Depressive Psychosis)

> *Then Big Harry said to me, "You know, Bobby, I think old Suicides was crazy." He was right, too, because when his family sent for him the man who came explained to Commissioner old Suicides had suffered from a thing called Mechanic's Depressive. You never had that, did you, Roger?*
> —Ernest Hemingway, *Islands in the Stream* (1970)

That manic and depressive symptoms are components of a single disorder was suspected even by Hippocrates in the fourth century B.C. Since that time, unipolar depression has been distinguished from bipolar disorder and is currently thought to result from different etiological factors (Goodwin & Jamison, 1990; Cullberg, 2006; McCullough, 2002; Whybrow, 1997).

The *DSM-IV-TR* lists the mean age of onset for Bipolar Disorder as the early twenties, but it is highly variable. The range of behaviors that typifies mania is broad and most commonly includes (1) hyperactive motor behavior; (2) variable irritability and/or euphoria; and (3) a speeding up of thought processes, called a "flight of ideas." Manic speech is typically loud, rapid, and difficult to understand. When the mood is expansive, manics take on many tasks (seldom completing them), avoid sleep, and easily ramble into lengthy monologues about their personal plans, worth, and power. When the mood becomes more irritable, they are quick to complain and engage in hostile tirades.

Psychotic manic reactions involve grandiose delusions, bizarre and impulsive behavior, transient hallucinations, and explosiveness; these reactions may be confused with schizophrenic episodes (Cullberg, 2006). However, whereas schizophrenics (and schizoaffectives) are distracted by internal thoughts and ideas, manics are distracted by external stimuli that often go unnoticed by others. Also, whereas schizophrenics (and schizoaffectives) tend to avoid any true relationships with others during an active phase, manics are typically open to contact with other people.

As with the case of Virginia Woolf, suicide is a frequent complication of bipolar depression. It is estimated that about 15 percent, if untreated, commit suicide. This is 30 times the rate in the general population and is higher than for any other psychiatric or medical risk group. As many as 82 percent of bipolar patients have suicidal ideation (Goodwin & Jamison, 1990).

Although the onset of discrete manic episodes may be sudden, the disorder has a generally slow onset in many cases; as with Virginia Woolf, the person's life history may evidence preliminary symptoms in childhood or adolescence that at some point become more intense and debilitating. Last, the presence of a bipolar disorder is not always seen as totally negative, as it is with schizophrenia, and it may indeed be a spur to creativity.

> *My candle burns at both ends;*
> *It will not last the night;*
> *But ah, my foes, and oh, my friends*
> *It gives a lovely light.*
>
> —Edna St. Vincent Millay, "A Few Figs from Thistles"

Creativity, Poetry, and the Bipolar Disorder

"Why is it," Aristotle asked 2,400 years ago, "that all men [i.e., people] who are outstanding in philosophy, poetry or the arts are melancholic?" Some 300 years ago, the English poet John Dryden wrote, "Great wits are sure to madness near allied; / And thin partitions do their bounds divide." Dryden's sweet couplet has since degenerated into the cliché, "There is a thin line between genius and madness."

As is evident, the concept that creativity may be a result of psychopathology is hardly new, and it is a persistent theme of certain authors, such as Arthur Koestler. Research (Goodwin & Jamison, 1990; Ludwig, 1996) offers impressive support for a creativity link in the particular instance of bipolar disorder (manic-depressive disorder), especially in relation to certain specific artistic endeavors. For example, Ludwig (1996) found that psychiatric disturbances were far more common among artists than nonartists, and that the rate of alcoholism was 60 percent among actors and 41 percent among novelists, but only 3 percent among those in the physical sciences and 10 percent among military officers. In the case of manic depression, 17 percent of the actors and 13 percent of the poets were thought to have had the disorder, whereas those in the sciences were believed to have suffered from it at a rate of less than 1 percent, comparable to the incidence in the general population.

The list of first-rank artists who appear to have suffered a bipolar disorder is impressive: painter Vincent Van Gogh; poet-painter Dante Gabriel Rosetti; playwright Eugene O'Neill; writers Herman Melville, William and Henry James, F. Scott Fitzgerald, Ernest Hemingway, Virginia Woolf (the next case), John Ruskin, and Honore de Balzac; and composers Robert Schumann, Hector Berlioz, and George Friederic Handel. Indeed, Handel wrote *The Messiah* in a frenetic 24 days during a manic high. But it is poets who are most often bipolars. Byron, Coleridge, Shelley, Tennyson, Poe, and Gerald Manley Hopkins were all bipolars, as are many of the major American poets, such as Hart Crane, Robert Lowell, Anne Sexton, Theodore Roethke, Sylvia Plath, and John Berryman.

Some might argue that poets tend to be bipolars because poetry often celebrates the inner turbulence of one's psyche. But even in the eighteenth century, a time in which poetry did not really focus on such inner upset, a high proportion of accomplished poets also appear to have been bipolars, and many others at least experienced subclinical hypomanic states during creative moments. The relationship of poetry and bipolar disorder, then, may more directly result from the fact that frenetic but sporadic effort is more effectively productive in poetry than in other areas and because the imagery inherent in poetry is more like the primitive thought found in severe emotional disruption. Also, the depressions of the bipolar mood swing provide the fuel of emotional depth to the productivity of the manic high. As a result, some artists so afflicted avoid therapy, out of a fear that successful treatment would curb their creativity. It appears that in some cases they may be correct.

Time . . . a device to prevent everything from happening all at once.
—Paul William Roberts (1995)

The Case of Virginia Woolf

A Specific Instance of Bipolar Creativity

Virginia Woolf is regarded as one of the most talented prose writers of the twentieth century, and was one of the first writers to describe the relativity of individual experience. In 1915, she published *The Voyage Out*, and in the next 30 years she wrote dozens of literary reviews, essays, stories, and 15 more books, including classics such as *To the Lighthouse* and *The Waves*. The most famous, *A Room of One's Own*, established her as an early leader of the women's movement. In that book are reflected the extremes of her own life: "The beauty of the world . . . has two edges, one of laughter, one of anguish, cutting the heart asunder" (Woolf, 1957). She was admired for fervently expressing all ranges of human emotion.

From childhood on, Woolf was afflicted with bipolar disorder, which those around her described as lapses into insanity. The emotional highs and lows of that disorder contributed to her passion in writing novels, yet ultimately destroyed her (Bell, 1972; Lehmann, 1975).

Childhood

Virginia Stephen was born in 1882, the second of four children, in Cambridge, England. Her father was Sir Leslie Stephen, a distinguished editor. She had two half-sisters. One was born to her father by his first wife, who was institutionalized most of her life for mental problems; and the other, Stella Duckworth, was born to her mother and her mother's first husband. She also had two Duckworth half-brothers. Virginia was exceptionally attractive, and she lived in a home where aunts, uncles, and cousins circulated constantly. The family was in the upper-middle professional class and emphasized intellectual achievement.

Virginia read everything she could find. At first, her father carefully chose what books she should read from their large library. However, by the time she was in her teens, she had read so much that he permitted her to read whatever she desired. During these times, this was a great amount of freedom for a girl. Virginia, who could not attend school because she was female, always envied her brother Thoby, who was educated at Cambridge. She taught herself English literature and received private lessons in Latin and Greek.

Virginia had been very close to her mother and described her mother's death, when Virginia was 13, as "the greatest disaster that could happen"(Lehmann, 1975, p. 13). Also, in reaction to her mother's death, Virginia's father became extremely demanding, unreasonable, and moody. Her stepsister, Stella Duckworth, took over their mother's role. This is when Virginia had her first breakdown. Her pulse raced and she felt uncontrollably excited (possibly a panic attack; see Chapter 3); later, she slipped into a deep depression. Her doctor prescribed outdoor exercise. Her lessons had been stopped, but she still read continuously.

Only two months after Virginia's mother died, Stella, whom Virginia also loved deeply, died. Without Stella, Virginia's father became tyrannical and full of self-pity. The next-oldest sister, Vanessa, then took their mother's place. Mr. Stephen was so inconsiderate and selfish to Vanessa that Virginia found herself torn between loving her father and despising him for the way he was behaving. When her father died in 1904, Virginia had an even more extreme breakdown. It started slowly, with headaches and moments of intense irritation, and then escalated into a severe manic state in which she felt intense guilt about her father. Virginia saw her nurses as evil, refused to eat, and tried to kill herself by jumping out a window. When she was able to lie down, she believed the birds were chirping in Greek and that King Edward VII was

swearing and hiding in the bushes. She lived in a time before effective treatment for this disorder had been discovered; therefore, the few doctors who examined her prescribed only rest.

Adult Years

Virginia's sexual development was deficient. Her two half-brothers had sexually abused her. Gerald examined her genitals when she was age 5, and George would periodically come into her bedroom and paw and fondle her when she was a teenager. Also, during her adolescence, Virginia fell deeply in love with her cousin, a girl named Madge. Later, an older woman friend who helped Virginia through her breakdowns became the object of Virginia's deepest love. Whether these women ever knew the extent of Virginia's affection is not clear.

With both parents deceased, Virginia and five of her siblings traveled to Greece. Vanessa, Violet, and Thoby contracted typhoid fever from impure milk, and from this disease Thoby died, another great blow to Virginia. Following this, Virginia's older sister married, leaving Virginia alone with her younger brother. Virginia and her brother took over a weekly social group that their older sister had started, and over many weeks Virginia became much more outgoing and willing to express her opinions, quickly becoming known for her sharp tongue. (Her fame in this regard, in concert with her pioneering role in the women's movement, inspired the title of the modern play by Edward Albee [later made into a movie], *Who's Afraid of Virginia Woolf?*)

Virginia began her career by writing book reviews for several well-respected magazines. During this time, she was pursued by many men, and she finally accepted the marriage proposal of Lytton Strachey. Immediately after proposing, however, he changed his mind and admitted his homosexuality to her. Leonard Woolf, a friend of Lytton, soon began dating Virginia. They married in August 1912, despite the fact that he was Jewish and she was at least at times anti-Semitic.

Leonard Woolf passionately loved Virginia; however, she did not respond to him

(continued)

The Case of Virginia Woolf Continued

sexually at all, as her sexual preference was for females. Then in March 1913, she began another breakdown. Leonard described Virginia's episodes as lapses into insanity wherein she lost complete contact with reality. She experienced wild excitement, intense guilt and depression, and delusions that her nurses were evil. During one episode, she talked rapidly for several days without stopping, after which she fell into a stupor. Virginia was able to remember most of what happened during her altered states.

Through the years, it seemed these episodes always occurred when Virginia was in the last stages of writing a novel. Through the 1920s, Virginia had no serious relapses, possibly because Leonard began enforcing total rest and quiet on Virginia when he detected another episode coming. Virginia was becoming famous, and over the years she was invited to the United States and Cambridge to give lectures and receive public honors, but she refused almost every invitation.

Finally, in the last stage of writing *Between the Acts* in 1941, she felt another attack coming. The fears and tormenting voices seemed real and endless. This time, she was convinced that the suffering would never stop. She wrote farewell letters to Leonard and her sister, filled her pockets with stones, and drowned herself in a nearby river. The letter to Leonard was as follows (Bell, 1972):

> Dearest,
>   I feel certain I am going mad again. I feel we can't go through another of those terrible times. And I shan't recover this time. I begin to hear voices, and I can't concentrate. So I am doing what seems the best thing to do. You have given me the greatest possible happiness. You have been in every way all that anyone could be. I don't think two people could have been happier till this terrible disease came. I can't fight any longer. I know that I am spoiling your life, that without me you could work. And you will I know. You see I can't even write this properly. I can't read. What I want to say is I owe all the happiness of my life to you. You have been entirely patient with me and incredibly good. I want to say that—everybody knows it. If anybody could have saved me it would have been you. Everything has gone from me but the certainty of your goodness. I can't go on spoiling your life any longer. I don't think two people could have been happier than we have been.

Etiology and Diagnosis

The *DSM-IV-TR* separates Bipolar Disorder into different categories depending on what the last episode was—Manic, Depressive, or Mixed. Bipolar I Disorder also is categorized according to (1) the long-term pattern of the illness (i.e., if there is interepisodic recovery); (2) whether there is a seasonal pattern to the depressive episodes; and (3) whether it is accompanied by rapid cycling (at least four occurrences in the last 12 months). Rapid cycling occurs in 10 to 20 percent of bipolars, and more often in females. At her death, Virginia's diagnosis would have been Bipolar I Disorder, Most Recent Episode Depressed. Requirements for this include currently having a major depressive episode and having had at least one manic episode in the past. The diagnosis also requires that other disorders with some similar features have been ruled out—for example, Schizoaffective Disorder and Delusional Disorder. The *DSM-IV-TR* also includes Bipolar II Disorder, which differs from Bipolar I by replacing the requirement for a Manic Episode with a Hypomanic Episode (milder than a full-blown manic state). If the individual experiences a polar shift, or if an interval of at least two months goes by between episodes, the disorder is specified as being *recurrent*.

Another aspect of this illness is the propensity for psychosis. When the bipolar illness is severe, according to *DSM* requirements, the subject may be classified as (1) severe without psychotic features; (2) severe with mood-congruent psychotic features (i.e., the delusions or hallucinations are consistent with feelings of inflated worth); or (3) severe with mood-incongruent psychotic features (i.e., the delusions or hallucinations do not involve themes of inflated worth or power). Virginia's psychotic delusions and hallucinations were of the third type.

A series of manic and depressive episodes with decreased durations of well intervals in later years is common over the lifetime course of this illness. In rare cases, patients experience only manic episodes, without evidence of depression. In the overwhelming majority, there is a bipolar pattern. Manic phases are characterized by elevated and expansive moods. The *DSM-IV-TR* defines manic episodes as periods of unusual and persistent mood elevation, expansiveness, or irritability that last at least one week (or any length of time if hospitalization is required). Three of the following symptoms are required (or four, if the mood is irritable instead of expansive): a decreased need for sleep, talkativeness or pressured speech, racing thoughts, distractibility, increase in goal-directed activities or agitation, and extreme involvement in pleasurable activities that have a high potential for painful consequences. Virginia experienced both the expansive and irritable variations of this disorder. She also had the pressured speech, distractibility, racing thoughts, and agitation.

Some episodes of mania or depression continue for months or years, and others make a complete bipolar circuit in a matter of minutes (*micropsychosis*). Still others have *mixed mania*, in which one experiences mania and depression at the same time. These patients feel euphoric and despairing, tired and energized, at the same time (Goodwin & Jamison, 1990; Ludwig, 1996). *Rapid cycling* indicates a poorer prognosis.

In mania, a bipolar patient's imagination seems to go into overdrive, and great significance is found in ordinary events. Common sense seems to desert the patient. Examples of consequences of poor judgment during mania include imprudent marriages, extravagant purchases, drastic career changes, and self-destructive sexual engagements. There is also a heightened risk of violence toward self or others (Bongar, 2002).

Mania eventually swings in the opposite direction. Ranging from sadness to despair, the pain of the depression is frequently nightmarish. Virginia described her depressions as extreme and unbearable; commonly, feelings during this phase often include hopelessness and exhaustion. Virginia's low self-esteem and self-deprecatory comments are also typical of this phase.

Predisposing Factors

Genetic transmission of bipolar disorder has been indicated by family studies, concordance in monozygotic and dizygotic twins, and correlations between adopted persons and their biological relatives (Dilalla, 2004; Nathan, 1995). The risk of having bipolar disorder increases with the proportion of genetic loading from either or both sides of one's family. Despite efforts to locate the genetic mode of transmission, no definitive conclusions have yet been drawn.

Treatment Options

Lithium is the standard treatment because of its ability to modify violent mood swings (Cullberg, 2006; Bezchlibnyk-Butler & Jeffries, 1999). It can be used prophylactically or during an active episode. Although there is tremendous support for lithium and its use, lithium may provide less protection to patients who already have had three or more episodes of the illness. Also, the benefits of lithium do not take effect immediately. Goodwin (1994) asserts that lithium should be taken for years before being evaluated for its effectiveness and concludes that, overall, lithium provides only minimal benefit. As much as 50 percent of the bipolar population does not respond to it. Lithium tends to be less effective if (1) a psychotic symptom (e.g., delusions) is the initial symptom; (2) there are problematic side effects or compliance problems; (3) there are comorbid physical or psychological disorders (including substance abuse—relatively common in manics); (4) there is evidence of more rapid cycles of mania to depression and back; and (5) there is a depression-mania–well pattern of symptoms (rather than mania-depression–well). Even normal expectations of successful lithium treatment are limited. While taking lithium, there are still occasions when one experiences a manic or depressive relapse. Lithium generally offers an approximately 70 percent probability against a relapse after one year, a 50 percent probability against relapse at three years, and only a 35 percent probability against relapse at five years.

Side effects of lithium include tremors, occasionally tardive dyskinesia, nausea, weight gain (especially in the first 6 to 12 months), memory impairment, concentration problems, an altered sense of taste, a decrease in sexual interest or ability, acne, hypothyroidism, lethargy, and a subjective feeling of sensory dulling. Some claim it reduces their creativity. Also, discontinuation of lithium, especially if abrupt, is associated with increased suicide risk. As a result of these limitations, other drug treatments (e.g., levetiracetam, oxcarbazepine, divalproexsodium, escitalopram oxalate, aripiprazole, carbamazepine, or a benzodiazepine) are combined, alternated, or substituted. When physical pain is part of the depression phase, duloxetine is a helpful adjunct drug.

Explanations for those who no longer find lithium effective are related to the kindling or sensitivity model of bipolar disorder. Also related to this model is the fact that psychosocial stressors are involved primarily in early episodes of bipolar illness, and later episodes typically occur without an environmental stimulus. This theory is that after a certain number of episodes, the bipolar illness gradually becomes more "well grooved" or autonomous. Post (1993) summarizes the model as follows:

As in the kindling model, a greater number of prior episodes may not only predispose to the phenomenon of spontaneity (where episodes emerge in the absence of psychosocial stressors or exogenous stimulation) but also to alter pharmacological responsiveness that appears to accompany this late-developing phase of the syndrome. (p. 88)

This explanation makes early institution and long-term maintenance of lithium therapy critical. If the treatment is timely, the disorder is not as likely to take such a severe neurobiological claim on the central nervous system (Post, 1993). Also, systems that support compliance are critical. In addition to being educated about medications, their side effects, and the natural course of the illness, families should learn how to recognize early signs of the episodes. Also, supportive psychotherapy and cognitive-behavior modification are required in most cases (Reinecke et al., 2008).

Comment

Virginia was fortunate to have married Leonard, who remained dedicated to her until her death. More often, this illness has a devastating impact on a marriage. The sense of trust, affection, and loyalty that accrues day by day may be traumatized by one bad day. Unpredictable behaviors create confusion and tend to elicit strong emotional reactions from spouses or children who do not understand why they are being treated so inconsistently (McCullough, 2002). Additional problems stem from the propensity of bipolar individuals in a manic state to threaten divorce, make inappropriate sexual advances to others, and actually engage in affairs. Thus, education for family and society is important.

The evolution of lithium as an effective treatment is a good example of the driving force of the profit motive in pharmacological research. Lithium is a chemical element that was first isolated in 1817 by John Arfwedson, a young Swedish chemistry student. He named it lithium because he found it in stone (*lithos* in Greek). John Cade, an Australian psychiatrist, discovered the positive effect of lithium on mania by chance in the 1940s, while studying whether an excess of uric acid might be the cause of manic-depressive episodes. Cade injected urea from the urine of guinea pigs into human subjects (that is, they were sort of guinea pigs as well). Expecting to learn that uric acid (a compound containing urea) increased the toxicity of urea, he added the most soluble salt of uric acid, lithium urate, and was surprised to find instead that the urea was less toxic as a result. Further experiments isolating lithium eventually indicated its curative properties.

However, it was a long time between initial discovery and the recent widespread marketing and use of lithium. In general, there had been little research on lithium, while more exotic, less widely available compounds received much attention. Two explanations for this seem plausible. First, there is reasonable concern about the significant side effects of lithium. Second, since lithium is a naturally occurring element, it cannot be patented. Drug companies are much more interested in researching new synthetic compounds that they can patent so that they can control the market and gain substantial profits.

8 The Psychosexual Disorders

When people mention the "sexual revolution," many recall the "hippies" of the 1960s and 1970s who preached sexual freedom. However, most agree that the sexual revolution in America began decades earlier when one man, Alfred Charles Kinsey, published his controversial findings about the sexual lives of American men and women. In his *Kinsey Reports*, he provided detailed accounts of the sexual behaviors allegedly practiced by mainstream Americans, but rarely acknowledged. Although he is recognized as a pioneer in our knowledge of sexual behavior, his personal life provided additional controversy about sexuality.

The Case of Alfred Kinsey

Alfred C. Kinsey was born on June 23, 1894, in Hoboken, New Jersey. His parents were extremely conservative evangelical Protestants. His father was very controlling and "acted as the head of the house and as God's spokesman to his family" (Jones, 1997, p. 14). His parents displayed very little affection toward one another and created a seemingly sexless household, leading him to question his own sexuality in adolescence and adulthood.

Kinsey was very sickly throughout his childhood and felt demeaned by his father. Having always felt inadequate in the eyes of his father, Kinsey sought validation through academic achievements. He excelled in the classroom and soon became interested in the subject of biology, gaining the title of a "second Darwin" from his high school classmates. In 1912, he graduated as valedictorian of his high school. Then, at the insistence of his

father, he attended the Stevens Institute of Technology in his hometown of Hoboken. After two unhappy years there, he transferred to Bowdoin College in Maine. After graduating magna cum laude with degrees in biology and psychology, he began graduate training in biology at Harvard's Bussey Institute. As part of his dissertation research, Kinsey collected and painstakingly labeled thousands of gall wasps, eventually gathering what was reputed to be the largest collection of gall wasps in the world. After earning his doctoral degree in 1919, he became an assistant professor of entomology at Indiana University in Bloomington.

Soon after his move to Indiana, he met Clara McMillan, ironically a self-declared virgin. They married in 1921 and eventually had four children. She also had a constricted hymen, making sexuality at the onset of their marriage problematic. After surgery normal sexuality was available. Determined that his family life would not replicate his own, Kinsey railed against the traditional family structure of patriarchic authority and sexual repression. He insisted on educating his children about sex, but did not limit this to talking with his children. Rather, he believed in teaching by example and often encouraged nudity in the home. As word got out about their stance on sex education, the Kinseys soon were perceived as the "authorities" in the area, although more negative terms were also used. He also often discussed explicit sexuality with his students, both in and out of the classroom.

These interests let him to gather information about others' sex lives while on traditional biological expeditions. However, his research on sexuality did not formally begin until 1938, when he offered a noncredit "marriage course." In conjunction with the course, Kinsey also offered "individual counseling sessions" that he used to gather information about his students' sex lives. Although the course was an instant success, the controversy generated by the counseling and the course led the university to cancel his class.

Kinsey continued to gather information in the form of questionnaires and interviews, and he inquired well beyond the scope of what were considered "normal" sexual practices of the times. Ultimately, his goal was to "discover every single thing people did sexually" (Gathorne-Hardy, 1998, p. 182). Then, in an attempt to gain a wider array of sexual experiences, he broadened his sample by including prison inmates and homosexuals, eventually conducting as many as 18,000 interviews, apparently working on the assumption that a huge data pool would override potential sampling biases.

After he received his first grant in 1940, his research assistants began traveling across

the country interviewing as diverse a population as possible about their sexual lives. In 1947, he opened the Institute for Sex Research on the campus of Indiana University and in 1948 published the first part of the *Kinsey Reports*, *Sexual Behavior and the Human Male*, followed by *Sexual Behavior and the Human Female* in 1953. Within two months of its publication, more than 200,000 copies of the "Male" volume had been sold.

Both books were controversial and outraged many average Americans. Also, statisticians harshly criticized Kinsey's sampling methods, accurately arguing that his sample was not representative of the general American population, for example, "Kinsey was not justified in generalizing his conclusions to the whole American population" (Gathorne-Hardy, 1998, p. 272). His sampling methodology also included a bizarre bias. Determined to gather as much information as possible regarding individuals' sexual practices, Kinsey began promoting sexual activity among his research team members. Again showing flawed judgment, Kinsey filmed and photographed his students in a variety of sexual acts.

Allegations continue to swirl regarding Kinsey's own sexual practices. There is a consensus that Kinsey was bisexual and also participated in masochistic sexual practices to the point that he was almost unable to experience pleasure without pain. Most striking, though, are allegations that Kinsey engaged in child sexual abuse during his data collection, specifically based on data he reported on the orgasms of pre-adolescent boys. Because the source of this information is still not clear, there are allegations that Kinsey had sexual contact with these boys. Not surprisingly, the Kinsey Institute (2007) denies this and claims that the "majority" of this information was gathered from one man who had engaged in numerous illegal sexual acts with children.

Controversy aside, the *Kinsey Reports* had a huge impact on American society. For the first time in America, mainstream society openly discussed a wide variety of sexual topics. In any case, all experts now agree that the variations in sexual behavior are limited only by an individual's imagination (Laws & O'Donohue, 2008; Sbraga & O'Donohue, 2004). The psychosexual disorders are equally varied patterns in which psychological factors are assumed to be of major etiological significance in the development of disrupted or deviant sexual behaviors. In the *DSM-IV-TR*, they include the Paraphilias, Gender Disorders, and Psychosexual Dysfunctions, and we describe a new syndrome not yet in the *DSM*, Sexual Addiction.

The Gender Disorders, commonly referred to as Transsexualism, are marked by felt incongruence between the actual physical sexual apparatus and gender identity. The essential feature of the Psychosexual Dysfunctions is inhibition in the appetitive or psychophysiological changes that accompany the complete sexual response cycle. Inhibitions in the response cycle may occur in one or more of the following phases: appetitive, excitement, orgasm, or resolution.

Current thinking generally regards the psychosexual disorders as the result of faulty socialization and learning, affected in certain cases by genetic and temperament variables. Thus, they are considered responsive to a variety of treatment approaches, such as pharmacological interventions, operant and classical conditioning, biofeedback, hypnosis, and/or sexual reassignment surgery. Outcome studies using these techniques have been generally encouraging, especially for the sexual dysfunctions, reasonably so for the gender disorders, but to a lesser degree for the paraphilias.

Sexual Addiction

The concept of sexual addiction first came to the attention of the public with the publication of a book by Patrick Carnes in 1992. The concept of sexual addiction gained even greater notoriety when applied by some observers to the behavior of the subject of our second case study, President William Clinton. Although not an official diagnostic category in the American Psychiatric Association's *Diagnostic and Statistical Manual of Mental Disorders (DSM-IV-TR)*, sexual addiction has gained increased acceptance as a legitimate psychological disorder (Sbraga & O'Donohue, 2004).

Traditionally, addiction is thought of as a person (the addict) being engaged in a pathological relationship with a mood-altering chemical, with accompanying physical changes (Andreassi, 2000). Therefore, generalization to sexual experiences, with their resulting release of pleasurable bodily chemicals and fulfillment of biological drives, is at least a logical step, and closer to the concept of addiction than is pathological gambling, which is also considered an addiction. How, then, does one conceptualize a "pathological relationship" between a person and his or her sexual experiences? First, the term *pathological* implies that the relationship is causing some type of impairment or distress. In the case of sexual addiction, impairment may mean not making it to work due to frequenting strip clubs. Distress may take the form of marital discord resulting from this pattern of behavior.

The *relationship* component can be thought of as the repetitive cycle of addiction. The initial stage consists of the person's obsessive occupation with sex. These thoughts can be very reinforcing in and of themselves, particularly when the person uses these thoughts, knowingly or otherwise, to alleviate tension (e.g., taking one's mind off work). The individual begins to associate the obsessional thoughts as a means of coping with stress. Eventually, the thoughts themselves often do not satisfy the addict's needs, and the thoughts begin to escalate into overt behaviors. This ritual phase is when an addict who is intrigued by thoughts of sex with young children may, for instance, begin to frequent playgrounds or cruise past schoolyards during recess. Other escalations may occur. For example, someone interested in very young children may begin to frequent prostitutes, even though people in that age range are not the object of the original obsession. Perhaps the most important step in the addiction cycle is the guilt experienced by addicts immediately following the compulsive sexual act, as the quality of that guilt will determine the possibility of behavior change.

As with any addiction, changes in the individual may indicate advancement of the addiction cycle into a more serious problem. A usually scrupulous individual may begin missing appointments or telling lies to friends, family, and co-workers. A "pillar of the community" may be arrested for soliciting prostitution, or even hedge on the truth during a Senate judicial inquiry. Thus, sexual addiction, a seemingly private concern, can become a more pervasive problem for the individual and society. The following case of William Clinton is based on public records, newspaper accounts, and a book by Maraniss (1996). It may be surprising how well Clinton's case fits the concept of sexual addiction, particularly regarding the contribution from genetics, early childhood turmoil, and modeling.

The Case of William Clinton

On August 19, 1946, William Jefferson Blythe, III, was born into a tumultuous world. The son of Virginia Dell Blythe—a flirtatious, socialite nurse—the baby was the topic of much discussion in the rural Arkansas town of Hope. The talk was of Bill's biological father. A soldier in the war, William Blythe, II, was known to some as a con artist. He had a past riddled with ex-wives and abandoned children, none of which he had included in his life history as told to Virginia. Townsfolk couldn't help but wonder how it was that William Blythe, II, was stationed overseas in the military nine months before the birth of baby Bill. This sug-

gested to some that William Blythe was not young Bill's biological father, an idea Virginia dismissed with a story of Bill being born prematurely.

Shortly following his return to the states, William planned to move his new family to Chicago, where he had secured work. But he was killed in a tragic car accident, and the widowed Virginia Blythe remained in Hope with her 3-month-old son, living in her parents' home. Bill's grandmother, "Mammaw," was very involved in his upbringing; Virginia even felt she was smothering. Mammaw was controlling, was easily angered, and

(continued)

The Case of William Clinton Continued

often downed a few drinks after a hard day's work. Virginia as well as Bill's grandfather also drank with regularity, and Virginia never seemed to sacrifice her affinity for young men. Yet, outside the home, the entire family was known for its exceptional work ethic.

It was during this period, some four years after the death of William Blythe, that Virginia met Roger Clinton. True to form with respect to Virginia's previous romantic interests, Roger was often in financial trouble and was an inveterate womanizer. Virginia even caught him in the act at one point during the early days of their dating. But Virginia was a woman who finished what she started and so she married Roger, against the advice of her family. Four-year-old Bill moved in with his mom and her new husband. Life in the Clinton household was in a constant state of uproar. Between Roger's drinking and socializing, he was rarely home, and rarely sober when he was. But Bill idolized Roger and called him "daddy" even though Roger seemed to pay little attention to Bill. Nights were often characterized by ferocious fights between Virginia and Roger.

The family moved to the nearby town of Hot Springs, Arkansas, when Bill was age 6. Hot Springs was a small tourist town known for its history of gambling and prostitution, a scene in which many Clinton family members had participated. Virginia and Roger joined in the Hot Springs social scene. Much of Bill's upbringing was now left to the nanny.

During his grade-school years, Bill consistently proved himself to be the top pupil in his class. Bill began using the Clinton name, and he established himself as a socially adept young man. Seemingly never having met a stranger, Bill had scores of friends. This trait would stay with him throughout most of his life. Most viewed Bill as distancing himself from his mother and Roger. Certainly this was so in that Bill regularly attended church, a value that was probably instilled in him by his nanny.

In high school, Bill continued on his quest of amassing scholastic awards, including serving as class president. The highlight of his high school political career came when at age 16 he won a mock senate seat, in a competition with 1,000 other boys, giving him a trip to Washington, DC, where he met then President John F. Kennedy, who became Bill's lifelong hero. Bill maintained his academic and social prowess throughout his school years, but he always had a bit of a wild side to him. Although he was never overly fond of drinking and wild parties, Bill was known as having a way (and often his way) with girls. He was known by his friends to date many young women, sometimes from other towns, sometimes having more than one "steady" girlfriend at a time. Most of the young women seemed aware of his reputation but didn't seem to mind. Although socially, Bill was an astounding success, life at home continued in turmoil.

Bill always remained close with his mother, and even though Roger Clinton's alcohol abuse was tearing the family apart, Bill still felt close to Roger. It was not until later during college that Bill would grow more distant from Roger. But for now, Bill took on the role of the family savior. He settled countless arguments between his mother and Roger, and helped get Roger home after many a drinking binge. Bill had made a good reputation for himself, which the family enjoyed vicariously through him. He did obtain some distance from this turmoil when he headed for Washington, to Georgetown University.

Here, he again made many friends, even among some of the aristocratic youth from more genteel backgrounds than his own. He could always be found somewhere on campus shaking hands and meeting people. Bill Clinton always seemed to be politicking for something, and won the position of Freshman Class President.

Also, he was near the top of his class academically, a position he would enjoy throughout his undergraduate career. It was also during his early years at Georgetown that Bill met his apparent first true love, Denise Hyland. But the relationship eventually faded, and they separated in the fall of their junior year at Georgetown, after which friends recounted that Bill dated "lots of women." Bill also allegedly used his dating life to further his political agenda. During a political campaign one summer, he and a Georgetown friend made political connections across the Arkansas countryside. Their method of getting to know all of the political bureaucrats was none other than to date their daughters.

In the summer of 1968, Bill found himself in one of his first political crises when he was put on "imminently draftable" status by the Arkansas draft board. Even though he had just won the prestigious Rhodes Scholarship to study at Oxford University in England, the discontinuance of graduate school draft deferments a few months earlier would seemingly allow Bill no reprieve. Accounts of just how Bill avoided being drafted vary from "luck" to a calculated use of hometown Arkansas politics. As with most rumors, the truth most likely lies somewhere in between.

Nevertheless, Bill did attend Oxford University. Although he would never officially complete his course of instruction there, he continued to expand his portfolio of sexual partners, including the daughter of one of his Oxford professors. Bill never showed much evidence of inhibition in the face of risk.

He eventually returned to the states to Yale Law School, where he continued his political (and sexual) quests. It was also during this time that he met a young law student, Hillary Rodham. Although this would be the beginning of Bill's most enduring relationship, there was continual evidence of sexual promiscuity on his part.

After law school, Bill went home to the University of Arkansas as a professor of law. He gradually developed his political career, despite rumors of his sexual misdeeds cropping up in each race. Although he suffered a few devastating political defeats during this

time, he would always pick up the pieces, analyze the problems, and begin the next campaign. His political prowess eventually gained him two nonconsecutive terms as the governor of Arkansas, beginning in 1978 as the youngest governor in the United States in 40 years, and Bill was termed the political "boy wonder." While Bill was governor, Hillary gave birth to Chelsea, but the marriage was often described as less than optimal. There continued to be evidence of womanizing on Bill's behalf. One state trooper assigned to the governor's mansion stated that he had been asked to solicit private meetings between Clinton and over 100 young women, characterizing Governor Clinton as someone with a "voracious sexual appetite."

During his second stint as governor, Bill had to confront his family's addictive predisposition. In the spring of 1984, Arkansas state troopers told Governor Clinton that his younger brother, Roger, had been picked up on charges of cocaine distribution. The Clinton family was devastated. Everyone took part in Roger's treatment process, attending group therapy and meetings.

On January 20, 1993, Bill Clinton was sworn in as the forty-second president of the United States. At 46 years of age, he was the youngest American president since the election of his childhood hero John F. Kennedy in 1960. Bill never seemed to falter in his ability as a politician. However, virtually everyone agrees that his sexual escapades and obsessions escalated beyond his control while in Washington. Charges of sexual harassment and misconduct persisted almost from day one. The sexual tryst with Monica Lewinsky and the resulting political turmoil led Bill Clinton to be only the second president in the history of the United States to be impeached (impeachment is the process, not the outcome). He will be forever associated with the saying, "I have never had sexual relations with that woman." When confronted with evidence to the contrary, President Clinton eventually conceded that although the two had engaged in oral sex, his claims were "technically, legally accurate," citing confusing

(continued)

The Case of William Clinton Continued

definitions in sexual terminology as the basis for the various discrepancies. It would be shown in the report by Independent Counsel Kenneth Starr that, according to Lewinsky's accounts, Bill's behavior was in fact enough to meet any legal definition of the term "sexual relations." And most observers perceived the pattern as having a strong element of compulsion. Even Hillary Clinton has stated that Bill's problems stemmed from childhood difficulties, but to his credit, he never overtly voiced this as an excuse.

Etiology

In general terms, the generic progression to being a sexual addict may take the form of the addictive cycle just discussed. With respect to why someone progresses into this dysfunctional state, the answer is most likely a mix of genetic predisposition, childhood turmoil, and behavioral modeling. In the case of Bill Clinton, there was likely a genetic predisposition to an addictive personality, evidenced by his parents' addictive propensities and his brother's legal difficulties and cocaine habit. While the hazy history regarding Bill's biological father precludes any analysis of paternal addictive genetics, the roots of addiction ran deep on Virginia Clinton's side of the family, with her mother and father both being alcoholics, along with a family history of gambling and sexual promiscuity.

It could be said that perhaps Bill had never been in a "normal," caring intimate relationship. At the very least, Bill's adolescent life seems devoid of any appropriate male role models, particularly when it came to how women were to be treated.

The conflict-based lifestyle in Bill's household was likely a stressor that exacerbated an addictive predisposition. Sexual behavior likely served a very adaptive role in Bill's adolescent life, as it helped to fill an emotional void brought on by the tumultuous life at home. Once set into motion, the sexual behaviors were most likely reinforcing enough to maintain the behavior well into adulthood. Again, the addictive predisposition probably set the stage for escalating preoccupation. Early accounts talk of Bill's aptitude with women in both high school and beyond, ever feeding the increasing need to satisfy his sexual desires. His lifestyle certainly seems consistent with the "preoccupation" and "ritualization" phases of addiction.

Although Clinton's development into a sexual addict was probably spurred on by his powerful political lifestyle and the sexual climate of the sixties, in general it is not unlike a similar path that others follow into the addictive cycle. In Bill Clinton's case, his addiction literally cost the American taxpayers millions of dollars, and it is likely that the final cost of this addiction to the Clinton family has yet to be played out. When the cycle continues without interruption, progression of the sexual desire continues into the "abnormal," as in pedophilia or serial rape, and the addictions impact on society can be much more costly.

Treatment Options

As with other disorders, a "wrap-around" approach to the treatment of sexual addiction is often recommended. The premise of "wrap-around" is to surround the client with as many services, pertaining to as many life domains, as feasible. However, the most popular treatment protocol to date has been the traditional 12-step approach popularized by programs such as Alcoholics Anonymous and Narcotics Anonymous (see also Chapter 9). This procedure addresses the spiritual, mental, emotional, and physical needs of both the recovering sex addict and the addict's family (Earle, Dillon, & Jecmen, 1998). There is, however, one fundamental difference between the treatment of sexual addicts and the treatment of those with substance abuse addictions: control versus abstinence.

Although it may be a productive endeavor for the substance addict to seek abstinence, sexual behavior is a fundamental biological drive from which abstinence would be difficult, if not impossible, to achieve, nor in less deviant cases (such as Bill Clinton's) would one necessarily want to achieve. This limits the use of aversion therapy and other behavior modification techniques that may be used in the treatment of chemical dependence. Therefore, through psychotherapy and family support, the sexual addict will strive to control the deviant nature of his or her sexual addiction. The family component of the 12-step program indicates that family members themselves will often require treatment, particularly the addict's spouse. Self-disclosure by the addict is needed to begin the healing process for the spouse. Although this can be a tricky undertaking at best, research has suggested an overall positive impact of self-disclosure on the relationship between addict and spouse (Sbraga & O'Donohue, 2004).

Too much of a good thing is wonderful.

—Mae West

Paraphilias

Paraphilia is the *DSM-IV-TR* term for the sexual deviations, and both terms will be used interchangeably. The deviation (*para*) is in that to which the individual is attracted (*philia*). In the *DSM-IV-TR*, all diagnoses of Paraphilia require fulfillment of (1) Criteria A—recurrent, intense sexually arousing fantasies, sexual urges, or behaviors (with the specificity required by the particular disorder), over at least a six-month period *and* (2) Criteria B—these fantasies, urges, or behaviors cause clinically significant distress or impairment in an important area of one's life. The specific paraphilia categories included in *DSM-IV-TR* are Fetishism, Transvestic Fetishism, Pedophilia, Exhibitionism, Voyeurism, Frotteurism, Sexual Masochism, and Sexual Sadism. Although the *DSM-IV-TR* does not directly provide for a diagnosis of sexual compulsion or sexual addiction, it is a factor in the case of Jeffrey Dahmer and in many of the previous diagnoses and is the focus of the second case in this chapter, that of President William Clinton.

Jeffrey Dahmer is one of the most infamous serial murderers in this country's history. Marked by his sexual obsession with dead and nearly dead bodies, Dahmer became proficient at drugging, murdering, dismembering, and consuming his victims. He is an excellent although unusual example of a paraphilia. The essential disorder in a paraphilia is an incapacity for mature, participating, affectionate sexual behavior with adult partners. Traditionally, these disorders have been far more common in males, but this discrepancy has decreased slightly in recent years.

The Case of Jeffrey Dahmer

Early Years

Jeffrey Dahmer was born on May 21, 1960. During most of his childhood, he lived on an estate in a wealthy suburb of Akron, Ohio. His father is a successful research chemist, and, consistent with that calling, now blames his son's aberrant behavior on the effects of medication Jeffrey's mother took during pregnancy. In the first grade, when his younger brother was born, Dahmer's teacher wrote a note to his parents saying that their son acted as though he felt neglected. Although Dahmer was not physically or sexually abused, he remembered his home as constantly filled with tension because of his parents' continuous fighting. Ironically, after Jeffrey's death, his parents fought bitterly over the custody of his remains. Dahmer reported feeling guilty for being born because his mother told him she had serious postpartum depression and a nervous breakdown after his birth.

There were reports of peculiar things Dahmer did as a child (as in many such cases, they were seen as more peculiar after his arrest than at the time). For example, his neighbors reported that he had a fascination with dead insects and animals, and his friends said he repeatedly listened to their hearts with his head on their chests. Dahmer collected animals that had been killed by cars, cut off their heads, and placed them on sticks. He also removed and dried out their skin.

There were several experiences in Dahmer's early life that suggested indifference to other's suffering. Of course, the issue is whether this was more than is found in the history of many "normal" boys. At age 5, Dahmer convinced a friend to put his hand in a wasp nest by telling him it was full of ladybugs. In grade school, Dahmer took some tadpoles to a teacher whom he liked. When he found out that his teacher had given the tadpoles to Dahmer's best friend, he felt rejected by the teacher and decided to punish his friend. So he poured motor oil into the bowl where his friend kept the tadpoles, killing them. One of Dahmer's favorite activities as a teenager was seeking out dogs and killing them with his car.

Dahmer reported that in the eighth grade he masturbated daily and fantasized about sex with boys his own age. His first sexual experience was in the ninth grade. The boy who lived next door came over and lay naked with Dahmer, kissing and fondling him. They stopped after doing this two or three times because of the risk of being caught. After Dahmer dissected a pig in biology class, he took the head home, removed the skin, and kept the skull. At this time he began thinking about using corpses for his sexual pleasure. In high school, Dahmer began drinking alcohol frequently, even during school hours. Although he took part in a normal assortment of high school activities and earned average grades, he was essentially a loner.

The only evidence available of his involvement with a female was when Dahmer went to the prom. He neither danced with nor kissed his date. Halfway through the prom, he left alone to get a hamburger.

Adult Years

When Dahmer was 18 years old, his parents were in a bitter divorce and in a custody fight for Dahmer's younger brother. It was at this time, in 1978, that Dahmer had one day walked into the woods with a baseball bat while fantasizing about having sex with a teenage jogger who Dahmer knew frequented that area. Fortunately, the boy did not show up that day, but the developing combination of aggression for control and sex is noted. Dahmer killed his first victim that same year, Steven Hicks, age 19. Dahmer had his own car and lived alone. He had been drinking and was driving home when he picked up a hitchhiker. Hicks agreed to go to Dahmer's parents' luxurious house, where they talked, drank beer, and smoked marijuana. Reports vary as to whether Dahmer and Hicks had sex. When it came time for Steven to leave, Dahmer tried to stop him and the two wrestled. Dahmer hit and strangled Hicks with a barbell.

After knocking Hicks out, Dahmer took off his clothes and masturbated while standing over the body, ejaculating onto the body. At dusk, Dahmer took the body to a crawlspace under his parents' house and cut it into pieces, placing the parts in plastic bags. At first, he carried the pieces with him in his car, but later he returned and placed them in the woods behind his parents' house.

After this first murder, Dahmer spent the next several years drifting, and he later reported he was trying hard to resist killing again. He attended Ohio State University for a few months, spent a couple of years in the army, and lived briefly on a beach in Florida. In 1982, Dahmer went to live with his grandmother in Wisconsin, where he got a job at a blood plasma center. He was fired for poor performance after a year. Later, he got a job in a chocolate factory. During the nine years after the first murder, Dahmer continued to experi-ence fantasies about capturing people but did not commit any homicidal acts.

When Dahmer returned from the army, he retrieved his first victim's body pieces and smashed them into fragments that he scattered in the woods. He began pursuing relationships in public places. As one of the early "date-rapists," he would go to a gay bathhouse or bar, meet a man, put drugs into his drink, and take the drugged man to a hotel room. When the man was in a sleep-like state, Jeffrey would have anal sex with him. He would then leave, and the man would awake the next morning with little recollection of what occurred. In what Dahmer described as an attempt to avoid killing, he once went to a funeral home to see the dead body of a young man whom he read had died. Dahmer tried to figure out how to dig up the body so that he could enjoy sex without killing. On another occasion, Dahmer stole a mannequin from a store and performed sexual acts on it. Dahmer's alcohol intake steadily increased.

In 1986, Dahmer was arrested for lewd and lascivious behavior when caught masturbating in front of two 12-year-old boys. Placed in therapy for this offense, Dahmer was described as being cooperative and willing to change.

Dahmer did not commit any murders from 1978 to 1987. In 1989, just after having killed three men, he pleaded guilty to second-degree sexual assault and enticement of a child for immoral purposes. Dahmer had approached a 13-year-old boy walking home from school and offered him $50 to come to his apartment to help him try his new camera. In the apartment, Dahmer persuaded the boy to remove some of his clothes, and then Dahmer kissed the boy's stomach, unzipped his pants, and pulled out his penis. Dahmer touched the boy's penis, explaining this would make him appear sexier for the pictures. While this was occurring, the boy drank coffee in which Dahmer had placed alcohol and a tranquilizer. When the boy returned home, his parents noticed his peculiar behavior and filed charges when the boy described his experience with

(continued)

The Case of Jeffrey Dahmer Continued

Dahmer. Despite his arrest and conviction for this offense, Dahmer's murders remained undiscovered.

During this period, Dahmer again was briefly exposed to therapy. At the same time that a Department of Probation and Parole psychologist informed the presiding judge that Dahmer was becoming more outgoing and relaxed, Dahmer was carrying the skull of his latest victim, which he had painted to resemble those bought in stores. He killed his fifth victim while waiting for sentencing. Another psychologist appointed by the court to examine Dahmer described him as uncooperative and unwilling to work on his problems. Therefore, the recommendation to cease requiring Dahmer to be treated for alcohol and sex offenses, which was supported by two more psychologists, was accepted. Dahmer appealed directly to the judge and said emphatically that he wished to change his behavior. The judge responded by staying Dahmer's five-year sentence and placing him on probation for five years. Even though Dahmer was directed to receive therapy, this was never carried out.

After he was released, Dahmer purchased a black table and made a temple on it of bleached and painted skulls. The temple, used to contain the skeletons of his victims, was to be an area of worship, to give him more energy and control in his life. In the summer of 1990, Dahmer was fired from his latest job for excessive absenteeism. His pace quickened as he killed 12 more men around that time and through the following summer.

Dahmer's Procedures with Victims

Dahmer was primarily interested in sex with unconscious men. He tried to make zombies out of his victims so they would forget their identity and stay with him. He did this in various ways, such as drugging them. He drilled holes in the heads of some men while they were alive and poured muriatic acid in the holes, hoping they would stay alive so that he could continue having sex with them. One victim walked around for three days in this condition before he died. Another way Dahmer tried to keep his victims was by storing and packaging their parts and eating the meat so that they would become a part of him. Dahmer had sex with every one of the 17 victims after they were dead. With 14 victims, Dahmer cut them open in the abdomen, placed his penis inside the cavity of the body, got an erection, and ejaculated while still inside the body. With 5 or 6 of the victims, Dahmer put his penis inside the mouth of the beheaded man, got an erection, and ejaculated. Dahmer also engaged in anal sex with 5 or 6 of the victims after they were dead. Dahmer talked about enjoying masturbating in front of and over the bodies.

Final Years

In May 1991, Dahmer gave his thirteenth victim a drugged drink, drilled holes in his skull, and filled them with acid. In the morning when the young man was sleeping, Dahmer went out to get a beer. As Dahmer was returning, he saw the man naked and sitting at the side of the road. Two women and the police and a firetruck were at the scene. Dahmer explained that the young man was a friend who had had too much to drink. The police then wrapped the man in a blanket, entered Dahmer's apartment, and laid him on the sofa. There was a body in Dahmer's bedroom that the police did not discover. When shown two pictures of Dahmer with the young man, a police officer said, "See, he is telling the truth." After the police left, Dahmer gave the man a final fatal injection. Dahmer proceeded to pose the victim, take pictures, perform anal sex with him, and masturbate on top of him. He acidified the flesh and skeleton and defleshed and saved the skull.

After killing four more men in less than three weeks, in July 1991, Dahmer approached Tracy Edwards, age 32. According to one account of what occurred that day, Dahmer offered Edwards the same opportunity he had presented to others: money in exchange for taking his picture. While Edwards was in Dahmer's bedroom watching *The Exorcist*, Dahmer handcuffed one of Edwards's hands and placed a knife at his chest. Dahmer began rubbing one of his skulls and said Edwards's skull would be staying with him, too. Edwards hit Dahmer, kicked him in the chest, and escaped. Edwards reported the incident to the police, who found the story so implausible that at first they were not inclined to investigate. Two police officers with extra time on their hands finally agreed to visit Dahmer.

It does appear that Dahmer deteriorated over time, and may have experienced psychotic and/or dissociative episodes. For example, when, on July 22, 1991, his last victim escaped from him, Dahmer made no attempt to leave his apartment or otherwise avoid apprehension. In fact, according to that victim's report, Dahmer seemed disconnected from reality and was shouting incantations as the victim left. When the police came, Dahmer did not ask about a search warrant or resist in any fashion, but simply let them in. One officer entered Dahmer's bedroom, where several body parts were resting. The other opened the refrigerator and found human heads. When put under arrest, Dahmer struggled a bit with the police and then he surrendered.

Dahmer readily confessed and supplied the police with detailed descriptions. He was charged with 2 counts of murder and 13 counts of first-degree intentional homicide. Dahmer pled insanity, probably because there was no other option. Because his demeanor was that of a quiet, sensitive, and intelligent college student, the jury was not impressed. He was found sane and sentenced to 957 years via 15 consecutive life sentences. After his capture, Dahmer repeatedly expressed remorse and was of the opinion that he did not deserve to live. In prison he refused all efforts available to protect him from being attacked by other prisoners. On November 28, 1994, while washing a bathroom floor in prison, Dahmer and another inmate were beaten to death with a 20-inch bar from an exercise machine. A third inmate, Christopher Scarver, was implicated in the murders. Scarver, who once claimed to be the son of God, said, "God told me to do it." Given the horrendous nature of Dahmer's crimes, there are some who might argue that Scarver wasn't delusional, that God might have told him to do it. According to the records released in March 1995 of the November 1994 autopsy of Dahmer, officials kept Dahmer's body shackled at the feet during the entire procedure, "such was the fear of this man," according to pathologist Robert Huntington.

Etiology

It is unusual for an individual to have just one diagnosis when the behavior involved is extreme like Dahmer's. For example, at one time or another, Dahmer has been described as having the following psychological diagnoses: pedophilia, borderline personality disorder, sadistic personality disorder, antisocial personality disorder, alcohol dependence, psychosis, marijuana abuse, and mixed personality disorder.

Ironically, testimony at his trial suggests that Dahmer had a "reverse conversion" (or "cognitive shift") after killing his second victim, which occurred after a long period of trying to resist killing. That is, he considered that there might not be a God and/or that he was being influenced by the Devil or some evil force and concluded that it was his destiny to kill. After that, he no longer exerted any strong conscious effort not to kill, as he reportedly had done up to that point, and the killings then came more easily and quickly.

Curiously, Dahmer does not appear to be a clear Factor 1 or primary psychopath (Boyd et al., 2007), an assumption many people might make in light of his horrendous crimes (see Chapter 11). All indications are that Dahmer could experience a form of guilt-related anxiety, and in spite of his successful deception of the police in May 1991, Dahmer's tendency to lie was not so pronounced that it was regarded as pathological. Dahmer was always surprisingly open about his behavior and motives after being captured. Also, most sophisticated observers said his expressions of remorse and his move toward religion and spirituality in prison were believable. In any case, the diagnosis most pronounced with Dahmer is paraphilia, as he clearly fit the criteria for the residual category, Paraphilia Not Otherwise Specified (NOS).

Dr. Judith Becker, a psychologist who is an expert in sexual deviations, testified as a defense expert at Dahmer's trial. She could find no reference in the literature for Dahmer's unique variation of necrophilia (i.e., his attraction to zombie-like human living bodies capable of little more than breathing).

Exclusivity, persistency, compulsivity, and pervasiveness, such as that exhibited by Dahmer, are the hallmarks of paraphilia. It is typically a driven, focused pattern, often seen initially in fantasy or behavior in mid-adolescence (LoPiccolo, 1993). Fantasies of sex with corpses first appeared in Dahmer's adolescence, with his pursuit of dead animals likely being a precursor to his full-blown variation of necrophilia.

Research does not support sex hormone or neurotransmitter abnormalities as the primary or major cause in the paraphilias (Laws & O'Donohue, 2008). Rather, it appears that Dahmer aptly fits the description given by LoPiccolo (1993):

> Paraphilias are complex, multiple determined conditions, and . . . any single-element theory of etiology is oversimplified and incorrect. Rather, we should realize that paraphilias clearly involve a host of factors, including arousal conditioned to inappropriate objects, lack of internalized moral values, inability to weigh long-term negative consequences against short-term sexual pleasure, distorted thinking about sexuality, lack of access to gratifying normal sexual outlets, lack of empathy for victim distress, disinhibition by alcohol or drugs, and, possibly, temporal lobe pathology. In individual cases, various combinations of these factors may be more or less important. (p. 340)

There is no evidence that one of these factors, temporal lobe pathology, applied to Dahmer, and nothing about Dahmer's past suggests there was any lack of access to normal sexual outlets. The rest of LoPiccolo's descriptors bear a close resemblance to Dahmer. Dahmer's ability to weigh long-term negative consequences against short-term sexual pleasure seems to have deteriorated as both his alcoholism and his experiences with dead and almost-dead bodies increased.

Treatment Options

Dahmer never pursued or received significant treatment for his disorder, which is not uncommon with paraphiliacs. The paraphilias range from disorders that involve passivity (sexual masochism) to those that involve coercive aggression and illegal actions (pedophilia), and treatments will differ as well. Indeed, anyone working in this area is constantly challenged by the creative diversity found in sexual preferences. For example, antisex crusader John Harvey Kellogg originated Kellogg's breakfast cereals to calm sexual lust and promote a generally healthy lifestyle in the general population. Kellogg himself avoided sex with his wife and obtained sexual gratification from enemas—a pattern known as *klismaphilia*. In general, all of the paraphilias are difficult to treat, success is often negligible and/or short term, and relapse is common (LoPiccolo, 1993). Castration is a time-honored treatment, or to quote from James W. Hall's 1996 novel *Buzz Cut*:

> Testicles. The Greek word was *orchis orchid*, from the shape of the flower's tuber. *Orchidectomy* being the technical term for castration. Cutting away the orchid's roots. Or in the Latin, *castrare*, from *castus*, which meant pure. Castration being used on the eastern slaves to keep women pure. *Castus*, as in the caste system, to keep the races pure. . . . And there was the other Latin term, *testiculus*, which referred to the ancient practice of swearing an oath by putting a hand on the nuts.

However, even physical castration is not always effective (Marvasti, 2004). Chemocastrators such as medroxyprogesterone acetate (Depo-Provera), which suppress all sexual arousal, not just the undesired forms, can be effective. Neurosurgical castration via temporal lobe ablation has been used in some countries.

Most paraphiliacs are best treated in a formal treatment program, usually referred to as a sex offender program. Several factors can optimize such a program. It is helpful if the program can be delivered in the context of a psychotherapy or counseling relationship wherein a degree of trust has been generated. However, the therapist must understand that, just as Dahmer behaved, these clients may well pretend sincerity, overstate gains, resist treatment, and prematurely terminate. One should be especially suspicious of a client's statements that he has spontaneously or quickly lost interest in deviant activities and/or has easily (or ever) become primarily interested in consensual sex with adult females. It almost never happens that way. The following are common components of a typical sex offender treatment program:

1. *Assessment of the offender* (e.g., phallometry, the measurement of sexual responses to suggested imagery or to actual pictures of various stimuli) is helpful in identifying the focus of the sexually deviant fantasies that are a key to treatment of the aberrant behavior. In a cooperative subject, direct measures of penile tumescence (usually, via changes in a tube encircling the penis) are often used. Less intrusive but reasonably effective is the Abel Assessment for Sexual Interest (referred to as the Abel Screen), which measures the length of time that a subject spends viewing a set of sexual stimuli. In some cases, thermography (measurement of temperature changes in the penis) has distinct advantages of ease of access and less embarrassment.

2. *Any necessary acute measures* (e.g., mandated residence changes, short-term chemocastration, etc.) and medications (e.g., antidepressants) may be necessary in some cases.

3. *Group and/or individual therapy* are necessary to clarify the individual's range of deviancy, level of disorder, and level of commitment to change. This is an appropriate place to deal with cognitive distortions (e.g., "Women may act like they don't, but I can tell they secretly like it when I _____").

4. *Various behavioral techniques* (Chambless et al., 1996), such as those noted here and in item numbers 5, 6, and 7, may be required. *Covert sensitization* is an imagery based counterconditioning procedure in which a client is instructed to imagine the relevant deviant sexual act or stimulus and then to imagine some negative reaction—usually severe anxiety, terror, or nausea—possibly assisted by a strongly noxious odor to develop a nausea response.

5. *Aversive conditioning* is when inappropriate sexual stimuli are presented to a client via computer-generated images or videotapes, followed by the presentation of noxious stimuli, such as electric shock or the inhalation of valeric acid or ammonia.

6. *Masturbatory satiation* therapy involves having the offender masturbate to an appropriate sexual fantasy while verbalizing it aloud. Following this, the offender is required to continue to masturbate for a period ranging from 45 minutes to two hours (or try, in some cases) while verbalizing deviant sexual fantasies. This should all be tape-recorded to check progress, possibility of malingering, and so on.

7. *Aversive behavioral rehearsal* attempts to decrease sexually deviant behaviors and arousal by making the behavior publicly observable. The offender describes in detail the types of offense committed and then, by use of mannequins, clothing, apparatus, and so on, reenacts the offense. This is narrated by the offender while discussing his plans, actions, feelings, and thoughts. Having victims, friends, and/or family members as an audience heightens the aversive effect.

8. *Education programs that focus on sexual education*, social-skills training, assertiveness training, and cognitive reeducation may be necessary.

9. A *support group*, such as Sexaholics Anonymous, or specialized group therapy is recommended.

10. In many cases, it is critical to develop an *ancillary surveillance* and *report group*, specific to the individual client. This may involve family, friends, and neighbors who are made aware of the situation on a need-to-know basis and who agree to report inappropriate or suspicious behaviors. A variety of other techniques that prevents relapse can be useful.

Social retraining toward an ability to attain mature heterosexual partners is often necessary. Unfortunately, recidivism is high with the paraphilias.

Pedophilia

Pedophilia literally—and ironically—means "love of children." For a diagnosis of pedophilia in *DSM-IV-TR*, sexual activity, fantasies, urges, or behaviors over a least a six-month duration toward a prepubescent child (generally age 13 or younger) are required. The person is at least 16 years of age and is at least 5 years older than the child. Pedophilia is rare in females, and although it is not a common behavior in any demographic group, it has traditionally been viewed as a disorder of middle-aged males. However, research indicates that a molestation pattern typically starts by age 15, and that most early victims are known to the pedophile. Boys are more likely to be victims than girls, although girls are more likely to be victims of "hands-off" crimes, such as exhibitionism. Over time, most pedophiles commit a wide range of crimes, including exhibitionism, voyeurism, and rape, and pedophiles who molest boys do so at a much higher rate than do those who molest girls. Nevertheless, the *DSM-IV-TR* mentions that pedophilia cases involving female victims are reported more often than those involving male victims.

Etiology

The etiology and the treatments discussed in the case of Jeffrey Dahmer are generally relevant here, as is the material in the cases of Charles and Abby in Chapter 13. In addition, as with physical abuse, having been a victim of sexual abuse makes one more susceptible to a broad spectrum of psychopathology, including sexual deviancy and/or dysfunction, and more specifically to becoming an abuser oneself. Other general factors that predispose one toward pedophilia (and many other forms of psychopathology) are a dysfunctional early or present family environment and general social or intellectual inadequacy. Factors that direct one toward pedophilia are social-sexual inadequacy; fantasy activity involving pedophiliac patterns, which is often facilitated by the use of pornography; and easy and practiced access to victims.

Treatment Options

Because of the disgust with which most people respond to this disorder, it is not surprising that the typical treatment approaches are somewhat coercive. Pedophiles rarely bring themselves into treatment and are typically coerced by sociolegal pressure. The techniques described in the Treatment Options section of the Dahmer discussion are particularly relevant. It is also critical to correct such common cognitive distortions as (1) "My sexual contact with children is not really bad for them, and may even be good for them," (2) "Children are able to reason, so if they consent to it, it is really not molesting," and (3) "If they don't resist [or strongly resist], they actually want the sexual contact." It is unfortunate that there is a high recidivism rate and that there is no good way to differentiate those who will relapse from those who won't (Marvasti, 2004).

Megan's Law

"Megan's Law" requires communities to be notified when convicted sex offenders move in. Several states passed such laws or administrative requirements, and President Clinton signed a national "Megan's Law" on May 17, 1996. Critics argue that such laws are an invasion of privacy and encourage the harassment of convicted offenders, and perhaps vigilantism. It is also argued that informing neighbors and schools unfairly punishes the offender, who has already paid his debt to society. The alternative position is that these crimes are already on the public record, such offenders have a high recidivism rate, and providing such information helps prevent these crimes. So far, the general thrust has been to uphold these laws (even the Supreme Court in February 1998) if applied to persons convicted of such crimes after the law was passed. As a postscript, the worm never seems to stops turning, as some released sex offenders who have received harassment from neighbors, such as signs and rallies in front of their houses, threatening phone calls, and so on, have retaliated with civil suits asking for monetary compensation for the harassment. Juries are seldom sympathetic.

Sexual Predator Legislation

Another critical sociolegal issue is whether convicted pedophiles and other sexual predators may be constrained once they have completed their prison sentence. Several states have passed legislation allowing these individuals to be institutionalized as dangerous, under some form of civil commitment. Civil commitment has traditionally required both (1) mental illness and (2) dangerousness to self or others, and typically the dangerousness had to be imminent and the "mental illness" had to be an Axis I disorder. The sexual deviations have never been construed as fulfilling the legal definition of mental illness. Hence, the legal challenge was whether legislation could be written somehow to allow a sexual predator pattern, absent another accompanying mental illness diagnosis, to be sufficient for commitment.

In 1997, the Supreme Court addressed this issue in *Kansas* v. *Hendricks* (117 S.Ct.; 65 L.W.4564, June 23, 1997). Leroy Hendricks, who had a history of sexual misconduct with children, was scheduled to be released to a halfway house in 1994, having served 10 years in prison for molesting children. Instead of releasing him, Kansas sought to apply its then newly enacted "Sexually Violent Predator Act," based on a similar statute enacted earlier in Washington state. The Kansas act established a civil commitment procedure for "any person who has been convicted or charged with a sexually violent offense and who suffers from a mental abnormality or personality disorder which makes the person likely to engage in the predatory acts of sexual violence." In several related decisions, for example, on January 23, 2002, the Supreme Court somewhat limited but generally upheld the validity of this Kansas statute. In *Kansas* v. *Crane* (534 U.S. 1009), the Supreme Court ruled that "the Kansas Predator Act was constitutional so long as it required proof that the offended had a 'serious difficulty' in controlling his behavior. The Act need not require an absolute loss of control (Meyer & Weaver, 2006, p. 295). In that same year, in *McCune* v. *Lile* (536.U.S. 24), the Court *allowed* that the first part of any sex offender treatment program "required a detailed description of all sexual behavior, the thoroughness of which was verified by polygraph" (Meyer &

Weaver, 2006, p. 203). Because the recidivism rate for crimes by sexual predators is very high, and because there is no clear way to discriminate those who will recidivate from those who will not, most decisions to release or not will present vexing dilemmas.

Transvestism

> *Strange diseases, he thought, demand strange remedies: he, her.*
> —John Updike, *Bech Is Back* (1982)

Transvestites, especially males who dress as females, receive much media attention. *Transvestism*, referred to as Transvestic Fetishism in the *DSM-IV-TR*, is one of the paraphilias. *Transvestic Fetishism* is defined in the *DSM-IV-TR* as recurrent and persistent cross-dressing that is initiated for the purpose of sexual arousal and that eventually becomes habitual. The transvestite experiences intense frustration when external circumstances interfere with cross-dressing.

The disorder is relatively rare and more predominant in males than in females. Indeed, the *DSM-IV-TR* limits the formal diagnosis of Transvestic Fetishism to cross-dressing heterosexual males. Most individuals who have been involved in transvestism have cross-dressed by the age of 10, and usually much younger. Often, the cross-dressing was significantly reinforced by parents, sometimes by "petticoat punishment," the humiliation of a boy by dressing him in girls' clothes. The cross-dressing behavior typically becomes paired with masturbation and eventuates in the classic transvestite pattern (Masters, Johnson, & Kolodny, 1991; Money, 1987). Transvestism is commonly confused with the next disorder to be discussed, Gender Identity Disorder, commonly referred to as *transsexualism*.

Gender Identity Disorder

> *Male and female represent the two sides of the great radical dualism. But, in fact, they are perpetually passing into one another. Fluid hardens to solid, solid rushes to fluid. There is no wholly masculine man, no purely feminine woman.*
> —Margaret Fuller, feminist author, literary critic, and journalist (1810–1850)

Historically referred to as Transsexualism, *Gender Identity Disorder*, as defined in the *DSM-IV-TR*, includes "a strong and persistent cross-gender identification" and "persistent discomfort with his or her sex or sense of inappropriateness in the gender role of that sex." Manifest symptoms of these criteria include a stated desire to be the other sex, attempts to "pass" as the other sex through cosmetic alterations, a desire to live as the other sex, and the wish to experience the typical emotions and reactions of the other sex. True cases of gender identity disorder are fairly rare and occur in only 3 to 5 percent of the U.S. population, although many cases go unreported due to the shame and embarrassment surrounding the condition. Exact percentages of males versus females with gender identity disorder are not known, but there appears to be more males diagnosed with the disorder than females (*DSM-IV-TR*, 2000).

Observable symptoms of gender identity disorder almost always begin in childhood, usually between the ages of 2 and 4. The male child with this disorder is often characterized by such feminine behaviors as wearing his mother's clothing, displaying a great interest in girls' toys, playing with girls, and showing distress over having male genitalia (Cohen-Kettenis & Gooren, 1999). Likewise, the female child with this disorder exhibits such prototypical male behaviors as displaying strong preferences for rough (masculine) games, refusing to wear dresses, becoming very athletic and strong, and identifying more with her father. Research also shows that these children have more trouble labeling the sexes correctly and identifying gender stability over time (Cohen-Kettenis & Gooren, 1999). These atypical behaviors must be demonstrated to be enduring and pervasive and not be confused with normal childhood play or occasional curiosity into the characteristics of the opposite sex.

The Case of Bruce/Brenda

The classic—and perhaps the most controversial and influential—case history within the field of gender identity development is the story of David Reimer, as was thoroughly documented by John Colapinto in his book, *As Nature Made Him: The Boy Who Was Raised as a Girl* (2000). David, who was originally christened Bruce Reimer, was born on August 22, 1965, in the town of Winnipeg in Manitoba, Canada. He was born one of a pair of identical twin boys through early labor and induced delivery. Although slightly underweight, both twins were born healthy and were named Bruce and Brian—Bruce being the eldest twin by 12 minutes.

Until 7 months of age, the twins lived a blissful, healthy existence in their modest, but caring and affectionate, environment. David's parents, Ron and Janet Reimer, were young, excited parents who were deeply in love with each other and their new babies. Yet, when the twins were about 7 months old, their mother noticed that the skin on the tip of her sons'

penises was sealing over, making the act of urination particularly painful and difficult. It was a condition called phimosis, a not uncommon problem among newborn boys. On the advice of their doctor, Janet took the twins to a local hospital to be circumcised in order to correct the problem.

A routine medical procedure, circumcision was hardly a concern to doctors or even to new parents, and the Reimers anticipated no problems. However, something went very wrong in the operating room and little Bruce's circumcision was botched, resulting in horrible burns to his penis. So botched was the surgical procedure that the sex organ resembled a burnt piece of flesh, rendering it useless as well as lifeless. Eventually, Bruce's penis dried up and flaked away until there was no sign that he had ever had any sort of genital appendage. Upon hearing the devastating news, the Reimers had to decide on the best course of action for their son's life. Their decisions would provide the fertile ground for the nature versus nurture debate that swept the field of gender identity.

At first, the Reimers were told that Bruce would need numerous intricate and painful surgeries throughout his youth in order to construct an artificial penis—a procedure referred to as phallic reconstruction or phalloplasty. This reconstructed organ would function only as a urine conductor, and would not be capable of sexual response to stimulation or have capacity for ejaculation, and thus reproduction. For a while, the Reimers were under the impression that a phalloplasty was their only option. They had, in fact, resigned themselves to this decision when another option presented itself by way of John Money, M.D., then and still one of the most famous researchers and clinicians in the area of sexual development and gender identity disorder.

Dr. Money took a very personal interest in baby Bruce's predicament. He encouraged the Reimers to meet with him at Johns Hopkins and discuss another option for Bruce before they decided to go through with the phalloplasty. Dr. Money suggested that Bruce be raised as if he had been born a female. Won over by Dr. Money's reputation, confidence, and charm, the Reimers decided to follow his advice and raise their biological son Bruce as their daughter, Brenda.

This complex process began with baby Brenda undergoing surgical castration, which succeeded in removing both testicles, as well as the construction of an exterior vagina. At this point, Brenda was 22 months old. Raising Brenda as a girl then became the main focus of the Reimers' life. Brenda was clothed in dresses, was given dolls and other feminine toys to play with, grew her hair long, and was encouraged to spend time and bond with her mother and to play with the other little girls at school. However, it became obvious to everyone that Brenda was fighting the forced femininity, desiring instead to play with trucks and soldiers, getting into fights at school, and rejecting the dresses and ladylike attire. She even insisted on urinating in a standing position. In fact, throughout her entire childhood,

into adolescence, Brenda rejected her female identity, displaying more and more tomboyish behaviors, and always feeling that something was wrong. The gender development community kept a close watch on Brenda's progress and development. She met regularly with Dr. John Money, who, despite Brenda's troubles at adapting to her feminine role, publicized the case as an unqualified success. He used the case as proof that sex reassignment surgery works to essentially create a successful sexual identity through the use of behavioral techniques and the powerful force of environmental factors.

As Brenda grew close to puberty, the pressure increased for her to undergo vaginal surgery, such as creating a full vaginal canal. Brenda's female genitalia needed more reconstructive surgery in order for her to be fully operational as a woman. However, Brenda vehemently objected to the surgery and would not consent to having the operations performed. At this point, Brenda had not been told any part of her past, of how she was really born a male child. (David explained later in his life that he felt that he would never be a girl, that this was the wrong gender for him, and so could not go through with the surgery, no matter how hard the doctors pressed him.)

Yet, when she was 12 years of age, Brenda agreed to begin a strict female hormone regimen. She was not told the exact purpose of the drugs and she often only pretended to take them, throwing them away instead. She took enough of them, though, to begin breast development, as well as hips that were beginning to shape and a layer of fat that began to feminize her figure. She was disgusted at the changes her body was going through. However, Brenda had reached a point of decision. For the first time, she decided to *be* a girl. She began wearing dresses and makeup, and taking pains to fix her hair and fit in with the other girls. She even went to a school dance and tried to dance with the boys, though she always felt awkward and deficient. She believed that convincing people that she was truly a girl was the only way to avoid the sur-

(continued)

The Case of Bruce/Brenda Continued

gery that her doctors were pressing upon her. This transformation did not improve Brenda's psychological state. She persisted in feeling trapped in her body, eventually becoming socially isolated and depressed. At this point in her life, she was still not privy to the critical events of her botched circumcision and resulting surgery. She had no answers for why she felt the way she did—she still did not know that she had been born a boy.

It was in this state of hopelessness and confusion that Brenda began therapy with a psychologist who would eventually change her life. Dr. Mary McKenty worked with Brenda from a psychoanalytic perspective to help her face her anxiety, depression, and confusion. Dr. McKenty was the first therapist (after a numerous string of unsuccessful therapeutic encounters) who succeeded in reaching Brenda, and she did not push Brenda toward any type of decision for surgery or efforts to be more feminine. After seeing Dr. McKenty for several months and just after she turned 14 years old, Brenda made the decision to cease her existence as a female. She now dressed as a boy, stopped all maintenance of her appearance, and tried to speak in a lowered tone of voice. She also started attending a vocational school where she learned auto mechanics. Even though she endured merciless teasing, and even violent threats from her classmates, it was still preferable to Brenda than feminizing her appearance.

As her parents realized that Brenda would never embrace her surgically reassigned sexual identity, they finally decided the time had come for a troubling, yet inevitable, confession. At 14 years of age, Brenda listened to her father explain the bizarre circumstances of her infancy and how they resulted in her being raised as a female despite her male birth. After processing such shocking information, Brenda reacted to the news with the decision to truly become a male. She opted for testosterone treatment to masculinize her fig-

ure, and to undergo surgery to construct an artificial penis. She also changed her name from Brenda to David.

The transformation was difficult for David. Depression set in after he was hospitalized numerous times due to complications with his surgery. Feeling betrayed by his parents, he attempted suicide twice during this period. He isolated himself from the world by moving into a cabin deep in the woods, trying to sort through the distressing details that comprised his life. It was not until he underwent more surgery—a second phalloplasty designed to improve performance, appearance, and sensitivity of the phallus—that he felt measurably better about his situation. At this point, he also met a woman with whom he fell in love. Due to the success of his new surgery, he was able to have sex with her, and for the first time have a fulfilling sexual relationship. His new love accepted him and his past unconditionally, with compassion and understanding. He married her in September 1990, happy and content in his new life as a male. However, this did not continue forever. David suffered from periodic depression which deepened markedly when his identical twin, Brian, killed himself in spring of 2002 by an overdose of antidepressants. David later became unemployed and was conned out of $65,000 by a scam artist. All of this contributed to increasing marital problems, and on May 2, 2004, his wife suggested they separate. On May 5th, David sawed off the end of a shotgun and then killed himself with it.

The Reimer case appears to provide strong evidence in favor of the nature side of the nature versus nurture debate. The case demonstrates that it is not enough to raise a child as one gender when the child is born into the opposite gender. Once hailed as an unequivocal success in the field of sexual reassignment, the case had been promoted as an example of how the environment sculpts a person's gender identity. However, once the true details of David's tortuous existence emerged, and how he simply refused to accept life as a female despite his upbringing, the scientific world realized that environmental effects were not as potent in these cases as had been assumed. The case was particularly unique in the fact that identical twins were involved. The twins' genetic blueprint was exactly the same and provided a singular opportunity to examine how monozygotic twins were raised in the same household but as different genders.

Etiology

The origins and causes of gender identity disorder remain somewhat of a scientific mystery. David Reimer's case of gender identity disorder is somewhat different from the typical case due to the fact that he actually was born a male—the sex that he was eventually surgically reassigned. The origin of his disorder was in the environmental efforts to raise him as a female, and not as his true biological sex. David always felt something was wrong with being female and, indeed, his instinct was correct. This case can be used as a metaphor for other cases of gender identity disorder, in that those suffering feel as if they, too, were actually born as the opposite sex. However, David's case is unique, as the great majority of clients diagnosed with gender identity disorder are born and raised as the sex they are uncomfortable with, not surgically transformed as a child into the opposite sex and then raised as that sex. Therefore, the question remains as to why certain individuals truly believe that they have been born as the wrong gender.

Theories of etiology stem from a range of theoretical orientations, such as parental/family, social learning, psychoanalytic, and biological. The first of these, parental and familial factors, have been researched extensively. The results of this research indicate that "extreme closeness to the mother, atypical psychosexual development of the parents, and father absence" have all been found to contribute to the development of gender identity disorder" (Cohen-Kettenis & Gooren, 1999, p. 317). The way in which children are raised has also been shown to contribute to the disorder. Male-to-female transsexuals report that their fathers were "less emotionally warm, more rejecting and more (over) controlling." Female-to-male transsexuals also report certain parental characteristics, such as their mothers being more overprotective and their fathers being more rejecting and less emotionally warm (Cohen-Kettenis & Gooren, 1999, p. 318).

Biological theories have focused on the amount and type of the antenatal hormones that come in contact with the fetus. Specifically, if the fetus is exposed to very high levels of testosterone, there is evidence that such a fetus will develop a male identity, even if the baby is born and raised as a girl. Also, if the fetus is exposed to an excess of androgens or a deficiency of androgen hormones, then gender-atypical behavior has been observed in research studies (Cohen-Kettenis & Gooren, 1999). The Reimer case can be used as a major source of support for research with such biological theories, as it was a clear example of nature versus nurture, where nature eventually triumphed. The question that it raises, however, is: If nature is so powerful, then why are gender disorder identity clients discontent with their biological genders in the first place?

To date there has not been a biological theory sufficient to definitively explain gender identity behavior, nor has any other branch of theories proved satisfactory in its explanative powers. Most research concentrates on how the child is raised, focusing on environmental cues, parental characteristics, and the interaction of child personality factors and parental personality and parenting factors.

Treatment Options

Take a knife and lop off that superfluous piece of meat?
—Juvenal, Roman satiric poet (c. 60–c. 130)

Since those individuals suffering with gender identity disorder truly believe that they were born the wrong sex, they often feel that the only remedy is to physically become their "true" sex. Therefore, the most widely prescribed treatment option for the disorder is sex reassignment surgery (SRS). This controversial treatment involves an extensive and intense series of surgeries designed to change anatomically the sex of the patient by surgical castration (for male to female) or phalloplasty (for female to male).

Before SRS takes place, many clinics require that the patient undergo a trial period designed to test his or her resolve about the decision before taking the typically irreversible step of SRS. The trial period, known as the "real-life test," involves several steps designed to simulate life as the opposite sex (Blanchard & Steiner, 1990). The steps usually include changing legal documents to reflect the opposite sex, as well as legally changing one's name to one of the opposite sex. Another required step is to provide proof that one can actually live as the opposite sex. Some clinics require that this must be done by enrolling in school as the opposite sex or working in a job as the opposite sex. Clinics may require clients to live in these roles anywhere from a period of months to five years before undergoing surgery. Other possible prerequisites of SRS are obtaining a legal divorce if married, being at least 21 years of age, showing no evidence or diagnosis of psychosis or mental retardation, and not being on parole or probation. The client must also undergo a strict regimen of hormone therapy, usually for about a year, in order to experience some of the drastic physical changes that occur before resorting to surgery (Blanchard & Steiner, 1990).

Once the client has passed successfully through the trial period and it is determined that he or she is fully committed to the surgical procedure, the SRS is performed. For males, SRS involves the castration of the male genitalia and the construction of a vaginal canal. For females, SRS involves the construction of male genitals, known as a phalloplasty, as well as having the labia fused together. However, since it is not possible to construct a penis that is fully functional, an erection may be achieved only through the use of removable implants made of bone, cartilage, or silicone. Sexual stimulation is still achieved through the clitoris, which is kept fully intact.

There are some serious drawbacks to sex reassignment surgery. First of all, the surgery is irreversible, hence the required trial period that will help target those who are steadfast in their conviction to become anatomically the opposite sex. Second, the surgery is very costly and is almost never covered by medical insurance as a legitimate medical illness or condition. Sex reassignment surgery is usually not the only medical procedure performed in the process of a sex change. Many male-to-female transformation patients opt for several or all of the following feminizing cosmetic procedures (from Blanchard & Steiner, 1990):

Steps Involved in SRS for Male-to-Female Transformation

- Surgical castration (required)
- Surgically shortening of the vocal chords (to raise pitch of voice)
- Thyroid cartilage shave (Adam's apple reduction)
- Augmentation mammoplasty (breast implantation)
- Rhinoplasty (nasal surgery)
- Electrolysis (removal of facial and body hair)
- Speech therapy to alter pitch of voice

The procedure that usually poses the greatest challenge involves raising the pitch of the male's voice to sound more like a female. The combination of speech therapy, castration, and hormones is usually enough to raise the pitch to a satisfactory level. However, some males cannot attain an acceptable feminine sound and opt to surgically shorten their vocal chords. Some experts express caution against this operation, however, as it is frequently unsuccessful (Blanchard & Steiner, 1990).

For those women desiring to transform to a male, breast reduction is usually performed, but not as much cosmetic surgery is necessary as with male clients. The following outlines the surgical procedures as well as the optional cosmetic procedures involved in SRS for female-to-male transformation patients:

Steps Involved in SRS for Female-to-Male Transformation

- Construction of an artificial penis from abdominal tissue that is transplanted and formed into a tube (must be able to pass urine, sense stimulation, and have intercourse)
- Fusion of the labia
- Clitoris left intact to be primary receptor of sexual stimulation
- Breast reduction surgery (optional)
- Creation of facial hair with theatrical makeup (optional)

Besides these cosmetic surgeries and procedures, clients usually also engage in other therapeutic interventions that are generally implemented in conjunction with SRS. These interventions help to ensure psychological health and well-being during a very stressful and challenging time (Dozois & Dobson, 2004). Such collateral treatments include peer support groups, group therapy, individual psychotherapy, and/or family counseling.

Sexual Dysfunctions

> *I was Romeo of the Roaches again, eating the lamb patties of her hands, licking her yellow hair. I grabbed her thigh ruthlessly, put my hand around the ankle of the other leg. I need you, I said. Bored, but having at it as the male of the species. I'd been trained.*
>
> —Barry Hannah, *Geronimo Rex* (1972)

As with the paraphilias, the sexual dysfunctions come in varied forms. It is generally estimated that most people have at least occasionally experienced some form of sexual dysfunction, and more enduring sexual dysfunction may affect as many as 50 percent of marriages (Masters, Johnson, & Kolodny, 1991). Overall, the determinants of any individual sexual dysfunction are often multiple—psychosocial, interpersonal, and/or neuro-physiological.

In the *DSM-IV-TR*, the Sexual Dysfunctions are differentiated into four subcategories, based on phases of the sexual response cycle: (1) Desire—Hypoactive Sexual Desire Disorder (302.71), Sexual Aversion Disorder (302.79); (2) Arousal—Female Sexual Arousal Disorder (302.72), Male Erectile Disorder (302.72); (3) Orgasm—Female (302.73) and Male (302.74) Orgasmic Disorder, Premature Ejaculation (302.75); and (4) Dyspareunia (302.76), Vaginismus (306.51). To earn a formal diagnosis, "marked distress or interpersonal difficulty" has to occur as a result of the condition.

In practice, one has to be somewhat arbitrary in assigning a label of psychosexual dysfunction. Masters and Johnson (1970) arbitrarily defined *erectile dysfunction* as a clinical problem if there are failures in 25 percent of the attempts at intercourse. Also, in most cases, *total erectile dysfunction* (the common term in the research literature) is fairly rare, and typically suggests a biological cause. Most often, the dysfunction is partial. An erection occurs, but it does not persist long enough to provide satisfaction for the partner or for one's own orgasm to occur (LoPiccolo, 1985).

Throughout the case history of Tim, the term *impotence* will be used, but note that there is a general pejorative connotation to this term. That is, *impotence* suggests general personality inadequacy and a weakness of character. The standard term for female psychosexual dysfunction, *frigidity*, in turn suggests a lack of emotional warmth. But there is no evidence that these implied traits occur more commonly in individuals who experience these problems (Doctor, 1998). It is interesting that the weakness in the male and the coldness in the female suggested by these terms are the exact opposites of the characteristics most clearly prescribed in the traditional sex roles of society—competence for males and sensitivity and warmth for females.

The Case of Tim

After suffering silently for some time, as is typical in this syndrome, Tim went to his personal physician and asked to be treated for impotence. The physician referred him to a urologist, who, through a careful medical examination, ruled out the various physical and endocrinological factors that can affect impotence. So he referred Tim to a clinical psychologist who specialized in the treatment of the sexual dysfunctions. The clinical psychologist listened to Tim's story of his background as a preparation for initiating appropriate treatment.

Tim is 33 years old, college educated, and makes a good first impression. He is handsome and in good shape physically, reflecting his prior occupation as a professional baseball player. He also dresses well, keeps himself well groomed, and relates to others with apparent warmth and interest.

Although he recently was promoted to assistant vice president in the bank in which he works, the general impression he gives is that he is not strikingly successful or interested in his work. Also, in spite of his good first impression, it is quickly evident that he is moderately anxious most of the time. On several occasions, he had trouble articulating his concerns, and he sometimes needed to get up and move about during the interview.

From his description of his parents, his mother seems to be best described as passive and pious, and his father as authoritarian and perfectionistic. Tim describes his upbringing as "standard middle-class Catholicism." Tim still attends church occasionally but is clearly not committed at any great depth to a religious orientation. The most important focus in his world still seems to be his relationship to sports. One of his most vivid early memories is of playing in a baseball game as a very young boy, possibly age 3 or 4, and hearing his parents' cheers as he ran from base to base. Yet, his parents were extremely demanding in the area of sports, in particular his father, but also his mother more subtly.

Tim's positive early images of his participation in sports are clouded by several other memories of his father's role in his early feelings about sports. His father coached his Little League team and harangued Tim if he made any errors. His father was also demanding of the other children on the team, but he certainly hollered more at his son when he made a mistake, possibly to avoid any accusations of favoritism. It was only when Tim performed competently that his father showed any positive response at all, and of course in the early years such moments were not common. Tim's father also demanded a great deal of off-the-field discipline and practice. Although these demands may have taken some fun out of growing up, Tim still refers to the discipline as "a necessary evil that allowed me to develop the skills I needed later."

The most disturbing aspect of his parents' attitudes in this area is that they still so highly value his life in sports, even though his professional career is over due to an injury from which Tim did not recover well. Both of his parents fixate on his role as a professional baseball player and often refer to his achievements in their discussions of him with family and friends, even though Tim makes his discomfort apparent when they do so. They seem to have stopped seeing him as a developing person, retaining their image of him as the successful and applauded athlete. Surprisingly, they allowed Jack, Tim's younger brother, to pursue an interest in music, possibly because they felt their needs in the sports area would be filled by Tim.

Tim himself was rather ambivalent about his inability to function any longer as a professional baseball player. His career was first curtailed when he injured his foot by sliding into a base. He returned and played earlier than he probably should have, before the foot was fully healed. He favored it slightly, which

(continued)

The Case of Tim Continued

caused a subtle change in his pitching motion, eventually leading to a chronically sore arm. The orthopedic surgeon he consulted told him that he had strained the arm such that it would never return to full functioning.

Several things made Tim's demise as a baseball player particularly painful to him and his parents. First, he had not made it to the big leagues until he was 29 years old, having spent more years in the minor leagues than is typical. It also appeared that before the injuries, he was on the edge of stardom. He had started to win consistently, and there was no reason to believe this would not continue. He also had the prospect of being on a championship team. His injury curtailed this not only for himself but for the team, as well. It was particularly galling to Tim when some sportswriters suggested that he did not have the courage to "stick with it" and make a success of his baseball career after the injury.

Tim married his first wife when he was a junior in college, just as he had moved into a star role on the college baseball team. She was a freshman at the university and obviously enjoyed the moderate degree of glamour that surrounded Tim at that time. They married after a short courtship and had a child almost immediately. Then it began to dawn on them that they had few mutual interests, as well as totally different views on child rearing. Although he indicated there were no episodes of impotence in the marriage, their sexual life was sporadic at best. She began an affair with an attorney at the office where she worked and eventually left Tim to marry him. When her new husband obtained a job with a prestigious firm in a distant city, she moved, taking the child with her. Tim still manages to see his son, now 11 years old, with some regularity. But the distance and the early separation have prohibited the development of a strong relationship. In recent years, Tim has dated Pam, a woman with whom he had initially enjoyed a satisfying sexual relationship. She moved in

with him a year and a half ago, six months before he decided not to continue with his baseball career. It is clear that Pam never saw Tim's career in sports as something she valued highly.

Tim has never been very clear as to whether he "loves Pam." Sexual attraction was a major part of their early courtship, and they had a very active sex life in the first several months of dating. Although Pam did not seem to respond specifically to his baseball career, Tim's overall athletic appearance was a strong factor in her initial attraction to him. They have talked of marriage, but neither feels confident about making that type of commitment. In the meantime, Tim's parents are upset that Pam and Tim are living together without being married, and they never mention Pam to any of their friends.

Tim personally links the first occasions of impotence with worries generated by sportswriters' criticisms about his alleged lack of desire to make a comeback. He remembers the first incident as occurring on a night when he had been drinking heavily, largely because he had been upset by reading an article noting how his absence had probably cost his former team a shot at the championship. He had also been feeling uncertain at that time about the permanence of his relationship with Pam. These factors together resulted in a distracted and apprehensive mental set. When he became aware that he did not have a full erection, he became even more anxious, thus deflating what erection he had obtained. Although Pam was not overtly critical at the time, she also was not very supportive, possibly because she also had drunk quite a bit. In any case, Tim saw this as a humiliating experience, and anticipated (at least unconsciously) a repeat. This expectation brought on anxiety, and Tim continued having problems obtaining or maintaining an erection.

Tim had been raised with prohibitions against virtually all types of sexual behavior, but he did not take his religious views seriously at a conscious level. He had been taught to masturbate by an older male friend. In high school, he engaged in much fondling and petting with Barbara, the first girl he dated with any consistency. But he had his first experience of intercourse with Carolyn, a good friend of Barbara's. It had been enjoyable, although at first it had been very anxiety provoking. It occurred in the living room of Carolyn's home, and just as they got started, Carolyn's father called down and asked if anyone was there, scaring Tim and temporarily deflating his erection. But his high drive level at that time came to his rescue, and they went on to finish.

Etiology

As noted, Tim had received a complete physical examination that ruled out physical causes of impotence. Also, he spent an evening at the university sleep lab. The tests indicated that he did show normal nocturnal penile tumescence (NPTs), or erections while sleeping, and these were of sufficient number, duration, and strength to suggest psychological rather than physical factors. Although not an infallible indicator, it has generally been found that men with physically based impotence show fewer or no NPTs (Masters, Johnson, & Kolodny, 1991).

The following cues are suggestive of erectile dysfunction in which organic factors play a major part:

Gradual onset

Sequentially deteriorating erections

Normal libido

Ability to initiate but not maintain erection

Loss of nocturnal and masturbatory erection

The following are generally indicative of psychogenic erectile dysfunction:

Episodic

Sudden onset

Acute, brought on by life stresses

Normal morning and nocturnal erections

Loss of libido

Several factors emerged from Tim's psychological evaluation that apparently contributed to impotence. Like his father, Tim had a strong need to control his environment, and he felt threatened by change he could not control. The divorce, the problems with his baseball career, and the ambivalence about his present girlfriend all suggested a loss of control to Tim and in turn generated anxiety. The impotence provided a physical focal point for the vague feelings of anxiety. But his focus on the sexual concerns created what Masters and Johnson (1970) have termed "performance anxiety." Under performance anxiety, persons take on a spectator role in the sexual act rather than letting themselves fully enjoy the pleasures of the response.

In addition to Tim's obsessive features, which generate a high need to control events, other characteristics could predict the impotence. Tim revealed that he perceived Pam as moving more heavily into the women's liberation movement than he would like. She had openly begun to discuss her need to "find herself" and "fulfill her own needs." She had begun to flirt while in his general vicinity, a behavior he allowed himself but frowned on in Pam. She had also insinuated that Tim had not really worked hard to recover fully from his injury. As a result of all these developments, Tim began to perceive Pam as threatening his self-esteem. When he experienced the impotence with her, these developing beliefs were strongly reinforced.

Residual guilt from his rather more strict than usual Catholic upbringing was also a factor with Tim. He had verbalized some concern about being divorced and now living with another woman, as he was still attempting to maintain a standard role in a church that at least in theory forbade such behavior. He struggled with the apparent hypocrisy in the church's stated position on divorce in light of the fact that priests and nuns who took "permanent vows" that included a vow of chastity were allowed to leave their calling and marry. Also, as Welch and Kartub (1978) found, the incidence of impotence is highest in societies in which sexual restrictiveness is high. In particular, a higher rate of impotence is likely if the society has had a restrictive belief system and also if it is now rapidly moving toward a more liberal value system.

As far as the specific instance that set off the impotence, Tim had experienced fatigue that day, had also overindulged in alcohol, and he and Pam were experiencing relationship problems—common factors when individuals first experience impotence (Doctor, 1998). Also, it is important to note that even though his early sexual experiences usually had been successful, they were often associated with a significant level of anxiety.

Treatment Options

A number of effective physical, chemical, and psychological techniques have been developed to treat erectile and orgasmic dysfunctions (Masters, Johnson, Kolodny, 1994; Meyer & Weaver, 2007). The first drug prescribed specifically for erectile dysfunction, sildenafil (Viagra), and the subsequent variations on this drug that have been developed are the most effective and efficient of these treatments. Indeed, they have become the only treatment in the great majority of cases. Administration of the hormone testosterone is not uncommon (although of questionable effectiveness for most cases). Penile artery bypass surgery can be used, although this is seldom needed. Various forms of revascularization are more likely to be useful. Certain prosthetic devices can be used for organically based cases and occasionally for severe psychogenic cases, as well. One is a semi-rigid rod that is implanted in the corpora cavernosa, the parts of the penis that engorge with blood in an erection. The consequent permanent erection can be an embarrassment, and it interferes with urological diagnostic procedures. An alternative is a hydraulic device that essentially inflates the penis.

It should be noted that the idea of a prosthesis is not a modern scientific invention, as is documented in this true anecdote reported by R. O'Hanlon in his book *Into the Heart of Borneo* (1984):

> "But Leon, when do you have it done? When do you have the hole bored through your dick?"
>
> "When you twenty-five. When you no good any more. When you too old. When your wife she feds up with you. Then you go down to the river very early in the mornings and you sit in it until your spear is smalls. The tattoo man he comes and pushes a nail through your spear, round and round. And then you put a pin there, a pin from the outboard motor. Sometimes you get a big spots, very painfuls, a boil. And then you die."
>
> "Jesus!"
>
> "My best friend—you must be very careful. You must go down to the river and sit in it once a month until your spear so cold you can't feel it; and then you loosen the pin and push it in and out; or it will stick in your spear and you never move it and it makes a pebble with your water and you die."
>
> "But Leon," I said, holding my knees together and holding my cock with my right hand, "do you have one?"
>
> "I far too young" said Leon, much annoyed; and then, grinning his broad Iban grin as a thought discharged itself: "But you need one Redmon. And Jams—he so old and serious, he need two!" (pp. 82–83)

Safe and generally quite effective treatments for both arousal and orgasmic disorders (that do not include a significant organic dysfunction factor) are the psychological "sensate focusing" techniques pioneered by Masters and Johnson (1970). They are now combined with more sophisticated cognitive therapies to help the client stop spectatoring (becoming too distanced from the act) (Meggers & LoPiccolo, 2002). These are particularly effective if carried out with a stable partner from the client's natural world. Sensate focusing is not a totally modern development. Sir John Hunter, a physician practicing around 1750, advised his clients to go home and lie in bed "a fortnight and caress and fondle." His only reported difficulty was that "no one ever completed the treatment."

Tim's actual treatment began with sessions with the psychologist to clarify his feelings about the relationship with his girlfriend, the guilt about sex he experienced at a less-than-conscious level, and his perfectionism. Tim gradually felt more confident of his relationship with Pam, and he asked her to participate in the latter part of the treatment program with him.

This phase of treatment proceeded along the lines suggested by Masters, Johnson, and Kolodny (1991). The therapist emphasized to Tim and Pam that they were to focus on the pleasures of fondling and petting, and for a period of time they were admonished not to proceed into intercourse. When they were doing well with this and also were becoming strongly aroused, the therapist suggested that they proceed to intercourse, but not attempt to reach orgasm. Eventually, as their arousal continued to be very high, intercourse was allowed and was successful. Other areas of their relationship continued to improve as they clarified the meaning and impact of their communications, and a year after the treatment they got married. The marriage helped with Tim's relationship with his parents, but he needed to work on clarifying his dependence on their approval. During some follow-up therapy sessions, he was able to distance himself from this need, while retaining a caring relationship for them.

Tim enrolled in some refresher courses related to his work and also took up painting. All of these changes helped his self-esteem, which in turn allowed him to initiate new behaviors, thus creating a positive cycle, the antithesis of the negative cycle often seen in psychopathology.

> *I have a coded list of 23 names and numbers in my billfold . . . each time is like the first time all over again, a strain. It's a job. I'll have to do well. I liked it better when they thought they were doing us a favor. I'm sorry they ever found out they could have orgasms too. I wonder who told them.*
>
> —Joseph Heller, *Something Happened* (1966)

Female Psychosexual Dysfunction

Many of the same treatment issues, as well as most of the diagnostic considerations, noted about the male psychosexual dysfunctions apply equally to the problems of female psychosexual dysfunction (Meyer & Weaver, 2007; Masters, Johnson, & Kolodny, 1991), and the reader is referred to the immediately prior sections. There is usually less significant personality pathology correlated with most cases of female psychosexual dysfunction. *Vaginismus*, on occasion a component of female sexual dysfunction, is a condition in which the vaginal musculature goes into intense involuntary spasms, primarily in the bulbocavernosus muscle and also in the leviator ani muscles. In some cases, even the anticipation of intercourse or other type of vaginal contact may suffice to elicit muscle spasms. As a result, intercourse is impossible or is accompanied by extreme pain (dyspareunia). Vaginismus is not necessarily associated with sexual inhibition or orgastic problems, although it is in some cases.

> *"Dear doctor . . . what I told you when I first became your patient was true. I had never had an orgasm . . . I can come by myself and with somebody else. So now I am a whole woman."*
>
> —Marilyn Monroe, 1962 (*Playboy*, 2005; p. 80)

The Case of Marilyn Monroe

On June 1, 1926, Gladys Pearl Monroe Baker gave birth to her third child, a baby girl she named Norma Jeane Mortenson, at Los Angeles General Hospital. The birth certificate listed Edward Mortenson, her mother's second husband, as the father. In reality, her biological father was probably Stanley Gifford, a co-worker of Gladys with whom she had a brief affair. In either case, Norma Jeane never knew her father. Gladys was reportedly mentally unstable, and Norma Jeane was soon sent to live in a foster home for the first seven years of her life. These foster parents were very devout Christian Scientists and strict with Norma Jeane. At the age of 7, she moved back in with her mother. However, this move was short-lived as Gladys's mental health deteriorated to the point that she was hospitalized with a diagnosis of paranoid schizophrenia. Psychological disorders apparently were common in Gladys's family. Both of her parents were characterized as "manic-depressive," and an unknown psychotic disorder contributed to the death of Gladys's great-grandfather as well as the institutionalization of her maternal grandmother. Norma Jeane's half-brother would eventually be diagnosed as schizophrenic (DePaulo, 2005).

Norma Jeane went to live with a close family friend by the name of Grace, who encouraged her to be a "movie star." But financial hardships resulted in Norma Jeane's being shuffled between seven foster families over the next four years before finally being reunited with Grace and her husband in 1941. In one foster home, an actor who rented a room there sexually assaulted Norma Jeane. When she tried to tell the family about it, her foster mother refused to believe her and told her never to mention it to anyone again.

In 1941, financial difficulties forced Grace and her husband to move; they were unable to take 16-year-old Norma Jeane with them. With Grace's encouragement, Norma Jeane married 21-year-old Jim Dougherty, the son of one of her neighbors, on June 19, 1942. Marilyn would later claim that although the marriage was boring, it was neither painful nor unhappy. In 1943, Jim joined the Merchant Marines and a year later was shipped off to fight in World War II. During that time, Norma Jeane worked at an aircraft and parachute-inspecting plant. She became lonely and insecure and turned to alcohol to escape.

In the middle of 1944, an army photographer named David Conover was working on a story for *Yank* magazine for which he was taking photographs of women who worked in factories that supported the war effort. He immediately recognized Norma Jeane's natural beauty and hired her to travel with him around California, taking pictures of her in different locations. The Blue Book Modeling Agency took note, and within a year she was on the cover of 33 national magazines. Norma Jeane was soon engaged in several extramarital affairs and filed for divorce in 1946. Approximately one month after her 20th birthday, she had her first interview with a casting director of 20th Century Fox, Ben Lyon. On August 26, 1946, 20th Century Fox hired her for $75 a week, with one stipulation: she needed to change her name to something catchier. Lyon suggested the first name "Marilyn," after his favorite actress at the time, Marilyn Miller. Norma Jeane chose her mother's maiden name "Monroe" as her last name. Marilyn Monroe was born (De Paulo, 2005).

Marilyn

Marilyn's career did not immediately take off. She played only bit parts in movies like *The Shocking Miss Pilgrim* and then her first musical performance in *Ladies of the Chorus*. In 1949, she agreed to pose nude in a calendar, which created a controversy only later when she became a superstar. Also in 1949, she took Johnny Hyde as a lover and mentor. Years later Marilyn reported to her psychologist that

(continued)

The Case of Marilyn Monroe Continued

after Hyde watched Marilyn give herself an enema (which she frequently did throughout her life to relieve chronic constipation), he exclaimed how much it turned him on. The two then engaged in anal sex for the first time. To please him, this became the focus of their sexual encounters from then on. Also, Johnny would frequently have her urinate in a glass so he could drink it.

Marilyn continued in a casual stance toward sex, engaging in numerous affairs during her adult life, including an episode when she masturbated a studio lackey simply because she was curious about his uncircumcised penis. Marilyn apparently at one time participated in a stag film, which Joe DiMaggio (the famous New York Yankee and Mr. Coffee spokesman) unsuccessfully attempted to purchase for $25,000 shortly after her death. Marilyn also engaged in sexual activity with women, including a one-night stand with actress Joan Crawford. Marilyn's name appeared in a government memo reporting multiple sex parties that had taken place at the Hotel Carlyle in New York. Other names on that list included both Robert Kennedy and President John Kennedy. These and other various affairs reportedly led to nearly a dozen abortions and multiple miscarriages, further adding to Marilyn's insecurities.

Marilyn's first serious acting job came in 1950, and over the next two years she began receiving more significant roles. Marilyn met Joe DiMaggio, and after two years together they married on January 14, 1954. That same year Marilyn was suspended by Fox for failing to appear on a movie set; she entertained 60,000 troops overseas in Korea; filmed the now famous "skirt blowing" scene in the film *The Seven Year Itch*; and divorced Joe DiMaggio after only nine months of marriage. Subsequently, she started her own production company and later married the noted playwright Arthur Miller on June 29, 1956. She converted to Judaism three days later (Miller was Jew-

ish). Marilyn and Miller moved to England, and she did not return to Hollywood until 1958. At this point, both her health and her marriage were rapidly deteriorating. She continued to work, but her addiction to barbiturates and tranquilizers had become so severe that she was often late for meetings and frequently forgot her lines. However, she was now the country's sexual icon, although ironically, she had never experienced an orgasm. When Marilyn was asked by DiMaggio's sister (and her close friend) June if she had at least achieved an orgasm during sex, Marilyn simply asked back, "What's that?" (Monroe, 2005, p. 82).

Early in 1960, Marilyn began seeing Dr. Ralph Greenson, a renowned psychoanalyst familiar to the Hollywood elite. Her orgasmic difficulties were a focus of their therapeutic relationship, and Marilyn reportedly told Dr. Greenson in the months before she died, "I never cried so hard as I did after my first orgasm. It was because I had fucked in every way there is and had men and women go down on me and never had an orgasm. What wasted years," (Monroe, 2005; p. 197). The relationship with Greenson lasted until she died, although she would credit him for bringing happiness to her life, their relationship took on atypical and seemingly unethical characteristics.

In January of 1961, Marilyn and Arthur Miller divorced. Marilyn now began to see Dr. Greenson virtually every day, often multiple times in one day in the beginning. It did not take long before Marilyn was Dr. Greenson's only patient. He even hired a live-in housekeeper to stay with Marilyn, allowing him to maintain his increasing control over her life. This unusual relationship was quite evident when Marilyn expressed to Dr. Greenson that since meeting him and his family, she had fantasized about how nice it would be if she were his daughter and not his patient. She stated, "I know you couldn't do it while I was your patient, but after you cure me maybe you could adopt me. Then I'd have the father I've always wanted, and your wife, whom I adore, would be my mother, and your children my brothers and sisters" (Monroe, 2005, p. 197). Dr. Greenson potentially added to this attachment by bringing her to his home for sessions.

About this same time Marilyn was first able to achieve orgasm through her work with Dr. Greenson. Greenson was a well-known psychoanalyst who practiced many of the ideas and techniques first posited by Sigmund Freud. Initially, Dr. Greenson encouraged Marilyn to "free associate," a technique commonly used by psychoanalysts. However, this was unsuccessful.

Marilyn's sexual difficulty did not improve until Dr. Greenson took the approach of explicitly telling Monroe how to masturbate and achieve orgasm on her own. Although such a direct approach can be useful (Haley & Richeport-Haley, 2008), it is an atypical approach for psychoanalysis as well as most forms of traditional psychotherapy. He also told her that after she learned to experience an orgasm with herself, she would soon be able to experience it with others. Ironically, this simplistic approach was effective. "Bless you, Doctor. What you say is gospel to me. By now I've had lots of orgasms" (Monroe, 2005, p. 197). Marilyn's breakthrough apparently came some time after she divorced Miller in early 1961. Although she was still in the grips of a severe addiction, paradoxically fueled by Greenson's routinely prescribing tranquilizers and barbiturates, things in Marilyn's life were looking up. She was seeing a lot of DiMaggio again, and the two had agreed to remarry on August 8, 1962. Additionally, Fox Studios agreed to rehire her at a salary of $250,000. By all accounts, although her mood would fluctuate due to her addiction, Marilyn was happy and by no means suicidal. Yet, on August 5, 1962, three days before she was to remarry DiMaggio, Marilyn Monroe was found dead in her Brentwood home.

The official cause of death was reported as a suicide, yet renowned medical examiner Thomas Noguchi, who performed the autopsy, listed the cause of death as "probable" suicide. What is not in dispute is that Marilyn Monroe died of an overdose of the barbiturate Nembutal. However, medical experts estimated that Marilyn would have had to ingest 30 to 40 Nembutal pills to reach the toxic levels found in her body. Yet there was no trace of any capsules or Nembutal crystals in her stomach at autopsy. Absolutely no needle marks were found on her body either, ruling out intravenous use. In fact, the only abnormality found during her autopsy was an area of pronounced bruising in the large intestines, or colon. This bruising would be consistent with Marilyn receiving a Nembutal-laced enema. But it would have been physically impossible for Marilyn to self-administer the full enema herself before passing out. Another curious fact about her death is that she reportedly had a phone in her hand at the time she was found. Thus, her death remains an enigma, allowing ample fodder for conspiracy theorists (Rebello, 2005).

Marilyn's Etiology

How is it that arguably the greatest American sex symbol who ever lived would go through the majority of her life without achieving an orgasm? The strict and repressive environment during the first seven years of her life no doubt contributed, as did the sexual assault at age 8, especially given the callous and rejecting response of her foster family. It's also unlikely that she ever received any adequate sex education, and she had little stability in her life even into early adulthood.

Certainly, having a bizarre and selfish individual like Johnny Hyde as her first sexual mentor and consistent partner was another factor.

A further contributor was the "casting couch" scenario, that is, the practice of studio executives sexually exploiting actresses in return for bestowing movie roles. Marilyn was not shy about doing whatever she had to, with whomever she had to, in order to further her career. "You know, that when a producer calls an actress into his office to discuss a script, that isn't all he has in mind. . . . I've slept with producers. I'd be a liar if I said I didn't" (Summers, 1985, pp. 34–35). This emotionally detached attitude would not facilitate learning how to be orgasmic. As in most cases of sexual dysfunction, both in men and in women, multiple causal factors are typical.

Unlike in Marilyn's case, the ultimate curative factor is seldom so straightforward.

Comment

The treatment for female sexual dysfunction can be fairly straightforward, even simplistic, as it was with Marilyn. Treatment may involve brief psychotherapy and possibly mild tranquilizers, as well as counseling on how to facilitate sexual functioning and cognitive-behavior modification to correct any distorted beliefs that contribute or have developed.

Like Marilyn (and the prior case of Tim), most sexually dysfunctional individuals are physiologically capable of adequate sexual performance. Most sexual dysfunction occurs when psychological factors inhibit what is normally a series of reflexive responses (Andreassi, 2000). A majority of individuals (male or female, or couples) who have any of the psychosexual dysfunctions often need to be challenged on underlying, yet common, problematic cognitive assumptions, such as (1) sex should be "perfect," "special," "ecstatic," "novel," "routine," and so on; (2) sex should occur "in bed," "in the dark," "somewhere exciting," "after a show of romance," "with all our clothes off," and so on; (3) without intercourse, it's not "real" sex; and (4) without both of us having an orgasm, it's not "real" sex.

Relapse among people treated for sexual dysfunction or inhibited sexuality is commonly reported. Success rates are much better when specific coping strategies for relapse have been taught and monitored. Such skills include role playing a discussion with a partner about a dysfunction occurrence; articulating and then replaying specific behaviors learned in therapy; using specific cognitive "mantras," such as "I was told this would happen, but I know it will pass," and the like (e.g., recovering heart attack victims may need to add mantras such as, "It's absurd to think I'd die because of intercourse—I'll feel better"); reading positive information books or pamphlets; generating a sensual, romantic, and/or erotic mind-set; and undergoing booster sessions.

9 The Substance Use Disorders

We have long had substances to abuse: "The use of alcohol, opium, and cannabis for various purposes was well recognized in the major centers of civilization . . . from at least 6000 years ago" (Durrant & Thakker, 2003, p. 66). Although Americans relish their combination of "Puritan" and "pioneer" traditions, the evidence is clear that the United States has an early tradition of substance abuse. In fact, a staggering amount of alcohol was consumed in early colonial times, in part abetted by the widespread and possibly accurate belief that drinking water in those days was hazardous to health. Hard apple cider was the accepted substitute. It is also noteworthy that in the 1770s, New York had almost 400 taverns, at a ratio of about 1 for every 12 adult males (compared to only 22 churches).

Unfortunately, modern America must deal with an increasing number of substances that are abused (Bartol & Bartol, 2008; Durrant & Thakker, 2003; Garner & Garfinkel, 1997), and this is reflected in the *DSM-IV-TR* (see Table 9.1). The first matrix in the *DSM-IV-TR* system refers to those drugs that are commonly abused—such as marijuana (cannabis), cocaine, amphetamine, and heroin (opioids)—and are given separate subcategories. Caffeine and nicotine use disorders are also included, the latter being especially important as a precursor to other forms of chronic substance abuse. Other categories in the *DSM-IV-TR* are hallucinogens; inhalants; phencyclidines; sedatives, hypnotics, and anxiolytics; polysubstance use; and "other." The three Es—effect, expense, and ease of access—are the critical determinants of drug use patterns.

The terms *dependence* and *abuse* are seen throughout the *DSM*'s substance abuse matrix, and they are defined similarly across substances. *Substance dependence* is a maladaptive pattern, signaled by impairment or distress, with three of the following seven occurring in a 12-month period; (1) tolerance (need for greater amounts to achieve similar results or diminishing effect with use of the same amount); (2) withdrawal (individual symptoms for each substance, or the use of the substance to relieve or avoid withdrawal symptoms); (3) unintended use of larger amounts or for longer than intended; (4) inability to control use or persistent desire for the substance; (5) high time cost to obtain, use, or recover from the substance; (6) giving up of important life activities because of use; and (7) continued use in the face of use-related psychological or physical problems.

TABLE 9.1   **Controlled Substances**

DEA Class	Characteristics	Examples
I	High abuse potential; no accepted medical use	LSD, heroin
II	High abuse potential with severe physical and psychological dependence	Amphetamines, opium, morphine, codeine, barbiturates, cocaine
III	Medium abuse potential with low to moderate physical dependence and high psychological dependence	Compounds containing codeine, narcotic analgesics, steroids
IV	Low abuse potential with limited physical and psychological dependence	Benzodiazepines, certain barbiturates, other sedative-hypnotics, non-narcotic pain meds
V	Lowest abuse potential	Preparations with low narcotic levels

A diagnosis of *substance abuse* presumes no prior diagnosis of dependence. It does require impairment or distress from a maladaptive pattern within a 12-month period as evidenced by at least one of the following: (1) failure in a major life role obligation in some recurrent pattern, (2) recurrent hazardous behavior such as driving impaired, (3) recurrent consequent legal problems, and (4) persisting use despite use-related sociointerpersonal problems.

Before proceeding further in this area, it is important to clarify several other terms that are common in the substance-abuse literature:

- *Synergy:* This compounded effect results from using a drug combination. The result is antagonistic if the effects of one or more of the drugs are reduced or canceled out, additive when the result is a sum of the effects of the separate drugs, or supra-additive when the result of the combination is greater than a sum of the separate drugs. A good example of supra-additive synergy is the lethal potential that results when relatively small amounts of alcohol and barbiturates are taken together.
- *Physiological Dependence:* This state occurs when a drug that has been used for some time alters the user's physiological functions in such a way as to necessitate continued use of the drug in order to prevent withdrawal symptoms, such as what happens with heroin, nicotine, and even caffeine.
- *Habituation:* This refers to dependence on a drug because of a strong desire to replicate the psychological state produced by the drug and/or from indirect reinforcement of psychological needs, such as oral needs and relief of depression.

The "danger signs" signaling possible abuse are disruption in job, marriage, or other significant relationships; deteriorating financial or physical health; frequent job changes; an arrest record; complaints of anxiety, depression, or insomnia; and direct signs of addictive personality and social patterns. Reports of significant others are very useful, as is knowledge of addictive patterns in blood relatives. For instance, young males who from early on showed a high tolerance to the effects of alcohol are much more likely to later become alcoholic, and having had an alcoholic father is a strong predictive factor for young males.

> *I swear, a certain amount of beer can make a man feel like he could beat cancer.*
> —Larry King, *Of Outlaws, Con Men, Whores, Politicians, and Other Artists* (p. 16)

Alcohol Dependence and Abuse

Alcohol has been used as long as any drug available today and is used and abused in most societies. As far back as 8000 B.C., in the Paleolithic Age, mead, an alcoholic beverage derived from honey, was used. Beer and berry wine were imbibed as early as 6400 B.C. Alcohol has almost certainly been abused for as long as it has been used, and the costs to the abuser, physiologically and psychologically, have always been high. Alcoholism is especially costly to society at large today, as it exacts an enormous toll through alcohol-caused accidents (especially auto accidents), disruption of family life, facilitation of violence in certain individuals, and inefficiency and loss in the business realm.

Alcohol is still the preeminent drug of abuse, as approximately 10 to 14 percent of Americans have problems with alcohol. Approximately 35 percent (these estimates vary considerably) of people with an alcohol problem have a comorbid mental disorder.

The psychological euphoria from alcohol is functionally a toxic response. Alcohol is not digested but absorbed through the stomach and intestinal walls and metabolized in the liver by the process of oxidation. In this process, alcohol fuses with oxygen, and the resulting pure grain alcohol, or ethanol, is converted by enzymes to acetaldehyde, which is further broken down to acetic acid (vinegar). The vinegar is then broken by enzymes into water and carbon dioxide, which are passed out of the body. The liver can break down only about 1 ounce of 100-proof whiskey per hour, assuming the person is of average weight. Any excess that cannot be broken down directly affects the brain, causing intoxication. Interestingly, even when males and females are of equal weight, this process is slower in females, making them more vulnerable to intoxication, for several reasons. Females have (1) more body fat, (2) less body water, and (3) a slower rate of alcohol metabolism. Also, given equal amounts of alcohol intake, females will develop liver cirrhosis faster. The *DSM* diagnosis for Alcohol Abuse requires fewer symptoms than for Alcohol Dependence. Manifestation of the latter includes physiological symptoms of withdrawal and increased tolerance, in addition to the general criteria for Substance Dependence. Whereas male alcoholics are more likely to carry a second diagnosis of antisocial personality disorder, female alcoholics are more likely to carry a second diagnosis of anxiety or depression. Women are more likely to drink in private and to show guilt about the behavior. A curious finding: On average, nonalcoholic women report taking their first drink at an earlier age than alcoholic women do.

Pharmacologically, alcohol acts as a depressant that first inhibits the higher brain centers and only later depresses the lower brain centers. The resultant decrease in control of overt behavior has led to the mistaken belief that alcohol is a stimulant. With continued alcohol intake, there is a loss of the more complex cognitive and perceptual abilities and eventually a loss in simple memory and motor coordination. It is interesting that part of the strength of the effect depends on whether people are getting drunk or sobering up. Because of a short-term tolerance effect, those who are sobering up generally appear less drunk and actually perform a bit better on short-term memory and perception tasks than those who have the same blood level of alcohol but who are getting high.

Long-term alcohol abuse is likely to result in central nervous system dysfunction or organicity (see Chapter 15 for relevant diagnostic considerations). This dysfunction is not simply a result of vitamin-B deficiencies from the poor diet that often accompanies chronic alcoholism, but is at least in part caused by the toxic effects of alcohol per se.

The Case of Betty Ford

Betty Ford is the widow of the thirty-eighth president of the United States, Gerald R. Ford. During her time as First Lady, she was a very influential positive force in America—speaking out about breast cancer and championing the women's movement. But it was not until Gerald Ford's defeat in the 1976 presidential election that Betty Ford's primary influence was manifest. On April 1, 1978, Betty Ford reluctantly admitted to her family that she was addicted to prescription drugs and alcohol. One week later, she was in a local hospital to begin a month-long treatment program. Inspired by this treatment program and with a desire to help others and put a positive note on her disorder, she made plans to open a clinic for people with similar addictions (Ford & Chase, 1978, 1988; Weidenfeld, 1979). On October 3, 1982, the Betty Ford Clinic for drug and alcohol addiction was dedicated. The Betty Ford Clinic is one of the most widely recognized names associated with the treatment of alcoholism and drug addiction today.

Betty was born in 1918 and grew up in Grand Rapids, Michigan. Her father, a traveling salesman, was gone from the family home quite often. Her adored mother was a strong and principled woman who was a perfectionist and demanded the same standards in each of her children. Betty viewed her mother as a strong role model in handling adverse situations with strength and courage, never asking for help or letting the children know of problems. Betty's childhood was positive, pleasant, and "normal," the only dark shadow over her youth being her father's death when she was 16 years old, in 1934. Despite the Depression, insurance helped Betty and her mother and two older brothers to survive comfortably. Betty learned after her father's death that he had been an alcoholic; she had never known because he drank only while traveling on business and never at home. Betty's brother Robert was also an alcoholic.

Betty's first experience with alcohol was when she was a young child and her mother would put a teaspoon of bourbon in hot tea to ease an ailment; however, she remembers being a prude about drinking up until she was about 18 years old. Betty developed into a socializer, enjoying late nights of dancing and partying with friends. She worked as a model for a while at a local department store, but her dream was to go to New York and become a famous dancer. She went to New York when she was 20 years old, but like the great majority with that same dream, did not succeed. Under peer pressure, she began to drink more at social gatherings in New York. At her mother's urging, she returned home to Grand Rapids for a trial period of six months that ended with her staying in her hometown permanently. A while after her return to Grand Rapids, at age 24, Betty met and married a young man she had known in her youth. Betty claimed that what had made their courtship so much fun (partying at the local bars) was the very thing that ruined their marriage. She was ready for settling down and he was not. They divorced after five years.

Not long after, Betty met Gerald Ford. Jerry (as Betty called him) was a lawyer with a good reputation in Grand Rapids who was just beginning his political career. Betty described him as "the most eligible bachelor in Grand Rapids . . . good-looking, smart, and from a good family." Their wedding plans were often dominated by Jerry's campaign for a seat in Congress—he was late for their wedding—and Betty received her first taste of what her life with Jerry Ford would be like. Jerry was an inexhaustible man who often put his work ahead of everything.

During the next several years, Betty became the mother of three boys and a daughter. Betty and her husband had a strong and loving relationship, and the couple shared an equally loving and strong relationship with the children. Betty often took the role of mother and father because Jerry was always busy with his job in Washington. It was during this time that Betty had the first of many medical problems. In 1964, she developed a pinched nerve in her neck that caused her excruciating pain. A hospital stay was needed and multiple treatments were applied—physical therapy, hot packs, and medications. Betty worried about her pain recurring after she went home from the hospital. When she voiced her fears to one of her doctors, she was told not to allow the

pain to even begin and was given strict orders to keep her medications close at hand. This was the beginning of a vicious cycle: Betty would develop a tolerance of one drug, and the doctors would simply prescribe a new one. Her pills became an avenue of escaping physical pain and made her more vulnerable to increased alcohol usage.

All of this had occurred just as her husband was beginning to gain a strong position in Washington. Betty began to feel lonely and unimportant. She tells of feeling like a doormat for her children and her husband and of her dreams of being someone important in the world being overridden by her role as her husband's behind-the-scenes support system. Her personal role models were always strong, independent women, like her mother, and when she compared herself to these "faultless" women, she felt like a failure. She often second-guessed herself, assuming that people could not like her or appreciate her for who she was. She was self-conscious that she had not made the grade as a dancer or obtained a college degree. She developed the attitude that "if I act smart and look smart, maybe people will think I'm smart." This attitude of "acting the part" helped her conceal her growing problem of addiction and alcoholism.

Over the years, Betty gave a few warning signals to many people that she had a problem. The first occurred in 1965, about a year after she began to drink alcohol while on her medication. She took her daughter to the beach and spent the whole day away from home, hoping that the rest of her family would become worried about her. As a plea for attention, the stunt worked enough to get her an appointment with a psychiatrist. However, this physician said nothing about her alcohol use and chose to look at her self-esteem problems instead. Another warning signal was a diagnosis of pancreatitis. The treating specialist told Betty to stay away from liquor for a while. Jerry asked this physician specifically if Betty's pancreatitis was caused by alcohol. The physician responded that it was a possibility, even though it was known that alcohol

(continued)

The Case of Betty Ford Continued

is one of the prime causes of pancreatitis. Like most alcoholics, Betty was surrounded by enablers, including her physicians, friends, and family.

When Gerald Ford became president of the United States on August 9, 1974, Betty realized that, as First Lady, she had a renewed opportunity to be that person she felt was lost years ago. She became happier than she had been in a long time. Her schedule was busy with public engagements defending important causes. During her stay in the White House, Betty was diagnosed with breast cancer and subsequently had to have a breast removed. This, surprisingly, seemed to cause Betty little emotional turmoil (as she was happy to be alive), and she used it as another vehicle to become a positive force to the public, to become an advocate of all cancer victims. The experience did not, however, help Betty's dependence on drugs. She was now at a point that any physical pain was associated with the temporary comfort medications or alcohol gave her.

Although Betty enjoyed her time in the White House, she admits that it was filled with pressure and that the pace kept was grueling. She describes nights when pills were the only thing able to bring on sleep and mornings when pills would get her started. During the "White House years," Betty often showed signs of the effects the pills and alcohol had on her. As her husband campaigned for reelection in 1976, Betty was constantly on the move, suffering from extreme pain caused by the pinched nerve in her neck and the emotional drain the campaign trail inflicted. Her medication and cocktails were the tenuous thread that kept her together during those final weeks.

After her husband's defeat and the move from the White House and the limelight in 1977, Betty's condition grew much worse. The couple had moved to California, into a new house they had built, and Jerry continued with his hectic schedule of public speaking

engagements and meetings all across the nation. Betty's youngest child had moved out on her own, and the other children had long been living out of the home. This was a time when Betty was truly alone. Further isolation occurred as she declined social invitations. Eventually, she had fewer close friends than she had in the past. She was on multiple medications and combined the pills with alcoholic beverages throughout the day. Her daughter, Susan, was distressed by her mother's illness and initiated a small "intervention" in which no other family members participated. This first intervention angered Betty and was a failure for the most part, but it gave the attending physician an idea of the magnitude of her illness.

The second intervention occurred just a few weeks after Betty's sixtieth birthday. This time, all family members were present. During this intervention, which took Betty completely off guard, each family member relayed with love an incident in which her addiction had caused them pain. This was desperately needed, for Betty felt that she did not have a problem because for so long everyone around her had covered up for her. Betty completely denied she had a drinking problem and justified her drinking by telling of the many cocktail parties she had been required to attend as First Lady. She argued that she wasn't an alcoholic because she kept herself neat and tidy, was not a falling down drunk, didn't drink in the morning, or didn't drink too much at the cocktail parties. She did admit a problem with the prescription drugs but resisted admitting to abusing alcohol. Each loved one took a turn talking to her. For example, Betty's middle son, Jack, told of how he did not like to bring friends home for fear of what kind of state she might be in on that particular day. Her husband talked about a recent fall in which Betty had cracked some ribs and chipped her tooth.

The physicians on hand at the intervention later brought out a blackboard and listed every drug Betty took each day, how many times she took it per day, how much the dosage was, and so on—the amount was staggering. There was some fear that the detoxification process would be brutal, if not fatal.

Faced with all of this, Betty still agreed that after a week-long detoxification (to be completed at the Ford home), she would check herself into a local naval hospital and begin a month-long treatment program.

Etiology

A review of information Betty has given in her autobiographies makes it evident that the substance abuse, especially her alcoholism, may have been caused by two key factors. First, there was a probable genetic predisposition for alcoholism, as Betty's father and brother were both alcoholics. Second, there were many psychological factors that may have been responsible for Betty's addictions. She lived many lonely years without a strong support system, due to her husband's absences, while raising four children. She endured time in the media spotlight for years, with her every move and word monitored, analyzed, and criticized. The stress was overwhelming. As the research of Baker, Piper, McCarthy, Majeskie, and Fiore (2004) has shown, avoidance of negative affect (or "feeling bad") is a primary component in maintaining an addiction.

Approximately 40 to 60 percent of the risk for alcohol dependence is genetic, although few researchers believe that there is one single gene involved or that genetics alone *compel* one into alcoholism. More likely, many genes together *predispose* a person toward abusing or depending on alcohol. For example, young men who have a low response to alcohol (which is apparently genetically determined)—in other words, they have to drink more than other people in order to feel any effect—are at a substantially increased risk of becoming alcoholic years later.

It is also known that peer pressure and exposure to dysfunctional models for drinking behavior, as well as any societal acceptance and affirmation of dysfunctional drinking, play a major part in facilitating an alcoholic pattern. Intrafamilial relationships are also important. Adolescents who don't have a good relationship with their father are at far greater risk of problem drinking, as well as smoking and using illegal drugs. Behavioral scientists have identified many traits that seem to affect a person's propensity to drink, but alcoholics may have countless combinations of these traits. Certainly antisocial personality factors predispose a person to substance abuse in general (Bartol & Bartol, 2008). Alcoholics tend to have different sensitivity to alcohol than nonalcoholics: They may eventually develop tolerance for large amounts of alcohol and dependence on its effects, and they may feel rewarded when they drink and suffer withdrawal when they don't. Temperament may also play a role in drinking. Alcoholics tend to be more aggressive, hyperactive, and prone to risky behaviors. Any or all of these traits may be inherited.

The general progression into alcohol dependence is as follows:

1. Prealcoholic Phase
   a. Social drinking and an occasional weekend drink are the major symptoms.
   b. Both tolerance and frequency of drinking increase, usually slowly.
   c. Alcohol use serves primarily as an escape from anxiety, mild depression, or boredom.
2. Initial Alcoholism
   a. Tolerance, frequency, and abuse increase.
   b. More is drunk per swallow; often there is a shift to more potent drinks.
   c. Disruptive-dysfunctional behaviors and/or depression often increase, along with loss of self-esteem over drinking patterns.
   d. Occasional blackouts occur.
3. Chronic Stage
   a. True loss-of-control patterns (such as drinking throughout the day and using any source of alcohol) predominate.
   b. Inadequate nutrition affects functioning and physical health.
   c. Signs of impaired thinking, hallucinations, and tremors emerge.

The disease model that is still influential today generally assumes that (1) substance abuse disorders, particularly alcoholism, reflect a physiological disorder, possibly genetically determined; (2) abusers have virtually no control over their intake of the substance because of this dysfunction; and (3) with some substances, especially alcohol, abusers permanently retain their status, even when they are able to abstain.

The assumptions in the disease model of substance abuse have been shown to be not entirely true in their implications. For example, some alcoholics are able to return to a pattern of social drinking even after many years of chronic alcohol abuse. In the 1960s, D. L. Davies, a British physician and alcohol researcher, published data to show that a few people who were treated for alcoholism eventually returned to a pattern of normal or moderate drinking, and did not relapse into alcoholism. Since that time, others have noted similar data, leading to an alternative goal to abstinence, but one that works with only a relatively small subset of "problem drinkers" (as opposed to true alcoholics). Those who are younger, are regularly employed, show only modest symptoms of problem drinking, and have a relatively unremarkable family history for drinking are candidates for a "reduction" rather than an abstinence approach. There is also clear evidence that many alcoholics, even while in the status of chronic alcoholism, can refrain from the first drink (a bedrock assumption in Alcoholics Anonymous).

Treatment Options

As with Betty Ford, most alcoholics who have been chronically imbibing will need an initial period of detoxification, especially in light of the mild confusion and memory and concentration problems commonly found as acute withdrawal symptoms in the one to three weeks following the cessation of drinking. In addition, a period of hospitalization or other controlled living environment may be necessary to keep them from giving in to strong immediate habits that would return them to drinking.

The first critical steps in the treatment of alcoholics are simply getting them to admit they have a problem and then getting them involved in any ongoing treatment program. Hence, some form of "motivational enhancement therapy," typically involving confrontation techniques, may be necessary. During consensual data gathering, it is good to write down critical agreements and pieces of data for the alcoholics to refer to later if short-term memory is temporarily impaired. Another helpful approach was first pioneered by Craigie and Ross (1980), who used videotape to model self-disclosing behaviors and treatment-seeking behaviors with a group of alcoholics in a detox unit, because, as with many disorders, people have to learn what it takes to be an effective "patient."

From a general treatment perspective (Durrant & Thakker, 2003; Garner & Garfinkel, 1997; Perkinson, 1997), several techniques can be employed:

- *Detoxification:* Many alcoholics need an initial period of detoxification to "dry out." This stay in a hospital or other controlled living situation also keeps them from giving in to compelling habits that would return them to drinking.
- *Medication:* Naltrexone, actually an opiate receptor antagonist, has proven to be effective in reducing the need for alcohol. More recently, varenicline has proven to be useful. Buprenorphine is also useful, especially as it continues to be effective (especially with opiate-based addictions) long after the drug has ceased to be administered. Buspirone, a nonbenzodiazepine anti-anxiety drug, is useful to control craving in long-term recovery, particularly if the individual has a propensity toward anxiety symptoms. Acamprosate has shown promise, and seems to have fewer side effects than other drugs that have been used in treatment. When depression is an issue, the SSRIs (selective serotonin reuptake inhibitors) appear to be most useful (Schuckit, 1996).
- *Antabuse:* Antabuse, which causes severe nausea if alcohol is consumed, can be helpful in controlling the immediate impulse to drink, although the effects of the medication can be easily bypassed by simply not taking it (this bypass could be eliminated by a time-release, implanted form). Antabuse helps adequately functioning alcoholics who want to change, but even with them, it is generally accepted that the drug is of little use as the sole or predominant intervention technique (Schuckit, 1996).
- *Self-Help Group:* Some form of a self-help facilitation process, such as provided by Alcoholics Anonymous or a similar group, is often highly beneficial. (The benefits of AA are discussed next.)
- *Family Therapy:* Because alcoholism is extremely disruptive to family life, family and/or marital therapy is often necessary to repair damaged relationships, as well as to help maintain abstinence.
- *Aversion Therapy:* Aversion therapy can help control specific problem behaviors unique to the client.

- *Relapse-Prevention Coping Skills:*   Cognitive-behavior approaches teach techniques for achieving and maintaining sobriety, such as coping with potential drinking situations, managing thoughts and urges about alcohol, and learning ways to refuse a drink. The critical first step is learning to recognize and prepare active coping strategies for high-risk situations. Most relapse occurs as a result of a negative emotional state, peer pressure, or a distressing interpersonal conflict.
- *Psychotherapy:*   Alcoholics commonly experience conflicts, anxiety, and self-esteem problems. A variety of psychotherapy techniques can be of help with these problems, especially in learning to cope with negative affect (Baker et al., 2004).

In recent decades, the consensus opinion on the appropriate primary psychotherapy treatment thrust was as follows:

1. People with greater alcohol dependency, greater desire to seek meaning in life, and a social environment that promotes drinking should do best with a *12-step facilitation*, such as AA, because it provides spiritual support and a new social network that encourages abstinence.
2. People with high cognitive impairment and people with severe psychological problems should improve most with *cognitive-behavioral therapy*, because it directly addresses these co-occurring problems. Because women experience these problems more than men, research indicates that they should also benefit best from this type of therapy.
3. People with low motivation to recover but without severe psychological problems or social pressures to drink should have the most success with *motivational-enhancement* therapy.

However, this consensus has been called into question. The largest clinical study of psychotherapies for alcoholism—Project MATCH (an eight-year, multisite study funded by the National Institute on Alcohol Abuse and Alcoholism [NIAAA] and completed in 1966)—randomly assigned 1,726 alcohol-dependent people to one of these three psychosocial treatments. The study concluded that all three of these treatments worked but that they all worked equally well with different types of alcoholics. The only significant effect of matching was for patients with few psychological problems, who did better in 12-step facilitation therapy than in cognitive-behavioral therapy. The NIAAA published three treatment manuals that detail the treatment protocols. For information on obtaining the manuals, contact NIAAA's Scientific Communications Branch at (301) 443-3860 or access its web page at www.niaaa.nih.gov.

There is no question that Alcoholics Anonymous is still a predominant treatment. Continued contact and long-term cognitive retraining are just two of the advantages of AA, founded in 1935 by New York stockbroker Bill Wilson and Ohio surgeon Bob Smith. A favorite AA saying is "Stinkin' thinkin' leads to drinkin'." In addition, AA forces alcoholics to acknowledge openly that they are in need of help, and it gives them a new social network composed of nondrinkers, as well as a strong support system they can call on when they are tempted to drink. Data supporting AA's claim of high rates of success are at times flawed methodologically. Yet, AA has clearly been helpful to persons who have trouble with impulse drinking, who need a new social network, and who are able to work within the somewhat rigid demands of the AA belief system.

Once alcoholism has developed, 9 to 15 months are usually needed to adjust to an alcohol-free lifestyle. But many alcoholics can achieve a relapse-resistant recovery within two to three years. For many alcoholics, the ability to have fun and enjoy life (and, as a result, to be more pleasant to have around) is a state-learned behavior (rather than a trait)—that is, it has become associated with the use of alcohol. Total abstinence means the loss of conditioned cues for enjoyment of life behaviors. Without relearning the "skills" to have fun and enjoy life, some recovered alcoholics become tedious to be around, further fraying relationships with friends and significant others. Helping recovered alcoholics develop these lost skills is an area ignored by most therapists.

Prevention of Alcoholism

The following should be included in any program for prevention of alcoholism at the family and community levels:

1. Recognize that alcohol abuse patterns start to consolidate in the 11- to 15-year age range, much earlier than most people imagine. Recognize that genetic and modeling factors are both important.
2. If children are to be allowed to drink alcohol at all in later life, introduce it to them relatively early and only in moderation.
3. Associate the use of alcohol with food and initially allow its use only on special occasions; deemphasize its value in controlling feeling states.
4. Provide a consistent model of low to moderate drinking; use beverages such as beer and wine that have a low-alcohol content, rather than hard liquor.
5. Make sure there is a thorough understanding of and agreement on the family rules for what is and is not allowed about drinking.
6. Never associate drinking behavior with evidence of attainment of adulthood or other identity accomplishments.
7. Label excess drinking behaviors as stupid and in bad taste rather than as "cool" or stylish.
8. Label help-seeking behaviors in people who have an alcohol problem as evidence of strength rather than weakness.
9. Encourage alcoholism education in community and public health programs, and, even more effectively, support restrictions on both the availability and use of alcohol in certain settings and age groups.

Before turning to the issue of prescription drug abuse, consider this specific and relevant pattern of the student alcoholic.

Alcohol is like love. The first kiss is magic, the second is intimate, the third is routine.

—Raymond Chandler, *The Long Good-bye*

The SA—Student Alcoholic

College people love to refer to people and phenomena by initials—GPA, RA, SATs, GREs, and so on—hence, the "SA" for the student alcoholic. College is a time when much learning takes place. Unfortunately, not all of it is positive.

A preeminent expert in this area is Dr. Alan Marlatt, a professor of psychology and a researcher at the Addictive Behaviors Research Center at the University of Washington. Recognized as an expert on alcoholism, in general, and for his "harm reduction" approach to substance-abuse treatment, for many years Marlatt has specifically studied drinking behavior in student populations.

Marlatt has found that for many students college is a place where drinking increases, for some students markedly so. He found that peer pressure and expectancies (often inaccurate) about sexual arousal and social acceptance increased the amount students drank and that, in addition to formal treatments, such practices as exercise, meditation, and involvement in community activities could decrease drinking. Also, even more than adults, young adults are most likely to relapse in the presence of nonabstinent peers.

One preventive intervention developed by Marlatt is a six-week cognitive-behavioral program that (1) challenges common beliefs about the "magical" effects of drinking, such as increasing confidence leading to sexual responsiveness; (2) teaches students how to drink more safely by being aware of their drinking habits, such as how much they drink, where they drink, and what they do when they drink; and (3) suggests alternatives to drinking, such as exercise, nonalcoholic parties, and community work. The program significantly reduced binge drinking among small groups of college students.

Such programs are especially useful with students identified early on as "at risk"—that is, those who have a family member(s) who is alcoholic or have shown predictive patterns such as consistent binge drinking, drinking before the age of 15, a high tolerance for alcohol, drinking when alone and/or depressed, or having had a DUI or other alcohol-related offense or problem.

Several anti-drinking measures at the student-community level can also be helpful:

- Responsible beverage service policies that include no pitchers, minimal happy hour, special promotions, and staff trained to be sensitive to excess drinking
- Controlled drinking in fraternities (and to a lesser degree, sororities), a high-risk place for binge drinking

- Programs to discourage liquor stores and parents from providing alcohol to people under age 21
- Beefed-up enforcement of drinking and driving laws
- Zoning to regulate the number of drinking establishments and their hours of operation

Prescription Drug Abuse

The *DSM-IV-TR* differentiates a number of substance-abuse patterns but does not specifically discuss a pattern called "prescription drug abuse." However, we feel that this is an important pattern because it is defined by a focus on the common characteristics of clients rather than on the specific drug that is abused—an approach that often cuts across personality patterns. Drug companies and physicians should openly acknowledge at least some degree of responsibility for the high level of prescription drug abuse in society.

The common signs of prescription drug abuse are (1) efforts to make sure prescriptions are quickly filled; (2) efforts toward developing back-up prescriptions and/or physician contacts; (3) resistance-avoidance toward any health care professional who begins to confront the pattern; (4) increased contacts with sympathetic health care workers; (5) an anxiety increase, especially if prescription refills are delayed or renewals are threatened; (6) withdrawal from standard interests, friends, and activities; and (7) increased use of alcohol to supplement the effects of the pills.

Polysubstance Dependence

The term *polysubstance abuse* is also not included in *DSM-IV-TR*, nor was it in prior versions of the *DSM*. However, there is in *DSM-IV-TR* the category Polysubstance Dependence, in which a person has used at least three different substances (not including caffeine or nicotine) for at least six months, with no substance predominating. The polysubstance abuse of nicotine, alcohol, and marijuana is often the "gateway" from adolescent drug abuse to dependence. The relative neglect of polysubstance abuse reflects an essential feature of U.S. society: the belief that there is a particular remedy for virtually any physical or psychological disorder that occurs (Garner & Garfinkel, 1997). The polysubstance abuser usually combines the expectancy that an external agent will take care of all problems with a high need for new experiences or sensation seeking. However, the arrest in summer 2007 of Albert Gore, III, the son of former Senator, Vice-President, and presidential candidate Al Gore, has focused attention on the increasing polysubstance abuse among high school and college-age individuals.

The Case of Elvis Presley

Elvis Aaron Presley is one of the most well-known and popular entertainers of all time. He became a cultural icon, which seems to require dying before your fans see you in old age, as was also the case with James Dean, Marilyn Monroe, John F. Kennedy, and others.

Elvis's music and charisma changed the music industry and left such an impression that he was later called "The King" of rock and roll. A curious testimony to his enduring popularity occurred in August 2001, when the prime minister of Japan released a compact disc "Junichiro Koizumi Presents: My Favorite Elvis Songs" to commemorate the twenty-fourth anniversary of Elvis's death. The prime minister commented, "My birthday is January 8, the same as Elvis. It's one of the things I'm so proud of."

From his first hit recording in 1956 to his untimely death in 1977 at the age of 42, Elvis Presley lived under heavy public scrutiny. It was not until just before his death that his public began to realize how significantly he was deteriorating. As a result of many destructive personal habits, the most devastating being the abuse of prescription drugs, Elvis's health had begun to fail at an alarming rate. On August 16, 1977, he died in his bathroom. The book he was reading at the time of his death was *The Scientific Search for the Face of Jesus*. Both an autopsy and toxicology test were administered; from the toxicology test it was determined that the key cause of death was an overdose of several prescription drugs. It is interesting to note that, even in the face of the evidence and personal history of Elvis's prescription drug use, several doctors testified in court that Elvis *did not* die of an overdose and, almost absurdly, that his drug usage was not out of the ordinary. The exact cause of and circumstances surrounding the death of Elvis Presley continue to be subjects of debate; however, the fact that The King severely abused prescription drugs is, without a doubt, fact.

Elvis Aaron (misspelled "Aron" on his birth certificate) Presley was born on January 8, 1935, in the small, rural town of East Tupelo, Mississippi. His only sibling, Jesse, his twin, was born stillborn 35 minutes before Elvis. His family was extremely poor and moved quite often. His father, Vernon Presley, was a friendly, vivacious man; his mother, Gladys, was considered a good mother and wife. When Elvis was about 4 years old, his father had some trouble with the law and spent three years in prison. As a result, Elvis's relationship with his father was distant. On the other hand, his relationship with his mother was extremely close. She was known to be obsessively protective of her only child. Many family members felt Gladys bonded so closely with Elvis because she had been pregnant with twins. Elvis became the center of her world, and she devoted all her love and energy to protecting and raising him. Family members remember Elvis's mother being very tense and anxious after the birth of Elvis and reported that she would often take medicine to calm "bad nerves" and to help her sleep.

Elvis had a reasonably happy childhood, aside from the problems already noted. In 1949, the Presley family moved to Memphis, Tennessee, in hopes of finding steady work. Elvis remained in Memphis until his music career took off. He graduated from high school, and his first recording, a 45 rpm recording of *Blue Moon of Kentucky* and *That's All Right (Mama)*, was published on July 14, 1954. In 1954, he debuted at the Grand Ole Opry, and by 1956, under the controlling hand of Colonel Tom Parker, Elvis Presley burst into the media and music scene. His first television appearance was on March 5, 1955, on the *Louisiana Hayride*, and his first national television appearance was on January 28, 1956, on Tommy and Jimmy Dorsey's *Stage Show*. From 1956 to 1958, Elvis had numerous hit records and made several movies. His stardom eventually reached unbelievable heights; he eventually had 142 gold records worldwide. However, in March 1958, just after completing the movie *King Creole*, he was drafted into the U.S. Army, and this marked a turning point—not in his career, as was first feared, but in his personal life. Elvis phoned his mother to tell her the news. She refused to speak with him. For the first time in his life, he was alone, without her support. Yet, to his credit, although the army wanted him to take the easy road of being a performer, he went in as a buck private and endured the same rigors as his fellow soldiers. After Elvis left for the army, his mother's physical and emotional health deteriorated. Over the next several months she was noted to be in a constant state of depression, broken only by fits of anger. She began drinking alcohol heavily, was eventually diagnosed with hepatitis, and died in August 1958.

The death of Gladys Presley marked a period of isolation for Elvis. After his release from the army in 1960, he made several unimpressive records and movies. He felt he had lost his creativity and consequently began to distance himself from fans and the world. In 1968, at age 33, he married Priscilla Beaulieu. Priscilla asserts, and is believed by many who knew both her and Elvis, that she slept with him in his bed for six years before they were married and that she was a virgin when she married. Nine months later, they had a daughter, Lisa Marie. Elvis had his first number-one hit in seven years, *Suspicious Minds*, in 1969. But by this time, he was an emotionally drained man whose living habits had become destructive. He began to be promiscuous sexually, and his sleeping schedule was out of sync. He would sleep from 8:00 A.M. until 4:00 P.M. and party from 4:00 P.M. until the early morning hours. His eating habits were poor, with big meals consisting of high-fat, fried foods. Perhaps most destructive of all was his increasing dependence and abuse of prescription drugs.

From the time Priscilla sued for divorce in 1973 until his death, Elvis's weight and drug use markedly increased. Many close friends felt that after Priscilla left, he simply gave up. Elvis had little privacy. He felt his life and des-

tiny were out of control; amid the love and admiration he received, he grew more and more alienated and alone. He experienced numerous physical disorders (a freak colon that was two feet too long, glaucoma, a slightly deformed leg, and, most important in the long run, a heart that skipped beats and sometimes awoke him with its pounding). He also had several drug-induced incidents, collapsing or behaving inappropriately on stage or just canceling tour shows. In 1973, after discovering that Priscilla was involved with another man, he had to be heavily sedated for several days. In the same year, he experienced problems with his throat that affected his singing. By 1974, he often spent days at a time in his room at Graceland in complete isolation. In 1975, he was admitted to a hospital for a liver problem, but it was rumored that it was for detoxification. For a while after this trip to the hospital, Elvis seemed to be content. However, in 1976, his drug use again increased.

During the years after his divorce from Priscilla, Elvis's behavior fluctuated from highly irrational to severely depressed. In 1974, he began going on wild spending sprees, often visiting car dealerships and buying every car on the lot, giving the cars away soon after. Gross amounts of money were also given to charities, with the amounts increasing over time. He began to have "giggle fits" on stage, not being able to control himself and often breaking into hysterical laughter for no reason at all. When a gun was thrown onto the stage at one of his concerts, he played with the gun for a while, much to the confusion and apprehension of the crowd. He often seemed confused, and he sweated profusely. He almost encountered a lawsuit when, at a late-night party, he was wrestling with a woman and "accidentally" broke her ankle. The crew at his shows reported that he was very irritable and always looking for a fight. All of these instances were offset by periods of seclusion and depression, and his drug abuse continued to increase.

In the 32 months prior to Elvis's death on August 16, 1977, his personal physician, Dr. George Nichopoulos, allegedly prescribed

(continued)

The Case of Elvis Presley Continued

nineteen thousand doses of drugs for Elvis. He asserted that many of the pills given to Elvis were placebos, and Nichopoulus was eventually acquitted of drug charges. Elvis relied on sympathetic doctors and pharmacists as well as friends in cities all over the United States to fulfill his demand for prescription drugs, such as codeine, morphine, Valium, Quaaludes, and Demerol. His common excuse for getting the prescriptions filled was "tooth problems," and he often explained late arrivals at concerts by telling the crowd he had a dentist appointment. One of his pastimes toward the end of his life was to study medical and prescription drug reference books; he did this to avoid deadly combinations of the pills he was taking. The day before his death, he had a dentist fill a prescription for Dilaudid, a painkiller.

Although the exact cause of Presley's death is still debated, there is no denying his extensive use of prescription drugs. Not surprisingly, Dr. Nichopoulos vehemently denies that his patient's death was caused by polypharmacy, but he will admit that Elvis's health was "controlled." He explains that Elvis took pills for sleep, a colon problem, and for high blood pressure and that these were not "happy pills." He may be accurate in the literal sense; there is little evidence that Elvis was very happy at this time. David Stanley, who worked closely with Elvis, feels that his death was most likely a suicide caused by drug

overdose, because in the bathroom where Elvis had just died, David saw three empty pill packets (called "attacks") lying near Elvis's body (Stanley & Loffey, 1994). Three of these pill packets contained a total of 33 pills and nine shots of Demerol. This is an enormous amount of medicine, even when taken at three- to four-hour intervals, yet it appeared that Elvis had taken the medicine in a shorter-than-normal period on this occasion.

In a decision supported by several physicians, the coroner ruled that Presley had died of a cardiac arrhythmia and not of a drug overdose, as the amounts of drugs in his body were alleged to be too low to point toward death by overdose. The autopsy report reads that he had heart disease, clogged arteries, and a distended liver. However, it is important to note that the toxicology report from the Bio-Science Laboratories in Van Nuys, California, states that Presley died of polypharmacy, a report strongly attacked by the autopsy physicians. But the evidence from the report is staggering. The report lists the following drugs as present in Elvis's body tissues: codeine, steroids/ACTH (used for colitis/bowel problems), Valium, ethchlorvynol (a sedative/hypnotic), Demerol, Amobarbital (a short-acting barbiturate used to help bring on sleep), phenobarbital (a sedative/hypnotic), and Methaqualone (Quaaludes—there was a very high amount of this drug found in the tissue).

Comment

There may be evidence of some predisposition for addiction from the accounts of Elvis's mother's drinking and dependency on pills to help her relax and sleep. His mother also showed signs of depression and anxiety—signs that Elvis showed as he became famous. And his father showed at least some antisocial patterns, and he likely abused alcohol. No doubt the immense pressure Elvis felt from his occupation and the consequent alienation and seclusion that accompanied his fame were also factors, as was the willingness of his physicians and dentists to provide medications.

As can be seen in this case, abusers could be described as psychotics without the loss of reality contact. They show deterioration of behavior in a wide variety of arenas (work, school performance, interpersonal relationships, and motivation), especially if they have been abusing drugs for a substantial length of time. Affect is generally flat, or, when emotion is manifest, it is quite labile. As with the alcoholic, there are often many protestations of future positive change, and, also like the alcoholic, the promises are seldom fulfilled. These protestations do not appear to be a manipulative deception, as the person seems intellectually committed to changing, yet the motivation and behavior necessary to actuate that change cannot be generated (Boyd et al., 2007). Such protestations did not occur with Elvis, as no one had enough influence or leverage to obtain such promises from him.

Nicotine Dependence

He fought a hard battle. Some of his last words were: "Take care of the children. Tobacco will kill you, and I am living proof of it."
—Louise McLaren, talking about her son Wayne McLaren (the first "Marlboro Man" of cigarette ads) when he died in July 1992 of lung cancer

In 1492, Luis de Torres and Rodrigo de Jerez, two of Columbus's crew, observed natives of Cuba drying and then smoking some plant leaves. De Jerez tried it himself, apparently becoming the first confirmed European smoker. When he tried it back in Spain, his countrymen were alarmed at the smoke coming out of his mouth, assumed him to be possessed by the devil, and imprisoned him via the Inquisition. Unfortunately, this did not prevent his legacy from being returned to North America. The first English settlement, at Jamestown, floundered economically until John Rolfe, the future husband of Pocahantas, planted some tobacco seeds. The plants flourished, and tobacco became the critical cash crop.

In general, smokers are about 50 percent more likely than nonsmokers to require health care each year, and the smoke they disperse is harmful to those around them. Historically, efforts to deter people from smoking, such as warnings from the Surgeon General's office, have had only limited effects, and those who do quit are extremely vulnerable to relapse. In the seventeenth century, even Turkish sultan Murad IV's campaign of torturing and executing those addicted to tobacco was not overwhelmingly effective, nor was a 1683 Chinese law that authorized beheading simply for possessing tobacco.

Seven major factors are usually considered to be crucial in initiating and maintaining tobacco addiction. The primary factor is the physiological addiction component, from nicotine, chemically "isolated by the German physician Wilhelm Posselt and the chemist Karl Reimann and named 'nicotine' after the Frenchman Jean Nicot, who had enthusiastically promoted tobacco in the sixteenth century"

(Durrant & Thakker, 2003, p. 73). Yet, researchers have found a small subgroup of smokers who can regularly and moderately smoke without becoming addicted. The addiction apparently stems from nicotine's role in speeding up and intensifying the flow of glutamate, a neurotransmitter that causes a sharp increase in the firing rate of synaptic signals flashing through the brain. The primary brain site for nicotine addiction is the insula, first noted when a man who had a stroke in the insula no longer smoked, and when asked about it said that he "forgot" that he smoked. Also, much of this neural intensification occurs in the limbic system whose physiological activation acts as a reward system for the brain. Other factors are (1) modeling and ease of access to tobacco, promoted by significant peers, authority figures, and media idols; (2) peer pressure, especially for early adolescents; (3) genetic predisposition; (4) habit and ritual; (5) the paradoxical tranquilizing effect of nicotine on the chronic smoker (pharmacologically, it is a stimulant); and (6) the fulfillment of personality needs (such as oral eroticism) (Petraitis, Flay, & Miller, 1995).

It is difficult to set out clear diagnostic-test correlates for nicotine abuse or dependence given (1) its legal acceptance by society, (2) widespread patterns of accepted daily usage, (3) society's traditional tolerance of smoking by adolescents, and (4) society's failure to clearly discriminate use from abuse. The *DSM-IV-TR* does offer a diagnosis of Nicotine Dependence, defined by the same criteria as other substance dependencies. Of those people who continue to smoke regularly through age 20, approximately 90 percent will become nicotine dependent.

The Case of Dr. S.

As a result of a severe flu attack at age 38, Dr. S. experienced an irregular heartbeat. His personal physician and colleague, Dr. F., told him that his habit of smoking cigars had caused it and advised him to stop smoking. When Dr. S. tried to do so, he became depressed and occasionally suffered an even worse pulse rate. After several attempts at stopping, he returned to smoking about 20 cigars a day. He developed cancer of the jaw at age 67. Despite 33 operations and the removal of his entire jaw because of various cancerous and precancerous conditions, Dr. S. continued to smoke. At age 73, he developed angina pectoris (chest pains from heart disease), which was relieved whenever he stopped smoking. Yet, although he continued to try to stop smoking, he could not. He died from cancer at age 83, after many years of severe suffering from operations, cancer, and heart disorder.

Comment

Unlike most of the cases in this book, this is not a recent case, as Dr. S. was born on May 6, 1856, in Freiberg, Moravia "(now known as Pribor and part of the Czech Republic), the son of a Jewish wool merchant, Jacob Freud, and his wife Amalie . . .

moved to Vienna when Sigmund was 4 years old . . . where he remained until he was forced to leave Austria to escape Nazi persecution in 1938" (Larson et al., 2007, p. 271). And the fact that Dr. S. is Sigmund Freud offers strong testimony to the difficulty of changing this behavior. In modern times, every tactic imaginable has been used. Most of these efforts have had either no or limited success; none has shown complete success. Even in an intensive resident (inpatient) program that combines all the techniques and medications that seem to help—for example, at the Mayo Clinic—the success rate is no better than 40 percent. The *DSM-IV-TR* indicates that each year, less than 5 percent of smokers who try to quit are successful. In many cases, individuals are able to control their smoking significantly during the treatment phase, only to remit gradually afterward. The relapse rate is very high. A single "lapse" that consists of smoking more than one or two cigarettes leads to a resumption of smoking almost 50 percent of the time, and virtually all who relapse twice eventually resume smoking. Heavy smokers are most prone to relapse.

Treatment Options

There is some consensus on what techniques (best delivered in the context of a psychotherapy) seem to help (Durrant & Thakker, 2003; Meyer & Weaver, 2007; Petraitis, Flay, & Miller, 1995):

- Increasing delay strategies, gradually but increasingly delaying smoking the first cigarette of the day up to the point of quitting and/or the use of a planned "quit day"
- Use of drugs such as naltrexone or buproprion to mute the "craving" and/or obsessive focus components
- Use of isolated nicotine to fade the addiction component. Evidence shows that the most effective combination of biologic treatments is the nicotine patch and the sustained-release form of buproprion (e.g., Zyban), and recent research has supported the use of varenicline.
- Use of a short-term and/or "as needed" prescription for psychotropic medication to mute anxiety, depression, and apprehension, especially during the first few weeks or months as well as a series of injections, usually five, of Nic-VAX which acts by blocking nicotine from reaching the brain thus muting the addiction component itself, thus making it easier to quit
- Use of hypnosis and/or relaxation training to develop long-term methods of coping with stress and situational anxiety, and to enhance motivation
- Counseling, along with follow-up queries or programs, from the primary care physician, with a continued emphasis on the need to quit
- Use of rapid smoking techniques to create aversion-extinction responses
- Attention to diet and exercise to enhance self-esteem and physiological health
- Direct treatment of any concomitant disorders such as depression or anxiety
- Participation in a support group
- Work with significant others to facilitate their support of attempts to change

A successful quit typically proceeds in the following stages:

- *Consideration of Change:*   The individual talks and thinks about the possibility of quitting and the personal ramifications.
- *Crystallization:*   A goal to actually quit is accepted. Cost-benefit analyses (e.g., health reasons) are explored. Lists should be prepared to concretize expectancies about annoyances, personal costs, and relapse traps.
- *Concrete Preparation:*   The commitment to quit is finalized and a time to quit is chosen, preferably a relatively stress-free period. Antistress mechanisms (e.g., hypnosis, yoga, prescription for benzodiazepines, contracts with significant others) can be put in place.
- *The "Just Do It" Phase:*   The move is made, with preparations put in action. New behaviors to fill "smoking time" are put in place. Smokers are avoided. Some coping strategies are activated to deal with the actual experience of the addiction, which continues for three to six months, and the change in metabolism, which can lead to weight gain.
- *Maintenance:*   A more healthful lifestyle (physically, emotionally, and spiritually) must be put in place.
- *Antirelapse:*   The possibility of some relapse is expected (approximately 45 percent do remit within one month), and coping for that is planned ahead of time. Enhanced mechanisms to avoid relapse are put in place (e.g., a public commitment to antismoking campaigns, allowing family members to destroy any tobacco products).

Continued success usually requires that the significant persons around the smoker be supportive of a change to nonsmoking. Friends and family (particularly if they are also smokers) often give lip service to the smoker's pledge to quit, only to subvert, consciously or unconsciously, such efforts. As with many other substance-abuse patterns, prevention is more efficient and effective than cure. This is especially important, as approximately 90 percent of people who smoke at age 20 become long-term smokers. The combined efforts at prevention and treatment have caused the smoking rate in U.S. adults to drop from 42.2 percent in 1966 to approximately 20 percent in 1997, and it has hovered somewhat below this percentage ever since. The smoking habit persists most strongly in lower socioeconomic classes.

10 The Eating Disorders

Anorexia Nervosa and Bulimia Nervosa

Eating disorders were hardly recognized as late as the 1960s. The first case in this chapter, that of Karen Carpenter, is important because it was her ultimate death stemming from this disorder that brought the significance of eating disorders into popular awareness. Eating disorders have become epidemic in the United States, even as obesity has increased to epidemic proportions (Agras, 1995; Garner & Garfinkel, 1977; Heffner & Eifert, 2004; Stice, Burton, & Shaw, 2004). The first case examines anorexia nervosa. The second case, of Christina Ricci, offers a somewhat different perspective on anorexia nervosa. The third case, that of Princess Diana, focuses on bulimia nervosa.

Ask your child what he wants for dinner only if he's buying.
—Fran Lebowitz, satirical humorist, *Social Studies*

Anorexia Nervosa

Anorexia nervosa is literally translated as "not eating because of nervous causes." The essential requirements for a diagnosis of Anorexia Nervosa, according to *DSM-IV-TR*, are refusal to maintain body weight at or above 85 percent of expected minimum normal weight for age and height or failure to meet that 85 percent minimum during periods of growth; intense fear of gaining weight or being fat, even though underweight; and related body image distortion or denial of seriousness of current low body weight. Generally, there is no actual significant loss of appetite in anorectics. Their fear of gaining weight persists and may even increase despite simultaneous weight loss. Postmenarcheal females who are anorectic experience amenorrhea. The *DSM* specifies the disorder as either one of two types: the Restricting Type or the Binge-Eating/Purging Type.

Anorexia nervosa was traditionally seen primarily in middle- and upper-socioeconomic classes of women. However, in recent years, anorexia, as well as bulimia, is increasingly observed in preadolescent girls, adolescent and young adult males, and older women (Grilo, 2006). It typically occurs first during puberty, as a young woman becomes more conscious of her self-image. Over 75 percent of cases originate between ages 12 and 18, about 1 in 200 to 250 females in this age range can be expected to develop the disorder, and follow-up studies estimate long-term mortality rates at between 5 and 15 percent. After the "violation" of eating, these women may resort to self-induced vomiting and laxatives to "cleanse" the body of food. Anorexia nervosa is less common in males. When it does occur, there are systematic differences from female anorectics. Males are less likely to diet or to use laxatives, are often less conscientious about school, are less likely to have had large appetites premorbidly, are more likely to overexercise and to report enjoyable sexual experiences, and are less likely to die from the condition. Anorectics who also show episodes of bulimia (binge eating), in general, are more disturbed than anorectics who do not (Agras, 1995; Heffner & Eifert, 2004; Grilo, 2006).

The parents of anorectics are typically very caring, yet very controlling, individuals. The anorectic appears to use the disorder as a statement of independence from the family in the narrow area that she can control. The salient personality characteristics are excessive dependency and sensitivity, introversion, perfectionism, and subtle but persistent selfishness and stubbornness (Bruch, Cyzewski, & Suhr, 1988).

Anorectics without bulimic characteristics are typically shy, passively controlling, perfectionistic, confused about sexuality, and stubborn. Bulimics who are also anorectic are more likely to be extroverted, industrious perfectionists who attempt to control their peers in direct ways. Many bulimics weigh in at normal levels, whereas others are obese; anorectics are almost always cadaverously thin. Both groups come from families in which food is a focus, as in socialization or recognition. Anorectics will often cook exotic meals for others, although they may eat only a small portion themselves. Bulimics do not usually like to cook because they are afraid they will eat all the food before the guests arrive.

> *We're still generally a hideously fat people with immense bubble butts.*
> —Julia Child, TV chef and cookbook author

The Cases of Karen Carpenter and Christina Ricci

Karen Carpenter

The case of Karen Carpenter in the 1960s brought anorexia nervosa into the public eye for the first time. Until her battle with anorexia, eating disorders were rarely recognized as such, and unfortunately it took the death of one of America's best-loved voices for the disease to be taken seriously for the first time. Karen was teased about being overweight at a young age and harshly called "Fatso" by her brother, whom she idolized. At 17, despite her mother's finality on the issue of big hips "running in the family," Karen lost 25 pounds and stayed around 120 through her late teens and early twenties.

Soon after, at 19, Karen and her brother were signed by Herb Alpert to record for A & M records. This seemingly wonderful opportunity signaled the beginning of Karen's years in the limelight as well as her increasing self-consciousness. Although it was her voice to the backdrop of her brother's music that made them stars, Karen always regarded her brother as primarily responsible for their enormous success. Karen's mother was extremely controlling and critical of Karen, and she made no effort to hide her obvious favoritism toward Karen's brother. The family was devoted to her brother and his career, and time for love and recognition of Karen's talents was rare. In fact, Karen's brother also thought himself the main reason for their success and kept Karen constantly under his control.

As her career soared, Karen received feedback, from both the media and her brother, that was critical of her weight. At age 24 she again began dieting. By 26 she was forced to take two months of bed rest due to exhaustion because she was exercising so excessively in the absence of any meaningful caloric intake. She began to miss shows due to illness as her immune system began to fail; and, still, she became addicted to laxatives and overdosed on thyroid pills in hopes of burning more calories. At age 30 she married a man whom she had known for only a few months. Less than 12 months later their marriage fell apart, and he openly admitted that he was too controlling with Karen.

Karen was finally treated for her anorexia and, with virtually no support from her family, managed to gain 25 pounds under her therapist's supervision in New York. However, after returning to California, Karen started taking ipecac every night in order to induce vomiting. She eventually increased her intake of ipecac to an entire bottle which very likely facilitated the heart failure that caused her death. Karen's story was the first to bring anorexia nervosa to the public forefront.

Christina Ricci

Christina Ricci's first film, at age 9, was *Mermaids* with Cher and Winona Ryder (see Chapter 12). However, she seemed to make more of an impression on moviegoers as Wednesday in *The Addams Family* movies. Much later, she also riveted audiences as the manipulative girlfriend of murderous hooker Charlize Theron in *Monster*. She is well known for her role in *Sleepy Hollow*, co-starring alongside Johnny Depp. Ricci prides herself on her preference for independent films and has been in a number, most notably *Prozac Nation*. Unlike Karen Carpenter, Christina Ricci has never been prized as one of America's sweethearts. Her gothic style and sarcastic nature as well as her virtually nonexistent nightlife have left her much more likely to be the subject of confusion than adoration or fantasy.

The Early Years

Christina Ricci was born on February 12, 1980, in Santa Monica, California. She was born as the youngest of four children. Her perfectionist mother had been a model, and her father was a primal scream therapist who saw fit to practice out of their home. Christina began making commercials for cereal and toys starting at age 5.

In 1993, when she was 13, Christina had just finished filming *The Addams Family* and started to enjoy her growing notoriety. The same year, her parents were divorced, and as a result her family was torn apart. If that were not enough stress for a 13-year-old girl living in Hollywood, she was soon cast into a role that brought her body image to the forefront.

In 1994, Christina was cast as a co-star in the film *Now and Then* with Rosie O'Donnell and Demi Moore. She had always been a cute, slightly chubby child, and for this film she was cast as the younger version of Rosie O'Donnell. Her friend and co-star Thora Birch was cast as the young Melanie Griffith. One would not have to be an overly sensitive teen to realize how her body type was being

(continued)

The Cases of Karen Carpenter and Christina Ricci Continued

portrayed—she was destined to grow up to be the overweight member of her peer group.

Early in her teens Christina became a good candidate for "most likely to rob a convenience store." She said off-the-wall things to the media about incest and being excited for her eighteenth birthday because she would be able to buy a gun. In fact, in an October 1997 interview, as a teenager, Ricci scoffed at the idea of doing a romantic comedy because "this is not a happy planet." She was also an avid smoker. She dealt with the media angrily and sarcastically during her teens, so it is hard to say which of her comments have merit, but it was clear that she was a girl who was having more trouble regulating herself than the average teenager. She has stated that by her mid-teens she felt completely removed from any ordinary semblance of reality.

Family and Fame

The divorce of her parents coupled with the unavoidable parallel drawn between Christina and Rosie O'Donnell, an overweight actress (especially by Hollywood standards), no doubt left this 13-year-old feeling a lack of control in her life. Her many neurotic behaviors morphed into anorexia in 1994 during the filming of *Now and Then*. She despised the way her body was and the way it was changing, and in order to show her self-hatred she began to burn herself with a cigarette lighter and continued to do so at least through her seventeenth birthday. She once proudly rolled up her sleeve, showing her burn marks to a reporter and explained that she wanted to see if she could handle pain.

Christina continued to become more and more obsessed with being thin. However, her anorexia seems due more to an addictive, neurotic personality than to the more typical perfectionistic personality, such as that of Karen Carpenter, that most anorectics portray (Forbush, Heatherton, & Keel, 2007). She was a rebel in the world of Hollywood, but the pressure to be thin became something she could not control in her tumultuous teenage world. At her lowest point, she ate one meal every three days and jogged six miles a day. At one point she weighed just 61 pounds.

In her mid-twenties, when Ricci began talking about her disorder, she said that television movies actually taught her how to become anorectic instead of warning her about the dangers of anorexia. Ricci claimed, "I did get all my tips from a Tracey Gold Lifetime movie on anorexia. It taught me what to do." She also admitted that burning herself and giving herself physical pain gave her justification for the emotional pain she was feeling.

Ricci has shown great courage in her fight against anorexia, and although she still continues to often play dark, disturbed roles, she says she is happy to be over that stage of her life and to have settled down. Now in her late twenties, she stays in most nights in lieu of competing with Hollywood's nightlife. She has just recently become pregnant and says she has been at peace with her body since her mid-twenties when she first felt that someone truly loved her.

Their Etiology

Although both Christina Ricci and Karen Carpenter suffered serious cases of anorexia nervosa, their diseases seem to have come about for importantly different reasons. Karen Carpenter was a perfectionist, and it was those closest to her, her family, who first drew attention to her weight. Ricci, on the other hand, was self-loathing, but not because she was perfectionistic, but more likely because she had a tumultuous family life. Yet, it was not her family who first drew her attention to her weight but rather her career and the sadly routine pressures of stardom. Ricci managed to stray from the cookie-cutter expectation of Hollywood and overcome her obsession with being thin, a feat that the perfectionistic Carpenter was never able to accomplish. Importantly, Christina, thanks in large part to Karen Carpenter's tragic story, had access to a much greater body of knowledge about and acceptance in dealing with her disorder.

Like Karen Carpenter and Christina Ricci, anorectics are usually talented, ambitious, young, white, and female. Karen was one of the older victims of this disorder; it typically appears during or just prior to puberty, as a young woman becomes more conscious of her appearance. Karen's anxiety over her appearance increased with public exposure. Karen had the Binge-Eating/Purging Type of anorexia nervosa, evidenced by her use of laxatives in the early years and her self-induced vomiting in the later years. The other *DSM-IV-TR* category, the Restrictive Type, is defined as an absence of bingeing and purging. To give the reader an idea of what a full *DSM-IV-TR* diagnosis would look like, here is Karen's probable diagnosis:

Axis I: 307.1 Anorexia Nervosa, Binge-Eating/Purging Type, Severe

Axis II: Dependent Personality Disorder (Provisional)

Axis III: Hypothyroidism, acquired; malnutrition, protein-caloric, severe

Axis IV: Severity of psychosocial stressors: moderate

Axis V: GAF = 80 (a general estimate of her level of functioning for the prior year—in this case, the year before death)

Anorectics consistently believe that they are too fat even when emaciated. Typically, the anoretic sets an ideal weight goal, and when that is reached, the goal shifts downward. Also typical of this illness is the anorectic's continuous fear of gaining weight (Heffner & Eifert, 2004). Even when audiences gasped at Karen's bony structure when she came on the stage, she continued to lose weight, yet kept her eating behavior a secret. She consistently denied she was ill and minimized the effects of her illness. Deception is central to maintaining this disorder.

One theory on how the cycle of self-starvation continues is that the person experiences a hurt, such as rejection, disapproval, or lack of control. Feelings of anger are turned inward and masked by an increased attempt to be perfect. Irrational thinking, similar in some ways to that of the obsessive-compulsive patterns, convinces the person that if he or she does more or better, things will improve. Perfectionistic living creates more stress, which further drives the person to escape through extreme eating behaviors (Forbush et al., 2007; Agras, 1995; Bruch, Czyzewski, & Suhr, 1988).

While growing up, Karen was teased for being fat, and her mother told her that being overweight ran in the family and that it was unlikely Karen would be any different. As an adult, Karen continued seeing herself as fat, even though she was severely underweight. Such a distorted body image is a prevalent characteristic of those who have anorexia nervosa.

A common theory of the origins of this illness focuses on the person's ability to control his or her life. Typically, anorectics feel powerless and overwhelmed by life and turn inward to exercise control over their bodies. The anorectic uses the disorder to establish independence in the one area over which she can keep control. There is also evidence that prenatal exposure to female hormones may predispose both males and females to anorexia.

Treatment Options

General goals include weight restoration, treatment of physical complications, and a change in the relentless pursuit of thinness. Because anorexia nervosa often results in very severe—even life-threatening—weight loss, an inpatient treatment program, possibly including forced and/or intravenous feeding, may be necessary. Nutritional counseling may be helpful, but one has to be careful to avoid moving into the anorectic's favorite battleground—food. At this stage a behavior modification program to develop feeding behaviors may be helpful, although the critical issue is deriving the reinforcements that can build up the feeding behavior (Agras, 1995). Megace ES (megestrol acetate) has proven useful in treating anorexia.

A more psychodynamic approach has been found to be useful as a person moves into more normal functioning, with a focus on the ambivalence over dependency, the high need for perfectionism, and, as trust develops, the subtle selfishness and narcissism that emerge (Bruch, Czyzewski, & Suhr, 1988). Family therapy is also likely to be necessary because so much of this pattern is related to interactions over dependency and control in the family.

Relapse prevention is critical with both anorexia nervosa and bulimia nervosa. Clients should receive exposure training for high-risk situations, as well as cognitive training to eliminate negative self-talk and to discriminate lapses from relapse (Dattillo, Davis, & Goisman, 2008; Heffner & Eifert, 2004).

Fortunately, most anorectics don't have the ultimately tragic outcome that happened to Karen Carpenter. Many do show problematic patterns over the long run, but in a number of cases, although they may have some residual symptoms, they can eventually function normally.

Any person with an eating problem needs counseling about diet facts and simple control of eating behaviors—counseling of the type used with the more common problems of binge eating without purging, general obesity, and persistent eating disorders. These facts can be modified to the specific eating disorder involved:

- Both a change in exercise amounts and energy-burning patterns and a restriction of caloric intake are critical in generating weight loss.
- There is a biological drive toward high-fat and very sweet foods, so control should be directed toward "what" as much as "when" and "how much."
- Weight loss is not hard to attain; maintenance of weight lost is.

- It is more difficult to lose weight during the second diet than the first.
- Most diets are broken in the late afternoon.
- Persons trying to lose weight must keep fluid intakes high. The body needs much more water and other fluids when undergoing weight loss.
- If activity level remains the same and there is a cessation of smoking, there will be a weight gain.
- For women, food cravings often increase in the days before their menstrual periods, so they are more vulnerable to lapses during these times.

Also, it is highly recommended that any person with an overeating or binge-eating disorder of any significance implement and monitor, via a diary, a day-to-day program based on general diet tips such as the following:

- Drink eight glasses of water each day, *at least*. This may be the single-most effective technique.
- Eat a high-carbohydrate breakfast and avoid eating anything at least two hours before going to bed.
- Eat a salad or have a low-calorie beverage or a cup of soup before a meal, then delay eating any main meal for an extra five minutes. Hot tea is effective for many people.
- Slow down while you eat, chew longer, and savor flavors.
- Don't eat standing up, in front of the TV, while talking on the phone, in the car, or on the run. Try not to eat alone.
- Try to eat two or three main (but not large) meals and two smaller snacks every day at predetermined times so you develop a feasible routine. Don't wait until you are extremely hungry to eat.
- Avoid drinks with alcohol or sugar.
- Be creative. For example, visualize yourself eating slowly before you even sit down for dinner.
- Use thought control. About to binge? Yell "Stop!" or at least whisper it if you are in a public place.
- Avoid keeping food around, other than planned food.
- Brush your teeth after every meal; you'll be less likely to snack.
- Identify times when you are prone to binge or overeat and plan alternative activities that are not compatible with eating.
- Avoid weighing yourself unless it is specifically prescribed.
- Develop an exercise program that is effective and that you can comfortably integrate into your life. Make a decision to walk rather than drive whenever possible.
- If you find yourself thinking too much about food or body image, this may be because you have a conflict you haven't dealt with and/or you are anxious or depressed. Try to identify what's going on and take some positive, coping measures.
- Plan ahead as to how you will handle "tough" situations like being in a supermarket, at a party, and so on. Drink a lot of water and a high-fiber snack a half-hour or so before you go.

- Set aside some time each day to reflect on how you are doing in this area and in life in general. Decide what you are doing well, affirm yourself for that, and visualize how you can improve in areas where you are not doing as well.
- Recruit help from family and friends and any other source of help that has meaning or usefulness to you. Be open about your decision to lose weight, ask them to help you, and then spell out how they can help.

I drink too much beer and eat too much ice cream, and if I don't swim, I will look like a little round bowling ball, and it will be disgusting.
—Newt Gingrich, politician

Bulimia Nervosa

Bulimia nervosa is a chronic pattern of binge eating. Bulimia (from the Greek words for "hunger of an ox") is known as the gorge-purge syndrome. The essential features, according to *DSM-IV-TR*, are recurrent binge eating, denoted by a sense of lack of control or eating, *and* eating within a discrete time period much more than others would normally eat; a minimum of two binge episodes a week for at least three months; recurrent, inappropriate compensatory attempts to control weight, for example, by diets, laxatives, or vomiting; and body and/or self-image distortion.

Binge eating may be triggered by episodes of dysphoria, extraneous stressors, intense hunger, and/or weight-related thoughts, and often has a dissociative quality (Grilo, 2006). Blouin and colleagues (1992) found that there are significant seasonal variations in bulimia. They found a high correlation of binge behaviors, but not purging behaviors or severity of depression, with number and occurrence of dark hours within the month, and a much higher overall rate of bingeing and purging in the winter months.

Bulimia nervosa affects individuals physically as well as emotionally (Agras, 1995). This is especially true when vomiting is the chosen method of purging. Essential nutrients are removed from the system during frequent vomiting, which increases the tendency to feel tired and depressed. Vomiting is reinforced because it alleviates both the pain of having too much food in the stomach and the guilt of having consumed too much food. In addition, the pain of vomiting causes the release of endorphins, which are chemicals that create a mild "high." Thus, the frequency of vomiting usually increases. After vomiting, the system attempts to return its pH balance to normal, but it is interrupted by the next bout of vomiting. All of this causes chaos in the system, which provides a basis for physical and emotional instability. Frequently, the bulimic will suffer from some related physical disorder.

Between bingeing episodes the sufferer usually diets, fasts, or vomits (Grilo, 2006). Typically, bingeing and purging are kept secret, and, as with Princess Diana, the secret is well kept, and the individual usually has a cheerful disposition and a demonstrated interest in helping others. Inside, however, there is often a great deal of unexpressed anger, as well as guilt and depression, both of which are apt to occur after bingeing. Also, as with other eating disorders, bulimics often have a distorted view of their body, seeing themselves as fat and ugly when in fact they are of normal weight. Individuals with bulimia nervosa may exercise excessively and may do it at atypical times and/or inappropriate places. This ritual is a compulsive attempt to compensate for prior binge-eating episodes.

The Case of Princess Diana

Princess Diana was a celebrity member of the royal family of Great Britain. From the outside, her life initially at least appeared to be the ideal story of a fairy princess. However, while facing tremendous turmoil in her private and public life, Diana struggled with bulimia nervosa and depression for years, particularly following her marriage to Prince Charles, the heir-apparent to the throne. The following description is based on Diana's own perceptions along with related accounts (Brown, 2007; Burrell, 2003; Campbell, 1993; Morton, 1992, 1994).

The Formative Years

On July 1, 1961, in Sandringham, Norfolk, in England, Honorable Diana Spencer, the third of four children, was born to Edward John ("Johnnie") and Frances Ruth Burke Spencer. Johnnie was not a kind husband. Frances, who married at age 18, stayed with him at least in part to give birth to a boy who, unlike a girl, would be able to inherit the vast Spencer fortune. Before Diana was born, Frances had given birth to a boy who lived only 10 hours. The parents were shattered by the baby's death. They convinced themselves Diana would be the boy they wanted so much, and they were bitterly disappointed that she was a girl. Diana sensed, then learned of her parents' disappointment, and she felt guilty for letting them down.

Diana grew up in an atmosphere of privilege and noble heritage. Despite this, she was not snobbish. She occasionally socialized with the Queen and family, who lived nearby.

Diana received a traditional upbringing, including christenings, godparents, and discipline. During Diana's early years, her family was very social. There were many birthday parties for the children and a yearly fireworks party. Despite these and other occasions that made Diana and her family appear ideal, at home Frances and Johnnie fought constantly. Diana remembers her mother weeping, her father not speaking, and her younger brother crying himself to sleep at night. With a tendency toward violence, Johnnie was known to have monumental rages as well as a drinking problem.

In 1967, when Diana was age 6, two major events changed her life. First, her two older sisters were sent off to boarding school. Second, Frances left her family to begin a trial separation from Johnnie. This devastated the family, and it was a shock to British society, as divorce was then considered embarrassing and extraordinary. Diana remembers having many nannies and many unanswered questions after her mother's departure.

Frances was branded as selfish for this move, but her children always cared a great deal for her. Her reason for leaving was that Johnnie was never good to her. Although he was a gentleman to outsiders and a kind father, he was emotionally abusive toward his wife. In addition, Frances had fallen in love with Peter Shand Kydd, a kind, witty, and wealthy man who was already married with children.

Frances was sensitive in explaining her departure, but she did not realize that except for a few occasional months with Diana and

(continued)

The Case of Princess Diana Continued

her 3-year-old brother Charles, this was to be a permanent separation. At that time, unless the mother was extremely incompetent, fathers were not usually given custody of the children. However, just by asserting her adultery, Johnnie was awarded custody. Frances then married Peter, who himself had just divorced. In part because of gossip in London, Frances and Peter moved to a distant part of England.

This parting and the subsequent divorce are topics that Diana would not discuss with others, even her close friends, until her adult years. Diana later reported that she felt rejected and alone and that her trust was violated. The formal atmosphere in the family may have exacerbated the sense of isolation, and neither Diana nor her parents were physically demonstrative.

Diana's distress was manifested in various ways, such as her tendency toward neatness, washing both herself and her clothes compulsively. She even offered to wash clothes for others. She dressed meticulously. She was constantly moving about, not staying with one activity for long. She began to be a compulsive talker and socializer.

Fortunately, Diana adored her school, which was small, private, traditional, and disciplined. She impressed her teachers as well behaved, cheerful, yet playfully mischievous. Diana did not excel academically, and she panicked when taking exams, sometimes failing them because her mind "went blank." Diana always had a large assortment of activities such as horseback riding and swimming available to her. She was an excellent athlete and talented dancer. Those who knew her were impressed with her positive, bubbly personality and her ability to get along with others.

Although some other girls at her school were anorectic, Diana never seemed to have this problem and loved to eat. She did notice that she could gain weight easily, and when she did, she simply cut back a bit on eating. Avoiding such temptations as smoking or drinking alcohol, Diana was not as successful at resisting sweets.

Diana was upset when her grandmother died in August 1972. In 1975, her grandfather died, which meant that Johnnie was given the official title of "Earl" and Diana became a "Lady." Her father was in the process of moving to the home he had inherited, a famous landmark with an art collection considered one of the finest in Europe. Because she had a difficult time saying good-bye to her home of many years, Diane escaped during the packing and went to a beach house where she gorged on food with a friend.

Another major change that upset Diana was her father's affair and subsequent marriage to Raine, Countess of Dartmouth, a charming and dominating woman. Raine succeeded at controlling Johnnie, but she could not control Diana. As a result of her feelings toward Raine, Diana began avoiding visiting her father, yet was generally respectful to her stepmother.

The Prince Arrives

Prince Charles had dated Diana's older sister Sarah, who was struggling through anorexia nervosa. In 1979, Sarah introduced Charles to Diana, then age 16. Despite her sophisticated background, the teenage Diana was shy in unfamiliar settings, wore no makeup, and dressed in clothes purchased by her mother. Diana decided to drop out before completing finishing school, making her a high school dropout.

After a frustrating attempt to teach dancing to groups of children, Diana decided to work at a kindergarten. She enjoyed this and also did cleaning or baby-sitting occasionally. By September 1980, however, the press had identified Diana as Charles's new love. Diana found Charles well settled (later, this would be seen as "rigid") in his daily routine. Charles seemed to enjoy his bachelor lifestyle, but many believed that the demands of his title compelled him to wed and produce an heir to the throne. Diana was excited by the attention he and others gave her when they were courting. Diana went wherever he directed. He called her "Diana"; she called him "Sir." She was certainly infatuated and probably in love; he probably never was in love with her. He proposed to her when she was age 19.

Before their wedding, on July 29, 1981, Diana moved into Buckingham Palace for three months. Her first night at the Queen Mother's London residence was spent alone, not welcomed by any of the members of the royal family. Although she had a brief lesson from the Queen Mother in royal protocol, Diana felt unprepared to take on the duties of a royal family member. Up to the wedding, Diana felt isolated and cried frequently in the face of demands of the public, the press, and the royal family. This is when Diana first began purging food from her body after eating, usually by vomiting. Her waistline dropped from 29 to 23 inches.

Things unraveled rapidly. Diane asserted that she learned two days before the wedding that Charles intended to give Camilla Parker Bowles, his former girlfriend and the wife of a member of the Queen's household, a bracelet with their nicknames, "Fred" and "Gladys," inscribed. The night before their wedding, Charles told Diana she should make the most of their last night of freedom. On their honeymoon Diana noticed that he was wearing cufflinks with Camilla's initials (Brown, 2007). She reported vomiting four or five times a day during her honeymoon.

Diana and Charles were gregarious in public, but in private, they argued continuously, frequently about Camilla. This, in addition to pressures from the press, caused Diana to continue vomiting. She sought counseling and refused recommended medication when she discovered she was pregnant. Allegedly, she sought Charles's assistance; however, she found him unresponsive. Finally, on New Year's Day in 1982, three months pregnant, she tearfully threatened to commit suicide. Charles did not take her seriously and began preparing to go riding. Diana then threw herself down to the foot of a wooden staircase, where she was discovered by a very shaken Queen Mother. Charles continued getting ready to go riding. Except for a few bruises, Diana and her unborn child were fine.

Diana's bulimic rituals became more frequent. Those around Diana continuously noticed her large appetite in stark contrast to her petite size. Examples include an evening when she ate a whole steak-and-kidney pie, and another evening when she consumed a pound of candy and later had a large bowl of custard. On one occasion Charles commented on Diana being chubby, which triggered her to induce vomiting to rid herself of her food. She later realized this helped her gain a sense of control and gave her a chance to express her anger.

Throughout the years of their marriage, Diana continued to feel threatened by Camilla, and, as time would tell, with good reason. Also, she continued to feel rejected by the royal family. Even though Prince Philip appeared sympathetic and tried to act as a mediator, "he rarely pulled punches . . . [and] upset and infuriated the princess with comments she described as brutal" (Burrell, 2003, p. 160). Diana reacted with more suicide attempts, which she considered to be cries for help. One time she hurled herself against a glass cabinet, and on a different occasion she slashed her wrists. Another time, while in an intense argument with Charles, she picked up a knife and cut her chest and thighs. Watching Diana bleed profusely, Charles only chided her. At the time, Diana explained these attempts as the result of having trouble adjusting to her new position. Actually, the trouble was the culmination of the bulimia, her problems with Charles, and the stress of consistent morning sickness. Although Diana was able to present herself well in public, she learned not to expect any praise from Charles or any other member of his family.

A major stressor involved dealing with the press. Diana consistently received more public attention than any other member of the royal family. At first, the press nicknamed her "Shy Di." To regain privacy, she did things

(continued)

The Case of Princess Diana Continued

such as fleeing out of a fire exit of a store and climbing over garbage containers to avoid the press. Despite her fear of and frustrations with the press, Diana remained courteous to them. At first, when there were no devastating surprises, Diana was able to treat the media attention as a joke. However, soon it made her feel panicky. One of Diana's early experiences was agreeing to be photographed while with a couple of children from her kindergarten. What the photographers did not tell Diana was that the light behind her shone through her skirt, exposing a clear outline of her torso and legs. Diana, horrified, was reduced to tears when she saw the photographs.

Diana carefully monitored her appearance, keeping herself photo-ready at all times. Her taste in clothes and personal grooming was impeccable, and she sought guidance in responding to crowds. However, on a face-to-face basis, she needed no help dealing with people.

Diana gave birth to William, her first son and the present heir to the throne after his father, in June 1982, and her bulimia temporarily ceased. Soon, however, some postpartum depression set in and the bulimia returned. She also believed Charles was becoming jealous of the attention she was getting from others and the press.

Diana's turmoil about Camilla increased. She panicked whenever Charles was absent unexpectedly. Once she heard him on the telephone saying, "I will always love you." Diana began to keep personal friends and family at a distance, and the royal family, already distant, began seeing Diana as a threat because of changes in Charles, such as his decisions to become a vegetarian and to quit shooting.

Diana was now chronically depressed. Her original infatuation with Balmoral, the Queen's highland retreat, waned. When she left Balmoral for Kensington, it was to seek psychiatric help, although the press accused her of returning so she could shop.

First Diana tried therapy with a Jungian therapist who primarily analyzed her dreams. This was not especially helpful for her, so she tried other therapists, who also did not seem to help. Her thoughts again turned to suicide, and she felt the press was persecuting her.

Despite her depression and bulimia, Diana slowly gained confidence as she toured the world and received abundant media attention. The media's focus on Diana seemed to increase the couple's already serious problems, and Diana was often physically ill. When Diana was pregnant with their second child, Charles made it clear he wanted a girl. When he saw the baby boy, Harry, he merely said a few words and then went off to play polo, which had a lasting impact on her feelings toward him.

Diana was visibly more confident in public. Once, while attending the ballet with Charles, she slipped away toward the end, put on a silk dress, and performed on stage, dancing to an arrangement of Billy Joel's song *Uptown Girl*. The audience went wild, and, in public, Charles seemed amazed and pleased. In private, he angrily told her she was undignified and too demonstrative. Her bulimia continued, and her self-esteem plummeted.

Charles left for extended periods of time, often spending time with Camilla, which was never mentioned by the press. Yet, any social encounter, no matter how innocent, that Diana had with members of the opposite sex was front-page news. At one point, after Charles had returned from a long trip, Diana voiced complaints about the pressures from the press. This time, his indifferent response caused her to decide that any hope of a loving relationship with him was gone. It no doubt also spurred her own involvement in a secret love affair.

When Diana heard from a friend that depression can result from mineral deprivation that occurs with bulimia, she again sought treatment. This time, therapy was somewhat successful. Consulting with a therapist specializing in eating disorders on a weekly basis, she began a slow recovery. At her therapist's recommendation, Diana read about her condition; she was reassured to learn that there were others like her. After six months, Diana's former ritual of vomiting four or five times a day changed to once every three weeks. Relapses occurred when she was exposed to increased stresses within the royal family.

Diana's slow recovery took many turns. Over time, she turned for help to a hypnotherapist, an astrological counselor, a deep-tissue masseuse, an aroma therapist, an acupuncturist, a cranial masseuse, a practitioner of osteopathy, a clinician who gives regular colonic irrigations (a water treatment that cleanses the bowels), and a new-age therapist (similar to Primal Scream Therapy) who encouraged her to shout, scream, and hit a punching bag. Her bulimia remained under control, probably aided by all these procedures. The relationship between Charles and Diana continued to deteriorate, and in 1992, Diana and Charles finally agreed to separate.

On February 9, 1996, Princess Diana agreed to a divorce, and the divorce became official on August 28, 1996. She received an estimated lump-sum settlement of $22.5 million, the right to keep her jewelry and to continue living in Kensington Palace, and approximately $800,000 a year to maintain her private office. Her most important loss in the divorce settlement was losing the right to be called "Her Royal Highness." Subsequent to this, she had a strong relationship with Hasmat Khan, a Pakistani heart surgeon, who Brown (2007) asserts was Diana's only true love ever. However, although Diana sought marriage with him, he eventually withdrew from the relationship, in part as a result of pressure from his family to do so.

Then, almost a year after the divorce, a fairy-tale life paradoxically full of conflict ended tragically. Attempting to elude paparazzi (photographers of celebrities for the tabloids), she died early in the morning of August 31, 1997, at age 36, after the 600 series Mercedes she was riding in went out of control, at 62 mph, and crashed in a tunnel near the Eiffel Tower. The chauffeur and her latest boyfriend, wealthy Egyptian playboy and film producer (e.g., the 1981 Oscar-winning *Chariots of Fire*), Emad "Dodi" Fayed, were also killed. A bodyguard survived. One of the paparazzi, who immediately started taking photographs of the accident, was beaten by horrified bystanders. There is evidence that the driver was legally drunk, with a blood alcohol level of .23, and had psychotropic medications in his blood.

Etiology

In addition to pressure from society to be thin, it is believed that the most immediate triggers for the onset of bulimia include unusual or extreme stressors and feelings of loss of control (Agras, 1995). Diana's initial symptoms coincided with sudden demands from the press, the public, and the royal family to present her best appearance and be on her best behavior while at the same time harboring fears about Charles's commitment to her (Brown, 2007).

Striegel-Moore, Silberstein, and Rodin (1986) found that although about 20 percent of bulimic women do not show any specific personality pattern, the other 80 percent are divided between those who show an obsessive-compulsive pattern and those who show more of a classic addictive pattern. Diana, with her constant cleaning and organizing, in addition to her continuously perfect appearance, fits into the obsessive-compulsive pattern.

In addition, several researchers (Stice, Burton, & Shaw, 2004; Striegel-Moore, Silberstein, & Rodin, 1986) have noted a number of other specific factors that increase the tendency to develop a bulimic pattern: (1) acceptance of a traditional feminine role; (2) middle- to upper-class social status; (3) attendance away at college or a boarding school; (4) early physical maturation; (5) a lower metabolic rate; (6) higher stress; (7) tendencies toward depression; (8) a prolonged history of dieting attempts; (9) family isolation; (10) a high valuing of appearance and thinness, (11) participation in a sport such as gymnastics or an activity such as ballet that reinforces significant weight loss, or a sport such as wrestling that encourages rapid weight loss, especially fluids, followed by bingeing; and (12) a high belief in the ability to use one's will to control the self and the world. Diana's history includes most of these factors.

Another explanation is that bulimia may be related to continuous dietary restriction. The "natural weight" of many women is higher than what is required to match society's ideal image. While the body naturally seeks one weight, the woman struggles with long-term dieting to maintain a different one. Bingeing may occur when food intake is constantly restricted over a long period of time. The binge brings satisfaction, but guilt soon follows. Purging then relieves the guilt. This becomes a self-perpetuating cycle that allows the bulimic to satisfy food cravings without suffering the consequences.

Diana especially seemed to fit Hilde Bruch's pioneering descriptions and Agras's (1995) later explanation of predisposing variables of eating disorders and specifically bulimia. Families of bulimics usually have higher socioeconomic status and make a good impression. Privately, problems are either not dealt with or are handled poorly. Bulimics and anorectics tend to be model children. They grow up believing they must live up to their parents' expectations and prove to their parents they were good role models. When circumstances require giving up control, the girl dutifully complies and then uses bulimia to regain personal autonomy. Just as during the early years Diana's family gave the impression of being ideal, Diana herself consistently exhibited perfect social skills and the appearance of happiness and showed no evidence of having any problems.

Treatment Options

Cognitive-behavioral psychotherapy, even in group settings, has shown positive results in treating bulimia (Dattillo et al., 2008; Agras, 1995; Garner & Garfinkel, 1997; Stice Burton, & Shaw, 2004). This involves assessing dysfunctional beliefs that perpetuate bingeing and purging. Examples of beliefs frequently found in those with bulimia are "Pleasing others is more important than my own needs"; "I must do this to maintain my weight so I will appear attractive to the opposite sex"; "In order to be attractive I must look like the models on television"; "My body is fat and ugly"; and "If I do not purge my food, I will gain weight and people will not like me." When the client learns the sources of these beliefs and their inaccuracy, an underlying force for this behavior is removed.

Behaviorists have not spent much effort trying to formulate the etiology of bulimia. Rather, they have focused on devising token economy, aversion therapy, and contracting programs that have been useful in an overall treatment package (Bongar & Beutler, 1995). Family therapy, which includes an acknowledgment that this disorder at least in part reflects a disturbed family system, is usually necessary if the bulimic is to recover. A particularly difficult task here is to get family members to see that they are not doing this for the bulimic; rather, that the bulimic's disorder is in large part the natural evolutionary result of a specific system of family expectations, values, and controls (Agras, 1995). For adolescent bulimics, group therapy is particularly effective (Chambless et al., 1996). This provides a sense of control as well as a source of feedback.

Another treatment model for bulimia focuses on the anxiety that occurs after bingeing due to the client's fear of gaining weight. Vomiting is reinforced by relieving the anxiety. The client brings food to a therapy session that is used to binge and then eats it to the point at which he or she would normally vomit. Then, instead of vomiting, the client deals with the anxiety and is able to observe that the anxiety declines over time. This treatment is thought to break the connection between vomiting and the relief of anxiety.

Although it is known that Diana's problem with bulimia substantially subsided after six months of therapy, it is not known exactly what type of therapy was used. One thing that her therapist recommended that Diana reported as being very helpful, however, was reading books about her condition. This alone has been shown to be effective in the healing process for those motivated to recover from bulimia.

Diana refused to take medication for her condition. The medication that is sometimes prescribed for those with bulimia is antidepressants. Selective serotonin reuptake inhibitors, such as Prozac, have been shown to be effective because in addition to alleviating symptoms of depression they also reduce feelings of hunger. Prozac was the first SSRI to be approved by the FDA for treating bulimia. When there are anorectic components combined with the bulimia, megestrol acetate is helpful.

It is difficult to determine which therapy is most effective because there are different ways to define improvement. Some believe that a higher self-esteem through more functional cognitions is the goal, whereas others believe the actual number of binge-purge cycles is the only way to determine improvement. Most likely, a successful recovery will involve elements of all the different conceptualizations of this disorder.

Bulimia is difficult to treat effectively (Grilo, 2006). Because of its secretive nature, the disorder is usually well entrenched before help is sought. Thus, a major problem with treatment is the dropout rate. Characteristics of bulimics that are associated with successful outcome include late-age onset, lack of prior hospitalization, shorter duration of the illness, less serious nature of the illness, fewer social stressors, and a good social or work history. Because bulimia can be life-threatening, it is important to be aware of how a focus on dieting and physical attractiveness, and conflict over self-expression, can meld into this disorder.

11 The Personality Disorders

The personality disorders are chronic, pervasive, and inflexible patterns of perceiving and responding to the environment that are sufficiently maladaptive to cause disruption in functioning and environmentally generated subjective distress. They are common patterns. People with a personality disorder are not typically as disturbed or as concerned by their behavior as are friends and relatives. Generally, they view their own particular personality traits as ego-syntonic—that is, as consistent with their self-perception. Thus, people with personality disorders are more likely to be brought to the attention of professionals by other people than by themselves, such as spouses, relatives, or the criminal justice system (Meyer & Weaver, 2006).

The personality disorders are listed here in the "appearance clusters" suggested by the *DSM*.

1. *Disorders That Appear Odd or Eccentric*

    Paranoid: Hyperalert, suspicious, litigious, and authoritarian

    Schizoid: Asocial "loners," not "schizophrenic-like"

    Schizotypal: "Schizophrenic-like" but no consistent hallucinations or delusions

2. *Disorders That Appear Dramatic, Emotional, or Erratic*

    Histrionic: Emotionally flamboyant and dramatic, though shallow

    Narcissistic: Chronically inflated sense of self-worth

    Antisocial: Chronic antisocial patterns; does not learn from experience

    Borderline: Irritable, anxious, sporadically aggressive and emotionally unstable

3. *Disorders That Appear Anxious or Fearful*

    Avoidant: Shy and inhibited, afraid to "risk" relationships

    Dependent: Seeks dependent relationships; naive, yet suspicious

Obsessive-Compulsive:	Controlled, formal, perfectionistic; "workaholics without warmth"
Passive-Aggressive:	Passively resistant through stubbornness, inefficiency, or threatened aggression (not included in *DSM-IV-TR* as an official diagnosis, but only as an optional, secondary descriptive category)

The personality disorders are coded on Axis II in *DSM-IV-TR*, which unfortunately can allow the implication that the personality disorders are not "clinical" syndromes, but rather are behavioral and psychosocial conditions, and thus are "less important." Although *DSM-IV-TR* does not always disallow these diagnoses in children, the diagnosis of a personality disorder in a person under age 18 is traditionally discouraged.

Personality Types and Their Potential Disorders

Genetic and other biological factors often play some part in predisposing an individual to a personality disorder (DiLalla, 2004). However, the specific disorder patterns are learned and refined because they are effective, at least in the short run, in coping with that person's individual environment and, most important of all, the environment he or she grew up in (Hersen & Ammerman, 2000; Horowitz, 2004). Of course, the more distorted or disturbed that environment is, the more likely it is that a distorted coping pattern will emerge and become reinforced. Yet, the behavior pattern is seen as within the normal range of adjustment. Within this perspective, a personality type is a way station on the developmental road toward a full-blown personality disorder. It is important to realize that all people fit reasonably well with one or more of these personality types. Table 11.1 describes the common personality types, along with the personality disorder they are most likely to become if they are exaggerated and crystallized.

The cases in this chapter were chosen to demonstrate the most important personality disorders; the reader is also referred to the case of John Hinckley, diagnosed as a Borderline Personality Disorder, in Chapter 16. The histrionic personality disorder, described in the case of Hilde, is a common pattern, and often critical to the development of marital and family distress, as well as to eventual personal unhappiness because of negative social feedback. The antisocial personality disorder, the case of Theodore Bundy, exemplifies what is arguably the most common personality disorder and certainly the most socially destructive pattern. The case of Theodore Kaczynski is a good example of the schizoid personality disorder. An extreme variation of the Narcissistic Personality Disorder, Malignant Narcissism, is discussed in the cases of Hitler, Stalin, and Hussein.

It ain't bragging if you really done it.
—Dizzy Dean, all-star pitcher for the St. Louis Cardinals

TABLE 11.1   Personality Types and Correlated Traits and Disorders

	Personality Types				
Types	**Controlling**	**Aggressive**	**Confident**	**Sociable**	**Cooperative**
Typical Behaviors	Manipulative Demanding	Bold Initiating	Poised Distant	Animated Engaging	Docile Submissive
Interpersonal Patterns	Authoritarian	Intimidating	Unempathetic	Demonstrative	Compliant
Thinking Styles	Calculating	Dogmatic	Imaginative	Superficial	Open
Mood-Affect Expression	Disappointment Resentment	Anger Distrust	Calm Unconcerned	Dramatic Labile	Tender Fearful
View of Self	Unappreciated	Assertive	Self-assured	Charming	Weak
Probable Personality Disorders	Passive Aggressive Sadistic Paranoid	Antisocial Sadistic Paranoid	Narcissistic Paranoid Antisocial	Histrionic Borderline Narcissistic	Dependent Compulsive Avoidant

Types	**Sensitive**	**Respectful**	**Inhibited**	**Introverted**	**Emotional**
Typical Behaviors	Erratic Responsive	Organized Formal	Watchful Preoccupied	Passive Quiet	Energetic Engaging
Interpersonal Patterns	Unpredictable	Polite	Shy	Withdrawn	Provocative
Thinking Styles	Divergent	Respectful	Repressed	Vague	Distracted
Mood-Affect Expression	Pessimistic Hurt	Restrained Content	Uneasy Wary	Bland Coolness	Intense Frenetic
View of Self	Misunderstood	Reliable	Lonely	Placid	Interesting
Probable Personality Disorders	Passive-Aggressive Borderline Avoidant	Compulsive Paranoid Passive-Aggressive	Avoidant Schizotypal Self-defeating	Schizoid Schizotypal Compulsive Avoidant	Borderline Schizotypal Histrionic Narcissistic

Source: Adapted in part from T. Millon and G. Everly, *Personality and Its Disorders* (New York: John Wiley, 1985).

The Histrionic Personality Disorder

The specific criteria that mark the Histrionic Personality Disorder (HPD) include dramatic and intense emotional expressions, efforts to gain the center of attention, and shallow, insincere, and disrupted interpersonal relationships (Kernberg, 1984). Such people are likely to overreact emotionally, even in everyday situations, and they are inclined toward suicide gestures as a manipulation of others. Somatic complaints such as "spells of weakness" and headaches are typical, and medical personnel often have difficulty diagnosing and treating these disorders (Johnson, 2008). Vanity and self-absorption are common traits.

Histrionic personalities appear to be emphatic and socially perceptive, so that they easily elicit new relationships. As they then turn out to be emotionally insensitive and with little depth of insight into their own role in relationships, they are likely to avoid any blame for the inevitable problems in the relationships. In this way, they are closer to the defense mechanism of paranoid patterns. Histrionic individuals are often flirtatious and seductive sexually, although there is little payoff if one follows these cues. The behavior of the histrionic personality often resembles some of the traditional concepts of ultrafemininity, so for that reason it is more common in females than in males. Indeed, the Greek root of the term is *hustera*, meaning "uterus."

Denial is a common approach to conflict in this pattern, often limiting intellectual accomplishment. In histrionics, intellectual accomplishment is often low relative to potential. Also, there is a deemphasis on analytic thought. As a result, histrionic individuals tend to be dramatic, yet gullible and impressionable.

> *Left to their own devices, the three networks would televise live executions. Except Fox—they'd televise live naked executions.*
> —Garry David Goldberg, television producer

The Case of Hilde

Hilde is a 42-year-old homemaker who sought help from her family physician for a combination of complaints, including headaches, mild depression, and marital difficulties. The family physician had attempted to treat her with quick reassurance and Valium. When these proved ineffective, he referred her to a private psychiatrist. In the initial interview, Hilde appeared to be motivated, although at times she rambled so much that he had to bring her back to the subject at hand. As one listened to her, it became apparent that she had not really reflected in any depth on the issues that she discussed and was only pumping out information much as a computer would. She delighted in giving extensive historical descriptions of her past, again without much insight (or even interest) as to how these

had any causal role in her present distress. When confronted with any irrelevancies in her stories, she first adopted a cute and charming manner, and if this proved ineffective in persuading her psychiatrist to change topics, she became petulant and irritated.

When she described her present difficulties, she was always inclined to ascribe the responsibility to some person or situation other than herself. She stated that her husband was indifferent to her and added that she suspected he had been seduced by one of the secretaries in his office. This situation, along with a "lot of stress in my life," was given as the reason for the headaches and depression. When pressed for more details, she found it hard to describe interactions with her husband in any meaningful detail.

(continued)

The Case of Hilde Continued

A parallel interview with her husband revealed that he "had simply become tired of dealing with her." He admitted that his original attraction to Hilde was for her social status, her "liveliness," and her physical attractiveness. Over the years, it became clear that her liveliness was not the exuberance and love of life of an integrated personality, but simply a chronic flamboyance and an intensity that was often misplaced. Her physical attractiveness was naturally declining, and she was spending inordinate amounts of time and money attempting to keep it up. Her husband admitted that, when he had married her, he had been reserved and inhibited. He was a competent and hardworking individual but had had little experience with the more enjoyable aspects of life. He viewed Hilde as his ticket to a new life. Now that he had established himself on his own, and had both matured and loosened up emotionally, he had simply grown tired of her childish and superficial manner. As he put it, "I still care for her and I don't want to hurt her, but I'm just not interested in putting up with all of this stuff too much longer."

It is interesting that when Hilde was asked about her children, she immediately responded that they were both "wonderful." They were now 14 and 16 years old, and Hilde's description of them suggested that they were exceptionally bright and happy children. She was adamant about this, saying, "They are doing fine, and it's my problems that I want to deal with here." Unfortunately, her husband's description of the situation suggested that both children showed patterns analogous to Hilde's. They were both spoiled, and the oldest boy in particular had some difficulties keeping up with his schoolwork.

Hilde was raised as a prized child of a moderately wealthy family. Her father owned a successful grain and feed operation. Her mother was active socially, joining virtually every socially prominent activity in the city.

She did not have much time for Hilde, yet delighted in showing her off to guests. Hilde was one of those individuals who is born with many gifts. She had potential for high intellectual achievement, easily adapted to all the social graces, and was almost stunningly beautiful. The sad part is that the family provided few if any rewards for achievements in the intellectual area. Hilde was expected to get decent grades, but there was no incentive for high grades, and the family often made fun of others in the town who were "intellectual snobs."

Her beauty was prized, and the response it received from friends in her parents' social circle also provided her with more than simple attention. Her mother delighted in having her stay up and greet guests at their parties, something she never consistently allowed Hilde's sisters to do. Also, Hilde soon discovered that if she misbehaved, a charmingly presented "I'm sorry" to her father usually voided any punishment.

As Hilde moved into adolescence, she developed a wide circle of friends, but she never attained much depth in any one relationship. Her beauty, social grace, and high status in the community made it easy for her to flit about like a princess among her court. Males came to her as bees come to a flower. She had a reputation for being loose sexually, but it is clear this was based on hopes and rumor rather than on actual behavior. As Hilde put it, "They like the promise; you don't really have to pay off."

Throughout high school, Hilde was active as a cheerleader and as an organizer of class dances and parties. She was usually elected to be class secretary and once was the class vice president. No one ever considered her as a candidate for class president, and she herself would not have cared for the position. She had little trouble with her coursework; although she seldom spent much time preparing, she usually obtained Bs and Cs, with an occasional A. Hilde remembers her junior high and high school years as "the happiest time of my life," an assessment that is probably accurate.

Hilde's college years were not unlike her high school years, except that some notes of discord began to creep in. She had to work harder to obtain the moderate grades she had always been pleased with, and she was not always able to carry through with the required effort, particularly as she was wrapped up in sorority activities and cheerleading. She dated many people, but rarely allowed dating to get to the point of a sexual experience. When it did happen, it was more to try it out than as a result of any strong desires on her part.

After college, she took a job in a women's clothing store whose clientele were primarily the rich and fashionable. One of her customers subtly introduced Hilde to her son, Steve, a young attorney with one of the most prestigious firms in the region. He courted Hilde in whirlwind fashion. They went out almost every night, usually attending the many parties to which they were both invited. Each was enraptured by the other, and they were married five months after they met. Both families had mild reservations about the short courtship. However, since each was from "a good family," no strong objections were lodged.

Over the years, Steve's practice developed rapidly. He not only had the advantage of being with an excellent firm but he was also intelligent and hard working. Hilde meanwhile moved into many social activities, although she sometimes abruptly found that they demanded more than charm and attractiveness. In spite of her best efforts, her beauty is naturally fading, and the bloom has worn off the romance that impelled them into marriage. She and Steve seldom do anything together that involves a meaningful interaction. Most of the time he is absorbed in his work, and they go out together only on ritual social occasions. They seldom have sex, and usually only after Steve has drunk a bit too much at a party. There is not much conflict in the marriage; there is not much of anything else, either.

Etiology

The Greek physician-philosopher Hippocrates provided one of the original explanations for this pattern, holding that the unfruitful womb became angry and wandered about the body, causing hysteria. As is obvious, Hippocrates thought the disorder occurred only in women, a conception that has since proven to be inaccurate. Freud saw conflict over the expression of sexual impulses as critical (Weston, 1998). Interestingly enough, both Hippocrates and Freud prescribed marriage as the cure. As marriage would provide a legitimate outlet for sexual desires, in some cases this medicine might be effective although, as with all medicines, there are side effects, some not so desirable. In Hilde's case, marriage exaggerated the problem instead of curing it.

Hilde's background has a number of factors that facilitate the development of a histrionic personality disorder. Hilde's mother showed little interest in her, except when she wished to show Hilde off, in essence responding to her as an object. A lack of consistent maternal attention commonly produces intense strivings for paternal attention as a replacement, and this appears to have been the case with Hilde. Although her father obviously cared for her, he had little time available to attend to her. As a result, he, too, responded primarily to the superficial aspects of her being. Indeed, HPDs have often been raised in households where "showy love" and "act as if we love each other" ethics were primary, appearance was reinforced, and indeed may have been the only means effective in eliciting attention from and/or controlling the caregiver. Sickness or weakness, as long as it was not too repulsive, often was similarly effective.

In addition, both parents allowed Hilde to use her charm and physical attractiveness as an excuse for not fulfilling the responsibilities that are expected of most children. Hilde learned that charm and statements such as "I'm sorry" would suffice to deflect punishment, so she never came to see her personality and decisions as the responsible agents in the problems she naturally encountered. As she grew up, other people would often give her the same allowance, although not to the degree her parents did. The inability to examine and respond effectively to the long-term consequences of her behavior was never reinforced and developed in Hilde.

As a result, Hilde made a wide range of friendships, but none with any real depth. They were oriented around social activities but involved little self-disclosure or sharing of personal vulnerabilities. Similarly, her parents never openly manifested their own personal vulnerability. They always put forth an optimistic and cheerful facade, even when it was apparent that they were having problems in their own lives.

It is most unfortunate that Hilde's potential for intellectual competence and analytic thinking withered in the face of the type of reinforcement she received from her family. The high level of attention to her physical attractiveness and social skills stood her in good stead during her adolescence. Physical attractiveness naturally decreases with age and does not carry one through the intricacies of any long-term relationship, however. Analogously, she had long ago learned to see her sexuality as a means of interpersonal manipulation and was never able to focus on the achievement of mutual intimacy and pleasure. It is as if she saw her responsibility ending at the point a male showed initiative behaviors toward her.

Steve came from a family that emphasized status, hard work, and vocational achievement. Hilde appeared to him as a guide to a new world, one in which pleasure, intimacy, and social activity were paramount. It was only when their whirlwind courtship, extravagant wedding, and expensive honeymoon were well behind them that the bloom went off the relationship. He gradually recognized the lack of depth in their relationship, and when he attempted to talk this out with Hilde, she became upset. She accused him of not loving her and of having another woman. She also responded by trying to make herself even more attractive. She did not age gracefully, and Steve even began to think of her as "pathetic" in this regard. Their meager sexual life dissipated even further. He eventually did start to see other women. Because he still cared for Hilde in a platonic way, he attempted to keep these affairs from her, and did so rather successfully.

By this time, Hilde's father had become a kind of patriarch in the area. He was a man of great wealth who still enjoyed indulging his favorite and most beautiful daughter. Hilde emotionally moved back toward her family, although like

Steve, she kept up the facade of the marriage. She also became depressed on occasion and periodically drank too much. The cycle spiraled, as if at some level of consciousness she realized her own role in her problems, as well as her inadequacy to deal with them.

Treatment Options

Over time, the following guidelines for intervention with HPDs are indicated:

1. Reward their product, not their presentation—the opposite of their behavioral history.
2. Reward any attention to reflective thoughts or efforts toward systematization or routine behaviors—again, a real change.
3. Emphasize appropriate assertiveness and mastery behaviors.
4. Avoid the role of rescuer, understanding that you will be guided toward that role and toward feeling frustrated and/or responsible for any of the HPD's failures.
5. Avoid the demands that HPDs be treated as "special"; they expect it.
6. Writing assignments help to develop analytic and problem-solving thought patterns (usually sorely lacking) and attention to detail.
7. The HPD needs to challenge such common underlying beliefs as (a) "Unless my emotions at least appear intense, they won't mean anything to others (and eventually even to me)," (b) "Being responsible or attending to details means the loss of 'zest for life,'" (c) "Rejection is disastrous," (d) "People won't love me for what I do but for what I pretend to be, or what I present to entertain/entice them," or (e) "Being 'special' means never having to say 'I'm sorry' (or at least I don't have to feel it or mean it)."

In Hilde's case, the first and most difficult task was to gain her trust. To that end, several sessions were held in which the therapist adopted a posture not unlike that employed with the paranoid individual. He listened to Hilde's discussion with empathy, yet at the same time bemusedly offered alternative explanations for her behavior. He did not confront her directly, as it had been her lifelong pattern, probably both as a result of temperament and parent training, to run away from any confrontation.

As trust developed, other therapeutic modes were tried in order to help Hilde's defenses gradually lessen. Bibliotherapy, or the reading of certain prescribed books, was used. She was asked to read various novels and plays that portrayed individuals who had grown up feeling as if they were appreciated for external rather than any ongoing essential personality factors. Of course, some of these individuals had developed coping strategies that were not unlike Hilde's. The works of Tennessee Williams, Edward Albee, and Jean Genet convey these concepts quite well. Hilde was then asked to write her own poetry or short stories that focused on characters who developed similar defenses. This led eventually to the use of role playing. Her therapist would take the role of Hilde's mother, for example, and Hilde would play herself in some typical childhood interaction. Since it is also effective to role play the opposite roles, at times Hilde would play her mother, and the therapist would play Hilde as a child. This role playing was expanded to include interactions with her father, her husband, and some of her friends.

Unfortunately, at approximately this time Hilde's husband told her that he had fallen in love with another woman and wanted a divorce. He refused to consider marital therapy, said that his decision had functionally been made long ago, and that he had waited only to find a woman with whom he could really become involved. Hilde made a mild suicide gesture, overdosing on a small bottle of aspirin, obviously hoping to manipulate her husband's decision. She was unsuccessful.

At this time, it was recommended to Hilde that she also enter group therapy (Saiger et al., 2008). Her first reactions were that "those people won't understand me" and "I don't have really bad problems like they do." After working through her defensiveness in this regard, the therapist asked Hilde to commit to go to at least three sessions. It was agreed that if Hilde felt as if she could not continue after that, she could leave the group. Hilde made the contract and went for the three sessions. Fortunately, the group was supportive of her—something she needed at this point, particularly because of the divorce. It is also ironically probable that Hilde enjoyed this forum in which she could dramatically replay many of the events in her life. She started to attend the group regularly and began to improve her ability to confront the responsibility she had for the events that happened in her life. She felt she could stop seeing her individual therapist, though at her last contact with her, Hilde was still struggling substantially with the problems of her world.

> *All universal moral principles are idle fancies.*
> —Marquis de Sade, *The 120 Days of Sodom* (1785)

The Antisocial Personality Disorder

The essential characteristic of the antisocial personality disorder (ASP) is the chronic manifestation of antisocial behavior patterns in amoral and impulsive persons. Persons with ASP are usually unable to delay gratification or to deal effectively with authority, and they show narcissism in interpersonal relationships. The pattern is apparent by mid-adolescence (usually earlier) and continues into adult life with consistency across a wide performance spectrum, including school, vocational, and interpersonal behaviors (Meyer & Weaver, 2006; Hare, Hart, & Harpur, 1991; Lykken, 1995).

DSM-IV-TR

The *DSM-IV-TR* term *Antisocial Personality Disorder* has evolved through a variety of terms and now supersedes the terms *psychopathic* and *sociopathic*, at least in formal diagnostic labeling. Pritchard's introduction of the term *moral insanity* in 1835 is considered by many to be the first clear forerunner to the present APD label. *Psychopath* first emerged in the label *psychopathic inferiority*, introduced by Koch late in the nineteenth century (Cleckley, 1964).

Terms incorporating psychopath were common until the *DSM-I*, published in 1952, used *Sociopathic Personality*. The *DSM-II*, in 1968, introduced the term *Antisocial Personality*, which is used in the *DSM-IV-TR*.

To apply the ASP diagnosis, the *DSM-IV-TR* requires that the individual be 18 years old, there is evidence that warrants an earlier diagnosis of Conduct Disorder, onset is before the age of 15, and a pervasive pattern of disregard or violation of others is evidenced by at least three of the following: (1) failure to conform to sociolegal norms, as denoted by repeated acts that are grounds for arrest; (2) irritability and aggressiveness, as seen in repeated fights or assaults; (3) consistent irresponsibility in work or financial obligations; (4) impulsivity or failure to plan ahead; (5) deceitfulness, as indicated in lying or conning; (6) reckless disregard for one's own or other's safety; or (7) lack of remorse. This category, as it is formulated in *DSM-IV-TR*, is probably best conceptualized as "a deviant child grown up." According to the *DSM-IV-TR*, the prevalence of APD in community samples is close to 3 percent in males and 1 percent in females.

> *When a man says he approves of something in principle, he means he hasn't the slightest intention of putting it into practice.*
>
> —Prince Bismarck of Germany

The Case of Theodore Bundy

Theodore (Ted) Bundy was born on November 24, 1946, in Burlington, Vermont. The illegitimate child never knew his father, nor did he remember ever wondering about him. Bundy spent his first three years in Philadelphia, where he remembered his grandfather with adoration. At age 4, he moved to Tacoma, Washington, to live with his uncles and family. Bundy was extremely upset when he and his mother moved away, leaving his grandfather behind. His mother met Johnnie Bundy, who worked at a local military base as a cook, at a church activity. His quiet, southern style attracted her to him. Like any child, Bundy reacted to his mother's romance with jealousy. In 1952, after Bundy's mother and Johnnie Bundy were married, they had their first child. Later, they had three more children. All Bundy knew about babies was that his mother's pregnancy had something to do with Johnnie Bundy and that his mother suffered extremely while giving birth.

Bundy idolized his first-grade teacher, and she wrote superlative evaluations of Bundy and his academic skills. When this teacher left to have a baby, Bundy was very upset. His second-grade teacher, however, was a different story. He despised her, and remembers her breaking a ruler over his hand because he had punched a schoolmate in the face during lunch. The peculiar sense of unease that Bundy later identified as growing into the "entity" that murders was already felt then, at age 7. He described it as simply a disturbing uneasiness.

Throughout his school years, Bundy did well in school, always receiving As in major projects. He recalled fondly his mother helping

(continued)

The Case of Theodore Bundy Continued

him with his homework, and he attributed his scholastic success to her diligent efforts. There was never any discussion between Bundy and his mother about personal matters such as sex. He felt that his mother just couldn't be open with him. He described his mother as someone who didn't enjoy socializing or gossiping with others. She never discussed her childhood, either. However, right after high school, Bundy's mother had become pregnant by a man who came and left. Bundy's status as illegitimate haunted him throughout his life, abetted by his mother's evident resentment.

Bundy went to Sunday school every week through high school. He studied the Bible extensively, but felt he retained none of it. He was politically oriented and remembers telling his mother about the hypocrisy of Christianity. His parents neither smoked nor drank. Johnnie Bundy, despite his quiet nature, had a violent temper when provoked.

From early on, Bundy often chose to be alone. He was enthralled with his radio and spent his spare time listening to it. In later years, Bundy found it difficult to integrate socially. When he was a child, Bundy would investigate neighborhood trash cans to find pictures of naked women. He took part in few organized sports activities because he felt that they were too serious and that he was too small. His stepfather never attended Bundy's games, and his mother disliked the sports because they cost money. Bundy found it traumatic when he could not get on the baseball and basketball teams. As a result, he became proficient at skiing. Bundy established a ticket forgery system that allowed him to ski free of charge. He was never caught.

Obsessed with material possessions, Bundy fantasized about being adopted by married movie stars Roy Rogers and Dale Evans, who would give him his own pony. He felt humiliated to be seen in his family's economy car. Instead of any physical or emotional abuse, Bundy depicted his childhood home life as empty. He felt overlooked and forgotten.

In junior high, Bundy had some friends and went to a few parties, but he failed to acquire good social skills. Unlike his experience in junior high, Bundy became shy and introverted in high school. He saw himself as a serious student who did not enjoy drinking. Others saw him as arrogant. In high school, Bundy never got into significant trouble. He felt inept with girls and had only one date during high school. Because his family had limited income, he always felt inferior to others who had more material possessions.

As a senior, Bundy volunteered to work in a local political race. A few years later, he drove the Republican candidate for lieutenant governor, and later he worked to help elect a candidate for governor. Through his political efforts, Bundy found friends with whom he could socialize.

Bundy described himself as having an entity in him that was not separate, which he sometimes referred to as "the malignant being," that compelled him to kill. He asserted that his desire during the killings was not the violence itself but that he wanted to have full possession of the victim. The sex was not extreme, and he claimed to have spared the victims as much pain as he could. The "entity" grew slowly within him, becoming stronger and more powerful after every deviant act. Of course, since Bundy was perceived by most experts to be a pathological liar, at least in adulthood, everything he said at that time that is not corroborated by collateral data has to be taken with a grain of salt.

Bundy's first documented murder occurred in Seattle in January 1974, where he smashed Sharon Clarke's head with a rod while she slept in her bed. After a lengthy coma, she survived, with no memory of the event. Sharon was a stranger to Bundy, and no explanation was ever given for the attack. Within weeks, a college student living a few blocks from Sharon, Lynda Ann Healy, disappeared. Thereafter, over a period of seven months, young women disappeared with appalling regularity. From March through June 1974, four more female college students disappeared while attending a concert or a movie, leaving a bar, or simply walking across campus.

On July 14, 1974, Bundy approached several young women with his arm in a sling, asking them to help him put a sailboat on top of his car. One woman went with him to his car, but when he said she needed to go with him in his car to get the boat, she refused. Others also refused. But Janice Ott agreed to help him, and she was never seen again. The same day, another young woman who was in the public washroom at the same lake disappeared. The remains of these and other unidentified women were later found in a forest near the lake. The killing spree continued in full force through October 1974. His victims tended to be college-age, white, attractive, and have long hair parted in the middle.

In November 1974, a young woman who believed Bundy was a police detective agreed to get into his car. After Bundy placed one handcuff on her, she screamed and fought her way out of the car. She caught a crowbar mid-air with which he tried to smash her skull, and she leapt in front of an oncoming car, which stopped and picked her up, and she escaped. The very same day, Bundy abducted and killed another victim and approached a third woman who turned him down.

In January 1975, Bundy began killing in Colorado. One woman was taken from her bed while sleeping; another disappeared on her way to meet a girlfriend in a bar; a third victim was found fully clothed except for her pulled-down jeans. More women disappeared—one from a gas station, another from a mine shaft. Finally, on August 16, 1975, Bundy was arrested for driving suspiciously slowly down a street and refusing to stop when ordered by an officer in a patrol car. The police found a hair in his car matching one of the victims, and a witness said he saw Bundy the night another victim disappeared. Bundy was tried for murder in Aspen, Colorado.

Bundy's charm, intelligence, sense of humor, and good looks soon convinced those in charge of him that he was special. He was exceptionally cooperative, and his captors showed him every courtesy, such as special health foods and no physical restraints when he attended court. Because he insisted on defending himself, he was provided law books as requested. During pretrial hearings, Bundy was allowed to wander through the Aspen law library as he pleased. It should have come as no surprise when he jumped out of a library window and escaped. Eight days later, he was recaptured and kept under heavy guard.

Bundy testified that he was a victim of circumstances and that there was no clear proof that he committed any of the murders. He also contended that many men had his same physical description. His legal skills helped him delay the case as he filed numerous motions. During this time, he lost weight and, with a hacksaw, carved a hole around the light fixture in his prison cell. He squeezed through a 12-inch opening and escaped again. From Aspen, Bundy went to Chicago, Michigan, and Atlanta, and then decided to stay when he reached Tallahassee, Florida, a few blocks from Florida State University sorority houses.

On January 15, 1978, five young women in a sorority house were severely beaten. Two of them died. They were bludgeoned, and at least two were raped. One month later, a 12-year-old girl disappeared after leaving her school. She was found strangled to death with her sexual organs mutilated. Bundy had been living under the pseudonym of Chris Hagen and survived by stealing a car and using stolen credit cards. On February 15, 1978, a police officer, suspicious of the slow, prowling manner that Bundy was driving at 1:30 A.M., began following him. As the officer was checking on his radio to learn if Bundy's vehicle was stolen, he turned on the car's blue pursuit light. Instead of stopping, Bundy accelerated, and then finally stopped. The officer ordered him to lie on the ground, and, just as one handcuff had been secured, Bundy knocked down the officer and ran. Eventually, the officer again had Bundy restrained. Bundy was arrested, and although he identified himself as

(continued)

The Case of Theodore Bundy Continued

Kenneth Raymond Misner, it did not take long to discover that he was the Ted Bundy wanted for murder in Colorado.

Bundy adamantly claimed innocence. One severely incriminating piece of evidence was matching his teeth with the teeth marks on the buttocks of one of his victims. At trial in Florida for two of the murders, Bundy again displayed his charm and intelligence before the jury. When he was found guilty and twice sentenced to death, the judge told him he would have made a good lawyer. When asked about Bundy as a child, his closest friends could think of nothing showing him to be anything other than quiet, bright, witty, handsome, and serious-minded. Bundy was flooded with attention from those wishing to interview him to find out what he was like. Using his legal skills and then over a long period almost teasingly admitting to 23 more murders, Bundy was able to keep himself alive for 10 years with his appeals. His charm continued, as he had many offers of marriage while in prison, and even fathered a child during that time. He died in the electric chair on January 24, 1989, in Florida. When those standing outside of the prison heard of his death, the crowd cheered, setting off firecrackers in celebration.

Bundy is a classic case of a high Factor 1 psychopath (see following discussion)—that is, high on the indices of true psychopathy. The major ways in which his case is atypical for psychopaths are (1) his higher level of intelligence (despite the myth of the bright psychopath, most are less intelligent than comparable normals) and (2) few indices of psychopathy early in life. This lack of early evidence may be explained by the fact that he was not under enough scrutiny, his mother probably covered for some of his deviance, and/or his intelligence allowed him to hide some of it. There is some evidence for an alternate explanation—that he was much more deviant earlier than has been assumed. First, there is some evidence that he often masturbated while peeping at women in the neighborhood as they undressed. Second, one of his biographers, Ann Rule (1999), tells a story about how, when Bundy was approximately 14 or 15 years old, an 8-year-old girl in his neighborhood disappeared from her first-floor bedroom and was never found. Bundy knew the little girl, and her house was on his paper route. Rule says that later, when Bundy was in jail, she asked him if he was responsible for that. He said "No," and then grinned and smirked.

Related Diagnostic-Etiological Considerations

In the nineteenth century, Caesare Lombroso advanced the theory that criminals manifest distinct physical markers, such as a low forehead. Although the theory has been discredited, much modern research (Bartol & Bartol, 2008; DiLalla, 2004; Lykken, 1995) supports the idea that biological factors, especially those that are derived genetically, influence the production of criminality, antisocial personality disorder, and, epecially, psychopathy. For example, even by the age of 2 weeks, babies are more alert and exploratory if they have a "novelty-seeking" gene that may influence sensation-seeking in adults. Babies with the gene DRD4 were more likely to follow a red ball with their eyes, respond to a human face, and pay attention to the sound of a rattle than were other babies. The novelty-seeking gene is controversial because some studies have failed to find a link to personality, whereas others have indicated connections to antisocial behaviors, addiction, and hyperactivity.

It is unclear how these biological factors translate into specific behaviors. Possibilities include deficits in specific types of intelligence or learning skills, brain dysfunctions, neurohormonal disorders, and so on. For example, Robert Hare (Hare, Hart, & Harpur, 1991) views psychopaths as language disordered at a neurological level; hence, they are weak at processing the emotional meaning of words. Others point to psychological factors as primary, such as patterns of parenting (i.e., arguing that harsh or abusive parenting or even permissive parenting can facilitate psychopathy, especially in predisposed individuals).

One major difference theoretically is between those like Hare who view psychopathy as stemming from some "defect" causing one to be "born bad" or "defective," and those (namely, Lykken [1995]) who view psychopaths as "born difficult." In the latter theory, a particular constellation of "normal" characteristics is inherited that predisposes one to psychopathy, and the degree and direction of disorder are then determined by how often and how intensely the factors occur, and/or the type of parenting received. I have devised the FUMES acronym to describe such characteristics:

Fearless

Unresponsive to pain

Mesomorphic (muscular)

Empathy-deficient

Stimulation-seeking

Although these can be reasonably termed "normal" characteristics, they require skill—indeed, great skill—in parenting in order to develop a conscience, prosocial habits, success in a standard classroom, avoidance of using power to manipulate others, and so on. In an environment with models for aggression, sexual or physical abuse, dishonesty, substance abuse, deviant sexual patterns, and the like, the flavor of the psychopathic "stew" is set into a particular direction.

The most influential modern conceptualization has viewed psychopathy as composed of two main factors (1 = Affective-Cognitive Instability, 2 = Behavioral-Social Deviance) (Hare, Hart, & Harpur, 1991). This view has helped generate and, in turn, has been facilitated by Hare's Psychopathy Checklist-Revised (PCL-R), a 20-item assessment technique that uses self-report and interview observation data, which are then cross-checked with collateral information. There has been considerable debate in the research literature about whether the material covered by the PCL-R could be better explained by three or even four factors (four factors now being favored by Hare), rather than the traditional two. However, in each of these scenarios factor 1 is similar to the traditional concept, and is most reflective of true psychopathy.

The following components contribute to factor 1 (the Affective-Cognitive Instability): glibness, a grandiose sense of self, pathological lying, conning-manipulative behaviors, lack of remorse, shallow affect, callousness and lack of empathy, and failure to accept responsibility. Components of the Behavioral-Social Deviance (factor 2) are a higher need for stimulation, a parasitic lifestyle, poor behavioral controls, early behavior problems, lack of realistic goals, impulsivity, irresponsibility, having been adjudicated delinquent, and a history of violating supervision or probation.

In general, research (Bartol & Bartol, 2008; Hare, Hart, & Harpur, 1991; Lykken, 1995) on the psychopath (much of which includes use of the PCL-R) indicates:

1. Although there is a decrease in criminal activity for psychopaths at about ages 40 to 45, this effect holds primarily for nonviolent crimes. There is only a slight decrease for violent crimes.
2. Concomitantly, while the Behavioral-Social Deviance factor starts to drop off somewhere in the age range of 35 to 45, the Affective-Cognitive Instability factor (closer to true "psychopathy") lessens only slightly with age.
3. Similarly, the Behavioral-Social Deviance factor 2 is a good predictor of general criminality and recidivism, is highly correlated with criminality, and is negatively correlated with socioeconomic status and, to a lesser degree, IQ. Factor 1 is a better predictor of violence, but it is virtually uncorrelated with socioeconomic status and IQ.
4. Although treatment may effect a positive change in the average criminal, it seldom does so with psychopaths, especially to the degree they are strong on factor 1, as was Ted Bundy. Indeed, there is evidence that psychopaths who are high on factor 1 may in some instances get worse with treatment, thus group and individual psychotherapy can be a "finishing school" for psychopaths (Rice, Harris, & Cormier, 1992). True to their nature, true psychopaths seem to learn little about themselves in therapy, but learn more about others, and then more boldly use such information. At least in part this is because they are language disordered, such that the emotional components of language are weak or missing, voiding the likelihood of empathy or remorse.
5. In general, socioeconomic and family background variables are good predictors of general criminal behavior, but they are relatively nonpredictive for psychopathy, especially where it is loaded on the Affective-Cognitive Instability factor.
6. Expect high factor 1s to be deceptive about virtually anything they report. To the degree feasible, independent corroboration of any critical questions about history or present behaviors is necessary (Boyd et al., 2007).

> *Identifying criminals is up to each of us. Usually they can be recognized by their large cufflinks and their failure to stop eating when the man next to them is hit by a falling anvil.*
>
> —Woody Allen, comedian and filmmaker

Proposed "Common Path" for the Development of Psychopathy

As described by Meyer (Meyer & Brothers, 2001; Meyer & Weaver, 2007), the following is an outline of the evolution of the psychopath-antisocial personality disorder:

Preexisting Risk Factors
1. Biological (genetic, prenatal, birth, or early childhood) disruption
2. Low SES (socioeconomic status)
3. Family history of vocational-social-interpersonal dysfunction
4. Family history of psychopathy
5. Characteristics of a FUMES child (see page 213) (i.e., fearless, unresponsive to pain, mesomorphic, empathy-deficient, stimulation-seeking)

From Birth to School Age
1. Child temperament factors
   a. Child's lack of emotional responsiveness and lack of social interest foster rejecting responses from parents
   b. Child's high activity levels may cause parental annoyance and elicit punitive responses
   c. Lack of responsiveness to physical punishment, emotional "numbness," and deficit in associating emotion in language learning result in failing to learn behavioral contingencies and the consequences of destructive behaviors on others
2. Parental factors
   a. Inconsistent parenting results in child's failing to learn behavioral contingencies
   b. Aggressive, punitive parenting and/or family interaction result in child's modeling aggression, experiencing hostility, becoming enured to punishing consequences, and developing a repressive defensive style (emotional "hardness")
3. Parent/child interaction
   a. Unreliable parenting, along with defective "expressed emotion," results in insecure attachment (i.e., interpersonally "avoidant" attachment style); child "goes it alone" rather than risk rejection and disappointment associated with unreliable and/or abusive parents
4. Environmental factors (can occur anytime during life span)
   a. High exposure from the media, to models (often likeable models) of violence, amorality, and a variety of other deviant behaviors can lead to imitation or at least disinhibition
   b. Although not common, toxic levels of heavy metals, especially lead, facilitate antisocial-aggressive patterns
   c. Although not common, trauma and/or disease that results in some forms of brain disorder, especially frontal lobe damage and especially if it occurs at a very young age, can facilitate a loss of inhibitory behaviors

School Age to Adolescence
1. Predisposing personality factors
   a. Low baseline level of brain stem arousal (i.e., Eysenck's biological extra-version) contributes to impulsive, undercontrolled, and stimulation-seeking behavior
   b. A combination of distorted physiological arousal, repressive psychody-namics, and habitual "numbness" to social contingencies results in child being insensitive to and unable to "condition" to environmental events; therefore, the child does not learn or "profit" from experience and does not relate to the experiences of others
   c. Mesomorphic (muscular) and energetic components lead to increased physical manipulation/control of others, and, along with stimulation seek-ing, lead to increased risk taking
   d. Commonly correlated Attention-Deficit Hyperactivity Disorder and/or "soft" neurological disorder may exacerbate behavior problems
2. Personality development
   a. Peer/teacher labeling may result in self-fulfilling prophecy effects
   b. School failure and social failure result in sense of inferiority and increased interpersonal hostility; child develops "moving against" interpersonal style
   c. Initial forays into antisociality (e.g., theft, fire setting, interpersonal vio-lence) occur, often with some "success"; evidence for diagnosis of conduct disorder mounts

Adolescence
1. The young psychopath hones exploitative style in order to express hostility and "rise above" feelings of inferiority; "proves superiority" by hoodwink-ing and humiliating teachers, parents, and peers
2. Continued antisocial behavior results in initial scrapes with the law
3. Increased use of physical and psychological aggression to control others
4. Physiological impulsivity, inability to profit from experience
5. A disordered cognitive-attentional style and interpersonal hostility and antagonism combine to make repeated legal offenses highly probable
6. Contact with other antisocials in the context of juvenile-criminal camps or prison results in "criminal education"; increased criminality results, accom-panied by a loss of the "time in place" that eventually brings accrued benefits to those who stay in the "mainstream" of life; criminal and antisocial behav-ior become a lifestyle at which the psychopath can "excel"

Adulthood
1. Antisocial behavior escalates through the psychopath's late twenties; increas-ingly frequent failure, rejection by others, and/or incarceration result in increased hostility and hardened feelings
2. Unable to profit from experience, lacking in insight and empathy, and unable to form therapeutic bonds, the psychopath becomes a poor therapy-rehab risk and bad news for society

3. There is a crystallization of these underlying cognitive beliefs:
   a. Rationalization: "My desiring something justifies whatever actions I need to take"
   b. The devaluing of others: "The attitudes and needs of others don't affect me, unless responding to them will provide me an advantage, and if they are hurt by me, I need not feel responsible for what happens to them"
   c. Low-impact consequences: "My choices are inherently good. As such, I won't experience undesirable consequences, or if they occur, they won't really matter to me"
   d. Entitlement: "I have to think of myself first; I'm entitled to what I want or feel I need, and if necessary, I can use force or deception to obtain those goals"
   e. Rule-avoidance: "Rules constrict me from fulfilling my needs"
4. Antisocial behavior decreases or "burns out" unevenly beginning in the mid-thirties (although less so with violent offenses); this may be due to lengthier incarcerations, to changes in age-related metabolic factors that formerly contributed to sensation-seeking and impulsive behavior, or perhaps to decrements in the strength and stamina required to engage in persistent criminal endeavors

Treatment Options

The treatment problem with all the personality disorders—getting the client to agree to therapy and then to become meaningfully involved—is acute with ASP, and success is rare. As the British prime minister William Gladstone (1809–1898) put it, "The disease of an evil conscience is beyond the practice of all the physicians of all the countries in the world," and this seems to include psychologists and psychiatrists as well.

A variety of treatment possibilities have been suggested as appropriate for the ASP. However, like Bundy, most have no interest in changing their behavior and are in a treatment program only because they have been forced by circumstances (Rice, Harns, & Cormier, 1992). Some antisocial personalities, usually those with less factor 1 psychopathy, are changed as a result of treatment, and, as noted, there are some changes as a result of aging. The great majority, however, are not changed markedly by either their environment or by treatment techniques (Bartol & Bartol, 2008).

The Schizoid Personality Disorder

People with schizoid personality disorder (SPD) are asocial, shy, introverted, and significantly defective in their ability to form social relationships and are usually described as loners. The essential feature of this disorder is impairment in the ability to form adequate social relationships; as author Joan Didion states in *The White Album*, they are "only marginally engaged in the dailiness of life" (p. 121). These individuals typically have difficulty directly expressing hostility and have withdrawn from most social contacts. But, unlike that of agoraphobia (see Chapter 3), the behavior is ego-syntonic—that is, the person is essentially accepting of it.

Usually, SPDs show shyness, although the concept of introversion may be more applicable. There is at least an element of avoidance of people because of fear-anxiety embedded in the concept of shyness, whereas introversion is more clearly a preference for avoidance of others. As a result of this introversion, SPDs gravitate to jobs that require solitude, such as work as a night guard. As they age or become vocationally dysfunctional, they are likely to move into a hermit-like existence or a "skid row," particularly if they are males. Even though they excessively fantasize and communicate in peculiar ways, they show no loss of contact with reality.

> *I think of him as a misguided very quixotic romantic figure of another era. . . .*
> *It's not that I'm sympathetic. I just feel I understand him.*
> —Joyce Carol Oates, author, commenting on Theodore
> Kaczynski, in the *New York Observer*

The Case of Theodore Kaczynski

Theodore John Kaczynski was apprehended by the FBI on April 3, 1996, and charged with being the "Unabomber," so named because many of the bomb attacks were directed to university-related persons or places. His 17-year endeavor, including 16 incidents resulting in three deaths and 23 wounded and maimed, first came to public notice on May 25, 1978, when a package found in a parking lot at the University of Illinois in Chicago was taken to Northwestern University because of the return address. It exploded the next day, injuring one person. The last known attack occurred on April 24, 1995, when a mail bomb was delivered to the Sacramento headquarters of the California Forestry Association, killing the president of the association, Gilbert Murray, when he attempted to open it. Kaczynski eventually received four life terms in a plea bargain that allowed him to avoid the death penalty.

Despite an elaborate intensive manhunt over 17 years, including the storing of at least 12 million bytes of information in computer databases, the efforts of a special 80-person task force of FBI, ATF, and Postal Service agents, extensive psychological profiling, and a sighting by an eyewitness, Kaczynski's apprehension came about only when his sister-in-law, Linda, began to suspect Ted might be the Unabomber. Subsequently, her husband, Ted's brother David, recognized parts of the 35,000-word manifesto published by the *New York Times* and the *Washington Post* as similar to writings of his brother that he came across at their mother's house, and turned Ted in.

David and Linda had already developed concerns about Ted's mental health. In a *60 Minutes* interview on September 15, 1996, David and Linda said that in 1991 they had taken two of Ted's letters to a psychiatrist, who said Ted was disturbed and could be violent. Civil commitment was considered, but they thought it would not be feasible. Later, they did contact a physician in Montana, presumably Ted's, and asked him to get Ted into psychotherapy, but nothing came of that.

Theodore Kaczynski was born on May 22, 1942. Even as a young child, Kaczynski was quiet and reclusive, but his early childhood was unremarkable, with apparently loving parents. His mother is said to have spent long hours reading passages from *Scientific American* to him when he was very young. He and his family were withdrawn socially. She did report concern that he played next to rather than with other children when he was a young boy, and she considered enrolling him in a study of autistic children. Instead, she depended on advice from Dr. Spock. A neighbor commented on the Kaczynski children, "They didn't mingle with the people on our street." He added that Ted didn't play with the other kids and would never respond to a hello.

Kaczynski graduated from Evergreen Park High School in a white, middle-class suburb of Chicago in three years. He was hardly remembered by most of his classmates. What perceptions do exist view him as quiet and reclusive, although he had been a member of the German, math, and biology clubs. He was remembered as a teenager for having a high interest in pyrotechnics and explosives. Yet, while he liked blowing things up, he never directly hurt anyone, and was not remembered as angry or sullen, but rather as shy and very immature.

A National Merit Scholarship finalist, at age 16 Kaczynski went on scholarship to Harvard University. He graduated just after he turned 20 years old. He earned only average grades and participated in no activities. For three years he lived in a seven-man suite in Eliot House, a Harvard dorm. One suitemate commented, "I don't recall 10 words being spoken to him in the three years." He apparently took some graduate courses at both Northwestern University and the University of Chicago, and then received a master's degree in mathematics in 1964 and a Ph.D. in 1967 from the University of Michigan. Somewhat ironically, his dissertation was titled "Boundary Functions." His professors generally remembered him as very bright, serious, and quiet. He published several outstanding journal articles before graduating.

While at the University of Michigan, Kaczynski visited a psychiatrist in 1966 to discuss the possibility of a sex change. But he felt humiliated about this in the waiting room and talked about other issues the psychiatrist saw as unremarkable. Although not likely to have ever been a true transsexual, he was evidently confused about his sexuality—not surprising, given his apparent lack of intimacy with anyone. After this meeting, Kaczynski wrote in his diary, "Why not really kill that psychiatrist and anyone else whom I hate?" This chronic anger evidently fueled his later actions. He had some other sporadic contacts with mental health professionals over the years, usually insomnia, concerns about meeting women, and/or mild depression.

Kaczynski's potentially brilliant future continued with his acceptance of an assistant professorship of mathematics at the University of California at Berkeley for the 1967–68 school year. But two factors melded to seemingly produce a major life change.

First, he was apparently unsuccessful in his role as a professor. He was reportedly a poor teacher and received some terrible evaluations, including the comment, "He absolutely refuses to answer questions by completely ignoring the students." He continued to be a loner; so again, most people's recollections of him are vague. Second was his high level of political activism in the 1960s. Certainly, Kaczynski was exposed to much of this at Berkeley. In this particular hotbed of radicalism, he had to have witnessed a wide variety of protests and riots, including the infamous People's Park riot of May 1969, which occurred one month before he resigned from his post at Berkeley, on June 30, 1969. Kaczynski lived only a few blocks from the People's Park, and that conflict was related to a number of environmental-social concerns. There was little evidence of radical concerns and ideas in Kaczynski prior to Berkeley. It was not unusual for disenchanted Berkeley activists to give up on society and "move back to the land," which is what Kaczynski eventually did in Montana. However, he strongly opposed various political views, and the focus in his attacks was on genetic engineering, airplanes, and computers.

(continued)

The Case of Theodore Kaczynski Continued

Kaczynski never gave anyone clear reasons for his resignation. As usual, information is sketchy. It is known that he lived in Utah and Montana in the 1970s and 1980s. His Harvard class's twentieth-anniversary report in 1982 listed his address as 788 Bauchat Pass, Khadar Khel, Afghanistan. No such place exists. He subsisted by way of odd jobs, menial labor, and a simple lifestyle. In 1990, his father, Theodore R. Kaczynski, who managed a small business, committed suicide after being diagnosed with cancer. There is no evidence that this had any significant effect on his son one way or another.

Eventually, Kaczynski settled into a spartan, mountainside cabin near the tiny town of Lincoln, Montana, on 1.4 acres purchased by him and his brother in 1971. The 10 foot × 12 foot cabin had a table, two chairs, a narrow bunk, and a woodburning stove, but no electricity, indoor plumbing, or phone. He grew some of his own food; hunted rabbits, squirrels, and porcupines for food; and about once a week, spent approximately $5 for provisions at the Blackfoot Market in Lincoln. He traveled on a dilapidated, one-speed bicycle, pieced together from mismatched parts, even occasionally riding 50 miles into Helena, Montana. He didn't drink or smoke; his only leisure activity was reading, as he frequented discount bookstores and the Lincoln library. Kaczynski rarely spoke more than a few polite words to anyone. He

was in part supported by periodic checks from his mother and received some money from his brother.

Shortly before he was apprehended, Kaczynski's life appeared to be fragmenting. His clothing was even more dirty and disheveled than before, if that was possible, and he looked depressed. Although he usually paid his property taxes on his 1.4 acres and cabin on time, he missed the November 30, 1995, deadline, and probably still owes $114.27. He even asked the owner of the Blackfoot Market for a job but was turned down. As far as anyone can remember, his last formal employment was in 1981.

In January 1998, Kaczynski was found competent to stand trial. Almost immediately thereafter, on January 22, 1998, he pled guilty to all federal charges stemming from the bombings, accepting the conditions that he would never be released and that he could not profit from his crimes. His attorneys stated that their client could not endure a trial that would portray him as, in Kaczynski's words, a "sickie." He received four life sentences plus 30 years and was immediately sent to Supermax, the so-called Alcatraz of the Rockies, in Florence, Colorado. There, he joined such noted felons as Oklahoma City bomber Timothy McVeigh; Ramzi Yousef, mastermind of the original World Trade Center bombing in 1993; and Charles Harrelson, the hitman father of celebrity Woody Harrelson.

Etiology and Diagnosis

Other diagnoses also likely applied to Kaczynski at various times, especially toward the end of his Unabomber career. However, the schizoid personality disorder (SPD) pattern was apparently lifelong. It is generally accepted that, of all the personality disorders, the SPD is one wherein substantial determination of behavior by genetic factors is clearest. The parallel research on introversion and shyness similarly points to a high genetic component (DiLalla, 2004). There are indications of at least mild schizoid tendencies in other Kaczynski family members. For example, David enjoyed spending long periods of time living in a tent outdoors, and for a time lived in a more remote part of Montana than did his brother.

In addition to the genetic predisposition toward shyness and introversion, Kaczynski's mother's general parental strategy to allow and even strongly facilitate intellectual, academic, and/or isolating behaviors turned out to be a factor. In Ted's Unabomber manifesto, he wrote, "It isn't natural for an adolescent human being to spend the bulk of his time sitting at a desk absorbed in study." Also, three specific situations may have contributed. When Ted was 9 months old, a severe allergy resulting in hives required that he be hospitalized for a week, and, as was customary in those days, he was allowed virtually no contact with any of his family. His family reports that he became much more unresponsive and withdrawn after that experience. Also, when Ted was age 7, his brother was born, and all reports are that Ted reacted very strongly to the consequent loss of attention. Their aunt commented that Ted used to snuggle up and talk to her, but he stopped doing that after David's birth. Ironically, David eventually received the million-dollar award for the information that led to Ted's arrest. Ted subsequently called him "Judas." In addition, when he was allowed to skip the sixth grade, an already emotionally immature boy was now even further distanced from potentially interacting with a peer group. A few years later, Ted skipped another grade, furthering the process.

Similarly, in the area of heterosexual relationships, Ted never developed emotionally. He never dated or even socialized with girls in grade school or high school. Just after his high school graduation, Ted had one or two dates with a girl, but he ended the relationship by expressing exasperation with her Catholic beliefs. There is no indication of any other consistent heterosexual socializing of any sort until 1974, when he made an overture to a 19-year-old waitress he worked with at the Kibbey Corner Truck Stop in Lincoln, Montana. She had no idea he had an interest in her until after she left the job and returned to school. Ted's first letter-overture invited her to move with him to Canada and be his squaw. A second letter contained a resumé, almost as if he were making a date application.

His next romantic foray, and in some ways his most successful, was in 1978, at age 36, about four months after the first Unabomber attack. He approached his work supervisor, Ellen Tormichael, when he happened to see her pumping gas at a store. He went with her to her apartment and played cards with her and her sister and her boyfriend. They had two dates, but she then told him she didn't want to see him again. Ted's brother, David, reported that Ted became very depressed, and, just as an emotionally immature adolescent might react, he wrote an insulting limerick about her and anonymously posted copies in lavatories and walls around the factory where they worked and in which his brother and father had managerial positions. Ironically, and possibly prophetically, he forced his brother to fire him by coming up to David at a water cooler and, as David watched, posting a copy on the wall in front of David. David told him to go home, and he was not allowed to return to work there. That's about it for this area of his social life.

As is characteristic of SPDs, Kaczynski never showed any evidence of directly confrontive aggression. Actually, most people with SPD don't even show high levels of passive aggression, in part because they usually show such low levels of overall interpersonal contact. In addition to the Unabomber activities, Kaczynski showed other patterns of "distant" and impersonal aggression as well as paranoid concerns—for example, see the following letter reportedly sent on October 1, 1974, to Joe Visocan, retired owner of the Kibbey Corner Truck Stop:

> Dear, sweet Joe:
>
> You fat con-man. You probably think I treated you badly by quitting without notice, but it's your own fault. You gave me this big cock-and-bull story about how much money I could make selling tires and all that crap. "The sky's the limit" and so forth. If you had been honest with me I would not have taken the job in the first place; but if I hadn't taken it, I wouldn't have quit without giving you a couple of weeks notice. Anyhow, I have a check coming. I am enclosing a stamped, self-addressed envelope in which you can send it. I had better get that check, because I know what authorities to complain to if I don't get it. If I have to complain about the check, then while I'm at it, I might as well complain about the fact that you don't have a proper cage for putting air in split-rim tires, which, if I am not mistaken, is illegal.
>
> Love and Kisses,
>
> Ted Kaczynski

From a cognitive perspective, the following are characteristic underlying assumptions that affect behavior of SPDs: (1) "Any disruption of my emotional routine (however minimal the emotions are) is scary and messy" (in this sense, the SPD's experience is analogous to the obsessive-compulsive's fear of disruption of external routines); (2) "People don't really mean anything to me"; (3) "I can survive alone (maybe not optimally, but at least predictably) and I need space to do that"; or (4) "It's necessary to be free and independent—other people are like Brer Rabbit's 'Tar Baby,' if you relate to them, you get stuck to them."

It is possible that at various points in his life Kaczynski might have earned more than one *DSM-IV-TR* diagnosis (e.g., paranoid personality disorder, avoidant personality disorder). He was apparently depressed enough to make a suicide attempt at some point in early January 1998, using his own underwear. Also, Dr. Sally Field, a federal prison psychiatrist, who found Kaczynski competent to stand trial, diagnosed him at approximately that same point in time as a paranoid schizophrenic (see Chapter 6). However, as evident from the following *DSM-IV-TR* criteria for schizoid personality disorder, the SPD diagnosis clearly applies.

According to the *DSM-IV-TR*, although SPDs have few if any friends, they show no communication disturbance, which is true of Kaczynski. It is required that SPD—which is marked by social-relationship detachment, introverted behavior, and constriction of expression or emotion in social settings—causes vocational or social disruption by at least four of the following: (1) does not desire or enjoy close relationships, including with family; (2) almost always seeks solitary pursuits; (3) has little or no interest in sexual experiences with another; (4) takes pleasure in only a few activities at most; (5) lacks close friends or confidants other than first-degree relatives; (6) appears indifferent to praise or criticism; or (7) is detached, cold, or flat emotionally. Although no one could make a definitive diagnosis without a formal, in-person contact evaluation, Kaczynski could easily be construed as fitting all seven.

Literary Obsessions and Violence

In Joseph Conrad's novel *The Secret Agent*, a brilliant but deranged professor abandons academia in disgust for the isolation of a tiny room—his "hermitage." There, clad in ragged, soiled clothes, he fashions a bomb to destroy an observatory derisively referred to as "that idol of science." In this novel, the Polish-born author created a character who wants to destroy an observatory he sees as a symbol of science, "the sacrosanct fetish of today." The professor, a brilliant but deranged man who walks around strapped with explosives and is committed to constructing "the perfect detonator," supplies the device. Describing a similar character, also nicknamed "the professor," in his short story "The Informer," Conrad wrote, "Explosives were his faith, his hope, his weapon and his shield."

The parallels fall neatly into place. Kaczynski, a brilliant man who was troubled most of his life, fled academia for a hermit-life existence in a Montana shanty. There, grossly unkempt, he lived for a time off turnips he grew behind his cabin. One of the anarchists in Conrad's novel lived on a diet of raw carrots. Further, the main character in Conrad's best-known work, *Heart of Darkness*, abandons European civilization for the jungle of the Congo. Ironically, in 1995, investigators sent *The Secret Agent* and other Conrad works to scholars, hoping for insights into the mind of a killer who eluded them for 18 years.

Investigators say they believe that Kaczynski used "Conrad" or "Konrad" as an alias on at least three occasions while staying at a hotel in Sacramento, California, where he went to mail bombs. By coincidence, literature reference books listed Joseph Conrad's birth-given name as either Teodore Jozef Konrad Korzeniowski or Jozef Teodore. Kaczynski's full name is Theodore John Kaczynski. Kaczynski's use of the initials "FC" on a number of bombs and in letters to news organizations is another similarity. The Unabomber's letters said the initials stood for "Freedom Club." In *The Secret Agent*, anarchists used the initials "FP," or "Future of the Proletariat," in their leaflets.

Kaczynski grew up with Conrad's complete works in his family's suburban Chicago home. During his 26 years in the Montana wilderness, he pored over Conrad's writings. In a 1984 letter to his family, "Ted said he was reading Conrad's novels for about the dozenth time," reported Washington attorney Anthony Bisceglie, counsel to Kaczynski's brother and mother.

If Kaczynski did indeed draw from Conrad's characters in plotting bombings, he would not be the first killer to find inspiration in literature or film. Mark David Chapman, who killed Beatles singer John Lennon, was obsessed with the novel *Catcher in the Rye*. Timothy McVeigh, who committed the Oklahoma City bombing, was fascinated by The Turner Diaries. John Hinckley, Jr., who shot President Ronald Reagan, was consumed by the film *Taxi Driver*. In our world today, it would more likely be an obsession with violent video games.

Treatment Options

The Kaczynski family was concerned enough about Ted's social development to consult school counselors, but apparently there was never any more sophisticated examination, and there is no indication he received any significant formal treatment. If he did, it was unsuccessful. People with schizoid personality disorder are not likely even to enter into therapy because such a relationship is the magnification of what is usually avoided. If for some reason they do become involved in therapy, the therapist must help them develop trust in that relationship and not overwhelm them with initial confrontations.

Like psychopathy, SPD is a condition in which efforts at early prevention will likely bring a greater payoff than will later treatment (Strupp, Lambert, & Horowitz, 1997). Shyness and/or introversion disrupt socialization and often require better than average parenting to avoid later dysfunctional patterns. The following are some ways a parent can help a shy/introverted child. Ted Kaczynski's parents were clearly well intentioned, but apparently violated a number of these guidelines:

- Use gentle encouragement rather than be too demanding or pushy. Consider whether a family ethic of perfectionism could be a factor.
- Openly discuss the situation. Make your child aware of your own struggles with shyness.
- Role play with your child to suggest ways to cope with difficult situations. Encourage the child to act out the positive patterns even if he or she denies being able to do it that way in real life.
- Ask your child what his or her "self-talk" is when "feeling shy." Usually, it is a negative self-statement such as, "I can't do it" or "If I go over there, they'll laugh at me." Try to get the child to say more positive things out loud about his or her potential behavior. Reward the child for doing so.
- Help your child develop friendships. Provide rides or a pleasant place for children to gather and play.
- Avoid criticism as well as any negative comparisons with siblings or playmates. Don't use shaming as a consistent disciplinary technique.
- Teach your child to reflect and empathize with how other people feel. This serves to blunt some of the self-centeredness that is often part of introversion.
- Look for positive ways to deal with the shyness. Instead of telling a teacher that your child is shy, use words such as *reflective* and *sensitive*. It may well be that your child is a good listener and not just shy. If so, play up that quality as a strength, not a weakness.
- Avoid making comparisons between your child and others who may be more extroverted, athletic, and/or intelligent. This is usually done to get a child to try harder, but it generally backfires and makes a child even less certain that extra effort will pay off. Also, the child, now intimidated, is inhibited around other children because of having been convinced of their superior abilities.

- Make sure that your child isn't lacking in basic social skills. Such skills often are taken for granted. However, not every child is equally adept at skills such as making eye contact, asking questions, talking clearly, appearing interested in others, and the like. Check these skills out by talking with your child and watching how he or she interacts with others.
- Be on the lookout for circumstances that are likely to increase a child's feeling of shyness. Few children are shy with everyone, but certain situations seem to bring out shyness. Among these are encountering strangers, being the center of attention (for good or bad), being with peers and members of the opposite sex, and less obvious things, such as in a group singing or being in a classroom play. Again, role playing ahead of time how to handle these situations can do a lot to lessen any problems.

Malignant Narcissism

Narcissism is generally defined as excessive love of self. Although there are narcissistic individuals in all cultures, the cultural historian Christopher Lasch points out in his 1978 book, *The Culture of Narcissism*, that it is not only more common in our modern culture but also at times encouraged by our strong emphasis on self and individualism. This may be why the personality disorder Narcissistic Personality Disorder (NPD) was not even added into the *DSM* until the third edition, in 1980. However, NPD is now also included in *DSM-IV-TR*, and is likely to be continued in future editions. The diagnostic requirements for NPD—which is a pervasive pattern of grandiosity, need for admiration, and lack of empathy, beginning in early childhood—must (according to *DSM-IV-TR*) include five of the following: (1) grandiosity, (2) preoccupations with fantasies of unlimited success, (3) belief in one's uniqueness and a consequent propensity to associate only with those who accept that, (4) a need for excessive admiration, (5) a sense of entitlement, (6) interpersonally exploitive behavior, (7) lack of empathy, (8) envy of others or beliefs that others are envious of him or her, or (9) arrogant and haughty behavior. It will be clear that all of the next three cases easily meet at least five of these criteria.

However, in 1984, Otto Kernberg extended the concept of NPD to a smaller subset of individuals whom he labeled malignant narcissists (MN), and in a book applied it to Hitler and Stalin. In an article in the May 4, 2004, edition of the *New York Times*, Erica Goode summarized the evolution of Kernberg's theory over the years and noted that experts agree it applies equally well to Saddam Hussein. In addition to having the NPD components previously noted, malignant narcissists show antisocial/psychopathic characteristics, paranoia, a lack of moral or ethical judgment, a lack of remorse for damage to others, and aggression (and in some cases, sadistic aggression).

The Case of Adolf Hitler

At 6:30 P.M. on the evening of April 20, 1889, Adolf Hitler was born in the small Austrian village of Braunau Am Inn just across the border from German Bavaria. Adolf was the middle child of five. Only Adolf and another sibling shared the same mother, Klara Polzl. Little is known about his early childhood. In 1895, Adolf entered the strict discipline of Austrian primary school. Concurrently, Adolf's father, Alois Hitler, took his retirement on a pension from the Austrian civil service. Adolf's father was both strict and an alcoholic. He had little tolerance for those who did not obey. Consequently, all family members suffered numerous physical and emotional beatings. However, Adolf enjoyed singing in the Catholic Church choir, for he had a fine voice. In his play time he would often dress up as a priest and even considered joining the priesthood.

In 1898, the Hitler family moved to the village of Leonding, close to Linz. Adolf obtained good grades with little effort and had a talent for architectural drawing. His favorite book was a picture book on the German/French war of 1870–1871, to the point that he states in his famous book, *Mein Kampf*, "It was not long before the great historic struggle had become my greatest spiritual experience. From then on, I became more and more enthusiastic about everything that was in anyway connected with war or, for that matter, with soldiering."

On January 3, 1903, Alois Hitler died of a lung hemorrhage. Financially, Adolf's father had left the family fairly well off. Adolf was even sent to a private boarding school but dropped out at age 16. He had hopes of becoming an artist, and in October 1907, he began attending the Vienna Academy of Fine Arts in Austria. In the meantime, Adolf's mother had been diagnosed with breast cancer by a Jewish doctor named Dr. Eduard Bloch. Adolf came home but then returned to the academy to take an important art exam. He failed the exam and was essentially told he

had little talent. This sent Adolf into a depression because he felt sure he had great talent, and he returned home. His mother was now in the painful late stages of her disease, and Adolf anguished over her suffering. She died on December 21, 1907. Adolf blamed Bloch, and this likely led in part to his developing hatred of Jews.

In February 1908, Adolf moved back to Vienna and roomed with his best friend, August Kubizek. Kubizek recalled that Adolf displayed an increasingly unstable personality with sudden outbursts of rage, especially whenever anyone disagreed with his ideas. In October of 1908, Adolf made a second attempt to be accepted by the Fine Arts Academy, but once again failed, helping to further destabilize him. On February 5, 1914, he was rejected for military service by Austria. He petitioned King Ludwig III of Bavaria and was enrolled in that army in August, and by December 1914 he had earned an Iron Cross, second class. When World War I ended on November 11, 1918, Adolf's rage was directed at German Jews, whom he felt had betrayed Germany. He became active in politics and in 1919 joined the Nazi party. A year earlier, in 1918, Hitler had suffered an episode of "hysterical blindness" and was treated by a Dr. Edmond Forster, who put Hitler under hypnosis and allegedly gave him a suggestion that he had to recover his sight in order to fulfill his mission to redeem Germany's lost honor. In any case, his sight returned.

On October 16, 1919, Hitler gave a speech at the Hofbrauhauskeller that marked the beginning of his political career. Over the next several years, he was imprisoned twice for his political activities, and on July 18, 1925, the first volume of *Mein Kampf* was published. The Nazi party was growing in power, based on making pledges to return honor to Germany and on blaming much of Germany's social and economic problems on the Jews. On January 30, 1933, Hitler became Chancellor, and upon the death of Hindenberg on August 1, 1934, he became both Chancellor and Fuehrer. Germany had been both secretly and openly rebuilding its military power and in 1936 invaded and reclaimed the Rhineland, then later Austria, Sudetenland, and Czechoslovakia. Britain had signed a pact with Poland on August 25, 1939. But, ignoring advice that Britain would go to war with Germany, Hitler ordered the invasion of Poland only a week later. Britain declared war on Germany on September 3, and France did so the following day. Again, against advice from his military experts, Hitler invaded Russia on June 22, 1941, expecting a quick victory. However, his army on the eastern front was eventually decimated by Russian soldiers and the Russian winter. This, along with the entry of the United States into the war in December 1941, turned the tide (Mosier, 2004). In spite of increasing defeats, Hitler insisted Germany would eventually win, and even came to believe the United States and Britain would eventually join Germany in order to stop the threat of Russian communism. Throughout this period his propensity toward rage reactions and tyrannical outbursts continued, as he seldom viewed any ideas but his own as valid.

Over the course of World War II, Hitler was ultimately responsible for the death of millions of Jews and others from captured countries, most dying in concentration camps, either from starvation, extreme labor, gas chambers, shooting, individual acts of cruelty, or medical experiments. Although there is little evidence anyone died by Hitler's own hand, he was the architect of this massive and horrific killing.

When Hitler finally came to realize that his enemies were about to capture him, he retreated with his household and closest advisors to a bunker under the Reich Chancellory in Berlin. There, he married his mistress, Eva Braun, on April 29, 1945. He had planned to commit suicide with her by taking prussic acid, supplied by Dr. Ludwig Stumpfegger. But, since he did not truly trust anyone, he had Stumpfegger first use the prussic acid to kill Blondi, Hitler's favorite dog. Then, the next evening, April 30, Hitler and Eva retired to their bedroom. When they were checked on hours later, the smell of bitter almonds indicated Eva had taken the prussic acid, but Hitler had apparently shot himself in the right temple with his 7.67mm Walther pistol just as he also took prussic acid. Following his orders, their bodies were taken out to the courtyard, doused with petrol that had been hoarded for that purpose, and burned to ashes. They were identified by parts of their jawbones that had not been incinerated.

The Case of Joseph Stalin

Joseph Stalin was born to a peasant family in the Georgian town of Gori in the Caucausus. His actual birth date was December 6, 1878, but for some reason when he came to power he listed his birth date as December 21, 1879. Joseph Stalin's father worked occasionally as a shoemaker and was a severe alcoholic. Stalin's family was very poor, and his father often violently beat his wife and children. His mother was a maid and a washerwoman, as well as an orthodox Christian, but she also often beat her son. Stalin later publicly expressed his devotion to his mother but was actually "coarse and cynical about his mother and gave orders for her to be constantly watched . . . there is no evidence to suggest that he ever felt any affection for her" (Medvedev & Medvedev, 2003, p. 310). Stalin's great-grandfather, Zara Dzhugashvili,

(continued)

The Case of Joseph Stalin Continued

was a model for Stalin as a politician, as Zara was the leader of a bloody (although unsuccessful) peasant revolt.

Stalin was extremely self-conscious about his looks. His face was scarred by smallpox, and a childhood accident left one arm shorter than the other. He was also very short for his age and often tried to wear high wooden shoes to hide this. In addition, Russians in the Soviet Union looked down on those born in other areas, such as Georgia, and this increased Stalin's sense of inferiority.

The concept that workers rather than the aristocracy should be in control fueled the political movement led by Lenin, called *Bolshevism* (see Chapter 5), later evolving into communism. Stalin joined with other Bolsheviks in committing robberies to fuel the cause, and Stalin very likely personally murdered individuals in those robberies. Stalin and his comrades were arrested many times by the tsar's police, eventually leading to years of exile for Stalin.

After the end of World War I, Russian morale was low. When the tsar was assassinated on July 17, 1918, a civil war ensued. The Bolsheviks prevailed, and Stalin was given the title of Commissar of Nationalities. Essentially, he was to enforce the party line, a job that was perfect for his ruthless personality. In 1918, Russian Communist leader Leon Trotsky sent Stalin a detachment of army specialists. However, Stalin did not trust him and so imprisoned the men on a boat that then mysteriously sank. He had many others executed, usually simply by shooting them.

Stalin married at a young age to Yekaterina Svandize, and she gave birth to their only child, Yakov. She died shortly afterward in 1907. Her family raised Yakov, and Stalin seldom saw him. At age 39, Stalin married again, to a young girl of age 17, Nadezhda Alliluyeva, who later killed herself in 1932. They had two children, Vasily and Svetlana, but Stalin was again seldom an active parent.

In 1920, Stalin was put in charge of the Soviet Secretariat, which allowed him to appoint people to the Communist Party and government positions. He appointed those who were "loyal" and eliminated those he distrusted. Stalin's circle was growing, but he knew that in order to gain more power he had to downgrade the influence of Trotsky. So, in 1927, Stalin demoted Trotsky and then exiled him, making Stalin essentially a dictator by the end of the 1920s. However, Russia then experienced a severe famine. Stalin took most of the available wheat from the peasants, causing more than 5 million deaths. He denied that there was a famine and made it against the law to even mention it.

To further support Stalin's views of a great and powerful Russia, the Soviets tried to increase industry, although Russia had a strong, traditionally rural economy, and the overall economy was still in a recession. Knowing that any failure would result in death, Stalin's accountants simply lied about productivity. Concurrently, Stalin created the Gulag camps that forced dissenters to work long and hard hours—work that often led to their death. In 1929, when the Russian economy recovered, Stalin was looked at as a god. The Russians believed that Stalin was responsible for the revolution. School children were taught that Stalin was infallible. His pictures and statues blanketed the Soviet Union. The worship of Stalin was the new Soviet religion.

Throughout the 1930s, Stalin killed anyone, including his own party members, whom he saw as a threat. Using torture, threats of repercussions to family members, and false promises, he forced them to falsely confess to crimes of treason so that Stalin would look blameless for any problems. Trotsky was the only one who could speak out against Stalin, so he was quickly again exiled and soon thereafter was secretly attacked and beaten to death. Whenever anyone spoke out against Stalin, he quickly had them killed and made others aware of their elimination.

Stalin admired Adolf Hitler and shared his anti-Semitism, hence he was willing to make an alliance with him. However, Hitler hated and feared communism and would soon betray Stalin (Montefiore, 2004), as noted earlier in the case of Hitler. When German troops invaded Kiev, they took many Soviets as prisoners, including Stalin's son, Yakov. When Nazi troops tried to negotiate a trade of Yakov's life for one of their fellow Germans, Stalin stated that he didn't have a son by that name, and Yakov was killed, sending a message to the Russian people that Stalin sacrificed his own son for them.

During and after the Second World War, Stalin ruled the Soviet Union with an iron fist, quickly exiling and/or killing anyone he distrusted or disliked. Yet, he constantly and successfully presented himself to the people as a benevolent patriarch and was commonly referred to as "Uncle Joe." However, the estimates of those killed by the forced famines, purges, Gulags, and suppression of revolutions and dissent go as high as 20 million people, although no one knows for sure. On February 28 and again on March 1, 1953, Stalin suffered a paralyzing stroke and slowly suffocated to death on March 5, 1953.

The Case of Saddam Hussein

Saddam Hussein was the president of Iraq from 1979 to 2003. His presidency was terminated when U.S. troops invaded Iraq and captured him in December 2003. His childhood, family background, and early acts of psychopathic violence all played a part in nurturing a future malignant narcissist—the most prominent of a number of diagnostic terms that could be applied to him.

Saddam Hussein suffered through an impoverished and unhappy childhood. He was born in al-Auja on April 28, 1937, growing up in a small village close to Takrit, Iraq. His father, Hussein al-Majid, either died around his birth or simply abandoned the family; his elder brother died while his mother, Subha, was pregnant with Saddam. She rejected him psychologically both before and after his father's death; in fact, she had attempted to abort him. Also both before and after Saddam's birth she had made several suicide attempts and for a while had others take care of him. His mother and stepfather, known as "Hassam the Liar," raised Saddam at various points in time (Coughlin, 2002). Although a sheepherder, Hassam was very violent; he

constantly insulted and abused Saddam, making him steal livestock that Hassam could sell or use himself. He also would not allow Saddam to go to school. Illiterate until the age of 10, Saddam was very angry that his cousin could read and write. His childhood friends characterized Saddam as constantly angry, yet quiet and lonely.

At the age of 10, Saddam was sent to Baghdad to live with his uncle, Khairallah Tulfah. There is evidence that Saddam was violent as a youth and he was clearly so by his early teen years. A clear sign of Saddam's ruthlessness came at the age of 14 when he claimed he had tried to kill his school teacher. While he was living with his uncle and attending school in Baghdad, Saddam was linked to the murders of a school teacher and a cousin. Tulfah encouraged him to dream of becoming a hero like Saladin, the Kurdish-born Arab who took on the Crusaders. Tulfah's political bitterness toward the British and then Westerners in general was modeled by Saddam, although when in power Saddam cooperated with the CIA on a number of occasions.

After finishing school at the age of 24,

(continued)

The Case of Adolf Hitler Continued

Saddam turned to political activity that would eventually lead him to power in the Baath party. In 1959, he attempted unsuccessfully his first political assassination—that of military ruler Abdul Qassim. Saddam was convicted for his attempt and sentenced to death, yet later escaped to Cairo, Egypt. During his time in Egypt, he was arrested on at least two occasions, once for threatening a fellow student and again for chasing another down the street with a knife. He returned to Iraq only when the Baath party rose to power through a military coup.

When his cousin, General Ahmed Hassan Al-Bakr, became president and head of the Revolutionary Command Council, Saddam became his deputy chairman in 1974. When Saddam finally became leader of Iraq, he remembered his uncle Tulfah and made him mayor of Baghdad. Saddam's inner circle was always filled with family members and old friends and those Baath members he trusted and felt he could control. However, he did not hesitate to eliminate, often sadistically, anyone who posed a threat to his power. He named his close cousin, Adnan Khairallah, defense minister, but then came to suspect him because he achieved a power base in the army. Saddam gradually eased him out of important areas like military intelligence, and in April of 1989, Adnan died in a "helicopter accident."

Saddam was thrown in jail in 1964 by anti-Baathist factions, yet while in jail, Saddam was appointed as the secretary general of the Baathist party. He escaped and, through a coup, became the leading member of the ruling Baath party. His older cousin, Ahmed Hassan al-Bakr, became the president of Iraq, and Saddam was officially the vice president by 1973. Shortly after he took full control as president of Iraq in 1979, he staged a Stalinist-style purge. Six days after Saddam was appointed, he condemned, to death, at least 20 of the leading members of the Baath party as well as a number of army officials. Even when former president al-Bakr died in 1982, it was widely suspected that Saddam had him killed. Hussein went against a 1975 peace agreement with Iran and invaded that country in September 1980, killing thousands over eight years. Simultaneously, he brutally killed thousands of his own citizens, especially the Kurds, on whom he used poison gas.

That Saddam gave himself numerous titles and widespread powers points to his narcissism. For example, he virtually blanketed Iraq with statues and visual images of himself, had numerous lavish palaces, and enjoyed showing off his gold machine gun. He created a lakeside vacation resort in Baghdad, where nearly every brick was engraved with his initials, as well as a 30-foot bronze statue of himself at the gateway.

The Iran-Iraq War caused a debt of about $75 billion that generated political pressure on Hussein, which in part led to his invasion of Kuwait on August 2, 1990. Although it quickly occupied the whole country, Iraq was eventually defeated. Hussein broke the peace terms in 1993, and in 1998 failed to abide by United Nations weapons inspector mandates. Saddam was given the ultimatum to leave Iraq in March 2003 by U.S. President George W. Bush, which Saddam ignored, resulting in the United States invading Iraq in search of Saddam, who went into hiding. In April of 2003, Saddam Hussein was captured by the United States and was subsequently executed by the Iraqi government.

Comment

Certainly Hitler, Stalin, and Hussein all fit the label of *malignant narcissist*. All three showed the narcissistic personality disorder characteristics of grandiosity, preoccupation with success and power, a sense of entitlement, a need for admiration, avoidance of those who do not accept the person's self-perception of uniqueness, lack of empathy, and arrogance, as well as the MN characteristics of antisocial factors (even to the point of psychopathy), lack of moral judgment, lack of remorse, paranoia, and aggression. The fact that all three men shared a history of physical abuse and a strong sense of inferiority early in life may play a part, and genetics no doubt contribute. But there are simply not enough data to fully explain the evolution of this thankfully rare disorder.

There are differences in the three, as well. Hitler was particularly marked by a sense of a unique mission, paranoia, and a lack of moral judgment. Aside from his service in the German army in World War I, there is no indication he killed anyone by his own hand. He was the architect of the death of millions of people, but this stemmed from a paranoid/delusional belief system rather than from sadism or the enjoyment of personal cruelty. Stalin was particularly ruthless, sadistic, deceitful, and somewhat paranoid, although he was more cunning and materialistic than Hitler. Hussein is marked more by a need for excessive admiration, even deification, psychopathy, and sadistic aggression (much of which his sons clearly inherited/modeled). The combination of comfort with personal aggression and the need for admiration is probably captured in his delight in brandishing his golden machine gun. His legacy of aggression was continued in Iraq on April 4, 2004, when the Shiite cleric Muqtada al-Sadr unleashed an army of his followers on occupation forces. This is ironic, since al-Sadr's father had been assassinated on the orders of Hussein.

It is important to note that one does not have to be a person of undisputed power to be a malignant narcissist, nor do MNs typically show characteristics of traditional mental illness—for example, severe psychosis with active thought disorder or severe depression. If the aggression/sadism predominates, they are likely to become criminal. (For example, Dr. Henry Holmes probably could be considered a malignant narcissist; see Chapter 13.) If there is little aggression or paranoia, but more of a lack of straightforward moral judgment, a high sense of uniqueness and entitlement, and the ability to manipulate others, the MN may be a success in a profession or corporation. A malignant narcissist may even have an apparently successful personal relationship if the significant other does not have much need for intimacy or personal loyalty and caring.

12 Disorders of Impulse Control

The extent to which an individual is in command of and can control urges to violate social rules is always an important consideration when evaluating emotional development. It is expected that young children will often find behavioral control difficult, but one is expected to achieve increasing mastery as socialization proceeds (Hersen & Ammerman, 2000). Inadequate impulse control is symptomatic of a wide range of disorders, including alcoholism, obsessive compulsive disorder, exhibitionism, and pyromania. Thus, the category of impulse control disorders could be so extensive and inclusive as to be meaningless (Johnson, 2008). As a result, disorders in which an absence of impulse control is only a component are classified in accordance with other symptoms (eating disorders, substance abuse, and paraphilias, for example). However, there are at least five disorders for which poor impulse control is the primary feature and that are not elsewhere classified: pathological gambling (the case of Fyodor Dostoyevsky), kleptomania (the cases of Winona Ryder and John Lennon), pyromania, intermittent explosive disorder (the case of Jack Ruby in Chapter 13), and trichotillomania (the recurrent pulling out of one's own hair).

Pathological gambling is characterized by chronic and maladaptive gambling behavior and/or irresistible urges to gamble. The essential feature of kleptomania is a recurring inability to resist impulses to steal things for reasons other than their usefulness or monetary value. In another impulse disorder pattern, pyromania, the individual cannot resist the buildup of tension and then the impulse to set fires, and is fascinated by fires. The intermittent explosive disorder is marked by incidents of inability to control aggression, resulting in serious attacks on others or destruction of property.

In all of the disorders of impulse control, a compelling impulse accompanied by a rising sense of tension is experienced. It may or may not be premeditated and/or consciously resisted. Then, when the act is committed, there is a sense of release, which may even be so intense as to be described as pleasurable or euphoric.

> *For though this exercise may be absorbing, it is not [harmful] in the hands of a man [who can] give it up when the chance comes along.*
> —Fernando Basurto, *Dialogue between a Hunter and a Fisher* (1539), speaking on the pleasures of fishing

Pathological Gambling

Gambling may be one of civilization's oldest recreational activities. Historical documents of the ancients are replete with examples of people's interest in wagering with friends and others. The verb *gamble* comes from the Old English and is related to the word *gambol*, meaning "sport" or "make merry." Legal gambling has not always enjoyed popularity. Lotteries were periodically banned in the United States, even though they had been used to finance the Revolutionary War and educational institutions such as Harvard University. Although a commonsense view of the gambling phenomenon has always led some to recognize its potential for pathological abuse, pathological gambling as a clinical phenomenon was not formally recognized until the third edition of the *DSM*, published in 1980. The *DSM-IV-TR* categorizes pathological gambling as a disorder of impulse control, with these primary features: (1) persistent and recurrent failure to resist an impulse to gamble or think about gambling; (2) an increasing sense of tension before committing the act; and (3) an experience of either pleasure or release at the time of committing the act.

As more states have moved toward various forms of legalized gambling, the prevalence of the disorder in the United States is constantly increasing (Hodgins & el-Guabaly, 2004). Indeed, many states now have a strongly vested interest in promoting gambling as state-operated lotteries are used to finance various activities that would otherwise require taxes to raise the money. In the United States, far more money is now spent on gambling than on movies, plays, and music events combined. Prevalence rates have steadily increased and will continue to do so as more states promote lotteries and allow casino gambling and as Internet use rises. And access is critical. People are twice as likely to be problem gamblers if they live within 50 miles of a casino. Addiction is a component, as pathological gamblers often manifest other addictions, such as alcoholism. Add to all this the increasing opportunities to gamble over the Internet and the enhanced effects made possible by virtual reality technology.

In general, the following factors can predispose a person to pathological gambling: family values that emphasize material symbols rather than savings and financial planning; an absent parent before age 16; an extroverted and competitive personality; personality traits of high stimulation seeking, self-centeredness, and low frustration tolerance; other addictive patterns, such as substance abuse; early opportunities for gambling or present access; and a gambling model in the family. Cultural acceptance of gambling also increases the number of abusers. For example, traditional Chinese cultural values strongly disapprove of alcoholism, but approve of gambling as an acceptable channel for stimulation seeking. As a result, the number of pathological gamblers is relatively high in traditional Chinese cultures (Marsella, De Vos, & Hsu, 1985).

Pathological gambling behavior can be confused with and be seen as another form of thrill-seeking behavior for the individual with the antisocial personality disorder (Bartol & Bartol, 2008). In contrast, the antisocial behavior that occurs as the result of the pathological gambling disorder invariably results out of desperation when no other avenues to obtain economic funds remain open to the gambler. Unlike relapse in substance abuse, where avoidance of "feeling bad" is a critical precipitant, in pathological gambling the critical precipitant appears to be rumination about making money, especially if alone and occurring in the early evening (Hodgins & el-Guabaly, 2004). Also, in contrast to the antisocial personality disorder, and as we see in Dostoyevsky's case, the pathological gambler usually has at least a reasonably stable work history until work also becomes disrupted by his or her gambling behavior.

Money is a vile intermediary.

—Fidel Castro

The Case of Fyodor Dostoyevsky

Fyodor Dostoyevsky is arguably the most well-known Russian novelist in the world, having authored such classics as *The Brothers Karamazov* and *Crime and Punishment.* He was born in Moscow on October 30, 1821, to a family of modest means and of Russian, Lithuanian, and Polish ancestry. There is some evidence of violence and sociopathy on the Dostoyevsky side of the family. Various legal documents describe forged wills, bloody feuds with neighbors, and the taking over of property belonging to the church and state. One of the wilder episodes occurred in 1606 when Marina Dostoyevskaya had one of her servants shoot her husband when he stepped out of a bathhouse. Wounded and bleeding, he stumbled to the house, but she had already bolted the door. While he begged to be let in, the servant followed Marina's orders and now attacked him with a sword. As the dogs and pigs lapped his blood, he died. Marina screamed, "Send him to hell" (Kjestsaa, 1987).

Fyodor's mother, Maria, had come from a family of some wealth. Ironically, given the family history, the father and grandfather of Mikhail, Fyodor's father, had both been clergymen, hence the modest means on that side of the family. Mikhail chose to become a physician and attained both success and respect in that field. Unfortunately, this did not translate into wealth since, in nineteenth-century Russia, physicians in Germany were perceived as the most skillful. Hence, the wealthiest clients would travel to Germany for treatment.

Money was a central theme in Mikhail's life course. The potential for strife here was heightened as Maria's sister, Alexandra, had married into the wealthy Kumanin family. This disparity in financial status was a constant source of contention for Fyodor's parents, and in relations with the rest of the family. When Mikhail was forced to accept the Kumanins' money, he was humiliated. His bitterness was evidently communicated to Fyodor, who himself referred to the Kumanins as "pitiful shopkeepers."

Disparity in financial status was also a theme in Fyodor's school life. Fyodor and his older brother were sent to one of Russia's most well-respected boarding schools, for "aristocratic male children." Fyodor's family was clearly one of the poorer ones represented at the school. His mother died from tuberculosis a few years after he had started at the school. His father became increasingly upset and paranoid about money issues and felt the boys could not continue at the school. He withdrew them and enrolled them in a vocational school, the Academy of Engineers in St. Petersburg. While Fyodor was at the academy, his father died at their tiny estate in the Russian countryside, allegedly killed by his own serfs. Fyodor did graduate from the academy in 1843, then served a short stint in the military, being discharged in 1844.

Fyodor's artistic interests, first nurtured at the boarding school, became focused into a passion for writing, and in 1846, he authored his first book, *Poor Folk*, which was well received. This resulted in advances from the publisher, which, along with earnings from other journalistic efforts, resulted in economic comfort. But this was short-lived. He became involved with a group of outspoken but essentially harmless radical intellectuals known as the "Petrashevsky Circle." The government acted to crush this group by arresting and sentencing its members to death. Their sentences were not commuted until the last moment, as they stood on the scaffold ready to be executed. But Fyodor was sentenced to four years in a Siberian prison followed by a forced period of military service in a desolate outpost near the Chinese border.

Because of his fame as a writer and some status as nobility, Fyodor was at least allowed to live off of the post. In this remote area, far from the tsar's watchful eyes, drinking and gambling were commonplace. Fyodor had no money with which to gamble but obtained a vicarious thrill by watching: "Oh, the way they played yesterday. The excitement was tremendous! If only I had some money. . . . This devilish gaming is a real downfall. . . . I can see very clearly that it is an abominable passion, but my desire is nearly irresistible" (Kjetsaa, 1987, p. 112). As events would show, he could have eliminated "nearly."

Soon after the death of the tsar in 1855, Fyodor was allowed to publish again. He married in 1857 and then returned to St. Petersburg in 1859. He began writing for a magazine that his brother had founded and was able to afford a trip to Europe in 1862. However, while on the trip Fyodor found his way to the gaming halls of Germany, where he reported that he had some big wins. He returned to Russia to visit his wife, who was ill with tuberculosis. But then, gambling still being illegal in Russia, he came back to Germany and the gaming halls, this time accompanied by his mistress Polina.

He particularly loved roulette. He approached it methodically, not surprising in an engineer, and like many heavy gamblers, he claimed to have a winning "system." For example, one technique in his system was to sit back and watch until the roulette ball had landed on red nine times in a row, and he would then jump in and bet on black. This is a classic "gambler's fallacy." (The theory assumes that the next spin of the wheel is statistically influenced by the prior spins. In fact, every scientific test of this assumption proves it to be a fallacy. Each spin is statistically independent of any other.)

Dostoyevsky reported often winning large sums of money; no doubt he did. But, as with many problem gamblers, his reports to others (and to himself) consistently glossed over the accompanying losses that diminished a day's big win. He attributed his eventual big losses to being overwhelmed by emotion or the effects of alcohol or just "bad luck." His tour eventually took him to Baden-Baden, a German resort town noted for its gambling halls frequented by the wealthy. There, Fyodor lost all his money, borrowed some from his siblings, and quickly lost it as well. About this time, he broke up with Polina, in part because of his impoverished state, and returned to Russia to be with his wife, who then died in 1864. It was just before this that his problems with gambling gave him the idea for one of his more famous books, which is somewhat autobiographical, *The Gambler*.

Telling himself he needed treatment because of the stress of his wife's death, Fyodor returned to Germany. Once again, he quickly went to the gaming tables and lost all his money. He obtained a loan from a friend, lost it all, and was thrown in a debtor's prison, returning to Russia only when a priest gave him enough money for the trip.

Shortly thereafter, while writing *The Gambler* and *Crime and Punishment*, he fell in love with Anna, a young woman he had hired as an assistant. They married and eventually decided to travel to Europe. They planned a three-month stay in Germany. However, Fyodor quickly returned to gambling, and they stayed

(continued)

The Case of Fyodor Dostoyevsky Continued

four years. In her memoirs, Anna describes what she saw then:

> Without a murmur I would give him the last of our money, well aware that my pawned effects would fall into disrepair and go missing, and that our landlady and creditors would come to lay claim to all that I possessed. But it was dreadful to see how Fyodor Mikhailvich suffered during this gambling. Pale and exhausted, he would return home and beg for more money. It was all he could do to stay on his feet. Then he would go back again, but after half an hour he would return even more depressed, and thus it continued until he had gambled away all that we owned. (Kjetsaa, 1987, p. 245)

However, Fyodor's poverty pushed him to write another of his classic works, *The Idiot*, which he amazingly completed in 28 days. Shortly thereafter, Anna gave birth to a daughter who died of pneumonia three months later.

Fyodor soon returned to the tables and his problem gambling. This continued until an external event apparently brought about a "cure." Germany outlawed gambling in 1872, and all of the halls were closed. No doubt this was an important factor. However, he could have traveled to other countries to gamble. What is evident from his letters at this time is his growing love and emotional dependence on Anna and his family. His fear of losing them was no doubt a factor. Also, as with most people, age was diminishing his need for stimulation, and maybe he was also just maturing.

Fyodor and Anna returned to Russia in 1871, where he continued his writing. They eventually raised a family and lived in relative comfort. During this period, he wrote what many consider to be his greatest work, *The Brothers Karamazov*. He died on January 28, 1881, at age 59, as a result of a hemorrhage resulting from emphysema.

Stages of Compulsive Gambling

Most compulsive gamblers go through some variation of the following stages:

1. *Winning Phase:* Occasional gambling is marked by heightened excitement when winning, along with a heightened ability to forget or ignore losses. "Big win" and "big shot" fantasies increase, and the occasional actual big win takes on an increased psychological focus.
2. *Losing Phase:* Fantasizing, actual gambling time, and losses increase, as do gambling alone, disruption of work and personal life, and debt and/or borrowing.
3. *Desperation Phase:* Monetary, vocational, and interpersonal difficulties become disruptive at a critical and/or clinical level. Allied patterns—such as depression, anxiety, and/or substance abuse—intensify. The addictive component is evident and controlling.

Therapeutic Intervention with Pathological Gambling

Therapeutic interventions favor treating compulsive gambling similarly to other types of impulse-habituation-addictive disorders, typically including the following phases of intervention:

1. Eliminate immediate opportunity to gamble by way of environment engineering (e.g., working with a spouse). In some cases, inpatient hospitalization may be necessary.
2. Immediately initiate an educational process about pathological gambling and the insidious role it takes on in every individual's life.
3. Participate in individual and group psychotherapy, including cognitive-behavior modification, to correct such cognitive biases as "Since I've lost a few times, the odds are with me now" and "I'm on a roll now, so I'll up my bets."
4. Regularly attend Gamblers Anonymous.
5. Seek economic counseling for living within a set income.
6. Participate in continued outpatient treatment in the form of weekly sessions that specifically deal with the issue of gambling. It may be necessary to focus on common accompanying patterns such as depression, substance abuse, and, in some cases, dissociative patterns.
7. Attend family and/or couples therapy when indicated.

Prevention of Pathological Gambling

As was so in Dostoyevsky's case, restriction of access to gambling is the most effective mode of prevention. The common impediment to decreasing access to gambling is that many states now try to profit from gambling while at the same time try to regulate it. Unfortunately, like gamblers, the state is often greedy; unlike gamblers, the state is betting on a sure thing. The following are other reforms that could be helpful:

1. Require all interests who profit from gambling to divert a reasonable but significant percentage of profits into programs of research and treatment related to gambling.
2. Ban all gambling before age 21, or at least age 18. Also, severely limit or ban Internet gambling. Disallow any "child-enticement" themes—for example, comic book characters or superheroes appearing in slot machines and video gambling.
3. Ban or strictly limit (with full public disclosure) political contributions from gaming interests.
4. Ban all betting on nonprofessional athletic events (for the record, Division 1-A college football and basketball are actually considered nonprofessional sports).
5. Ban automatic teller machines from gambling sites. Strictly limit the amount for cashing checks or the advancement of credit at these sites.

> *If I make a set of rules, then a guy goes out and steals an airplane. He comes back and says, "It wasn't on the list of rules."*
>
> —Abe Lemons, college basketball coach

Kleptomania

Kleptomania refers to a recurrent inability to resist the impulse to steal. And it commonly occurs in those who clearly can afford the items stolen. The *DSM-IV-TR* emphasizes that the stealing is done to gain the strong feelings of gratification that occur with the release of tension from anger and/or stress that the act brings in such an individual. These acts are seldom accompanied by significant preplanning, are primarily impulsive, and usually carried out alone.

Although kleptomaniacs (the use of the subterm *mania* is unfortunate) may have problems in interpersonal relationships, their general personality functioning is likely to be within the normal range. Kleptomania can begin as early as the first school years, and it is likely to be chronic without some kind of direct intervention. Anxiety, substance abuse, and depression, as well as guilt over the fear of being apprehended, may accompany this condition.

Stealing is a common behavior in society. About 1 out of every 12 shoppers is a shoplifter, but less than 5 percent of shoplifters are kleptomaniacs. Most shoplifters steal to get something they want for free. Also, a substantial proportion of shoplifting occurs in isolated acts, and the person does not repeat the behavior very often. Some people, particularly adolescents, shoplift in a group to gain peer acceptance, which can act as a precursor for later kleptomania. But stealing in kleptomania is not motivated by anger or vengeance and is not the result of delusions or hallucinations.

> *All my possessions for a moment of time.*
> —Queen Elizabeth I (1533–1603) on her deathbed

The Case of Winona Ryder

Winona Laura Horowitz entered this world on October 29, 1971, in Winona, Minnesota. Her parents, Michael and Cindy Horowitz, grew up in the sixties, and both did their fair share of experimenting with mind-altering drugs. Winona insists that her parents are intellectuals and not "hippie-like," which is hard to believe considering that Michael's good friend and Winona's godfather is none other than the notorious LSD guru Timothy Leary. Michael is an editor, publisher, and writer. His enterprise, Flashback Books, deals with the history, science, and literature of psychedelic drugs and their effects. Cindy is a writer, editor, and video producer. It is easy to see that with parents like Michael and Cindy, Winona's childhood was anything but traditional.

Upon the success of her father's first book, *Moksha: Aldous Huxley's Writings on Psychedelics and the Visionary Experience*, and the birth of their second child, Yuri, the Horowitzs decided it was time to move. Winona, only 7 years old, was uprooted and taken to a small town in northern California. Without the luxuries of running water or electricity and television, the Horowitzs found other ways to pass the time. Cindy created her own private movie theater in the barn and charged others to come and watch movies, generating Winona's love of theatrics. Although the Horowitzs enjoyed the privacy and the outdoors, the family moved to Petaluma, California, in 1982.

Winona described the other kids in her high school as "cliquish," but she did little to generate friendships. Her experiences point to early and severe episodes of interpersonally generated anxiety (Dozois & Dobson, 2004). Ridiculed for being thin and boyish, she was often mistaken for a gay boy and was bullied. Eventually, her parents removed her from public school and home schooled her until she graduated. Winona immediately joined a nearby theater school. A short time later she was cast in her first movie, *Lucas*, in 1986 and took the name Winona Ryder.

After *Lucas* came Winona's big hit, *Beetlejuice* (1988), and then other movies, such as *Heathers* (1989) and *Great Balls of Fire* (1989). She then received Academy Award nominations for her roles in *Little Women* and *The Age of Innocence*. But problems began for Winona in the early 1990s. At age 19, Winona found herself engaged to and living with actor Johnny Depp. They were the targets of endless media harassment. It was all too much for Winona to handle, and soon the couple drifted apart. Their eventual break-up was very hard on Winona, and she checked herself into a psychiatric ward. She had severe anxiety attacks and was suffering from insomnia. All of the stress and negative attention caused extreme physical exhaustion and was most likely the cause of her abrupt departure from the movie *Godfather III*. Her doctor prescribed her sleeping pills, and she reported that she was "eating them like candy." She had also periodically abused some illegal drugs.

Despite a continuation of her personal problems, Winona starred in several movies over the next few years, including *Dracula* (1992), *Reality Bites* (1994), *Simone* (2001), and the major hit *Girl Interrupted* (1999). Then in December of 2001, she was arrested and charged with felony grand theft, burglary, and vandalism for stealing $5,560.40 worth of merchandise from Saks Fifth Avenue in Beverly Hills. Curiously, she had shopped there earlier in the day and had bought and paid for $3,700 worth of merchandise. When caught shoplifting, she told the security guard that she was preparing for a movie role.

As the investigation developed, other problems emerged, especially Winona's substantial drug addiction. When she was arrested, the officers found eight different kinds of painkillers in her purse, including liquid Demerol and a syringe. Some of the prescriptions were for her alias, Emily Thompson. The police discovered that between 1996 and 1998, Winona filled 37 prescriptions for painkillers that were written by 20 different doctors.

Unfortunately, the prosecution had evidence that this was not Winona's first shoplifting incident. There were videotapes of prior similar behavior. The first incident occurred in Barneys in New York on May 14, 2000, and again at the same store on October 10, 2001. In Los Angeles, on November 29, 2001, Winona was caught on security tape wearing a hat around a Neiman Marcus store, then leaving without paying for it. All of these incidents ended without arrest.

Since her arrest, Winona was sentenced to three years' probation, 480 hours of community service, and drug abuse counseling, using the same attorney, Mark Geragos, who was the lead attorney for Michael Jackson and Scott Peterson. She appeared in court again in December 2003, when the judge praised her for the positive reports he received about her. She complied with all three conditions. Her drug counselor reported in court that her therapy is coming along, and he has had no problems with her. She returned to the silver screen in 2007 in the movies *The Ten, Sex and Death 101*, and *The Lost World*.

Winona's case is a classic pattern of kleptomania. There is a compulsive and irrational component, it is associated with other substantial addictive patterns, and the catalyst for the kleptomaniac episodes appears to be an increase in anxiety or depression.

In the following case of John Lennon, the pattern has kleptomaniac components, a degree of compulsivity, and some psychological distress that generated the shoplifting. However, it falls in the gray area between classic kleptomania and simple shoplifting, as it was largely peer generated (Horowitz, 2004) and was part of a broader picture of behavioral acting-out.

The Case of John Lennon

Along with Elvis Presley (see Chapter 9), the Beatles are generally considered the most influential figures in modern popular music, and although all four of the Beatles were talented, most consider John Lennon to be the musical genius of that group. In December 1938, Alfred "Freddy" Lennon and Julia Stanley were married after dating periodically for about 10 years. Freddy claims it was to be a joke even though they were formally married. Two years later, on October 9, 1940, John Winston Lennon was born in Liverpool, England, amidst the horrendous bombing of England early in World War II. Freddy worked for a shipping company and spent most of his days away at sea. During John's first 18 months of life, Freddy was there for about three of those months. Julia stayed home to care for John and went to collect Freddy's paychecks regularly. However, in December 1943, Julia went to the shipping company to collect as usual, and they told her that Freddy jumped ship in New York, deserting his 18-month-old son and his new wife. Julia was distraught. She moved in with her parents, began drinking and partying a lot, and then in 1944 became pregnant again. Due to the urgings of her family, she gave up the little girl for adoption. No one was ever able to find her. While Lennon continued to live with Julia, it is clear that his early life was filled with turmoil, as is well documented in Ray Coleman's excellent 1992 biography, *Lennon*, published in New York by Harper Perennial.

When Lennon was only 5 years old, Julia met John Dykins. Julia and John quickly fell in love, got married, and moved to a small apartment, bringing Lennon along. Suddenly Lennon's dad, Freddy, reappeared and took Lennon for the day. During that time, Freddy tried to persuade Lennon to leave the country with him. An altercation ensued in front of Lennon, and so Freddy and Julia told Lennon to decide with whom he would rather live. Lennon, only age 5, ultimately chose to live with his father. Julia was naturally upset and stormed out of the house. After the door slammed shut, Lennon became frantic, screaming, "Mummy, mummy, don't go." Julia returned and took Lennon with her. Shortly after this, Lennon began experiencing behavior problems to the point that he was eventually expelled from kindergarten.

Julia's sister, Mimi, became concerned and felt that Julia was an unfit mother. Mimi obtained a social advisor and successfully gained custody of Lennon. Aunt Mimi was strict and not violent but was inconsistent. Mimi would often shout at Lennon and at other times ignore him when he misbehaved. Yet, she as also extremely overprotective. When Lennon began school at Dovedale Primary, Mimi insisted that she accompany him every day. Eventually she gave in and let Lennon go alone, but she continued to follow him in secret and spy on him. While at Dovedale, Lennon continued to misbehave and emerged as the ringleader of his own little gang. Lennon and his friends took pleasure in shoplifting, fighting, and "pulling down girls' knickers." Around the age of 10, Lennon began seeing his mother again. Julia, her husband, and their two children moved in down the street from Mimi and Lennon. Lennon began sneaking out of the house to go visit his mother because Mimi didn't approve of it and was angry when she found out about the secret visits. According to childhood friends of Lennon, Mimi wasn't too far off base. Julia was emotionally disturbed and actually often encouraged Lennon to smoke, drink, and rebel.

In 1952, Lennon started attending Quarry Bank High School, where his grades began to drop. His report cards often described him with the words *hopeless* and *class clown*. Lennon was bored with school; he preferred drawing and writing stories. He continued shoplifting, smoking, and skipping classes with his friends. He had always wanted a guitar, and in 1955, Mimi finally bought him one. In 1956, Mimi took Lennon's drawings to the Liverpool College of Arts, and he was accepted. He started classes there in September 1957, but he still didn't take school seriously and mainly focused on his band, The Quarrymen, which included Paul McCartney. On July 15, 1958, Julia was hit by a drunk driver and killed while walking home from Aunt Mimi's house.

In the summer of 1960, The Quarrymen changed their name and booked their first shows as the "Beatles" in Hamburg, Germany. Over the next year they played hundreds of times throughout Hamburg and referred to it as "The Hamburg Experience." During 1961, the Beatles' popularity grew immensely in Liverpool. Lennon continued shoplifting on occasion even after the formation of the Beatles, but this behavior faded over time, supporting the fact that it was primarily peer generated. In 1962, he married Cynthia Powell after finding out she was pregnant, and their son Julian was born August 23, 1962. The Beatles recorded their first LP, *Please Please Me*, in 1963, which was just the beginning. Over the next seven years the Beatles recorded dozens of albums, including *Abbey Road* and *Sgt. Pepper's Lonely Hearts Club Band*. In 1966, Lennon met Yoko Ono and left Cynthia for her. Three years later, they married and in 1975 his second son, Sean, was born. After the Beatles dissolved around 1970, Lennon began recording music on his own. His albums were successful, and he was constantly the center of media attention. On December 8, 1980, Mark David Chapman went to Lennon's New York home and asked him to autograph an album, which he did. But Chapman continued to wait in front of Lennon's home for his return that evening and shot him because he felt Lennon was a "phony." Lennon was pronounced dead at the scene, and Chapman is currently serving 20 years to life.

Etiology

As is evident from these cases, a pattern of apparent kleptomania can emerge from very different background experiences. John Lennon's pattern likely emerged from a broader spectrum of behavioral acting-out and was specifically cultivated by peer modeling and maintenance. It is arguable whether he was a true kleptomaniac. His pattern did continue beyond the years where his peers were influential and into a time where other forms of behavioral acting-out had apparently dissipated. And it does appear that at least for a period of time there was a compulsive quality to the behavior. Yet, the shoplifting seemed to cease without therapeutic intervention and with little evidence of significant relapse.

Winona Ryder presents a more classic pattern of kleptomania—that is, where the stealing seems to offer relief from some form of psychological distress, such as anxiety or depression. She typically shoplifted alone, took blatant risks, was clearly compulsive in her pattern, often took items that she had little actual use for, and did not stop her behavior even when her kleptomania came into public awareness. Although not all kleptomaniacs show substance abuse, it is not uncommon and was likely a factor in Winona's case as it could obviously contribute to a loss of inhibition of behavior. Note that although many kleptomaniacs may have allied psychological problems, in most cases the severity of these problems does not rise to the level of a formal diagnosis, such as Major Depression. However, virtually all kleptomaniacs report a pattern wherein there is an increase of stress or distress, accompanied by increasing compulsion to steal something, even if the person has plenty of money available and no need of the item. They then report that the stealing causes a strong sense of relief, and the compulsion ceases until the cycle begins again.

Treatment

As with most of the impulse disorders, it is critical to help the individual gain immediate control over the behavior, especially as there are often potential legal complications. At the same time, there should be a thorough evaluation of the individual's personality so that one can also focus on any contributing psychopathology (in Winona's case, her psychological distress and substance abuse).

Cognitive-behavior modification is helpful in eliminating subconscious thoughts that may allow the person to be more likely to engage in the behavior (for example, "This is a big national store, and what I'm taking won't really have any effect on anybody") (Dattillo & Freeman, 2008). In severe cases, medication to control anxiety or depression may be needed, possibly facilitated by medication to control the sense of craving, such as buproprion.

Kellam (1969) pioneered an interesting aversive conditioning procedure that has proven helpful with chronic kleptomaniacs. While being videotaped, the individual is asked to simulate the shoplifting sequence in a room made up as much as possible to look like a store. The individual is asked to amplify her imagination of the shoplifting sequence as she watches the replay of the video. At critical points an electric shock is administered, which acts to suppress the thoughts and behaviors. To enhance the effect, the person is asked to imagine herself in a shoplifting sequence at various points in her daily life and to hold her breath until discomfort occurs, which strengthens the suppression effect generated during the therapy sessions. The person is trained to use the breath-holding technique whenever the craving emerges.

If the impulse is not suppressed and she finds herself in a store ready to steal, she is instructed to pick up a fragile item, such as a vase, and then deliberately drop it on the floor near a number of customers. She is also instructed to stay around as long as the item is being cleaned up and to insist on paying for it. Certainly these measures are often successful with kleptomaniacs. But, as with all impulse disorders, relapse is a consistent risk, and periodic booster sessions are advisable. In that vein, in order to have a sense of support, the person is also advised to join Shoplifters Anonymous.

13 Disorders with Violence

Violence in America has become rampant and seems to be increasing (Bartol & Bartol, 2008). Many experts believe violence will continue increasing because of gangs, drugs, terrorism, availability of powerful weapons, and a growing tolerance of violence in society. Understanding the cause of violence is an ongoing challenge among mental health professionals. The classic debate is whether personality traits or social stressors predict violence (Hillebrand & Pallone, 1995). There is evidence supporting both theories. Several other cases in this book also discuss patterns of violence, such as the cases of O. J. Simpson (Chapter 1), Joseph Westbecker (Chapter 7), Jeffrey Dahmer (Chapter 8), Ted Bundy (Chapter 11), John Hinckley (Chapter 16), and, to a lesser degree, some of the other cases. Here, the focus is on the causes of violence. The first case of Jack Ruby looks at violence in general; the second case looks at the first well-documented case of a serial killer in the United States; and the third and fourth cases consider patterns of violence and abuse in the family.

> *Liberals have invented whole college majors—psychology, sociology . . .*
> *[etc.]—to prove that nothing is anybody's fault.*
> —P. J. O'Rourke, *Give War a Chance*

Causes of Violence

As demonstrated by the quote above, there are many differing theories into the causes of violence. Because of the incredible public attention it received, the case of Jack Ruby has provided theorists with fodder for much thought and discussion (scientific and otherwise) on the matter.

The Case of Jack Ruby

On Friday, November 22, 1963, while in a motorcade with his wife, Jacqueline, and others going through the streets of Dallas, Texas, President John F. Kennedy was assassinated. The individual captured for this murder was Lee Harvey Oswald, who was imprisoned in a Dallas jail.

Two days later, on November 24, Jack Ruby entered the basement of the jail where Oswald was in the process of being transferred to a different facility. Somehow Ruby was able to penetrate a legion of police to fatally shoot Oswald. Great controversy still surrounds Jack Ruby because his connections with crime created grave questions about possible motives for Kennedy's assassination. There are several approaches that can be taken in diagnosing Ruby's mental status. The early years of Ruby's life will first be presented, followed by alternative theories that focus on different facts from Ruby's adult life (Kantor, 1978; Scott, 1994; Summers, 1980).

Jacob Rubenstein was born in Chicago in 1911, the fifth of eight children. Jacob's parents' marriage had been arranged through a traditional Jewish Polish marriage broker. His mother, Fanny Rubenstein, who came with a dowry, was uneducated, emotionally unstable, and, like Jacob, an incessant talker. His father, Joseph Rubenstein, was short, stocky, and mean. He had no trade and was known for cursing, drinking, and beating women. Joseph beat Fanny regularly. The couple had come from Poland to America and settled in Chicago in 1905.

Jacob's home was poor and unhappy. His parents had violent fights that frequently resulted in Fanny filing assault and battery charges against Joseph. Joseph also regularly slapped his children, and he insisted they end their education after grade school.

When Jacob was 10, his parents separated. He and his siblings were placed in foster homes. Occasionally, he stayed with his mother, who abused him physically and emotionally. She was demanding, ate compulsively, was lazy, threw temper tantrums when things didn't go her way, and often announced that she did not like any of her children. Finally, in 1937, at age 61, she was committed to a mental hospital and diagnosed as having deteriorating paranoia, a term that probably reflected some degree of organic deterioration.

At age 11, Jacob became noticeably defiant and depressed. He constantly skipped school and was disobedient to anyone in authority. The welfare department described him then as having an adequate IQ, being impulsive, unable to pay attention, and self-centered. Jacob quit school in the eighth grade at age 16 and began spending all of his time in the streets. He was unsuccessful at his attempts to hold a regular job because of tardiness and his violent disposition. Some of his ventures included selling race track tip sheets, novelties from a pushcart, peanuts at athletic games, and chocolates in strip shows. He also scalped tickets and ran errands for Al Capone. Later, he was a nightclub bouncer and waiter. He worked out regularly, wore expensive clothes, and saw himself as a ladies' man.

Jacob soon gained a reputation for engaging in senseless violence. It appeared he was determined to prove to the world he was a man and a Jew. He frequently got into fights with those who expressed anti-Semitic feelings. Before he was a teenager, Jacob had already fought in a gang against others who taunted Jews.

As is often the case, the facts in a case may support more than one theory. The following sections present several theories that might explain Jacob Rubenstein's (who later changed his name to Jack Ruby) murder of Oswald, along with the facts of the case relevant to each theory.

Social Psychology Theories

Social psychology views behavior as resulting from interactions between the person and his or her environment. One explanation for Ruby's tendency toward crime and violence is that he learned this behavior from his parents when he was a child. He also probably learned that his parents did not love him. Cognitive dissonance theory maintains that a person with two conflicting beliefs feels tension or stress and is motivated to find ways to remove the conflict. As a child, Ruby may have had conflicting ideas along the line of "I love my parents and they love me" and "Both of my parents are cruel to me and say they do not like me." One way to resolve this conflict is to conclude "I don't really need my parents, so it doesn't matter what I think of them or they think of me." Perhaps Ruby learned not to care about society's values, leaving him more apt to resort to criminal activities.

At age 26, Ruby became a union organizer for scrap iron workers. This position evolved into working with Jimmy Hoffa, an underworld leader and head of the Teamsters Union, who was known to have threatened the life of John F. Kennedy. By age 28, Ruby was entrenched with the most notorious criminal leaders of Chicago.

The influence of stress on behavior is a related theory. The diathesis/stress theory of behavior is that everybody has weaknesses and strengths, and when stress increases, a person's weak area is more likely to surface. For example, in his twenties, Ruby was in another gang that attacked anti-Semites, and in his thirties, he beat up a sergeant who called him a Jew bastard. Here, the diathesis is being a Jew while knowing there are people who hate Jews. Another diathesis is a predisposition to violence, triggered when the stress of being taunted or hated as a Jew becomes too great.

In modern times, there has been an increasing awareness of the role of the media in facilitating a violent society. Researchers such as Edward Donnerstein have found that rates of physical aggression in TV programming has held steady at about 60 percent for several years and often escalate to higher rates in prime time. A consensus from such studies also finds that (1) "good" characters, or heroes, the attractive/role models that children often emulate, commit more than nearly 40 percent of violent acts; (2) more than one-third of programs feature bad characters who are not punished and physical aggression that is condoned, and younger children oftentimes don't make the connection when the bad guy is punished in the end; (3) more than 70 percent of aggressors show no remorse for their violence and experience no criticism or penalty when it occurs; and (4) approximately half of TV violence produces no evident physical injury and no pain and suffering in the victim or any negative impact on the family or the community.

Organic/Biological/Genetic Theories

The condition of deteriorating paranoia in Ruby's mother indicates that Ruby may have inherited some genetic predisposition to a form of organic dysfunction that resulted in delusions. For example, in his mid-fifties, while in jail, Ruby believed Jews would be tortured as a result of his shooting Oswald. This became most apparent after Ruby was found guilty of first-degree murder and during his subsequent time in jail. Similarly, Ruby's mother's delusions increased as she became older.

An organic explanation for Ruby's actions offered at trial (possibly because the attorneys had no other option) that he used in trying to prove he was innocent by reason of temporary insanity was psychomotor epilepsy. Epileptic seizures are subdivided into two major groups: partial or generalized. *Partial epilepsy*, also called *focal epilepsy*, is a type of seizure that begins in a limited area of the brain and either stays in that area or spreads adjacently. It may or may not be associated with loss of consciousness. *Generalized epileptic* seizures involve large areas of the brain from the beginning and invariably involve loss of consciousness.

(continued)

The Case of Jack Ruby Continued

Psychomotor epileptic seizures are complex partial seizures. These involve experiences of illusions and behavioral responses to the illusions. Applying this diagnosis to Ruby would construe his behavior immediately before and during the shooting of Oswald as outside of his normal consciousness. He may have experienced visions that he thought were real and to which his shooting responded. Testimony at his trial described the shooting as occurring during an epileptic blackout.

However, there were problems with this diagnosis—for example, evidence suggesting that he planned this act. In addition, psychomotor epilepsy has a particular physical course that was not exhibited by Ruby. Even if it could be persuasively argued that this was the very first seizure he had ever had, which would be unusual, there was no evidence that he experienced any subsequent seizures. Psychomotor epilepsy takes a kindling course, which means that after one seizure occurs, it takes less stimulation to produce future seizures. Finally, there is no evidence that Ruby was ever prescribed anticonvulsant drug therapy for this condition. However, there was some evidence at autopsy of a brain tumor, which could support the diagnosis.

If testimony in support of psychomotor epilepsy was along the lines of there being a disruption in Ruby's consciousness, a more appropriate diagnosis may have been a dissociative disorder (see Chapter 4), a condition in which the predominant feature would be an interruption in the usually integrated mechanisms of consciousness. However, this diagnosis would also be difficult to prove in light of there being no prior or subsequent events similar to the alleged dissociative experience. Thus, with psychomotor epilepsy as Ruby's main defense, it is not a great surprise that Jack Ruby was found guilty of first-degree murder and sentenced to death.

There is another interesting and alternative biological perspective on violence. For centuries, many theorists have held to the hypothesis that only humans deliberately kill others of their own species without survival reasons. However, in the early afternoon of January 7, 1974, as Richard Wrangham and Dale Peterson reported in *Demonic Males: Apes and the Origins of Human Violence* (New York: Houghton Mifflin, 1996), in Gombe National Park in Tanzania, eight chimpanzees purposefully traveled to the border of their range, entered a neighboring chimpanzee territory, attacked and mortally wounded a young male from another community, then returned home—the first recorded instance of lethal raiding among chimpanzees. The event was significant not only as an example of another species that killed its own deliberately and without apparent purpose but also because the species happened to be the one most closely related to humans. Subsequent research has found gratuitous violence in other species.

Affective Disorder Theory

An intriguing possibility is that Ruby suffered from an affective disorder such as atypical depression, bipolar disorder (major mood swings), or cyclothymia (less intense mood swings) (see Chapter 7). Information is insufficient to determine if Ruby was prone to have periods of time when he was uncharacteristically active (manic). There were times, however, when he was depressed; for example, the welfare department described him as being depressed as a child. Ruby admitted that as an adult he overate in order to ward off depression, a not uncommon pattern (Williams et al., 2008). He then took medication to suppress his appetite and give him energy. Later, Ruby stopped taking his weight-loss medication when he worried that it was making his hair thinner.

Unlike some diagnoses, such as antisocial personality disorder (ASP), that are manifest throughout a person's life, the diagnosis of depression or a related affect disorder leaves open the opportunity for remission. Something like this occurred in 1944, the same year that Ruby's mother died, when he joined the U.S. Army Air Force. Ruby's experience in the Army Air Force was in contradiction to his previous behavior patterns: He was an aircraft mechanic who seldom got into fights and earned a good conduct metal. When he was discharged in 1946, he was a private first class.

Ruby did not necessarily seek out the life of a criminal. When he returned to civilian life, he struggled for eight years in a business distributing punch boards, key chains, and other miscellaneous items with his brothers, with whom he fought constantly. For a few years following this venture, Ruby did not speak to two of his brothers. This experience may have caused Ruby's mood swings to return. It was after this that Ruby allegedly responded to instructions from organized crime to go to Dallas.

Depression can be accompanied by psychosis (DeBattista, 1998). When Ruby heard the verdict of electrocution, he likely lost all hope. His delusions about all Jews being killed took control, and he realized he would never see his dogs again, whom he considered to be his wife and children. Expecting electrocution at any time, he tried several times to kill himself in different ways, such as by crashing his head against the wall, hoping to split his skull. At this point in his life, all would agree that Ruby was very depressed.

Psychopathy: Antisocial Personality Disorder Theory

Ruby's life of crime that began as a child supports the diagnosis of psychopathy and/or ASP (see Chapter 11). His connections with Cuba linked him with the U.S. government and the underworld. Six years before the assassination, he began smuggling guns and ammunition to Cuba in support of Fidel Castro. Organized crime supported Castro to ensure good relations when the revolution ended. However, the same group later turned against Castro because he would not endorse their activities. It may not have been a coincidence that the head of the underworld wished Kennedy dead.

Examples of additional activities characteristic of the antisocial personality disorder abound. For example, Ruby's name became associated with the expansion of organized crime into Dallas. He became involved with smuggling narcotics and operating bootleg whiskey. In addition, he opened nightclubs where underworld figures attended regularly. He beat up those who crossed him, but he never was punished. Throughout the nightclub years, Ruby was arrested nine times for various acts of violence, but the only thing he ever received a punishment for was a traffic violation. This probably reflects his manipulativeness as well as the extent of his contacts among local law enforcement officials and judges.

The antisocial personality might be willing to kill for money, and that is what many believe caused Ruby to kill Oswald. In 1963, before Kennedy's assassination, Ruby was in financial trouble. Debts and unpaid taxes forced him to sell one of his nightclubs. He agonized over finances, and then suddenly, immediately before the assassination, he behaved entirely differently, confident that his financial troubles would soon end. On November 19, 1963, three days before Kennedy's assassination, Ruby told his tax lawyer he was going to be able to pay his debts as a result of a connection. There is some evidence that he received large sums of cash payments immediately after Kennedy's assassination.

Another characteristic of ASP is deceitfulness (Boyd et al., 2007). Immediately following the assassination, Ruby showed up at a variety of public places and displayed an exaggerated amount of grief about Kennedy's death (although this could reflect a dissociative process, as well). The possible deceit continued, as, after killing Oswald, Ruby denied any connections with the underworld or Cuba.

(continued)

The Case of Jack Ruby Continued

His verbalized motive for killing Oswald was allegedly to save Mrs. Kennedy from the pain of attending Oswald's trial.

However, there were facts that contradict the psychopathy-antisocial personality disorder theory. The most striking is the way Ruby killed Oswald. He was certain to get caught and be punished—something a psychopath would try to avoid.

Conclusion

Despite the appropriateness of any of these theories to his case, Jack Ruby was found guilty of the first-degree murder of Lee Harvey Oswald on March 14, 1964, and was sentenced to death. Ruby died in 1967 of cancer while awaiting a new trial after his death sentence conviction was overturned.

Interventions

As noted, there are numerous potential causes of violent behavior. The following gives an overview of the common causes, along with consensus intervention strategies:

1. *Violence as an Inherent Part of Human Nature:* (a) individual psychotherapy to modify basic personality patterns; (b) medications to diminish anxiety and minimize inappropriate reactions; (c) psychosurgery to change or interrupt patterns of brain functioning
2. *Violence as a Consequence of Social Learning:* (a) family therapy to change home environment or facilitate coping in the family setting; (b) group therapy to enhance appropriate coping in social situation; (c) assertiveness training and social-skills training to give concrete training in self-assertion without violence; (d) systematic desensitization (SDT) to desensitize client to the precipitating stimuli, so as to diminish inappropriate or excessive reactions; (e) token economy, time out, social isolation to extinguish violent behavior through removal of environmental reinforcers, as well as to strengthen appropriate responses; (f) classical conditioning to extinguish violent behavior, as in aversive conditioning; (g) parent effectiveness training, Parents Anonymous to enhance adequate coping skills and provide a supportive peer group
3. *Violence as a Consequence of Frustration and Other Situational Factors:* (a) traditional psychotherapy to release frustrations and to change coping patterns; (b) family therapy (see 2a); (c) group therapy (see 2b); (d) assertiveness training, social-skills training (see 2c); (e) token economy, providing opportunities for positively reinforcing experiences while extinguishing the violent behavior; (f) parent effectiveness training (see 2g)
4. *Violence as a Means of Communication:* (a) expressive therapies to substitute alternate means of expression of feelings underlying violent acting out; (b) assertiveness training (see 2c); (c) SDT (see 2d); (d) parent effectiveness training (see 2g)

5. *Violence and Aggression as Protection of Territorial Integrity and Body Space:* (a) SDT (see 2d); (b) assertiveness training (see 2c); (c) individual psychotherapy to improve the sense of self and self-esteem

Prediction of Violent Behavior

The prediction of violent behavior is perhaps one of the most formidable tasks asked of any mental health professional, and because it cannot be consistently accurate, it is better termed *risk assessment*. At a personal level, it may be viewed as an unpleasant and anxiety-producing situation that brings the psychologist too close to the darkest side of the human condition. On a professional level, Monahan (1981) was one of the first to thoroughly describe many of the problems inherent in making such judgments. The difficulties for the professional were heightened even more when, in 1976, a major precedent was set by the California Supreme Court in *Tarasoff* v. *Regents of the University of California* (551 P.2d 334 [Cal. 1976]). Tatiana Tarasoff had become the romantic obsession of Prosejit Poddar after she gave him a ritual New Year's Eve kiss. In therapy at the counseling center, Poddar told the therapist that he felt like killing Tarasoff. The campus police were sent to pick Poddar up, but he convinced them he would not be a problem, so they left. He later killed Tarasoff. Her estate sued, and the California Supreme Court held that the therapist had a "duty to warn" Tarasoff (later amended to a "duty to protect"). Unfortunately, given the low base rates of severe aggressive behaviors (and suicide, as well), making an accurate prediction of specific actual behavior is virtually impossible, and overprediction is common (Meyer & Weaver, 2006).

The Problems of Prediction and Overprediction

Five factors primarily contribute to problems of prediction and to overprediction. First, predicting rare events is an inherently difficult task, and violence (and suicide) is something of a rare phenomenon. Any attempt at predicting a low base rate event will guarantee a significant number of false positives. A second bias toward overprediction stems from the relative costs of mistaken predictions. Mistakenly labeling an individual dangerous (i.e., a false positive) may result in continued confinement to a hospital or treatment program, with little potential for adverse consequences for the therapist. By comparison, incorrectly labeling someone safe who later commits a violent act (i.e., a false negative) exposes the predictor to public outcry and civil liability. The high costs of false negatives create a bias to overpredict out of self-defense.

Third, although one can develop lists of factors that contribute to some type of dangerousness (e.g., to others in general, to a spouse, to self, etc.), one cannot and likely will never be able to develop an accurate predictive equation in which to plug these lists of factors. That is, definite weights cannot be assigned to each factor, and each case is likely to show variations of a pattern of contributing factors. Fourth, most studies on the prediction of dangerousness to self or others are based on long-term follow-up, usually for many years and seldom for less than one year. Yet, in the real world, the requested predictions are usually for "imminent" predictions (i.e., for that day or a few days). Fifth, "dangerousness" is not a simple trait or predisposition. People vary along many dimensions; they may be dangerous or violent at some point, but no one is invariably and constantly dangerous. Under the right conditions, nearly any individual may become assaultive, while even very impulsive, hostile individuals are not violent most of the time. Unlike other characteristics that are viewed as highly stable, dangerousness fluctuates over time in accordance with a variety of environmental factors, maturation, changes in level of adjustment, and so forth. Violence and dangerousness may be viewed most parsimoniously as an interaction of personality and environmental factors. It is the second group, environmental factors, that greatly confounds the prediction problem due to its constant variation.

Specific Indicators of Aggression   Early on, Monahan (1981) pinpointed eight of the most critical demographic predictor variables for aggression. Violence is more common if the potential perpetrator (1) is young (this variable correlates strongly up until the 30–35 age range, after which the correlation is close to random), (2) is male, (3) is of a lower socioeconomic class, (4) is from a disadvantaged minority, (5) is less educated, (6) has a lower intellectual level, (7) has an unstable school and/or vocational history, and (8) has a history of juvenile violence and/or alcohol and/or drug abuse.

Other demographic indicators of a potential for violence that have been noted throughout the literature are (1) a prior history of violent behaviors; (2) a prior history of suicide attempts; (3) a history of family violence; (4) soft neurological signs; (5) bipolar disorder or schizophrenia, especially if the schizophrenia includes command hallucinations; (6) fascination with weapons; (7) histrionic personality traits; (8) a pattern of cruelty to animals as a child or adolescent; (9) a rejecting or depressed father; and (10) recent stress, especially if associated with low levels of serotonin.

Serial Killers

Although public interest seems to be insatiable, Schechter (2003) has pointed out that "serial killers always existed . . . many . . . for whatever reason . . . never achieve lasting notoriety . . . there's nothing new about the interest in serial murder . . . only the technology has changed" (p. 3). A reasonable consensus definition includes (1) premeditation, (2) three or more victims, and (3) a cooling-off period between killings. In the United States during the frontier days up to the Civil War, and in the chaos that followed, there were likely people who fit that definition. However, the following is the first well-documented case of a serial killer in America—an individual so horrific that the fictional character of Hannibal Lector in *The Silence of the Lambs* pales by comparison. Erik Larson integrated some truthful components of Hermann Mudgett in his somewhat fictionalized novel, *The Devil in the White City*, published in 2003 by Vintage Press. Both Leonardo

DiCaprio and Tom Cruise are allegedly working on movies depicting aspects of his life. An excellent 64-minute documentary film by John Borowski is available at www.hhholmesthefilm.com.

The Case of Hermann Mudgett (Dr. Henry Holmes)

Hermann Webster Mudgett was born into a strict Methodist family on May 16, 1860, in Gilmanton, an isolated village in New Hampshire's Lake District. His father, Levi, was a strict disciplinarian. Hermann was a "delicately built boy, blue-eyed and brown haired, with a reputation as 'the brightest lad in town' . . . his father . . . beat the boy with savage regularity" (Schechter, 2003, p. 180). The beating was often followed by a day of confinement in the attic with neither food nor speech. Hermann was also often bullied by his peers. On one occasion they grabbed him, dragged him into the office of the village doctor, who was out on a call, and forced his face into the hands of the skeleton the doctor used for demonstrations. Though hysterically traumatized, Hermann later said this incident led to his interest in anatomy. By age 11, he was "experimenting" by dissecting live animals and keeping a collection of their bones. His closest and possibly only childhood friend was killed in a suspicious "fall" while the two of them were playing in an abandoned house. Hermann was standing just behind him before he fell.

Hermann graduated from high school at age 16 and at age 17 married Clara Lovering, who had some wealth. He used much of her money and rather quickly abandoned her. Hermann decided to become a physician. He enrolled in a small college in Burlington, Vermont, but quickly transferred to the University of Michigan when he learned they had begun using the then-controversial practice of dissecting cadavers. While there, he developed a scam wherein he would purchase insurance policies on a faked individual, steal a corpse, and then claim the settlement when these "family members" suffered disfiguring "deaths," preventing accurate identification of the bodies. After

graduating in 1884 with a medical degree from Michigan, he moved around, first running a business, working as a "keeper of an insane asylum," and then working as a pharmacist. As he traveled around, an uncommon number of unexplained deaths occurred in his vicinity, but he was never suspected.

He eventually settled in Chicago. At age 26, he formally registered himself as Henry Howard Holmes when he passed the licensing exam as a pharmacist and used that name from then on. He started to work at the Holton Pharmacy in Englewood, a section of Chicago. Eventually, he bought the business from Mr. Holton's widow but reneged on the payments. She took him to court, but then, although she was old and frail, he reported that she suddenly "moved out West," never to be heard from again.

Holmes then bought the land across the street in order to build his "Castle." He employed over 500 workers in order that, with the exception of his "assistant" Benjamin Pitezal, no one worker had any real idea of the purpose of the Castle. The Castle had many hidden peepholes, various soundproof chambers, hidden gas jets in the guest rooms, several rooms ideal for surgery, a 3' × 3' × 8' oven that would fire at 3,000 degrees Fahrenheit "for bending glass," various body-sized chutes leading to the cellar, which had several steel-lined acid vats and a lime pit. He obtained most of his victims (most commonly young females) through want ads, or he killed those visiting the Castle, including at least 50 visitors to the Colombian Exposition (or World's Fair) in 1893. He eventually killed most of the people who were close to him at one point or another. Although no one knows for sure, it is estimated that he killed at least

(continued)

The Case of Hermann Mudgett (Dr. Henry Holmes) Continued

200 people. Many were used in his insurance scams or were rendered down to bones that were then reassembled as skeletons and sold to physicians or medical schools or were simply killed and discarded, which he later admitted was for the pleasure of killing.

Dr. Holmes's many scams and his consistent avoidance of paying his bills finally caught up with him in the fall of 1893. A collection agent arranged a meeting with Holmes and over 20 of his creditors. He was charming and responsive during the meeting and then left Chicago the next day. He moved from city to city until he was arrested in Boston in November 1894. During the period he moved about, he killed numerous people, including the person who had been closest to him, Benjamin Pitezal. He had taken out an insurance policy on Pitezal, telling him he would fake his death. Instead, he poured gasoline on Pitezal, burned him alive, then poured a caustic solvent on his face and left him in the sun to make it look like an accident. He went on to kill Pitezal's three children separately, over a period of time. Shortly thereafter, Holmes was arrested but

was relieved to realize it was for insurance fraud and not murder. He pled guilty on May 28, 1895, and faced only a few months in jail.

Meanwhile, however, a Philadelphia police detective, Frank Geyer, continued the investigation of Pitezal's missing children. He visited various cities Holmes had moved through, including Fort Worth, Cincinnati, Philadelphia, Indianapolis, Toronto, and several smaller cities. Geyer was able to find evidence that the children had been killed in separate cities, and based on this evidence the Chicago police searched the Castle. In addition to the horrors included in the original building, they found that Dr. Holmes continued to devise and use new torture devices, including an "Elasticity Determinator" designed to stretch the human body to twice its normal size. Holmes did confess to killing 27 people (Schechter, 2003) but as noted here, it was likely many, many more. Philadelphia indicted and convicted Holmes for killing Benjamin Pitezal and hanged him on May 7, 1896. As the hangman prepared the noose, Holmes joked to him, "Take your time, old man. I'm in no hurry."

Comment

Only in recent years have there been attempts to collect scientific data on such individuals (Schechter, 2003). For example, the FBI has traditionally categorized serial killers as either organized or disorganized. But so far, such categorizations have proven to be too simplistic. Indeed, there are several problems in obtaining adequate data. First, it is a low base rate phenomenon. Also, most of these individuals are very deceptive and much of the data that have been collected are either from hindsight or self-reports; hence what little data that are available are significantly tainted (Boyd et al., 2007).

The Death Penalty

A discussion of the death penalty may be appropriate at various junctures in this book. But it is probably most applicable here because serial killers are almost always considered for it if the relevant state's law allows the death penalty. The first critical case in modern times was *Furman* v. *Georgia* (408 U.S. 238, 1972), wherein the Supreme Court held that the death penalty was unconstitutional as it was being applied at that time but might be constitutional if juries or judges were not given complete discretion in imposing death; that both mitigating (e.g., horrific childhood, etc.) and aggravating (more than one person was killed, another felony such as rape was included in the crime, etc.) circumstances should be allowed to be presented; that the death penalty could never be mandatory; and that imposing a death penalty for rape or kidnapping was disproportionately severe, that is, no life was taken, under the Eighth Amendment's "cruel and unusual" clause. Then, a few years later, the Supreme Court in *Gregg* v. *Georgia* (428 U.S. 153, 1976) found the death penalty to be explicitly constitutional. Related to the issue of aggravating circumstances, the Supreme Court in *Payne* v. *Tennessee* (501 U.S. 808, 1991) allowed "victim impact" statements to be used in the penalty phase (rather than the guilt or innocence phase) of a death penalty trial.

The issue as to whether children may be executed has long been controversial. In colonial times children as young as 12 were executed, although rarely so. In modern times, *Thompson* v. *Oklahoma* (487 U.S. 815, 1989) established that children under age 16 at the time of the crime could not be executed. It was assumed that persons over the age of 18 at the time of the crime could be executed, and then the Supreme Court in *Stanford* v. *Kentucky* (492 U.S. 937, 1989) held that children ages 16 to 18 could be executed. The Court then revisited the issue in *Roper* v. *Tennessee* (125 S. Ct. 1183, 2005) and held that children ages 16 to 18 could not be executed, citing the concept from the admonition in *Trope* v. *Dulles* (1957) that judges should be guided by "evolving standards of decency that mark the progress of a maturing society" (p. 4). It is of course debatable whether our society is maturing. In a related vein, in *Ford* v. *Wainwright* (477 U.S. 399, 1986), the Supreme Court held that a person must be "competent to be executed," that is, he must be able to comprehend why he is being executed. The issue of competency and mental retardation is discussed at length in the case of Daryl Atkins in Chapter 15.

The controversy over the death penalty centers on the taking of a life. What other alternative is available for those horrific individuals like Dr. Henry Holmes? In various papers and presentations, the senior author (Dr. Meyer), has reported on data that suggest there are two options in which no one is executed, but people generally perceive these options as having greater deterrent value than the death penalty or life without parole. The first is *banishment*, wherein the person is forever in solitary confinement but is allowed no human contact except for medical or legal purposes, that is, no television, Internet, letters, visits, and so forth. The second option is *permanent coma*, with the choice of making it revocable or irrevocable (the latter only if all appeals have been exhausted). In addition to avoiding actually taking a life, a second advantage of permanent coma is that it would be extremely economical. All such inmates would be in morgue-like drawers, monitored physiologically, with a technician on site and a physician on call. No treatment or correctional staff or even lights or standard meals would be necessary. All could be housed in a rather small building, placed in an inexpensive real estate site. The majority of those sampled said banishment has the most deterrent value, with permanent coma not far behind and well ahead of the death penalty. The legal issues would be sticky but not insurmountable.

Family Violence: Physical and Sexual Abuse of Children and Spouse Abuse

Throughout history, as well as across cultures, the abuse of children has been clearly documented (Laws & O'Donohue, 2008; Finkelhor & Dzuiba-Leatherman, 1994; Melton et al., 1997). It is ironic that the first formal legal intervention in a child abuse case, that of Mary Ellen in New York in 1875, had to be prosecuted through animal protection laws and primarily as a result of the efforts of the Society for the Prevention of Cruelty to Animals. However, all 50 U.S. states have now established legislative routes to identification of abusive families and to intervention. As a result, the number of identified cases has grown enormously. Because of the private nature of abuse and the reluctance of both perpetrators and victims to reveal it, clearly identified cases of child abuse are still generally believed to represent only a portion of actual cases. Estimates vary widely, and debate over incidence of child abuse will doubtless continue. However, whatever the true incidence rates, the problem is obviously substantial.

The consequences of abuse to children are usually extensive and debilitating (Chu et al., 1999; Finkelhor & Dzuiba-Leatherman, 1994). And the effect goes beyond consequences to the child to encompass consequences to others with whom the child later interacts—for example, abused children are prone to grow up to be abusers, as will be seen in the following case of Abby. Most experts believe that the problem is of massive proportion.

Spouse Abuse

As the data indicate, there's no place like home, for either happiness or violence. As a marriage breaks down, the potential for violence soars (Kubany, McCaig, & Laconsay, 2004). It may be directed toward a child or toward the spouse. Estimates of the percentage of couples who experience physical violence at some time in the course of a marriage range from 30 to 60 percent, and it is clear that the amount of reported violence is far less than the amount of actual violence. In most cases, the wife is the victim, although there are a few reports of the husband being abused. Family therapy can sometimes be helpful, although often by the time the abuse pattern has been made public, the bonding between the two parties has been so violated that reconciliation is highly improbable. As is noted in the subsequent case of Abby, many spouse abusers were themselves abused as a child by one or both of their parents.

Recognizing a Potentially Abusive Adult Relationship

Cases such as O. J. Simpson's (see Chapter 1) and recognition of such patterns as "date rape" bring home the need to be aware of the cues that help one recognize a potential abusive adult relationship and/or a potential batterer, especially when entering a relationship. The following pattern may suggest potential abuse behavior:

- Having been a participant in, a victim of, or witness to (in that order of predictive power) abusive patterns or, to a lesser degree, an abusive or violent episode
- Violence toward pets, other animals, or even inanimate objects
- General problems with anger control or evidence of a "temper"
- Problems in impulse control
- "Playful" use of force during sex
- Threats of violence and/or use of force or threats to manipulate arguments
- Evidence of control issues, especially when there are problems of relinquishing control in relationships, and especially when this is combined with tendencies to avoid responsibility for behaviors or project blame on others
- Evidence of possessiveness toward persons, or jealousy
- An increasing dependency on the relationship
- Substance abuse in either party
- Verbalizations of strong adherence to traditional male/female roles in relationships
- Evidence of psychopathy or sadistic personality patterns
- Feelings of being possessively controlled, jealousy, or anger easily elicited by the person potentially abused
- Indicators of emotional or physical isolation or vulnerability, or being prone to masochism or excessive dependency in the person potentially abused

Child Abuse

I was coming home from kindergarten—well, they told me it was kindergarten. I found out later that I had been working in a factory for ten years. It's good for a kid to know how to make gloves.
—Ellen DeGeneres

First is a classic pattern of child sexual abuse, the case of Charles, followed by one of physical abuse, the case of Abby.

The Case of Charles

Charles is a 39-year-old civil engineer who lives in a medium-sized city in Kentucky. He works for a large construction business, makes a good salary, and would certainly be characterized as a model citizen by most who know him. He is a long-time member of a church (although he doesn't profess or practice any strong religious beliefs) and belongs to a number of civic organizations. All indications are that he had a normal childhood. He has never sought help for any psychological disorder.

Charles married at age 25. The marriage was certainly a good one at the outset, and both he and his wife were delighted when she had a baby girl, Vicki, when Charles was 30. Unfortunately, the marriage started to deteriorate

(continued)

The Case of Charles Continued

shortly thereafter. Charles's wife enjoyed the status of being a mother but not the functions. She returned to her job as a secretary as soon as she could after Vicki's birth and often hired babysitters in order to escape the routine demands of child care. She had always been a regular social drinker but now began to drink more secretively and more often, probably to dissolve both guilt and anxiety. Within several years, she had developed a true alcoholic pattern. She was just barely able to hold on to her job and was almost nonfunctional as a wife and mother.

Charles, on the other hand, enjoyed fathering and developed a strong bond with Vicki. He had few friends or interests away from home. He and his wife now simply tolerated each other, with only rare sexual or emotional encounters. He satisfied his sexual needs in several ways: an occasional affair, a visit to a prostitute, or by masturbation to stimulation from pornographic magazines and videotapes.

Charles had always allowed Vicki to lie down next to him or put her head in his lap for 15 minutes or so before she went off to bed. One night, when Vicki was 8 years old, he let her lie next to him on the couch for almost an hour, enjoying the closeness to her—a closeness that seemingly was not available to him elsewhere. He became aroused sexually and responded by sending Vicki off to bed. Several nights later, he was again lying with Vicki and again became aroused. This time, he just lay there. After a while, as Vicki moved around a bit, he suddenly had a strong orgasm. He felt some upset at this time but allowed a repetition on a couple of subsequent occasions.

A week later, the situation escalated further. When Charles had become very aroused, he raised the back of Vicki's nightgown and gently rubbed his penis against her buttocks, again having a strong orgasm. He told Vicki everything was all right and not to be upset, and she wasn't. This, however, was the first time that he had acted to directly cause a sex-

ual act, and this seemed to break down any remaining inhibitions. He would sometimes have Vicki reach behind her and rub his penis. Also, he would now touch her occasionally on her genitals and would bring on his orgasm by rubbing his penis between her legs. He eventually asked her to "lick it" at a point of high arousal and would ejaculate on her face, all the time presenting all of this to Vicki as a sort of game, though always emphasizing her need to keep secret about it. He tried to penetrate her vagina a couple of times but quickly backed off when Vicki complained that it hurt.

This pattern went on for about six months. There was some reason to believe that Charles's wife may have been at least vaguely aware what was happening. But she did nothing and in fact had been using alcohol even more heavily over the last year or so. Then, one day while Vicki was playing with a neighbor girl, the word *penis* came up, and Vicki blurted out, "Well, Daddy lets me lick his." The friend's mother overheard this, asked Vicki what she meant, and Vicki described it all in vivid detail. The neighbor called her husband, who, as a physician, knew it had to be reported, and where, and did so.

When confronted by a worker with the child protective services division, Charles broke down and confessed. He was later convicted. But based on his history and the recommendations of a psychologist and social worker, his sentence was probated, with a stipulated requirement for community service and treatment.

Treatment was successful in the sense that Charles never sexually abused Vicki again. But he and his wife could never reconcile their feelings about this and were divorced within the year. It's not yet clear how much psychological damage Vicki has incurred. However, it was probably quite a bit; indeed, it is very likely that over time she will pay the highest price of all.

Then spare the rod and spoil the child.

—Samuel Butler, *Hudibras* (1663)

The Case of Abby

Abby was born to a poor family in the mountains of West Virginia. When she was age 4, the family moved to Akron, Ohio, in hopes of her father getting work in a tire factory, where her uncle already had a job. Unfortunately, this was at the time when such jobs were drying up. After struggling for several years, often surviving only on welfare, the family moved to Tennessee to try to find work at a new General Motors plant being built there.

There were no dramatic problems or incidents in Abby's childhood. However, child care was minimal, and there was little value placed on education or achievement. She seldom had any interaction with her father, who spent his time away from home when he could. When he was home, he spent his time eating, sleeping, drinking, or beating Abby's mother or one of the five children if they gained too much of his attention. Abby's mother loved the children, but her emotional, intellectual, and physical resources were overwhelmed to the point that she could do little more than meet their basic needs.

Eventually, Abby made it through high school, though with close to failing grades. She had become pregnant in her junior year but aborted without letting her parents know. One month after getting out of high school, she discovered she was again pregnant, but this time she maneuvered the father into marrying her. They moved to a nearby city, and she delivered a healthy girl and almost immediately became pregnant again. This pregnancy and labor were difficult, and the child, a boy, soon showed some signs that he had incurred brain damage.

Abby's husband soon had enough of fatherhood and left town, to be seldom heard from again. Abby was not especially attractive and was neither very bright nor had any marketable skills. With two young children and no money, she did not attract the most eligible of men. She had a string of live-in boyfriends, and several of them would beat whichever child bothered them in some way, and it was usually the youngest child.

Abby herself was confused and overwhelmed by the tasks of child care. Her daughter was quiet and docile, almost to the point of being withdrawn, so she caused Abby few problems. However, as her youngest became more mobile, he became more difficult to control. Abby had few skills or resources to bring to the task, and more and more she quickly resorted to beating this child. A week after yet another boyfriend had abruptly walked out on her, her son broke a small vase that Abby had received years ago from a much loved grandmother. Abby started shrieking at her son, grabbed him roughly, dragged him by the arm into the kitchen, and started hitting him and beating him. When she finally stopped, he was bleeding and bruised, and it became evident he could hardly move his arm. He was still not moving the arm the next day, and Abby took him to a hospital emergency room, where attendants quickly recognized the probability of child abuse. At first, Abby tried to deny it, but she eventually admitted what had happened. She was diverted into treatment and a parents' training group and began to make some progress in handling her children. But there were repeat incidents, and then Abby left town with a new boyfriend. No follow-up information is available, but it is probable that the abuse occurred again, becoming a legacy her children would carry into their own world as parents.

Etiology

Many overall factors contribute to the ultimate emergence of an episode of physical and/or sexual child abuse (Laws & O'Donohue, 2008; Kubany, McCaig, & Laconsay, 2004; Finkelhor & Dzuiba-Leatherman, 1994). These factors are found within three contributing systems: sociocultural, familial, and individual. To the degree these factors are present, the probability of an occurrence of child abuse is increased. At the most basic level are the following *sociocultural* factors that facilitate an increase in episodes of child abuse:

1. Lack of affirmation and support of the family unit
2. Lack of emphasis on parent training skills as a prerequisite to parenting
3. Acceptance of and high media visibility of violence
4. Acceptance of corporal punishment as a central child-rearing technique
5. Emphasis on competitiveness rather than cooperation
6. Unequal status for women
7. Low economic support for schools and child-care facilities

Sociocultural factors heighten the probability of abuse in conjunction with the following *familial* factors:

1. Low socioeconomic and educational level
2. Little availability of friends and extended family for support
3. A single parent or merged parent family structure
4. Marital instability
5. Family violence as common and traditionally accepted
6. Low rate of family contact and information exchange
7. Significant periods of mother absence
8. High acceptance of family nudity
9. Low affirmation of family member privacy
10. "Vulnerable" children—that is, to the degree they are young, sick, disturbed, retarded, or emotionally isolated

The probability of abuse in a specific instance is then in turn increased by the following *individual* factors:

1. History of abuse as a child
2. Low emotional stability and/or self-esteem
3. Low ability to tolerate frustration and inhibit anger
4. High impulsiveness
5. Lack of parenting skills
6. High emotional and interpersonal isolation
7. Problems in handling dependency needs of self or others
8. Low ability to express physical affection
9. Unrealistic expectancies for child's performance
10. Acceptance of corporal punishment as a primary child-rearing technique
11. Presence of drug or alcohol abuse

As with most cases, many but not all of these factors are found in the cases of Charles and of Abby. Some predict more to physical abuse and some to sexual abuse, but most factors predict to either type of abuse. However, from an overall perspective, the following general factors were evident in the cases of Charles and of Abby:

1. *Impulsivity:* The actual incident often occurs in persons in whom either training or temperament (or both) has predisposed to immediately act on impulse, not bring inhibitory belief systems to bear on impulse, or delay gratification. In a similar vein, the demands of child rearing are too much for an immature personality, who lashes out in retaliation at the cause for these demands. Remorse may follow, but the damage is done.

2. *Incompetence:* As with Abby, far too many parents come to this crucial task with little preparation or support (e.g., poverty markedly increases the potential for child abuse). When the task overwhelms them, they react with harsh punishments in an attempt to regain control.

3. *Disturbance:* Psychological and physical disturbances (not in the child), such as schizophrenia, drug and alcohol abuse, mental retardation, or, as in the case of Charles, a disrupted marriage generate problems that facilitate child abuse.

4. *Modeling:* The child who has been abused or who has witnessed a pattern of spouse abuse is much more likely to become an abuser than the average child.

5. *Characteristics of the Child:* As was the case with Abby's younger child, children who have characteristics that make frustration or disappointment more likely (e.g., ADHD, physical or psychological disabilities) are more likely to be abused. The amount of parental bonding and the vulnerability of the child are also relevant; thus, stepchildren and younger children are more often the victims. Indeed, live-in boyfriends are a common source of child abuse.

Physical Abuse

Mothers physically abuse more in absolute terms; fathers physically abuse more in number of abuse events per contact hours. Predictors of physical abuse of children (with the greatest applicability to mothers who become physical abusers) are (1) single parent, (2) younger, (3) less educated, (4) lower SES, and (5) a history of abuse. These are the best predictors, but demographic predictors are not usually responsive to intervention. Mediating-causative variables, which offer more potential for intervention, are (1) higher physiological reactivity to a crying child, to children in general, and probably just in general; (2) a higher proclivity to label negative child behaviors with internal and stable attributions and positive events with external and transient attributions; (3) acceptance of fewer mitigating factors for problematic behavior (thus facilitating judgments of "badness" and subsequent punishment); (4) unrealistic expectations before and after birth for a child's performance, especially regarding more complex behavior sequences; (5) more rigid attitudes; (6) higher than normal rates of physical illness, stress, and depression; (7) lower self-esteem; and (8) lack of empathy. Surprisingly, physical abusers show only slightly higher levels of precipitating substance abuse. They generally like their children less (some research indicates this is not usually based on objective fact), and they attend to and track their children's behavior less often (Milner, 1998).

Sexual Abuse

The factors that generate physical child abuse are also often relevant to cases of sexual child abuse. However, a number of specifically relevant factors are also critical (Laws & O'Donohue, 2008; Marvasti, 2004). For example, psychodynamic features here include the interaction of such parental factors as marital discord, personality disorder, loss of an important relationship or fear of disintegration of the family, and emotional deprivation. Other factors include the equating of sexuality and affection, the importance of heterosexual success to self-identity, a focus on sexual acts rather than on relationships, and any acceptance of younger and smaller sexual partners. See also the discussion of pedophilia in Chapter 8.

The seriousness of consequent disorder in the child resulting from sexual abuse appears to depend on several factors. More serious problems are likely if (1) the offender is in a close relationship to the child, such as the father; (2) the sexual activity included genital contact, and especially if this includes penetration; (3) the child is older (e.g., adolescent) at the time of abuse; (4) the abuse is frequent and/or of long duration; (5) the child has strong negative feelings about the abuse and/or is somehow aware of its wrongness; and (6) much upset and/or distress occurs around the event (e.g., court testimony).

Diagnostic Problems in Sexual Abuse

The following list is adapted in part from the review of research and clinical data by Michael P. Maloney, Ph.D., the lead defense psychologist in the McMartin trial, the first "false memories of abuse" trial that attained national notoriety. The research presents the levels of confidence or quality of inference allowed by various types of evidence often employed in assessing allegations of child sexual abuse:

1. Personal involvement/personal observation	Typically Conclusive
2. Pregnancy; DNA testing	Typically Conclusive
3. Photographic documentation	Minimal Inference
4. Sexually transmitted disease	Minimal Inference
5. Confession by offender in context of child accusation	Minimal Inference
6. Physical/medical findings with disclosure	Minimal/Moderate Inference
7. Physical/medical findings without disclosure	Moderate Inference
8. Inappropriate sexual behavior or knowledge with disclosure	Moderate Inference
9. Sexualized responses to anatomical dolls with no contextual behavior	High Inference
10. Nonsexual inappropriate behavior with disclosure	High Inference

11. Sexualized drawings with no contextual   High to Extreme Inference
    behavior
12. Inappropriate behavior with no disclosure   High to Extreme Inference
13. Examiner/therapist "hunches"   Extreme Inference

Note that a determination of moderate to extreme inference does not suggest that abuse did not occur, but rather that such a conclusion is based on limited critical data. These cases necessitate a careful analysis of a variety of contextual factors. Any conclusions must be carefully weighed and documented.

Treatment Options

The interventions noted in these two classic patterns of Charles and Abby are those typically employed (Marvasti, 2004; Kubany, McCaig, & Laconsay, 2004). The emphasis is obviously going to differ depending on issues in an individual case. However, in addition to individual psychotherapy, there are three core approaches that are potentially useful in almost all such cases:

1. *Family Therapy:*   Since the family is virtually always disrupted, family therapy is necessary. Even when the family system eventually changes, as in the case of Charles, family therapy can help to mute the damage to all concerned.
2. *Parent Training:*   When the abuse comes from a parent, parent training is necessary to deal with not only the problems that led to the abuse but also those generated by the abuse.
3. *Support Systems:*   As in the cases of both Charles and Abby, abuse often comes where there has been a sense of having been emotionally isolated. In this vein, a community-based counseling and support group is helpful both to victims and abusing parents.

These three approaches can be supplemented by other interventions, such as attempts to change the person's employment possibilities or social skills (both would be important for Abby). When there is a couple involved, marital therapy is likely to be necessary if the marriage is to continue. Last, and from a moral perspective, it is emphasized that the most deserving of specific treatment attention is the child victim or other siblings who may be vicarious victims.

Comment

Treatment may help in a specific case. But the greatest changes will come with efforts at prevention (e.g., parent training before becoming parents, the reduction of the percentage of very young and/or single parents without enough skills or resources, educational programs in the schools) or cultural change (e.g., efforts to reduce the acceptance of the common use of physical discipline).

14 Disorders of Childhood and Adolescence

This chapter documents cases that are characteristic of the earlier years of life. As in all the chapters of this book, representative cases have been chosen to sample the relevant range of disorders and age ranges. Symptoms of the first three cases—Developmental Language Disorder, Attention Deficit/Hyperactivity Disorder, and Early Infantile Autism—are usually evident in early childhood. As with many of the childhood disorders, however, they may not cause a major disruption in the child's and/or family's world until the child moves into the structured social demands of day care and formal schooling (Kronenberger & Meyer, 2001). The first case of an actual disorder, Delano, a child with the Developmental Language Disorder, is a particularly good example of this phenomenon. Although the disorder did not emerge until he went to school, there was hard evidence of disorder as early as 18 months of age. Even though all three of these disorders may take a severe toll on a child's later adjustment, Delano's symptomatology is subtle when compared to that seen in the Autistic Disorder case.

The next two disorders discussed, the Separation Disorder and the Oppositional Defiant Disorder, are more characteristic of middle childhood, particularly the early school years, although again the initial symptoms may appear much earlier. These disorders present contrasting styles of coping with a major developmental task—the establishment of a new and separate sense of identity. In the Separation Disorder, a too-fearful coping style makes adequate separation very difficult and results in a School Phobia, whereas in the Oppositional Defiant Disorder, uncontrolled assertiveness blocks an adequate adjustment. The next case considers a case of school shooting, a seeming epidemic in recent years. The final case, that of Mr. E., demonstrates the potential complexities of identity development in adolescence and adulthood. However, before we deal with these cases, let us consider a case in which people apparently speculated disorder without definitive data, that of Albert Einstein.

The Case of Albert Einstein

"Words or Language, as they are written or spoken, do not seem to play any role in my mechanism of thought."

—Albert Einstein (Cited
in *Calaprice*, 2000, p. 301)

An accurate diagnosis is especially important when the subject is a child. A child's developmental path can be altered with a clinical diagnosis, whether that diagnosis is correct or not. Too often parents, teachers, and even clinicians make judgments regarding children's abilities or disabilities using incomplete data sets, and this is the issue here.

As a scientist, Albert Einstein was one of the most influential figures of modern time. His ideas were not limited to physics alone, and the influence of his theories reaches far beyond the scientific community. He was best known for his specific theory of relativity, as well as the equation describing the relationship between mass and energy ($E = mc^2$). His interest in physics was evident as early as 16 years old, when he sent an essay to his uncle that suggested interest in the subject of luminiferous aether, an important precursor to his theory of relativity. This began a decades-long passion for science that would eventually peak in 1922 when he was awarded the Nobel Prize for Physics. Though this was the most prestigious public recognition for his work, his influence has continued in science, politics, and philosophy beyond his death in 1955 and will continue for the foreseeable future. For example, in 1936 he predicted that when incoming light is interrupted by a massive object such as a galaxy, space is warped and the light is bent, sometimes so markedly that it appears to form a circle around the galaxy. This is referred to as an "Einstein ring" (was he the Lord of the Rings?), but it was not until the 21st century that scientists had the technology to test the theory and have now identified at least 19 instances of Einstein rings.

But could it be that one of the world's greatest minds was learning disabled? Many have suggested that Einstein displayed characteristics of a variety of disorders. Some have reported that he had developmental delays in speech and reading, while others have claimed that he was dyslexic. Those who believe these speculations to be true often cite his difficulties in both school and his later employment as supporting evidence.

Einstein was born on March 14, 1879, in Ulm, Germany. One myth that still circulates is that he was unable to speak until the age of 4 and did not read until he was 9. Although there was some delay in speech initially, he was speaking in whole sentences between the ages of 2 and 3 (Thomas, 2000). Einstein entered school at the age of 6, and within a year his mother was quoted in a letter to his grandmother, saying, "Yesterday Albert got his grades, once again he was ranked first" (Thomas, 2000, p. 154). Given the time and place of his initial schooling, it is not hard to imagine why a boy with a rapid thought process and dislike for authority in general would be classified as a poor student (Goldsmith & Libbon, 2005). German standards in the late nineteenth century would have called for a child to sit still and endure large amounts of rote memorization, in addition to only answering the teacher's questions, instead of the other way around. One of his teachers was quoted as saying that he was "forever adrift in his foolish dreams," a clear indication that Einstein's ideas were beyond the comprehension of even those who were supposed to be educating him (Thomas, 2000, p. 151).

Again, proponents of the notion that Einstein was learning disabled point to his work history as evidence to support their claim. Following college, he did go through three jobs in 2 years, but two of these were temporary positions, a detail normally left out. The third position was as a teacher in a boarding school, a job for which he was no more suited than he was suited to be a dutiful student. This information, coupled with his living the next 50 years with gainful employment, clearly contradicts

(continued)

The Case of Albert Einstein Continued

the notion that he had an unstable employment history (Thomas, 2000).

Retroactive diagnosis is often problematic; however, the consequences for this type of misdiagnosis are relatively benign when compared with improper pathologizing of children who do not "fit the mold" during their schooling. Many children have subclinical difficulties that parents and teachers feel compelled to address as if they are catastrophic to the child's future achievement potential. These children may just be different enough to cause concern but are not necessarily at risk. Still others may have perfectly legit-

imate diagnoses yet are more than capable of succeeding in many areas. The lesson we learn from the case of Albert Einstein (see also the case of Temple Grandin later in this chapter) is that an individual who is not a perfect student is not by definition a failure and may even become markedly productive.

> *"Do not worry about your difficulties in mathematics; I can assure you that mine are still greater."*
> —Albert Einstein to junior high school student, Barbara Wilson, on January 7, 1943
> (Cited in *Calaprice*, 2000, p. 252)

> *We spend the first 12 months of our child's lives teaching them to walk and talk, and the next 12 telling them to sit down and shut up.*
> —Phyllis Diller, 1980

Developmental Language Disorder

Children with language and other skill achievement problems are likely to show signs of the disorders from early on. However, it is when these become manifest in school-related problems that there is often a referral for psychological assessment (Odom, Horner, Snell, & Blacher, 2008). In such cases, the psychologist's role often focuses on evaluating the child's level of cognitive and intellectual skills and on making recommendations for intervention within the school system. Such intervention often requires the integration of a great deal of history from a variety of sources, with the consequent problem of organizing a small mountain of information into a diagnostic impression of the child (Naar, Ellis, & Frey, 2004).

The term *learning disabled* is often used to describe children who encounter more than the usual degree of difficulty in mastering basic school subjects. Any implication that such children have central nervous system impairment is not accurate. A 1980 federal law, *Education for All Handicapped Children* (P.L. 94-142), incorporates a definition of the learning disabled child that is useful here, as it is broad enough to encompass many of the types of school-related problems that clinical psychologists are called on to handle. Implicit in such a definition is that a child with a learning disability possesses skills in other areas and is not simply deficient in performance abilities across the board.

"Specific learning disability" means a disorder in one or more of the basic psychological processes involved in understanding or in using languages, spoken or written, which may manifest itself in an imperfect ability to listen, think, speak, read, write, spell, or to do mathematical calculations. The term includes such conditions as perceptual handicaps, brain injury, minimal brain disfunction, dyslexia, and developmental aphasia. The term does not include children who have learning problems which are primarily the result of visual, hearing, or motor handicaps, or mental retardation, or of environmental, cultural, or economic disadvantage. (P.L. 94-142, sect. 121a. 5(9))

In a general way, the *DSM-IV-TR* aids in the identification of school-related disorders owing to its expanded treatment of childhood disorders, including the common problems of the disorders of reading and language. The former condition is diagnosed when there is a significant discrepancy between a child's IQ score and a standardized assessment of reading proficiency. Reading disorders are generally first identified after a child has been in school for some time—long enough for a discrepancy between reading and intellectual skills to develop. In many instances, however, reading disorders may be preceded by disorders of language, which are included in the *DSM-IV-TR* under the Communication Disorders.

The following case of Delano illustrates a situation in which both a receptive language disorder and a reading disorder were concurrently diagnosed. In this case, a comprehensive psychological evaluation revealed evidence of specific developmental disorders affecting both receptive (and some expressive) language and reading ability. Although the child's problems became most obvious once he had started school, their origin could be traced to evidence of central nervous system impairment evident at a very early age, when epileptic seizures first occurred.

The Case of Delano

Delano ("Del") was referred to a local psychology clinic for a series of tests to determine his overall ability level. Although 7½ years old, he was still in first grade, having failed the first time through. Del's parents could not understand his poor school performance and had been of the impression that he possessed at least average intelligence. They described him as a quiet, well-mannered child who was well liked by his classmates and his teacher.

According to the developmental history supplied by the parents, Del, one of three children, was the product of a planned pregnancy and normal delivery. He was described as a "good baby" but manifested a series of medical problems, including allergies, ear infections, pneumonia, and psychomotor seizures—the

latter first diagnosed when Del was about 18 months old. At this time, both parents had noticed that Del would occasionally become preoccupied with the movement of his hands and also seemed to withdraw from social contact and take on a glassy-eyed stare. These episodes were reported as occurring before sleep or on first waking, then later began to occur during the day as well. According to the parents, these trance-like states could usually be interrupted by calling Del's name.

Shortly after these episodes began, Del was taken to the family pediatrician, who recommended a neurological examination. As part of the exam, an electroencephalogram (EEG) recording was made. In this technique, small electrodes placed on various parts of the

(continued)

The Case of Delano Continued

head are used to monitor electrical activity in brain tissue immediately underneath. Because certain characteristic brainwave patterns emanate from various locations, any abnormalities are readily evident.

In Del's case the EEG report indicated "mild dysrhythmia," with evidence of a "focal discharge" in the posterior region of the temporal lobe of the left hemisphere. That is, electrical activity in Del's brain was mildly irregular and also was comparatively uncontrolled in one specific location. Numerous studies have demonstrated that this region of the brain plays a significant role in understanding speech and language. The presence of irregular electrical activity in this portion of Del's brain suggested some disruption of brain structures involved in the ability to understand language. The seizure activity and the underlying irregular brain wave activity were subsequently controlled with a medication called phenobarbitol, and at the time of the assessment, Del had not had a seizure in years. Nevertheless, it was apparent that the early brain trauma associated with the seizures somewhat curtailed his development of certain skills during the critical early formative years.

Thus, it was not surprising to discover that Del's speech and language skills were slow to develop. He did not speak clearly until he was almost 3 years old, and his parents reported that it was often necessary to repeat instructions endlessly, after which time there was still no guarantee that he would do what he had been told. At the age of 3 years old, he was enrolled in a nursery school, where he displayed a behavior pattern characterized by a short attention span, low frustration tolerance, and social immaturity. This pattern continued into first grade. Despite attending a summer tutoring program before entering school, he did not do well in first grade, which he was repeating when the psychological assessment was made.

One of the most obvious things about Del was that he was a likable child. During the psychological testing, he proved easy to get along with and worked industriously if given clear structure. He was attentive to task instructions but occasionally misunderstood the examiner, especially when asked to define words. For example, he confused the word *donkey* with *doggie* and repeated the word *diamond* several times, as if trying to form the memory of a word that he had never heard, yet he knew what a diamond was. It seemed that tasks such as word definitions gave Del the most problem; he did best on test items that provided contextual cues that aided comprehension. Del adopted a rather passive stance toward testing, almost timid at times. He was reluctant to ask for repetitions of test questions, even when it was evident that he did not clearly understand them.

In addition, Del created the general impression of a somewhat shy child, less talkative than many children of similar age. As it turned out, Del had developed this style as a result of feeling sensitive about having to ask people to repeat things that he did not understand the first time; he felt that others thought him stupid. Indeed, several of the kids at school, with their unerring ability to focus on other children's weaknesses, had taken to calling him "Spaceman" because he seemed to be "out of it" much of the time. Nonetheless, despite the reserve apparent in Del's behavior, he was an appealing child.

The results of the psychological assessment revealed that Del did possess average intellectual skills, or the overall mental ability necessary to handle normal academic demands. Even this level was felt to be an underestimate of his actual potential, due to the language disturbance, which inhibited the expression of intelligent behavior. Not surprisingly, a standardized test of intellectual abilities revealed that Del's verbal skills were less highly developed than abilities that made use of nonverbal activity, such as visual-motor coordination. The examiner had access to Del's scores on the same test when it had been administered about one year earlier; it was notable that Del's language skills were not keeping pace with his development in other areas. One of the most significant revelations of the assessment was that Del's performance improved markedly whenever he was able to process test information visually. For example, he performed rather poorly on a vocabulary test in which the examiner read words for Del to define. His performance improved dramatically when vocabulary was assessed by having the examiner show Del pictures of objects or events and ask him to select those that corresponded to the words read.

Performance on a number of the tests revealed that Del was adept at using contextual cues to obtain meaning from what was going on around him. In this regard, it was fascinating to find that, despite markedly subaverage performance on measures that evaluate basic reading skills (e.g., word and letter identification and word comprehension), Del was able to read and comprehend passages in grade-school readers at nearly a second-grade level. It appeared that Del had developed a reading strategy in which he used contextual cues to understand much of what he read. For example, he appeared to search for familiar words in a passage and then try to fit them together with words whose meaning he was unable to decipher. In the absence of such contextual cues, as when word comprehension was tested, he was at a considerable disadvantage because he was not able to sound words out effectively. (Word sounding is an invaluable skill that helps many readers trigger acoustic memories that are associated with the visual images of words.) Del, in contrast, relied almost solely on visual cues to make sense out of what he read and was thereby clearly handicapped in his efforts to read all except materials that were familiar to him.

The overall results of the psychological assessment indicated that, despite possessing visual comprehension skills and reasoning abilities well in excess of his current grade level, Del manifested a significant deficit in auditory processing—specifically, in comprehension. It was found that Del required frequent repetitions of task instructions and items and that his ability to remember auditorily presented information for immediate recall was markedly below average.

The results of the assessment helped tie together a number of observations that had been made about Del. It became evident that his difficulty in comprehending spoken language went back a long way to the early stages of language development and as a result may have reduced the amount of information about his surroundings that Del was able to assimilate. His difficulty in understanding others led him to become somewhat shy and withdrawn in social situations. He preferred to appear as if he understood what was going on rather than to risk peer censure (comments such as "Earth to Del, Earth to Del . . ."), which inevitably followed his attempts to have people repeat things. The language impairment became a real handicap when he entered school, where he was forced to repeat first grade despite possessing average intelligence. He appeared to have developed moderately effective compensatory strategies in school-related areas, including the use of visual and other contextual cues. However, the numerous indications that receptive language development had not kept up with relatively normal development in other cognitive skills made this a prime target for remediation recommendations. Using *DSM-IV-TR* terminology, primary diagnoses of Mixed Expressive-Receptive Language Disorder and Reading Disorder were made.

The Treatment of Delano

A number of specific recommendations were made to help Del overcome the effects of his language disability. First, it was recommended that he receive intensive training in basic auditory encoding skills necessary for reading. For children who need work in this area, a format such as that provided by the classic television program *Sesame Street*, in which sounds are accompanied by visual representations in animated form, is often quite effective. This format permitted Del to apply his visualization skills to aid him in such auditory encoding skills as word attack and comprehension. As he became more familiar with the basic sound combinations, the use of visual prompts was gradually phased out.

Second, it was felt that Del should participate in second-grade reading classes, because his overall comprehension level was considerably in advance of his first-grade placement. Much of the second-grade reading material used extensive pictorial cues, so Del would be able to use these in understanding what he read. Moreover, as the additional training in auditory encoding began to have an effect, it was thought that his reading skills would increase even more. Efforts were also made to develop rewards for reading, including giving Del access to appropriate comic books and other texts that employed a lot of visual cues. Del's parents were encouraged to spend time with him going through magazines and other such materials, giving Del additional reading experience as well as access to the modeling of adult reading behavior.

An issue related to developmental language delays concerns Del's difficulty in organizing his approach to various tasks. Children with this sort of problem profit from several strategies (Odom et al., 2008). First, they learn from exposure to role models who provide visual cues about task performance and also talk their way through tasks, explaining each step in turn, with frequent repetitions. Second, it is often helpful to sit down with such children before beginning a new task and have them verbally rehearse the steps to be followed, while perhaps jotting them down either in written or pictorial form. Many situations existed both at school and at home in which it was possible to build such routines into Del's daily activities. For example, his father began to work with Del in building plastic models and adopted an approach in which he would explain, rehearse, and demonstrate the sequences of necessary steps for Del as a means of helping him develop a more organized, less impulsive approach. Model building soon became a favored activity and provided the basis for more emotional closeness between father and son.

If the list of recommendations seems extensive, it is because deficits in language skills have so many far-reaching implications that must be addressed in planning intervention. In Del's case, every effort was made to keep him in a regular classroom, in order to avoid further stigmatizing him. Both school officials and parents responded positively to the recommendations and were able to implement most of them without significantly altering Del's daily activities. Within six months, Del showed marked improvement in basic reading skills and continued to do well in his second-grade reading class. His parents reported that he was becoming socially more responsive around other children and less defensive about his difficulties in understanding. At last report, he was doing well in school, and the administrators were considering a phased promotion plan that would permit Del to move gradually into more advanced classes as his abilities permitted.

Comment

Children who manifest early indications of biological vulnerability and developmental delays are often slow to develop socially and interpersonally. They frequently feel themselves to be somehow different from other children, although they are often unable to articulate their concerns. Prompt recognition and treatment of conditions that compromise a child's development and contribute to the child's sense of psychological vulnerability assure the greatest potential for subsequent adequate adjustment.

> *Children nowadays are tyrants. They contradict their parents, gobble their food, and tyrannize their teachers.*
>
> —Socrates (circa 425 B.C.)

Attention Deficit/Hyperactivity Disorder

The term *Attention Deficit/Hyperactivity Disorder (ADHD)* is used to describe a condition that involves (1) the persisting inability to keep one's attention focused in a sustained manner and (2) an impulsive, hyperactive-motoric factor. Children with ADHD are presumed to possess adequate basic cognitive capabilities, but they are typically unable to focus themselves effectively enough to get things done. It is important to note that rather than being distracted by other stimuli, most experts believe the ADHD child's brain is understimulated; hence, children with ADHD are highly stimulation seeking. That is, rather than being distracted, they lose interest in stimuli and move on to others. Studies have shown that ADHD children and teens may have slightly smaller brains than children without ADHD, although this does not appear to affect IQ. It is likely related to problems in attention, as is the finding that those children with significantly higher exposure to television in their early years are more at risk for attention problems (Novak & Pelaez, 2004).

The current recognition of ADHD in the *DSM-IV-TR* reflects the belief of physicians, teachers, and psychologists over the years that persisting problems in regulating both attentional processes and motor behavior make up a distinct syndrome frequently seen in clinical settings (Kronenberger & Meyer, 2001; Wender, 1995). Originally, terms such as *hyperactivity, hyperkinesis*, and *minimal brain dysfunction* were used to characterize the condition, which was believed to involve various forms of mild central nervous system (CNS) impairment. So strong was the assumed association between excessive activity and underlying brain impairment that the corresponding diagnostic terms were used interchangeably for years. In practice, the nature of this deficit was seldom clearly specified, owing to the wide range of disorders and conditions that may have hyperactivity as an associated symptom. This caused endless confusion among professionals and considerable anxiety on the parts of parents whose children were labeled as having "minimal brain damage" or the "hyperkinetic syndrome."

Modern research, however, strongly suggests that neither attentional problems nor hyperactivity should *necessarily* be assumed to involve CNS damage, although maturation and integration of CNS components are involved. Current research has amply documented the fact that genetic, physiological, nutritional, motivational, social, and environmental factors all may play important roles in the regulation and allocation of attentional capabilities (Odom et al., 2008; Barkeley, 1998; Hersen & Ammerman, 2000; Kronenberger & Meyer, 2001).

The *DSM-IV-TR* recognizes a pattern of ADHD in which attentional problems are primary, a pattern in which hyperactive-impulsive patterns are primary, and a mixed pattern. Findings of field trials confirmed differences among the subtypes: (1) the predominantly hyperactive impulsive youth was significantly younger (by three to four years) than the predominantly inattentive and combined types; (2) the greater occurrence of ADHD in males than females was most characteristic of the combined type and least characteristic of the predominantly inattentive types; (3) scores on a global rating of impairment demonstrated the worst impairment for the combined type and least impairment for the inattentive type; (4) on the basis of teachers' and parents' ratings, the inattentive and combined types had significantly greater academic impairment than the hyperactive-impulsive type; and (5) social impairment was greater among the hyperactive-impulsive type than the inattentive and combined types. By *DSM-IV-TR* estimates, some 3 to 5 percent of children show ADHD. Note that ADHD often continues, in varying degrees, into adulthood (Wender, 1995). There is a 5:1 ratio of males to females, with an even higher ratio of the more active and aggressive forms. Approximately 25 percent of first-degree relatives of children of ADHD show some clear indices of this disorder. ADHD is prognostic of a heightened chance for a variety of psychological dysfunction patterns later in life, as well as criminality and nicotine and cocaine abuse. However, it is important to note that consistently aggressive children are much more likely later on to have criminal problems involving aggression than are ADHD children.

Assessments of children with ADHD in school and clinical settings have often been somewhat imprecise, due in part to the difficulty of specifying the criteria for attention and of determining just how active a child should be before being considered hyperactive. Very often, physically aggressive children are perceived as ADHD kids. In recent years, however, a number of advances have been made in diagnostic procedures, resulting in more clearly defined and more stringent criteria for assessing the presence of ADHD (Naar, Ellis, & Frey, 2004).

Appropriate assessment practices go beyond simple behavioral ratings. A thorough assessment (Kronenberger & Meyer, 2001; Naar, Ellis, & Frey, 2004) includes an evaluation of the following factors: (1) the child's overall behavioral repertoire and patterns of interactions with the environment, (2) patterns of motor activity, and (3) how the child typically approaches and works through tasks. Frequently, by the time an evaluation has been completed, a child with attentional problems may have been assessed by pediatricians, teachers, psychologists, and parents. Each of these individuals has a specific perspective on the child's behavior that often must be taken into account in designing appropriate intervention strategies.

The Case of Matt

It was not until Matt was nearing the end of first grade that his inattention and poor concentration became apparent. He was a bright child, according to the results of school-readiness testing, who began the year with predictions of great accomplishments. At first, he seemed to live up to his promise, but as the months passed, he seemed to have persisting difficulty absorbing new information and finishing his daily lessons. His teacher felt from the outset that Matt had been considerably more active than his classmates but attributed this to a high level of curiosity that constantly led him into new undertakings.

At home, Matt had never been considered to be a problem child. The second of five children, he had grown up in a family that encouraged independence and imposed minimal constraints on the children's behavior. He was not watched especially closely by his parents but was instead encouraged to develop his own interests and keep himself occupied. With four other children around the house, the level of ongoing activity was rather high, and Matt's behavior did not seem markedly atypical by his parents' standards.

The problem that emerged at school involved the fact that Matt found it extremely difficult to focus his attention effectively on his work. Moreover, he seemed to be restless and physically agitated much of the time. Accustomed as he was to working on things that interested him and at a pace that suited his somewhat high-strung temperament, Matt found it difficult to work under the constraints imposed by his teacher at school. He constantly fidgeted in his seat, was easily distracted by things going on around him, and seldom completed his assignments on time. Because his behavior was not especially disruptive to others, it initially received little attention. But after the first few months of school, his teacher had become aware that the quality of his work consistently failed to measure up to the standards she felt were reasonable based on his aptitude test scores.

By the end of the first grading period, Matt was passing all his academic subjects, but he received several "Unsatisfactory" ratings in such areas as Paying Attention, Completing Work on Time, General Work Habits, and Ability to Work Independently, which surprised his parents. A meeting with Matt's teacher achieved no particular resolution, mostly because it was difficult to specify precisely just what Matt needed to do in order to work more effectively. His teacher did suggest that he have a physical examination, however, as she felt that his restlessness might have a physical basis.

Matt's physical health had been generally good throughout his early development. His mother's pregnancy was free of major complications, and although the labor had been difficult, he was born without incident. He was sometimes colicky as an infant and seemed more demanding than her other children had been. She viewed him as more active than the other children right from the start and recalled that his attention was constantly being diverted from one thing to another. But this did not create any particular problems at home, and prior routine physical examinations had uncovered no major health problems. Thus, the first real suggestion that anything might be amiss did not occur until after Matt had started school.

The physical exam done at his teacher's suggestion once again found Matt to be basically in good health, although on the basis of the teacher's report and his own observations, Matt's pediatrician felt that the boy's behavior might warrant a consideration of "hyperactivity." Until Matt's behavior was evaluated more precisely, however, the pediatrician was reluctant to prescribe any medication. He recommended that Matt be evaluated by a clinical psychologist in private practice and that a decision regarding medication be postponed until the assessment was completed.

Matt's parents were perplexed and somewhat upset by the lack of clear definition

(continued)

The Case of Matt Continued

of Matt's problems. They were also distressed by the apparent insinuation that Matt's problems might have a psychological, rather than physical, basis. Despite these reservations, they proceeded with the recommendation and had the evaluation performed. A clinical psychologist saw the entire family together as a unit after an initial interview with the parents. She also carried out basic psychological testing on Matt, using tests designed to assess general mental abilities, school achievement levels, work habits, and basic personality dimensions. Finally, she visited Matt's school to observe his reported problems firsthand. The results of the assessment indeed suggested that Matt had greater difficulty than most children with respect to sustained concentration and attention. In addition, his typical activity level at school appeared markedly higher than that of the other children.

Evidence came from several sources. First, Matt's performance on the most recent revision of a Wechsler intelligence test designed specifically for children was marked by (1) an overall above-average level of performance but (2) relatively poor performance on a group of component measures that collectively forms a "Freedom from Distractibility" factor. Each of these tests demanded sustained, careful attention to a fairly complex task—an undertaking that was beyond Matt's powers of concentration. On portions of the Wechsler IQ

scale, Matt's performance was at a level indicative of above-average general abilities. Further testing revealed that, although he possessed sufficient basic academic skills to master the demands of his schoolwork, Matt seemed at a loss in controlling the process of analyzing the various parts of any complex task and working systematically toward a solution.

Classroom observations by the psychologist tended to corroborate the test data. Matt seemed unable to work out and stick to a plan for getting his work done. He dawdled, played with objects in his desk, looked around the room, and accomplished little during the study time allotted. Some part of his body seemed to be perpetually in motion, even during rest periods when many of the other children were napping.

The available information suggested that Matt's inattentive behavior fit the *DSM-IV-TR* criteria for ADHD. It was stressed to Matt's parents that he was a child of above-average abilities whose problems involved chiefly his method of approaching tasks and an excessively high level of activity. The psychologist developed a program for Matt's teacher and parents designed to help him focus his attention on tasks more effectively. She also referred the parents to the pediatrician for a trial of Ritalin, which was to be used in conjunction with an activity rating form completed daily by the teacher.

The Treatment of Matt

In addition to the Ritalin that was prescribed, Matt's intervention program involved elements of both behavioral and cognitive approaches. Biofeedback training was helpful, as was a technique of teaching Matt to "talk to himself" as a means of keeping his attention focused on a particular task. This involved modeling on-task behavior in which the therapist performed an activity while describing exactly what she needed to do each step of the way. At first, his tendency was to ignore the instructions and to work inconsistently as he had habitually done. But gradually, through a combination of judiciously selected activities and an animated, often humorous, style of verbal modeling, the therapist succeeded in capturing Matt's attention and engaging his participation.

One activity that Matt particularly enjoyed involved assembling model autos and trucks. Normally, he worked so quickly and haphazardly that the finished product bore little resemblance to its namesake. With the therapist's assistance, Matt learned to slow his pace down, plan each step of the assembly in advance, gather the necessary materials before starting, and work at a slow but steady pace. At the outset, the therapist had him talk himself through each step before actually doing anything. Often, at first she either had to prompt him directly or remind him to prompt himself. But gradually the use of language as a task mediator became more habitual, to the point that eventually Matt was able to work systematically without having to say anything audible at all.

This procedure was combined with a behavioral program at school in which Matt was issued periodic rewards for staying in his seat and working on his assignments. The combination of these techniques achieved the basic goal of engaging Matt's attention more consistently than had been the case before. More important, his added powers of concentration contributed to a demonstrable improvement in the quality of his work. As this occurred, the satisfaction derived from good schoolwork provided a source of intrinsic motivation that further engaged his interest.

In a matter of weeks, Matt had made considerable gains in three important areas: First, he became much more effective at planning and monitoring his work. Second, his ability to work both productively and independently improved markedly. Third, his overall grades improved to the point where his performance was beginning to approach the potential his parents and teachers had known he possessed all along. In addition to these gains, Matt's motor activity diminished somewhat as a result of the Ritalin. He was described by his teacher as somewhat calmer but fortunately seemed to have lost none of the curiosity and alertness that characterized his previous behavior.

Comment

Matt's situation is in part one that is commonly experienced by young school children. Paying attention is a skill that is generally taken for granted but one that is much too important to go unevaluated. Matt had no lack of basic intelligence; rather, he was unable to harness it effectively to get things done at school. Having been raised without many rules and regulations, he had perhaps never really learned effective work habits. In terms of the underlying etiology, no single specific factor came to light, although in many similar cases genetic or birth defects appear to be causal (Barkley, 1998; Duncan et al., 1995; Wender, 1995). Yet, it did appear that, in their effort to let their children be independent of adult authority, Matt's parents may have erred somewhat by not providing effective role models.

Most experts believe that structural differences (not defects or deficits) in the brain, particularly those that link the prefrontal cortex with the basal ganglia's caudate and globus pallidus, which are nearer the center of the brain, appear to operate as "accelerator and brakes" on behavior. In most cases, the cause of such differences is genetic, although some types of trauma or toxin could conceivably be the cause.

As it is with most ADHD children, Ritalin was helpful with Matt. A number of other medications, such as methylphenidate, dexmethylphenidate hydrochloride, or atomoxetine, may also be effective. But medication is not a panacea—it does not boost IQ, has what so far appears to be only a minimal effect on long-term academic success, and does not take away the learning disabilities that affect the some 15 to 20 percent of ADHD youngsters. Unfortunately, treatment using only medication, especially Ritalin, is still common. In fact, the production of Ritalin for use in the United States increased fivefold between 1975 and 1995. For some pediatricians, it is a response that (choose one or more) (1) is easy and quick, (2) is financially efficient, and (3) is the only one that they know anything about. Also, many people, including some pediatricians, assume that a positive response to Ritalin indicates that the child does have ADHD. This is bad scientific logic; stimulants sharpen the focus of any active child.

Matt's case illustrates the effective application of a multimodal intervention program. A combination of psychological and medical procedures was employed to treat a problem that, years ago, would probably have been diagnosed and treated exclusively from a medical standpoint. Viewing problems such as ADHD from a broader perspective that encompasses both psychological and physical factors makes it feasible to consider a wide range of intervention techniques, each of which makes a unique contribution to the problem's solution.

If the child really isn't lovable, you simply have to fake it.

—B. F. Skinner

Autistic Disorder

Autistic Disorder is a pervasive, debilitating disorder having its onset prior to 3 years of age. The term *autistic* connotes a failure to relate effectively to one's environment. People described as autistic are viewed as being absorbed in a private world of their own that is inaccessible to others. Historically, the term *autism* was used by Bleuler to describe one of the cardinal symptoms of schizophrenia. However, it has since been associated with other forms of psychopathology, most notably with the pattern of disturbed behavior in childhood first described by Leo Kanner in the 1940s and named "early infantile autism" (Kanner, 1943). The children studied by Kanner manifested a pattern of detachment and severe communication impairment.

Detailed studies of these children have revealed a number of additional symptoms as well, including restricted, repetitive, and stereotyped behaviors; emotional withdrawal; cognitive impairments; and unusual behavioral mannerisms (Atkinson & Goldberg, 2004; Hersen & Ammerman, 2000; Whitman, 2004). Among the latter, echolalia and self-stimulation are especially notable. Children with echolalia continuously repeat words and phrases uttered by another person, making effective communication all but impossible. Self-stimulation may take any of several forms. A child may sit for hours waving a hand in front of his or her face, transfixed by the constant movement. Other children engage in more destructive behaviors, such as head banging or pinching or biting themselves. Observations of such behaviors have led to the suggestion that autistic children are especially sensitive to what is termed *proximal* stimulation, which is very tangible and immediate. In contrast, these children are less responsive to *distal* stimulation, emanating from sources that are physically more remote (such as the sound of someone speaking from a distance of several feet).

In terms of cognitive functioning, some autistic children are frequently found to possess "splinter skills" within a broader context of impaired mental functioning. Splinter skills are isolated capabilities possessed by autistic children that in some instances are developed to exceptionally high levels (dramatically portrayed by Dustin Hoffman in the movie *Rain Man*). Mathematical, artistic, and various other skills have all been found in autistic children whose behavior is otherwise globally impaired. In fact, children with Autistic Disorder are often oblivious to others' distress or needs. They may react dramatically to even minimal alterations in their environment. Children with autism are generally fascinated by parts of objects as well as by movement. Their focused interests usually involve nonfunctional and unreasonable routines.

Kanner's work with autism led him to believe that the disorder was essentially the result of severe emotional deprivation. He noted that the parents of these children seemed, in general, to be intellectually and analytically oriented, while lacking in emotional warmth. The term *icebox parent* resulted from characterizations such as this and fostered the impression that autism was essentially an acquired condition. According to this theory, unremitting exposure to nonnurturing parents brought about progressive withdrawal from the world and increasing self-absorption.

In retrospect, it is clear that this conclusion was erroneous, being the result of biased sampling procedures (Kronenberger & Meyer, 2001). The most telling criticism of this theory comes from the increasing evidence that symptoms of autism are in fact present at birth, in the form of neurological and related abnormalities. This in turn suggests that parental aloofness, when present, is essentially a defensive reaction to a child whose behavior is atypical and frequently characterized by unresponsiveness.

Asperger's Syndrome

In early stages, autism may be hard to differentiate from Asperger's Syndrome (AS), which was first described in 1944 by Hans Asperger, a Viennese pediatrician. Like autism, there is often repetition in play, need for routine, and a lack of interest in other children. However, unlike children with autism, AS children have high intelligence, good verbal skills, and an organized approach to their often specialized or esoteric interests such as stamp collecting. Also, they seem to like attention from other people, especially if they can give a monologue on one of their esoteric interests. No wonder Asperger termed them "little professors." The dysfunction in autism seems primarily lodged in the left brain, whereas AS is mainly a right brain dysfunction.

Let us now turn to the case of Temple Grandin, an interesting case of Autistic Disorder.

> *Books: these are great to fill empty wall units. Designers keep stacks of these on reserve for this purpose. Watch for sales sponsored by local libraries that need to clear stacks for new books. The covers of the books can relate to the color scheme of the room. Books also look nice stacked on a coffee table.*
> —From the Jacksonville, Florida, *Times-Union*, as quoted in *The New Yorker*

The Case of Temple Grandin

In most cases of autism the disorder is very debilitating, especially for those individuals who develop little or no speech. However, the outcome is not always negative (consider, for example, the character in the 1988 movie *Rain Man*). A real-life example is Temple Grandin, who was diagnosed with autism as a child but went on to graduate from college, receive her Ph.D. in cattle and animal science, and become internationally renowned in the development of designs and equipment for livestock handling.

Temple was her parents' first child. Her mother was initially concerned when Temple failed to begin speaking like that of other 2-year-olds. However, doctors failed to find any physical problem, and unfortunately she was subsequently labeled as "brain-damaged." It was not until a few years later, around age 5, that she was formally diagnosed with autism. However, by age 2, she did manifest classic autistic symptoms. She had no speech, made little eye contact, withdrew from social interaction, and spent large amounts of time staring into space.

In her autobiography (Grandin, 1995), Temple recalls the frustration of her inability to speak. She understood other people's speech but was unable to verbalize a response. Instead, she would throw tantrums and scream, as this was her only way of communication. After intensive speech therapy she finally learned to speak at age 3½, thus allowing her to use phonics, the sounding out of words to learn to read. Determined to keep her from being institutionalized, her mother would spend 30 minutes every day teaching Temple to read; she also employed a speech therapist. When Temple's attention would lag, her speech therapist was able to bring her back to the here and now by taking her chin and directing Temple to look at her. Temple states that this was pivotal in her learning to speak and read, as many autistic children become habitually preoccupied in their own world.

Temple also had many of the sensory problems consistent with autism. Although she craved the pressure stimulation of a hug, she was unable to accept hugs because the other movements and the emotional stimulation were too overwhelming for her. Because of the desire for the relaxation that pressure itself created, she spent much time as a youth imagining a machine that would apply pressure without being stimulating. She first got the idea for the "squeeze machine" at her aunt's ranch in Arizona while watching cattle being restrained in an apparatus for a veterinary procedure. She noticed that when restrained, the cattle would relax somewhat. A few days later, after having a panic attack, she got into the squeeze chute and asked her aunt to slowly squeeze her. For the first few seconds she was rushed with anxiety, but what soon followed was a sense of relief and relaxation that remained for the 30 minutes she stayed in the cattle chute. Thus, the idea for the "squeeze machine" was born—an apparatus now routinely used in the treatment of autism. Temple made her first squeeze machine from plywood panels. Over the years, the design has greatly improved. More advanced designs have foam-padded panels to apply pressure that is controlled by an air valve lever, which is under the control of the autistic individual.

Although Temple excelled in school, she always had difficulties understanding verbal concepts until she could visually comprehend them. To do this, she would use symbols for concepts. For example, she thought of peace as a dove, and honesty was represented in her mind as a person placing his or her hand on the Bible in a courtroom. She later turned this "deficit" to a positive advantage in her work as a livestock equipment designer.

Upon graduating from high school, Temple went to Franklin Pierce College. She graduated in 1970 with a degree in psychology and then went to Arizona State University to pursue a Ph.D. in psychology, but she soon realized that her interests lay elsewhere and she subsequently obtained her Ph.D. in cattle and animal science. Temple was able to meet these challenging transitions in her life by using her visual imagery skills. For instance, when transitioning schools, she represented each school as a "door," then would mentally practice going through each door prior to the transition she was about to make.

Temple no longer uses "door" images but now describes her thinking as similar to "full-color movies, complete with sound, which run like a VCR tape" in her mind

(Grandin, 1995, p. 19). She is able to conceptualize entire livestock systems in her mind without writing or drawing a rough draft. She calls it "thinking in pictures," similar to a "computer graphics program" (p. 20). She is able to view the equipment from any angle by mentally rotating the equipment. She has what she calls a "video library" (p. 20) in her memory, which consists of video images of every single piece of livestock and farm equipment with which she has ever worked. By using parts of the different images in her mind, she can bring them together to create new images and thus test the equipment in her mind for possible problems. One of the first instances in which she used her video library was for the development of a cattle dip vat. The problem was that cattle would often get spooked when entering the liquid of the dip vat, causing them to panic and even drown on occasion. Temple's job was to develop a more efficient dip vat. She considered various designs in her mind and then mentally tested each design, modifying it until she had developed a design that would allow cattle to calmly descend into the dip vat without panicking.

Temple continues to develop innovative livestock equipment and structures. She has developed such equipment as cattle chutes for use during veterinary procedures and truck loading and sorting facilities. Nearly one-third of the cattle and pigs in the United States have at one point passed through equipment developed by Temple. There are some downsides, though, even for Temple. She has never married and doubts that she will, saying she is not sure she could handle the emotional complexity of such a relationship, although other high-functioning autistics have successfully married. Yet, Temple Grandin is clear proof that although autism can be a very debilitating disorder, a number of autistics go on to lead productive, even notable, lives.

Comment

It is often difficult for pediatricians to make a diagnosis of Autistic Disorder early on, especially since most pediatricians seldom see such cases (Johnson, 2008). However, it is generally agreed that if the following four markers are noted at age 1, the observer should be sensitized to the possibility of autism: (1) failure to make eye contact with others, (2) a general failure to point, (3) failure to show objects to others, and (4) failure to orient to one's name being called. Other commonly observed patterns are as follows: more likely to mouth objects and less use of visual information, little engagement in reciprocal or functional play, and less copying of movements by peers (Whitman, 2004). Neuroimaging techniques, such as positron emission tomography (PET) and magnetic resonance spectroscopy (MRS), show potential for aiding in early diagnosis (e.g., autistics often show large brains).

Unlike Temple, most autistics are permanently left with problematic language and social skills. This, along with the fact that autistics tend to think in pictures rather than with abstract words, makes it hard for them to participate in regular classroom settings. This is consistent with a significant shift in attitudes about the causes of autism. The preponderance of recent research data points to either genetic or possibly prenatal factors as likely explanations for the condition. Interest has focused on chromosomes 7 and 15 as the source of the genes that most contribute to autism, but mutations in as many as 20 genes may contribute in any one case of autism. Interest also focuses on the autistic's commonly elevated blood levels of serotonin as well as on secretin, a hormone that has been found to improve language and cognitive abilities in children with autism. Because of this attitude change, parents with autistic children are now less likely to develop guilt about their child's condition and are more likely to become involved in a collaborative treatment effort.

> *To be adult is to be alone.*
> —Jean Rostand, French biologist, *Thoughts of a Biologist*

Separation Anxiety Disorder Associated with School Refusal

The term *separation anxiety* was coined by Johnson and associates in 1941 to describe the acute distress and attachment behavior exhibited by some children when separating from their mothers to go to school and then related to pioneering work on attachment of Bowlby (1973). In more current use, the term refers to a more general disorder of childhood in which excessive anxiety occurs when a child is separated from major attachment figures or from home (Atkinson & Goldberg, 2004). Anxiety reactions may range from displays of anger and protest to symptoms of panic. Discussions in the clinical literature suggest that the disorder is fairly common, affecting about 4 percent of children (American Psychiatric Association, 1994), with approximately equal prevalence among boys and girls. When separated from parents or other attachment figures, the children often become obsessed with fears of accidents or illnesses befalling themselves or significant others. These fears may be expressed openly and verbally or may be manifested in nightmares and fantasy. Sometimes fears are displaced onto animals, strangers, or surroundings. Sleep disorders, including nightmares and sleep terror, are common; children may experience great difficulty falling asleep alone and require that someone, usually a parent, be with them when they fall asleep. Somatic complaints are also common in response to the threat of separation.

The relationship between separation anxiety and school first described by Johnson and colleagues (1941) is still important, although the term *school phobia* to describe the disorder is frequently misapplied. It is usually not the stimulus of school from which the child retreats that is of clinical significance, but the attachment to parents or others that he or she seeks. Thus, the term *school phobia* is a bit of a misnomer; the term *school refusal* is generally more appropriate.

The clinical literature is in substantial agreement regarding the personalities and behaviors of children with separation anxiety and their parents (Atkinson & Goldberg, 2004; Bowlby, 1973; Johnson et al., 1941). With the exception of the symptoms associated with the disorder, these children are generally well behaved, although they often appear shy, overly anxious, and socially inhibited. Families are often intact, with close relationships between parent(s) and children, and family members have often not experienced long or frequent separations from home. Upon separation from their family or home, individuals with Separation Anxiety Disorder express a fear of being lost and permanently stripped away from home. A clear distinction can be drawn between children with Separation Anxiety Disorder and children with conduct disorder, who may also refuse to attend school or other activities but typically come from highly unstable families with a long history of separations. Whereas children with conduct disorder characteristically do not stay home when truant and engage in a variety of antisocial behaviors (Bartol & Bartol, 2008), the school refuser is generally quiet and cooperative once in school.

The problem of school refusal may appear to be clear and straightforward when first addressed in treatment. However, the dynamics of separation anxiety are often deeply enmeshed in a larger family context and may involve a variety of issues of clinical significance, as in the case of Julie, described here.

> *Your mother can't be with you anymore.*
> —Felix Seton, *Bambi*, the Great Prince speaking to Bambi

The Case of Julie

Julie P., an 8-year-old second-grader, was court-referred for outpatient treatment because of school truancy. During her first year in school, Julie had refused to enter her classroom without her mother and would scream and throw herself on the floor if her mother tried to leave her at school. As a result, Mrs. P. accompanied Julie to her classroom each day and stayed with her for the remainder of the morning. If Mrs. P. tried to leave the

(continued)

The Case of Julie Continued

classroom, Julie would again throw her "mad fits" and only Mrs. P. was able to calm her. Because Mrs. P. held a job during the afternoon, she devised a plan in which she would accompany Julie to the lunchroom and leave her while she was eating her lunch. Although Julie resisted at first, she gradually became accustomed to it, and this pattern was maintained for the remainder of the school year. In her mother's absence during the afternoons, Julie was generally well behaved, although she was extremely shy and interacted little with the other children She also consistently refused to complete any schoolwork without her mother.

In second grade, Julie's teacher would not allow Mrs. P. to remain with Julie in the classroom. Julie began to miss an excessive number of days in school for a variety of somatic complaints, including headaches, nausea, and stomachaches. The school insisted that the child be seen by a physician, who reported no apparent physical basis for Julie's problems. The school then insisted that Julie take the school bus to school each day and maintain regular attendance. Although Mrs. P. reported that she tried to force Julie to take the school bus, Julie refused to do so for fear that it would crash, and her attendance did not improve.

After numerous attempts were unsuccessful to encourage Mrs. P. to force Julie to go to school, the school filed a truancy petition with the court. In accordance with an alternative-to-court program, a caseworker was assigned to the family. When Julie's attendance did not improve, the case was brought to court. On the recommendation of the caseworker, Julie was ordered to attend school, and Mrs. P. was ordered to seek treatment for her.

During intake, a number of clinical symptoms were reported along with school refusal that suggested a diagnosis of separation anxiety. Julie was plagued with obsessive ruminations of catastrophe befalling her mother, her grandmother, or herself, and she

frequently personalized news stories, fearing that whatever disaster or tragedy was reported on the television news would soon befall the P. family. She also reported ongoing fears of being kidnapped or killed in a motor vehicle accident, such as a school bus crash.

In addition to these conscious fears, Julie experienced terrifying nightmares in which she or another family member would mysteriously disappear, become lost, or be killed. She usually awoke from these dreams in a panic state; as a consequence, she reported a great fear of sleeping and insisted that sleep was not very important anyway.

Julie also experienced a variety of somatic complaints, always on the mornings of school days. Samples of her somatic complaints, as well as her "mad fits" in which she shrieked, cried, and banged her hands on the floor and table, were observed on several occasions at the clinic where she was seen when her mother was encouraged to leave her for brief periods of time. Once separated, Julie would regain her composure, sometimes dramatically, although she generally remained withdrawn and unable to concentrate on tasks for more than a few moments.

A series of family interviews revealed a number of significant events in the history of the P. family, although only Gary, Julie's brother, was willing to discuss these in any detail. Julie and Mrs. P. were more likely to argue about issues such as Julie's clothes or Mrs. P.'s mother, who had been living with the P. family for the past three years.

Mr. and Mrs. P. were divorced when Julie was age 4 and Gary was age 7, with Mrs. P. retaining custody of both children. Shortly after the divorce, when Julie was in the care of her father one weekend, she was allegedly sexually abused by a friend of her cousin's, who reportedly took her clothes off and had her "play games" with him. Mrs. P. reported that Julie had told her of this the following week while she was taking a bath. Mrs. P.

would not discuss this in the presence of the children and reported that it had never been mentioned since the bath. Following this incident, which Mr. P.'s family insisted could not have happened, Mrs. P. refused to allow Julie's father or anyone else in his family to see the children. Some three weeks after the incident, a heated family argument was carried on regarding Mrs. P.'s decision. Mr. P. was killed in a motor vehicle accident. Mrs. P. reported that she did not bring the children to the funeral or cemetery because she believed that they would not understand, and she stated that they seemed to cope with their father's death very well, particularly Julie. Gary, on the other hand, began to steal things for no apparent reason. Not long after, Gary's stealing behavior stopped of its own accord, and he did not exhibit any behavior problems in school or at home thereafter. Julie, like her brother, rarely mentioned her father during the year following his death, but recently she had begun to insist that she be taken to visit him in the cemetery.

When Julie was 5 years old, her maternal grandmother moved in with the family. Mrs. P. described her mother as a demanding, helpless woman who always complained of her health and rarely got out of bed. She also reported that her mother was an extremely anxious and fearful woman who had not left her apartment for 15 years following her husband's death, suggesting the possibility of an agoraphobic condition.

As Julie reached school age, Mrs. P. became involved in a protracted dispute with the local board of education over the correct school district for Julie, and as a result, Julie's entrance into first grade was delayed for a year. Once Julie started school, the problems began to surface. When Mrs. P. brought Julie to the outpatient clinic for intake, she described herself as a "nervous wreck," fearing on the one hand that the court might take Julie away from her and on the other hand that Julie "might be crazy." Mrs. P. reported that she had had a "nervous breakdown" herself when Julie was 2 years old and that Mr. P. had started a new job that required extensive travel away from home.

Etiology

The history and symptoms of this case suggest several issues of etiological significance. First, as Bowlby (1973) suggested early on, fears of separation and loss are generally traceable to real loss events in the history of the individual. In Julie's case, it is certainly important to note the loss of her father, the alleged sexual abuse, and the subsequent cutoff of her father's family in the development of her presenting symptoms, including her nightmares, her fears of catastrophe befalling her mother, and her fears that she herself would be kidnapped or killed in an automobile accident. All of these symptoms involved themes of separation and loss of attachment figures, which reflected unresolved issues of grief and an underlying feeling of insecurity regarding the stability of the world around her. The development of anxious attachment behaviors, such as a reluctance to sleep alone, school refusal, and agitation at times of separation, reflected Julie's fear that she might suddenly be left alone. In this sense, they were adaptive responses in that they served to promote attachment to significant others and to prevent further loss (Atkinson & Goldberg, 2004).

It is generally believed that a child's model of self is a function of stable parent/child or other attachment bonds. Thus, a child who experiences severe instability in her relationships with major attachment figures is likely to develop feelings of personal inadequacy and interpersonal insecurity. Thus, Julie's difficulties in establishing peer relationships, participating in play, and concentrating on purposive behaviors such as school work likely reflected a poor self-image that was based in the losses and family instability she had experienced. It is also clear that Julie's refusal to attend school was as much a function of her mother's unwillingness to let her go as it was a function of her own fears. Despite her insistence that she had tried to force Julie to attend school, Mrs. P. had implicitly condoned and reinforced Julie's "problem" behaviors from the start. On a typical day, Julie would wake up, complain of feeling ill, and then refuse to meet the school bus for fear that it might crash. If her mother tried to insist, Julie would become extremely agitated, scream, and throw things about the house. Once the school bus had come and gone, she would quiet down, Mrs. P. would fix her a nice breakfast, and they would watch the soap operas and game shows on television for the rest of the day while taking care of Julie's grandmother.

In one sense, both Julie and her grandmother provided a means for Mrs. P. to meet her own needs for adequacy and self-worth by playing the roles of inadequate persons who required Mrs. P.'s attention. Thus, despite Mrs. P.'s verbal protests about Julie's school refusal, it is clear that Julie's symptoms resulted in secondary gain for both parties and that Julie's behaviors reflected a well-established family pattern of separation and dependency issues, as well as her own fears and anxieties.

Finally, the history of anxiety-related problems in Julie's mother and grandmother suggests both a role model for her symptomatology as well as a possible biochemical or neurological predisposition for an anxiety disorder. Certainly, the overall level of anxiety and overt tension was high among all members of the P. family, supporting the possibility that genetically weighted variables may have increased the overall risk.

Treatment Options

Cases of separation anxiety like Julie's offer an opportunity for treatment from a variety of theoretical perspectives, largely due to the range of clinical symptoms that arises and the nature of etiological factors (Duncan et al., 1995; Kronenberger & Meyer, 2001). From a behavioral perspective, treatments involving contingency management programs and systematic desensitization (SDT) have been found to be successful in reducing symptoms of anxiety and improving school attendance. In these treatments, emphasis is placed on developing a relaxation response in association with a feared stimulus—such as school, separation from mother, or riding a school bus—in an attempt to reduce and eventually eliminate fear responses. At the same time, there is an assessment of the system of overt and covert reinforcers that is maintaining the target behaviors. In Julie's case, school refusal was clearly being reinforced by her mother when she prepared Julie a nice breakfast and allowed her to watch television following her school refusal. In a contingency management program, reinforcers such as these would be used to reward school approach behaviors rather than school avoidance behaviors, and school refusal would result in punishments such as time out, loss of privileges, or extra household chores.

From a psychodynamic or developmental perspective, symptoms of separation anxiety may be seen as mechanisms of defense that function to reduce the anxiety generated from intrapsychic conflict. In Julie's case, unconscious conflicts involving object loss and individuation would need to be worked through using the therapeutic relationship as a mechanism of change, and perhaps involving techniques such as psychodynamic play therapy, fantasy storytelling, and art therapy to express unconscious material indirectly.

A family systems model would attempt to restructure family boundaries and communication patterns. In Julie's case, attempts might be made to strengthen the parental boundary between Mrs. P. and Julie and to more clearly establish family roles for all family members, including the grandmother.

The Treatment of Julie

In the case of Julie, family treatment was recommended and accepted by Mrs. P. The P. family was subsequently seen weekly for approximately two months. Despite the therapist's early efforts, the grandmother never joined the family for sessions, which consisted of Julie, Gary, and Mrs. P.

During the first sessions, great effort was expended by the therapist to side with Mrs. P. on all issues in an effort to support her role as executive of the family. To this end, the seating arrangement placed the children together on one side of the room, Mrs. P. on the other, and the therapist in the middle, frequently moving over to physically side with Mrs. P.

Interventions initially included encouraging Mrs. P. to view Julie's school refusal and other behaviors as misbehaviors rather than problems or signs that she was "crazy." In keeping with this, a system of punishments was devised to make staying at home less favorable for Julie. Although this met with early success in improving Julie's attendance, she soon began to fear the school bus again and Mrs. P. did not enforce the punishment system out of sympathy for Julie's fears.

At this point, Julie was paradoxically praised by the therapist for not going to school and in so doing keeping the family together. Mrs. P. was praised at the same time for recognizing Julie's authority to do this out of respect for Julie's role as the holder of all family problems. These paradoxical approaches were designed to generate sufficient anger in Mrs. P. so that she would begin to govern the family more forcefully. This began to have a dramatic effect on family dynamics when Mrs. P. refused to feed her mother one evening, insisting that she feed herself. Not long after this, Julie's attendance began to improve significantly.

However, as family boundaries began to change and Julie's school attendance continued to improve, Mrs. P. began to cancel sessions. The school and court again intervened, as the school year was drawing to a close and Julie would not have completed the requisite number of days of attendance to be passed on to third grade. Although Julie's attendance had improved, the improvement was not great enough to keep the P. family out of court, where removal from the home was threatened before Mrs. P. agreed to voluntarily sign Julie into an inpatient treatment facility.

After two weeks of inpatient treatment and near-perfect school attendance, Julie convinced her mother (by promising her that she would never miss school again) to sign her out of the treatment facility against the strong recommendations of the treatment staff. When she returned home, Julie again refused to go to school and, sobbing and frightened, begged her mother never to let anyone take her away again.

At this time, the P. family's caseworker became so angry with Mrs. P. that she dropped the case, and it was returned to court, where removal from the home was to be considered.

Comment

Along with the diagnostic and treatment issues raised here, this case also highlights the need for carefully planned, well-organized intervention programs when several social systems are involved. The P. family might likely have never sought treatment had it not been for the insistence of the school system and the courts. Thus, while it would appear on the one hand that the courts, the school system, and the mental health system were working at cross-purposes in this case, the goals of each were reasonably equivalent. The observation that similar goals can at times result in conflicting intervention attempts is an important factor to remember when dealing with cases that involve a number of social systems in a community mental health setting.

> *Give to a pig when it grunts and a child when it cries, and you will have a fine pig and a bad child.*
> —Old Danish proverb

Oppositional Defiant Disorder

The Oppositional Defiant Disorder (ODD) is marked by negativistic, hostile, and defiant behaviors, often elicited by the attempts by parents or other authority figures to control the behavior of the child or adolescent. Stubborn and/or hostile resistance is manifested in a variety of behavior patterns, including consistent violation of minor rules and pouting with an occasional temper flare-up. When it emerges most strongly in adolescence, as it often does, similar behaviors usually have been evident in the child's earlier behavioral history.

Adolescence is commonly a stressful period for teenagers, their families, and school officials. Pubertal changes, the task of identity formation, the renegotiation of relationships with parents, and rapid changes in the social environment can precipitate a variety of problematic behaviors (Petraitis, Flay, & Miller, 1995). Certain adolescents are unable to effect a logical or objective break from their earlier emotional bonds with parents, and thus teenagers' struggles for an autonomous relationship with parents may be a significant source of problems. Teenagers may become rebellious, emotional, or hypercritical in order to convince parents that they are no longer "children," and so must be accorded greater independence.

Oppositional teenagers, while emotionally unpredictable and argumentative, may elicit a generally positive response from others, as individuals with ODD may mask their disorder out in community settings but consistently manifest it at home. They may evidence stubbornness and emotionality rather than an antisocial value system or deliberate disregard for the feelings of others. Also, oppositional behavior usually has a compulsive component, which maintains the problematic behavior despite detrimental (and undesired) consequences. Oppositional behavior is consistent with the traditional concept of the neurotic paradox; that is, the behavior is goal directed (aimed toward emotional autonomy and independent thinking) but not goal attaining (usually resulting in descriptors such as "immature" or "irresponsible"). As in the case of Phyllis, compulsive violations and seemingly reflexive negative responses elicit mistrust and anxiety, resulting in criticism and further restrictions of freedom, to which the oppositional person responds with intensified negativism. Consequently, relationships with authority figures deteriorate and become increasingly conflict-ridden.

The Case of Phyllis

Throughout Phyllis's childhood, her parents were embassy officials in several South American countries. When Phyllis entered high school, her parents moved back to the States and joined the political science department of a small private college. Phyllis attended public high school for two years and was suspended four times. Her parents enrolled her in a private girls' academy, hoping the structured atmosphere would "settle her down." However, Phyllis was suspended from the academy twice in the first semester, and the principal threatened permanent expulsion if her school behavior did not improve. The school had a weekly "detention hall" for students who had broken rules. Phyllis's suspensions resulted primarily from noncompliance with detention hall and the sheer number of outstanding detentions. The infractions for which she received detention were generally minor, such as talking during class, violations of dress code, and tardiness for detention hall.

The youngest of five girls, Phyllis was the only daughter who still lived with her parents at the time she was referred by her school's guidance counselor to a clinical psychologist. Four years separated Phyllis and the next-youngest sister. Phyllis's parents described the family as close and loving. They said that the older girls had gone through brief periods of rebellion during adolescence but that they all grew out of it. The family was very achievement oriented, and everyone except Phyllis had distinguished academic records.

Phyllis's behavior had been normal through childhood, although she had been very stubborn and difficult as a preschooler and had often been prone to temper tantrums, causing her father to semi-affectionately dub her as "the little witch." Phyllis had always

(continued)

The Case of Phyllis Continued

produced an inconsistent academic perform-ance. Throughout grammar school, she often earned above-average grades, yet her teachers consistently concluded that her potential was higher. Junior high school was characterized by a particularly erratic performance.

Similar inconsistencies were observed in Phyllis's social relationships. She had several "personality conflicts" with teachers, on whom she blamed her low grades, and her parents described her as "moody and difficult to get along with" as she neared adolescence. Frequent arguments erupted at home. When the tension in the home became intolerable, Phyllis would visit one of her sisters. However, these visits were often prematurely ter-minated by some disagreement with her sister concerning Phyllis's curfew.

In grade school, Phyllis apparently got along fairly well with her classmates. The family moved every two or three years, however, and Phyllis had not continued any of her child-hood friendships. In high school, she moved from one close girlfriend to another, often within a few weeks. These friendships seemed to die from lack of interest on the other girls' parts and seldom resulted in an actual argu-ment. Phyllis dated frequently but did not have a steady boyfriend. This was an addi-tional source of conflict in the family, because her mother suspected, without any hard evi-dence, that Phyllis was sexually active.

Etiology

Eric Erikson (1959) described adolescence as a period in which one must resolve the crisis of self-definition by committing oneself to a role and adopting an ideol-ogy (attitudes, beliefs, moral values). The apparent ideology and role adopted by Phyllis are ones of counter-dependence. That is, although her behavior is directed toward demonstrating autonomy, she remains defined by the external environ-ment because her coping strategy is generally limited to acting in the opposite direction of perceived external forces. These dynamics are generally frustrating for everyone involved, including Phyllis. In addition to provoking predictable nega-tive reactions from parents, peers, and teachers, the oppositional adolescent's behavior does not result in feelings of autonomy or independence. Rather, the individual is likely to feel that emotionally charged situations escalate too quickly and that he or she is unable to control his or her behavior. Phyllis said, "Sometimes I just get mad because someone's ordering me around. So I just don't do it, and then I get in trouble I'm sorry for later."

How adolescents arrive at maladaptive ideologies and roles is a process about which there is considerable speculation and scant empirical data. Generally, behavior problems in adolescents are attributed to predisposing family dynamics and/or deficient coping skills on the part of the teenager (Novak & Pelaez, 2004). In Phyllis's case, both groups of variables contributed to her poor adjustment. She was the youngest in her family and was no doubt accustomed to relatively uncon-ditional affection, despite implicit expectations of high achievement. In addition to the typical problems experienced by adolescents with successful older siblings, Phyllis's process of self-definition was hampered by her family's indulgence and overprotection, which resulted in her lack of experience with problem solving. Phyllis was able to meet the social and educational demands of grammar school with minimal effort, but her level of effort and coping ability did not step up to the increased demands of adolescence.

Moreover, because of the family's many moves and the age gap between her and her sisters, Phyllis's only stable relationships were with her parents (who had become part of the problem). Sullivan (1953) was a pioneer in noting that an important predictor of problematic interpersonal relationships is the absence of a close same-sex relationship in preadolescence, as these friendships provide experiences with intimacy, essential reality testing, and a broader perspective from the combined experiences. Phyllis had missed this significant experience in childhood, and the constantly changing environments and associated behavioral norms (complicated by cultural differences among her numerous schools) had interfered with her development of a consistent set of attitudes and behaviors. It is not surprising that she adopted a rigid approach to the environment that was defined by being against the expectations of her parents and teachers.

Treatment Options

A useful technique for oppositional children, as well as for conduct-disordered children, is Parent Management Training (PMT). In PMT, the therapist provides a brief overview of underlying social learning concepts, models, and techniques and then coaches parents in implementing the procedures.

> Procedures and interaction patterns practiced in the sessions are then used in the home. Parents usually are taught how to define, observe, and record behavior at the beginning of treatment because once behaviors (e.g., fighting, engaging in tantrums) are defined concretely, reinforcement and punishment techniques can be applied. The PMT therapist details the concepts and procedures derived from positive reinforcement (e.g., contingent delivery of attention, praise, points) and punishment (e.g., time out from reinforcement, loss of privileges, and reprimands). Reinforcement for prosocial and nondeviant behavior is central to treatment. Parents are taught how to use reinforcement and punishment techniques contingent on the child's behavior, to provide consequences consistently, to attend to appropriate behaviors and to ignore inappropriate behaviors, to apply skills in prompting, shaping, and fading, and to use these techniques to manage future problems. There is an extensive amount of practice and shaping of parent behavior within the sessions to develop skills in carrying out the procedures (Feldman & Kazdin, 1995, p. 3).

The therapist maintains close telephone contact with the parents between sessions. These contacts encourage parents to ask questions about the home programs and give an opportunity for the therapist to prompt compliance with the behavior-change program, to reinforce parents' use of the skills, to strengthen the therapeutic alliance, and to help the parents immediately confront and solve problems.

Because persons with an oppositional disorder often avoid accepting responsibility for the difficulties they encounter in their world, the classic Reality Therapy techniques that William Glasser (1980) developed while working with delinquent adolescent girls, who are especially inclined to avoid responsibility, can be appropriate here. Adlerian therapy, which melds some analogous approaches into a traditional psychodynamic therapy, is also successfully applied.

Once some of the oppositional tendencies are muted, either client-centered or nondirective therapies (variations of the original explorations by Carl Rogers [1961]) can be used to explore the conflicts over defining one's identity while adjusting to parental constraints. Similarly, Gestalt therapy techniques (Perls, Hefferline, & Goodman, 1958) can help the oppositional disorder confront the underlying feelings toward parental figures, often via the "empty chair technique." Here, the adolescent pretends the parent is in a chair and holds a dialogue by taking both parts, which helps the teenager get in touch with the parent's perspective.

The Treatment of Phyllis

Phyllis's treatment took place over 10 individual therapy sessions, which included Adlerian and Gestalt techniques, followed by weekly adolescent group therapy for three months. Her parents were given advice on reactions to Phyllis's behavior and a list of books and magazine articles written especially for parents of teenagers. Phyllis was slow to disclose spontaneously with the therapist, although she was willing to answer questions and negotiate contracts for more appropriate behaviors. She was motivated both by the threat of expulsion from school and by her desire to effect more harmonious relationships with her parents, teachers, and peers. As is often the case with adolescents, a major portion of Phyllis's problems stemmed from inadequate social skills and an inability to communicate feelings in socially appropriate ways. Consequently, individual sessions concentrated on more appropriate assertive behaviors for Phyllis, including contracts for in vivo trials with parents and peers. These strategies dramatically reduced the intense tension between Phyllis and her parents.

The therapy group that Phyllis participated in consisted of 8 to 10 teenagers who had similar problems in relationships with authority figures, school achievement, and maintaining stable peer relationships. This group functioned like the intimate preadolescent friendships described by Sullivan (1953). Group members assisted one another in problem solving and reality testing within an accepting atmosphere. The group was open ended; members could enter and then "graduate" as their individual needs were met. Some of the group members became close friends and continued their relationships even after they left the group. Phyllis was more disclosing in the group setting and was relieved to discover similarities with the experiences of other group members.

After three months, Phyllis's improvement was evidenced by more pleasant interactions with her parents, significant decreases in school detentions, and better grades. She has maintained the friendships formed in the group, enjoys more stable relationships with schoolmates, and is no longer threatened with expulsion. Also, Phyllis now reports that she simply is happier and more confident.

Comment

Phyllis's case is an example of how seemingly unremarkable life circumstances can combine to predispose adjustment problems in adolescence. Phyllis's childhood experiences, although superior in many ways, did not include adequate practice in frustration tolerance or in the maintenance of long-term peer relationships. Also, her status as the family's youngest and later as the only child in the home combined with deficits in social skills to restrict her socially. Phyllis did not know how to rely on the support of peers or siblings for credible feedback about her behavior, and she was forced to use the expectations of her parents and teachers as guidelines for judgments.

School Violence

Although society has had at least a dim recognition for some time that serial killers have existed among us for at least centuries (also see Chapter 13), for example, Jack the Ripper, we have no good data to refute the concept that school shooters are more of a modern phenomenon. The *Report of the Review Panel* (2007, Appendix L) finds that from 1966 to 2007 we have had approximately 45 school shootings, probably the most horrific being the Virginia Tech shootings of 2007 (discussed next). Curiously, our society tends to reframe serial killers as having some interesting/positive characteristics, and at the same time we perceive school shooters as almost totally pathetic/unlikable individuals. Nevertheless, the concept of serial killers does include the data that these were calculating, often psychopathic, unredeemable individuals who deserve the gravest of punishments and the least empathy. School shooters, however, are typically more like most of us; they had significant moments of normality, and their acts were not calculated over long periods of time. Rather, as in the next case, the shooting is often the culmination of a long developmental process.

The Centers for Disease Control (CDC)'s (2001) Youth Risk Behavior Survey, which is a survey of school children in grades 9 through 12, reported that 5.9 percent of high school students carried a gun with them during the 30 days before the survey. The survey also reported that 7.4 percent of respondents had been threatened or injured with a weapon on school property in the past year, with males (10.2 percent) more likely to have been threatened than females (4 percent). Approximately 4 percent of students were absent for one or more days of school in the preceding 30 days of the survey due to feeling unsafe at school.

Given the frequency of guns in school and the likelihood of disagreements between students, the nation has become extremely interested in understanding and preventing school violence. Events such as the shootings in Columbine (Colorado), Paducah (Kentucky), Jonesboro (Arkansas), Springfield (Oregon), and, more recently, the Virginia Tech massacre have brought the issue of school violence to the forefront, causing parents, children, and administrators to search for answers.

The Case of Seung-Hui Cho

April 16, 2007, is now known as being the day of not only the largest school shooting but also the largest mass murder by one person in the history of the United States. Although some of the material for this article was first gathered from articles in the *Washington Post*, it is now referenced as the *Report of the Review Panel* (2007), the independent panel report submitted to Governor Raines of Virginia and released to the public on August 29, 2007. Seung-Hui Cho was apparently up early on April 16, as was now his pattern, and the horror became manifest at 7:15 A.M. when a call was made to report that there had been a shooting at West Ambler Johnston Hall. When police arrived at the scene they found that freshman Emile Hilscher and resident assistant Ryan Clark had been shot. The two were pronounced dead at the hospital. The police began to secure the area and thought they had a boyfriend-girlfriend scenario. At 9:26 A.M. Virginia Tech authorities sent the first of many e-mails to students, staff, and faculty alerting them of the shooting and listing precautions they should take. Many never saw the e-mail.

No one is clear what Cho did immediately after this, except to mail a videotaped confession to NBC. But approximately two hours after the first attack Cho entered Norris Hall, where he chained all exit doors. He went from one classroom to another, shooting rapidly and without hesitation, killing people in consecutive classrooms. Students across the hall from one of the rooms opened the door to see what was happening. As soon as the door opened they saw the shooter leaving the classroom across the hall. They swiftly closed the door. One student realized that there was a heavy rectangular table that could be used as a barricade. Moments later Cho was at the door. With the table in place and students pushing against the door, the gunman was unable to enter but instead fired a couple of shots through the door, hitting no one. Cho moved on, and the killing continued,

but at some point before the police stormed the building, Seung-Hui Cho shot and killed himself.

In the end Cho killed a total of 33 people (27 students, 5 faculty, and himself) and injured 17 others. The attack in Norris Hall was estimated to have lasted no more than 9 minutes. Officials have stated that Cho had fired more than 170 shots and had brought 17 ammunition magazines with him.

The *Report of the Review Panel* (2007) concluded that one problem was the delay in sending out a general notification about the attack on the first two students killed. In part the delay occurred because police viewed that first attack as a boyfriend-girlfriend scenario. A related issue was the result of classic bureaucracy. Only two administrators had the ability to send out campuswide e-mails, and whatever message was sent out had to first be approved by the Policy Group. This group was chaired by President Steger and included nine vice presidents and several vice provosts; not surprisingly it took at least a half-hour to get this group together. A more significant problem was the lack of communication and a lack of adequate response, from as early as high school, between persons and agencies concerning the warning signs of disorder in Cho that portended violence (Depue, 2007), with its possible consequences.

Background and Warning Signs

Seung-Hui Cho was born in South Korea in January of 1984. Cho developed whooping cough at 9 months of age, then pneumonia and was hospitalized, during which time doctors diagnosed a heart problem, either a "hole in the heart" or a heart murmur. Two years later, doctors performed "a procedure (probably either an echocardiograph or a cardiac catheterization). This caused the 3-year-old emotional trauma. From that point on, Cho did not like to be touched. . . . According to his mother, he cried a lot and was constantly sick" (*Report of the Review Panel*, 2007, Ch. 4, pp. 31–32). Although his family was not severely deprived, as were many postwar Koreans, the family was financially struggling, and at the instigation of a relative who had already immigrated to the United States, they moved here in 1992 when Cho was 6. Neither Cho nor his parents could read or speak English. Although he was already withdrawn when in Korea, it became much worse as children taunted Cho for his shyness and his unusual accent. Some students did try to make friends with him, but they were rebuffed. So far there had been no mention of his ever having any friends.

Relatives state that Cho was abnormally quiet as a child. Interactions with family members were often distant. Cho seldom responded to greetings, let alone any physical contact. At the same time, Cho excelled in academically. In elementary school it became apparent that Cho had a gift for math and English. Often his teachers would refer to him while talking to other children in the class. However, students who knew Cho in middle school remember him as being uncommunicative to other students and avoiding talking to his teachers. When called on by a teacher he would typically just sit there until the teacher finally moved on, or he would just mumble a reply. Similarly, in high school Cho remained uncommunicative.

Contrary to early impressions, Cho showed clear problems as early as grade school, and his parents did seek help for him. In July 1987, the Chos took their son to a mental health services facility, and after working with "a Korean counselor with whom there was a poor fit, Cho began working with another specialist who had training in art therapy [and] a psychiatrist who participated in the first meeting" (*Report of the Review Panel*, 2007, Ch. 4, p. 34), who offered a diagnosis of "social anxiety disorder." Cho seemed to do well, but his therapist noted a change for the worse in the eighth grade, and after the April 1999 Columbine High School murders, Cho wrote that "he wanted to repeat Columbine," resulting in an evaluation by another psychiatrist who diagnosed Cho with "selective mutism"

and "major depression, single episode" and prescribed paroxetine, 20 milligrams, which Cho took for a little over a year. Selective mutism is a variant of anxiety disorder in which the person does not speak in social situations in which there is a reasonable expectancy of a response. The fall of 1999 he entered high school and generally did well as he continued with his therapy until the eleventh grade and was given special needs considerations for his communication deficits. He graduated with a 3.52 GPA and SAT scores of 540-verbal and 620-math and was accepted at Virginia Tech, which does not require letters of recommendation, personal interviews, or an essay.

Cho started as a business information major, and although he had problems with roommates and became increasingly withdrawn, he managed a 3.00 average but inexplicably changed his major to English. He managed to get through his sophomore year, but in the fall of his junior year in 2005 he took a definite turn for the worse. Nikki Giovanni, a poetry instructor, had difficult interactions with him and finally had enough when several of her other students quit attending class; some women students complained of Cho taking pictures of them with a cell phone during class. Giovanni then went to Lucinda Roy, a co-director of the writing program at Virginia Tech, and asked if she could tutor him. Roy also became alarmed at Cho's writings and odd behavior, and she spoke to officials about the matter. Information bounced around bureaucratic channels with the ultimate conclusion that the legal issues would be too great, and that there were no explicit threats. Cho had also harassed at least two women, resulting in police confrontations. On November 30 Cho did call the Cook Counseling Center, resulting in several phone interviews but no actual therapy.

In December, Cho was seen stabbing a carpet at a party. He also harassed a female student, leading to police contact that in turn stimulated Cho to send "an instant message to one of his suitemates stating 'I might as well kill myself'" (*Report of the Review Panel*, 2007, Ch. 4, p. 47), eventually leading to police

The Case of Seung-Hui Cho Continued

contact and an evaluation that recommended involuntary hospitalization. He was hospitalized, but evaluators had different opinions, and only written opinions (rather than any witnesses) were available the next day when Cho appeared in front of the special justice to be considered for involuntary commitment. "The special justice ruled that Cho 'presents an imminent danger to himself as a result of mental illness' and ordered 'O-P' (outpatient treatment)'" (*Report of the Review Panel*, Ch. 4, p. 48). Under supervision Cho made an appointment for treatment but was only evaluated and did not make any further appointments.

In all of his classes, his writings disturbed teachers and fellow students. In the fall of 2006, in a screenwriting class, Cho's writings were so gruesome that many of the students gathered before class began to discuss the possibility of Cho becoming a school shooter. Although opinions of others' writings were required, students chose their words carefully when discussing Cho's. After opin-

ions are given, the student is expected to give a closing statement about the comments. However, the professor did not pressure Cho to provide one. This same issue continued in the next two semesters. Then, in the spring semester, 2007, students recall that Cho changed drastically in the month(s) before the shooting. He began to work out; he shaved his head, began wearing contact lenses, and began to awaken very early in the morning. Also, Cho gradually ceased to attend class, which is inconsistent with his academic history. On February 9, 2007, Cho purchased a gun, a Glock 9, at a pawn shop across from the Virginia Tech campus. One month later on March 16 he bought his second gun, a .22-caliber Walther. In a phone call to his parents on August 15, the night before the shooting, Cho "appeared his 'regular' self. He asked how his parents were, and other standard responses: "No, I do not need any money.' His parents said, 'I love you'"(*Report of the Review Panel*, 2007, Ch. 4, p. 52). He then carried out the killings the next day.

Comment

In hindsight, from a very young age Cho manifested clear schizoid traits. Seemingly as he grew older he became increasingly interpersonally distant and inappropriate, depressed and/or angry, and paranoid. The schizoid personality pattern and the apparently increasing anger and paranoia made it unlikely he would seek help again or cooperate if he was forced into treatment (Meyer & Weaver, 2007). These factors, combined with an increasing fascination with violence and the unwarranted access to guns (he had been found mentally ill), made a lethal event a not-surprising outcome.

In Appendix M of the *Report of the Review Panel* (2007, pp. M-2–M-4), Depue provides an overview of the warning signs associated with school shooters in the United States. These are (1) violent fantasy content, (2) anger problems, (3) fascination with weapons and related materials, (4) boasting and practicing of fighting and combat proficiency, (5) loner-schizoid patterns, (6) suicidal ideation, (7) homicidal ideation, (8) stalking behavior, (9) noncompliance and disciplinary problems, (10) imitation (and/or admiration) of other murderers, and (11) interest in previous shooting situations.

Identifying Violent Children and Adolescents

How does one identify children and adolescents at risk for violent behavior? Mulvey and Cauffman (2001) discussed the difficulties in the identification of violent adolescents, such as the low base rate of school violence and the possibility of false positives; the developmental aspect of a child's personality, which is constantly changing and evolving; and social and situational aspects that may increase the likelihood of violence. Another challenge is to understand the differences between school shooters who perform alone and those who act out in collaboration with other children. However, there have been common traits among the perpetrators of the many school shootings in the United States. Most are white males who come from middle-class families, are of average intelligence, have an unclear history of mental illness, are being bullied and or perceived as "geeks" or "nerds," and are, on average, around 16 years of age.

Other possible indicators include:

1. Threats of violence
2. Broken home and/or family problems
3. Recent stressor, such as a break-up or perceived rejection
4. Preoccupation with violent or gruesome movies, stories, etc.
5. Depression
6. Drug or alcohol abuse
7. Brain dysfunction
8. Access to guns
9. Cruelty to animals
10. Extreme interest in weapons, explosives, or the military
11. History of violent behavior
12. Dramatic change in mood or behavior
13. Intense dislike for school
14. Feelings of loneliness and isolating behaviors
15. Complaints about being treated badly
16. Suicidal thoughts

It is important to remember that (1) many risk factors are not static, (2) no single risk factor is compelling enough to definitely predict that a child will become violent, and (3) there is no equation available that would even remotely begin to accurately predict a school shooting event.

Preventing School Violence

There is no easy way to prevent future school violence. However, the following are problem-solving initiatives for violence prevention:

1. Intervention should start at the most basic level. Parents should attempt to prevent brain damage connected to low birth weight and early head injury and recognize that if it does exist, anger management techniques may be useful.

Behavioral techniques to develop prosocial behaviors and to deter violent behavior should be used throughout the child's development.

2. Parents should be aware of and modify activities, situations, and places that promote violent behavior. They should know what their children are doing and where they are.

3. Decrease risk factors by eliminating access to firearms, alcohol, and drugs. Education about the lethality of guns and the effects of drugs and alcohol is also helpful.

In addition to these recommendations, the following are suggestions that, when used in combination, may help to eliminate future school shootings and reduce the likelihood of school violence in general (Fassler, 2001):

1. As early as feasible, identify kids with problems. (See the previous indicators of potentially violent children.)

2. Improve awareness and communication. Encourage children to talk about their problems and to ask for help when necessary. This also includes allowing and encouraging children to discuss their friends' problems.

3. Reduce access to guns. Even a gun in a locked cabinet can be obtained by a persistent child.

4. Reduce class size. Smaller classes will give the teacher more control over the classroom and will also increase teacher/child interactions. It will also assist in the identification of at-risk children.

5. Promote tolerance and socialization, and teach problem-solving skills. Children must learn how to resolve conflicts without using violence. These problem-solving skills should be taught early during the child's development and practiced and improved throughout the school years.

Another area of concentration is the relationship between violent behavior and previous school discipline problems. The rationale for this focus is the supposition that past behavior is the best indicator of future behavior. Some schools are implementing a multiple gating technique to screen at-risk students. One such screening program presented by Sprague and colleagues (2001) includes a four-level process. The first level involves recommendations from teachers of students who evidence antisocial behavior. The second level requires teachers to rate the identified students in areas of social skills, previous discipline problems, and study habits. A review of student records is the third level of the process. It involves using a standardized evaluation of all previous discipline actions. The last level is a search of records, such as corrections and public safety files, for information about previous offenses and arrests.

Identity Development Crisis or Disorder

Almost everyone has encountered and endured both adolescents and adolescence. Thus, most have experienced and witnessed the developmental period that is most intense for identity issues. As shown in the following case study, going through this critical developmental period without successfully working through these issues can result in a crisis of identity in the adult years.

The Case of Mr. E.

Mr. E. was born June 15, 1902, near Frankfurt, Germany. He was born to a Danish Jewish mother who had traveled to Frankfurt to be with friends after being abandoned by Mr. E.'s father, who died shortly thereafter.

During Mr. E.'s first years, he lived alone with his mother, an artist who traveled frequently. When Mr. E. was age 3, he became ill, and his mother took him to a pediatrician, Theodore Homburger, whom she subsequently married. Mr. E. grew up as a child believing Dr. Homburger was his biological father. He eventually learned differently, but he kept the secret until he was 68 years old that he was the product of an extramarital affair.

While growing up in Karlsruhe, Germany, Mr. E. received other critical identity-related mixed messages. Because his stepfather, Dr. Homburger, was Jewish, Mr. E. went to the temple, where he was referred to as "goy" because of his blonde hair and blue eyes, which reflected his Danish biological parentage. In school, he was referred to as the "Jew" because his stepfather and name were Jewish.

Added to this confusion was the natural role rebellion of adolescence. Although loved and indulged by his parents, Mr. E. rebelled against the "bourgeois" aspects of his family. He even voiced the familiar refrain, "I set out to be different." He decided to become an artist, spent a year or so wandering around Europe, then enrolled in an art school in Karlsruhe. He soon went to Munich to study art, then to Florence, then back to Karlsruhe.

As often happens in identity development, a pull from the environment rather than a conscious choice provides direction. In his mid-twenties, Mr. E. was asked by a friend to come to Vienna to teach in a progressive school set up for English and American children by Dorothy Burlingham. Burlingham had studied with Sigmund Freud, and this opened up an interest in psychological issues for Mr. E. During Mr. E.'s Vienna years (1927–1933), he came to the attention of Anna Freud, Sigmund Freud's daughter, who was well on her way to becoming a prominent theorist-therapist with children. Mr. E. became one of her training analysands (a combination of student and patient). He then met and married Joan Serson, a fellow analysand-trainee and an artist and dancer.

Because of the political turmoil in Europe in 1933, especially considering Mr. E's perceived Jewishness, he and his wife tried to settle in Copenhagen, but, ironically, he was not allowed Danish citizenship, so they traveled to America.

Due to his ability as well as the scarcity of child psychoanalysts, Mr. E. soon received many prestigious academic and medical school appointments. He was Boston's only child psychoanalyst in the early 1930s. He enrolled in the Ph.D. program in psychology at Harvard, but he never finished. Interestingly, although he was soon lauded (and still is) for his academic achievements, he had no degree beyond high school.

Mr. E. moved from Boston to New Haven, Connecticut, in 1936, then to the Pine Ridge Sioux Indian Reservation in South Dakota for fieldwork, then to San Francisco in 1939, then to Berkeley, California, then to Stockbridge, Massachusetts, in 1950 (with weekly commutes to Pittsburgh), then back to Harvard and New Haven in 1960. In 1970, Mr. E. retired, dividing his retirement time between Marin County, California, and Cape Cod, Massachusetts, until his death on May 12, 1994.

Identity Challenge

Mr. E.'s life provided much fodder for identity crises: confusion and rejection related both to his parentage and to his ethnicity, as well as issues around vocational choice, educational achievement, where "home" was, and so on. Thus, it is not surprising that "Mr. E." (Erik Homburger Erikson) himself coined the term *identity crisis* and was the pioneer of this research area (Hopkins, 1995). Even his eventual personal choice for his last name, Erikson, reveals identity questions. He gave some indication that his choice was an attempt to acknowledge his biological father in naming himself after the early Danish explorer, Leif Eriksson.

Erik Erikson certainly confronted and surmounted his own identity crisis in grand style. He is revered as one of the greatest theorists and also synthesizers across theories and disciplines in the behavioral sciences. One colleague described Erikson as "Freud in sonnet form" (Hopkins, 1995). He authored many well-known books and articles, such as the classic *Identity, Youth and Crisis* (1968) and the psychobiography *Gandhi's Truth*, for which he won a Pulitzer Prize.

Treatment Options

For most people, physiological maturation, education, contact with mentors, life experience, and time are all the therapy they need for their identity crises. It is important to remember that although the majority of the work is done early in life and in bits and pieces, it is nevertheless a lifelong process for all people. In most instances, it is a process of normal development rather than a disorder. This reflects the modern trend to see these issues less as disorder, maybe as crisis, and always as a normal developmental challenge. In this vein, although prior *DSM*s included "identity disorder" as a standard disorder, in the *DSM-IV-TR*, there is only an "identity problem," and the diagnosis is applied only as an "other condition that may be a focus of clinical attention."

However, whether it is called a *disorder* or a *problem*, a number of individuals require some formal intervention to get through the identity challenge. Some high school counselors try to take on this task, but they seldom have enough time to do much. Counseling centers in universities do much of this work. Approaches such as client-centered therapy, existential therapy, and the cognitive therapies (see Chapters 1 and 2) are most often useful here.

15 Organic Mental Disorders and Mental Retardation

The title of this chapter can be a bit misleading in that most mental disorders have accompanying biological conditions, contributing causes, and/or results. What this chapter deals with are those consistent behavioral, affective, and intellectual patterns of disturbance that result when there has been damage to the normal brain. Brain cells can be functionally impaired or destroyed by a wide variety of injuries, diseases, and toxic chemicals. Damage to brain structures involved in cognition, affect, and/or impulse control can lead to inadequate psychological functioning. The extent to which a person's psychological functioning is impaired depends on the location and extent of neural damage, the person's prior psychological adjustment, and the quality of the person's lifestyle (Andreassi, 2000; Ricker, 2004). The effects of an organic mental disorder can range from mild memory disturbances to severe psychotic reactions.

This chapter presents a rather incredible case in which a person (Harry) had an entire hemisphere (one-half of the brain) surgically removed in his youth. Not only did he survive to live a somewhat normal life but also he actually achieved an overall adjustment at well above the average level. The second case study focuses on the development of a variant of Parkinson's disease in one of the most famous boxers of all time, Muhammad Ali. The third case is a case of Alzheimer's disease in the late U.S. President Ronald Reagan. This chapter concludes with a discussion of mental retardation and, in the case of Daryl Atkins, whether mental retardation disqualifies one for the death penalty.

Most fighters have some type of trauma. Hey, we're in the traumatizing business.
—James "Bonecrusher" Smith, after being denied a boxing license in
England in April 1994 because of trauma to his brain from boxing

Recovery of Functions following Removal of Dominant Brain Hemisphere

Although the human brain can be fragile, it is at the same time a remarkably adaptable organ. People have been known to sustain massive amounts of brain damage due to motor vehicle accidents, tumors, and other lesions, yet show remarkable degrees of recovery. Of course, the eventual level of recovery depends on a number of factors, including age at the time of injury, severity of damage, affective response to the injury, and the particular region (or regions) of the brain that sustained damage. The psychological assessment of people who have sustained brain injuries should therefore consider changes in performance that are likely to occur for some time after the original insult (Kay & Franklin, 1995). For this reason, many clinical neuropsychologists make it a habit to follow up on their clients and to retest them periodically in order to document changes that occur over time.

The processes by which the brain recovers from injury are being studied by a number of investigators, most of whom emphasize the capacity of nondamaged brain areas to help compensate for injury to other areas by assuming new functional roles. This line of reasoning implies that there is not a strict one-to-one correspondence between brain structures and behavioral or mental activity, even though under ordinary circumstances certain regions of the brain appear to exert dominant influence over specific functions.

Many years ago, it was believed that there existed a strict correspondence between brain regions and behavior (Harrington, 1985). According to this model, popularly called phrenology, discrete regions of the brain controlled very specific behaviors or mental processes. Thus, specific brain regions allegedly were responsible for such states as euphoria, anger, and intellectual superiority. An implication of this view of brain functions is that damage to a given region would be expected to affect only certain psychological functions, leaving others relatively intact. Indeed, early anatomical studies lent some support to this theory. For example, in the late nineteenth century, French neurologist Paul Broca discovered that impairment of expressive speech followed damage to a relatively circumscribed region of the left (or dominant) cerebral hemisphere.

Subsequent attempts to localize brain centers that control particular functions have met with varying degrees of success. At present, it is evident that even though there is certainly a general relationship between brain structures and psychological functions, the correlation is by no means exact (Harrington, 1985). It is well known, for example, that the two cerebral hemispheres each control some relatively distinct functions. In healthy and mature right-handed persons, the left cerebral hemisphere plays the dominant role in meditating language skills. The right cerebral hemisphere exerts correspondingly more control over what are known as visuospatial abilities, which are manifested in activities such as drawing, following directions, and being able to visualize spatial arrangements such as one might encounter in geometry problems. At a more general level, a distinction between the hemispheres emphasizes the capacity of the left hemisphere for rational, logical, and analytic thought processes, in contrast to the right hemisphere's role in more holistic, intuitive processes.

The axis of the brain extending from front to back is referred to as the *anterior-posterior dimension*. The front-most regions play a significant role in planning and executing behavior patterns. Structures in the posterior regions appear to be more involved in processing information taken in by the various sensory systems.

A third part of the brain extends inward from the surface of the brain. Surface regions, collectively called the *cortical mantle*, appear to mediate most of what are called *higher mental processes*, such as language, abstract thought, and reasoning abilities. Areas of the brain beneath the cortical mantle, by contrast, control a wide range of activities, including vegetative (life support), reflexive, appetitive, and emotive functions. From an evolutionary standpoint, these regions are the oldest, most primitive regions of the brain, collectively referred to as the *allocortex*, in contrast to the outermost cortical regions, known as the *neocortex*.

Regarding the functional localization and implications for recovery processes, it is evident that regions, or zones, of the brain are usually responsible for mediating certain psychological functions. These functions can be grouped according to three dimensions: left/right, anterior/posterior, and brain surface/inner regions. Although these dimensions do imply a degree of functional specificity, there is by no means a precise correspondence between circumscribed regions of brain tissue and specific behavior patterns or thought processes.

It is interesting to note that this absence of a strict correspondence holds true to a greater degree for the so-called higher functions than for the lower functions. For example, lesions in regions of the visual system concerned with basic perceptual processes may have very pronounced and permanent effects, such as blind spots or reductions in the visual fields (the area of sight from one visual periphery to the other). By contrast, brain lesions in areas controlling cognitive activities, such as language, may disrupt certain linguistic processes, without such clear-cut effects, however. There are several possible explanations for this. One explanation holds that because language is such a complex process, it is mediated by a greater proportion of brain tissue than are relatively less complex functions (Andreassi, 2000). As a result, focal damage is less likely to affect adversely all of the regions involved in this skill. A second possibility is that higher-level functions, such as language, may be reduplicated in adjacent or even in more distant brain regions. Thus, damage to a zone that ordinarily controls or mediates may be compensated for by other structures, which provide a sort of back-up coverage.

However, depending on the individual, both the right and left cerebral hemispheres manifest language capabilities, although to different degrees; ordinarily the left hemisphere is considered dominant. Until recently, the role of the right hemisphere in language activity was not well understood. However, the results of studies of patients who have undergone certain surgical procedures have made it clear that the right (or nondominant) hemisphere has a capacity for language-related activity. In one such procedure (termed a *hemispherectomy*), an entire cerebral hemisphere is removed, leaving the individual with essentially only half a brain. Understandably, relatively few of these operations are performed. Those that are done have been carried out either to arrest malignant tumors that have infiltrated one hemisphere or to control severe seizure activity that has not responded to less dramatic therapy.

The case of Harry is one of the most dramatic instances reported in the literature. Early in childhood, the left hemisphere of Harry's brain was removed. The removal was followed by a remarkable recovery of speech and language functions, as assessed by follow-up evaluations years later. Originally described in an article by Smith and Sugar (1975), Harry (not his real name) was briefly observed some three years later, at which time a follow-up evaluation was being performed.

The Case of Harry

The product of a full-term pregnancy and a Caesarean birth, Harry soon afterward began to manifest signs of significant brain impairment in the form of seizures. These seizures increased to nearly a dozen per day by the time he was 5 years old. A left hemispherectomy was performed shortly thereafter. Within a few months, the seizure activity had abated. Testing prior to surgery had revealed distorted speech, doubtless due to the disruptive effects of damage in the left hemisphere.

Remarkably, Harry's performance on tests of language and other abilities improved significantly in the months and years following surgery, despite nearly complete removal of the cerebral hemisphere that normally mediates language skills. In fact, follow-up testing of Harry 15 and 21 years after surgery revealed that he was performing in the high-average range of intelligence, with a verbal IQ score in the superior range.

Subsequent contact with Harry suggested that these high performance levels had been sustained and that he was adjusting extremely well. He successfully graduated from college and, at last report, had worked in an executive-level position for an industrial company and at age 80 was still doing daily crossword puzzles. He had compensated remarkably well for the aftereffects of surgery, which included loss of sight in the right visual field and motor control problems on the right side. (It is characteristic of damage to either hemisphere that control of the contralateral side of the body is affected.) Harry was a talkative, quick-witted person who undoubtedly was functioning very effectively with half of his brain intact.

Comment

The case of Harry contains several important implications about the long-term effects of brain injury on behavior. First, the development of above-average language capabilities following removal of the cerebral hemisphere that normally mediates these functions suggests that the nondominant hemisphere may possess greater linguistic capabilities than previously realized. More generally, it is at least evident that brain-behavior relations do not correspond to strict one-to-one functional relations. Instead, compensation for or reduplication of control mechanisms appears to exist for certain cognitive processes.

Second, in Harry's case, it may be concluded that right hemisphere structures were responsible for subsequent development of language skills, despite the fact that the right hemisphere's role in language skills is normally thought to be comparatively minor. Finally, the radical changes and improvements in Harry's mental functions underscore the importance of assessing the effects of brain injury over time and emphasize the recuperative powers of the central nervous system in certain situations. As noted earlier, the brain and related nervous system structures make up an incredibly complex yet flexible and adaptive system.

Changes in mood or emotion are quite common in cases of central nervous system (CNS) trauma (Ricker, 2004). Perhaps the most commonly reported reaction is one of depression, and Harry showed some of this at first. This probably reflects both an overall slowing of responsiveness due to the impact of trauma on the brain and a personal reaction as the individual becomes aware of loss of abilities and of newly imposed limitations on behavior. Generally, as recovery proceeds, depression is succeeded by a more optimistic outlook and by the gradual return of cognitive and behavioral capabilities. Of course, not everyone recovers from the effects of CNS trauma. Factors such as severity, region or regions of the brain affected, and the age of the individual all play a role in determining the likelihood of subsequent recovery.

As far as Harry is concerned, it is likely that the early age at which surgery occurred enhanced his recovery potential, as brain structures do become more rigid as one ages. Furthermore, the degree of recovery may indicate that Harry possessed exceptional potential to begin with, and for this reason, a truly representative picture of recovery potential is not given. Nonetheless, a discussion of this case is important as a means of counteracting tendencies either to view various functions as being strictly localized in the brain or to assume that any brain damage results in a corresponding permanent loss in psychological abilities.

> *Human life nearly resembles iron. When you use it, it wears out. When you don't, rust consumes it.*
>
> —Marcus Porcius Cato, Roman statesman (234–149 B.C.)

Parkinson's Disease and Pseudo-Parkinson's Disease

Parkinson's disease is a degenerative disease that affects the nervous system. Named and first described by James Parkinson in 1817, Parkinson's disease was initially thought of as having no impact on cognitive functioning; however, this notion was subsequently refuted (Nicholi, 1999). Although the exact etiology of Parkinson's disease is unknown, and initial diagnosis is difficult (Johnson, 2008), research indicates that individuals suffering from Parkinson's disease typically display a loss of brain cells in the region of the brain that produces the neurotransmitter dopamine. Approximately one-third of individuals suffering from Parkinson's disease go on to develop dementia, which progressively affects memory, language, attention, and problem solving. An individual who develops Parkinson-like symptoms but does not display all symptoms traditionally associated with Parkinson's disease is typically diagnosed as having Parkinsonism or Pseudo-Parkinsonism. Also, Pseudo-Parkinsonism appears to be more directly related to accumulated head trauma, as we see in the case of Muhammad Ali. Typical symptoms associated with Parkinson's disease and Parkinsonism are:

- Marked tremors while active and while resting
- Muscular stiffness or rigidity
- Weakness in throat and facial muscles
- Stiffness in legs, neck, and other muscles
- Talking as well as swallowing may be taxing on the individual
- Gait disturbances

- Slowness in goal-directed movement (bradykinesia)
- Poor balance and postural instability

Other symptoms may include:

- Reduced dexterity
- Speech difficulties
- Urinary and digestive problems
- Difficulties with involuntary motor activities
- Drooling
- Sleep disturbance
- Flat affect
- Fatigue

Float like a butterfly, sting like a bee.

—Muhammad Ali

The Case of Muhammad Ali

In October of 1983, Muhammad Ali, one of the greatest boxers of all time, was diagnosed with Parkinson's disease to the dismay of his many fans around the world (Hauser, 2005). Although physicians were initially ambivalent about attributing the etiology of his symptoms to boxing, it was ultimately concluded that Ali suffered from pugilistic Parkinson's syndrome or Pseudo-Parkinsonism. Many had observed an obvious decline in Ali's boxing skills and maintained the sentiment that Ali fought too long.

Muhammad Ali was born on January 17, 1942, to Cassius and Odessa Clay in Louisville, Kentucky, the eldest of two boys (Hauser, 2005). Although his given name was Cassius Clay, Ali would later change his name to Muhammad Ali due to his eventual conversion to the Nation of Islam some 22 years later. Ali's childhood was described as normal. He always struggled academically, at least in part as a result of undiagnosed dyslexia. However, a rather trivial event that occurred when he was 12 years old would change the course of his life. His bicycle had been stolen, and Ali told the reporting police officer that he would beat up the responsible party if he ever found out who did it. Noticing Ali's imposing stature, the police officer suggested that Ali begin boxing. Ali complied and ultimately won six Kentucky Golden Gloves, two national Golden Gloves titles, an Amateur Union Championship Title, and the light heavyweight gold medal in the 1960 Rome Olympics. Ali's final amateur record was 100 wins and 5 losses, which marked a stellar, albeit very long, amateur career.

Although Ali won the gold medal at the Rome Olympics, his homecoming was not as welcoming as one would expect because he was not excluded from the racism that still existed in the United States. Upon returning to Kentucky, Ali was denied service at a "Whites Only" restaurant and subsequently got into a physical confrontation with a white street gang. Ali was so outraged at his maltreatment that he threw his gold medal into the Ohio River.

Ali then began his professional boxing career in Louisville, and he attained a record of 19-0. Although undefeated and arguably untested, Ali was the next opponent for the heavyweight champion at that time, Sonny Liston. Ali was a sizeable underdog prior to this fight and had developed a reputation as a cocky fighter who often predicted the exact round in which he would knock out his opponent. Ali's famous quote, "Float like a butterfly, sting like a bee," was first documented at the prefight conference between Ali and Liston, and Ali did just that in this fight (Remnick, 1999). He shocked the world, as he stated he would, as Liston was unable to return to the ring after the seventh round, thus Ali won his first heavyweight championship of the world. Following this victory, Ali became an extremely controversial figure due to his ring antics, trouble with the U.S. government, and lifestyle. Following the Liston fight, Ali announced that he was now a Black Muslim, again shocking the world. Ali subsequently dodged the U.S. military draft and was stripped of his WBA heavyweight title, sentenced to five years in prison, and barred from boxing. Ali remained free due to numerous appeals but was still unable to fight until 1970, when he fought and knocked out Jerry Quarry in Atlanta, Georgia, where there was no boxing commission at the time. Ali's conviction was reversed by the U.S. Supreme Court on June 28, 1971, in *Clay v. United States*.

Ali went on to lose and regain his title over a span of about 16 years. During this time, Ali's deterioration would become increasingly salient, specifically markedly decreased hand speed and swiftness in the ring. Many boxing enthusiasts mark the famous "Thrilla in Manila" match as the point at which the possibility of a significant physical decline in Ali's skills first became evident, and Ali periodically struggled in the ring from this point on. Although sustaining 14 rounds of grueling blows to the head, Ali went on to win on a technical knockout due to Joe Frazier's corner not allowing him to fight after the fourteenth round. Ali fought Joe Frazier three times, winning two of these bouts, with all three fights going at least 14 rounds. The physical damage arguably sustained in these fights was evidenced in both fighters; Joe Frazier permanently retired after two more fights, and Ali would have significant difficulties with subsequent fights. Ali would go on to fight several unknown fighters, winning some of these bouts by decisions after the fifteenth round, thus accumulating many more blows to the head. It was during this time that Ali's ring doctor, Ferdie Pacheco, left Ali's camp due to his professional opinion that Ali was damaging himself by continuing to box. Ali continued to fight despite these warnings. In February of 1978, Ali lost his title by a split decision after 15 rounds to Leon Spinks, the 1976 Olympic champion who had only seven previous professional fights; he regained his title from Spinks seven months later. Ali announced his retirement on June 27, 1979, but later challenged the WBC champion, Larry Holmes, in an attempt to become the first boxer in history to win the heavyweight title four times. Many boxing enthusiasts viewed this fight as a mistake because they deemed Ali as well past his prime and already damaged. However, he did fight Holmes and was knocked out in the eleventh round. Ironically, this fight was promoted as "the last hurrah."

Following the Holmes fight, it was revealed that Ali had been physically examined at the Mayo Clinic. The results of this examination supported the notion that Ali had fought too long and had been deteriorating in brain function. The results showed a hole in the membrane of his brain, and Ali admitted to slurring of speech and tingling in his extremities, commonly reported symptoms of Parkinson's disease. Despite compelling evidence of deterioration, Ali fought the up-and-coming Trevor Berbick on December 11, 1981. The match was touted as the "drama in the Bahamas," but relatively few watched this fight, accepting the notion that Ali had physically deteriorated to the point of obvious decreases in effectiveness in the boxing ring. Ali lost a unanimous decision to Berbick and then stated that he would permanently retire following this fight.

In October of 1983, Ali was diagnosed with Parkinsonism, although it has not been

(continued)

The Case of Muhammad Ali Continued

definitively determined whether Ali's symptoms are entirely due to head trauma sustained from boxing. Not surprisingly, he was ultimately diagnosed with pugilistic Parkinson's syndrome, which is also referred to as Parkinsonism or Pseudo-Parkinsonism, due to repeated head trauma. Yet, Ali is still an occasionally visible public figure, role model, and sports icon. Ali carried the torch in the 1996 Olympic Games held in Atlanta, Georgia, and was symbolically given a new gold medal to replace the one that he threw into the Ohio River. He was given the Presidential Medal of Freedom in November of 2005, and named the Kentucky Athlete of the Century by the Kentucky Athletic Hall of Fame. The Muhammad Ali Center in Louisville, Kentucky, was opened in 2005. However, he paid a high price. Ali currently displays significant Parkinson's disease symptoms such as marked tremors, soft, unintelligible speech, muscular stiffness and rigidity, and a slow, unsteady gait.

Where's the rest of me?
—Ronald Reagan, referring to his missing limbs in the movie *King's Row* (1942)

Alzheimer's Disease

Alzheimer's disease is a form of dementia caused by the progressive deterioration of brain cells. It is referred to as a *presenile dementia* because the age of onset can occur even before the age of 50. This distinguishes Alzheimer's disease from other forms of neural deterioration associated with the latter phases of the life span, which are collectively referred to as the *senile dementias*. In actual practice, the distinction between presenile and senile dementias is problematic, because there is some disagreement about the age at which the term *senile* should first be used.

Unlike certain forms of central nervous system impairment, Alzheimer's disease involves widespread deterioration of brain tissue so that a broad range of cognitive, behavioral, and physical capabilities eventually becomes affected. Nerve tissues are invaded by pathogenic structures, known as *neuritic plaques* and *neurofibrillary tangles*, that interfere with nerve conduction impulses. The course of the disease varies but can be fairly rapid, with death often occurring within four to five years from the time of onset.

Diagnostic Signs

At the beginning, manifestations of Alzheimer's disease are typically rather subtle (Ricker, 2004). Often, the first indications take the form of slight but persisting memory difficulties or of a perceptible loss of efficiency in going about one's day-to-day activities. Gradually, a more severe and generalized impairment of intellectual capabilities becomes evident. Cognitive skills—such as reading, writing, and reasoning—begin to show impairment as an increasing number of brain centers are affected. Signs of neurological impairment begin to become evident, with abnormalities in visual evoked potentials being reliably reported. Changes in emotional status are evident as well, as bouts of depression, lability (fluctuating mood states), and heightened irritability become increasingly frequent. Eventually, the disease progresses to a point at which the patient becomes persistently confused, incoherent, and disoriented. At this stage, there is usually a failure to recognize even such familiar family members as spouses and children. Self-care and basic hygiene skills deteriorate, and an almost total dependence on others ensues.

In some instances, a confirming diagnosis can be made only by postmortem examination. However, the *functional* behavioral and neurological manifestations of Alzheimer's disease become increasingly pronounced as the disease progresses, leaving little doubt as to the presence of underlying CNS impairment.

Psychological Assessment

Psychological assessments of patients with Alzheimer's disease are of greatest help during the early stages of the disorder (Ricker, 2004). There are three major ways in which these evaluations contribute to the diagnosis and management of the disease. First, early manifestations of Alzheimer's disease often include subtle changes in memory, mood, and cognition that can frequently be detected or validated via psychological testing (Kay & Franklin, 1995). In conjunction with a neurological evaluation, this information may provide some of the earliest indications of the impending changes in mental status that result from the disease. Second, a thorough assessment of psychological capabilities can help both patient and family develop realistic strategies for coping with the impact of the disease. Significant issues such as employment status and disability determination must be confronted, and psychological assessments can provide useful information to aid in making informed decisions in these areas. Finally, periodic psychological assessments can be useful in helping evaluate the patient's ongoing status, much as repeated physical and neurological examinations do.

Effects on Victim and Family

Victims of Alzheimer's disease, as well as their families, must confront a variety of psychological stressors, and crisis counseling may be very useful (Rainer & Brown, 2008). The patient must deal with the progressive deterioration of mental capabilities that eventually can turn even routine activities into confusing ordeals. A particularly stressful period comes when a tentative diagnosis has been made while the patient continues to be basically alert and oriented. At this phase, the prospect of facing an ultimately fatal illness following the gradual loss of behavioral and mental control is highly stressful and frequently triggers secondary disorders such as depression.

Family members face several key stressors and often need help at this point. Many report that the increasing inability of a parent or spouse to recognize them as the disease progresses is especially disturbing. Related to this is the distress of adapting to the inevitable changes that transform a previously healthy, vital individual into someone who becomes chronically debilitated, frequently depressed and irritable, and eventually totally dependent on others. At this point, the victim will typically manifest dementia (often less accurately referred to as senility). Dementia is diagnosed when there is evidence of significant intellectual decline, plus evidence of more specific cognitive deficits, one of which involves memory loss. Finally, families of patients with Alzheimer's disease frequently must endure extraordinary financial hardships, as well. This is most evident when the patient has been the chief economic provider and is afflicted with the disease at a point in his or her career when earning power is nearing its peak.

Many of these issues are relevant to a discussion of Ronald Reagan, whose physicians diagnosed him as having Alzheimer's disease six years after the end of his second term as U.S. president.

> *Near or above the age of fifty the elasticity of the mental processes, on which the treatment depends, is as a rule lacking—old people are no longer educable.*
> —Sigmund Freud, at age 48

The Case of Ronald Reagan

On November 5, 1994, an announcement was made to the American people that Ronald W. Reagan, the fortieth president of the United States, had been diagnosed with Alzheimer's disease (Morris, 1999). Due to the difficulty of accurately diagnosing Alzheimer's disease in living patients, Reagan's team of five personal physicians carefully administered extensive tests and conducted close observations during the several weeks leading up to the announcement; they had suspected the possibility of Alzheimer's for over a year. After all the tests and observations were completed, the team ruled out virtually all other possibilities. The knowledge that Reagan's mother had died of Alzheimer's disease also aided somewhat in making the diagnosis. According to many newspaper articles in which friends and co-workers were quoted, most of those who had contact with Reagan over the past year

were aware that something was not right mentally with the former president.

Ronald Reagan was born on February 6, 1911, in Tampico, Illinois. In his autobiography, he described his mother as loving and attentive. He credited her with nurturing his acting ability. His father, John, was much loved by Ronald Reagan and was described as "restless, ambitious, and constantly frustrated" by the difficulties he faced as a shoe salesman. John Reagan was an alcoholic, which Ronald Reagan cited as his father's "only weakness." Although John Reagan was much revered and his alcoholism was written off as a simple weakness, his problem left a deep impression on his son. When Ronald was 11 years old, he came home one winter day to find his father passed out on the front porch of the family home; he pulled his father into the house and put him to bed. Whenever asked to recall memories from his childhood, this was a memory that Reagan often described. And although he pleaded no resentment toward his father, it is evident by the sheer lasting power of the memory that the alcoholism was a source of pain to Ronald Reagan.

Throughout his life, Reagan experienced several illnesses and traumas. As a very young boy, he had bronchial pneumonia; his mother also came down with influenza at about the same time and was delirious with high fevers and chills. Later in his life, at around the age of 37, Reagan developed viral pneumonia and almost died. He, too, experienced high fevers, delirium, and chills with this illness. On March 30, 1981, President Reagan was shot by John Hinkley, Jr., in an assassination attempt. The bullet struck Reagan in the chest; he lost a great deal of blood and after surgery experienced high fevers and appetite loss. He also underwent surgeries for prostrate gland trouble and colon cancer. In 1989, just after leaving the White House and finishing his second term as president, Reagan suffered a subdural hematoma when he was thrown from a horse in Mexico; this, too, required surgery.

In 1962, Reagan's mother died of Alzheimer's disease after years of torment and pain. It was not known that she had the disease until long after her death. Reagan never hid the fact that his mother was "senile," freely giving the information to reporters who questioned his mental health and age as he campaigned for the presidency. He requested to be tested yearly for senility before he even won the election. Because Ronald Reagan was the oldest president, his health had always been an issue, especially while he was in office. Some experts have said that it is probable that President Reagan was significantly affected by Alzheimer's in his final months in the White House. This idea has been strongly opposed by Reagan's physicians and supporters, who assert that Reagan was monitored and tested yearly for any signs of senility or Alzheimer's disease and that his memory and mental acuity were very sharp

during his White House years. However, rumors were heard that Reagan needed cue cards to get through speeches, would doze off during White House meetings, and so on. Whenever President Reagan forgot things or became unsure of himself, however, he would joke, for example, that it was because of the deafness in his right ear or put himself into a flattering position that emphasized his physical fitness.

The possibility of his Alzheimer's disease clearly emerging toward the end of his second term as president would certainly clarify the confusion felt by many about Reagan's "memory lapses" at the Iran-Contra hearings. He failed to recall not only events that occurred but also the name of an important staff member. Yet, one must be cautious in interpreting some of Reagan's memory lapses (Morris, 1999). Occasionally, it no doubt reflected his easygoing indifference to the world around him, including episodes before he was older when had trouble recognizing some of his own family members. His son Michael relates an eerie story of his boarding school graduation when his father did not recognize him and genially put out his hand and introduced himself. When Maureen Reagan found out that her 7-year-old half-sister, Patti, did not know they were siblings, Reagan shrugged, "Well, we just haven't gotten there yet." His children often commented in public that he shut out virtually everyone from his emotional life.

However, now even close friends and associates admit that they detected a slowing of Reagan's mental sharpness and memory much earlier than the doctors' final diagnosis (Morris, 1999). The general consensus among many friends and associates was that, consistent with Alzheimer's, President Reagan had been fading slowly. Some even claim that as far back as 1986 there was a definite decline in Reagan's mental health. At a press conference in June of that year, Reagan responded with muddled answers (that aides had to continually "clarify"), and he appeared very disoriented. Subsequently, he was periodically described as

(continued)

The Case of Ronald Reagan Continued

"less engaged" and "slowing down," and he occasionally expressed concern about the deterioration of his thought processes. On March 2, 1987, an emergency transition paper was drafted for observation of the president because of his evident disorientation (Morris, 1999). President Bill Clinton recalled talking with Reagan after winning the presidency in 1992. He said that in the middle of a discussion about the job of the presidency, Reagan completely forgot what he was talking about and admitted frustration with himself. During times of forgetfulness, Reagan had been known to wonder if he had inherited Alzheimer's disease from his mother.

It is ironic that, in 1982, President Reagan signed into law a designation of November as National Alzheimer's Disease Month. It was in November 1994 that President Reagan disclosed in a heart-wrenching letter his own diagnosis of Alzheimer's. He called it the start of "the journey that will lead me into the sunset of my life." After the announcement of his illness, he was rarely seen in public. He did continue a somewhat active life for a few years, then became essentially housebound, but under the loving care of his family. By 2004, he was apparently consistently unable to recognize himself or anyone around him, including his wife Nancy. President Reagan died peacefully at home in Los Angeles on June 5, 2004, from pneumonia and complications from his Alzheimer's disease.

Etiology

Many factors may have played a role in Ronald Reagan's diagnosis of Alzheimer's disease. Primary consideration must be given to the genetic component in his mother having died of Alzheimer's. Several genes may be involved. For example, the gene termed *apoE-4*, carried by 4 to 8 percent of Americans, appears to determine the age at which some forms of late onset Alzheimer's emerge. Other genes, such as *A2M-3*, increase the risk of the development of the disorder itself.

John Reagan's alcoholism may have also been a factor, as it was a primary component in an early life of almost constant stress. And President Reagan grew up in an alcoholic and financially struggling home environment, worked for many years as a famous actor, and later went into politics to end up with the most stressful job of all, president of the United States of America. He also experienced many physical traumas, including several that affected the brain (hits to the head in sports, subdural hematoma, delirium from fevers, etc.). Any of these factors may have contributed to the individual pattern of Reagan's Alzheimer's disease.

Issues of both causation and the value ethics of seeking earlier evidence of potential Alzheimer's are highlighted in one of the most elegant "field" studies (see the section on research in Chapter 1) ever devised. Dr. David Snowden and colleagues (2001) first decided to study a group of 93 cloistered nuns, all born before 1917 and in their eighties at the time of the study, hypothesizing that nuns who had spent their lives teaching would show less Alzheimer's than those who mainly did household chores. This did not prove to be true.

Fortuitously, all of these nuns had been asked to write a short autobiography four years after they entered the convent, just before taking their permanent vows. In a stunning finding that surprised even these researchers, a rating of these autobiographies allowed a prediction, with 90 percent accuracy, as to whether these nuns would or would not develop Alzheimer's some 50 years later. In addition to this validity, they also assessed the raters' reliability in scoring these autobiographies and found that to be nearly 90 percent.

Overall, the researchers found that nuns whose sentences were grammatically complex and showed the highest amount of the psycholinguistic feature termed *idea density* did not develop Alzheimer's. Idea density is the number of written ideas per 10 written words. For example, the two nuns in the study whose writings were at the extremes when rated for idea density were both 20 years old when they wrote their autobiographies, and both had high school degrees. One wrote: "At the time of my entrance, I was in good health and had had no serious illnesses before this time." The other nun wrote: "Now I am wandering about in 'Dove's Lane' waiting, yet only three weeks to follow in the footprints of my Spouse, bound in Him by the Holy Vows of Poverty, Chastity, and Obedience." The first nun obtained a bachelor's and a master's degree and died of Alzheimer's disease about six decades later. The second nun got a bachelor's degree and is still alive, her mind keen and her memory intact. In studies with other groups of nuns, it also became clear that the amount of positive emotion expressed in these early letters predicted less likelihood of an earlier onset of Alzheimer's.

This study generally fits with the hypothesis that genetics plays a substantial part in the development of Alzheimer's disease, especially early Alzheimer's. It also correlates with the findings of German researchers headed by Tomas G. Ohm (1996) of J. Gutenberg University in Mainz, who examined 887 brains of people 20 to 104 years old. He concluded that neurofibrillary tangles, the pathological changes characteristic of Alzheimer's disease, are present in some individuals as early as 20 years old. The German group concluded that the roots of Alzheimer's disease may even extend into adolescence.

Snowden's (2001) studies have the "natural event" value of all field studies—that is, the lives of these nuns were not manipulated by an experimenter, nor were the nuns asked to write their autobiographies by experimenters, with informed consent, or in a "lab" setting. Yet, it has many of the benefits of a controlled experiment; the subjects were all white, female, from similar socioeconomic-religious backgrounds, and lived together in the same environment for almost 60 years.

Several ethical implications are interesting. Should people be examined early on and then told of their probabilities of developing this or other diseases? Should candidates for political office, especially the presidency, be examined on such early variables? Remember that one of the characteristics many people liked in President Reagan was that his ideas were clear, straightforward, and even simple at times.

Outcome Issues

At present, Alzheimer's disease, perhaps the best known of the presenile dementias, is a condition for which there is no known cure. Various medications, such as memantine, galantamine, and rivastigmine, have been found to slow the progress of the disorder, and some show potential for delaying the onset or possibly eliminating the disorder. Genetic reprogramming offers similar possibilities. Research on the Notch receptor, first described in studies at Yale University in the 1940s, has recently shown the potential to regenerate adult brain cells, which would allow a direct antidote to the Alzheimer's disease process. Snowden (2001) also has suggested ways to help delay the onset of Alzheimer's: (1) keep mentally stimulated, (2) avoid head trauma (e.g., from strokes, engaging in a risk endeavor without proper protection, such as bicycling without a helmet); (3) keep blood folate levels high by taking folic acid supplementation (a less clearly supported recommendation is to supplement with vitamins C and E); and (4) stay emotionally positive and physically active.

> *Jesus said . . . I tell you the truth . . . when you are old you will stretch out your hands and someone else will dress you and lead you where you do not want to go.*
>
> —John 21:18

Mental Retardation

About 1 percent of the population falls into the category of mental retardation. The *DSM-IV-TR* requires indication of significantly subaverage intellectual functioning (Criterion A), an IQ of 70 or below—although testing measurement error, approximately 5 points, would allow a diagnosis up to an IQ of 75 in a standardized, individually administered test—and onset before the age of 18 (Criterion C). Also required (Criterion B) is evidence of significant limitation in adaptive functioning in at least two of the following skill areas: communication, self-care, home living, social/interpersonal skills, use of community resources, self-direction, functional academic skills, work, leisure, health, and safety. (It's good that an IQ score is required, as it appears that many in the population would qualify on Criterion B.) The criteria for severity and descriptors and interventions, by age, are found in Table 15.1.

A wide variety of interventions is necessary to deal effectively with mental retardation and its associated problems. Those with less impairment profit most from psychoeducational and social skills interventions, and the greater the degree of impairment, the more necessary are the various behavioral interventions.

TABLE 15.1   Criteria for Severity of Mental Retardation by Age

Level	Preschool Age (birth to 5 years)	School Age (6 to 12 years)	Adult (over 21 years)
Mild Retardation (IQ of 50-55 to 70—by *DSM-IV-TR*) (about 85% of retarded persons)	Can develop social and language skills; less retardation in sensorimotor areas. Seldom distinguished from normal until older. Referred to as educable.	Can learn academic to approximately sixth grade level by late teens. Cannot learn general high school subjects. Needs special education, particularly at secondary-school levels.	Capable of social vocational adequacy with proper education and training. Frequently needs guidance when under serious social or economic stress.
Moderate Retardation (35-40 to 50-55) (10% of retarded persons)	Can talk or learn to communicate. Poor social awareness. Fair motor development. May profit from self-help; can be managed with moderate supervision.	Can learn functional academic skills to approximately fourth-grade level by late teens if given special education.	Capable of self-maintenance in unskilled or semi-skilled occupations. Needs supervision and guidance when under mild social or economic stress.
Severe Retardation (20-25 to 35-40) (3-4% of retarded persons)	Poor motor development. Speech is minimal. Few or no communication skills. Generally unable to profit from training in self-help.	Can talk or learn to communicate. Can be trained in elemental health habits. Cannot learn functional academic skills Profits from systematic habit training.	Can contribute partially to self-support under complete supervision. Can develop self-protection skills to a minimally useful level in a controlled environment.
Profound Retardation (IQ of 20-25 or below)	Minimal capacity for functioning in sensorimotor areas. Needs nursing care.	Some motor development present. Cannot profit from training in self-help. Needs total care.	Some motor and speech development. Totally incapable of self-maintenance. Needs complete care and supervision.

Source: Adapted in part from J. M. Sattler, *Assessment of Children's Intelligence and Special Abilities* (Boston: Allyn and Bacon, 1982), p. 426.

The Case of Daryl Renard Atkins

Daryl Renard Atkins was born on November 11, 1977. He never graduated from high school. Even though he was placed in special education, he managed to achieve a grade-point average of only 1.26 out of 4.0. Report cards to the family documented significant behavior problems and lack of motivation in academic activities (*Atkins* v. *Commonwealth*, 2000).

On a mid-August afternoon in 1996, 18-year-old Daryl was hanging out at his father's

(continued)

The Case of Daryl Renard Atkins Continued

house with his friend, William Jones. By this time, Daryl had on his record a series of prior felony convictions, including robbery and maiming. The pair were "drinking and smoking weed" while various friends of Daryl's came and went. Daryl would later claim that he was also using crack cocaine that day. The crew made various trips to the local convenience store to buy beer when there were enough people present to pool money. About 10:30 that evening, while Daryl was begging for change in the store parking lot, a stranger by the name of Myles (not his real name) pulled up in his pickup. Myles was a 21-year-old airman working at Langley Air Force Base. Upon leaving the store, Myles got into his truck and began to leave the premises, at which time Daryl whistled to him from across the parking lot. Myles stopped his truck while Daryl and his friend approached—a decision he would no doubt regret for the short remainder of his life (*Atkins* v. *Commonwealth*, 1999). The two friends abducted Myles and forced him to make a $200 withdrawal at his bank ATM. The machine's security tape showed Daryl holding the pistol to Myles as he leaned across William in the driver's seat to operate the machine (*Atkins* v. *Commonwealth*, 1999).

William Jones would later recount that, at his urging, he and Daryl had agreed to tie Myles up somewhere so the two could make their escape. It was Daryl himself who changed the plans when he shot Myles eight times in a secluded area near Interstate 64. The two left Myles at the scene to die. The police, following up on the images captured on the bank ATM, soon found and arrested both assailants (*Atkins* v. *Commonwealth*, 1999).

The Commonwealth of Virginia put up a convincing case. Citing his prior felony convictions and testimony by victims of some of these crimes, as well as testimony from Myles's mother, the prosecutor argued for imposition of the death penalty on the bases of future dangerousness and the "vileness" of the crime (*Atkins* v. *Commonwealth*, 1999).

However, a forensic psychologist from the Richmond area, Dr. Evan Stuart Nelson, testified at the trial that Atkins had a full-scale IQ of 59. Nelson also testified that it was unlikely that Atkins would be violent in prison, having proven his ability to maintain his behavior in such a setting before. Yet, perhaps damning to the defense's case, Nelson also testified that he could offer no reason as to why Atkins should not be able to appreciate the wrongfulness of his act, despite his limited mental abilities (*Atkins* v. *Commonwealth*, 1999).

The Virginia jury returned a verdict of guilty and found that Daryl represented a continued risk for violence and that the crime had been "outrageously or wantonly vile." The jurors recommended the maximum penalty of death, and the judge agreed. Defense counsel's objection was renewed on appeal to the Supreme Court of Virginia, and a second trial was granted. In this hearing, the veracity of Nelson's diagnosis of mental retardation was to be hotly contested.

At the time of the hearings, the *Diagnostic and Statistical Manual of Mental Disorders*, 4th edition (*DSM-IV-TR*; American Psychiatric Association, 1994) served as the basis for mental disorder diagnoses in courts of law. Diagnosis of Mental Retardation under *DSM-IV-TR* requires the finding of three characteristics:

1. Valid measurement of an IQ below 70
2. Impairment in more than one area of adaptive functioning and
3. Onset of the disorder before the age of 18

Although not argued in court, of interest here are citations by the defense that Atkins had scored "below the 20th percentile in *almost* every standardized test he took" (emphasis added; p. 8). By definition, an IQ of below 70 represents mental ability at or below the 2nd percentile, significantly worse than the 20th.

The prosecution would attack the diagnosis on each of the three grounds. Dr. Nelson himself had admitted in court that Atkins's performance on the IQ test would likely have been better were it not for "depression" he was suffering due to the trial proceedings. Nelson also explained that Atkins met diagnostic criteria for Antisocial Personality Disorder, some key traits of which are manipulation and disregard for rules and law. In addition to Nelson's testimony, prosecutors brought in their own expert witness, another forensic psychologist by the name of Dr. Stanton Samenow. Samenow testified that he "sharply disagreed" with the diagnosis of Mental Retardation, claiming Atkins to be of at least average intelligence. Although Samenow had not given Atkins a formal IQ test, he cited Atkins's use of complex words and knowledge of current events as evidence supporting his findings. Furthermore, Samenow stated that he had given Atkins select questions from psychological tests during the assessment. Dr. Samenow elaborated on Atkins's history of poor motivation in academic settings, proffering this as the reason for his seemingly limited mental abilities.

Samenow also attacked the diagnosis on the basis that Atkins's deficits in adaptive functioning did not extend beyond academic settings (recall that a proper diagnosis requires deficits in more than one setting). Again, Samenow described a history in which Atkins chose not to excel, rather than lacked the capacity to do so (*Atkins* v. *Commonwealth*, 2000).

After hearing this testimony and being instructed to consider the evidence of mental retardation as a mitigating factor, the jury again recommended imposition of the death penalty. Judge Prentis Smiley agreed, and Daryl Atkins, now age 21, was again sentenced to death. This time on appeal, the Supreme Court of Virginia deemed in a 5-to-2 decision that all previous concerns had been adequately addressed and upheld the ruling that Daryl Atkins be put to death. With regard to the defense's objection that a mentally retarded offender would be executed, the Virginia Supreme Court cited the lack of clarity in diagnosis in its statement: "We are not willing to commute Atkins' sentence of death to life imprisonment merely because of his IQ score" (*Atkins* v. *Commonwealth*, 2000 p. 7).

On September 25, 2001, the U.S. Supreme Court agreed to hear the appeal of Daryl Atkins, further limiting the appeal on October 1 to the issue of whether execution of mentally retarded offenders violates the Constitution's Eighth Amendment protection against cruel and unusual punishment. The Supreme Court held that the death sentence could not be imposed on someone who is truly mentally retarded. Unfortunately, the Court did not define the criteria for deciding whether or not a person is mentally retarded, and to this day that issue is still unclear in the legal arena.

Comment

If there is good reason to believe that significant intellectual retardation is present with functioning at least below an approximate IQ of 70 and for some reason the individual is untestable, the diagnosis of Mental Retardation, Severity Unspecified (319) is used. The diagnosis of Borderline Intellectual Functioning (V62.89) encoded on Axis II requires evidence of problems in adaptive coping and an IQ of 71 to 84.

A wide variety of interventions is necessary to deal effectively with mental retardation and its associated problems. Those with less impairment profit most from psychoeducational and social skills interventions, and the greater the degree of impairment, the more necessary are the various behavioral interventions.

16 Legal Issues and Psychological Practice

Legal decisions and processes depend more and more on psychological information, as has already been suggested in the case studies of O. J. Simpson, Jeffrey Dahmer, Jack Ruby, Ted Bundy, and several others in this book. There are many ways in which psychology and its related disciplines may provide input or impact into the legal system (see Table 16.1). Some of the most common and important input comes in the areas of evaluating criminal responsibility, competency to stand trial, or competency to handle one's affairs; gauging potential dangerousness and its relationship to involuntary civil commitment; and the appraisal of honesty or truth telling by participants in the criminal justice system (as well as in other areas). The chapter begins with discussions about malingering, the factitious disorders, Munchausen by Proxy (in the case of Marna), and then the issues of deciding on a person's competence to stand trial and his or her level of criminal responsibility and potential for dangerousness. These issues are discussed through the well-publicized but not always well understood case of John Hinckley, the individual who attempted to assassinate President Reagan.

Courtroom: A place where Jesus Christ and Judas Iscariot would be equals, with the betting odds in favor of Judas.

—H. L. Mencken, American essayist

Malingering, Factitious Disorder, or True Disorder?

Whenever the factitious disorder is considered as a diagnosis, the possibility of malingering must also be considered. Each label refers to a voluntary production of symptoms on the part of the client in an attempt to be labeled physically sick or psychologically disturbed. The primary differences arise from the motivations for this presentation (Johnson, 2008). The malingerer tries to appear ill to gain some logical goal, such as exemption from criminal responsibility or financial compensation for alleged injuries (or skipping a test?).

In its less common form, the factitious disorder is manifested by psychological symptoms. More often, in the case of factitious disorder the symptoms are

TABLE 16.1   Taxonomy of Psycholegal Issues

Legal Context	Reconstructive Context	Contemporaneous Context	Predictive Context
Defendant Issues	Competency to confess (at past arrest) Criminal responsibility NGRI, GMBI *Mens rea:* intent purpose v. reckless Special defenses:	Competency to consent to evaluation Competency to stand trial Competency to plead guilty Competency to waive counsel Competency to refuse NGRI Competency to waive	Restoration to CST Bond release •Flight •Danger to community Presentence probation risk Death penalty issues:
Criminal Issues	•Battered wife syndrome •Involuntary intoxication •Duress •Infancy (on mental age) Death Penalty Mitigation mentality (OBS, MR) under domination of other "emotional disturbance"	*Miranda* (at present arrest) Competency to testify Competency to refuse medicine for CSI restoration Competency to be executed Juvenile waiver; sophistication and maturity	•Future danger •Prison adjustment Inmate classification Parole release Juvenile waiver Amenability for treatment Special sentencing: •Sex offenders •Youthful offender act
Victim Issues	"Validation" of child's molestation Rape trauma syndrome in rebuttal to consent Victim impact statement		
Civil Issues	Testamentary capacity (testator deceased) Personal injury (proximate cause) Workers' Compensation (work relatedness) Substituted judgment: patient's consent to Rx Malpractice: •Negligent release •Failure to commit/warn •Liability for suicide •Abandonment •Failure to consult/refer •Wrongful commitment •Sexual harassment/ contact •Breach of confidentiality Mental illness defenses: •Impaired professional •At-fault divorce grounds •Prior contact(s)	Involuntary commitment (need for treatment now) Guardianship Conservatorship Competency to contract Competency to consent •Voluntary treatment •Refuse treatment •Research participation Testamentary capacity (testator alive) Competency to die (?) (assisted suicide) Competency to testify (child) Competency of child to choose custodial parent Termination of parental rights (implementation) Child in need of supervision Malpractice; license supervision/revocation	Involuntary commitment (danger self/others) Inpatient disposition: •Suicide watch •Less restrictive care discharge Parental competence: •Child custody •Visitation •Foster care/adoption •After domestic abuse Psychological autopsies Termination of parental rights; treatment Response to mediation Relicensure of Ph.D, M.D. Return to work; duty Personal injury; damages (Rx costs)

Source: From "Taxonomy of Legal Issues" by Geoffrey McKee, 1994, *Bulletin of the American Academy of Forensic Psychology, 15,* 2–4. Used with permission.

physical, a pattern also known as *Munchausen's syndrome*. The Munchausen syndrome was named after Baron Von Munchausen, an eighteenth-century German equivalent of America's Paul Bunyan, both of whom are associated with tales of exaggeration (Janofsky, 1994). In either case, the motivation to appear needful of treatment stems from the client's own peculiar psychology, rather than from an easily shared goal, which is malingering. Thus, although there is conscious deception, it is not technically malingering. The range of symptomatology is limited only by one's imagination and by the degree of sophistication about medical information (Boyd et al., 2007).

Some experience with hospitals or medical situations, either through previous hospitalizations or knowledge from family members who were involved in the medical profession, can contribute to this disorder. These persons rely on ill behaviors to elicit care from others, including physicians, nurses, and psychologists. Not surprisingly, most persons with factitious disorder lack close personal relationships that might provide alternative supports. At least one skilled patient, a Mr. McIlroy, was able to obtain over 200 separate hospital admissions in Britain, during which he was subjected to thousands of diagnostic procedures and hundreds of treatments, many of them quite painful (Pallis & Bamji, 1979). The willingness of these persons to submit to such rigors reveals the strength of their compulsion to be seen in the patient role. Though the disorder is relatively rare, it has been reported consistently since the first published systematic description in 1951 by Richard Asher (1951).

The following are the major characteristics of Munchausen's syndrome:

1. The patient makes a dramatic presentation of one or more complaints, usually physical.
2. The patient exhibits "Pseudologia Fantistica"—contrived, exaggerated, and intriguing accounts of the supposed illness.
3. The patient uses hospitals, clinics, and physicians in different geographical areas, so as to minimize communication among them.

Munchausen by Proxy Syndrome (MBPS)

Munchausen by Proxy syndrome (MBPS) is a form of factitious disorder in which a caregiver, usually the mother, fabricates or actually induces physical or psychological symptoms in her child, for which she then seeks extensive medical testing and/or hospitalizations. In 1977, Dr. Roy Meadow, a pediatrician in Leeds, England, was the first to describe this disorder and recognize it as a serious and often fatal form of child abuse. This form of child abuse is different from others in the sense that the mother (the majority of the perpetrators in these cases are female) typically presents herself as a model parent and the behavior is clearly premeditated rather than impulsive. This disorder, like the overall form termed *Munchausen syndrome*, is coded in the *DSM-IV-TR* as a factitious disorder but is referred to specifically as Factitious Disorder by Proxy. Not much is known about the etiology of this disorder, but it appears that this abusive behavior somehow meets a variety of psychological needs for the caregiver. Also, it is important to note that many

Munchausen by Proxy perpetrators have also suffered at some point from Munchausen syndrome themselves. The guidelines and indicators noted further along in this chapter are evident in the following case.

The Case of Marna

Marna, a 37-year-old housewife and former nurse, was arrested the day after her 6-year-old daughter, Prudence, was admitted to the hospital with severe vomiting. Marna was charged with aggravated child abuse and fraud and could face as much as 45 years in prison if convicted. This had been Prudence's sixty-eighth hospital/medical center contact over the past 2½ years. She was Marna's fourth child and had been generally healthy until she was about 4 years of age. Prudence had two older brothers who had both been chronically ill as youngsters, with symptoms similar to hers. They had seemed to recover around the time that the third child, Penny, had come along, and they were now healthy. Penny died when she was 3 months old, presumably of Sudden Infant Death Syndrome. Less than a year later, Prudence was born.

Early during the course of Prudence's illness, Marna had brought her to the emergency room several times, reporting that she had suffered from seizures. In response, the attending physician had prescribed medication and periodically increased its dosage when the seizures seemed to worsen. When the seizures did not cease after several months on the medication, the prescription was discontinued. It was shortly after that time that the first of eight different occasions occurred when Marna said she saw symptoms that led her to believe that Prudence might be suffering from sepsis, a rare and severe, often fatal, blood infection. However, other than her claim of symptoms that were consistent with sepsis, there were no symptoms observed at the hospital that would allow this diagnosis.

Between the ages of 4 and 6, Prudence would eventually be treated for various chronic conditions, including gastrointestinal problems, immune system deficiency, and seizure disorders. Prudence was unable to eat normally and eventually had to have a tube surgically implanted in her stomach. However, this would not be the last surgery for her. She would endure 27 more, including additional tubes in her stomach and intestines and exploratory surgery around her heart. In total, she spent over 600 days in the hospital and underwent over 700 other minor procedures.

Marna's presentation in the face of these severe medical problems was one of intense concern yet relative calm and collectedness, always verbalizing her confidence in the competence of the physician and the hospital. Her only overt distress emerged when it was time for her to leave Prudence, as she would always make a stop at the nurses' station to remind staff to "take care of her baby." She quickly became familiar with most of the staff. She became particularly attached to Lynne, the charge nurse on the children's ward. Marna would often bring her gifts and talk about how much they had in common because of her own background as an RN. As time went on, the medical bills piled up, and Medicaid had paid out close to one million dollars in claims for Marna's daughter. Marna organized fund raisers in the community for Prudence's "mystery illness" and even went so far as to have local celebrities and even a few professional athletes come and visit Prudence in the hospital.

The medical staff at the hospital naturally became suspicious over time because of the abnormal frequency of Prudence's symptoms. Eventually, the staff noted that Marna would sometimes draw the curtains and close the door, and then sometime later on Prudence's symptoms would worsen. They also began to observe that an increase of symptoms would typically occur within a day or two of a planning discharge. In addition, staff eventually

(continued)

The Case of Marna Continued

became aware of information about Marna's past that was contradictory to what she was reporting. By happenstance, Lynne had lunch with a nurse on another floor who had worked with Marna at another hospital. During their conversation, this person informed Lynne that Marna was an LPN, not an RN like she had said. Further, she told Lynne that Marna often talked about how wonderful her husband was, yet she had never seen him at any hospital functions, and Lynne had never heard any mention of a husband.

Finally, upon Prudence's final admission, nursing staff submitted a sample of her vomit for a more extensive lab analysis. The lab results showed a toxic level of the previously discontinued antiseizure medication. It was at this point that Marna was arrested and Prudence was placed in foster care. Prudence immediately improved and did not deteriorate again. During the subsequent investigation, authorities examined thousands of documents that made up Prudence's medical records. They observed further evidence of abuse in

that they found dozens of doctors' orders that were clearly in Marna's handwriting. Added to this, when interviewing nursing staff and checking documents, investigators discovered that on several occasions when Marna and Prudence were likely alone together, the speed on her IV pump had been tampered with. During her trial, expert witnesses testified that Prudence had not exhibited any of the symptoms indicative of the claimed illnesses, which could not be explained by Marna's interventions. Additionally, expert witness testimony established that it was unlikely that someone would suffer from problems with so many different systems. Marna was found guilty of both aggravated child abuse and Medicaid fraud and was sentenced to five years in prison. Later, while her case was under appeal, the case of the death of her other daughter, Penny, was reopened. It was clear she had been poisoned. Marna was indicted and convicted of Penny's murder and sentenced to life in prison. As is evident, Marna's case is clearly consistent with the guidelines listed below.

Munchausen by Proxy syndrome is often difficult to diagnose, particularly because many medical professionals have little awareness of the disorder or are reluctant to apply such a diagnosis (Johnson, 2008). Using a multidisciplinary team with some familiarity with MBPS, diagnosis is facilitated by using a set of guidelines, such as those suggested by Day and Parnell (see Parnell, 1997, pp. 48–50). The guidelines are divided into three categories: child-victim features, mother-perpetrator features, and family features. The practitioner should consider these guidelines upon initial suspicion of MBPS to determine if intervention is appropriate and then again to confirm or refute the diagnosis once all the data have been compiled.

Guidelines for Identifying Munchausen by Proxy Syndrome Cases

Child-Victim Features

1. Persistent or recurrent illness that cannot readily be explained by the consulting physician despite thorough medical workup
2. A "diagnosis" that is merely descriptive of the symptoms, or a diagnosis of an extremely rare disorder

3. Symptoms that do not respond to the usual treatment regimen
4. Physical or laboratory findings that are not consistent with the reported history
5. Physical findings and reported symptoms that are at odds with the child's generally healthy appearance
6. A temporal relationship between the child's symptoms and the mother's presence
7. Pertinent medical history that cannot be substantiated
8. Presenting complaints that include bleeding seizures, unconsciousness, apnea, diarrhea, vomiting, fever, and lethargy

Mother-Perpetrator Features
9. Reluctance to leave the child while the child is in the hospital
10. Development of close personal relationships with hospital staff
11. Educational or employment background in the medical field or the desire to be employed within the medical field
12. Unusual calm in the face of problems with the child's care
13. Medical problems similar to those of the child or other unusual symptoms
14. Fabrication of information about many aspects of her (mother's) life

Family Features
15. Unexplained illness or death of a sibling of the victim or of another child in the mother's care
16. A marital relationship that is emotionally distant
17. Perpetrator's family of origin marked by emotional, physical, or sexual abuse
18. Perpetrator's family of origin exhibits a pattern of illness behavior (e.g., family history of unusual or frequent medical ailments)

Treatment Options

The Child-Victim. After making the diagnosis of MBPS, both the medical team and the mental health professionals should work in close collaboration to share important information and formulate treatment goals. Psychotherapy is essential for victims of MBPS who are at least 3 years of age. The focus of treatment differs slightly depending on the age at which the child is rescued from the mother (Ayoub, Deutsch, & Kinscherff, 2000). Generally 3- and 4-year-olds tend to blame themselves for being taken away from their mother or father. It needs to be made clear to these children that they were removed from their home for their own safety, not because they did anything wrong. Many victims at this age have grown accustomed to illness. Hence, they develop the identity of the "sick child." The goal of therapy in this instance is to help the child gain autonomy, become competent, accept health, and form a healthy identity.

Children who are age 7 and older often develop an enmeshed relationship with the perpetrator that is not easily altered. One reason for this is that the parent has isolated the child, thus limiting his or her normal social interaction with other children. Instead of playing and attending normal social functions, the child is consumed with the fabrication and/or induction of sickness. When rescued from their situation, these children often experience a conflict of loyalty.

Adolescents who are victims of MBPS have little or no identity formation independent of that associated with their mothers. Adolescence is supposed to be a time of identity development and separation from caregivers. In cases of MBPS, however, the relationship with the mother is characterized by extreme dependence rather than autonomy. The child may, in fact, feign illness without being in the presence of the mother. The dysfunctional core belief that the child is helpless and irreparably medically impaired must be addressed in therapy. It is also important that the child's therapist provide services only to the victim and not to other members of the family, as the role of the therapist is so central to the improvement of the victim.

The Parents.   Unfortunately, psychotherapy for mother-perpetrators of MBPS is often ineffective (Ayoub et al., 2000). In fact, the worst, or most extreme, perpetrators, such as Marna, will continue their behavior while in or even after participating in the legal system and/or extensive psychotherapy. Treatment is not recommended for cases in which a mother has induced, rather than simply fabricated, illness in her child. In such cases, the child typically should be removed from the mother's care. Although successful therapy is unlikely, it is possible. Reunification may even be feasible for some, but only if the following conditions have been met (Ayoub et al., 2000):

1. The mother and other relevant family members acknowledge the MBPS.
2. The mother has participated in intensive individual therapy with a mental health expert who has experience in treating MBP.
3. Other family members, particularly fathers, have participated in treatment, they understand the nature of the disorder, and they have made repeated attempts to protect and support the child(ren) victim(s).

Improvement in therapy depends on recognizing the inappropriate behaviors, ceasing those behaviors, and creating alternative methods to cope with feelings of abandonment. Marital therapy may be used to build support and lessen the sense of isolation felt by the perpetrator. Family therapy may be initiated only if younger children remaining in the home do not feel threatened. It may also be necessary to have the child-victim participate with his or her individual therapist present. The treatment of fathers, particularly those who remain in the marriage and often allow the abusive behavior to occur, is crucial for success and reunification (if that is the ultimate goal). Fathers who are separated or divorced by the time the abuse comes to light are often more willing to acknowledge the abuse of their child. Thus, the goal of their therapy is to encourage them to maintain support for their children, especially if the perpetrator continues to deny the abuse. The safety of the child is the primary concern; therefore, if a child is at high risk for serious injury or death, termination of parental rights should be considered.

> *Listen . . . I don't know how accurate they are, but I know they scare the hell out of people.*
>
> —Ex-President Richard M. Nixon, speaking of "lie detectors"

Comment

A number of approaches to detecting deception through physiological measurements have been popularized (Boyd et al., 2007). Sometimes the process is simple. For example, in his 1940 book, *Behind the Scenes of Murder,* Joseph Cotton described how he added whiskey to the food of a person who had remained persistently mute and who was now a patient subsequent to being arrested for murder while intoxicated. Cotton commented, "The insanity defense was dissolved in five ounces of the same liquid that precipitated the killing." It's seldom that easy, though.

The most widely used method of detection is the polygraph, sometimes called the "lie detector." In fact, the polygraph measures physiological arousal that can arise from a variety of emotional experiences, including the distress of lying, but also including fear, anger, and even sexual arousal. The polygraph is so named because it actually involves measurement of several bodily functions, usually including respiration, heart rate, and blood pressure. The results obtained through a polygraph examination are strongly influenced by (1) the questioning techniques employed, (2) the skill of the examiner in getting the client to believe deception will be detected, and (3) the client's willingness to accept this belief. Because the polygraph may "detect" such a variety of sources of arousal, it is often inaccurate to infer that a subject is being dishonest on the basis of polygraph records. Although professional polygraphers claim extraordinarily high rates of accuracy in making such judgments, methodologically sound research indicates only modest validity (Boyd et al., 2007).

> *I feel the insanity defense should be retained. I bear no grudge against John Hinckley, but I sure don't hope he wins the Irish Sweepstakes.*
> —James Brady, presidential news secretary, victim of John Hinckley

Criminal Responsibility, Competency to Stand Trial, and Dangerousness, and a Case of Borderline Personality Disorder

As violent crime plagues U.S. society, citizens strive to accept judicial decisions while living in a world in which they fear for the welfare of their friends and families. Perhaps no other legal concept raises as many moral ambiguities as the concept of "criminal responsibility," popularly known as the *insanity defense* (Meyer & Weaver, 2006). Rightly or wrongly, the insanity defense is often portrayed as a choice between liberty and security, for both the accused and society. Despite the behavioral sciences' strongest efforts to draw a firm line of distinction between "madness" and "badness," this boundary continues to shift under the interwoven social, political, economic, and other pressures of society.

When an individual is charged with a crime and an insanity defense is raised, each juror (or, in some cases, solely the judge) must determine culpability.

Such a determination is never easy, not only because of the real ramifications for the defendant(s), victim(s), family members, and others but also because the legal concept of criminal responsibility raises the broadest of ethical questions about the limits of one individual's responsibility to another (Bartol & Bartol, 2008).

Although the issue of criminal responsibility can be reviewed as a singular concept, in judicial application it is nearly always interwoven with the defendant's competency to stand trial. Indeed, the issues of criminal responsibility and competency to stand trial are often confused by mental health experts involved in the judicial process. *Criminal responsibility* refers to the state of the defendant's mind at the time of the alleged crime, and includes such concepts as insanity, diminished capacity, and "automatism." *Competency to stand trial* refers to the defendant's psychological state at the time of his or her trial. Such a temporal distinction is of crucial importance in the assessment of these issues. There is actually a variety of areas in which psychologists are frequently called on to address the issue of an individual's mental competence (Meyer & Weaver, 2006). *Competence* in the legal arena can also refer to competence to manage one's day-to-day affairs, competence to make a will, competence to be a witness at trial (often an issue in child abuse cases; see Chapter 13), and even competence to be executed, as required by the Supreme Court in *Ford v. Wainwright* (1986) (477 U.S. 399).

However, note that not everyone appreciates the contributions of psychologists to the assessment of competency. In its 1995 session, the New Mexico legislature pondered and passed a bill that set limits on the testimony of psychologists regarding competency. Senate Bill 459, written by Richard Romero, included the following language, quoted in the newsletter *Dispatches:*

> When a psychologist or psychiatrist testifies during a defendant's competency hearing, the psychologist or psychiatrist shall wear a cone-shaped hat that is not less than two feet tall. The surface of the hat shall be imprinted with stars and lightning bolts.
>
> Additionally, a psychologist or psychiatrist shall be required to don a white beard . . . and shall punctuate crucial elements of his testimony by stabbing the air with a wand. [Apparently there are only male shrinks in New Mexico.] [Before the expert's testimony about competency], the bailiff shall contemporaneously dim the courtroom lights and administer two strikes to a Chinese gong.

Although the Senate passed the bill by a voice vote, and the House voted 46-to-14 to make it official, New Mexico Governor Gary Johnson vetoed it.

Criminal Responsibility

For a punishable criminal act to occur, two related but independent factors must be present. First, an act or behavior legally defined as illegal must occur—that is, the *actus rea* or the act itself. Second, the individual committing the act must have the general intent to do so—that is, the *mens rea*. Except for a few criminal statutes (e.g., some product liability laws), both an illegal act and a guilty mind must be present before a punishable crime has occurred.

Consideration of both the act and the intent has occurred for at least the last 2,000 years of recorded history. The U.S. judicial process has historically encompassed a variety of criminal responsibility standards. The McNaughten rule was borrowed from English case law (Daniel McNaughten's Case, 1843) and states the following:

> If as a result of mental disease or defect, the defendant did not understand what he did or that it was wrong, or if he was under a delusion (but not otherwise insane), which, if true, would have provided a good defense. Thus, if one does not understand what he was doing at all or did not know that it was wrong, he is excused. He is also excused if due to an insane delusion he thought he was acting in self defense or carrying out the will of God. (Often called the right/wrong test.)

The criminal responsibility standard continued in this form until the irresistible impulse or volition test was added (*Davis* v. *United States*, 1897). The question became whether the individual had been robbed of his or her free will to control his or her behavior due to mental disease or defect, despite knowing such behavior was wrong.

In 1954, the Durham rule was set forth (*Durham* v. *United States*) in which Judge David Bazelon greatly widened the standard. In the face of much criticism, in 1972, Judge Bazelon rejected his own Durham Rule (*United States* v. *Brawner*) and adopted the Model Penal Code created by the American Law Institute (ALI; 1962). In general, the ALI standard asserted that an individual is not criminally responsible if, by reason of mental disease or defect, the person lacked substantial capacity to appreciate the wrongfulness of his or her conduct or lacked the substantial capacity to conform his or her behavior to the requirements of law. The ALI standard thus narrowed the Durham rule but was not as restrictive as the older McNaughten rule. The next important change in criminal responsibility came about as a result of the Hinckley trial, via changes in the federal law (see Table 16.2).

Competency to Stand Trial

As previously noted, the issue of *competency to stand trial* deals with the defendant's current state of psychological functioning, whereas *criminal responsibility* refers to the defendant's status at the time of the crime. The concept of criminal responsibility may trace its roots to English case law and beyond, but the principle of competency to stand trial is based firmly in the Sixth Amendment of the U.S. Constitution, as follows:

> In all criminal prosecutions, the accused shall enjoy the right to a speedy and public trial, by an impartial jury of the state and district wherein the crime shall have been

TABLE 16.2   Comparison of Insanity Defenses

Test	Legal Standard	Final Burden of Proof	Who Bears Burden of Proof
McNaughten	"Didn't know what he or she was doing or didn't know it was wrong"	Varies from proof by a balance of probabilities on the defense to proof beyond a reasonable doubt on the prosecutor	
Irresistible impulse	"Could not control conduct"		
Durham	"Criminal act was caused by mental illness"	Beyond reasonable doubt	Prosecutor
A.L.I.—Brawner	"Lacks substantial capacity to appreciate the wrongfulness of the conduct or to control it"	Beyond reasonable doubt	Prosecutor
Present federal law	"Lacks capacity to appreciate the wrongfulness of his or her conduct"	Clear and convincing evidence	Defense

Source: Adapted in part from "Insanity Defense" by Norval Morris, *National Institute of Justice Crime File Study Guide* (Washington, DC: U.S. Department of Justice, National Institute of Justice/Criminal Justice Reference Service, 1986).

committed, which district shall have been ascertained by law, and to be informed of the nature and cause of the accusation; to be confronted with the witnesses against him, to have compulsory process for obtaining witnesses in his favor, and to have the assistance of counsel for his defense.

Case law provides specific guidelines for the determination of competency to stand trial. *Dusky* v. *United States* (1960), which provided the standards used in most jurisdictions after 1960, states that the accused must generally fulfill three broad criteria. First, he or she must have some factual understanding of the judicial proceedings. Second, the accused must have a rational understanding of the proceedings. Third, he or she must also be able to consult with an attorney with a reasonable degree of rational understanding. It should be noted that forensic opinions (i.e., from a psychologist or psychiatrist) regarding competency to stand trial are only clinical opinions and the final determination is a judicial decision. Should a defendant be found not competent to stand trial, then he or she may not be confined for further treatment for an indeterminate period of time, as set forth in *Jackson* v. *Indiana* (1972).

> *Reply to a plaintiff who claims his cabbages were eaten by your goat: You had no cabbages. If you did they were not eaten. If they were eaten, it was not by a goat. If they were eaten by a goat, it was not my goat. And, if it was my goat, he was insane.*
>
> —I. Youngner, quoted by J. E. McElhaney,
> *Trial Notebook,* American Bar Association (1987)

The Case of John Hinckley

On March 30, 1981, shortly before 2:30 P.M., a gunman aimed and fired six shots from a 22-caliber revolver. Four of the six Devastator bullets found human targets, with tragic results. The first shot struck presidential press secretary James Brady. Although the exploding bullet did extensive neurological damage, Brady lived and began a long rehabilitation process. The second shot struck Washington, DC, police officer Thomas Delahanty; he also survived his back wound. The third bullet hit a building across the street from the Washington Hilton. No human damage resulted. The fourth bullet struck secret service agent Timothy McCarthy. His chest wound was serious, but Agent McCarthy survived. The fifth bullet struck the glass in the presidential limousine but also did no human damage. The sixth and final bullet ricocheted off the rear panel of the limousine and entered the chest of Ronald Reagan, president of the United States. Like the others, President Reagan survived.

The entire attack lasted only a few seconds. A Secret Service agent later testified to his feeling of desperation as he attempted to stop the gunfire: "I came down on top of the assailant, with my right arm around his head. . . . He was still clicking the weapon as we go down." Understandably, such violent and senseless brutality raised many questions about psychological motivation, history, and stability of the gunman, John Hinckley. Testimony in Hinckley's seven-week trial indicated his ultimate goal was to capture the love and respect of Yale University student and movie star Jodie Foster. Although unsuccessful in this goal, Hinckley's behavior did lay the foundation for major revisions in criminal responsibility statutes at both federal and state levels.

Background Data

John Hinckley was born in Oklahoma in 1955. His childhood was not unlike that of most children. At the age of 4, he moved to Dallas, Texas. Recreational activities included quar-

terbacking his elementary school football team and playing basketball in high school. At the age of 9, Hinckley became a fan of the Beatles. His interest in music and possible identification with John Lennon continued into his adulthood. When he was age 12, Hinckley moved with his family to a prominent Dallas neighborhood and almost immediately lost social status. He was no longer the "king pin."

Graduation from high school in 1973 prompted a move to Evergreen, Colorado. Soon after, he decided to attend Texas Tech University in Lubbock, Texas. Although Hinckley's future dreams frequently included pursuit of a college degree in Lubbock, repeated efforts over the next five to six years were generally unproductive. Around 1974, Hinckley quit school at Texas Tech and moved to Dallas. He wanted to be on his own and "dreamed of future glory in some undefined field, perhaps music or politics" (Caplan, 1984, p. 34). A move to Hollywood in 1976 to sell his music did not have the desired result, but he did see the movie titled *Taxi Driver* some 15 times that summer. In the spring of 1977, Hinckley returned to Lubbock.

Roesch (1979) reported that Hinckley's overall adaptation and emotional adjustment were apparently beginning to decline at this point. In the next year, he began to experience a number of minor health problems and received medical treatment. In October 1978, he became interested in the American Nazi movement via the National Socialist Party. In August 1979, he purchased his first firearm and in September of that year began to publish the "American Front Newsletter." He appointed himself national director of the American Front and fabricated membership lists from 37 states. By now, he had moved 17 times since high school.

In 1980, Hinckley, who had gained 60 pounds since high school, experienced his first anxiety attack. He bought another gun. In May 1980, *People Magazine* announced that Jodie Foster, star of *Taxi Driver* (later of *The*

(continued)

The Case of John Hinckley Continued

Silence of the Lambs), would be attending Yale University. This was very important to Hinckley, who appears to have fueled his belief that he could win Foster's attention and love. After a disappointing telephone conversation with Foster on September 20, 1980, Hinckley wrote this in his diary: "My mind was at the breaking point. A relationship I had dreamed about went absolutely nowhere. My disillusionment with everything was complete" (Caplan, 1984, p. 38).

Subsequently, the infamous Devastator exploding bullets were purchased, along with six more guns. There were numerous flights to distant places, including Colorado, Washington, DC, Ohio, Nebraska, and Tennessee. Perhaps the most serious development was Hinckley's decision to begin following—perhaps stalking—both President Carter and President Reagan.

During psychiatric treatment by John Hooper, M.D., between October 1980 and February 1981, Hinckley failed to divulge his thoughts, fantasies, or planned activities. Without this information, Dr. Hooper and the patient's family formulated a plan to encourage their son's independence and emotional stability. Despite these efforts, Hinckley took a bus from Los Angeles to Washington, DC, arriving on March 29, 1981. After breakfast on the morning of March 30, Hinckley learned of President Reagan's schedule, and, having written a final love letter to Jodie Foster, he loaded his Devastator bullets and began his vigil outside the Washington Hilton Hotel. In seconds, his plan to obtain glory, and thereby the love of Jodie Foster, was enacted.

The Trial

The trial of John Hinckley was well publicized. The 13 criminal charges included the attempted assassination of the president. Lawyers for the prosecution and defense differed little on the factual events. Considerable disagreement existed over the defendant's true psychological condition. The raising of the insanity defense resulted in a trial that lasted slightly over seven weeks. The costs incurred were impressive. Mental health experts testifying or assisting the prosecution received over $300,000 in fees. Defense experts received fees in excess of $150,000. Defense attorneys may have received between $500,000 and $1,000,000. Such bills did not include salaries for court officials, ancillary staff, public relations, and so on (Caplan, 1984).

After two to three days of jury deliberation, Hinckley was found not guilty by reason of insanity on all 13 counts. He was automatically committed to Saint Elizabeth's Hospital in Washington, DC, for treatment, to stay there until he is viewed by the hospital as no longer dangerous as a result of his mental illness.

Aftermath

In the following weeks, 26 different bills were introduced to modify the federal statute that covers the insanity defense. As a result of these efforts, two important changes occurred in federal law pertaining to the issue of criminal responsibility. First, the volitional component (i.e., the irresistible impulse concept) was removed from the original McNaughten model. At present, a successful insanity defense is solely based on the defendant's inability as a result of mental disease or defect to appreciate the criminality of his or her alleged conduct. Second, the burden of proof (i.e., whose responsibility it is to demonstrate the viability of the defendant's psychological state) was shifted from the prosecution to the defense. The level of proof required for the prosecution was also reduced from "beyond a reasonable doubt" to "clear and convincing evidence" when applied to the defense. Thus, the level of certainty required of the jury when viewing the evidence was reduced from an estimated

90 to 95 percent (an estimate) to somewhere below that (see the O.J. Simpson case in Chapter 1). Although these changes in federal law were significant, they served only as models to state courts, who hear by far the greater number of insanity defenses each year.

The difficulty for the professionals who are evaluating insanity is that they are typically making their assessment long after the act was committed, yet the most relevant data set is objective information as to how the person was functioning around the time of the crime. The second most relevant data set is the person's mental health history prior to the crime. The least relevant data set is the person's mental status at the time of the evaluation. But mental health professionals often focus on this last data set because it is so readily available. Unfortunately, such data are often likely to be contaminated by several factors: (1) the person may have spent time in jail or some other institution, which in itself could affect one's mental state; (2) the person may have received psychotropic medications; (3) the person might have some emotional reaction to increasing or continuing awareness of whatever damage he or she perpetrated; (4) the person is no doubt aware that he or she is making a plea of insanity and would be inclined, either consciously or unconsciously, to provide data, whether true, enhanced, or false, to support that plea; (5) the person may have received subtle or direct coaching from his or her attorney to further the goal discussed in item 3; and (6) if the person has spent time in jail, he or she has likely received advice/coaching from other inmates.

It should be noted that in May and November of 1981, Hinckley's defense attorneys offered to have their client plead guilty to all counts if the prosecution would agree to recommend to the court that penalties on all counts run concurrently, rather than consecutively. Under this arrangement, Hinckley would be eligible for parole in 15 years. The prosecution declined this plea offer because, among other reasons, it was viewed as improper and unseemly to plea bargain a case involving the attempted assassination of the president of the United States.

John Hinckley is still undergoing treatment at Saint Elizabeth's Hospital. He may be released at the recommendation of the hospital and with approval of the presiding judge. Such a recommendation will occur only if the hospital feels that Hinckley no longer poses a threat to society or himself. The political issues amplify the dilemma in all such cases—when to release an individual who has been proven dangerous in the past, may well be dangerous at some point in the future, but who is probably not "imminently" dangerous. Add to that the fact that Hinckley's evident mental disorder symptoms were likely lessened by psychotropic medication and other interventions, and one sees the complexity inherent in determining to make such a recommendation.

His behavior in recent years has generally been without substantial blemish, whereas in earlier years he provided plenty of material to argue for retaining him in the hospital. In 1986, he exchanged letters with Ted Bundy (see Chapter 10); according to a psychiatrist, Hinckley wrote Bundy to "express his sorrow" for the "awkward position he must be in." In 1988, his obsession with Jodie Foster was still evident as he wrote a mail-order company to order a nude drawing of her; the year before, a search of his hospital room had uncovered 57 photos of the actress. However, a 1999 federal appeals court allowed Hinckley to take supervised day trips off hospital grounds, and in 2004, he was allowed to make unsupervised overnight visits with his family.

In 1984, Hinckley's father, John Sr., sold his oil and gas prospecting company, the Vanderbilt Energy Corporation, reportedly for $26 million. He and his wife spent about $1 million during the 1980s on a national advertising campaign to increase public awareness about both mental disorders and the insanity defense.

You couldn't even prove the White House staff sane beyond
a reasonable doubt.

—Edwin Meese, counselor to Ronald Reagan

Borderline Personality Disorder

Several different diagnoses of Hinckley were offered at his trial. However, there was a consensus from a substantial group of these experts that one diagnosis that would apply to him was that of Borderline Personality Disorder (BPD). The BPD diagnosis, first incorporated into the *DSM-III* in 1980, has consistently proven to be a meaningful and useful category (Strupp, Lambert, & Horowitz, 1997; Widiger et al., 1991). Although the *DSM-IV-TR* does not specifically mention it, BPD seems to be in part a resurrection of an old term at one time much favored by clinicians: *emotionally unstable personality*. People with BPD show significant emotional instability, are impulsive and unpredictable in behavior, are often antisocial, are irritable and anxious, often show "soft" neurological signs, and avoid being alone or experiencing the psychological emptiness or boredom to which they are prone (Atkinson & Goldberg, 2004). There is some evidence that as these individuals improve, they show more predictable behavior patterns, yet this is combined with increasingly evident narcissism. An occasional additional feature of BPD is *pseudologia phantastica*. This lying is often an attempt to control or to enhance self-esteem rather than the conning malingering seen in the antisocial personality disorder.

In the *DSM-IV-TR*, BPD is described as a pervasive pattern of mood, self-image, impulse control, and interpersonal instability beginning by early adulthood, evident in such behaviors as: (1) frantic efforts to avoid actual or imagined abandonment; (2) an unstable and intense interpersonal relationship pattern, with extremes of idealization and devaluation; (3) persistent and markedly disturbed or unstable identity or sense of self; (4) impulsive self-damaging behaviors (excluding item 5); (5) recurrent suicidal behaviors, gestures, threats, or self-mutilation; (6) mood instability; (7) chronic feelings of emptiness; (8) inappropriate, intense anger or lack of anger control; and/or (9) transient, stress-related paranoid ideation or severe dissociation. BPD is thought to be relatively common, affecting approximately 1 to 2 percent of the general population.

Husband and wife, in the language of the law, are styled baron and feme. . . .
[I]f the baron kills his feme it is the same as if he had killed a stranger, or
any other person; but if the feme kills her baron, it is regarded by the laws as
a much more atrocious crime, as she not only breaks through the restraints
of humanity and conjugal affection, but throws off all subjection to the
authority of her husband. And therefore the law denominates her crime
a species of treason, and condemns her to the same punishment as if she
had killed the king. . . . The sentence of woman was to be drawn and
burnt alive.

—W. Blackstone, *Commentaries on the Laws of England*, 1897, Bk. 4, p. 1602

Treatment of People with BPD

Typically, people with BPD have been the target of and/or witnessed a chaotic, soap-opera early life, often mixed with some form of abuse wherein love was equated with pain and loss of control. Attempts at self-definition received random reinforcement, at best. Crises such as sickness were the keys to attention and some nurturance, although abandonment was always an understood option. Reflecting such chaos, BPD is truly a polyglot syndrome and will therefore require equally variable treatment responses (Kroll, 1993).

Multiple hospitalizations are not uncommon. Medication may be necessary (e.g., for any depressive components), and the SSRIs have been useful to generally calm and stabilize extreme response patterns. Since there is usually some disordered autonomic-emotional functioning, biofeedback and relaxation training may be appropriate. Group therapy can be helpful if the person will allow the development of trust in the group, but such clients are often unwilling to share the attention of the therapist and are so emotionally unpredictable that they are difficult to work with. They can exert such a high cost on the progress of the group that they make it unwise to include them.

Also, the following beliefs have to be challenged and corrected (e.g., as in dialectical behavior therapy,) pioneered by Linehan, which has been proven effective for people with BPD (Chambless et al., 1996): (1) "I'm afraid I'll be alone forever, as no one who really gets to know me will stay with me or love me"; (2) "If I ignore my own needs, I can entrap some people into relationships, but since I can't control my feelings and I need the relationships, I'll be very unhappy"; (3) "Although I need people, they will eventually hurt or reject me, so I must protect myself"; (4) "People and/or relationships are usually all good or all bad, and often at different times in the same relationship"; (5) "I deserve any bad things that happen to me"; or (6) "My misery (and/or "badness") is how people recognize me as a unique self."

Legal Perspectives and Prescriptions for Reform

The case of O. J. Simpson and, to a lesser degree, the case of John Hinckley highlight several overall perspectives on the legal system (Meyer & Weaver, 2006). The two primary criteria by which a legal system should be judged are effectiveness and efficiency. Is our legal system effective? The clearest conclusion is that no one knows, because, unlike other systems in society, such as financial or medical systems, the legal system has no method of accountability, no way of determining whether it actually finds the truth. Interestingly enough, the percent of time the jurors in the O. J. Simpson criminal trial spent in formal deliberation was 0.06 percent (4 hours of deliberation divided by 6,384 hours in sequestration).

It is clear that many legal maneuvers restrict or void certain pieces of useful information from reaching the jury, thus constricting the potential for gaining any ultimate truth. During the Simpson trial, 16,000 objections were raised, with approximately 9,000 overruled and 7,000 sustained. Incidentally, the number of other cases completed in some fashion by the Los Angeles Superior Court between the time Simpson was arrested and the end of his first trial was 51,769. Also, the legal system has very little allowance for interactive assessment—a method used in other systems to maximize effectiveness, in which jurors, for example, could ask the questions they really wanted answered at about the time they needed the information most. This restricts both effectiveness and efficiency. So, the belief shared by many people that the legal system is not especially effective is probably accurate.

As to the other criterion, the criminal trial of O. J. Simpson made it clear that the legal system is appallingly inefficient. Cost accountability appears to be a concept that is foreign to the legal system. Aside from the costs to Simpson himself (estimated at $2.75 million), the costs to the taxpayers of Los Angeles County were absurd, even estimated as high as $9,100,000. Who profited? Certainly the attorneys did. The fact is that if any other profession were in such complete control of a system that brought such high profits from such questionably effective endeavors, they would eventually have to answer to people outside their own profession. For all other professions they would eventually go to our legal system. But, when this happens to attorneys, they go before other attorneys, as the judicial system is housed almost entirely by attorneys. And most lawmaking bodies and legislatures are dominated by attorneys. Any ultimate reform will at the very least require that the actions of the attorneys be reviewed by boards in which the great majority of members are not attorneys and are not somehow biased in favor of attorneys.

> In the trial of the century, the specter of mistrial arose when it was reported that some jurors, in between recesses and sidebar conferences, might have heard some actual testimony. An angry Judge Ito sternly told them to disregard it.
> —Dave Barry, "Windows on the World," *Miami Herald*, December 31, 1995

Assuming the jury system is retained, reform should include the following:

1. Simplify the language and concepts used in the legal system, and provide uniform definitions to any vague and/or complex terms (e.g., "clear and convincing," "beyond a reasonable doubt," etc.).
2. Provide for effective penalties for people who avoid or do not respond to a jury summons.
3. Markedly reduce the number of people (especially those of higher intelligence and/or socioeconomic status) who are excused from jury duty.
4. Set higher minimal competency requirements to become a juror (e.g., intelligence, education, etc.) and especially so in complex issue trials.
5. Markedly reduce (or even eliminate) the availability of peremptory challenges (i.e., those that do not require a cause).
6. Expand the types of trials that do not require a jury verdict (i.e., the judge can decide guilt or innocence).
7. Give judges (or even juries in some fashion) greater powers to reduce or eliminate repetitive or questionably useful testimony.

8. Use very stringent criteria for the admission of expert testimony (see the year 1923 in Historical Development in the Introduction).
9. Eliminate the requirement for unanimous decisions in all trials except capital cases; and even there, consider allowing 11–1 decisions to avoid having the decision controlled by the one individual who is more likely to be biased, bought, or bizarre, rather than the principled hero portrayed in some movies. In *Ballew* v. *Georgia* (1978) (435 U.S. 223), the Supreme Court established six as the minimum number of jurors necessary to guarantee a person the constitutional right to a jury trial.
10. Provide for a legal category or easier legal recognition of "frivolous" suits (e.g., by a board similar to a grand jury). When there is such a finding, make the party responsible for bringing such a suit responsible for all of the other party's costs (including some form of punitive damages).
11. Allow juries to order the plaintiff to pay the defendant's costs (e.g., attorney fees and expert witness fees) in any civil trial.
12. Allow jurors to take notes and to ask questions (through notes to the judge) during the trial (e.g., so they can get the information they want, when they want it). Allow them to discuss the evidence together at various points during the trial.
13. Consider "level playing field" requirements (e.g., each side may spend only so much money, including all types of costs, or each may use no more than some maximum allotted time at trial, such as 20 hours, including the time to have all witnesses, objections, motions, and so on heard).
14. Last, and most important, redesign the system so that jurors are not treated as fragile, gullible drones (e.g., in the Simpson trial when there was concern the jurors might see billboards with the words *guilty* or *innocent* on them). Avoid sequestering juries except in the most extreme circumstances. When judges make a guilty or not guilty decision in a "bench" trial, they are not required to be sequestered or protected. Are judges somehow "better" at anything other than a knowledge of the law? If so, then the jury system is a bad system.

The U.S. jury system has been referred to as an antiquated legacy from the Vikings. As some experts have pointed out, if people were trying to come up with a good system, it's not likely they would come up with the idea of pulling in 12 people off the street (who had no excuse) to make the decisions. A number of countries that adopted the jury system later dropped it (e.g., India and Japan). Supporters of the jury system point to Britain's retention of the system. Yet, in Britain only about 5 percent of criminal trials are heard by juries, and only about 1 to 2 percent of civil trials are heard by juries. The U.S. military, as well as the nations of continental Europe, rely on panels of professional or lay jurors, or just judges.

> *[An expert] is somebody who is more than 50 miles from home, has no responsibility for implementing the advice he gives, and shows slides [or today uses PowerPoint].*
>
> —Former Attorney General Ed Meese

CHAPTER

17 Postscript Positive Mental Health

I don't want to achieve immortality through my work, I want to achieve immortality through not dying.

—Woody Allen

The preceding chapters have focused on negative mental health conditions. However, there are ways that people can improve their psychological functioning, not just as an antidote to psychological disorder but also as a way to get more enjoyment out of life. Many psychologists, writers, and philosophers have tried to communicate what leads to positive mental health, but it is only in recent years that psychologists have begun to focus research on the "positives" of life (Schneider & Leitner, 2002; Seligman & Csikszentmihalyi, 2000). For a quick snapshot of positive mental health, consider this one from a young woman from a small town in rural Kentucky:

> You are responsible for your own happiness, and you can do anything you want to do, no matter what your handicap is. Don't worry about what you can't do, just concentrate on what you can do, and make your life count! . . . I believe that I can choose to use my mental capacity and emotional strength to make my life count, to reach out to others in their time of need, and to share the abundant good God has given me.

This statement was made some years ago by a young woman who, 11 years earlier, was in the midst of a miscarriage with her first pregnancy and was diagnosed as having amyotrophic lateral sclerosis, more commonly known as Lou Gehrig's disease. As had happened with her, people with this disease gradually lose the ability to move their arms and legs and to talk. Eventually, they lose the ability to swallow and to breathe; they usually die in two to five years. She spent the last part of her time using her computer, typing into it by moving her head, to write letters to encourage and support others with difficult diseases. Throughout this book, a number of facts and opinions may have allowed the reader to infer more specific conclusions as to how a person could lead a happy life across the life span. In closing, I present a number of formal principles that may help in that endeavor:

1. As noted elsewhere in this and other books, I believe that the first true law of psychology is that "behavior predicts behavior." Remember that—not only in your dealings with others but also in reflecting on yourself. Yes, people

can change, leading to the second law of human behavior, "behavior predicts behavior, without intervention." The intervention need not be formal, as in psychotherapy; it may even have self- or other-generated "conversion" qualities.

2. Note the many times that exposure treatment is recommended as central to change, as in the treatment of the anxiety disorders (Chapter 3). In more common terminology, "When you fall off the horse, get right back on." And if you are afraid of riding the horse, face that directly and work directly until you overcome that avoidance. Consciously, or mindfully (Williams et al., 2008) and behaviorally confronting the sources of your fears until you feel they are mastered is the only way to overcome them, and it's important to keep facing the conflict or disturbing stimulus, even if it makes you uncomfortable while doing so.

3. The anticipation of a situation is often more distressing or important to a person than is the actual situation itself. When you expect to fail in a situation, you are very likely to avoid the situation or take inadequate steps to cope with it. The predicted failure is therefore more likely to occur. This in turn decreases self-esteem, increases depression, makes you now even less likely to do what is needed, and therefore makes future failure more likely.

4. Your interpretation of your experience is often more important than the actual experience itself. Unfortunately, that interpretation may at times be less than conscious, leading you to behave in ways even you don't understand.

5. Develop and cherish friendships and other forms of social and moral support. Be there when you are needed, be quick to ask for help when you need it, and be appreciative of that help.

6. Recognize the importance of relationships in your life. Try to heal any bruised or fractured relationships with significant others (significant in potentiality or by blood). Plan so that people relationships will be in place.

7. Do not ruminate or even focus on missed opportunities and past mistakes. Emphasize your positive achievements and pleasures, be optimistic, and work to accept the fact that you do the best you can.

8. Some problems are best solved by "letting go" and relaxing, adopting a posture of acceptance, humor, and perspective.

9. Some factors in every person are strongly influenced by genetics (heredity), and it is more effective to develop ways to cope with these factors rather than trying to directly change them.

10. Ambiguity or uncertainty about life situations is anxiety producing and aversive. Most people will go to great lengths to impose understanding or meaning on a situation even where there is none or it is not yet available, which may lead them to a quick and sometimes less than optimal solution. As one client put it in a moment of frustration while waiting for the results of a biopsy, "I almost wish they would go ahead and tell me I had cancer, rather than making me wait around so long to find out."

11. The belief that you are in control of a situation may decrease anxiety, even if that belief is false and even if you have never actually done anything to change the situation.

12. The spiritual life, in whatever form it takes in your life, affects psychological health. If you are religious, develop an association with a church, synagogue, etc. Make at least a minimal plan for spiritual development.
13. Physical health affects mental health. Get regular exercise, and consider doing it with others, to satisfy your social needs and to fuel your motivation to continue with the exercise. Plan a sound nutritional program and work to change any destructive health habits, such as drinking too much or smoking. Be aware of the side effects of any drugs you are taking.
14. Prevention (of psychological and physical disorder) is always less costly and distressing, both emotionally and financially, than are the efforts it takes to cure disorder.
15. Purposefully accumulating positive experiences and then preserving them in memory and in symbols (such as photographs) lead to a positive self-image and protect the "self" from the effects of negative experiences.
16. Realize that to learn from your own experience is wisdom; to learn from the experience of others is genius.

Happiness (or at least contentment) and a positive mental health are attained by working directly and purposefully toward the components of positive mental health, which include the following:

1. A clear and accurate picture of your world (good reality testing)
2. An ability to clearly and rationally analyze problems and challenges and a willingness to take well-considered risks in order to meet these challenges
3. Flexibility and the ability to adapt in the face of change and stress
4. Elimination of most emotionally and physically draining internal conflicts by a willingness to take responsibility for your own life and life choices and to make sure your own needs are taken care of but also to make several selected others a close second to your own needs (and on occasion, ahead of those needs), with the rest of the world not too far behind
5. Controlling and reducing both internal and external sources of stress—for example, periodically asking yourself, "Will this matter a year from now?" reminding yourself that when you die your "in-basket" won't be empty—and learning meditative mindfulness-relaxation techniques
6. The capacity to sublimate, to direct your developed or instinctive hostile energy into creative and constructive outlets
7. A positive personal identity that includes a sense of self-worth and some unique competencies
8. Mutually satisfying interpersonal relationships, friendships, and loves
9. A good sense of humor
10. The capacity to relax and enjoy life
11. The ability to be more of a "giver" than a "taker"; the capacity to love and to make commitments to other people, interests, and causes; and the desire to become spiritually and psychologically involved with something outside and beyond yourself

As you work to develop these or similar principles in your life or in the lives of your children, remember that all of us must strive (although not without relaxation and humor), because we never fully succeed. Yet, as the senior author's daughter once said, "The best advice you ever gave me was that you should always try to do your best, but when you do fail, and at times you will fail, *forgive yourself*, right any wrong you did, and start over again."

> *Once I wasn't*
> *Then I was*
> *Now I ain't again*

—From a Cleveland cemetery

REFERENCES

Abraham, K. (1916). "The first pregenital stage of the libido." In *Selected papers on psychoanalysis*. New York: Basic Books.

Agras, W. S. (1995). "Treatment of eating disorders." In A. Schatzberg & C. Nemeroff (Eds.), *Textbook of pyschopharmacology*. Washington, DC: American Psychiatric Press.

Alford, B., & Beck, A. (1997). *The integrative power of cognitive therapy*. New York: Basic Books.

American Law Institute Model Penal Code, Section 4.01 (1962).

American Psychiatric Association. (1994). *DSM-IV: Diagnostic and statistical manual of mental disorders* (4th ed.). Washington, DC: American Psychiatric Press.

American Psychiatric Association. (2000). *DSM-IV-TR: Diagnostic and statistical manual of mental disorders* (4th ed. text revision). Washington, DC: American Psychiatric Press.

Amir, N. (1998). "Anxiety." In H. Friedman (Ed.), *Encyclopedia of mental health*. San Diego: Academic Press.

Amminger, G., Pope, S., Rock, D., Roberts, S., et al. (1999). "Relationship between childhood behavioral disturbance and later schizophrenia in the New York High-Risk Project." *American Journal of Psychiatry*, 156, 525–530.

Andreassi, J. (2000) *Psychophysiology*. Mahwah, NJ: Lawrence Erlbaum.

Asher, R. (1951). "Munchausen syndrome." *Lancet*, 1, 339–341.

Atkins v. Commonwealth of Virginia. (1999). 257 Va. 160, 510 S.E. 2d 445.

Atkins v. Commonwealth of Virginia. (2000). 260 Va. 375, 534 S.E. 2d 312.

Atkinson, L., & Goldberg, S. (2004). *Attachment issues in psychopathology and intervention*. Mahwah, NJ: Lawrence Erlbaum.

Ayllon, T., & Azrin, N. (1968). *The token economy: A motivational system for therapy and rehabilitation*. New York: Appleton-Century-Crofts.

Ayoub, C. C., Deutsch, R. M., & Kinscherff, R. (2000). "Psychosocial management issues in Munchausen by Proxy." In R. M. Reece (Ed.), *Treatment of child abuse: Common ground for mental health, medical, and legal practitioners* (pp. 226–235). Baltimore: Johns Hopkins University Press.

Baker, T., Piper, M., McCarthy, D., Majeskie, M., & Fiore, M. (2004). "Addiction motivation reformulated." *Psychological Review*, 111, 33–51.

Bandura, A., & Walters, R. (1963). *Social learning and personality development*. New York: Holt, Rinehart.

Barkley, R. (1998). "Attention Deficit Hyperactivity Disorder (ADHD)." In H. Friedman (Ed.), *Encyclopedia of mental health*. San Diego: Academic Press.

Barlow, D. (2002). *Anxiety and its disorders*. New York: Guilford Press.

Barrett, C., & Meyer, R. (1992). "Cognitive behavioral therapy for inpatient alcoholics." In J. Wright, A. Beck, M. Thase, & J. Ludgate (Eds.), *Inpatient cognitive therapy*. New York: Guilford Press.

Bartol, C., & Bartol, A. (2004). *Forensic psychology*. Thousand Oaks, CA: Sage.

Bartol, C., & Bartol, A. (2008). *Criminal Behavior*. Belmont, CA: Wadsworth.

Baumeister, R. (1998). "Impulse control." In H. Friedman (Ed.), *Encyclopedia of Mental Health*. San Diego: Academic Press.

Beck, A. (1976). *Cognitive therapy and the emotional disorders*. New York: International Universities Press.

Beck, A., Freeman, A., & Associates (1990). *Cognitive therapy of personality disorders*. New York: Guilford Press.

Beck, A., & Valin S. (1953). "Psychotic depressive reaction in soldiers who accidentally killed their buddies." *American Journal of Psychiatry, 110,* 347–353.

Bell, Q. (1972). *Virginia Woolf: A biography*. New York: Harcourt Brace Jovanovich.

Bezchlibnyk-Butler, K., & Jeffries, J. (1999). *Clinical handbook of psychotropic drugs* (9th ed.). New York: Hogrefe & Huber.

Bickman L. (2005). "A common factor approach to improving mental health services." *Mental Health Services Research, 7(1),* 1–4.

Blanchard, R., & Steiner, B. W. (Eds.). (1990). *Clinical management of gender identity disorders in children and adults*. Washington, DC: American Psychiatric Press.

Blatt, S. (2004). *Experiences of depression*. Washington, DC: American Psychological Association.

Bleuler, E. (1911). *Dementia praecox oder die gruppe der schizophrenia*. Leipzig: Deuticke.

Blouin, A., Blouin, J., Aubin, P., Carter, J., et al. (1992). "Seasonal patterns of bulimia nervosa." *American Journal of Psychiatry, 149,* 73–81.

Bongar, B. (2002). *The suicidal patient*. Washington, DC: American Psychological Association.

Bongar, B., & Beutler, L. (Eds.). (1995). *Comprehensive textbook of psychotherapy*. New York: Oxford University Press.

Boss, M. (1963). *Psychoanalysis and Dasein analysis*. New York: Plenum.

Bostwick, J. M. (2000). "Affect disorders and suicide." *American Journal of Psychiatry, 157,* 1925–1932.

Bowlby, J. (1973). *Attachment and loss: Separation anxiety and anger* (vol. 2). New York: Basic Books.

Boyd, A., McLearen, A., Meyer, R., & Denney, J. (2007). *The assessment of deception*. Sarasota, FL: Professional Resource Press.

Briere, J. (1997). *Psychological assessment of adult post-traumatic states*. Washington, DC: American Psychological Association Books.

Bruch, H., Czyzewski, D., & Suhr, M. (1988). *Conversations with anorexics*. New York: Basic Books.

Buckley, P., & Meltzer, H. (1995). "Treament of schizophrenia." In A. Schatzberg & C. Nemeroff (Eds.), *Textbook of psychiatry*. Washington, DC: American Psychiatric Press.

Burrell, P. (2003). *A royal duty*. New York: Putnam.

Calaprice, A. (2000). *The expanded quotable Einstein*. Princeton, NJ: Princeton University Press.

Campbell, L. C. (1993). *The royal marriages*. New York: St. Martin's Press.

Caplan, L. (1984). *The insanity defense*. Boston: Godine.

Carnes, P. (1992). *Out of the shadows: Understanding sexual addiction*. Center City, MN: Hazelden.

Chambless, D., Sanderson, W., Shoham, V., & Johnson, S. (1996). "An update on empirically validated therapies." *The Clinical Psychologist, 49(2),* 5–18.

Chiles, J., & Strosahl, K. (1995). *The suicidal patient*. Washington, DC: American Psychiatric Press.

Chu, J., Frey, L., Ganzel, B., & Matthews, J. (1999). "Memories of childhood abuse." *American Journal of Psychiatry, 156,* 749–755.

Clayton, R., & Heard, D. (1994). *Elvis up close: In the words of those who knew him best*. Atlanta, GA: Turner.

Cleckley, H. (1964). *The mask of sanity* (4th ed.). St. Louis, MO: Mosby.

Clum, G. (1998). "Phobias." In H. Friedman (Ed.), *Encyclopedia of mental health*. San Diego: Academic Press.

Cohen, S., Kessler, R., & Gordon, L. (1995). *Measuring stress*. New York: Oxford University Press.

Cohen-Kettenis, P. T., & Gooren, L. G. J. (1999). "Transsexualism: A review of etiology, diagnosis and treatment." *Journal of Psychosomatic Research, 46*(4), 315–333.

Colapinto, J. (2000). *As nature made him: The boy who was raised as a girl*. New York: Harper-Collins.

Colby, K. (1977). "Appraisal of four psychological theories of paranoid phenomena." *Journal of Abnormal Psychology, 86*, 54–59.

Coleman, R. (1994). *The Carpenters*. New York: HarperCollins.

Coughlin, C. (2002). *Saddam: King of terror*. New York: HarperCollins.

Craigie, F., & Ross, S. (1980). "The use of a videotape pre-treatment training program to encourage treatment-seeking among alcoholic detoxification patients." *Behavior Therapy, 11*, 141–147.

Crowther, J. H., Wolfe, E. M., & Sherwood, N. E. (1992). "Epidemiology of bulimia nervosa." In J. H. Crowther, D. L. Tennenbaum, S. E. Hobfoll, & M. A. P. Stephens (Eds.), *The etiology of bulimia nervosa: The individual and family context* (pp. 1–26). Washington, DC: Hemisphere.

Cullberg, J. (2006). *Psychoses*. New York: Routledge.

Curtin, J. E. (1992). *Unseen Elvis: Candids of the king*. New York: Little, Brown.

Dangel, R., & Polster, R. (1986). *Teaching child management skills*. New York: Pergamon Press.

Daniel McNaughten's case. (1843). 10 C1, and Fin. 200, 8 Eng. Rep. 718.

Datillo, F., Davis, E., & Goisman, R. (2008). "Crisis intervention with medical patients." In F. Dattillo & A. Freeman (Eds), *Cognitive-behavior strategies in crisis intervention*. New York: Guilford.

DeBattista, C. (1998). "Mood disorders." In H. Friedman (Ed.), *Encyclopedia of mental health*. San Diego: Academic Press.

Dell, P. F., & O'Neil, J. A. (Eds.). (2008). *Dissociation and the dissociative disorders: DSM-IV and beyond*. New York: Routledge Press.

DePaulo, L. (2005). "The strange, still mysterious death of Marilyn Monroe." *Playboy, 52*(12), 76, 78, 82, 195–195.

Depue, R. (2007). "Red flags, warning signs and indicators." In *Report of the Review Panel, Mass shootings at Virginia Tech*. Blacksburg, VA: Office of the Governor of the Commonwealth of Virginia.

DiLalla, L. (2004). *Behavior genetics principles*. Washington, DC: American Psychological Association.

Diliberto, G. (1985). "Karen Carpenter was killed by over-the-counter drug some doctors say may be killing many others." *People Weekly, 23*, 67–70.

Doctor, R. (1998). "Sexual disorders." In H. Friedman (Ed.), *Encyclopedia of mental health*. San Diego: Academic Press.

Dozois, D. J., & Dobson, K. S. (2004). *The prevention of anxiety and depression*. Washington, DC: American Psychological Association.

Duncan, M., Bregman, J., Weller, E., & Weller, R. (1955). "Treatment of childhood & adolescent disorders." In A. Schatzberg and C. Nemeroff (Eds.), *Textbook of psychopharmacology*. Washington, DC: American Psychiatric Press.

Durham v. *United States*. (1954) 214 F. 2d 962, 874–875 (D.C. Circuit).

Durkheim, E. (1951). *Suicide*. New York: Free Press.

Durrant, R., & Thakker, J. (2003). *Substance use and abuse.* Thousand Oaks, CA: Sage.

Dusky v. *United States.* (1960) 362 U.S. 402.

Earle, R. H., Dillon, D., & Jecmen, D. (1998). "Systemic approach to the treatment of sex offenders." *Sexual Addiction and Compulsivity, 5,* 49–61.

Ellis, A. (2002). "Rational emotive behavior therapy." In M. Hersen & W. Sledge (Eds.), *Encyclopedia of psychotherapy.* San Diego: Academic Press.

Endicott, J., Nee, J., Cohen, J., Fliess, J., & Simon, A. (1986). "Diagnosis of schizophrenia." *Archives of General Psychology, 43,* 13–19.

Erikson, E. (1959). "Identity and the life cycle." *Psychological Issues, 1,* 18–64.

Escobar, J. (1998). "Somatization and hypochondriasis." In H. Friedman (Ed.), *Encyclopedia of mental health.* San Diego: Academic Press.

Esposito, J., & Oumano, E. (1994). *Good, rockin' tonight.* New York: Simon & Schuster.

Everly, G. S., & Lating, J. M. (2004). *Personality guided therapy for PTSD.* Washington, DC: American Psychological Association.

Eysenck, H. (1985). "Incubation theory of fear/anxiety." In S. Riess & R. Bootzin (Eds.), *Theoretical issues in behavior therapy.* Orlando, FL: Academic Press.

Fassler, D. (2001). *A common sense 10 point plan to address the problem of school violence.* American Academy of Child and Adolescent Psychiatry. Online: www.aacap.org.

Fawcett, J. (1992). "Suicide risk factors in depressive disorders and in panic disorder." *Journal of Clinical Psychiatry, 53* (Suppl.), 9–13.

Feldman, J., & Kazdin, A. (1995). "Parent management training for oppositional and conduct problem children." *The Clinical Psychologist, 48(4),* 3–5.

Fenichel, O. (1945). *The psychoanalytic theory of neurosis.* New York: Wiley.

Fenigstein, A. (1998). "Paranoia." In H. Friedman (Ed.), *Encyclopedia of mental health.* San Diego: Academic Press.

Fernald, D. (1984). *The Hans legacy.* Hillsdale, NJ: Lawrence Erlbaum.

Ferster, C., & Culbertson, S. (1982). *Behavior principles* (3rd ed.). Englewood Cliffs, NJ: Prentice-Hall.

Finkelhor, D., & Dziuba-Leatherman, J. (1994). "Victimization of children." *American Psychologist, 49,* 173–183.

Ford, B., & Chase, C. (1978). *The times of my life.* New York: HarperCollins.

Ford, B., & Chase, C. (1988). *A glad awakening.* Boston: Hall.

Forbush, K., Heatherton, T., & Keel, P. (2007). Relationships between perfectionism and specific disordered eating behaviors." *International Journal of Eating Behaviors, 40(1),* 37–41.

Frankl, V. (1975). *The unconscious god: Psychotherapy and theology.* New York: Simon & Schuster.

Friedman, M., Keane, T., & Resick, P. (Eds.). (2008). *Handbook of PTSD.* New York: Guilford.

Frost, R. (1998). "Obsessive-Compulsive Disorder." In H. Friedman (Ed.), *Encyclopedia of mental health.* San Diego: Academic Press.

Garfield, S. (1981). "Psychotherapy: A 40-year appraisal." *American Psychologist, 36,* 174–183.

Garner, D., & Garfinkel, P. (Eds.). (1997). *Handbook of treatment for eating disorders.* New York: Guilford Press.

Gathorne-Hardy, J. (1998). *Kinsey: Sex the measure of all things.* Bloomington, IN: Indiana University Press.

Gilmore, J. (1991). "Murdering while asleep." *Forensic Reports, 4,* 455–459.

Glasser, W. (1980). "Two cases in reality therapy." In G. Belkin (Ed.), *Contemporary psychotherapies.* Chicago: Rand McNally.

Goldsmith D., & Libbon, R. (2005). *Einstein: A relative history*. New York: Ibooks.

Goodwin, F. K., & Jamison, K. R. (1990). *Manic-depressive illness*. New York: Oxford University Press.

Goodwin, G. M. (1994). "Recurrence of mania after lithium withdrawal." *British Journal of Psychiatry, 164,* 149–152.

Gottesman I., & Shields, J. (1972). *Schizophrenia and genetics: A twin study vantage point*. New York: Academic Press.

Grandin, T. (1995). *Thinking in pictures and other reports from my life with autism*. New York: Doubleday.

Greenberg, S., Shuman, D., & Meyer, R. (2004). "Unmasking forensic diagnosis." *International Journal of Law and Psychiatry, 27(1),* 1–15.

Grilo, C. (2006). *Eating disorders*. New York: Routledge.

Haley, J., & Richenport-Haley, M. (2008) *Medically unexplained illness*. Washington, DC: American Psychological Association.

Hare, R., Hart, S., & Harpur, T. (1991). "Psychopathy and the *DSM-IV* criteria for antisocial personality disorder." *Journal of Abnormal Psychology, 100,* 391–398.

Harrington, A. (1985). "Nineteenth-century ideas on hemisphere differences and 'duality of mind.'" *The Behavioral and Brain Sciences, 8,* 617–660.

Harsh, J., & Ogilvie, R. (Eds.). (1995). *Sleep onset: Normal and abnormal process*. Washington, DC: American Psychological Association.

Hauser, T. (2005). *Muhammed Ali: His life and times*. London: Robson Books.

Heffner, M., & Eifert, G. (2004). *The anorexia workbook*. Oakland, CA: New Harbinger.

Hersen, M., & Ammerman, R. (2000) *Advanced abnormal child psychology* (2nd ed.). Mahwah, NJ: Lawrence Erlbaum.

Hillebrand, M., & Pallone, N. (Eds.). (1995). *The psychobiology of aggression*. Binghamton, NY: Haworth.

Hodgins, D., & el-Guabaly, N. (2004). "Retrospective and prospective reports of precipitants to relapse in Pathological Gambling." *Journal of Consulting and Clinical Psychology, 72,* 72–80.

Hopkins, J. R. (1995). "Erick Homburger Erikson (1902–1994)." *American Psychologist, 50,* 796–797.

Horowitz, L. (2004). *Interpersonal foundations of psychopathology*. Washington, DC: American Psychological Association.

Ingram, R. (1998). "Depression." In H. Friedman (Ed.), *Encyclopedia of mental health*. San Diego: Academic Press.

Jackson v. *Indiana*. (1972). 406 U.S. 715.

Jaffee v. *Redmond*. (June 13, 1996) 116 S.Ct., 64 L. W. 4490.

Janofsky, J. (1994). "The Munchausen syndrome in civil forensic psychiatry." *Bulletin of the American Academy of Psychiatry and the Law, 22,* 488–489.

Johnson, A., Falstein, E., Szurek, S., & Svendsen, M. (1941). "School phobia." *American Journal of Orthopsychiatry, 11,* 702–711.

Johnson, S. (2008). *Medically unexplained illness*. Washington, DC: American Psychological Association.

Jones, J. (1997). *Alfred C. Kinsey: A public/private life*. New York W. W. Norton & Company.

Jones, M. C. (1924). "A laboratory study of fear: The case of Peter." *Journal of General Psychology, 31,* 308–315.

Kanner, L. (1943). "Autistic disturbances of affective content." *Nervous Child, 2,* 217–240.

Kansas v. *Hendricks*. (June 23, 1997). 117 S.Ct.; 65 L. W. 4564.

Kantor, S. (1978). *Who was Ruby?* Bethesda, MD: Everest House.

Katon, W. (1993). "Somatization disorder, hypochondriasis, and conversion disorder." In D. Dunner (Ed.), *Current psychiatric therapy*. Philadelphia: Saunders.

Kay, J., & Franklin, S. (1995). In R. Mapor & J. Spector (Eds.), *Clinical neuropsychological assessment*. New York: Plenum.

Kellam, A. (1969). "Shoplifting treated by aversion to a film." *Behavior Research and Therapy, 7*, 125–127.

Kelly, G. (1955). *The psychology of personal constructs* (2 vols.). New York: Norton.

Kelly, W. (Ed.). (1985). *Post traumatic stress disorder and the war veteran patient*. New York: Brunner/Mazel.

Kendler, K., Heath, A., Martin, N., & Eaves, L. (1986). "Symptoms of anxiety and depression in a volunteer twin population." *Archives of General Psychiatry, 43*, 213–221.

Kernberg, O. (1984). *Severe personality disorders*. New Haven, CT: Yale University Press.

Kessler, R., Berglund, P., Demler, O., Jin R., & Walters E. (2005). "Lifetime prevalence and age of onset distributions of *DSM-IV* disorders in the National Comorbidity Survey Replication." *Archives of General Psychiatry, 62*, 593–602.

Kinsey Institute. (2007). www.indiana.edu/-kinsey/.

Kjetsaa, G. (1987). *Fyodor Dostoevsky: A writer's life*. New York: Viking Penguin.

Kluft, R. (1998). "Dissociative Disorders." In H. Friedman (Ed.), *Encyclopedia of mental health*. San Diego: Academic Press.

Kluft, R., & Fine, C. (1993). *Clinical perspectives on multiple personality disorder*. Washington, DC: American Psychiatric Press.

Knable, M., Kleinman, J., & Weinberger, D. (1995). "Neurobiology of schizophrenia." In A. Schatzberg & C. Nemeroff (Eds.), *Textbook of psychiatry*. Washington, DC: American Psychiatric Press.

Kohut, H. (1977). *The restoration of the self*. New York: International Universities Press.

Kraeplin, E. (1899 [1919]). *Dementia praecox and paraphrenia* (8th Ger. ed.). R. Barclay & G. Robertson (trans.). Edinburgh: Livingstone.

Kroll, J. (1993). *PTSD/borderline in therapy*. New York: Norton.

Kronenberger, W., & Meyer, R. (2001). *The child clinician's handbook* (2nd ed.). Boston: Allyn and Bacon.

Kubany, E., McCaig, M., & Laconsay, J. (2004). *Healing the trauma of domestic violence*. Oakland, CA: New Harbinger.

Larson, R., Graham, E., & Baker, K. (2007). *A history of psychology*. Upper Saddle River, NJ: Prentice-Hall.

Lasch, C. (1978). *The culture of narcissism*. New York: Norton.

Laws, D. R., & O'Donohue, W. (2008). *Sexual deviance* (2nd ed.) New York: Guilford.

Lazarus, A. (1971). *Behavior therapy and beyond*. New York: McGraw-Hill.

Lehmann, J. (1975). *Virginia Woolf and her world*. New York: Harcourt Brace Jovanovich.

Lezak, M. (1995). *Neuropsychological assessment*. New York: Oxford University Press.

LoPiccolo, J. (1993). "Paraphilias." In D. Dunner (Ed.), *Current psychiatric therapy*. Philadelphia: Saunders.

Ludwig, A. (1996). *The price of greatness*. New York: Guilford Press.

Lydiard, B., Brawnmen-Mintzer, O., & Ballenger, J. (1996). "Recent developments in the pharmacotherapy of anxiety disorders." *Journal of Consulting and Clinical Psychology, 64*, 660–668.

Lykken, D. (1995). *The antisocial personalities*. New York: Lawrence Erlbaum.

Maraniss, D. (1996). *First in his class: The biography of Bill Clinton*. New York: Simon & Schuster.

Margolis, R., & Zweben, J. (1998). *Treating patients with alcohol and other drug problems*. Washington, DC: American Psychological Association.

Marsella, A., De Vos, G., & Hsu, F. (Eds.). (1985). *Culture and self: Asian and western perspectives*. New York: Tavistock.

Marvasti, J. (2004). *Psychiatric treatment for sexual offenders*. Springfield, IL: Charles Thomas.

Maslow, A. (1954). *Motivation and personality*. New York: HarperCollins.

Massie, R. K. (1967). *Nicholas and Alexandra*. New York: Atheneum.

Masters, W., & Johnson, V. (1970). *Human sexual inadequacy*. Boston: Little, Brown.

Masters, W., Johnson, V., & Kolodny, R. (1991). *Human sexuality* (4th ed.). Glenview, IL: Scott, Foresman.

Masters, W., Johnson, V., & Kolodny, R. (1994). *Heterosexuality*. New York: HarperCollins.

Maultsby, M. (1998). "Behavior therapy." In H. Friedman (Ed.), *Encyclopedia of mental health*. San Diego: Academic Press.

May, R. (1981). *Existential psychology*. New York: Random House.

McCullough, J. (2002). *Skills training manual for diagnosing and treating chronic depression*. New York: Guilford.

McElhaney, J. E. (1987). *Trial notebook* (2nd ed.). Chicago: American Bar Association.

Medvedev, R., & Medvedev, Z. (2003). *The unknown Stalin*. Woodstock, NY: Overlook.

Meggers, H., & LoPiccolo,, J. (2002). "Sex therapy." In M. Hersen & W. Sledge (Eds.), *Encyclopedia of psychotherapy*. San Diego: Academic Press.

Meichenbaum, D. (1977). *Cognitive behavior modification*. New York: Plenum.

Meichenbaum, D. (1986). *Stress inoculation training*. New York: Pergamon Press.

Meister, R. (1980). *Hypochondria*. New York: Taplinger.

Melton, G., Petrila, J., Poythress, N., & Slobogin, C. (1997). *Psychological evaluation for courts* (2nd ed.). New York: Guilford Press.

Meyer, R. (1998a). "Antisocial personality disorder." In H. Friedman (Ed.), *Encyclopedia of mental health*. San Diego: Academic Press.

Meyer, R. (1998b). "Personality disorders." In H. Friedman (Ed.), *Encyclopedia of mental health*. San Diego: Academic Press.

Meyer, R., & Brothers, A. (2001). "A common path for the development of psychopathy." In J. Aponte & R. Meyer (Eds.), *The psychopath and the mental health professional*. Mahwah, NJ: Lawrence Erlbaum.

Meyer, R., & Salmon, P. (Forthcoming). *Clinical hypnosis*. Sarasota, FL: Professional Resource Press.

Meyer, R., & Weaver, C. M. (2007). *The clinician's handbook: Integrated diagnostics, assessment, and intervention in adult and adolescent psychopathology* (5th ed.). Long Grove, IL: Waveland Press.

Meyer, R. G., & Weaver, C.M. (2006). *Law and mental health: A case-based approach*. New York: Guilford Press.

Miklowitz, D., Strachan, A., Goldstein, M., Doane, J., Snyder, K., Hogarty, G., & Falloon, I. (1986). "Expressed emotion and communication deviance in the families of schizophrenics." *Journal of Abnormal Psychology*, 95, 60–66.

Milner, J. (1998). Personal communication.

Mischel, W. (1969). "Continuity and change in personality." *American Psychologist*, 24, 1012–1018.

Mischel, W. (1986). *Introduction to personality* (4th ed.). New York: Holt, Rinehart and Winston.

Mitchell, S. (1817). "Mary Reynolds: A case of double consciousness." *Transactions of the College of Physicians of Philadelphia*. Third series 10, 1888.

Monahan, J. (1981). *Predicting violent behavior*. Thousand Oaks, CA: Sage.

Money, J. (1987). "Sin, sickness, or status: Homosexual gender identity and psychoneuroendocrinology." *American Psychologist, 42,* 384–399.

Montefiore, S. S. (2004). *Stalin: The court of the Red Tsar*. New York: Weidenfeld and Nicholson.

Morel, B. (1857). *Traite des degenerescences physiques, intellectuelles et morales*. Paris: Bailliere.

Morgillo-Freeman, S. (2008). "Acute and chronic pain." In F. Dattilo, & A. Freeman (Eds.), *Cognitive-behavioral strategies in crisis intervention*. New York: Guilford.

Morris, E. (1999). *Dutch: A memoir of Ronald Reagan*. New York: Random House.

Morrison, A. (2002). "Somatoform disorders." In M. Hersen & W. Sledge (Eds.), *Encyclopedia of psychotherapy*. San Diego: Academic Press.

Morton, A. (1992). *Diana: Her true story*. New York: Simon & Schuster.

Morton, A. (1994). *Diana: Her new life*. New York: Simon & Schuster.

Mosier, J. (2004). *The Blitzkrieg myth*. New York: HarperCollins.

Mulvey, E. P., & Cauffman, E. (2001). "The inherent limits of predicting school violence." *American Psychologist, 56(10),* 797–802.

Munich, R. (2002). "Schizophrenia and other psychotic disorders." In M. Hersen & W. Sledge (Eds.), *Encyclopedia of psychotherapy*. San Diego: Academic Press.

Naar, S., Ellis, D. A., & Frey, M. A. (2004). *Assessing children's well-being*. Mahwah, NJ: Lawrence Erlbaum.

Nathan, K., Musselman, D., Schatzberg, A., & Nemeroff, C. (1995). "Biology of mood disorders." In A. Schatzberg & C. Nemeroff (Eds.), *Textbook of psychiatry*. Washington, DC: American Psychiatric Press.

Nicholi, A. M. (1999). *The new Harvard guide to psychiatry* (3rd ed.). Cambridge, MA: Belknap Press.

NMHA (National Mental Health America). (2006) "Postpartum disorders." www.nmha.org/go/get-info/depression/postpartumdisorders.

Nolan, S., Strassle, C., Roback H., & Binder, J (2004). "Negative treatment effects in dyadic psychotherapy." *Journal of Contemporary Psychotherapy, 34(4),* 311–330.

Novak, G., & Pelaez, M. (2004). *Child and adolescent development*. Thousand Oaks, CA: Sage.

Odom S., Horner R., Snell M., & Blacher, J. (2008). *Handbook of developmental disabilities*. New York: Guilford.

Oren, D., Moul, D., Schwartz, P., Brown, C., et al. (1994). "Exposure to ambient light in patients with winter seasonal affective disorder." *American Journal of Psychiatry, 151,* 591–593.

Pallis, C., & Bamji, A. (1979). "McIlroy was here, or was he?" *British Medical Journal, 1,* 973–975.

Parnell, T. F. (1997). "Guidelines for identifying cases." In T. E. Parnell & D. O. Day (Eds.), *Munchausen By Proxy Syndrome: Misunderstood child abuse* (pp. 47–67). Thousand Oaks, CA: Sage.

Pasqualone, G. A., & Fitzgerald, S. M. (1999). "Munchausen by Proxy Syndrome: The forensic challenge of recognition, diagnosis, and reporting." *Critical Care Nursing Quarterly, 22,* 52–64.

Pate v. Robinson. (1966). 383 U.S. 375, 86 S.Ct., 83C, 15 L. Ed. 2d 815.

Perkinson, R. (1977). *Chemical dependency counseling*. Thousand Oaks, CA: Sage.

Perls, F., Hefferline, R., & Goodman, P. (1958). *Gestalt therapy*. New York: Julian.

Peselow, E. D., Fieve, R. R., Difiglia, C., & Sanfilipo, M. P. (1994). "Lithium prophylaxis of bipolar illness." *British Journal of Psychiatry, 164,* 208–214.

Petraitis, J., Flay, B., & Miller, T. (1995). "Reviewing theories of adolescent substance abuse." *Psychological Bulletin, 117*, 67–86.

Pfefferbaum, B., et al. (November 1999). "Posttraumatic stress responses in bereaved children after the Oklahoma City bombing." *Journal of the American Academy of Child & Adolescent Psychiatry, 38*(11), 1372–1379.

Phelps, L., Brown, R., & Power, T. (2002). *Pediatric psychopharmacology*. Washington, DC: American Psychological Association.

Phillips, D. (1974). "The influence of suggestion of suicide." *American Sociological Review, 39*, 340–354.

Phillips, D., Lesyna, K., & Paight, D. (1993). "Suicide and the media." In R. Maris, A. Berman, & J. Maltsberger (Eds.), *Assessment and prediction of suicide*. New York: Guilford Press.

Pike, J. (1993). *The death of rock 'n' roll*. Boston: Faber and Faber.

Piper, W., Joyce, A., McCallum, M., Hassam, A., & Ogrodniczuk, J. (2002). *Interpretive and supportive psychotherapies*. Washington, DC: American Psychological Association.

Pitman, S., & Orr, S. (1993). "Psychophysiologic testing for PTSD." *Bulletin of the American Academy of Psychiatry and the Law, 21*, 37–52.

Pollard, C. A., & Zuercher-White, E. (2003). *The agoraphobia workbook*. Oakland, CA: New Harbinger.

Post, R. M. (1993). "Issues in the long-term management of bipolar affective illness." *Psychiatric Annals, 23*, 86–93.

Pressman, M., & Orr, W. (Eds.). (1997). *Understanding sleep: The evaluation and treatment of sleep disorders*. Washington, DC: American Psychological Association.

Prochaska, J., DiClemente, C., & Norcross, J. (1992). "In search of how people change." *American Psychologist, 47*, 1102–1114.

Rainer, I., & Brown, F. (2008). *Crisis counseling and therapy*. Binghamton, NY: Haworth Press.

Ray, O. (2004). "How the body hurts and heals the body." *American Psychologist, 59(1)*, 29–40.

Rebello, S. (2005). "Somebody killed her." *Playboy, 52*(12), 79, 186–190.

Reinecke. M., Washburn, R., & Becker-Weidman R. (2008). "Depression and suicide." In F. Dattillo, & A. Freeman (Eds.), *Cognitive-behavioral strategies in crisis intervention*. New York: Guilford.

Remnick, D. (1999). *King of the World: Muhammad Ali and the Rise of an American hero*. New York: Random House.

Report of the Review Panel. (2007). *Mass shootings at Virginia Tech*. Blacksburg, VA: Office of the Governor of the Commonwealth of Virginia.

Reynolds, D. (1984). *Constructive living*. Honolulu: University of Hawaii Press.

Rice, M., Harris, G., & Cormier, C. (1992). "An evaluation of a maximum security therapeutic community for psychopaths and other mentally disordered offenders." *Law and Human Behavior, 16*, 399–412.

Ricker, J. H. (2004). *Differential diagnosis in adult neuropsychological assessment*. New York: Sage.

Robins, L., & Regier, D. (1990). *Psychiatric disorders in America*. New York: Free Press.

Roesch, R. (1979). "Determining competency to stand trial: An examination of evaluation procedures in an institutional setting." *Journal of Consulting and Clinical Psychology, 47*(3), 542–550.

Rogers, C. (1961). *On becoming a person*. Boston: Houghton Mifflin.

Rogers, R., & Shuman, D. (2000). *Conducting insanity evaluations*. New York: Guilford.

Rosenbaum, R. (1998). *Explaining Hitler*. New York: Harper Perennial.

Rosenhan, D. (1973). "On being sane in insane places." *Science, 179*, 250–258.

Roth, D., Eng, W., & Heimberg, R. (2002). "Cognitive behavior therapy." In M. Hersen & W. Sledge (Eds.), *Encyclopedia of psychotherapy*. San Diego, CA: Academic Press.

Ruggiero, K. J., Morris, T. L., & Scotti, J. R. (May 2001). "Treatment for children with post-traumatic stress disorder: Current status and future directions." *Clinical Psychology-Science & Practice, 8(2)*, 210–227.

Saiger, G., Rubenfeld, S., & Dluhy, M. (Eds). (2008). *Windows into today's group therapy*. New York: Routledge.

Salmon, P., & Meyer, R. (1986a). "Neuropsychological assessment: Adults." In M. Kurke & R. Meyer (Eds.), *Psychology in product liability and personal injury law*. New York: Hemisphere.

Salmon, P., & Meyer, R. (1986b). "Neuropsychological assessment: Children." In M. Kurke & R. Meyer (Eds.), *Psychology in product liability and personal injury law*. New York: Hemisphere.

Sbraga, T., & O'Donohue, W. (2004). *The sex addiction workbook*. Oakland, CA: New Harbinger.

Schechter, H. (2003). *The serial killer files*. New York: Ballantine.

Schmidt, C. (1995). "Sexual psychopathology and *DSM-IV*." In J. Oldham & M. Riba (Eds.), *Review of psychiatry*. Washington, DC: American Psychiatric Association.

Schneider, K., & Leithner, L. (2002). "Humanistic psychology." In M. Hersen & W. Sledge (Eds.), *Encyclopedia of psychotherapy*. San Diego: Academic Press.

Schuckit, M. (1996). "Recent developments in the pharmacotherapy of alcoholism." *Journal of Consulting and Clinical Psychology, 64*, 669–676.

Schwartz, J., Stoessel, P., Baxter, L., Martin, K., & Phelps, M. (1996). "Systematic changes in cerebral glucose metabolic rate after successful behavior modification treatment of obsessive-compulsive disorder." *Archives of General Psychiatry, 53*, 109–113.

Scott, P. D. (1994). *Deep politics and the death of JFK*. Los Angeles: University of California Press.

Seidman, S., & Rieder, R. (1994). "A review of sexual behavior in the United States." *American Journal of Psychiatry, 151*, 330–341.

Seligman, M. E. (1995). "The effectiveness of psychotherapy." *American Psychologist, 50*, 965–974.

Seligman, M. E., & Csikszentmihalyi, M. (2000). "Positive psychology: An introduction." *American Pyschologist, 55*, 5–14.

Seltzer, L. (1986). *Paradoxical strategies in psychotherapy*. New York: Wiley.

Shields, B. (2005). *Down came the rain*. New York: Hyperion.

Shneidman, E. (1985). *Definition of suicide*. New York: Wiley.

Silverman, I., & Geer, J. (1968). "The elimination of a recurrent nightmare by desensitization of a related phobia." *Behavior Research and Therapy, 6*, 109–111.

Slovenko, R. (1995). *Psychiatry and criminal culpability*. New York: Wiley.

Smith, A., & Sugar, O. (1975). "Development of above normal language and intelligence 21 years after left hemispherectomy." *Neurology, 25*, 813–818.

Smith, M., Glass, G., & Miller, T. (1980). *The benefit of psychotherapy*. Baltimore: Johns Hopkins University Press.

Snowden, D. (2001). *Aging with grace*. New York: Bantam.

Spanos, N. (1996). *Multiple identities and false memories*. Washington, DC: American Psychological Association.

Spanos, N. P., Weekes, N. P., & Bertraud, L. D. (1985). "Multiple personality: A social psychological perspective." *Journal of Abnormal Psychology, 94(3),* 362–376.

Sprague, J., Walker, H. M., Stieber, S., Simonsen, B., Nishioka, V., & Wagner, L. (2001). "Exploring the relationship between school discipline referrals and delinquency." *Psychology in the Schools, 38,* 197–206.

Stanley, D., & Loffey, F. (1994). *The Elvis encyclopedia.* Santa Monica, CA: General Publishing Group.

State v. *Grieg* (Yellowstone County, Montana, 1877).

Stice, E., Burton, E., & Shaw, H. (2004). "Prospective relations between bulimic pathology, depression, and substance abuse." *Journal of Consulting and Clinical Psychology, 72,* 62–71.

Striegel-Moore, R., Silberstein, L., & Rodin, J. (1986). "Toward an understanding of risk factors for bulimia." *American Psychologist, 43,* 246–263.

Strupp, H., Lambert, M., & Horowitz, L. (Eds.). (1997). *Measuring patient changes in mood, anxiety and personality disorders.* Washington, DC: American Psychological Association.

Sullivan, H. S. (1953). *The interpersonal theory of psychiatry.* New York: Norton.

Summers, A. (1980). *Conspiracy.* New York: McGraw-Hill.

Summers, A. (1985). *Goddess: The secret lives of Marilyn Monroe.* New York: Scribner.

Taylor, W. S., & Martin, M. (1944). "Multiple personality." *Journal of Abnormal Psychology, 39,* 281.

Thigpen, C., & Cleckley, H. (1984). "On the incidence of multiple personality." *International Journal of Clinical and Experimental Hypnosis, 32,* 63.

Tollefson, G. (1993). "Major depression." In D. Dunner (Ed.), *Current psychiatric therapy.* Philadelphia: Saunders.

Thomas, M. (2000). "Albert Einstein and LD: An evaluation of the evidence." *Journal of Learning Disabiligies, 33(2),* 149–157.

United States v. *Brawner.* (1972). 471 F. 2d. 969, D.C. Circuit.

Van Oppen, P., Hoekstra, R., & Emmelkamp, P. (1995). "The structure of obsessive-compulsive symptoms." *Behavior Research and Therapy, 33,* 15–23.

Wachtel, P. (1997). *Psychoanalysis behavior therapy, and relational world.* Washington, DC: American Psychological Association.

Walker, E. (1998). "Schizophrenia." In H. Friedman (Ed.), *Encyclopedia of mental heath.* San Diego: Academic Press.

Watson, J., & Rayner, R. (1920). "Conditioned emotional reactions." *Journal of Experimental Psychology, 3,* 1–14.

Weidenfeld, S. R. (1979). *First Lady's lady: With the Fords at the White House.* New York: Putnam.

Weissberg, M. (1993). "Multiple personality disorder and iatrogenesis: The cautionary tale of Anna O." *International Journal of Clinical and Experimental Hypnosis, 41(1),* 15–34.

Welch, M., & Kartub, P. (1978). "Socio-cultural correlates of incidence of impotence: A cross-cultural study." *Journal of Sex Research, 14,* 218–230.

Wender, P. (1995). *Attention deficit hyperactivity disorder in adults.* New York: Oxford University Press.

Weston, D. (1998). "The scientific legacy of Sigmund Freud: Toward a psychodynamically informed psychological science." *Psychological Bulletin, 124,* 333–371.

Whitman, T. (2004). *The development of autism.* New York: Jessica Kingsley Books.

Whybrow, P. (1997). *A mood apart: Depression, manic depression and other afflictions of the self.* New York: Basic Books.

Widiger, T., Frances, A., Pincus, H., Davis, W., & First, M. (1991). "Toward an empirical classification for the DSM-IV." *Journal of Abnormal Psychology, 100,* 280–288.

Williams, M., Teasdale, J., Segal, Z., & Kabat-Zin, J. (2008). *The mindful way through depression.* New York: Guilford.

Winer, D. (1978). "Anger and dissociation: A case study of multiple personality." *Journal of Abnormal Psychology, 87,* 368.

Wolpe, J. (1958). *Psychotherapy by reciprocal inhibition.* Stanford, CA: Stanford University Press.

Wolpe, J. (1973). *The practice of behavior therapy.* New York: Pergamon Press.

Wrangham, R., & Peterson, D. (1996). *Demonic males: Apes and the origins of human violence.* New York: Houghton Mifflin.

INDEX